INSPIRE / PLAN / DISCOVER / EXPERIENCE

FRANCE

FRANCE

CONTENTS

This page: Vintage shoemaker's sign in the south of France
Previous page: Lavender fields of Provence
Front cover: Through the vineyards to Riquewihr village

DISCOVER 6

EXPERIENCE PARIS 70

EXPERIENCE FRANCE 164

NEED TO KNOW 550

DISCOVER

The historic town of Dinan in Brittany

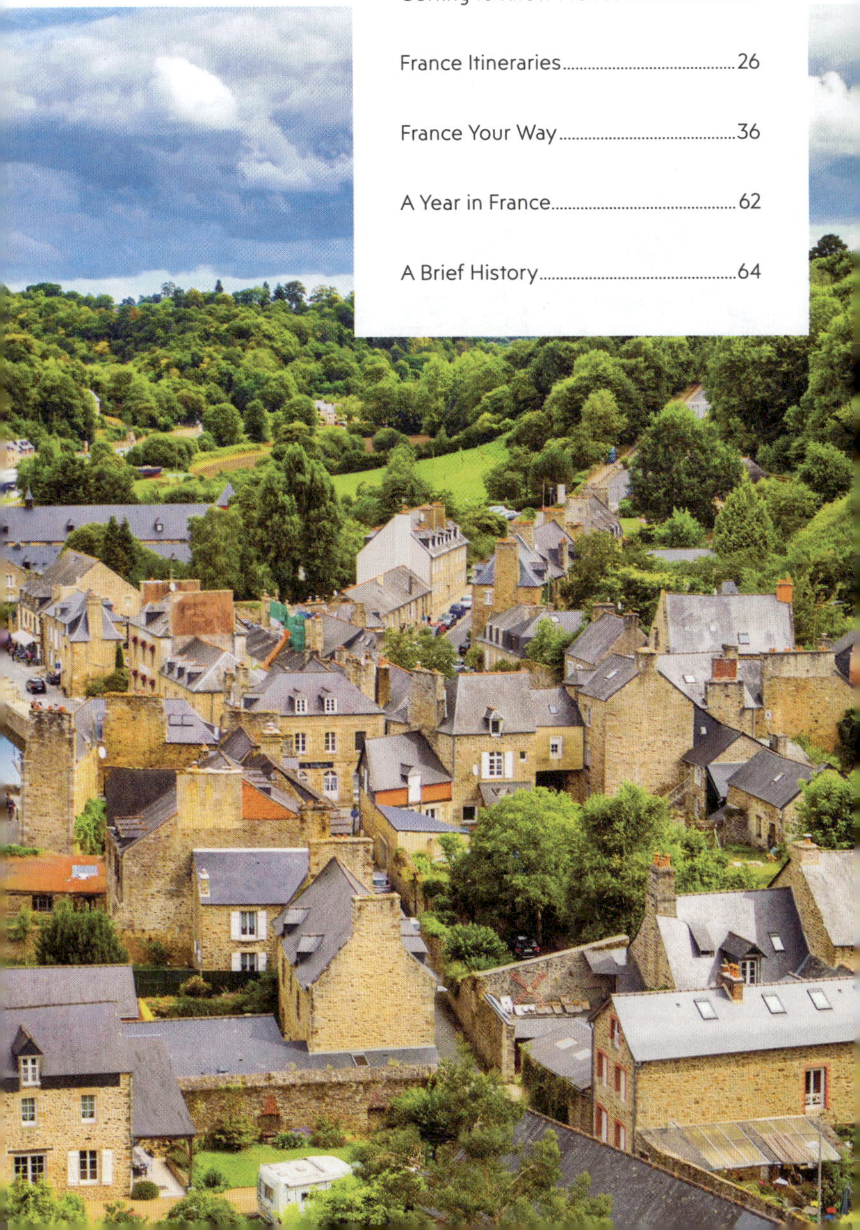

WELCOME TO
FRANCE

Fairy-tale châteaux and inspiring landscapes. Superb cuisine and outstanding wines. World-renowned art museums and stunning prehistoric monuments. France provides it all, with a dash of that characteristic *je ne sais quoi*. Whatever your dream trip to France includes, this DK Eyewitness Travel Guide is the perfect companion.

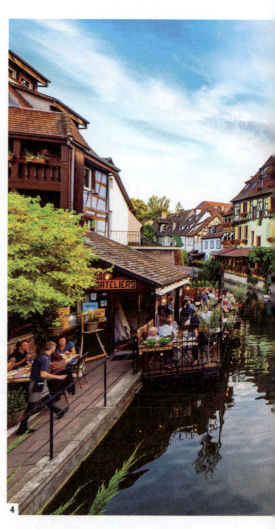

1 Rustic al fresco dining in Auvergne.

2 Wandering the streets of Paris.

3 The glorious Château de Sully-sur-Loire.

4 Relaxing canalside in colourful Colmar

Few countries capture the imagination like France. Synonymous with romance, fine dining and inimitable style, this huge country also boasts spectacular landscapes: the wave-lashed cliffs of Brittany, the deep gorges of the Massif Central, the lavender fields of Provence, sun-kissed Mediterranean beaches and lofty Alpine peaks. These glorious landscapes have been immortalized in iconic artworks found in the country's world-famous museums and galleries.

The cities and villages, too, are not to be missed. Lyon is one of the world's hottest foodie scenes. Paris has some of the best art galleries the country has to offer. To the east, the colourful village of Riquewihr was immortalized in Disney's *Beauty and the Beast*. In the west, wine festivals attract visitors to vibrant Bordeaux, while Nice dazzles in the south.

France's long and thrilling history is evident across the country in prehistoric monuments, Roman ruins, magnificent castles and chât-eaux, and awe-inspiring abbeys, cathedrals and churches. Yet, not content to rest on its historic laurels, France continues to innovate and inspire. There is a festival for every occasion, ready to showcase the best France has to offer.

With so many different experiences and regions on offer, France can seem overwhelming. We've broken the country down into easily navigable chapters, with detailed itineraries, expert local knowledge and colourful, com-prehensive maps to help you plan the perfect visit. However long you plan to stay, this Eyewitness guide will ensure that you see the very best that *la belle France* has to offer. *Bienvenu!* Enjoy the book, and enjoy France.

REASONS TO LOVE
FRANCE

Its cuisine is delightful. It's steeped in culture. Its history pops up round every corner. Ask anyone from France and you'll hear a different reason why they love their country. Here, we pick a few of our favourites.

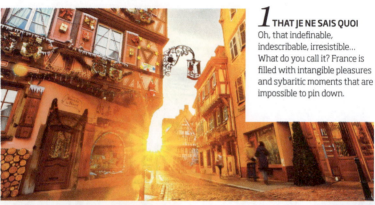

1 THAT JE NE SAIS QUOI

Oh, that indefinable, indescribable, irresistible... What do you call it? France is filled with intangible pleasures and sybaritic moments that are impossible to pin down.

MONT BLANC 2

At 4,800 m (15,770 ft), Mont Blanc is France's highest, most dangerous mountain, and a magnet for mountaineers, skiers and anyone who enjoys winter sports.

3 FRENCH HISTORY

The French countryside is littered with the debris of its extraordinary past, from battlefields and cathedrals to prehistoric cave paintings and ancient amphitheatres.

4 MEANDERING AROUND MARKETS

Rain or shine, the markets of France spring to life each day. Bustling farmer's markets fill village squares, while vintage treasures await to be uncovered in flea markets.

CHÂTEAU DE CHAMBORD 5

Built to wow the world, France's opulent châteaux and gardens are the stuff of fairy tales, none more so than the beguilingly lavish Château de Chambord *(p294)*.

CLASSIC FRENCH CUISINE 6

The timeless rituals of French cuisine are unrivalled – dining in a restaurant is an immersive experience, where service is an art and every dish is perfectly paired with its ideal wine.

LAVENDER FIELDS 7

Come summer, the rolling fields of Provence *(p490)* transform into a bee-buzzing purple haze of blossoming lavender, the "blue gold" that makes its way into soaps, honey and sorbets.

WORLD-CLASS ART 8

From tiny specialist galleries to the incomparable Musée du Louvre *(p106)*, France is home to some of the best art in the world. It's easy to lose hours admiring your favourites.

9 CITY OF LIGHT

Millions of lights set Paris aglow after dark, but that's not all that makes it dazzle. Monumental landmarks and glorious galleries compliment laid-back boulevards and cosy *café-terrasses*.

THE CÔTE D'AZUR 10

The spectacular landscapes and clear, soft light of the south coast have inspired a myriad of artists. Its pretty hill villages and harbours remain hotbeds of glamour and creativity.

WINE TASTING IN BORDEAUX 11

Bordeaux is a wine-lover's paradise. The vineyards surrounding the city *(p400)* are the perfect place to meet master winemakers and learn what makes a noble vintage.

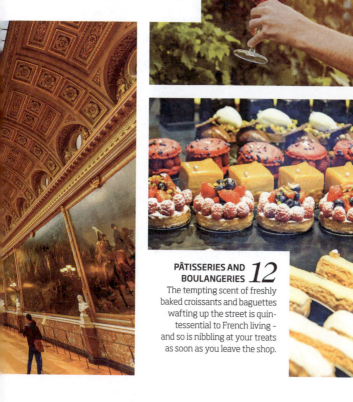

PÂTISSERIES AND BOULANGERIES 12

The tempting scent of freshly baked croissants and baguettes wafting up the street is quintessential to French living – and so is nibbling at your treats as soon as you leave the shop.

EXPLORE
FRANCE

This guide divides France into 17 colour-coded sightseeing areas, as shown on this map. Find out more about each area on the following pages.

UNITED KINGDOM

English Channel

Cherbourg

Le Havre

Caen

NORMANDY
p232

St-Malo   Avranches

Brest   St-Brieuc   Alençon

Châteaulin   **BRITTANY**   Fougères

Quimper   *p258*   Laval   Le Mans

Rennes

Lorient   Vannes   **THE**
                                    LOIRE VALLEY
                         p286   Tours

St-Nazaire

Nantes

Atlantic Ocean

Châtellerault

Poitiers

Niort

La Rochelle

Saintes

Angoulême

POITOU AND
AQUITAINE   Périgueux
p392

Bordeaux

Bergerac

Agen

Mont-de-Marsan   **THE**
                  DORDOGNE
                  p416

Biarritz   Pau   Tarbes

THE PYRÉNÉES
p448

Pamplona

SPAIN

Tudela   Huesca

Zaragoza

WESTERN EUROPE

SWEDEN

North Sea   DENMARK

IRELAND   UNITED KINGDOM   POLAND

GERMANY

CZECH REP.

Atlantic Ocean   FRANCE   AUSTRIA
                    SWITZ.

PORTUGAL   SPAIN   ITALY

Mediterranean Sea

MOROCCO   ALGERIA   TUNISIA

0 kilometres   150

0 miles   150

N

Antwerp

Ghent

Brussels

Cologne

BELGIUM

Frankfurt

Dunkerque

Calais

Boulogne

Lille

Arras

LUX.

GERMANY

Dieppe

LE NORD AND PICARDY
p184

Charleville-
Mézières

Sedan

Rouen

Amiens

Beauvais

St-Quentin

Thionville

PARIS
p70

Reims

Verdun

Metz

Sarreguemines

Strasbourg

Stuttgart

PARIS

Châlons-en-
Champagne

Nancy

Dreux

ÎLE-DE-FRANCE
p166

CHAMPAGNE
p204

**ALSACE AND
LORRAINE**
p216

Chartres

Sens

Troyes

Chaumont

Mulhouse

Orléans

Auxerre

Vesoul

Zürich

Blois

Dijon

Belfort

Zug

Vierzon

Besançon

Bern

SWITZERLAND

Bourges

Nevers

**BURGUNDY AND
FRANCHE-COMTÉ**
p312

Dole

Lausanne

Châteauroux

Moulins

Mâcon

Geneva

Montluçon

Bourg-en-
Bresse

Annecy

Milan

Limoges

Clermont-
Ferrand

Lyon

Chambéry

Brive-la-
Gaillarde

**THE MASSIF
CENTRAL**
p338

St-Étienne

Vienne

Grenoble

Turin

ITALY

Aurillac

**THE RHÔNE VALLEY
AND FRENCH ALPS**
p360

Briançon

Genoa

Rodez

Montélimar

Gap

Montauban

Alès

Avignon

Nice

Menton

Albi

Nîmes

**PROVENCE AND THE
CÔTE D'AZUR**
p490

Monaco

Toulouse

Montpellier

Arles

Cannes

**LANGUEDOC AND
ROUSSILLON**
p468

Aix-en-Provence

Carcassonne

Narbonne

Marseille

Toulon

Bastia

Perpignan

ANDORRA

*Mediterranean
Sea*

CORSICA
p532

Girona

Ajaccio

Barcelona

Bonifacio

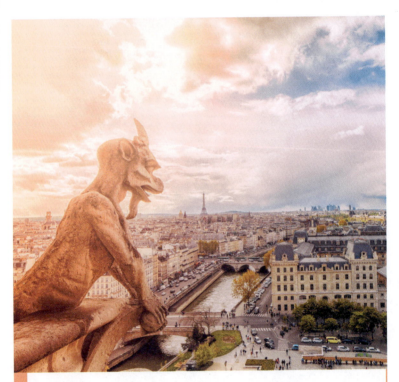

GETTING TO KNOW
FRANCE

Ah, *la belle* France! The world-famous food and wine is as rich and varied as the country's glorious landscapes, which range from alpine peaks to Mediterranean beaches. Each region has its own robust history and a lively, unique culture that entices many visitors to return again and again.

PARIS

PAGE 70

A patchwork of neighbourhoods, Paris is known for its utterly irresistible charm. The historic heart of the City of Lights lies on the banks of the Seine, where its medieval core, the Île de la Cité, still pulses with life. Further westwards, the cafés and bohemian bars of the Left Bank and world-class art galleries of Tuileries rub shoulders with iconic landmarks such as the Eiffel Tower and Arc du Triumphe. Beyond the centre, hilly Montmartre is a fashionable destination for diners and boutique shoppers, while leafy Cimetière du Père Lachaise is an oasis of calm.

Best for
Culture, fashion, nightlife, literature, romance

Home to
Musée du Louvre, Notre-Dame, Centre Pompidou, Ste-Chapelle, Arc de Triomphe, Eiffel Tower, Sacré-Coeur, Cimetière du Père Lachaise, Musée d'Orsay

Experience
Ambling across the Pont des Arts at sunset

ÎLE-DE-FRANCE

PAGE 166

Spreading out from Paris and its densely packed suburbs, the Île-de-France is a peaceful region of tranquil towns, forests and fields which once inspired artists like Corot and Cézanne. Royals and aristocrats came here to escape the city hubbub, and it's still home to fairy-tale châteaux, such as Versailles and Fontainebleau. You'll find more princesses – including Cinderella and Sleeping Beauty – at Disneyland®, Europe's most popular theme park.

Best for
Châteaux, churches and abbeys

Home to
The Palace and Garden of Versailles, Disneyland®, Château de Fontainebleau

Experience
Strolling through the breathtaking ornamental gardens at Fontainebleau

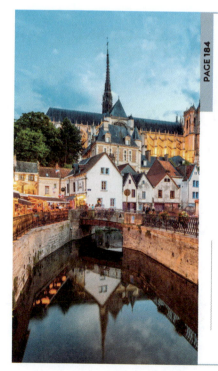

PAGE 184

LE NORD AND PICARDY

Gabled houses and delicious beer bear testament to the Flemish influence on northern France. It's a region of contrasts, with cool, urban Lille, full of independent boutiques and superb modern art museums, nestled against the belle époque seaside resorts such as fashionable Le Touquet, with their bathing huts and pretty villas. Calais remains France's most bustling sea port, while further south, superb Gothic cathedrals soar skywards in Amiens and Beauvais. Across the Somme Valley rise haunting memorials to the World Wars.

Best for
Beer, Gothic cathedrals, glamorous seaside towns

Home to
Amiens Cathedral

Experience
Touring the World War battlefields

→

CHAMPAGNE

Everyone knows what the Champagne region is famous for. Its eponymous – and delectable – sparkling wine conjures images of celebration around the world. Pop a cork or two in Epernay, Châlons-en-Champagne and Reims, known as the "sacred triangle" of Champagne. Reims also has one of the finest Gothic cathedrals in all France. Champagne's rolling hills are covered with snaking vines, historic towns, and serene lakes and rivers that invite leisurely exploration. To the east, the mysterious, ancient forests, valleys and ravines of the Ardennes beckon.

Best for
Champagne, historic towns

Home to
Reims Cathedral

Experience
Sipping champagne after a day hiking trails in the Ardennes forest

ALSACE AND LORRAINE

Nudged up against the German border, Alsace and Lorraine straddle French and German culture and cuisine. Strasbourg, elegant and cosmopolitan, is its biggest city, but much of the region is dotted with medieval villages set amid verdant hills. Alsace is famous for its wines, best tried in a cosy *winstub* (wine cellar), but also produces more than half of the beer made in France. Neighbouring Lorraine feels more traditionally French, and is sleepier but just as enticing. It's historic capital, Metz, is known as the Green City, because of its expansive green spaces.

Best for
Wine cellars, medieval villages, unspoiled countryside

Home to
Strasbourg

Experience
Sampling local vintages at a buzzing wine harvest festival

PAGE 232

NORMANDY

Normandy conjures up a bucolic idyll, with its gentle hills, villages full of half-timbered houses and apple orchards. Monet painted his famous *Water Lilies* series in the garden at Giverny, still one of the most alluring attractions in the region. Off its dramatic coastline rises the ethereal island of Mont-St-Michel, an ancient fortification accessed by a tidal causeway. Bicycle is the best way to explore the picture-postcard harbour towns and seaside resorts that line the pretty Côte Fleurie, where the menus are filled with delicious local treats like Camembert and calvados.

Best for
Cider and cheese, half-timbered houses, sweeping beaches

Home to
Mont-St-Michel, Caen, Rouen

Experience
Strolling through Monet's garden at Giverny

PAGE 258

BRITTANY

Wild and beautiful, Brittany's wave-whipped cliffs jut into the Atlantic, while wolves still roam its remote primeval forests. In this untamed region, Brittany's ancient Celtic heritage is celebrated in song, in the Breton language and, of course, in regional specialities from crêpes to cider. Head to the perfectly preserved harbour towns of St-Malo and Roscoff to uncover Brittany's long seafaring tradition and tasty fish dishes. Inland, the capital, Rennes, boasts a beautifully maintained medieval centre, while the prehistoric megaliths of Carnac and the Golfe du Morbihan lure visitors to discover their secrets.

Best for
Stunning coastline and islands, Celtic culture, prehistoric megaliths

Home to
St-Malo, Côte de Granit Rose

Experience
Exploring the towering cliffs and wild beaches of the Côte de Granit Rose

$\rightarrow$

PAGE 286

THE LOIRE VALLEY

Glorious châteaux straight from a fairy tale are scattered across the lush, green Loire Valley. Long the playground of French aristocracy, 42 of the finest châteaux have been designated UNESCO World Heritage Sites. Chambord, constructed for François I to designs by Leonardo da Vinci, is the most famous, but Azay-le-Rideau is perhaps the most romantic. For many, the gorgeous gardens will be just as much of a draw. Beyond the châteaux, beautifully preserved historic towns and villages produce the region's celebrated wines.

Best for
Wine, châteaux, gardens

Home to
Tours, Château de Chenonceau, Château de Chambord, Chartres Cathedral

Experience
A night visit to the illuminated gardens of the lovely Château de Chenonceau

PAGE 312

BURGUNDY AND FRANCHE-COMTÉ

All the things that France does best – world-class wines, delicious food, dreamy countryside and exquisite historic towns – are found in Burgundy and Franche-Comté. Magnificent towns, such as Beaune and Dijon, and the remarkable Romanesque architecture at Vézelay, Fontenay and Cluny attest to Burgundy's historic importance. Franche-Comté provides a sleepy contrast, with forests, waterfalls and alpine peaks that offer countless opportunities for hiking, canoeing and other outdoor sports.

Best for
Superb food and wines, Romanesque architecture, gorgeous countryside

Home to
Abbaye de Fontenay, Basilique Ste-Madeleine, Dijon

Experience
Swimming in natural pools and waterfalls in Franche-Comté

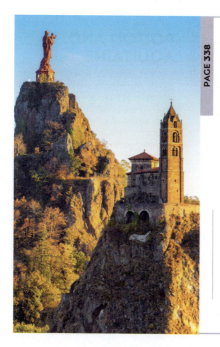

PAGE 338

THE MASSIF CENTRAL

The Massif Central is the huge central plateau in the heart of France, surprisingly little visited. This beautiful region rewards adventurous travellers with medieval castles, Romanesque churches and volcanic landscapes. Explore some of France's most secret corners, like the untouched Auvergne, or the wild uplands of the Cévennes. It's a stunning hiking destination, with ancient pilgrim paths and one of France's deepest gorges.

Best for
Outdoor activities, remote and dramatic landscapes, hearty regional food and wine

Home to
Le Puy-en-Velay, Abbaye de Ste-Foy, gorges du Tarn

Experience
Hiking down into the gorges du Tarn

→

THE RHÔNE VALLEY AND FRENCH ALPS

The mighty River Rhône makes its majestic descent from the snowcapped peaks of the Alps through the fertile plains and farmland of eastern France. Long a vital artery between north and south, all along its banks, you'll find the vineyards of the renowned Beaujolais and Côtes du Rhone, and the ravishing, art-filled city of Lyon, which is France's undisputed gastronomic capital. Chic resorts in the French Alps offer a dazzling array of winter sports, or you could take the waters in one of the charming historic spa towns.

Best for
Outstanding food and wine, unspoiled landscapes, historic spa towns, winter sports

Home to
Lyon, Grenoble

Experience
The local flavours and foodie flights of fantasy of Lyon's thriving restaurant scene

POITOU AND AQUITAINE

Sublime beaches, the world's finest brandy, pilgrim paths and timeless villages are all found in this beautiful region. Dramatic cliffs, islands and vast sandy beaches dot the magnificent Atlantic coastline, a paradise for sailors and watersports' enthusiasts. Bordeaux, home to world-renowned wine châteaux, has a pulsing restaurant scene. Inland is a different story, with medieval villages and forests providing a tranquil escape.

Best for
Glorious beaches, world-class wine, lush countryside, traditional villages

Home to
Poitiers, Bordeaux

Experience
Touring the celebrated wine châteaux of Bordeaux

PAGE 416

THE DORDOGNE

These verdant valleys have been inhabited for tens of thousands of years, as the many prehistoric cave sites attest. The hunting scenes painted some 20,000 years ago at Lascaux seem to leap from the walls, while the "Venuses", prehistoric statutes of women, have been found in caves all around Les Eyzies. The Dordogne river makes its sinuous progress through gorges and farmland, overlooked by ancient towns like lofty Rocamadour, which have barely changed in centuries. Earthy local specialities such as *magret de canard* are delicious paired with the robust wines from Cahors.

Best for
Regional cuisine, beautiful valleys and rivers, superb prehistoric cave paintings

Home to
Sarlat, Rocamadour, Abbaye du St-Pierre, Toulouse

Experience
Spelunking to discover extraordinary prehistoric art

→

PAGE 448

THE PYRÉNÉES

Stretching all the way from the Atlantic to the Mediterranean, the Pyrenees present a formidable natural border between France and Spain. The craggy peaks and snaking valleys are home to rare flora and fauna, and fantastic hiking trails where walkers can try to spot these rarities. Castles and fortresses such as those of Foix and Montségur are reminders of the region's strategic importance and centuries of siege. The Basques, the most ancient inhabitants of these mountains, display their unique language and culture in towns like Bayonne and St-Jean-de Luz.

Best for
Mountain scenery, wildlife, historic citadels, regional food and wine

Home to
Parc National des Pyrénées

Experience
Soaking up the Basque culture and food in Bayonne

PAGE 468

LANGUEDOC AND ROUSSILLON

Sun-kissed Languedoc and Roussillon boasts miles of heavenly sandy beaches along the Mediterranean coast, while fields of sunflowers and vineyards stretch over inland hills. There are plenty of enticing sights to explore. Pocket-sized Montpellier is one of the most seductive little cities in France, while the perfectly preserved citadel of Carcassonne and a string of vertiginous Cathar castles vie with remarkable Roman monuments – including the astonishing Pont du Gard.

Best for
Arty beach towns, Cathar castles, Roman ruins

Home to
Carcassonne, Montpellier, Nîmes

Experience
Climbing the craggy peaks and into deep-forested valleys of stunning Cathar country

PROVENCE AND THE CÔTE D'AZUR

PAGE 490

Provence conjures up images of endless lavender fields and villages of honey-coloured stone. Ancient cities such as Orange and Avignon burst with Roman monuments and medieval palaces. Along the Mediterranean coast, the bite-shaped coves of white sand beaches and turquoise-coloured sea are synonymous with glamour, and chic resorts like Cannes and St-Tropez are a magnet for celebrities and the ultra-rich. The intense light has drawn artists for centuries, and their legacy lives on in magnificent art museums in Nice and elsewhere.

Best for
Glamorous resorts, beautiful beaches, art museums, Mediterranean landscapes

Home to
Arles, the Camargue, St-Paul-de-Vence, Nice, Monaco, Palais des Papes

Experience
Horse riding and flamingo-spotting in the Camargue

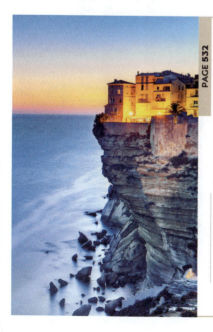

CORSICA

PAGE 532

Corsica feels like nowhere else in France. It's a wild, beautiful island, bisected north to south by a dramatic mountain chain, with forests giving way to vineyards and citrus groves on the lower slopes. The beaches are breathtaking, whether you want secret coves tucked into cliffs or endless golden sands. Ajaccio and Bastia are lively harbour towns, while Bonifacio is in a sublime setting on the island's southern tip.

Best for
Stunning beaches, outdoor sports and activities

Home to
Bonifacio

Experience
A boat trip to the remote Réserve Naturelle de Scandola

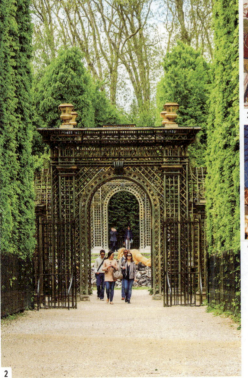

1 Notre-Dame cathedral from the bridge to Île de la Cité.

2 The gardens at Versailles.

3 The Bayeux tapestry.

4 Inside the glass pyramid at the Louvre.

France is a treasure trove of things to see and do. Travelling the length of the country and taking in vibrant cities and beautiful natural spaces, these itineraries will help you make the most of your trip.

2 WEEKS

Tour de France

Day 1

Start on the bridge to Île de la Cité for a fabulous view of Notre-Dame cathedral (*p86*). Nip north a few blocks for lunch at quirky workers' canteen Chartier (*p111*), then backtrack towards the river to delve into the Louvre (*p106*) and see the *Mona Lisa*. Come evening, check into the family-run Hôtel Saint-Marcel (*p151*).

Day 2

To avoid the crowds, get an early start at Louis XIV's Château de Versailles (*p170*), the epitome of French royal grandeur. Wander through the Sun King and Queen's bedchambers and the extravagant Hall of Mirrors. Later, stop to eat at one of the bistros in the grounds, then take a stroll through the magnificent gardens to the fountains, the Trianon palaces and Marie Antoinette's village.

Day 3

Set out early to Bayeux (*p251*), and the stunning Bayeux Tapestry. This colossal piece portrays William the Conqueror's invasion of England in 1066. Bayeux is home to the Bayeux War Cemetery, the largest Commonwealth cemetery of World War II in France. At the end of the day fall into bed at the aptly named L'Hôtel Churchill (*p255*).

Day 4

Carry on from Bayeux to Mont-St-Michel (*p240*), a monument to medieval ambition. Soaring up out of the sea, the car-free island dominates the horizon. Climb the steep hilly streets to visit the abbey; later, walk along the ramparts, and watch the ebb and flow of the galloping tides.

Carry on to overnight at St-Malo (*p268*). Wend through the narrow streets to La Chalut (*p285*) for the freshest seafood, then watch the sun set over the sea.

Day 5

Arrive in riverside Tours (*p290*) by mid-morning, to check into Hôtel de Biencourt (*p290*), then continue straight on to the serene Château de Chambord (*p294*) to see its fairy-tale-esque towers reflected in the languid waters of Le Cosson. Choose from one of its tea rooms, and tuck into *tarte tatin*, a Loire specialty, then spend a few hours touring the château and its marvellous gardens. Back in Tours, as dusk falls, roam this walkable city on foot, past the soaring Cathédrale St-Gatien (*p291*), and into the atmospheric old quarter, around place Plumereau (*p290*).

Day 6

Journey north east to the Château de Chenonceau (*p292*), often described as the "ladies' château" due to the number of aristocratic women who have put their mark on the building. On the way back to Tours, stop in Amboise (*p304*) to visit Le Clos Lucé, where Leonardo da Vinci spent the last three years of his life, and the compelling Château Royal d'Amboise, which dominates the town centre.

Day 7

Arrive in Poitiers (*p398*) for morning coffee and a moment of stillness at the Notre-Dame-la-Grande (*p398*). Then spend the day driving through countryside and vineyards, stopping to buy fruit at roadside stalls and dip into tiny villages, before ending up at Toulouse.

→

Day 8

The university and aerospace metropolis of Toulouse *(p430)* has a charming old town and historic buildings, such as Basilique St-Sernin *(p431)*, France's largest Romanesque church, and Les Jacobins *(p430)*, famed for its 22-ribbed palm-tree vault. It takes a bit over an hour to drive to Carcassonne *(p472)*, a carefully restored medieval city with concentric walls and winding alleys. Explore the Château Comtal and walk atop the ramparts, then enjoy a traditional Occitan dinner at family-run restaurant La Marquiere *(p473)*.

Day 9

Set off for Nîmes *(p476)* to experience some of France's most impressive Roman monuments. Drop by the Maison Carrée *(p477)*, an elegant Roman temple, and Les Arènes *(p477)*, an amphitheatre with seating for 24,000; both are extraordinarily well-preserved. After picking up edibles at Les Halles (the food market), have a picnic at Les Jardins de la Fontaine *(p476)*. Have dinner on or around the lively place du Marché, then drive to Marseille for dinner at tiny Café des Épices *(p523)*.

Day 10

Discover the fascinating cross-cultural currents of the Mediterranean basin at Marseille's Mediterranean culture museum, MuCEM, then walk around the adjacent Villa Méditerranée, spectacularly canti-levered. Follow the scenic D559 via Calanques National Park, its jagged inlets accessible only by sea, to the vibrant town of Cassis *(p518)* and tuck into inspired seafood dishes at Angelina *(p523)*.

Day 11

Take an ambling route along the coast to Nice *(p506)*, capital of the Côte d'Azur. Check out the artists' impressions of the interplay between light and colour at the Musée Matisse *(p507)* and the Musée National Marc Chagall *(p506)*. Watch the sun set above the bay from the elegant, seafront promenade des Anglais, then dine at Paper Plane *(14 rue Gubernatis)*.

Day 12

Avignon *(p511)*, three hours northwest of Nice, is perhaps the archetypal southern French city, with its golden stone walls,

1 Carcassonne's soaring cathedral.

2 The narrow streets of Nice.

3 The calm water at Calanques.

4 A Lyonnais *bouchon*.

5 Paris's glorious Panthéon.

relaxing squares and warm sunlight, not to mention the hallowed halls of the 14th-century Palais des Papes *(p510)*. In the afternoon, carry on up the Rhône Valley to the thriving market town of Valence *(p382)*. Visit the Romanesque Cathédrale St-Apollinaire and inspiring Renaissance-era Maison des Têtes, embellished with the sculpted heads of ancient Greeks. End the day with dinner at innovative restaurant Têtedoie *(p371)* in Lyon *(p370)*, France's sophisticated second city. Fall asleep at Le Royal *(www.lyonhotel-leroyal.com)*, a 19th-century boutique hotel which hosted the Beatles and Sophia Lauren in its day.

Day 13

Awake with perfectly prepped barista coffee at La Boîte à Café *(3 rue Abbé Rozier)*. Lyon is one of France's culinary capitals *(p366)*, with several marvellous markets and cute little *bouchons* (bistros) lining every street. Wander around medieval and Renaissance Vieux Lyon (Old Town) and the city-centre Presqu'île, a narrow peninsula at the confluence of the Saône and Rhône rivers, then duck

into Les Halles de Lyon market *(102 Cours Lafayette)* to gather everything you might need for a picnic. Walk east, across Pont Lafayette, and drop into the Musée de l'Imprimerie where the history of printing is documented through fascinating, millennia-spanning exhibits *(p370)*.

Day 14

Spend the morning wandering the galleries of Lyon's marvellous Musée des Beaux-Arts *(p372)* – don't miss Paul Gauguin's evocative *Nave nave Mahana* - meaning "delicious days" in Māori. Later, savour a leisurely lunch at the late Paul Bocuse's acclaimed restaurant L'Auberge du Pont de Collonges *(p371)*. When you've had your fill, hop on the fast train to Paris. Arrive at Paris Gare de Lyon in late afternoon and pass across the Pont d'Austerlitz into the Latin Quarter and the soft gloom of the Panthéon *(p142)*. Head west across the city to finish your journey at the top of the Eiffel Tower *(p122)* at sunset. As the City of Lights begins to twinkle in the falling dusk, reminisce over everything you've seen and done on your tour of France.

8 DAYS
in the Wine Country

Day 1

Start your tour in the centre of Reims at Cathédrale Notre-Dame *(p208)*, where 30 French kings were crowned over eight centuries. Swing past the Art Deco Café du Palais *(p215)* for a coffee and pastry under its inspiring stained-glass ceiling, then drive south through Montagne de Reims Natural Regional Park to Épernay *(p210)*, self-proclaimed capital of fizz. Pop into La Cave à Champagne *(p215)* for simple Champenoise dishes and locally produced champagnes.

Day 2

After a quick breakfast, get on the road for Troyes. Stop for a *petit pause* at Chez Gus *(29 rue Molé)* and a wander through the city's quaint half-timbered centre. By the late morning, you will have arrived in the lovely hilltop village of Vézelay *(p318)*. Check into SY La Terrasse hotel *(www.vezelay-laterrasse.com)* and ask for a room overlooking the imposing Basilique Ste-Madeleine. Come evening, head back to the hotel's restaurant for a home-cooked dinner made with local produce.

Day 3

Pick up a croissant from a *boulangerie*, then drive an hour west through Auxerre *(p322)*, which bears the scars of 20th-century wars. Continue west to Orléans *(p308)*, the city Joan of Arc was famous for liberating. In the old quarter, head to Les Becs à Vin *(www.becsavins.com)* to enjoy a dinner of *rillons* (slow-cooked pork belly) with a glass of expertly paired wine. A 15-minute walk past the statue of Joan of Arc in place du Martroi takes you to Hôtel de l'Abeille *(p305)* and bed.

Day 4

Fuel up on pastries and freshly squeezed orange juice in the hotel's art-filled dining room, then drive 45 minutes southwest to the magnificent Château de Chambord *(p294)* for a glimpse of castle life (be sure to walk up the magnificent double-helix staircase to the roof). Enjoy lunch at a café overlooking the village square a short walk from the château, then clear the cobwebs with a walk through the grounds. Stay on the estate overnight in a self-catering *gîtes (www.chambord.org)*.

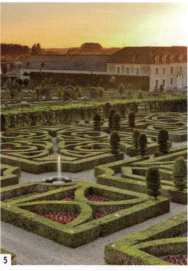

1 A verdant vineyard.

2 The old walls of Vézelay.

3 The magnificent Château de Chambord on Le Cosson canal.

4 Amboise's bustling central square.

5 The garden at Château de Villandry.

Day 5

Take one last walk around the château's lovely estate, then follow the curve of the Loire river to the attractive riverside town of Amboise (p304), where the gorgeous Château Royal d'Amboise has a bloody history and panoramic views. On Sunday morning, Amboise hosts an unmissable 200-stall food market along the river. Come evening, take a noctural ramble through the vineyards of nearby Château de Chenonceau (p292). Return to Amboise for a well-deserved rest.

Day 6

Enjoy a relaxing morning at Amboise's Le Clos Lucé, Leonardo da Vinci's home during the last three years of his life; its lovely gardens display models of the great Italian's many extraordinary inventions. Spend the afternoon brushing up on tasting notes at the wine cellar Cave Duhard (www.caves-duhard.fr); set in a troglodyte cave, there are bottles from as far back as 1874. Put everything you've learned to the test over a delicious meal at Restaurant le 36 (36 Quai Charles Guinot).

Day 7

Indulge in a sweet breakfast of *puits d'amour* (flaky pastry filled with custard cream and rum) at Pâtisserie Bigot (2 Rue nationale), and then drive downriver to admire the gardens of Château de Villandry (p302). Continue on towards Saumer, where Bouvet Ladubay (www.bouvet-ladubay.fr) offers bicycle tours of their subterranean wine caves, along with the chance to sample their wines. Return to Saumur for a night at the elegant, riversider Hôtel Anne d'Anjou (www.hotel-anneanjou.com).

Day 8

A leisurely drive through the countryside is just the way to say farewell to wine country. Stop off to admire vineyards along the way to the dynamic university city of Nantes (p299), one-time capital of Brittany. There, spend the morning at the Château des Ducs de Bretagne, which chronicles the city's rich history. Linger over dinner at the storied restaurant La Cigale (www.lacigale.com) where the meal is elevated to a masterpiece.

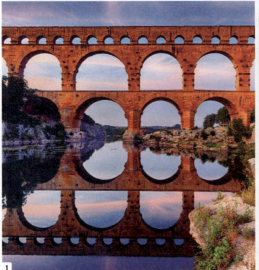

7 DAYS
Coast to coast

Day 1

Arrive in Marseille *(p528)* and get to know the city on foot before dipping into the Musée des Civilisations de l'Europe et de la Méditerranée. Stroll around the adjacent villa, then walk to quai du Port and board a boat out to the Château d'If. Spend a few hours exploring the prison island made famous by Alexander Dumas' *The Count of Monte Cristo* (1844). For dinner, return to the mainland and sample the seafaring city's signature dish at Chez Madie les Galinettes in Vieux Port.

Day 2

Set out early to drive to Nîmes *(p476)*, 90 minutes away. Here you'll find France's most complete set of Roman monuments; visit the Maison Carrée, an ancient temple, and Les Arènes, the city's amphitheatre. After picking up a picnic lunch at Les Halles (the city's food market), drive to the university city of Montpellier *(p474)*. Spend the afternoon taking in the city centre sights, then check into Domaine Bar, an 18th-century folie. Mingle with other guests over dinner around a shared table.

Day 3

Pick up some croissants and local jam for breakfast, and spend the morning in the one-time Cathar (Albigensian) stronghold of Béziers *(p482)*. Next, continue to Narbonne *(p482)* to visit Roman sites such as the 14th-century Gothic cathedral and cloister. Sample the local favourite, a *vin citronné* (white wine with lemon), and admire the "coral sea" – blush-coloured salt pans stretching away from the city. Pull up in Carcassonne *(p472)* at dusk for dinner in La Marquiere *(p473)* and a lavish night's rest at Hotel de la Cité *(p481)*.

Day 4

Get out your walking shoes and enjoy the battlement-wreathed city of Carcassonne on foot. Walk through the forbidding Port Narbonnaise, the city's main gate, and into the winding stone alleys, lined with very modern eateries and souvenir shops. Spend a couple of hours admiring the Château Comtal and the Gothic Basilique St-Nazaire. Arrive in Toulouse *(p430)* in time for a treat at Michel Sarran, where the chef's tasting menu is exceptional.

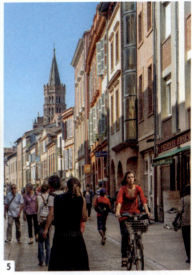

1. Pont Gard, Nîmes.
2. Medieval Carcassonne.
3. Marseille's signature *bouillabaisse*.
4. Bordeaux's La Cité du Vin.
5. The old city streets of Toulouse.

Day 5

Toulouse owes much of its modern-day dynamism to its university and Airbus, the European aeronautics conglomerate (advance-booked factory tours are available), but most visitors come to explore the city's centuries-old centre. Start at Basilique St-Sernin, France's largest Romanesque church, then stroll to the southern French Gothic-style Couvent des Jacobins. In the afternoon, peruse the sculptures and paintings of the Musée des Augustins, in a medieval Augustinian convent. Have dinner and a nightcap at bustling Brasserie Flo, a local institution with a huge menu.

Day 6

Start early and head northwest through plum orchards – producing the celebrated pruneaux d'Agen – to the river town of Agen (p444), just over an hour away. Visit the Musée Municipal des Beaux-Arts, whose prize exhibits include paintings by Goya and the Vénus du Mas, a marble statue from the 1st century BC. Set out on a meandering drive towards Bordeaux, dipping in and out of picturesque villages. Stop in Bergerac (p434) to explore the extraordinary Musée du Tabac, and take a short detour to the charming village of St-Émilion (p413). When you arrive in Bordeaux (p400), dine by candlelight at Tante Charlotte (p401). It's open late, so linger for a cocktail or three afterwards.

Day 7

Explore Bordeaux's 18th-century Grand Théâtre before strolling east to place de la Bourse. Admire its impressive Classical buildings reflected in the Mirroir d'Eau ("water mirror"), then head north along the quay to CAPC Musée d'Art Contemporain (p400), a contemporary art museum housed in a two-century-old warehouse. Stop for simple, seasonal lunch at Le Café Madd, in a cobblestoned courtyard next to Musée des Arts Décoratifs (p401). Later, take the riverside tram to La Cité du Vin, a museum dedicated to the "living heritage" of wine. Celebrate the end of your journey with dinner at La Brasserie Bordelaise, where farm-fresh duck and tasty profiteroles lure locals.

←

1 Riverside mansions, Lyon.

2 Palais des Papes, Avignon.

3 Exquisite morsels at Maison Pic, Vienne.

4 A Chateauneuf-du-Pape vineyard at sunrise.

4 DAYS
on the Rhône

Day 1

Morning After your coffee and *pain au chocolat*, explore Lyon (*p370*) on foot. Aim for the old quarter on the west bank of the Saone, or the grand Renaissance mansions that line the rue du Boeuf and rue Juiverie. When you've worked up an appetite, pick a neighbourhood *bouchon* (bistro) for a light lunch.

Afternoon Stroll up Fourviere to visit the Roman-era Grand Théâtre, before popping into the Musée de la Civilisation Gallo-Romaine for further insight into Roman Lugdunum (Lyon). Afterwards, walk to the Basilique Notre-Dame de Fourviere for breathtaking views.

Evening Indulge in a gourmet feast at the late Paul Bocuse's Auberge du Pont Collonges (*p371*). Retaining three Michelin stars in 2018, this is the temple of gastronomy against which all other great French restaurants are judged.

Day 2

Morning Set off early for Vienne (*p378*), where you'll discover a treasury of Roman and medieval architecture, including the Temple d'Auguste et Livie and the Romanesque-Gothic Cathédrale de St-Maurice. Reach Valence (30 minutes south of Vienne) in time for a cheerful lunch at L'Épicerie.

Afternoon Stroll through Valence's historic centre, pausing to take photos at the Kiosque Peynet. It was the inspiration for Raymond Peynet's sweetly romantic image of two young lovers, *Les Amoureux* (1942).

Evening Savour an aromatic feast at Maison Pic, Anne-Sophie Pic's highly regarded restaurant. Tastebuds satisfied, roll upstairs to one of the plush bedrooms for the night; ask for a room overlooking the Mediterranean garden.

Day 3

Morning Travel through the lush slopes of Côtes du Rhône to Orange (*p512*), where you can treat yourself to an ice cream from Regal Tendance. Then spend an hour or so marvelling at the Roman Théâtre Antique, a UNESCO World Heritage Site.

Afternoon Drive on to Châteauneuf-du-Pape (*p513*), surrounded by vines that produce world-renowned vintages. There's a superb view of the vineyards from the ruined Château des Papes at the top of the village. Enjoy a late afternoon vineyard and wine cellar tour at Château Fortia, thought to be the world's first wine-producer, and sample some of their vintages made from hand-picked grapes.

Evening A 30-minute drive brings you to Avignon (*p511*). Dine at La Vielle Fontaine, where the menu is dazzlingly eclectic, before spending the night at the deliciously intimate Au Cœur d'Avignon.

Day 4

Morning Set your alarm for an early start to beat the crowds to the Palais des Papes (*p510*) and drift about the serene halls with a self-guided audio tour. Afterwards, stroll to Les Halles, Avignon's covered market, for a fabulous seafood lunch at La Cabane d'Oleron.

Afternoon Cross the river to Villeneuve-lez-Avignon, a well-kept secret just across the Rhône from the tourist hustle of Avignon itself. Here you can climb the 176 steps to the top of the Tour Philippe le Bel for an unbeatable view.

Evening Arrive hungry at Naturabsolu, for fresh, belly-hugging vegan takes on French classics and more. Spend the final night of your tour at L'Atelier, a charming and great-value boutique hotel that features a leafy courtyard.

Wander Through Neighbourhood Markets

Local markets are a staple of every town and village across France, and a visit to the market is a social occasion – even major cities have regular markets in every neighbourhood. There's nowhere better to sample regional specialities, from pungent blue cheeses in Auvegne and toothsome canistrelli in Corsica, to the lavender-studded biscuits, honeys and liqueurs that make their way onto Provençal market stalls during summer.

→

A stall selling local meats and cheese in Ajaccio, Corsica

FRANCE FOR
FOODIES

The scent of freshly baked baguettes wafting down cobbled streets; the cheerful pop of bubbles in a champagne flute; the salty tang of just-caught oysters: in France, foodie dreams are made. Get ready to discover delicious regional dishes, mouthwatering markets and cook-it-yourself courses.

WORLD INTANGIBLE HERITAGE

Back in 2010, "the gastronomic meal of the French" *(le repas gastronomique)* was awarded World Intangible Heritage status by UNESCO. This social custom of gathering friends and family over a splendid meal to celebrate special occasions reveals just how deeply the French identify with their cuisine. Starting with the apéritif, this gastronomic gathering usually features four courses, accompanied with wine and culminating with liqueurs. The ritual is as important as the cuisine.

Take a Cookery Course

Learn how to make macarons in Paris, try your hand at haute cuisine or give traditional home cooking a go at a local farm. Often, courses include a visit to local markets with the chef, who will then show you how to use the ingredients to make iconic French dishes, such as in a hands-on class at La Cuisine in Paris *(www.lacuisineparis.com)*.

→

A fine-dining cookery course in Paris

Follow Michelin's Stars

Great food can be found across France, but the best eateries are those that earn that fateful accolade: the Michelin star. There were 621 awarded in 2018, with the highest concentration bestowed to restaurants in Paris, though gastronomic Lyon was not far behind. This city has a foodie heritage that has garnered an international reputation for excellence *(p366)*, and the Michelin judges agree. From five-star feasts to delicately plated masterpieces, in Lyon you're never far from a Michelin-starred delight.

Fine dining at L'Auberge du Pont de Collonges in Lyon

(p366)

TOP 5 FRANCE'S BEST CHEESES

Maroilles
This stinky orange-skinned cheese is eaten at breakfast.

Comté
Steeped in alpine air, this fruity hard cheese is ideal for tired hikers.

Époisses
An intense soft cheese best paired with Burgundy wine.

Roquefort
This iconic blue cheese is matured in the caves of the Larzac Plateau.

Camembert
A gloriously mellow cheese of Normandy.

A Dish for Every Region

Everywhere you go in France you'll find distinctive local cuisines which have developed over many centuries. In Normandy, fabulously fresh seafood dishes – such as *moules marinieres* (mussels in white wine sauce) – are *de rigueur*, while in the east, *tarte flambée* is found in every tavern. In the Alps, carbs rule: join locals in a warming *pot-au-feu*, a hearty stew where the meat, vegetables and broth are served separately.

A delicious plate of the Normandy classic *moules marinieres*

Festivals of Song

Perhaps the best time of year to soak up *chansons* is the summer. A host of festivals spring up across the country, showcasing new talent and celebrating the songs of the past. Whatever your tastes, you're more than likely to find something right for you. Throughout July, join *chanson* enthusiasts at the Festival de Montjoux, Pause Guitare in Albi, Francofolies de La Rochelle and Chansons de Parole in Barjac. In August, the place to be is Chansons et Mots d'Amou, a three-day festival of song with sing-alongs, banter and good humour. Among the biggest is the annual Festival de la Chanson Française du Pays d'Aix, where up to 10,000 fans flock to Aix-en-Provence in early October to hear the voices of their favourite *chanteurs*, as well as up-and-coming artists in the genre.

→

A crowd reaching for the stage at the Francofolies de La Rochelle festival in 2016

FRANCE FOR
CHANSONS

French *chansons* – poignant, lyrical, passionate songs – are the country's most beloved musical tradition. This distinctive style emerged in the early 20th century to become the soundtrack to French life. From sold-out stadiums and festivals to tiny cafés, the air is filled with the moving sound of *chansons*.

Catch Dreamy Gigs

Cafés and bars are a breeding ground for *chansons*, and even non-French speakers love to hear the voice of a *chanteur* or *chanteuse* rise above the crowd. In Paris, Montmartre, Pigalle and Edith Piaf's old haunt Belleville have the best bars for *chansons*. Beyond the City of Lights, melancholy crooning and artistic cabaret can be found everywhere from Tulle, self-proclaimed City of the Accordion, to Narbonne, home of Charles Trenet, who penned the dreamy ode "La mer".

←

Belgian-born singer-songwriter Tamino in concert at Café de la Danse in Paris

TOP 5 GREATEST CHANSONS

"La mer" (1946)
Charles Trenet

"La vie en rose" (1946)
Edith Piaf

"Tous les garcons et les filles" (1962)
Françoise Hardy

"Je t'aime… moi non plus" (1968)
Serge Gainsbourg and Jane Birkin

"Les Champs-Élysées" (1970)
Joe Dassin

→

A collection of mementos in the Musée d'Edith Piaf in Paris, and *(inset)* Jane Birkin and Serge Gainsbourg

PRESERVING THE HERITAGE: LE HALL DE LA CHANSON

Le Hall de la Chanson, or "Le Hall", preserves the heritage of France's most cherished musical style. Located in the Parc de la Villette, it is an ideal spot to seek out concerts, talks, seminars and other events in its 140-seat auditorium. You can even sing along at the weekly Café Chantant event held in Le Hall's new cabaret restaurant.

Discover Origin Stories

In Paris, Gainsbourg fans pay homage at his former home *(5 bis rue de Verneuil)*; the inside has remained untouched since his death in 1991, but it remains private and accepts no visitors. Across the river, near Cimetière du Père Lachaise, Edith Piaf is remembered in the intimate Musée Édith Piaf *(5 rue Crespin du Gast)*; full of mementos, it is opened by appointment only. Further south, you can follow in the footsteps of chanteuse Mireille Mathieu, who still lives in Avignon, while in the nearby fishing village of Sète, the streets are filled with the sounds of the legendary singer Georges Brassens, who made his home there.

Bask in the Sun King's Legacy

Louis XIV was one of the most powerful kings to rule France. He built the opulent palace and gardens at Versailles *(p170)*; the gold decorations and ornate Hall of Mirrors reflect his unlimited power. Take time to visit his birthplace at Saint-Germain-en-Laye - it's now the National Museum of Archaeology.

←

The overwhelmingly excessive Hall of Mirrors, symbol of Versailles

FRANCE FOR
HISTORY BUFFS

France is home to magnificent prehistoric cave paintings, mysterious megalithic sites, spectacular Roman theatres, lavish Renaissance châteaux and haunting memorials to those killed in both world wars. Everywhere you turn, inspiring sights attest to the country's long and colourful history.

Ramble Through Roman Ruins

France is strewn with superb Roman monuments, particularly in the south. Nîmes *(p476)* has a fantastic Roman history museum, and a well-preserved Roman amphitheatre, which is the setting for the Festival of Nîmes in summer; don't miss tickets to major acts. The Roman theatre in Orange also puts on concerts. Nearby, climb to the top tier of 2,000-year-old aqueduct Pont du Gard *(p489)* for tremendous views.

Did You Know?

Napoléon ordered trees to be planted along French roads so that his armies could march in the shade.

Prehistoric Monuments

Discover a remarkable record of early humanity in Vezere Valley, where the Lascaux caves *(p434)* are filled with spellbinding paintings created 20,000 years ago. In Brittany, walk among the more than 3,000 hand-hewn standing stones at Carnac *(p279)* – it's the world's largest megalithic site.

 HIDDEN GEM
Playing Roman

At the MuseoParc Alésia, you can explore a reconstructed Roman camp, watch thrilling Gallic-Roman battle reconstructions and take part in great family-friendly workshops and other events.

↑ Marvelling at some of France's oldest art in the Lascaux caves

Visit World War Memorials

Millions of soldiers died in World Wars I and II – and many lost their lives along the Western Front, which extended along northern France. Thousands flock to the region each year to remember and to search for information about ancestors lost in the fighting, at sites such as the Thiepval Memorial in the Somme *(p191)* and the Meuse-Argonne American Cemetery in Montfauc.

 ← Gravestones at the moving Pozieres memorial in the Somme

On the Trail of Napoléon

Revolutionary superstar turned despot Napoléon Bonaparte escaped forced exile in 1815 and returned to Paris before being defeated at Waterloo. Load up the car and trace his journey along the Route Napoléon, a 325-km (202-mile) stretch of road that winds through the mountains of Provence to Grenoble *(p376)*, where the general gathered his armies.

→ Napoléon looming large near Laffrey along the Route Napoléon

↑ The amphitheatre at Orange, mixing Roman and medieval styles

Cheer on the Cyclists

France is criss-crossed with cycle paths, so it's no surprise that cycling is more than just a pastime here. The world's most celebrated cycle race, the Tour de France, has 21 tough stages that take place over 23 days in July. Each year, the race takes a different route through France and neighbouring countries, although it always scales parts of the Pyrenees and the Alps, before finishing in Paris. Follow the riders to cheer on your favourites or create your own Tour and see the highlights of the country by bicycle.

Cyclists jostling for position during the Tour de France, the famous cycle race

Did You Know?

A polka-dot jersey is given to the cyclist who first reaches the mountain summits in the Tour de France.

FRANCE FOR
SPORTS FANS

France is sports mad. Here, football is the national obsession, with rugby and tennis also enormously popular. Quintessentially French traditional sports like snail racing and – perhaps the most uniquely French of all – pétanque still enjoy avid support, while the Tour de France draws a fanatical following.

Allez les Bleues!

Nothing rouses French passions like rugby, particularly in southern France. The Six Nations championship is a highlight on the country's sporting calendar, closely followed by the Rugby World Cup. The French team has won multiple times, and is affectionately known as "Les Bleus". Six Nations matches are held in the Stade de France in Paris, the largest stadium in Europe, where the atmosphere is always electric.

England battling France during the Six Nations, one of rugby's main championships

TOP 5 CURIOUS SPORTS

Gouren
Breton wrestling with barefoot contenders.

Jeu de Paume
There is still an annual championship held for this precursor of tennis.

Ballon au Poing
A handball game, hugely popular in Picardy.

Bont
Points are awarded for driving the ball through a croquet-style hoop.

Snail Racing
Losers are tossed into a pot and eaten.

Enjoy a Serving of a French Grand Slam

The French Open is one of the world's most prestigious tennis championships. Watch from the stands or, inspired, hit the courts at Nice's Lawn Tennis Club *(www.niceltc.com)* or atop Gare Montparnasse *(www.paris.fr)*

→

Daria Kasatkina playing on the famous clay courts during the 2018 French Open in Paris

Play Pétanque

Ah, the click of pétanque on a balmy summer evening – it's the sound of France. This bowling game's current form originated in Provence in the late 19th century. Settle in at a traditional café and watch the locals, or perhaps join in yourself. In the Basque country, you're more likely to see pelota, a handball game played on a court, being enjoyed.

←

Locals bowling during summer in Cannes

Glorious Galleries

Beyond Paris, France boasts a line-up of extraordinary art museums and galleries. Exhibitions of contemporary art flourish in the Pompidou in Metz *(p228),* while in the Roubaix area of Lille *(p200)* the curious La Piscine is home to Musée d'Art et d'Industrie. Set in a former Art Deco swimming pool, the latter gallery displays 19th- and 20th-century artworks throughout the refurbished building, including around the ornate pool. In Nice, the glorious Musée Matisse *(p505)* and Musée Chagall *(p504)* are devoted to two of France's most beloved artists.

→

The intriguing La Piscine museum, with artworks arranged around a swimming pool

Did You Know?

Many of the major galleries offer free entry on the first Sunday of each month.

FRANCE FOR
ART LOVERS

Unsurprisingly, the array of world-class art on show in France is dazzling. Here you can visit the beautiful landscapes that inspired such artists as Cézanne, Picasso and Van Gogh, as well as take in some of the finest art museums in the world.

Sketchpad in Hand

Most major French museums allow you to sketch and paint in the galleries, although you may need prior permission to bring an easel. Surprisingly few offer workshops, but there are artist-led drawing and painting classes in the Louvre and other top museums. Monet's home at Giverny draws thousands annually to sketch, as does the extraordinary light of the French Riviera. Painting and photography tours can be arranged through tourist offices – or follow in Monet's footsteps and paint at local attractions.

←

An artist at work in the gardens of Claude Monet's home, Giverny

IMPRESSIONISM

The most famous art movement to have originated in France, Impressionism emerged in the late 19th century. Among the earliest advocates of this style were Monet, Degas and Renoir, who were inspired by Manet and broke with the formal tradition that previously dominated. Painting outdoors, they used delicate brush work, as well as light, movement and colour to capture a fleeting moment.

Outdoor Artworks

From murals to stunning statues, graffitti to light installations, public art in France is a great way to indulge in a bit of culture on the cheap. Enormous murals by the CitéCreation collective are found in numerous French cities, including Lyon, Marseille and Paris, while the bold Le Voyage à Nantes festival brings new art to Nantes *(p298)* every year.

↑ Rodin's famed *Le Baiser* in the Jardin des Tuileries

French Artists at Home

The homes of some of France's most revered artists, including Monet and Rodin, have been converted into museums where artworks are complemented by a glimpse into the artist's process. The French Riviera is especially flush with such museums, featuring abodes that once belonged to Picasso and Van Gogh, while Monet's Giverny *(p255)*, is a magical place most known for its breathtaking gardens.

↑ Visitors studying a piece at the Musée Picasso in Antibes

Champagne Caves and Cellar Tours

A glass of bubbly is central to the local heritage of the Champagne region, and the best way to get to know both is to visit some of the 250 km (155 miles) of cellars and Gallo-Roman galleries where the good stuff is aged. Reims is the epicentre of champagne houses, home to world-famous producers such as Veuve Cliquot and Taittinger. Ruinart, established in 1768, is the world's oldest; take a walk through its *crayères* (chalk cellars, where the wines are aged) – the view is spectacular. For biodynamic wines, visit the boutique de Sousa cellars in the charming village of Avize.

INSIDER TIP
Cheers!

When toasting, the French commonly wish each other "*Santé*", or "good health", before they clink glasses. You might also hear "chin-chin" (which mimics the sound the glasses make when they touch).

Visitors wandering one of the many champagne cellars in Reims ↑

FRANCE
UNCORKED

France's vineyards have a longstanding reputation for yielding some of the world's finest wines – but that's not all. The fruits of orchards and hops fields are also pressed and distilled into heady brews, and maybe even a signature cocktail designed to pack a punch. Raise a glass to the country's beverages!

Cocktail Hour

The spiritual home of the *bon viveur*, France is the perfect destination for cocktail connoisseurs. In Paris, seek out the fashionably louche Lulu White (p159), while the top address in Nice is Le Negresco (p505). For those keen to create rather than simply imbibe, there are many workshops available. Learn the tricks of the trade from mixologists across Paris, from the Four Seasons' Georges V to the Ritz, home of the mimosa.

←

A bartender crafting a pale lemon cocktail at a top Parisian restaurant

Go Beyond the Grape

France is home to a vast array of beer, cider, liqueurs and *eaux de vie* (brandies made with fruit other than grapes). Round out an evening with a smooth Cognac in Normandy, or a glass of *eau de vie* in Alsace. In Brittany, join the locals by pairing cider with crêpes; and on a balmy summer evening in the south, take to an outdoor table to sip a glass of *pastis* (an aniseed-flavoured liqueur) before dinner.

← Men sampling amber glasses of Cognac

Come Harvest Time

Festivals celebrating a bountiful year abound across France. The best of the wine festivals must be the epic Bordeaux Wine Festival and its Marathon du Medoc counterpart. The latter winds through the region's vineyards, with runners marking every mile with a glass.

→ Athletes pounding past vineyards in the Marathon du Medoc

The Rural Heart of France

Right in the middle of France, yet largely unknown by visitors, the mountainous Auvergne is mainly rural. It's an ideal destination for outdoor activities such as hiking and biking, and there are even a couple of small ski resorts. If that sounds too much like hard work, set up camp in the genteel spa town of Vichy *(p350)*.

→

A hiker surveying the sunrise in the Auvergne

FRANCE
OFF THE
BEATEN PATH

There's no shortage of world-famous sights in France, but there are also plenty of opportunities to escape the crowds. Plunge into the great outdoors, feast on delicious regional cuisine and succumb to an appealingly slower pace of life – this is France at its most authentic.

The Second Face of the South

Penetrate the interior of Provence and you'll discover a different world from the celebrity haunts along the coast. Here you can explore dreamy villages like ochre-hued Roussillon and endless perfumed lavender fields around Gordes *(p513)*.

A traveller taking in the lavender fields surrounding the abbey in Gordes

Sweet Valley Living

The Vallée du Lot *(p357)*, more mellow neighbour of the Dordogne, is perfect for an unhurried taste of authentic French life. Drift through sleepy stone villages like Puy l'Évéque or Saint-Cirque-Lapopie, or the handsome medieval town of Cahors *(p436)* with its glorious sunflower fields. Throughout the valley, fabulous riverside cycling paths lead to child-friendly beaches.

→

Saint-Cirque-Lapopie, a hilltop village in the Lot Valley

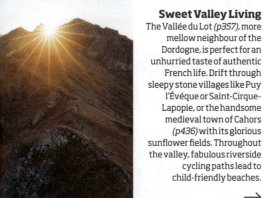

A Rustic Haven for Foodies

Stretching along the Swiss border, Franche-Comté is a pristine paradise that's bursting with rustic French specialities – think excellent charcuterie, cheeses and some delicious wines. The biggest draw is Besançon *(p337)*, a city famed for clock-making that is crowned by a UNESCO-listed citadel. Tiny villages dot rural valleys, ideal for slow, meandering exploration.

←

A tempting cheese board, ubiquitous in Franche-Comté

FRANCE'S SECRET PASTIME

In the summer months, the cities empty as the French pour into the countryside to return to nature. Camping is enormously popular in France, with both rugged sites for the self-sufficient and chic glamping spots housed in yurts or treehouses. One of the best ways to experience camping in France is to seek out the *camping à la ferme* sites *(www.camping france.com)*. These are tiny campsites on local farms, where there are just a handful of pitches and your only neighbours will be curious hens.

Unpopulated Pyrénées

For mountains, valleys and waterfalls minus the crowds, make for the Pyrénées Orientales. The sacred Catalan mountain of Canigou *(p478)* is well off the tourist track; or further south, head to artsy little Collioure *(p480)*, which is little changed from the anchovy port beloved of Matisse and André Derain.

↑ Families hiking the beautiful landscapes of the Pyrénées Orientales

Music in the Air

France's most famous music festival – the 24-hour Fête de la Musique, held annually on 21 June – has now spread to more than 120 countries, and remains extraordinarily popular throughout France itself. Bands take over the streets and squares, and street parties and food stalls keep the party going all night long. Alternatively, the Nuits Sonore in Lyons (held in late May/early June) is one of the coolest electronic music festivals anywhere in Europe, or you could rock till you drop at the Rock en Seine festival in Paris (late August).

→

Musicians performing as part of the renowned Fête de la Musique in Marseille

10 million
—
The average number of people who join the celebrations at Fête de la Musique.

FRANCE FOR
FESTIVALS

Village festivals honouring a patron saint or the wine harvest or a local food. Lavish city festivals celebrating music, theatre and the performing arts. Celebrations of cinema or the circus. Whenever and wherever you are in France, there's always something going on.

Celebrating Circus Arts

The French adore circuses – and not just the old-fashioned kind. They are renowned throughout the world for new-generation circuses, which combine theatrical performance with a 21st-century take on traditional circus skills. Join thousands of visitors in the big top at the biggest, the Festival International du Cirque de Massy each January – just stick to the human acts.

←

Trapeze artists balancing at the Festival International du Cirque de Massy

TOP
5
JAZZ
FESTIVALS

Nice Jazz Festival (Jul)
A glitzy event.

Paris Jazz Festival (Jun & Jul)
Held in the Parc Floral
on summer weekends.

Jazz in Marciac (Jul & Aug)
A three-week festival
with big-name acts.

Jazz à Juan (Jul)
Always features New
Orleans jazz bands.

Jazz à Vienne (Jun & Jul)
Hosted in the town's
Roman theatre.

Traditional Carousing

Celebrations of traditional French culture abound, and are a great way to discover more about France's minority cultures. Experience authentic Breton culture at Lorient's Festival Interceltique, a celebration of song and dance in traditional costumes. In the Pyrénées, Les Fêtes de Bayonne is hosted each July, inviting visitors to join the *festayres* (revellers) and paint the town red.

→

A parade at the Festival
Interceltique in Lorient

Fabulous Film Festivals

Cannes might be the industry highlight, but France boasts several other prestigious film festivals. Open to anyone, the week-long Lyon Festival of Light revels in films new and old, with screenings and themed evenings that make it a favourite for families and night owls. The Clermont-Ferrand Short Film Festival, with the second-largest audience after Cannes, shows only short films, while the Annecy International Animation Film Festival has free open-air screenings.

←

Watching a short at
Clermont-Ferrand

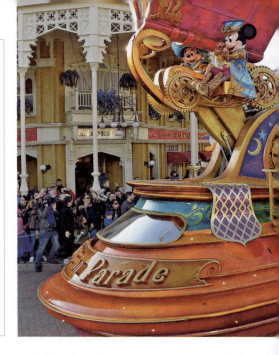

TRAVELLING WITH LITTLE ONES

Travelling with young children in France has certain challenges, as there are often limited facilities for breast-feeding or nappy changing. French children are bafflingly well behaved, and are often kept to a tighter schedule of naps and snacks than yours may be used to. Luckily there are lots of parks where kids can let off steam, and you'll find plenty of family-friendly restaurants. High chairs are not widely available, so you may wish to bring a travel version.

FRANCE FOR
FAMILIES

Home to fairy-tale castles, fun parks and circuses, France is a great family destination. Even in big cities, there's always a nearby green space to run around in, and most attractions are kid-friendly. Whether you're canyoning in the Alps or relaxing on the Riviera, there's plenty of family fun to be had.

The Great Outdoors

France's landscapes beg to be explored. Coastal rock pools and glaciers like Mer de Glace will fascinate smaller children. Bigger kids can enjoy snorkelling in the picturesque bays of the Calanques or try their hand (and legs) at surfing in Biarritz (p458), where Jo Moraiz Surf School (www.jomoraiz.com) offers lessons for kids. On dryer land, the Voies Vertes network of converted train lines in Brittany are ideal for young cyclists.

A family looking over the Mer de Glace glacier in the Alps

Epic Theme Parks

Disneyland® Paris (p174), just outside the French capital, is the most visited theme park in Europe. All the family favourites are here, from parades featuring beloved characters such as Mickey Mouse and Cinderella, to some truly hair-raising rides, including the famous Star Wars Hyperspace Mountain and the Rock 'n' Roller Coaster. It's actually two parks in one: Disneyland (based on the US theme parks) and Disney Studios (dedicated to cinema and TV), so thrill-seekers will be spoiled for choice. Further south, Futuroscope (p404), on the outskirts of Poitiers, is a cinematography-themed park that packs in the wow factor for technophiles of all ages with its vision of the future and rides. Many attractions change every year, so you'll need no excuse to keep coming back for more.

←

Popular Disney characters topping a colourful parade float in Disneyland® Paris

Rainy-Day Favourites

If the sun doesn't shine, you'll still find plenty to entertain the whole family. Here, there are scores of child-friendly museums, including Paris's enormous Cité des Enfants at the Cité des Sciences et de l'Industrie (p157) or Le Petit Musée Fantastique de Guignol in Lyon (p370). You could also explore the spooky catacombs in Paris, or head to a performance by Cirque du Soleil.

→

Interactive display at the Cité de Sciences et de l'Industrie

Teenage Kicks

Arty adolescents will be thrilled by museums and galleries, from Paris's Centre Pompidou (p90) to converted swimming pool La Piscine in Lille (p200); adrenaline junkies can indulge the need for speed by, surfing, canyoning or heli-skiing; and music fans can take their pick of fantastic festivals (p50), from chilled-out Calvi on the Rocks in Corsica to the countrywide Fête de la Musique on 21 June.

←

Canyoning though caves in Provence

Glitz and Glamour

The French Riviera has long been a byword for glamour. The villas along the stunning southern coast are now the homes of billionaires and film stars, while the marinas at St-Tropez *(p520)* and Cannes *(p521)* are full of super yachts – especially during the Cannes film festival. Away from the fray, idyllic coves are ideal for dropping anchor and enjoying a bellini onboard.

A string of yachts bobbing gently in the calm waters of a calanque near Marseille

FRANCE FOR
BEACH LIFE

With more than 2,000 miles of coastline, France has enough sandy shores for everyone. Take your pick, from glamorous beaches – perfect for celeb-spotting – on the French Riviera, to wild, dune-backed strands on the islands of Ré or Oléron. You'll even find beaches in Paris once the summer heats up.

The Great Escape

Shake off the crowds in magical Brittany, which has scores of breathtakingly unspoiled beaches. The Côte de Granit Rose *(p270)* gets its name from the pink-tinged cliffs that tumble to the sea. A walking path, the Sentier des Douaniers, links the villages of Ploumanac'h and Perros-Guirec, with a host of coves to explore en route.

↑ Ploumana'h Lighthouse, guarding the rocky coastline of Brittany

The Old Resorts

The resort town of Deauville was once the jewel of the "Parisian Riviera", where wealthy Parisians flocked in the late 19th century. This golden spot on the Côte Fleurie (p252) still oozes vintage charm. It shares glorious beaches with nearby Trouville, more down-to-earth but no less appealing. Up the coast, dreamy Étretat inspired the Impressionists with its endless alabaster strands and soaring cliffs.

The stylish Art Deco beach huts at Deauville

 INSIDER TIP
City Beach

Each summer without fail, landlocked Paris transforms the banks of the Seine and the Canal St Martin into a family-friendly beach, with open-air pools and activities for kids.

Sunkissed Strands

If you're looking for sun, sea and sand, France delivers in spades. There are tourist hotspots aplenty on the Med – the best sandy beaches are in Argelès and Narbonne (p482) in Languedoc. The Grand Plage in St-Jean-de-Luz (p466), meanwhile, is a heavenly golden beach on the Atlantic coast, great for kids. And there are other first-rate strands in the north, such as those in Le Touquet (p202) or genteel Cabourg, Proust's old haunt.

 TOP 4 SECRET BEACHES

Îles Lavezzi
Head to southern Corsica for granite shores and translucent waters.

Calanque de Saint-Barthélémy
A spectacular stretch of coastline, dotted with miniature beaches.

Plage de la Bastide Blanche
Golden sands matched with crystal waters.

Plage de Notre Dame
A blissfully quiet beach on the island retreat of Porquerolles.

↑ Bird's-eye view of turquoise water on the French Rivieira, and children playing (inset)

Epic Public Spaces

The Centre Pompidou *(p90)* inspired love and hate in equal measure when it opened in 1977; today visitors marvel at its revolutionary design with its exposed mechanical workings. In Rennes, Christian de Portzamparc also pushed the boundaries of public architecture with his futuristic Champs-Libres cultural centre *(www.leschampslibres.fr)*.

The eye-catching Centre Pompidou with its "inside-out" design

FRANCE FOR
MODERN
ARCHITECTURE

In a country renowned for its châteaux and historic buildings, France is a surprisingly heavy hitter when it comes to modern architecture. From Le Corbusier to Jean Nouvel, luminaries have created extraordinary buildings across France, delightfully redefining the very function of architecture.

Astounding Feats of Engineering

The world's tallest bridge at 343 m (1,125 ft), the ethereal Millau Viaduct spans the gorges du Tarn *(p346)* in southern France, and has won numerous accolades for its innovative design. In the French Alps you'll find the Tignes Dam. Once the world's largest dam, nowadays it's famous for its enormous mural of Hercules.

The piercing spires of southern France's spectacular Millau Viaduct

Wondrous Residential Design

Iconic residential designs that draw architecture pilgrims to France include the E-1027 in Roquebrune-Cap-Martin *(p527)*. Completed in 1929, this diaphanous, light-drenched villa is considered a Modernist masterpiece. Light also plays a starring role in Pierre Chareau's Maison de Verre *(31 rue Saint-Guillaume)* in Paris, which boasts a stunning transparent façade.

←

The striking modernist villa E-1027, designed by Eileen Grey

↑ Visitors exploring the spectacular MuCEM in Marseille

JEAN NOUVEL: GALLIC MODERNIST

By "dematerializing" space in unexpected ways, Jean Nouvel's buildings break moulds. The first building by this celebrated architect to gain international acclaim was the Institut de Monde Arabe *(www.imarabe.org)* in Paris; its façade – inspired by the latticework windows of traditional Arabic architecture – is covered in mechanical "oculi" that open and close in response to sunlight. Nouve was awarded the prestigious Pritzker Architecture prize in 2008.

↑ The striking façade of La Fondation Louis Vuitton in Paris

Extraordinary Exhibition Spaces

Architect Rudy Ricciotti described his design for the MuCEM museum *(p528)* in Marseille as a building of "stone, water and wind". The stunning seafront museum is encased in a filigree skin that filters gorgeous light into the galleries. At night, it is dramatically illuminated by Yann Kersalé's light installations. Paris is home to La Fondation Louis Vuitton *(p150)*, which contains a world-class contemporary art collection and occupies an undulating, glass-and-titanium edifice by Frank Gehry.

TOP 4 ICONIC FRENCH NOVELS

Candide by Voltaire
Published in 1759 and widely banned for years.

The Three Musketeers by Alexandre Dumas
A swashbuckling epic, this is Dumas's most famous title.

Madame Bovary by Gustav Flaubert
This 1856 novel has an enduringly famous female protagonist.

The Stranger by Albert Camus
A novel that examines the fundamental absurdity of life.

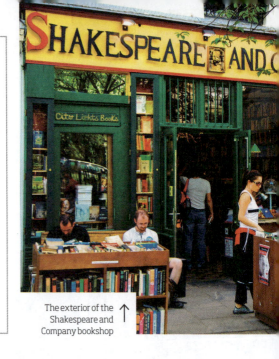

The exterior of the Shakespeare and Company bookshop ↑

FRANCE FOR
BOOKWORMS

If you like literature, you'll love France. There's plenty for writers and readers to celebrate, with literary festivals, inspiring bookshops and numerous opportunities to walk along the real streets that inspired your favourite work of fiction. Few countries reward the bibliophile so richly.

Literary Festivals

The Paris Book Fair is France's largest literary event, drawing huge crowds and fantastic writers across all genres. Fans of crime fiction should head to Lyon *(p370)* for the atmospheric Quais du Polar, an international festival that combines books, cinema and art. The Charroux's *(p408)* eponymous Literary Festival is a wonderful bilingual event in southwest France, which brings together English- and French-speaking writers.

←

The bustling stands of Paris Book Fair, which is held in spring every year

A Bounty of Bookshops

France offers an array of second-hand stalls to browse, from rare-book specialists to niche book boutiques. Shakespeare and Company has an expanded premises and even a new address in the Left Bank *(p132)*, and remains the city's most famous English-language bookshop and a mecca for writers and literary enthusiasts. Librairie Maupetit, Marseille's oldest bookshop, hosts events and workshops for readers of all ages. In Strasbourg *(p220)*, Librairie Kleber organizes stimulating salon-style debates between writers, psychoanalysts, historians and artists.

INSIDER TIP
Book Vendors

Forget fizzy drinks, vending machines in France can spit out a free short story to go. The first machine was installed in Grenoble in 2015, but they have now spread across France.

Plot It Out

Literary tours abound across France. Trace the plots of novels and the lives of your favourite authors, whether that's raising the ghost of Emma Bovary in Ry, or seeking out the childhood home of Colette *(p323)* in St-Sauveur-en-Puisaye. Self-guided tours are ideal on a budget.

→

Inside the home of the novelist Colette, now a museum

Cities of the Written Word

There are eight *villages de livre* (book towns) scattered across France. These medieval villages are a hub for bookish pursuits, with schools for binding restoration, calligraphy and more. Montmorillon *(p405)* is France's largest *cité de l'ecrit*, attracting hundreds of visitors to its book fair every year, while the Breton town of Bécherel is perhaps the prettiest, and is home to fantastic bookshops.

→

Writing display in Montmorillon

Monumental Mountains

Mont Blanc (4,809 m/15,777 ft) is the highest mountain in the Alps and the 11th-highest on earth. Its craggy silhouette – often snow-capped, even in August – is instantly recognizable. The Barre des Ecrins is France's second-highest peak, and a mecca for winter sports, as well as summertime climbing and hiking. The French Pyrenees are equally beautiful, and feature some spectacular natural sights, such as the magnificent Gavarnie Falls in the Pyrénées National Park.

A lone climber crossing the towering snowy peak of Mont Blanc

FRANCE FOR
INSPIRING
LANDSCAPES

France has few rivals when it comes to spectacular scenery. It's bounded by the Alps to the east, the Atlantic to the west and the Mediterranean to the south; a dramatic geography that results in an array of breathtaking landscapes, from glowing fields of lavender to wave-pounded Breton cliffs.

Fields of Flowers

All summer long, powder-puff bushes of lavender bloom across France, a blaze of pale purple with a heady scent. The charming village of Sault is considered the epicentre of lavender production, but you can find these picture-perfect fields throughout the countryside, surrounding rocky hills like Grignan *(p384)* and medieval villages such as Gordes *(p513)*.

The sun sinking below the horizon of a purple lavender field in Sault, Provence

Great Gorges

France is scored with stunning gorges and canyons. The Gorges du Verdon are the deepest and perhaps the most spectacular: the intensely green river carves a narrow canyon through pale limestone cliffs. The Gorges du Tarn are just as impressive, its looming cliffs studded with tiny stone villages to explore. Both are fantastic areas for outdoor activities.

→

A kayaker tackling the narrow waters of the Gorges du Verdon

MONET'S STUDY OF LIGHT IN ROUEN

In the 1890s, Claude Monet made almost 30 paintings of Rouen's cathedral, several of which can be seen in the Musée d'Orsay (*p136*). He studied the effects of changing light on the west façade, putting colour before contour. The leading Impressionist painter said he conceived the series when watching light hit a country church, "as the sun's rays slowly dissolved the mists... that wrapped the golden stone in an ideally vaporous envelope".

↑ Dramatic cliff formations in Étretat, along the northern coast of France

Gorgeous Coastlines

Perhaps the most glamorous coastline in the world, the stunning Côte d'Azur stretches along the Mediterranean from Menton to Toulon. It's a favourite retreat for the rich and famous, as the lavish mansions and glossy, yacht-filled marinas attest. If you prefer something wilder, head to the Côte de Granit Rose in Brittany, or the gloriously craggy Basque coast around Biarritz.

A YEAR IN
FRANCE

JANUARY

△ **Paris Fashion Week** (*mid–late Jan*). The world's top designers and models strut their stuff.

Truffle Festival (*mid–late Jan*). The black Périgord truffle is celebrated in its home town of Sarlat-la-Canéda with huge feasts.

FEBRUARY

△ **Nice Carnival** (*mid-Feb–early Mar*). The biggest street event in the Riviera, with elaborate floats, feathered costumes, and dancing day and night.

Six Nations Rugby (*early and late Feb*). One of France's most important sporting fixtures, with Europe's best playing France at home.

MAY

△ **Cannes Film Festival** (*mid-late May*). The world's premier film industry event.

Night of the Museums (*mid-May*). Over 1,200 French museums stay open to 1am, with free admission and special activities for night owls.

Roland Garros (*late May–early Jun*). The French Open tennis tournament, one of the world's four Grand Slam events.

JUNE

24 Hours of Le Mans (*mid-Jun*). A gruelling test of both car and driver, one of the world's most important motor races.

△ **Marche des Fiertés** (*last two weeks*). At the culmination of the Fortnight of Pride, thousands flock to the capital to celebrate the LGBT+ community in style.

SEPTEMBER

Braderie de Lille (*early Sep*). Dating from the 12th century, this is Europe's biggest flea market, with 10,000 vendors and millions of bargain hunters.

△ **Heritage Days** (*mid-Sep*). All across France some 16,000 landmark buildings normally closed to the public are opened for free.

OCTOBER

△ **Nuit Blanche** (*5 Oct*). The Paris art scene stays up all night. Galleries, museums and restaurants host free dance and music events.

Tous au Restaurant (*first two weeks*). A nationwide movement "to get everybody to a restaurant". Promotional menus, cooking classes and new culinary creations abound.

MARCH

Mulhouse Carnival (*mid-Mar*). Celebrating the end of winter, France's most outlandish carnival rivals those in Germany and Switzerland.

△ **Paris International Book Fair** (*mid-Mar*). One of the largest book fairs in Europe, avidly attended by British and American writers.

APRIL

△ **Paris Marathon** (*mid-Apr*). Over 40,000 long-distance runners throng the streets of Paris for the biggest foot race in the country.

Roman Games (*last weekend*). Actors in Roman garb re-enact gladiatorial combats In the Nîmes arena, complete with dancing girls.

JULY

△ **Tour de France** (*late Jun–late Jul*). The single most-attended sport in the world, with 15 million spectators lining the roadways to cheer on cyclists chasing the yellow jersey.

Paris Plage (*early Jul–end of Aug*). For those who cannot get to the beach, the city of Paris brings sand to the Seine for the whole summer.

Bastille Day (*14 Jul*). The French national day, celebrating the storming of the Bastille prison.

AUGUST

△ **Soöruz Lacanau Pro Surf** (*mid-Aug*). Europe's oldest pro-surfing competition, near Cap Ferret on the west coast. Riders come from all over the world to put themselves to the challenge.

Summer holidays (*all month*). Many factories shut down for the whole month and it seems like the entire country heads for the beaches. Attractions and museums extend hours accordingly.

NOVEMBER

△ **Beaujolais Nouveau** (*3rd Thu*). The new vintage is released at 12:01am, with parades and ceremonies and a great deal of "tasting".

Les Trois Glorieuses (*3rd Sun*). The "Three Glorious Days" in Burgundy draw fine-wine enthusiasts from all over the world for tastings of new vintages, processions and an auction.

DECEMBER

△ **Christmas Markets** (*to 24 Dec*). Hundreds of towns and villages have special markets, but the most outstanding are those in Colmar and Strasbourg in Alsace to the east.

Critérium de la Première Neige (*early Dec*). Snow flies at the first skiing competition of the season, hosted in Val-d'Isère.

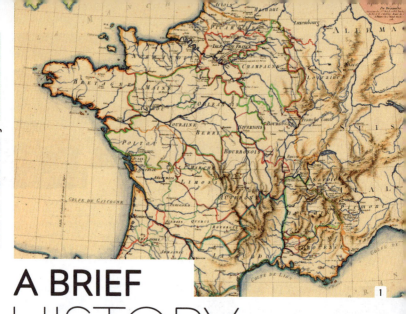

A BRIEF
HISTORY

One of Europe's oldest nation-states, France has been a cultural melting pot for millennia and subject to a particularly rich variety of influences. It has survived thousands of years of invasion, revolution and plagues, and emerged on the world stage with a style now very much its own.

Prehistoric France

Artifacts found in the Hérault Valley (southern France) indicate that early humans inhabited France at least 1.5 million years ago. About 400,000 years ago, Neanderthals started spreading across France, leaving behind tools in places like the gorges du Verdon. A skull dated to c. 28,000 BC found at Cro-Magnon gave its name to the earliest known *Homo sapiens*, who left behind extraordinary art in caves like Lascaux. Around 6000 BC, after the end of the Ice Age, a major shift in lifestyle occurred, as people started settling down to herd animals and cultivate crops.

Did You Know?
———
The caves at Cro-Magnon were excavated by Édouard Lartet, widely considered the father of paleontology.

Timeline of events

28,000 BC
The first Venus sculptures are created, which possibly represent fertility goddesses.

15,000 BC
Prehistoric artists begin painting the caves of Lascaux.

7000– 4500 BC
The Celts arrive from the west.

600 BC
The Greeks establish a colony at Marseille.

500 BC
Celtic nobles bury their dead with riches such as the Vix treasure.

Roman Gaul

Celts trickled in from the east in the first millennium BC and developed a hierarchy of druids, warriors, farmers and artisans. They became known as Gauls to the Romans, who conquered all of what is now France between 125 and 51 BC. The Romans built roads, bridges and aqueducts, as well as temples and amphitheatres, but the empire in Gaul collapsed in the second half of the 5th century AD, as rival barbarians battled for supremacy.

The Frankish Realm

Out of these dark ages emerged the Frankish realm, dominated by the Merovingian dynasty (486–751), then by the Carolingians (751–987), whose power was threatened for several centuries by Arab invasions from Spain. The Carolingian empire reached its apogee in 800 when Charlemagne (742–814), king of the Franks, was anointed Holy Roman Emperor. He expanded his empire across western Europe, but in 843, after years of civil war between rivals for the throne, it was carved up between his three grandsons, one of whom, Charles the Bald (823–877), became king of West Francia, the nation that would become known as France.

1 A historical map of France from 1787. ↑

2 Prehistoric painting of an ox, part of the stunning wealth of art at the Lascaux caves in southwestern France.

3 An amphitheatre in Orange, built by the Romans in the 1st century AD.

4 Oil portrait of the Holy Roman Emperor Charlemagne by German painter and theorist Albrecht Dürer, dated to around 1512.

31 BC
Augustus establishes the Three Gauls (*Gallia Celtica, Gallia Aquitania* and *Gallia Belgica*).

AD 508
Paris made capital of Frankish kingdom.

AD 843
The Treaty of Verdun creates West Francia, the forerunner of modern France.

125–51 BC
The Romans conquer and colonize Gaul.

AD 43
Lugdunum (Lyon) becomes the capital of the Three Gauls.

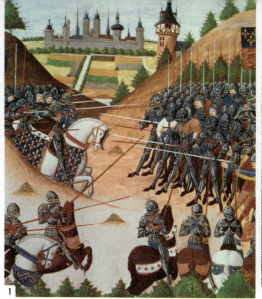

1

2

Medieval France

Clovis, baptized in 496, was the first Frankish ruler to convert to Christianity. As the Frankish realm evolved into a medieval nation-state, great abbeys like Cluny *(p332)* and Fontenay *(p316)* became wealthy and influential. The French fought the Angevin–Plantagenet rulers of England during the Hundred Years' War (1337–1453), while also battling to subdue Occitanie and the ambitious dukes of Burgundy, who sought to create a kingdom of their own between France and Germany.

Renaissance France

Following the French invasion of Italy in 1494, the ideals and aesthetic of the Italian Renaissance spread to France, reaching its height during the reign of François I, who invited artists such as Leonardo da Vinci and Cellini to his court. Catherine de Medici, widow of François's son Henri II, virtually ruled France through her sons, François II, Charles IX and Henri III. During their reigns, the Wars of Religion between Catholic and Protestant factions tore France apart, until a compromise was reached with the Edict of Nantes (1598) by Henri IV, first of the Bourbon line of kings.

↑ Catherine de Medici of Italy, who ruled France by proxy for years

Timeline of events

1337
The start of Hundred Years' War, which finally ends in 1453, with only Calais still in English hands.

1415
French defeated by Henry V of England at the Battle of Agincourt.

1593
Henri IV converts to Catholicism, ending the 30-year Wars of Religion.

1154
Henry Plantagenet, count of Anjou and (as Henry II) king of England, creates the Angevin realm, straddling France.

1348–52
The Black Death kills half the population in some cities.

The Sun King

France in the 17th century quickly became a major player on the world stage. Colonies were established in Canada, Indochina and the Caribbean. As powers behind the throne, Cardinals de Richelieu and Mazarin paved the way for Louis XIV, the "Sun King" whose court at Versailles (p170) became the glory of Europe. Louis built mighty citadels as he embarked on a series of wars with Spain, the Netherlands, England, Austria and Savoy.

Revolution and Empire

Louis XIV made France a great power, but his wars cost France dearly. In the 18th century, philosophers such as Voltaire and Rousseau challenged the aristocracy, but the monarchy's refusal to address the grievances of the people ultimately led to the revolution of 1789, followed by the execution of Louis XVI and his queen, Marie Antoinette, and the "Reign of Terror", in which thousands of aristocrats were sent to the guillotine. A young military genius, Napoléon Bonaparte, emerged from the chaos of the republic to make himself emperor in 1804. His empire lasted until 1815 and covered much of Europe at its peak.

① Depiction of the Battle of Formigny, 1450.

② Henri IV signing the Edict of Nantes.

③ Interior of the Château de Versailles.

④ Napoléon on horseback in the 1814 campaign.

Did You Know?

While popular myth says that Napoléon was particularly short, he was in reality around 5 ft 7 inches.

1682

The Royal Court moves to Versailles.

1756–63

France loses Canada and other overseas possessions to England.

1789

The French Revolution begins and feudal laws are abolished.

1792

Louis XVI is overthrown and the First Republic is established.

1804

Napoléon is crowned emperor; 11 years later, he is defeated at Waterloo.

The Turbulent 19th Century

The restoration of the Bourbon monarchy following the defeat at Waterloo ushered in a century of much change. In 1830, Charles IX was overthrown and replaced by his cousin, Louis Philippe, who ruled until he was ousted in 1848, giving way to the Second Republic. Its president, Louis-Napoléon Bonaparte, declared himself Emperor Napoleon III in 1852. Under his "Second Empire" France expanded its overseas colonies in North Africa. Nice and Savoy were annexed to France, but defeat in the 1870–71 Franco-Prussian War led to the loss of Alsace and Lorraine to Germany. Another revolution saw the creation of the Third Republic in 1871, and more colonial expansion. The belle époque, a time of arts and culture, emerged at the end of the century.

World Wars I and II

France suffered terribly during World War I (1914–18), as almost 1.5 million French soldiers died. In World War II, France was defeated and occupied by German forces. Resistance fighters carried on the fight against the occupiers until France was liberated by US, British and Free French forces in 1944.

1 Scene from the French Revolution.

2 Ruins of St-Lô, August 1944.

3 Last flight of the Concorde, 2003.

4 Eiffel Tower lit up after the 2015 attack in Paris.

Did You Know?

As French forces approached Paris in 1944, Hitler ordered the city be razed – but he was disobeyed.

Timeline of events

1848
The July Monarchy is overthrown and the Second Republic is established.

1870–71
Defeat in the Franco-Prussian War leads to the loss of Alsace.

1889
The Eiffel Tower is built in Paris

1914–1918
WWI breaks out with the German invasion of France.

1940–44
Germany occupies France during World War II.

4

Modern France

Following World War II, France fought unsuccessfully to retain its colonial possessions. From the 1960s onward, old industries declined while new technology grew dramatically, and France became a world leader in aviation. Political turmoil in 1968, led by left-wing students and trade unions, almost toppled the government. In 1994 the Channel Tunnel opened, connecting Britain and France. France was among the six founding nations of the European Economic Community in 1957 and is now among the most influential members of the European Union.

France Today

In the 21st century France faced new threats from international terrorism, with more than a dozen attacks in Nantes, Nice, Marseille and Paris, leading to an increase in support for the far-right Front National. The party was, however, defeated in the 2017 presidential elections by the centrist En Marche party, led by Emmanuel Macron, suggesting that, at the heart of the country's framework, there remain the republic's principles of *liberté*, *égalité* and *fraternité*.

↑ Emmanuel Macron celebrating his 2017 election victory

1954

French colonial rule in Cambodia, Laos and Vietnam comes to an end.

1945

World War II ends and the Fourth Republic begins. Women are given the vote.

2003

The supersonic British-French Concorde makes its last flight.

1957

France helps found the EEC, forerunner of the EU, with five other nations.

2018

France wins the FIFA World Cup, beating Croatia 4-2.

EXPERIENCE
PARIS

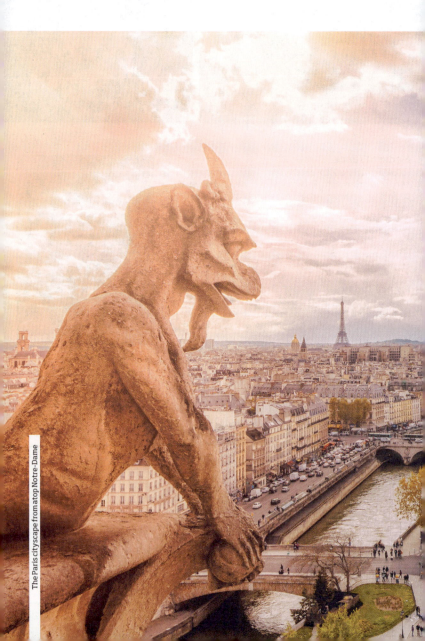

The Paris cityscape from atop Notre-Dame

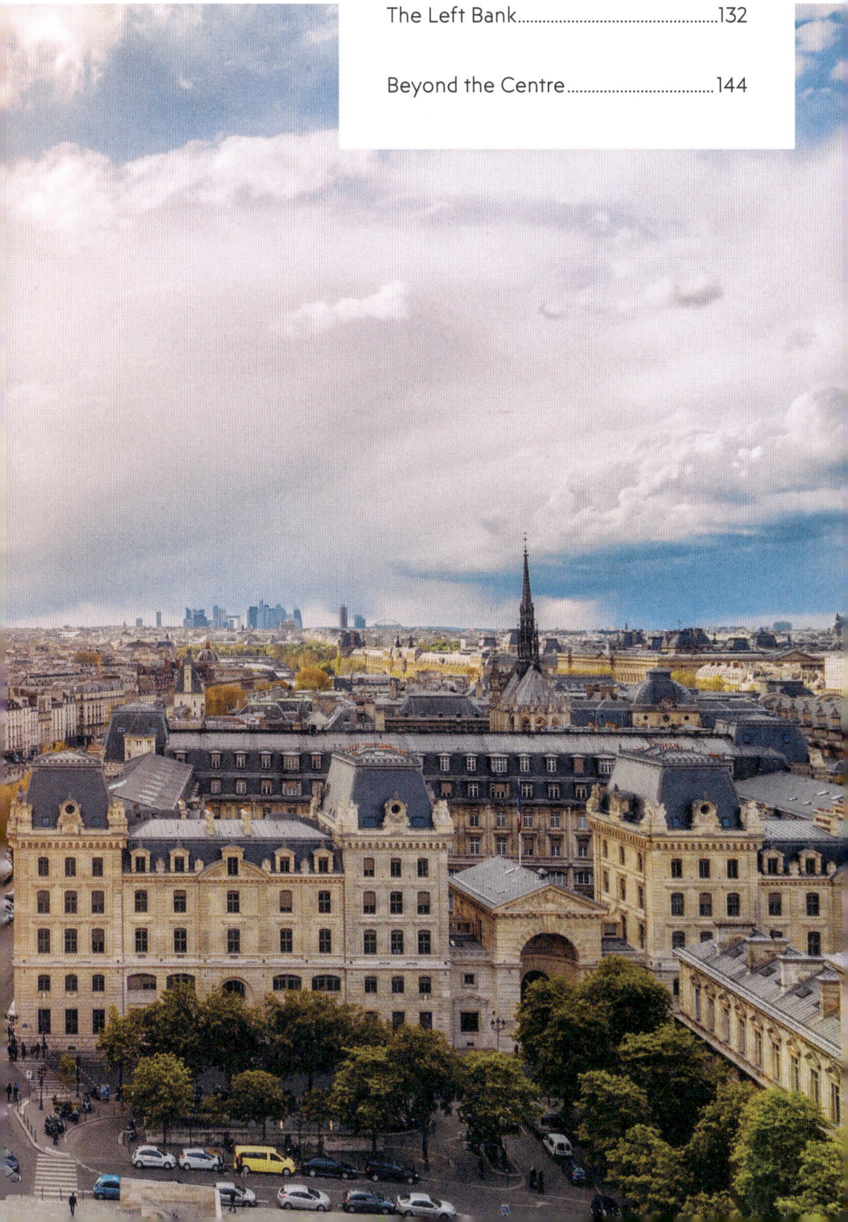

EXPLORE
PARIS

This guide divides Paris into four sightseeing areas, as shown on the map below, plus an area beyond the city centre. Find out more about each area on the following pages.

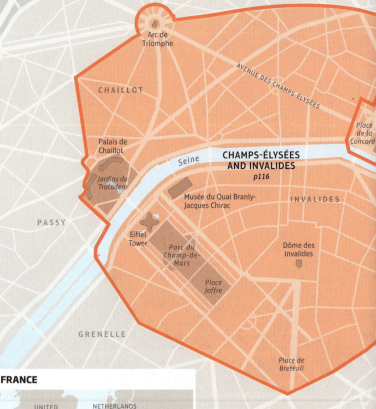

BATIGNOLLES

Parc Monceau

Arc de Triomphe

CHAILLOT

AVENUE DES CHAMPS-ÉLYSÉES

Place de la Concord

Palais de Chaillot

Seine

CHAMPS-ÉLYSÉES AND INVALIDES
p116

Jardins du Trocadéro

Musée du Quai Branly-Jacques Chirac

INVALIDES

PASSY

Eiffel Tower

Parc du Champ-de-Mars

Dôme des Invalides

Place Joffre

GRENELLE

Place de Breteuil

MONTPARNASSE

FRANCE

UNITED KINGDOM

NETHERLANDS

BELGIUM

GERMANY

Lille

PARIS

Strasbourg

Rennes

FRANCE

SWITZERLAND

Atlantic Ocean

Lyon

ITALY

Bordeaux

Toulouse

Marseille

SPAIN

Mediterranean Sea

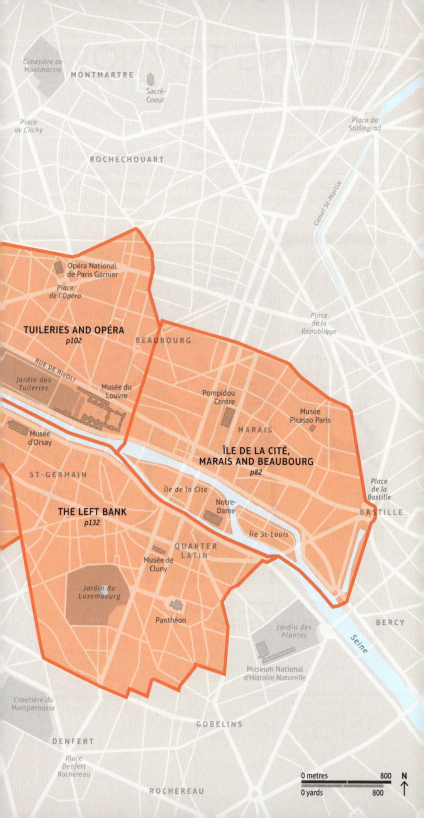

Cimetière de
Montmartre

MONTMARTRE

Sacré-
Coeur

Place
de Clichy

ROCHECHOUART

Place de
Stalingrad

Canal St-Martin

Opéra National
de Paris Garnier

Place
de l'Opéra

TUILERIES AND OPÉRA
p102

BEAUBOURG

Place
de la
République

RUE DE RIVOLI

Jardin des
Tuileries

Musée du
Louvre

Pompidou
Centre

Musée
Picasso Paris

Musée
d'Orsay

MARAIS

**ÎLE DE LA CITÉ,
MARAIS AND BEAUBOURG**
p82

ST-GERMAIN

Île de la Cité

Place
de la
Bastille

THE LEFT BANK
p132

Notre-
Dame

BASTILLE

Île St-Louis

**QUARTIER
LATIN**

Musée de
Cluny

Jardin du
Luxembourg

BERCY

Panthéon

Jardin des
Plantes

Seine

Museum National
d'Histoire Naturelle

Cimetière du
Montparnasse

GOBELINS

DENFERT

Place
Denfert
Rochereau

ROCHEREAU

0 metres   800

0 yards   800

N
↑

GETTING TO KNOW
PARIS

Paris is a patchwork of neighbourhoods, each with a history and essence all of its own. The Seine runs through the heart of the city, creating its Right and Left banks, and most sightseeing areas are enclosed by the Périphérique, a ring road that separates the city centre from the suburbs.

PAGE 82

ÎLE DE LA CITÉ, MARAIS AND BEAUBOURG

Located at the heart of Paris, the Île de la Cité is a cornucopia of must-see sights from the Notre-Dame to Sainte-Chapelle, masterpieces of gothic architecture. Former royal palaces double as administrative buildings – it's not a place to mingle with the locals, who instead flock to the grand streets and intriguing alleys of the Marais and Beaubourg. This area, on the Right Bank, is full of fashionable boutiques and restaurants, and the air entices with smells of falafel and pastries.

Best for
Epic sightseeing, history, shopping, dining, LGBT+ life

Home to
Notre-Dame, Centre Pompidou, Sainte-Chapelle

Experience
The awe-inspiring Gothic architecture of Notre-Dame and Sainte-Chapelle

PAGE 102

TUILERIES AND OPÉRA

The Musée du Louvre, with its infamous glass pyramid and *Mona Lisa*, bookends the stately Tuileries. At the other end of the district, with the famous eponymous manicured gardens and its cafés and art galleries in between, is the opulent Opéra Garnier. The area around this storied building is studded with theatres and grandly epitomizes Baron Haussmann's plans for Paris, with monuments at every intersection. Its broad avenues, lined with exquisite churches and wallet-emptying department stores, are filled with bustling crowds of Parisians. This is the place to stroll, shop and repeat, whether it's for rose-flavoured macarons from Ladurée's original shop or a luxury bag from Printemps.

Best for
The grand monuments of Parisian art and culture, shopping, entertainment

Home to
Musée de Louvre

Experience
Coming face to face with the Mona Lisa *before sampling pastries along Rue Montorgueil*

$\rightarrow$

PAGE 116

CHAMPS-ÉLYSÉES AND INVALIDES

This corner of town is grandiose and ornate, with the gold-topped Dôme des Invalides soaring against the skyline. Full of history and artifacts, it plays second fiddle to the neighbourhood's real star: the Iron Lady herself, the Eiffel Tower, rises at the edge of the river. Just across the river is the grand boulevard of Champs-Élysées, where the Arc de Triomphe sits. Away from the chaos of tours and lines, this district offers fine – and expensive – shopping and dining.

Best for
Sightseeing and fine dining

Home to
Arc de Triomphe, Eiffel Tower

Experience
A dip into the Petit Palais exhibition hall before splashing out on a terrace coffee on the Avenue des Champs-Élysées

PAGE 132

THE LEFT BANK

From Romans ruins to Hollywood backdrops, the Left Bank is beloved by Parisians and travellers alike. Every block seems to have a bookstore, and peppered among the tiny twisting streets are crêpe stands and dive bars, all offset by the grandeur of stunning sights such as the Panthéon, Musée de Cluny and St-Étienne-du-Mont church. In iconic St-Germain-des-Prés, cafés line the streets and squares – the chocolates and pastries are some of the city's best. While a smattering of museums and churches attracts tourists, locals continue to lay claim to this bohemian enclave.

Best for
People watching and history lovers

Home to
Musée d'Orsay

Experience
Local life at one of the legendary cafés while nibbling macarons and discussing philosophy like a student

BEYOND THE CENTRE

PAGE 144

More than just major monuments, Paris is a living, breathing city – particularly beyond the centre. Look past the famous landmark of the Moulin Rouge to the fashionable cobbled and quaint streets of Montmartre and Pigalle, where you can join the locals queuing for the best pastries in town, or head to the warren of alleys around the Canal St-Martin for artisan coffee. Further out, the natural parks of Bois de Vincennes and Bois de Boulogne are the city's green lungs; breathe deep before heading down into the Catacombes, where an artfully macabre labyrinthe awaits.

Best for
Getting off the beaten track in your own style

Home to
Sacré-Coeur, Cimetière de Père-Lachaise

Experience
The sound of buskers on the steps in front of the Sacré-Coeur while watching the sun set over the city

1

2

3

4

① The opulent Hall of Mirrors in the palace of Versailles.

② Cruising the Seine at sunset.

③ A classic French breakfast.

④ Art for sale in Place du Tertre in Montmartre.

3 DAYS

Day 1

Morning Start the day in St-Germain-des-Prés with coffee and a croissant at a café, then take a leafy stroll through the nearby Jardin du Luxembourg (p140). Dip into St-Sulpice church (p143) to inspect the paintings by Eugène Delacroix before shopping along Boulevard St-Germain.

Afternoon Follow rue de Seine towards the river, stopping for lunch at La Palette, a traditional café serving delicious *croque monsieur*. Stroll the Île St-Louis, popping into Notre-Dame (p86) before taking the Metro west to spend the rest of the afternoon exploring the iconic Eiffel Tower (p122). Dare to walk the stairs if the elevator line is too long.

Evening Have dinner nearby at Café Christian Constant (p129), which serves classic French dishes. Follow this with a boat ride down the Seine as the sun sets.

Day 2

Morning Begin in hilly Montmartre, with a quick visit to the Sacré-Coeur basilica (p146). Browse the work of artists selling their wares in the open-air gallery of place du Tertre (p162), then visit the Musée de Montmartre (p162) for a quick lesson on the 19th-century artists that made the district famous.

Afternoon Have lunch at Le Sancerre on rue des Abbesses before heading down the hill towards rue des Martyrs, laden with pastry shops and boutiques. Consider a late afternoon jaunt through the Louvre (p106) to see the highlights, including *Mona Lisa* and the *Venus de Milo*. Soak up the views of the grand exterior with a coffee stop at the Café Marly, under the arcades of the Richelieu wing.

Evening Head to Les Halles for dinner at Champeaux *(rue Rambuteau)*. Sip wine and people-watch for the rest of the evening along bustling rue Montorgueil, or see what shows are playing at nearby venues in the Opéra district, such as the historic Olympia music hall.

Day 3

Morning Travel less than an hour out of the city to Versailles (p170). Wander the world-famous gardens and 17th-century château, renowned for its opulent Hall of Mirrors.

Afternoon Splurge on lunch at Ore, an ornate little restaurant situated inside the château. Be sure to visit the outer estates, including Marie-Antoinette's fairy-tale hamlet with a working farm.

Evening Head back to Paris and share a bottle at an intimate venue like Willi's Wine Bar on rue des Petits Champs, near the Louvre. If you've still got room after your lunch, have dinner in style at one of the city's glamorous and iconic belle époque brasseries, such as La Rotonde *(105 blvd du Montparnasse)*.

Did You Know?

A million "love locks" were removed from Pont des Arts in 2015 – they were straining the bridge.

PARIS FOR
ROMANTICS

Paris is the ultimate romantic city. Its very fabric seems made for romance, from enchanting gardens to beautiful riverside walks, while the city's pavement cafés invite intimacy and lingering tête-à-têtes. Everywhere you look there is a heady mix of elegance, passion and culture.

Intimate Spaces

There's little more romantic than escaping the crowds in a peaceful hideaway. With its cobbled streets, dreamy Montmartre *(p162)* is full of secret staircases and little squares affording scenic glimpses of the city spread out below. Or flee the crowds with a trip to the slopes of Parc des Buttes-Chaumont *(p157)*. One of the few parks in Paris where you can actually sit on the grass, it's an ideal spot for a leisurely picnic – and afterwards there's a rowing lake to drift upon while reading a book of poetry aloud.

→

An idyllic Corinthian temple in Parc des Buttes-Chaumont

Idyllic Views

Take the hand of the one you love for a stroll along Paris's picturesque riverside. Along the Left Bank east of the Musée d'Orsay (p136), a delightful traffic-free stretch called the Parc Rives de Seine enjoys sigh-worthy views of two of the city's most romantic bridges, the Pont des Arts and Pont Neuf (p94). Break on one of the benches to admire the view, or hole up at a window table in a moored barge-restaurant and let the world pass you by.

← The Eiffel Tower, as glimpsed from the embankment

TOP 4 ROMANTIC THINGS TO DO IN PARIS

Musée de la Vie Romantique
This sweet art museum has a delightful café.

Candlelit Cocktails
Sip cocktails in a dimly lit bar such as Lulu White (p159).

Hot Air Balloon
Take to the skies in a tethered balloon in the Parc André-Citroën.

Secret Cinema
Snuggle up in one of the "loveseats" at the MK2 Bibliothèque cinema.

↑ A champagne toast to *l'amour* overlooking the skyline of Paris

Romance on a Plate

After an afternoon mooning about the dark nooks of Paris's galleries, even the staunchest romantics need replenishing. The garden café at the Petit Palais (p125) is tucked away from prying eyes, while Loulou at the Musée des Arts Décoratifs (p114) enjoys an unbeatable location in the Tuileries gardens.

↑ An ornately decorated restaurant in Paris, perfect for indulgent meals

ÎLE DE LA CITÉ, MARAIS AND BEAUBOURG

The Île de la Cité is where Paris began. This tear-drop-shaped island on the Seine was settled by Celtic tribes in the 3rd century BC; one of them, the Parisii, eventually gave its name to the city. The island offered a convenient river crossing on the route between northern and southern Gaul and was easily defended. In later centuries the settlement was expanded by the Romans, the Franks and the Capetian kings to form the nucleus of today's city. Connected to the island by bridge is the tiny Île Saint-Louis, named after King Louis IX.

Situated to the north of the Île de la Cité on the Seine's right bank is the Marais district, encompassing the neighbouring Beaubourg area. Once an area of marshland (*marais* means "swamp"), this district grew steadily in importance from the 14th century, by virtue of its proximity to the Louvre, the preferred residence of Charles V. Its heyday was in the 17th century, when it became a fashionable area for the monied classes. Abandoned by its royal residents during the 789 Revolution, the Marais descended into an architectural wasteland before being rescued in the 1960s. Today its lively streets are packed with contemporary art galleries, cutting-edge design boutiques and handsome town houses, as well as the eye-catchingly eclectic Pompidou Centre.

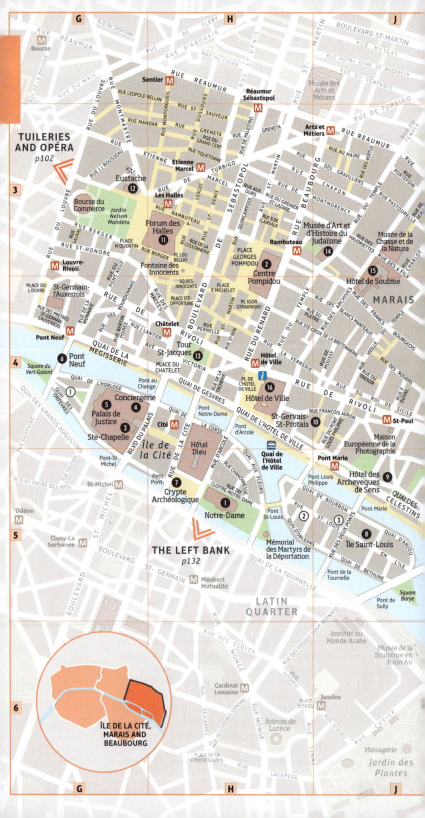

ÎLE DE LA CITÉ, MARAIS AND BEAUBOURG

Must Sees

1. Notre-Dame
2. Centre Pompidou
3. Ste-Chapelle

Experience More

4. Conciergerie
5. Palais de Justice
6. Pont Neuf
7. Crypte Archéologique
8. Île St-Louis
9. Hôtel des Archeveques de Sens
10. St-Gervais-St-Protais
11. Forum des Halles
12. St-Eustache
13. Tour St-Jacques
14. Musée d'Art et d'Histoire du Judaïsme
15. Hôtel de Soubise
16. Hôtel de Ville
17. Musée Picasso
18. Musée Carnavalet
19. Place des Vosges
20. Maison de Victor Hugo
21. Place de la Bastille

Stay

1. Paris Perfect Flat Place Dauphine
2. Saint-Louis en l'Isle
3. Hôtel du Jeu de Paume

NOTRE-DAME

H5 **Pl du Parvis Notre-Dame** **Cité** **21, 38, 47, 58, 70, 72, 81, 82**
Notre-Dame **8am-6:30pm Mon-Fri, 8am-7:15pm Sat & Sun** **1 Jan,**
1 May, 25 Dec **notredamedeparis.fr**

No other building is more associated with the history of Paris than
Notre-Dame (Our Lady). The "heart" of the country, both geographically
and spiritually, the cathedral rises majestically at the eastern end of the
Île de la Cité. A Gothic masterpiece, it is famed for its stained glass and
rose windows, towers, flying buttresses and gargoyles.

Notre-Dame is built on the site of a Roman
temple. After Pope Alexander III laid the first
stone in 1163, an army of architects and craftsmen toiled for 170 years to realize Bishop
Maurice de Sully's magnificent design. At
the time it was finished, in about 1334, it
was 130 m (430 ft) long and featured flying
buttresses, a large transept, a deep choir
and 69-m- (228-ft-) high towers.

Within the cathedral's hallowed walls,
kings and emperors were crowned and royal
Crusaders were blessed. But Notre-Dame was
also the scene of turmoil. Revolutionaries
ransacked it, banished religion, changed it into
a temple to the Cult of Reason, and then used
it as a wine store. Napoléon reinstated religion
in 1804 and architect Viollet-le-Duc later
restored the building, replacing missing
statues, as well as raising the spire and fixing
the gargoyles. Both the pointed arch and the
rose window were made elsewhere in Paris,
but Notre-Dame is the finest Gothic church in
the city, and the most impressive of the early
French cathedrals.

> **After Pope Alexander III laid the
> foundation stone in 1163, an army of
> architects and craftsmen toiled for
> 170 years to realize Bishop Maurice
> de Sully's magnificent design.**

↑ Jean Ravy's spectacular flying
buttresses, with a span of 15 m (50 ft),
at the east end of the cathedral

↑ The cathedral's legendary gargoyles
(chimères), hiding behind a large upper
gallery between the towers

1163
▲ Foundation stone
laid by Pope
Alexander III.

1708
▲ Choir remodelled by
Louis XIV, fulfilling his
father's promise to
honour the Virgin.

1793
▲ Revolutionaries loot
the cathedral and
rename it Temple
of Reason.

2013
▲ The cathedral
celebrates its
850th anniversary.

INSIDER TIP
Organ Recital

There are free organ recitals every Saturday at 8pm. The organ is one of the largest in France, with five keyboards and nearly 8,000 pipes.

The West Front, featuring superb statuary, a central rose window and an openwork gallery ↑

Inside Notre-Dame

Notre-Dame's interior grandeur is instantly apparent on seeing the high-vaulted central nave. This is bisected by a huge transept, at either end of which are medieval rose windows, 13 m (43 ft) in diameter. Works by major sculptors adorn the cathedral. Among them are Jean Ravy's old choir screen carvings, Nicolas Coustou's *Pietà* and Antoine Coysevox's Louis XIV statue.

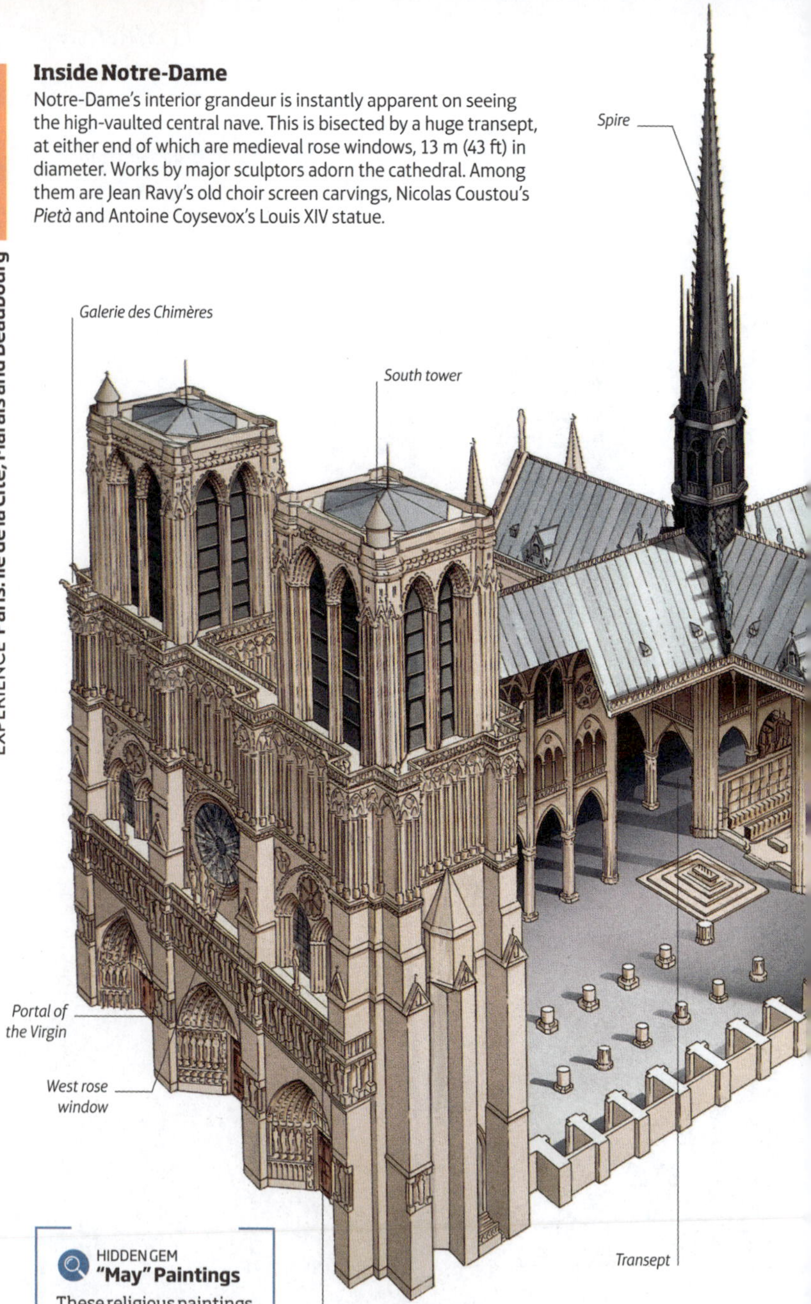

Spire

Galerie des Chimères

South tower

Portal of the Virgin

West rose window

Transept

The Kings' Gallery

🔍 HIDDEN GEM
"May" Paintings

These religious paintings hang in the side chapels, and include works by Charles Le Brun. In the 17th and 18th centuries, the Paris guilds presented a painting to the cathedral on May day each year.

↑ Illustration of the Notre-Dame, a monument of national importance

387

steps up the north tower lead to the famous gargoyles.

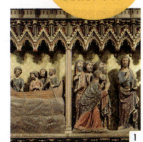

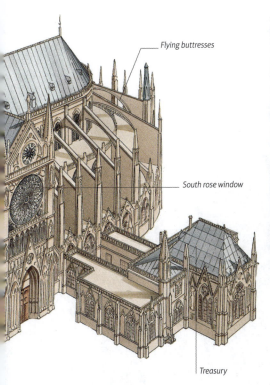

Flying buttresses

South rose window

Treasury

① A 14th-century screen enclosed the chancel, offering canons at prayer some peace from noisy congregations.

② Behind the high altar is Nicolas Coustou's *Pietà*, standing on a gilded base.

③ Only the north window retains its stunning 13th-century stained glass.

A MEDIEVAL ROMANCE

The 12th-century romance between the monk Pierre Abélard and the young Héloïse began in the cloisters of Notre-Dame. Abélard was hired as a tutor to the 17-year-old niece of a canon, and a love affair soon developed between the teacher and his pupil. In his wrath, Héloïse's uncle had the scholar castrated and Héloïse took refuge in a convent.

CENTRE POMPIDOU

◉ H3 ⌂ Pl G Pompidou Ⓜ Rambuteau, Châtelet, Hôtel de Ville.
🚌 21, 29, 38, 47, 58, 69, 70, 72, 74, 75, 76, 81, 85, 96 ◷ MNAM:
11am–10pm Wed–Mon (to 11pm Thu); library: noon–10pm Wed–Mon
(from 11am Sat, Sun and public hols); Atelier Brancusi: 2–6pm Wed–Mon
🌐 centrepompidou.fr

Home to the Musée National d'Art Moderne (MNAM), with over 60,000
works of art from over 5,000 artists, the Pompidou holds Europe's
largest collection of modern and contemporary art. Looking like a
building turned inside out, its exterior is as eye-catching as the works
on display within.

Blue: air conditioning

Did You Know?

Centre Pompidou's collection was originally housed in the Palais de Tokyo.

← *With the Black Arc* (1912) by Vassily Kandinsky

← *Le Rhinocéros* (1999) by Xavier Veilhan

Exploring the Museum

The "historical" collections bring together the great artistic movements of the first half of the 20th century, from Fauvism to Abstract Expressionism. The rich collection of Cubist sculptures is displayed, as well as examples of the great masters of the 20th century. Matisse, Picasso, Braque, Duchamp, Kandinsky, Léger, Miró, Giacometti and Dubuffet command large areas at the heart of the collection, which also shows the groups and the movements on which the history of modern art is based, or by which it has been affected, including Dada, Abstract Art and Informal.

The contemporary art section occupies the fourth floor. The collection starts with works by leading French artists of the second half of the 20th century: Louise Bourgeois, Pierre Soulages, Jean-Pierre Raynaud, François

↑ The striking escalator overlooking the piazza

Morellet and Bertrand Lavier. The display is organized around a central aisle from which the rooms lead off. Certain areas have been designated to bring together different disciplines around a theme such as minimalist painting or conceptual art rather than a school or movement, while other rooms are artist-specific. Design and architecture are also covered, and there is a "global" room bringing together major pieces by African, Chinese, Japanese and American artists. A graphic arts exhibition room and a video area complete the collection.

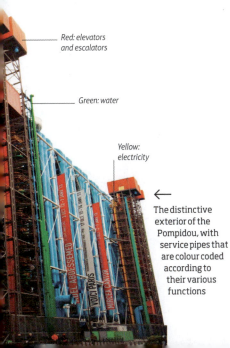

———— Red: elevators and escalators

———— Green: water

Yellow: electricity

← The distinctive exterior of the Pompidou, with service pipes that are colour coded according to their various functions

BRANCUSI'S STUDIO

The Atelier Brancusi, on the piazza, is a reconstruction of the workshop of the Romanian-born artist Constantin Brancusi (1876–1957), who lived and worked in Paris from 1904 until his death. He bequeathed his entire collection of works to the French state on condition that his workshop be rebuilt as it was on the day he died.

3

STE-CHAPELLE

📍G4 🏛8 blvd du Palais 75001 🚇Cité 🚌21, 27, 38, 85, 96 to Île de la Cité
Ⓡ St-Michel ◉ Notre-Dame ⏰Apr–Sep: 9am–7pm daily; Oct–Mar: 9am–5pm daily 🚫1 Jan, 1 May, 25 Dec 🌐sainte-chapelle.fr

Ethereal and magical, Ste-Chapelle has been hailed as one of the greatest architectural masterpieces of the Western world. In the Middle Ages, the devout likened this church to "a gateway to heaven". Today, no visitor can fail to be transported by the blaze of light created by the 15 magnificent stained-glass windows.

The chapel was built in 1248 by Louis IX to house Christ's purported Crown of Thorns (now housed in the Notre-Dame treasury). A Gothic masterpiece, its stunning stained-glass windows – the oldest still surviving in Paris – are separated by narrow columns that soar 15 m (50 ft) to the star-studded, vaulted roof. The windows portray more than 1,000 biblical scenes, from Genesis to the Crucifixion, in a kaleidoscope of red, gold, green, blue and mauve. Servants and commoners worshipped in the Lower Chapel, while the Upper Chapel was reserved for the use of the king and the royal family.

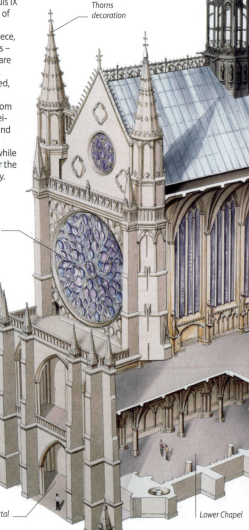

Spire

Crown of Thorns decoration

Rose window

Main portal

Lower Chapel

↑ The rose window, telling the story of the Apocalypse

Did You Know?

The spire is 75m (245 ft) high. It was erected in 1853 after four previous spires burned down.

Angel

Upper Chapel

① The Lower Chapel is not as light and lofty as the Upper Chapel, but is still magnificent.

② The windows of the Upper Chapel contain 600 sq m (6,458 sq ft) of stained glass.

③ Carved stone statues of the Apostles adorn the pillars of the Upper Chapel.

↑ Illustration of Ste-Chapelle, a landmark of national importance

ST LOUIS'S RELICS

Louis IX was extremely devout, and was canonized in 1297, not long after his death. In 1239, he acquired the Crown of Thorns from the Emperor of Constantinople and, in 1241, a fragment of Christ's Cross. He built this chapel as a shrine to house them. Louis paid nearly three times more for the relics than for the construction of Sainte-Chapelle. The Crown of Thorns is now kept at Notre-Dame.

EXPERIENCE MORE

4

Conciergerie

📍 G4 🏛 2 bd du Palais 75001 Ⓜ Cité 🕐 9:30am–6pm daily 🚫 1 Jan, 1 May, 25 Dec 🌐 paris. conciergerie.fr

Forming part of the huge Palais de Justice, the historic Conciergerie served as a prison from 1391 to 1914. Henri IV's assassin, François Ravaillac, was imprisoned and tortured here in 1610.

During the Revolution, the building was packed with over 4,000 prisoners. Its most notorious inmate was Marie Antoinette, who was held in a tiny cell until her execution in 1793. Others included proto-feminist Charlotte Corday, who stabbed revolutionary leader Jean-Paul Marat. The Conciergerie has a splendid four-aisled Gothic hall, where guards of the royal household once lived. Renovated during the 19th century, the building retains its 11th-century torture chamber and an ornate 14th-century clock tower.

5

Palais de Justice

📍 G4 🏛 4 bd du Palais 75001 Ⓜ Cité, Châtelet 🕐 9am–5pm Mon–Fri 🚫 Public hols & Aug recess 🌐 cours.appel.justice.fr

This huge block of buildings making up the law courts of Paris stretches the entire width of the Île de la Cité. It is a charming sight with its Gothic towers lining the quays.

The site has been occupied since Roman times, when it was the governors' residence. It was the seat of royal power, until Charles V moved the court to the Marais following a bloody revolt in 1358. In April 1793 the notorious Revolutionary Tribunal began dispensing justice from the Première Chambre Civile (or first civil chamber). Today the site is emblematic of Napoléon's great legacy – the French judicial system.

6

Pont Neuf

📍 G4 🏛 75001 Ⓜ Pont Neuf, Cité

Despite its name (New Bridge), this bridge is the oldest in Paris and has been immortalized by major literary and artistic figures. The first stone was laid by Henri III in 1578, but it was Henri IV (whose statue stands at the centre) who inaugurated it and gave it its name in 1607.

> **INSIDER TIP**
> **Ticket Savings**
>
> If you plan on visiting both the Conciergerie and Ste-Chapelle on the same day, you can save money by buying a combined ticket, which is also valid for a year, at either sight's website.

↑ The Conciergerie, with its medieval turreted towers, overlooking the River Seine

Did You Know?

Henri IV's nickname, Vertgalant, means "old flirt". The king was infamous for his womanizing.

7

Crypte Archéologique

📍 H5 🏛 Parvis Notre-Dame-7 pl Jean-Paul II 75004 Ⓜ Cité, Saint Michel ⏰ 10am–6pm Tue–Sun 🚫 Public & religious hols 🌐 crypte.paris.fr

Situated beneath the *parvis* (main square) of Notre-Dame and stretching 120 m (393 ft) underground, the crypt was opened in 1980. There are Gallo-Roman streets and houses with an underground heating system, sections of Lutetia's 3rd-century BC wall and remains of the cathedral. Displays show the origins of Paris as a Parisii settlement, the Celtic tribe who inhabited the island 2,000 years ago.

↑ The ornate interior of the Baroque church of St-Louis-en-l'Île

8

Île St-Louis

📍 J5 🏛 75004 Ⓜ Pont Marie, Sully Morland St-Louis-en-l'Île 19 rue

Across Pont St-Louis from Île de la Cité, Île St-Louis is a little haven of quiet streets and riverside quays. Replacing the cattle pasture and wood stock of old, today's luxurious restaurants and shops include the famous ice-cream maker Berthillon, at 29-31 rue St-Louis-en-l'Île. Almost everything on the Île was built in Classical style in the 17th century. The church of **St-Louis-en-l'Île**, with its marble-and-gilt Baroque interior, was completed in 1726 from plans by royal architect Louis de Vau. Note the 1741 iron clock at the church entrance, the pierced iron spire and a plaque given in 1926 by the city of St Louis, Missouri.

The church is twinned with Chapelle Saint-Louis de Carthage in Tunisia, where St Louis is buried.

St-Louis en l'Île

🏛 3 rue Poulletier ⏰ 9:30am-1pm & 2-7:30pm daily (to 7pm Sun, public hols) 🌐 saint louisenlile.catholique.fr

9

Hôtel des Arche-veques de Sens

📍 J5 🏛 1 rue du Figuier 75004 Ⓜ Pont Marie ⏰ 10am-7:30pm Wed & Thu; 1-7:30pm Tue, Fri & Sat 🚫 Public hols

One of just a few medieval buildings still standing in Paris, the Hôtel de Sens is home to the Forney arts library. During the period of the Catholic League in the 16th century, it was turned into a fortified mansion and occupied by the Bourbons, the Guises and Cardinal de Pellevé.

10

St-Gervais-St-Protais

📍 J4 🏛 Pl St-Gervais 75004 Ⓜ Hôtel de Ville ⏰ 7:30am-12:30pm & 1-5:30pm Mon-Fri (to 2am Thu), 8:30am-12:30pm & 1-5:30pm Sat & Sun

This church has magnificent origins, which go all the way back to the 6th century. It boasts the earliest Classical façade in Paris, dating from 1621, with a triple-tiered arrangement of Doric, Ionic and Corinthian columns. Composer François Couperin (1668–1733) arranged his two Masses for the organ of this late-Gothic church.

The great glass-and-concrete Forum des Halles, and the sheltered "Canopy" *(inset)* ↑

⓫ Forum des Halles

📍 H3 🏠 101 Porte Berger 75001 Ⓜ Les Halles, Châtelet 🚉 Châtelet-Les-Halles ⏰ Complex: 10am–8:30pm Mon–Sat, 11am–7pm Sun; restaurants/cinemas: 9am–11:30pm 🌐 forumdeshalles.com

Known simply as Les Halles and built amid controversy on the site of a famous fruit-and-vegetable market, this large underground complex is covered by an undulating glass-and-steel roof, known as "La Canopée", unveiled in 2016. Shops and restaurants abound, and there are two multi-screen cinemas, a gym and swimming pool, and a cinema resource centre, the **Forum des Images**. At the forum, you can choose from thousands of cinema, television and amateur films, many featuring footage of the city of Paris, which illustrates the city's history since 1895. Above ground are peaceful gardens, pergolas and mini-pavilions.

Forum des Images

🏠 2 rue du Cinéma ⏰ 12:30–9pm Tue–Fri, 2–9pm Sat & Sun 🌐 forumdesimages.fr

⓬ St-Eustache

📍 G3 🏠 2 impasse St-Eustache 75001 Ⓜ Les Halles, Châtelet 🚉 Châtelet-Les-Halles ⏰ Hours vary, check website 🌐 saint-eustache.org

With its Gothic plan and Renaissance decoration, St-Eustache is one of Paris's most beautiful churches. Its interior is modelled on Notre-Dame, with five naves and side and radial chapels. The Renaissance style flourished over the course of the 105 years (1532–1637) it took to complete the church, as evident in the magnificent arches, pillars and columns.

St-Eustache has hosted many ceremonial events, including the baptisms of Cardinal Richelieu and Madame de Pompadour, and the funerals of fabulist La Fontaine. It was here that Berlioz first performed his *Te Deum* in 1855. Today, talented choir groups perform regularly, and organ recitals are often held.

⓭ Tour St-Jacques

📍 H4 🏠 Sq de la Tour St-Jacques 75004 Ⓜ Châtelet ⏰ Tower: Jun–Nov: 10am–5pm Fri–Sun; gardens: year-round 🌐 desmotsetdesarts.com

This late-Gothic tower, dating from 1523, is all that remains of a church used as a rendez-vous by pilgrims on the road to Compostela in Spain. The church itself was destroyed by revolutionaries in 1797.

Earlier, Blaise Pascal, the 17th-century mathematician, physicist and writer, used the tower for barometric experiments. His statue is at the base of the tower, now used as a meteorological station.

→

Admiring the works in the Musée d'Art et d'Histoire du Judaïsme

Did You Know?

Every winter the large square in front of the Hôtel de Ville is transformed into an ice rink.

14

Musée d'Art et d'Histoire du Judaïsme

J3 Hôtel de St-Aignan, 71 rue du Tempe 75003 Rambuteau 11am–6pm Tue–Fri, 10am–6pm Sat–Sun Jewish hols mahj.org

Housed in a Marais mansion, this museum brings together collections formerly scattered around the city, commemorating the culture of French Jewry from medieval times to the present. Visitors learn about the sizable Jewish community in France since Roman times. Much exquisite craftsmanship is displayed, with elaborate silverware, Torah covers, fabrics, and items of fine Judaica and religious objects for use both in the synagogue and in the home. There are also photographs, paintings, cartoons and historical documents, including some on the anti-Semitic Dreyfus Affair around the turn of the 20th century.

15

Hôtel de Soubise

J3 60 rue des Francs-Bourgeois 75003 01 40 27 60 96; tours: 01 40 27 60 29 Rambuteau 10am–5:30pm Mon, Wed–Fri, 2–5:30pm Sat & Sun Public hols

This mansion, built from 1705 to 1709 for the Princesse de Rohan, holds the Musée des Archives Nationales. It boasts a majestic courtyard and 18th-century interior decoration by some of the best-known artists of the time. Notable items include Natoire's *rocaille* work in the princess's bedchamber, and Napoleon's will.

16

Hôtel de Ville

H4 Pl de l'Hôtel de Ville, 29 rue de Rivoli 75004 Hôtel-de-Ville Hours vary for exhibitions Public hols, official functions paris.fr

The 17th-century town hall was burned down by insurgents of the Paris Commune in 1871. It was replaced by a 19th-century building, an example of Third Republic architecture.

STAY

Paris Perfect Flat Place Dauphine

Apartments with hotel service make this ideal for visitors who want to feel like a local.

G4 25 place Dauphine 75001 parisperfect.com

€€€

Saint-Louis en l'Isle

Elegantly decorated, it offers comfort without going over the top.

H5 75 rue Saint-Louis-en-l'Île 75004 saintlouisenlisle.com

€€€

Hôtel du Jeu de Paume

Wooden beams in this 17th-century building, along with the great location, make it a draw.

J5 54 rue Saint-Louis-en-l'Île 75004 jeudepaumehotel.com

€€€

17

Musée Picasso

📍 J4 🏠 Hôtel Salé,
5 rue de Thorigny 75003
Ⓜ St-Sébastien Froissart,
St-Paul, Chemin Vert
🕐 10:30am–6pm Tue–Fri;
9:30am–6pm Sat, Sun &
hols 🚫 1 Jan, 1 May, 25 & 31
Dec 🌐 museepicassoparis.fr

On the death of the Spanish-born artist Pablo Picasso (1881–1973), who lived most of his life in France, the French State inherited a quarter of his works in lieu of death duties. In 1986, it used them to create the Musée Picasso in the beautifully restored Hôtel Salé.

Comprising 5,000 works, including over 200 paintings, 158 sculptures, 88 ceramic works, and 3,000 sketches and engravings, this unique collection shows the huge range and variety of Picasso's work, including examples from his Blue, Pink and Cubist periods. Highlights include his Blue period *Self-portrait*, painted at age 20; *Still Life with Caned Chair*, which introduced collage to Cubism; the Neo-Classical *Pipes of Pan*; and *The Crucifixion*.

The museum frequently loans canvases for exhibitions elsewhere, so some works will be on show in other galleries.

18

Musée Carnavalet

📍 J4 🏠 16 rue des Francs-Bourgeois 75003
Ⓜ St-Paul, Chemin Vert
🔒 Closed for major renovations until 2020
🌐 carnavalet.paris.fr

Devoted to the history of Paris since prehistoric times, this vast museum is in two adjoining mansions. The interiors include fully decorated rooms with gilded panelling, furniture and objets d'art; many works of art, such as paintings and sculptures of prominent personalities; and engravings showing Paris being built.

PICASSO IN FRANCE

Born in Spain, Pablo Picasso first moved to Paris in 1904 as a young artist, drawn by the city's bohemian art scene and raucous nightlife. Later he settled in the south of France. After 1934, Picasso's rejection of Franco's regime meant he would never return to his homeland. Nonetheless, throughout his life in France he used Spanish themes in his art, such as the bull and the guitar, which he associated with his Andalusian childhood.

PICASSO'S THE HEAD OF A WOMAN

The main building is the Hôtel Carnavalet, which was built as a town house in 1548 by Nicolas Dupuis. The literary hostess Madame de Sévigné lived here between 1677 and 1696, entertaining the intelligentsia of the day and writing her celebrated *Lettres*. Many of her belongings are in the first-floor exhibition covering the Louis XIV era.

The 17th-century Hôtel le Peletier, opened in 1989, features reconstructions of early 20th-century interiors and artifacts from the Revolution and Napoleonic era. The Orangery houses a section devoted to Prehistory and Gallo-Roman Paris. The collection includes pirogues discovered in 1992, during an

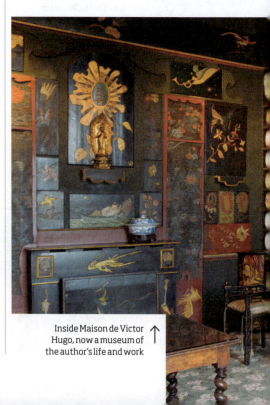

Inside Maison de Victor Hugo, now a museum of the author's life and work ↑

archaeological dig in the Parc de Bercy, which unearthed a Neolithic village.

19

Place des Vosges

📍**K4** 🏠**75003, 75004** Ⓜ**Bastille, St-Paul**

A perfectly symmetrical square, Place des Vosges was laid out in 1605 by Henri IV and is considered among the most beautiful in the world. Houses, nine on each side, are built over arcades that accommodate antiques shops and fashionable cafés. The square has hosted many historical events over the centuries, including a three-day tournament in celebration of the marriage of Louis XIII to Anne of Austria in 1615.

> **A perfectly symmetrical square, Place des Voges was laid out in 1605 by Henri IV and is considered among the most beautiful in the world.**

20

Maison de Victor Hugo

📍**K4** 🏠**6 pl des Vosges 75004** Ⓜ**Bastille** 🕐**10am–6pm Tue-Sun** 🚫**1 Jan, 1 May, 25 Dec; May 2019 to May 2020** 🌐**maisonvictor hugo.paris.fr**

The French poet, dramatist and novelist Victor Hugo lived on the second floor of what was once the Hôtel de Rohan-Guéménée, the largest house on the square, from 1832 to 1848. It was here that he wrote most of *Les Misérables*. On display are reconstructions of some of the rooms in which he lived, complete with his desk, his mementos and drawings from key periods of his life, from his childhood to his exile between 1852 and 1870.

💬 **INSIDER TIP**
Marais Mansions

Several of the former mansions in the Marais are open to the public. If the doors are open, you can step in and discover what's inside.

21

Place de la Bastille

📍**K5** 🏠**75004** Ⓜ**Bastille**

Nothing remains of the prison stormed by the revolutionary mob on 14 July 1789, thus sparking the French Revolution.

The 50-m (164-ft) Colonne de Juillet stands in the middle of the traffic-clogged square to honour the victims of the July Revolution of 1830. On the south side is the 2,700-seat Opéra National de Paris Bastille, completed in 1989.

To the south of the square is Bassin de l'Arsenal marina, with bars, restaurants, galleries and the Jardin de l'Arsenal.

A SHORT WALK
ÎLE DE LA CITÉ

Distance 1.5 km (1 mile) **Nearest metro** Cité
Time 20 minutes

The origins of Paris are on the Île de la Cité, the boat-shaped island on the Seine first inhabited over 2,000 years ago by Celtic tribes. There is no older place in Paris, and remains of the first buildings can still be seen today in the archaeological crypt under the square in front of Notre-Dame. A stroll of this part of the city takes you from one Parisian icon – the great medieval cathedral – to another: the Gothic masterpiece that is Ste-Chapelle.

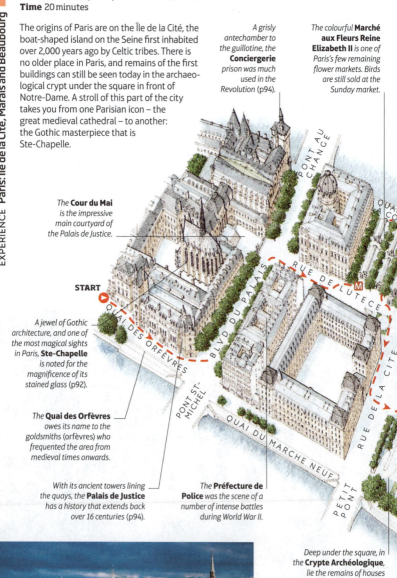

A grisly antechamber to the guillotine, the **Conciergerie** *prison was much used in the Revolution (p94).*

The colourful **Marché aux Fleurs Reine Elizabeth II** *is one of Paris's few remaining flower markets. Birds are still sold at the Sunday market.*

The **Cour du Mai** *is the impressive main courtyard of the Palais de Justice.*

START

A jewel of Gothic architecture, and one of the most magical sights in Paris, **Ste-Chapelle** *is noted for the magnificence of its stained glass (p92).*

The **Quai des Orfèvres** *owes its name to the goldsmiths (orfèvres) who frequented the area from medieval times onwards.*

With its ancient towers lining the quays, the **Palais de Justice** *has a history that extends back over 16 centuries (p94).*

The **Préfecture de Police** *was the scene of a number of intense battles during World War II.*

PONT AU CHANGE

QUAI COR

RUE DE LUTECE

QUAI DES ORFÈVRES

BLVD DU PALAIS

RUE DE LA CITE

PONT ST-MICHEL

QUAI DU MARCHE NEUF

PETIT PONT

Deep under the square, in the **Crypte Archéologique**, *lie the remains of houses from 2,000 years ago (p95).*

← A riverside view of the Conciergerie, a former prison

↑ Patrons sitting outside one of the delightful cafés on the quaint Rue Chanoinesse

ÎLE DE LA CITÉ AND ÎLE ST-LOUIS

Locator Map
For more detail see p72

For more detail see p72

Did You Know?

Tourists often drop coins on Point Zéro's plaque or spin around on one foot for good luck.

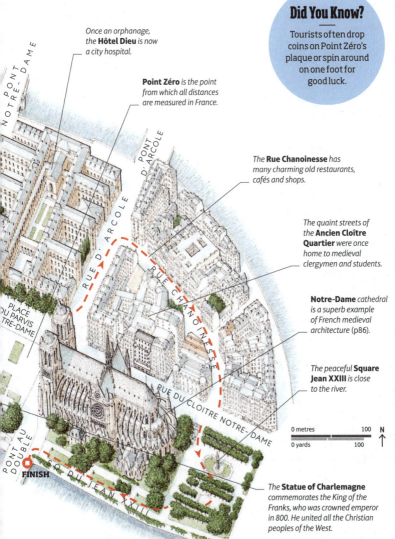

Once an orphanage, the **Hôtel Dieu** *is now a city hospital.*

Point Zéro *is the point from which all distances are measured in France.*

The **Rue Chanoinesse** *has many charming old restaurants, cafés and shops.*

The quaint streets of the **Ancien Cloître Quartier** *were once home to medieval clergymen and students.*

Notre-Dame *cathedral is a superb example of French medieval architecture (p86).*

The peaceful **Square Jean XXIII** *is close to the river.*

The **Statue of Charlemagne** *commemorates the King of the Franks, who was crowned emperor in 800. He united all the Christian peoples of the West.*

NOTRE-DAME
PONT

PONT D'ARCOLE

RUE D'ARCOLE

RUE CHANOINESSE

RUE DU CLOITRE NOTRE-DAME

PLACE DU PARVIS NOTRE-DAME

PONT AU DOUBLE

FINISH

SQ DU JEAN XXIII

0 metres   100
0 yards   100

N ↑

TUILERIES AND OPÉRA

Philip II, the first king of France, built a defensive fortress on the outskirts of medieval Paris in 1190 which became known as the Louvre Castle. This was soon surrounded by a dense urban settlement. Francois I took up residence here in 1528 and destroyed the castle in favour of a larger residence, inaugurating centuries of specially commissioned gardens and buildings. The formal gardens of the Tuileries, running alongside the Louvre, were created by Marie de' Medici in 1564 on the site of medieval tile factories, exclusively for royal use. Following the French Revolution of 1789, they were opened to the public. That year, the revolutionary government erected a guillotine in the grandiose place de la Concorde, at the westernmost end of the garden, and it was there that King Louis XVI and his wife, Marie-Antoinette, were executed. In 1793 the palace was opened to the public as a national museum.

Following the downfall of the monarchy, the area remained affluent. Its broad leafy grands boulevards and elegant squares were part of Baron Haussmann's extensive 19th-century modernization of the city. The iconic Opéra National de Palais Garnier is another landmark in the area.

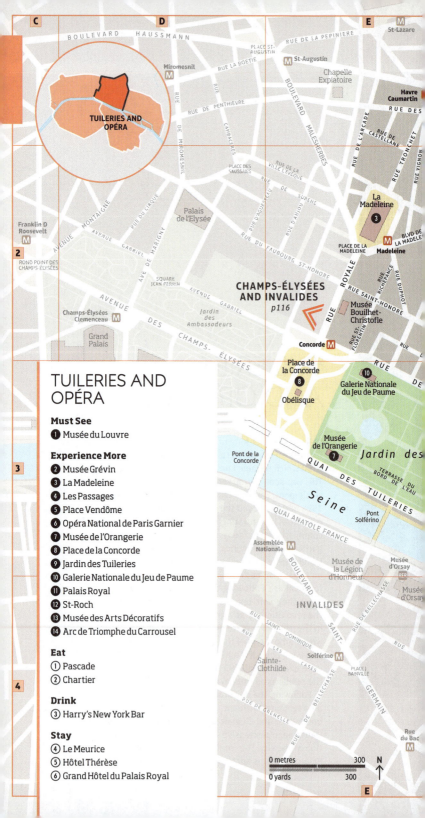

TUILERIES AND OPÉRA

Must See

① Musée du Louvre

Experience More

② Musée Grévin
③ La Madeleine
④ Les Passages
⑤ Place Vendôme
⑥ Opéra National de Paris Garnier
⑦ Musée de l'Orangerie
⑧ Place de la Concorde
⑨ Jardin des Tuileries
⑩ Galerie Nationale du Jeu de Paume
⑪ Palais Royal
⑫ St-Roch
⑬ Musée des Arts Décoratifs
⑭ Arc de Triomphe du Carrousel

Eat

① Pascade
② Chartier

Drink

③ Harry's New York Bar

Stay

④ Le Meurice
⑤ Hôtel Thérèse
⑥ Grand Hôtel du Palais Royal

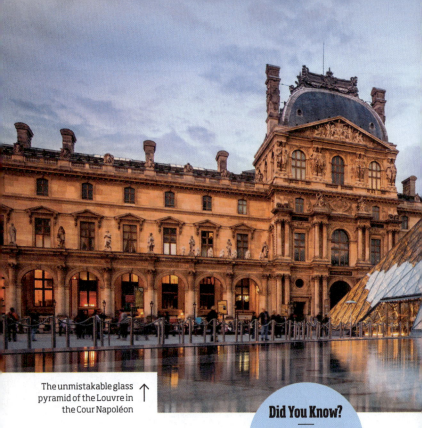

The unmistakable glass pyramid of the Louvre in the Cour Napoléon ↑

Did You Know?

Napoleon temporarily renamed the museum after himself and hung the *Mona Lisa* in his bedroom

❶ 〽 〽 🍴 🛍

MUSÉE DU LOUVRE

📍 F3 🏠 Pl du Louvre Ⓜ Palais-Royal Musée du Louvre 🚌 21, 24, 27, 39, 48, 68, 69, 72, 81, 95 🚆 Châtelet-Les-Halles ⓒ Louvre 🕐 9am–6pm Wed–Mon (to 9:45pm Wed & Fri) 🗓 1 Jan, 1 May & 25 Dec 🌐 louvre.fr

First opened to the public in 1793 after the Revolution, the Louvre contains one of the most important art collections in the world. Its stunning architecture makes it an icon of Paris.

Constructed as a fortress in 1190 by King Philippe-Auguste to protect Paris against Viking raids, the Louvre lost its imposing keep during the reign of François I (1514–47), who replaced it with a Renaissance-style building. Thereafter, four centuries of French kings and emperors improved and enlarged it. A glass pyramid designed by I M Pei was added to the main courtyard in 1989, from which all of the galleries can be reached.

The Louvre's treasures can be traced back to the 16th-century collection of François I, who purchased many Italian paintings, including the *Mona Lisa (La Gioconda)*. At the time of Louis XIV's reign (1643–1715) there were a mere 200 works, but donations have augmented the collection ever since.

GALLERY GUIDE

Eight departments are spread over four floors: Near Eastern antiquities; Egyptian antiquities; Greek, Etruscan and Roman antiquities; Islamic art; sculptures; decorative arts; paintings; and prints and drawings.

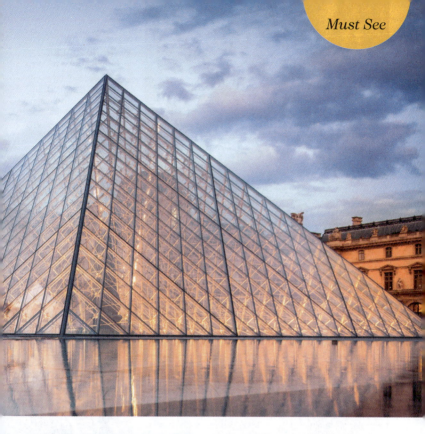

① This sculptural spiral staircase forms part of the modern entrance hall designed by Chinese American architect I M Pei.

② The Marly Horses by Guillaume Coustou once stood near the Place de la Concorde.

③ *The Coronation of Napoléon* by Jacques-Louis David is an impressive 6.2 m (20.5 ft) high by 9.8 m (32 ft) wide.

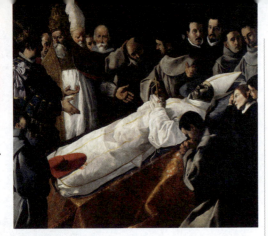

↑ *Lying-in-State of St Bonaventura* (c 1629) by Francisco de Zurbarán

EUROPEAN PAINTING: 1200 TO 1850

Painting from northern Europe is well covered, with works by Flemish, Dutch, German and English artists including Jan van Eyck, Vermeet, Hans Holbein and J M W Turner. The Spanish collection tends towards depictions of the tragic side of life, although several portraits by Goya are in a lighter vein.

The large collection of Italian paintings covers the period 1200 to 1800. Key figures of the early Renaissance are here, including Giotto and Raphaël. Several paintings by Leonardo da Vinci are as enchanting as his *Mona Lisa*.

The French collection ranges from the 14th century to 1848. There are superb works by Jean Fouquet, George de la Tour and J A Watteau, as well as J H Fragonard, master of the Rococo.

THE NOTORIOUS MONA LISA

Acquired by King François I, this portrait of a mysterious woman was one of the first paintings displayed in the Louvre when the museum opened. For many years it was simply one da Vinci work among many, but that all changed when the painting was stolen in 1911. The much-publicized theft pushed the artwork into the public eye, with reproductions appearing around the world. Its popularity has not dwindled since.

EUROPEAN SCULPTURE: 1100 TO 1850

← *Saint Mary Magdalene* (c 1515–20) by Gregor Erhart

Early Flemish and German sculpture in the collection has many masterpieces including an unusual life-size nude figure of the penitent Mary Magdalene by Gregor Erhart (early 16th century). The French section opens with early Romanesque works, such as the figure of Christ by a 12th-century Burgundian sculptor, and a Head of St Peter. With its eight black-hooded mourners, the Tomb of Philippe Pot is one of the more unusual pieces.

The works of Pierre Puget have been assembled inside the Cour Puget, while the Cour Marly houses the Marly Horses and other master-pieces of French sculpture.

The Italian sculpture collection includes pre-Renaissance work by Duccio and Donatello, and later masterpieces such as Michel-angelo's *Slaves* and Cellini's *Nymph of Fontainebleau*.

DECORATIVE ARTS

The Louvre has well over 8,000 "decorative art" objects, including jewellery, silver and glassware, bronzes, porcelain, snuffboxes and armour. Many of these precious objects are from the Abbey of St-Denis, where the kings of France were buried. The treasures include a serpentine stone plate from the 1st century AD with a 9th-century border of gold and precious stones, and the golden sceptre made for King Charles V in about 1380.

↑ Serpentine stone plate (1st century/ 9th century AD)

> **The French crown jewels include the coronation crowns of Louis XV and Napoleon, and the Regent, one of the purest diamonds in the world.**

The French crown jewels include the coronation crowns of Louis XV and Napoleon, and the Regent, one of the purest diamonds in the world.

The large collection of French furniture ranges from the 16th to the 19th centuries. On display are important pieces by prominent furniture-makers such as André-Charles Boulle, who was cabinet-maker to Louis XIV.

In 2012, the Islamic Art Department opened in the Cour Visconti, with around 18,000 objects on display covering 3,000 years of history from three continents. The museum also has a number of decorative art galleries dedicated to objects from the reign of Louis XIV and the 18th century.

NEAR EASTERN, EGYPTIAN, GREEK, ETRUSCAN AND ROMAN ANTIQUITIES

The range of antiquities is impressive, with objects from the Neolithic period to the fall of the Roman Empire. Important works of Mesopotamian art include the seated figure of Ebih-il, from 2400 BC, while the warlike Assyrians are represented by delicate carvings and a spectacular reconstruction of part of Sargon II's (722–705 BC) palace. A fine example of Persian art is the enamelled brickwork depicting the king of Persia's personal guard of archers (5th century BC).

Most Egyptian art was made for the dead to take to the afterlife. One exquisite example is the tiny carved funeral chapel built for a high official in about 2500 BC. A special crypt dedicated to the god Osiris contains some colossal sarcophagi and mummified animals.

The departments of Greek, Roman and Etruscan antiquities contains some exceptional pieces. The two most famous Greek statues in the Louvre, the *Winged Victory of Samothrace* and the *Venus de Milo*, belong to the Hellenistic period (late 3rd to 2nd century BC), when more natural-looking human forms were beginning to be produced. The star of the Etruscan collection is the terracotta *Sarcophagus of the Cenestian Couple*, while the many fine pieces in the Roman section include a bust of Agrippa and a splendid, powerful bronze head of Emperor Hadrian from the 2nd century AD.

→

Winged Victory of Samothrace (c 190 BC)

EXPERIENCE MORE

2

Musée Grévin

📍 G2 🏠 10 bd Montmartre 75009 Ⓜ Bourse, Grands Boulevards 🕐 9am–5pm Mon–Sat 🗓 7 Jan–8 Feb 🌐 grevin-paris.com

Founded in 1882, this is a Paris landmark, on a par with Madame Tussauds. The historical scenes include Louis XIV at Versailles and the arrest of Louis XVI. Notable figures from the worlds of art, politics, film and sport are also on display. On the first floor is a holography section devoted to optical tricks. The museum also houses a 212-seat theatre that stages recitals, follies and poetry events.

3

La Madeleine

📍 E2 🏠 Pl de la Madeleine 75008 Ⓜ Madeleine 🕐 9:30am–7pm daily 🌐 eglise-lamadeleine.com

Modelled after a Greek temple, La Madeleine was begun in 1764, but not consecrated until 1845. Before that, there were proposals to turn it into a stock exchange, a bank or a theatre.

Corinthian columns encircle the building, supporting a sculptured frieze. Three ceiling domes crown the inside, richly decorated with rose marble and gilt sculptures.

4

Les Passages

📍 G2 🏠 75002 Ⓜ Bourse

The early-19th-century *galeries* or *passages,* (the glass-roofed shopping arcades), are found mainly between boulevard Montmartre and rue St-Marc. They house an eclectic mixture of small stores selling anything from designer jewellery to rare books and art supplies. One of the most charming is Galerie Vivienne (off rue Vivienne or rue des Petits Champs) with its mosaic floor and excellent wine bar.

5

Place Vendôme

📍 F2 🏠 75001 Ⓜ Tuileries

Perhaps the best example of 18th-century elegance in the city, the 17th-century architect Jules Hardouin-Mansart's royal square was begun in 1698 and remains largely intact. The original plan was to house academies and embassies behind its arcaded façades, but instead bankers moved in and created sumptuous mansions for themselves. The most famous residents include Frédéric Chopin, who died here in 1848 at No 12, and César Ritz, who established his famous hotel at No 15 in 1898.

← Marochetti's sublime *Mary Magdalene Ascending to Heaven* in La Madeleine

An audience enjoying a performance at the Opéra National de Paris Garnier, and star ballerina Aurélie Dupont *(inset)*

Opéra National de Paris Garnier

F1-2 **Place de l'Opéra 75009** **Opéra** **10am–5pm daily** **1 Jan, 1 May & special events** **operade paris.fr**

Sometimes compared to a giant wedding cake, this lavish building was designed by Charles Garnier for Napoleon III in 1862. The Prussian War and the 1871 uprising delayed the opening until 1875. Its unique appearance is down to a mixture of materials, including stone, marble and bronze, and styles, ranging from Classical to Baroque with a number of columns, friezes and sculptures on the exterior.

Inside, the opera house is famous for its Grand Staircase made of white Carrara marble, topped by a huge chandelier (weighing 8 tonnes and bearing 340 lights), and the Grand Foyer, its domed ceiling covered in mosaics. The five-tiered, horseshoe-shaped auditorium is adorned in red velvet, gold leaf and plaster cherubs, with a false ceiling painted by pioneering artist Marc Chagall in 1964. It is primarily used for dance, but shares operatic productions with the Opéra National de Paris Bastille.

> Inside, the opera house is famous for its Grand Staircase made of white Carrara marble, topped by a huge chandelier, and the Grand Foyer, its domed ceiling covered in mosaics.

EAT & DRINK

Pascade
Discover innovative crêpes, stuffed with gourmet fillings.

F2 **14 rue Daunou 75002** **Sun & Mon** **pascade.fr**

€€€

Chartier
A budget-friendly favourite for tasty French classics.

G2 **7 rue du Faubourg Montmartre 75009** **bouillon chartier.com**

€€€

Harry's New York Bar
Birthplace of the Bloody Mary, it's tradition to make a stop here.

F2 **5 rue Daunou 75002** **harrysbar.fr**

Did You Know?

Monet made some 250 paintings of the water lilies. About 60 are on view in the Musée de l'Orangerie.

7

Musée de l'Orangerie

📍 E3 🏛 Jardin des Tuileries, place de la Concorde 75001 Ⓜ Concorde ⏰ 9am-6pm Wed-Mon 🗓 1 May am, 14 Jul, 25 Dec 🌐 musee-orangerie.fr

Paintings from Claude Monet's crowning work, representing part of his water lily series, fill the two oval upper floor rooms. Known as the *Nymphéas*, most of the canvases were painted between 1899 and 1921.

This superb work is complemented by the Walter-Guillaume collection, including 27 Renoirs, notably *Young Girls at the Piano,* works by Soutine and 14 Cézannes, including his evocative *The Red Rock.* Pablo Picasso is represented by works including *The Female Bathers*, and Rousseau by nine paintings, notably *The Wedding.* Other works include paintings by the likes of Matisse, Derain, Utrillo and Modigliani.

8

Place de la Concorde

📍 E3 🏛 75008 Ⓜ Concorde

One of most magnificent and historic squares in Europe, the place de la Concorde was a swamp until the mid-18th century. It became the place Louis XV in 1775, when royal architect Jacques-Ange Gabriel was asked by the king to design a suitable grand setting for an equestrian statue of himself. The monument, which lasted here less than 20 years, was replaced by the guillotine (the Black Widow, as it came to be known), and the square was renamed place de la Révolution. On 21 January 1793 Louis XVI was beheaded, followed by over 1,300 other victims, including Charlotte Corday (Marat's assassin), Marie Antoinette, Madame du Barry and revolutionary leaders Danton and Robespierre. The blood-soaked square was optimistically renamed place de la Concorde, after the Reign of Terror finally came to an end in 1794. In the 19th century a 3,300-year-old Luxor obelisk was presented to King Louis-Philippe as a gift from the viceroy of Egypt (who also donated Cleopatra's Needle in London), and two fountains

 → People enjoying a mild summer evening in the Jardin des Tuileries

Visitors admiring Monet's Water Lilies *(Nymphéas)*, in the Musée de l'Orangerie

and eight statues personifying French cities were added to the square.

Flanking rue Royale on the north side of the square are two of Gabriel's Neo-Classical mansions, the Hôtel de la Marine and the exclusive Hôtel Crillon.

↑ The Galerie Nationale du Jeu de Paume, housed in the former royal court where nobles played handball

9 Jardin des Tuileries

⦿ F3 ⌂ 75001 Ⓜ Tuileries, Concorde ⊙ Apr, May & Sep: 7am–9pm; Jun–Aug: 7am–11pm; Oct–Mar: 7:30am–7:30pm

These Neo-Classical gardens once belonged to the Palais des Tuileries, which the Communards razed to the ground in 1871. Forming part of the landscaped area between the Louvre and the Champs-Elysées, they were laid out in the 17th century by André Le Nôtre, who created the broad central avenue and geometric topiary. Ongoing restoration has created a new garden with lime and chestnut trees, and modern sculptures.

10 Galerie Nationale du Jeu de Paume

⦿ E3 ⌂ Jardin des Tuileries, 1 place de la Concorde 75008 Ⓜ Concorde ⊙ 11am–9pm Tue, 11am–7pm Wed–Sun ⊘ 1 Jan, 1 May, 25 Dec ⓦ jeudepaume.org

The Jeu de Paume – literally "game of the palm" – was built as two royal tennis courts by Napoleon III in 1851 on the north side of the Tuileries Gardens. When *réal* (royal) tennis was replaced by lawn tennis, an Impressionist museum was eventually founded here. The courts were later converted into an art gallery and exhibition space, which now hosts rotating exhibitions of photography, video and film, and talks with photographers.

JEU DE PAUME

Nobles used to play a version of handball, *jeu de paume*, in the former royal court that today houses the Galerie Nationale du Jeu de Paume. French players would yell "tenez" or "take it" to their opponents. As the game evolved, the word did, too, and the English began to call it tennis, or real tennis, and used racquets instead of their hands. Later, the Jeu de Paume became a storehouse during World War II, where Nazis stashed stolen art. Those deemed offensive, for example many Picasso and Dalí paintings, were burned in front of it in 1942.

⓫
Palais Royal

📍F3 🏛Palace: Pl du Palais Royal 75001; gardens: 6 rue de Montpensier Ⓜ Palais Royal ⏰ Apr-Sep: 8am-10:30pm daily; Oct-Mar: 8am-8:30pm daily 🌐 domaine-palais-royal.fr

This former royal palace, built by Cardinal Richelieu in the early 17th century, passed to the Crown on his death and became the childhood home of Louis XIV. Under the 18th-century royal dukes of Orléans, it became the epicentre of brilliant gatherings, interspersed with periods of gambling and debauchery. It was from here that the clarion call to revolution roused the mobs to storm the Bastille on 14 July 1789.

Today the south section of the building houses the Councils of State and the Ministry of Culture. Just to the west is the Comédie Française, established by Louis XIV in 1680. The gardens are about one-third smaller than the original ones, laid out by the royal gardener for Cardinal Richelieu in the 1630s. This is due to the construction, between 1781 and 1784, of 60 uniform houses that border three sides of the square.

These days, restaurants, art galleries and specialist shops line the square, which has counted such luminaries as

Did You Know?

Daniel Buren's striped columns in the Palais Royal's courtyard are the artwork that Parisians love to hate.

Jean Marais, Jean Cocteau and Colette among its famous former residents.

The courtyard contains the black-and-white stone columns that form conceptual artist Daniel Buren's *Les Deux Plateaux*, installed here in 1986, despite opposition about their suitability for the space. Today, they are loved by children and skateboarders alike.

⓬
St-Roch

📍F3 🏛296 rue St-Honoré 75001 Ⓜ Tuileries, Pyramides ⏰ Sep-Jun: 8:30am-7pm daily; Jul-Aug: 9am-7pm Tue-Sun 🚫Non-religious public hols 🌐 paroisse saintroch.fr

This remarkably long church, unusually set on a north-south axis, was designed by Jacques Lemercier, the renowned architect of Paris's iconic Louvre museum, and its foundation stone was laid by Louis XIV in 1653. The church is a treasure trove of exquisitely preserved

→

Displays of art and design at the Musée des Arts Décoratifs

religious art, much of it surviving from now-vanished churches and monasteries. Contained within its peaceful walls are the tombs of the playwright Pierre Corneille, the royal gardener André Le Nôtre and the Enlightenment philosopher and art critic Denis Diderot.

⓭
Musée des Arts Décoratifs

📍F3 🏛Palais du Louvre, 107-111 rue de Rivoli 75001 Ⓜ Palais Royal, Tuileries ⏰ Museum: 11am-6pm Tue-Sun (to 9pm Thu); library: 1-6pm Mon & Thu, 10am-6pm Tue, Wed, Fri 🚫1 Jan, 1 May, 25 Dec 🌐 madparis.fr

Occupying the northwest wing of the Palais du Louvre (along with the Musée de la Publicité and the Musée de la Mode et du Textile), this museum offers an eclectic mix of decorative art and domestic design ranging from the Middle Ages to the present

→

The Arc de Triomphe du Carrousel, crowned by Victory riding a chariot

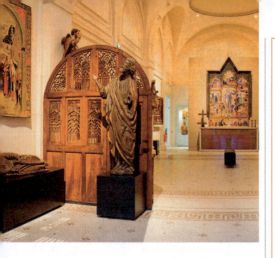

day. The Art Nouveau and Art Deco rooms include a reconstruction of couturier Jeanne Lanvin's home. Other floors show Louis XIV, XV and XVI styles of decoration and furniture. Works by contemporary designers and artists, such as the Bouroullec brothers, are represented. Fashion, advertising and graphic design collections are displayed at temporary exhibitions. The restaurant has amazing views over the Jardin du Tuileries.

14

Arc de Triomphe du Carrousel

F3 🏠 **Pl du Carrousel 75001** Ⓜ **Palais Royal**

This vast rose-marble arch, at the entrance to the Jardin des Tuileries, was built by Napoleon to celebrate various military triumphs, notably the Battle of Austerlitz in 1805. The crowning statues, added in 1828, are copies of the famous Horses of St Mark's, which Napoleon had stolen from Venice and was subsequently forced to return after his defeat at Waterloo in 1815.

STAY

Le Meurice
Rococo luxury sits side by side modern comforts at this palace hotel with Michelin-starred restaurant.

E3 🏠 **228 rue de Rivoli 75001** ⓦ **dorchestercollection.com**

€€€

————————

Hôtel Thérèse
A chic boutique-hotel with cocooning rooms individually decorated in a soothing palette.

F3 🏠 **5 rue Thérèse 75001** ⓦ **hoteltherese.fr**

€€€

————————

Grand Hôtel du Palais Royal
Overlooking the Palais Royal gardens, this luxury hotel has a secluded feel.

G3 🏠 **4 rue de Valois 75001** ⓦ **grandhoteldupalaisroyal.com**

€€€

CHAMPS-ÉLYSÉES AND INVALIDES

Bisected by the River Seine, this area was a suburb of Paris during the Middle Ages. The rue du Faubourg St-Honoré began as a medieval dirt road, connecting outlying western villages to the city market. In 1616, Queen Marie de' Medici commissioned a tree-lined approach road through the countryside to the former Palais des Tuileries. Named the Champs-Élysées in the 18th century, its crowning glory, the Arc de Triomphe, was commissioned by Napoleon I in 1806, after his great victory at the Battle of Austerlitz. The Baroque construction of the Hôtel des Invalides, built to house wounded military veterans, brought about subsequent urbanization. The neighbourhood was especially popular with nobles, who built impressive palaces, and has strong military connections as the home of the École Militaire. In 1889, its parade ground staged the Universal Exhibition, to commemorate the 100th anniversary of the Revolution, with the main draw then and now – the Eiffel Tower.

D **E** **F** **G**

Église St-Augustin

Gare St-Lazare
Ⓜ St-Lazare

HAUSSMANN

Miromesnil

St-Augustin
Ⓜ

Chapelle Expiatoire

Haussmann St-Lazare

Galeries Lafayette

1

PLACE DES SAUSSAIES

Opéra National de Paris Garnier

CHAMPS-ÉLYSÉES AND INVALIDES

❺ Palais de l'Élysée

Madeleine
Ⓜ

BLVD DES CAPUCINES

Opéra
Ⓜ

Quatre Septembre

2

Espace Pierre Cardin

CHAMPS- ÉLYSÉES

❼ Petit Palais

Obélisque

PLACE DE LA CONCORDE

Musée de l'Orangerie

Jardin des Tuileries

TUILERIES AND OPÉRA *p102*

3

COURS LA REINE
Port des Champs-Élysées

Pont Alexandre III

Invalides QUAI D'ORSAY

Pont de la Concorde

QUAI DES TUILERIES

Pont Solférino

QUAI ANATOLE FRANCE

Musée d'Orsay

Invalides
Ⓜ

Assemblée Nationale
Palais-Bourbon

Ⓜ **Assemblée Nationale**

INVALIDES

SAINT-DOMINIQUE

BLVD SAINT-GERMAIN

THE LEFT BANK *p132*

4

Sainte-Clothilde

Ⓜ **Solférino**

Ⓜ Varenne

❻

Musée Maillol

Ⓜ **Rue du Bac**

⑱ **Musée Maillol**

⑭ Musée Rodin

Hôtel Matignon

BOULEVARD DES INVALIDES

St-François Xavier
Ⓜ

Jardin Catherine Labouré

Le Bon Marché

Square Boucicaut

5

Vaneau
Ⓜ

Duroc
Ⓜ

RUE DE SÈVRES

St-Placide
Ⓜ

6

Falguière
Ⓜ

BOULEVARD DU MONTPARNASSE

CHAMPS-ÉLYSÉES AND INVALIDES

Must Sees

❶ Arc de Triomphe
❷ Eiffel Tower

Experience More

❸ Pont Alexandre III
❹ Avenue des Champs Élysées
❺ Palais de l'Elysée
❻ Grand Palais
❼ Petit Palais
❽ Palais de Chaillot
❾ Les Egouts
❿ Musée d'Art Moderne de la Ville de Paris
⓫ Jardins du Trocadéro
⓬ Église du Dôme
⓭ Hôtel des Invalides
⓮ Musée Rodin
⓯ École Militaire
⓰ UNESCO
⓱ Musée du Quai Branly
⓲ Musée Maillol

Eat

① L'Astrance
② Pierre Gagnaire
③ Relais de l'Entrecôte
④ Café Christian Constant
⑤ David Toutain
⑥ Arpège

Drink

⑦ Le Bar at the Four Seasons George V Hotel
⑧ Bar de l'Hôtel Belmont
⑨ Bar Kléber at the Peninsula
⑩ Le Bar Botaniste at the Shangri-La
⑪ Le Bar du Bristol

30

shields just below the Arc's roof each bear the name of a victorious Napoleonic battle.

The golden tones ↑
of the Arc's stonework,
highlighted by the sunset

❶ ⟨icons⟩

ARC DE TRIOMPHE

📍 B1 🏠 Place Charles de Gaulle 75008 Ⓜ️ⓇⒺⓇ Charles de Gaulle-Étoile 🚌 22, 30, 31, 52, 73, 92 to pl Charles de Gaulle 🕐 Apr–Sep: 10am–11pm daily; Oct–Mar: 10am–10:30pm daily 🕐 All day 1 Jan, 1 May, 25 Dec; mornings only 8 May, 14 Jul, 11 Nov 🌐 paris-arc-de-triomphe.fr

Situated at the heart of Place Charles de Gaulle, overlooking the Champs-Élysées, the Arc de Triomphe was commissioned by Napoleon to celebrate France's military might. The exterior is adorned with sculptures depicting various battles, while the viewing platform at the top affords one of the best views in Paris.

After his greatest victory, the Battle of Austerlitz in 1805, Napoleon promised his men they would "go home beneath triumphal arches". The first stone of what was to become the world's most famous triumphal arch was laid the following year, but disruptions to architect Jean Chalgrin's plans and the demise of Napoleonic power delayed completion of this monumental building until 1836. Standing 50 m (164 ft) high, the Arc is now the customary starting point for victory celebrations and parades.

← The twelve avenues radiating from Place Charles de Gaulle

→ The symbolic torch at the Tomb of the Unknown Soldier

NUPTIAL PARADE

In 1809, Napoleon divorced his wife Josephine because she was unable to bear him children. A diplomatic marriage was arranged in 1810 with Marie-Louise, daughter of the Austrian emperor. Napoleon was determined to impress his bride by going through the Arc on their way to the wedding, but work had barely started, so Chalgrin built a full-scale mock-up of the arch on the site for the couple to pass beneath.

Timeline

1806
▽ Napoleon commissions Chalgrin to build the triumphal Arc following the Battle of Austerlitz in the previous year.

1815
Napoleon abdicates after defeat at the Battle of Waterloo, causing work on the Arc to cease.

1919
Allied armies parade through the Arc to celebrate the end of World War I.

1836
King Louis-Philippe completes the Arc during the Bourbon Restoration.

1944
△ De Gaulle leads the crowd from the Arc following the liberation of Paris.

2

EIFFEL TOWER

📍 B4 🚩 Quai Branly and Champ-de-Mars Ⓜ Bir-Hakeim 🚌 42, 69, 72, 82, 87 to Champ-de-Mars 🚈 Champ-de-Mars 🚢 Tour Eiffel 🕐 Sep–Jun: 9:30am–11:45pm daily (6:30pm for stairs); Jul & Aug: 9am–12:45am 📅 14 Jul 🌐 toureiffel.paris

An impressive feat of engineering and the most distinctive symbol of Paris, the Eiffel Tower stands 324 m (1,063 ft) tall and offers unrivalled views over the city.

Originally built to impress visitors to the 1889 Universal Exhibition the Eiffel Tower (Tour Eiffel) was meant to be a temporary addition to the Paris skyline. Built by the engineer Gustave Eiffel, it was fiercely decried by 19th-century aesthetes – it is said that the author Guy de Maupassant frequently ate lunch at the tower as it was the only place he could avoid seeing it. The world's tallest structure until 1931, when New York's Empire State Building was completed, the tower is now an icon of Paris and attracts 7 million visitors a year. The glass-floored first level houses a visitor centre and an interactive museum chronicling the history of the tower.

THE TOWER IN FIGURES

276 m (905 ft): the height of the viewing gallery on the third level.

1,665: the number of steps leading up to the third level.

2.5 million: the number of rivets holding the tower together.

7 cm (2.5 in): the maximum amount the tower ever sways.

10,100 tonnes: the tower's total weight.

60 tonnes: the amount of paint needed to decorate the ironwork.

18 cm (7 in): how far the top can move in a curve under the effect of heat.

↑ The view from the tower, ranging up to 72 km (45 miles)

← The Eiffel Tower under construction in April 1888, less than halfway complete

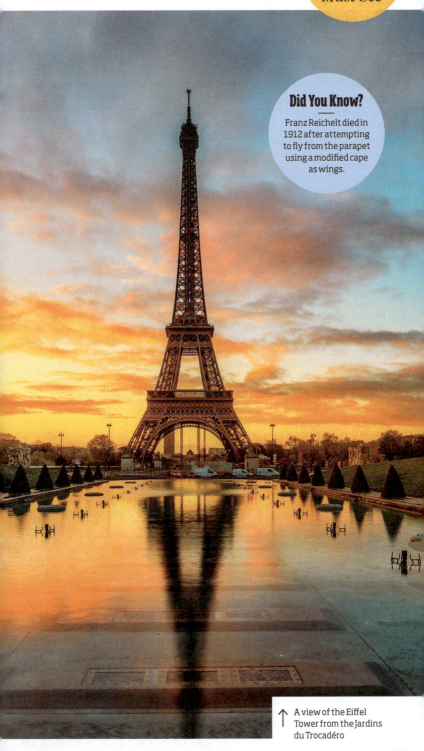

Did You Know?

Franz Reichelt died in 1912 after attempting to fly from the parapet using a modified cape as wings.

↑ A view of the Eiffel Tower from the Jardins du Trocadéro

EXPERIENCE MORE

3

Pont Alexandre III

 D3 75008 M Champs-Elysées-Clemenceau, Invalides

This is Paris's prettiest bridge, with exuberant Art Nouveau decoration of gilt and bronze lamps, cupids and cherubs, nymphs and winged horses at either end. It was built between 1896 and 1900 to commemorate the 1892 French–Russian alliance, and in time for the Universal Exhibition of 1900. Pont Alexandre III was named after Tsar Alexander III (father of Nicholas II), who laid the foundation stone in 1896.

The style of the bridge reflects that of the Grand Palais, to which it leads on the Right Bank, and the construction is a marvel of 19th-century engineering. It consists of a 6-m- (18-ft-) high single-span steel arch across the Seine. The design was subject to strict controls that prevented the bridge from obscuring the view of the Champs-Elysées or the Invalides, so today you can still enjoy the views.

4

Avenue des Champs-Élysées

 C2 75008 M Charles de Gaulle-Etoile, George V, Franklin D Roosevelt, Champs-Elysées-Clemenceau, Concorde

The majestic tree-lined "avenue of the Elysian Fields" (the mythical Greek heaven for heroes), first laid out in the 1660s by the landscape designer André Le Nôtre, forms a 3-km (2-mile) straight line from the huge place de la Concorde to the Arc de Triomphe. The 19th century saw it transformed into an elegant boulevard (pedestrian-only on the first Sunday of every month), lined with cafés and restaurants.

The Champs-Elysées keeps a special place in the French heart. National parades are held here, and the finish of the annual Tour de France cycle race is always on the Champs-Elysées. Above all, ever since the homecoming of Napoleon's body from St Helena in 1840, it has been the place where Parisians congregate at times of major national celebration. The famed Christmas market normally held on the Champs-Elysées was relocated to the Tuileries for 2018 and 2019.

5

Palais de l'Elysée

 D2 55 rue du Faubourg-St-Honoré 75008 M St-Philippe-du-Roule To the public W elysee.fr

Built in 1718 and backing onto splendid English-style gardens, the Elysée Palace has been the official residence of the French President since 1848. Several occupants left their mark. Louis XV's mistress, Madame de Pompadour, had the whole site enlarged. After the Revolution, it became a dance hall. In the 19th century, it was home to Napoleon's sister, Caroline Murat, and his wife Empress Josephine. The President's Apartments are today on the first floor. General de Gaulle gave press conferences in the Hall of Mirrors.

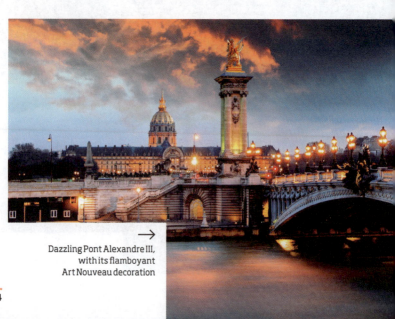

→ Dazzling Pont Alexandre III, with its flamboyant Art Nouveau decoration

→

The soaring Neo-Classical entrance to the Petit Palais, topped with cherubic statues

Grand Palais

📍 D2 🏛 Porte A, 3 av Général Eisenhower 75008 Ⓜ Champs-Elysées-Clemenceau ⏰ For exhibitions only 🌐 grandpalais.fr

Built at the same time as the Petit Palais opposite, this huge, glass-roofed palace housing the Galeries Nationales has a fine Classical façade adorned with statuary and Art Nouveau ironwork. Bronze flying horses and chariots stand at the four corners. The Great Hall and the glass cupola can be seen during the palace's exhibitions. On the west side, the **Palais de la Découverte** is a child-oriented science museum with fun workshops and great interactive exhibitions.

Palais de la Découverte

🏛 Av Franklin D Roosevelt Ⓜ Franklin D Roosevelt ⏰ 9:30am–6pm Tue–Sat, 10am–7pm Sun 🚫 1 Jan, 1 May, 14 Jul, 25 Dec 🌐 palais-decouverte.fr

Petit Palais

📍 D3 🏛 Av Winston Churchill 75008 Ⓜ Champs-Elysées-Clemenceau ⏰ 10am–6pm Tue–Sun (to 9pm Fri for temporary exhibitions) 🚫 Public hols 🌐 petitpalais.paris.fr

Designed by architect Charles Girault for the Universal Exhibition in 1900, this jewel of a building now houses the Musée des Beaux-Arts de la Ville de Paris. Arranged around a pretty courtyard, the palace is similar in style to the Grand Palais, and has Ionic columns, a grand porch and a dome.

Permanent exhibits, housed on the Champs-Elysées side, include the Dutuit Collection of medieval and Renaissance objets d'art, paintings and drawings; the Tuck Collection of 18th-century furniture and objets d'art; and the City of Paris collection, with work by Ingres, Delacroix and Courbet, and the landscape painters of the Barbizon School.

Well-curated temporary exhibitions are housed in the Cours de la Reine wing.

EAT

L'Astrance
This Michelin-starred restaurant reinvents French cooking daily.

📍 A4 🏛 4 rue Beethoven 75016 🌐 astrance restaurant.com

€€€

Pierre Gagnaire
One of Paris's best chefs wows diners with a contemporary menu.

📍 B1 🏛 6 rue Balzac 75008 🌐 pierre gagnaire.com

€€€

Relais de l'Entrecôte
Great steak and chips at this family favourite.

📍 C2 🏛 15 rue Marbeuf 75008 🌐 relaisentrecote.fr

€€€

8

Palais de Chaillot

📍 A3 🏛 Pl du Trocadéro 75116 Ⓜ Trocadéro

Designed in Neo-Classical style for the 1937 Paris Exhibition, the Palais de Chaillot is adorned with bas-reliefs and has curved, colonnaded wings each culminating in a vast pavilion. It houses the **Théâtre National de Chaillot**, famed for its experimental dance.

In the west wing, the **Musée de l'Homme** is an anthropological and ethnographic museum, tracing the history of human evolution. Next door is the Musée National de la Marine, devoted to the French navy (closed for renovations until 2021). The east wing contains the **Cité de l'Architecture et du Patrimoine**, which charts French architecture through the ages.

Théâtre National de Chaillot

🏛 1 place du Trocadéro
🌐 theatre-chaillot.fr

Musée de l'Homme

🏛 17 place du Trocadéro
🕐 10am–6pm Wed–Mon
🌐 museedelhomme.fr

Cité de l'Architecture et du Patrimoine

🏛 1 place du Trocadéro
🕐 11am–7pm Wed–Sun (to 9pm Thu) 🔒 1 Jan, 1 May, 25 Dec 🌐 citechaillot.fr

---

9

Les Egouts

📍 C3 🏛 Pont de l'Alma, opposite 93 quai d'Orsay 75007 Ⓜ Alma-Marceau
🚉 Pont-de-l'Alma 🕐 11am–5pm Sat-Wed (to 6pm in summer) 🔒 Until early 2020

One of Baron Haussmann's finest achievements, most of Paris's sewers (*égouts*) date from the Second Empire. One-hour walking tours of this attraction are limited to an area around the quai d'Orsay entrance. Visiting the sewers without a guide can be dangerous, and is against the law.

Did You Know?

If laid end to end, the city's 2,100 km (1,300 miles) of sewers would stretch from Paris to Istanbul.

Visitors can discover the mysteries of underground Paris in the sewer museum.

10

Musée d'Art Moderne de la Ville de Paris

📍 B3 🏛 Palais de Tokyo, 11 av du Président-Wilson 75116 Ⓜ Iéna, Alma-Marceau 🕐 10am–6pm Tue-Sun (to 10pm Thu for temporary exhibitions) 🔒 Public hols 🌐 mam.paris.fr

This large, lively museum covers trends in 20th-century art and is located in the east wing of the Palais de Tokyo.

← Looking down across the Palais Chaillot from the Eiffel Tower viewing platform

masterpiece is without a doubt one of the greatest examples of 17th-century French architecture, the period known as the *grand siècle*. After Louis XIV's death, plans to bury the royal family in the church were abandoned.

The main attraction is the tomb of Napoleon; 20 years after his death on the island of St Helena, his body was returned to France and then installed in this grand crypt, encased in six coffins in a vast red porphyry sarcophagus.

DRINK

Here are five of the best hotel bars where you can enjoy a decadent sundowner (or two) around the spectacular Champs-Elysées.

Le Bar at the Four Seasons Hotel
📍B2 🏠31 av George V 75008
🌐four seasons.com

Bar de l'Hôtel Belmont
📍B2 🏠30 rue de Bassano, 75116
🌐belmont-paris hotel.com

Bar Kléber at the Peninsula
📍A2 🏠19 av Kléber 75116
🌐peninsula.com

Le Bar Botaniste at the Shangri-La
📍A3–B3 🏠10 av d'Iéna 75116 🌐shangri-la.com

Le Bar du Bristol
📍D2 🏠112 rue du Faubourg-St-Honoré 75008
🌐oetkercollection.com

The Fauves and Cubists are well-represented here among the 10,000 works. Two of the museum's highlights include Raoul Dufy's gigantic mural, *The Electricity Fairy* (created for the 1937 World Fair), and Matisse's *The Dance* (1931–3). There is also a collection of Art Deco furniture.

Jardins du Trocadéro

📍A3 🏠75016 Ⓜ️Trocadéro
☎Cinéaqua: 01 40 69 23 23
🕐24 hrs daily

The centrepiece of these beautiful gardens is a long rectangular ornamental pool, bordered by stone and bronze-gilt statues and sculptures. It is a spectacular sight at night, when the fountains are illuminated. Among the works are *Woman* by Daniel Bacqué and *Horses and Dog* by Georges Lucien Guyot. On either side of the pool, the slopes of the Chaillot hill lead gently down to the Seine and the Pont

d'Iéna. Cinéaqua, the high-tech aquarium here, has over 25 sharks and a petting pool for children.

Eglise du Dôme

📍D4–5 🏠Hôtel des Invalides, 129 rue de Grenelle, 75007 Ⓜ️La Tour Maubourg, Varenne, Invalides 🚌28, 63, 69, 80, 82, 83, 87, 92, 93 🚈Invalides 🕐10am–6pm daily (to 9pm Tue Apr–Jun & Sep; to 7pm Jul & Aug) 🗓1st Mon of month, 1 Jan, 1 May, 25 Dec 🌐musee-armee.fr

Jules Hardouin-Mansart was asked in 1676 by Louis XIV to build the Eglise du Dôme to complement the existing buildings of the Invalides military refuge, designed by Libéral Bruand. The Dôme was to be reserved for the exclusive use of the king and as the location of royal tombs. The resulting

Hôtel des Invalides

D4 **6 bd des Invalides 75007** **M La Tour Maubourg, Invalides, Varenne** **RER Invalides** **Hours vary, check website** **w musee-armee.fr**

This impressive building, with its harmonious Classical façade, was commissioned by Louis XIV in 1670 to be a home for his wounded and homeless veterans. Designed by Libéral Bruand, it was completed in 1676 by Baroque master architect Jules Hardouin-Mansart. He later incorporated the Église du Dôme *(p127)*, with its golden roof, which was built to serve as Louis XIV's private chapel. Nearly 6,000 soldiers once filled the building's halls; today there are fewer than 100 who live here.

The building houses several museums, including the Musée de l'Armée, one of the most comprehensive museums of military history in the world. One exhibition features on France's victories and defeats. Also on display here are Francois I's ivory hunting horns and a model of the 1944 Normany landing.

On the south side of the complex is the cathedral of St-Louis-des-Invalides, also built from 1679 to 1708 by Hardouin-Mansart, to Bruand's design. The stark Neo-Classical interior has a 17th-century organ, on which the first performance of Berlioz's *Requiem* was given on 5 December 1837.

Musée Rodin

D4 **77 rue de Varenne 75007** **M Varenne, Invalides** **RER Invalides** **10am–5:45pm Tue–Sun** **1 Jan, 1 May, 25 Dec** **w musee-rodin.fr**

Auguste Rodin (1840–1917), regarded as one of the greatest French sculptors, lived and worked in the Hôtel Biron, an elegant 18th-century mansion, from 1908 until his death. In return for a state-owned flat and studio, Rodin left his work to the nation, and it is now

↑ Auguste Rodin's haunting sculpture *The Three Shades* at the Musée Rodin

exhibited here. Some of his most celebrated sculptures are on display in the garden: *The Thinker*, *The Gates of Hell* and *Balzac*. Indoors, the exhibits span Rodin's entire career, including *The Kiss* and *Eve*.

École Militaire

C5 **1/21 pl Joffre 75007** **01 80 50 14 00** **M École-Militaire** **During European Heritage Days in September**

The Royal Military Academy was founded in 1751 to educate 500 sons of impoverished

The splendid Hôtel des Invalides seen from
↓ Pont Alexandre III

officers. Louis XV and Madame de Pompadour commissioned architect Jacques-Ange Gabriel to design a building that would rival Louis XIV's Hôtel des Invalides. One of the main features is the central pavilion – a magnificent example of the French Classical style, with ten Corinthian columns and a quadrangular dome.

A cadet at the academy, Napoleon's passing-out report stated that "he could go far if the circumstances are right".

UNESCO

📍 C5 🏠 7 pl de Fontenoy 75007 Ⓜ Ségur, Cambronne 🕐 Visits suspended until further notice 🌐 unesco.org

This is the headquarters of the United Nations Educational, Scientific and Cultural Organization (UNESCO). Its aim is to contribute to international peace through education, science and culture. UNESCO is a treasure trove of modern art, including a mural by Picasso, and sculptures by Henry Moore.

Musée du Quai Branly

📍 B4 🏠 37 quai Branly 75007 Ⓜ Alma-Marceau 🚆 Pont-de-l'Alma 🕐 11am–7pm Tue, Wed & Sun, 11am–9pm Thu–Sat 🚫 1 May, 25 Dec 🌐 quaibranly.fr

Built to give the arts of Africa, Asia, Oceania and the Americas a platform as great as that given to Western art in the city, Musée du Quai Branly has more than 300,000 objects. It is particularly strong on Africa, with stone, wooden and ivory

↑ The eye-catching glass wall exterior of the Musée du Quai Branly

masks. The Jean-Nouvel-designed building, which is raised on stilts, is a worthwhile sight in itself, while the ingenious use of glass allows the surrounding greenery to act as a natural backdrop.

Musée Maillol

📍 E4–5 🏠 61 rue de Grenelle 75007 Ⓜ Rue du Bac, Sèvres-Babylone 🕐 10:30am–6:30pm daily during exhibitions (to 8:30pm Fri) 🌐 musee-maillol.com

This museum was created by Dina Vierny, muse to Aristide Maillol. His work is exhibited here in all its diverse forms: drawings, engravings, paintings, sculpture and decorative objects. Allegorical figures of the city of Paris and the four seasons adorn Bouchardon's fountain outside.

EAT

Café Christian Constant

Tasty French classics, reasonably priced and near the Eiffel Tower – a rarity.

📍 B4–C4 🏠 139 rue Saint-Dominique 75007 🌐 maisonconstant.com

€€€

David Toutain

This relaxed Michelin-starred experience is great value. It's worth booking at lunchtime.

📍 C4 🏠 29 rue Surcouf 75007 🚫 Sat & Sun 🌐 davidtoutain.com

€€€

Arpège

Alain Passard's three-Michelin star restaurant, with a focus on fresh produce, is a worthwhile treat.

📍 D4 🏠 84 rue de Varenne 75007 🚫 Sat & Sun 🌐 alain-passard.com

€€€

> Built to give the arts of Africa, Asia, Oceania and the Americas a platform as great as that given to Western art in the city, Musée du Quai Branly has more than 300,000 objects.

A SHORT WALK
CHAMPS-ÉLYSÉES

Distance 2 km (1 mile) **Nearest metro** Invalides
Time 30 minutes

The formal gardens that line the Champs-Élysées from the Place de la Concorde to the Rond-Point have changed little since they were laid out by the architect Jacques Hittorff in 1838. The Grand Palais and Petit Palais, which were created as a showpiece of the Third Republic for the Universal Exhibition of 1900, sit on either side of an impressive vista that stretches from Place Clémenceau across the elegant curve of the Pont Alexandre III to the Invalides.

There are plaques on the back door of the **Théâtre du Rond-Point** *representing Napoleon's many campaigns.*

Metro Franklin D Roosevelt

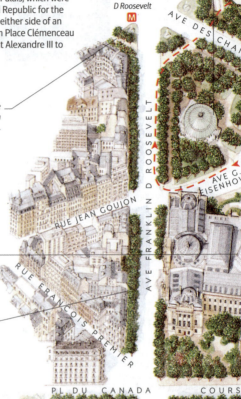

Christian Dior and other haute couture houses are based on the chic **Avenue Montaigne**.

Designed by Charles Girault, and built between 1897 and 1900, the 19th-century **Grand Palais** *is still used for major exhibitions (p125).*

The **Lasserre** *restaurant is decorated in the style of a luxurious ocean liner from the 1930s.*

AVE DES CHAMPS
AVE FRANKLIN D ROOSEVELT
AVE G. EISENHOWER
RUE JEAN GOUJON
RUE FRANÇOIS PREMIER
PL DU CANADA
COURS L
PONT DES INVALIDES

← The interior of the Palais de la Découverte, a museum of scientific discoveries

Avenue des Champs-Élysées
was the setting for the victory parades following the two World Wars, and for the bicentennial parade in 1989 (p124).

Metro Champs-Élysées-Clemenceau

Locator Map
For more detail see p118

CHAMPS-ÉLYSÉES AND INVALIDES

The **Jardins des Champs-Élysées***, with their fountains, flower beds, paths and pleasure pavilions, became very popular towards the end of the 19th century. Fashionable Parisians, including Marcel Proust, often came here.*

AVE GABRIEL

ELYSEES

AVE DE MARIGNY

AVE DES CHAMPS ELYSEES

M

PL CLEMENCEAU

FINISH

AVE WINSTON CHURCHILL

PONT ALEXANDRE III

SEINE

START

↑ Strolling through the tree-lined Jardin des Champs-Élysées

Lit by natural light, **Petit Palais** *is as much a work of art as the wide-ranging collections it contains, from antiquity to the belle époque (p125).*

Pont Alexandre III*'s four columns help to anchor the piers that absorb the immense forces generated by such a large single-span structure (p124).*

| 0 metres | | 100 | N |
| 0 yards | | 100 | ↑ |

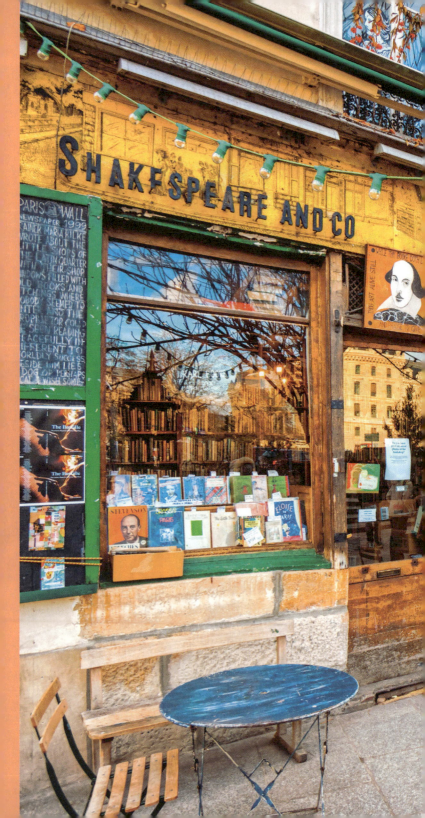

THE LEFT BANK

The Left Bank is one of the city's oldest areas – the site of the ancient Paris Mint, founded in 864 AD, and ruined Gallo-Roman baths, now hidden beneath the medieval Hôtel de Cluny. The Sorbonne, France's first university, was founded in 1253 in the Latin Quarter, which cemented its position as a centre of learning. In the 16th century, Marie de' Medici built the Jardins du Luxembourg, with its Baroque palace, designed to remind her of her native Florence. She was also a fervent patron of the arts and under her care the area's reputation as a bohemian enclave flourished. As a result, in the centuries that followed, the Left Bank became a beacon for poets, philosophers, artists – and radical thinkers. It was, then, a natural home for the centre of the Paris Commune, the revolutionary government that ruled the city for two months in 1871. Following World War II, this district once again became synonymous with Parisian intellectual society, fuelled by its many pavement cafés, and politics. In 1958, the French Senate moved into the Palais du Luxembourg. Ten years later, the Left Bank became the scene of student riots, but since then has become better known for the diverse shops and avant-garde theatres that line its labryinthine streets.

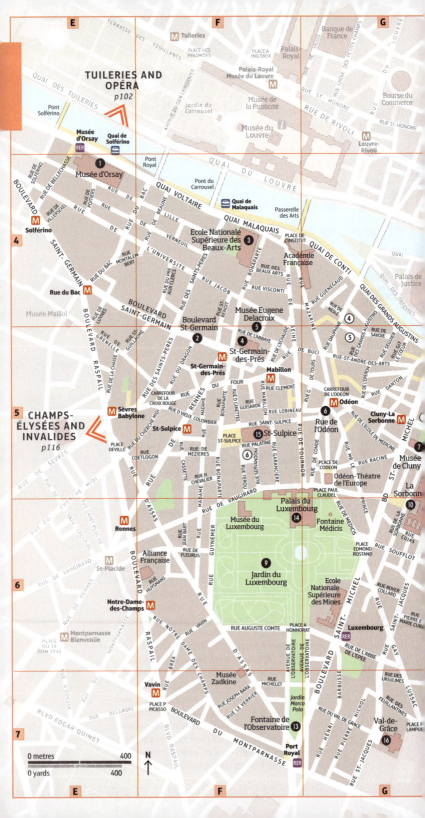

THE LEFT BANK

Must see

① Musée d'Orsay

Experience more

② Boulevard St-Germain
③ Ecole Nationale Supérieure des Beaux-Arts
④ St-Germain-des-Prés
⑤ Musée Eugène Delacroix
⑥ Rue de l'Odéon
⑦ Musée de Cluny
⑧ St-Séverin
⑨ Jardin du Luxembourg
⑩ La Sorbonne
⑪ St-Etienne-du-Mont

⑫ Panthéon
⑬ Fontaine de l'Observatoire
⑭ Palais du Luxembourg
⑮ St-Sulpice
⑯ Val-de-Grâce

Drink

① Monk le Taverne de Cluny
② Le Piano Vache
③ Le Bombardier

Stay

④ Hôtel d'Aubusson
⑤ Relais Christine
⑥ Hôtel Récamier

❶ Ⓜ Ⓨ 🖥 🛍

MUSÉE D'ORSAY

📍 E4 🏠 1 Rue de la Légion d'Honneur Ⓜ Solférino 🚌 24, 68, 69, 84 to Quai A France; 73 to Rue Solférino; 63, 83, 84, 94 to Bd St-Germain 🚃 Musée d'Orsay 🕒 9:30am–6pm Tue–Sun (to 9:45pm Thu) 🚫 1 Jan, 1 May, 25 Dec 🌐 musee-orsay.fr

The Musée d'Orsay picks up where the Louvre ends, showing a variety of art forms from 1848 to 1914. Its star attraction is a superb collection of Impressionist art, which includes famous works by Monet, Renoir, Manet and Degas, as well as pieces by Georges Seurat, Gaugin and Van Gogh.

In 1986, 47 years after it had closed as a mainline railroad station, Victor Laloux's truly superb late-19th-century building was reopened as the Musée d'Orsay. Originally commissioned by the Orléans railway company to be its Paris terminus, the structure avoided demolition in the 1970s after being classified as a historical monument. During the conversion into a museum, much of the original architecture was retained. The collection was set up to present each of the arts of the period from 1848 to 1914 in the context of contemporary society and other forms of creative activity happening at the time. In 2009–2011 the top-level galleries were renovated, improving the display of Impressionist works.

↑ The light and spacious entrance hall, with its curved glass ceiling

GREAT VIEW
City Panorama

Make your way to the building's rear escalator, ride it all the way up, and then head to the small rooftop terrace for a great bird's-eye view of the city.

1 The clock face on the fifth floor provides views over the Seine to the Jardin des Tuileries.

2 The nudity in Manet's *Le Déjeuner sur l'herbe* (1863) caused a scandal when first exhibited.

3 Monet's *Le Déjeuner sur l'herbe* (1865–6) was a tribute to the work of the same name by Manet.

GALLERY GUIDE

The collection occupies three levels. On the ground floor, there are works from the mid-to late 19th century. The middle level features Art Nouveau, decorative art, and a range of paintings and sculptures dating from the second half of the 19th century to the early 20th century, as well as Neo-Impressionist art. The upper level has a great collection of Impressionist art.

←

The former railway station, designed by Victor Laloux for the Universal Exhibition in 1900

EXPERIENCE MORE

2

Boulevard St-Germain

📍F5 🏛75006, 75007
Ⓜ Solférino, rue du Bac,
St-Germain-des-Prés,
Mabillon, Odéon, Cluny-La
Sorbonne, Maubert-
Mutualité

The most celebrated street
on the Left Bank slinks across
three districts from the Île
St-Louis to Pont de la Concorde.
Its architecture is the result
of Baron Haussmann's bold
strokes of urban planning, but
it encompasses a wide range
of lifestyles.

💬 INSIDER TIP
Macaron Mecca

Sample the city's most
innovative macarons,
such as chestnut-rose,
white truffle-hazelnut,
and raspberry-lychee,
at Pierre Hermé's flag-
ship patisserie, on rue
Bonaparte *(www.
pierreherme.com).*

Starting from the east, it
passes the Musée de Cluny
and the Sorbonne, and is
most lively from boulevard
St-Michel to St-Germain-des-
Prés, with its café culture.

3

Ecole Nationale
Supérieure des
Beaux-Arts

📍F4 🏛14 rue Bonaparte
75006 Ⓜ St-Germain-des-
Prés 🕐Public Open House
days during Jun & Jul,
check website for details
🌐beauxartsparis.fr

The main French school of
fine arts has an enviable
position at the corner of rue
Bonaparte and the riverside
quai Malaquais. It is housed
in several buildings, the most
imposing being the 19th-
century Palais des Etudes.
A host of budding French
and foreign painters and
architects have crossed the
courtyard, which contains a
17th-century chapel, to learn

in the ateliers of the school.
Many American architects
have also studied here.

4

St-Germain-des-Prés

📍F5 🏛3 pl St-Germain-
des-Prés 75006 Ⓜ St-
Germain-des-Prés 🕐9am-
8pm Mon, 8:30am-8pm
Tue-Sat 🌐eglise-sgp.org

The oldest church in Paris
originated in 542 as a basilica
to house holy relics. It grew
into a powerful Benedictine
abbey, was rebuilt in the 11th
century, was mostly destroyed
by fire in 1794, and was fully
restored in the 1800s. One of
the three original towers survives, with one of France's oldest belfries. The interior is a
mix of styles, with 6th-century
marble columns, Gothic vaulting, Romanesque arches and
19th-century frescos. Tours
take place between September
and June at 3pm on Tuesdays,
Thursdays and the third
Sunday of each month.

Musée Eugène Delacroix

📍 F4-5 🏠 6 rue de Fürstenberg 75006 Ⓜ St-Germain-des-Prés, Mabillon 🚌 39, 63, 70, 86, 95, 96 🕐 9:30am–5:30pm Wed-Mon (to 9pm 1st Thu of month) 🚫 1 Jan, 1 May, 25 Dec 🌐 musee-delacroix.fr

The leading Romantic painter Delacroix lived here from 1857 until his death in 1863. His *The Way to Calvary* and *The Entombment of Christ* hang in the museum. He also created murals for a chapel in nearby St-Sulpice church *(p143)*. In the apartment and studio are a portrait of George Sand and some self-portraits. There is free entry to the museum on the first Sunday of the month.

---

⑥ Rue de l'Odéon

📍 G5 🏠 75006 Ⓜ Odéon

Opened in 1779 to improve access to the Odéon Theatre, this was the first street in the

↑ Paintings in Musée Eugène Delacroix, the artist's former home

city to have gutters and it still has many 18th-century houses. Sylvia Beach's original Shakespeare & Company bookshop stood at No 12, patronized by writers such as James Joyce, Ezra Pound and Hemingway.

TOP 5 **SHOPPING STREETS**

Rue Lobineau
Home of the St-Germain covered food market and shopping centre.

Rue Bonaparte
Full of swanky shops, including the Pierre Hermé flagship store.

Rue du Bac
Full of shops selling pastries and other tasty confections.

Rue de Sèvres
The location of Le Bon Marché, the first department store in Paris, which opened in 1852.

Rue de Buci
A former market street that today houses cafés and cute shops.

↑ Shoppers and strollers on the elegant and leafy boulevard St-Germain

← Heads from statues of the kings and queens of Judah in the Musée de Cluny

 7

Musée de Cluny

📍G5 🏛6 place Paul-Pain-levé, 75005 Ⓜ St-Michel, Odéon, Cluny 🚈St-Michel ⏰9:15am–5:45pm Wed–Mon 🚫1 Jan, 1 May, 25 Dec 🌐musee-moyenage.fr

Officially the Musée National du Moyen Age, this is a unique combination of Gallo-Roman ruins, incorporated into a fine medieval mansion standing in recreated medieval gardens, and one of the world's finest collections of medieval art and crafts. Its name comes from Pierre de Chalus, Abbot of Cluny, who purchased the ruins in 1330.

The present building dates from 1485–98 and its star exhibits include tapestries, remarkable for their quality, age and state of preservation. The highlight of the sculpture section is the Gallery of the Kings, while one of Cluny's most precious objects, the Golden Rose of Basel, from 1330, is found in the collection of jewellery and metalwork.

300,000
books are held in the green *bouquinistes* boxes along the River Seine.

Other treasures here include stained glass, woodcarvings and books of hours.

8

St-Séverin

📍G5 🏛1 rue-des-Prêtres-St-Séverin 75005 Ⓜ St-Michel ⏰11am–7:30pm Mon–Sat, 9am–8:30pm Sun 🌐saint-severin.com

One of the finest churches in Paris, St-Séverin is named after a 6th-century hermit who lived locally. A perfect example of the Flamboyant Gothic style, it was begun in the 13th century and finished in the early 16th and includes a double aisle encircling the chancel. The garden contains the church's medieval gable-roofed charnel house.

9

Jardin du Luxembourg

📍F6 🏛Blvd St-Michel/rue Guynemer 75006/rue de Vaugirard/ Ⓜ Odéon 🚈Luxembourg ⏰Dawn-dusk daily 🌐senat.fr/visite

A green oasis covering 25 ha (60 acres) in the heart of the Left Bank, the lovely Jardin du Luxembourg is one of the most popular parks in Paris. Beautifully sculpted gardens are centred around the Palais du Luxembourg, home of the French Senate, and feature an octagonal basin, often lined by children sailing toy boats.

The garden was created at the request of Marie de' Medici, who had it designed to be a fitting reminder of the Boboli Gardens in her home town of Florence. Statues were placed throughout the park around 1848. They include those of the queens of France, famous French women – that of Sainte Geneviève is an impressive example – and, later, famous writers and artists were added, making a total of 106 statues.

The garden is a great space for children, with activities such as the puppet theatre, a safely fenced playground, the carousel and tennis courts.

→ Statuary and lawns around the pond in the Jardin du Luxembourg

Adults can also play tennis, or chess or bridge, take a stroll through the open-air photography exhibitions that are sometimes held here, or relax in one of the heavy green metal chairs that are scattered about for just that purpose.

 10

La Sorbonne

📍 G6 🏠 1 rue Victor Cousin 75005 Ⓜ Cluny-La Sorbonne, Maubert-Mutualité 🕐 By appt Mon-Fri & one Sat a month 🌐 paris-sorbonne.fr

The Sorbonne, which is one of the oldest universities in the world, was established in 1253 by Robert de Sorbon, confessor to Louis IX, for the benefit of 16 poor scholars, so they could study theology. It went on to become the centre of scholastic theology.

In 1469, three printing presses were brought from Mainz, and the first printing house in France was founded. The college's opposition to liberal 18th-century philosophical ideas led to its suppression during the Revolution. In 1806 it was re-established by Napoleon, and the 17th-century buildings replaced. In 1969, the Sorbonne split into 13 separate universities, but some lectures are still held in the old building.

---

11 Ⓜ 🏛

St-Etienne-du-Mont

📍 H6 🏠 Place Ste-Geneviève 75005 Ⓜ Cardinal Lemoine 🕐 Hours vary, check website 🌐 saintetiennedumont.fr

This remarkable church, with its notable stained-glass, is home to the shrine of the patron saint of Paris, Sainte Geneviève, and also holds the remains of literary figures Racine and Pascal.

Some parts of the church are in the Gothic style, while other sections date from the Renaissance, including a magnificent rood screen that crosses the nave like a bridge.

STAY

Hôtel d'Aubusson
Offering a cosy lobby and refined rooms.

📍 G4 🏠 33 rue Dauphine 75006 🌐 hoteldaubusson.com

€€€

Relais Christine
Enjoy top-notch service and amenities.

📍 G5 🏠 3 rue Christine 75006 🌐 relais-christine.com

€€€

Hôtel Récamier
Elegance is on offer at this hidden gem.

📍 F5 🏠 3B place St-Sulpice 75006 🌐 hotelrecamier.com

€€€

← The interior of the Panthéon, looking up into the 43.5-m- (143-ft-) wide diameter dome

the fountains in Paris. The central sculpture, by Jean-Baptiste Carpeaux, which was erected in 1873, is made of bronze. It features four women holding aloft a globe that represents four of the continents – Oceania, the fifth, was left out for reasons of symmetry. There are some subsidiary figures, including dolphins, horses and a turtle.

 14

Palais du Luxembourg

F6 **15 rue de Vaugirard 75006** **Odéon** **Luxembourg** **Hours vary, check website** **senat.fr/visiteor museeduluxembourg.fr**

Now home of the French Senate, this palace was built to remind Marie de' Medici, the widow of Henri IV, of her native city of Florence. It was built to a design by Salomon de Brosse in the style of the

12

Panthéon

G6 **Pl du Panthéon 75005** **Maubert-Mutualité, Cardinal-Lemoine** **Luxembourg** **21, 27, 38, 82, 84, 85, 89** **Apr–Sep: 10am–6:30pm daily; Oct–Mar: 10am–6pm daily** **1 Jan, 1 May, 25 Dec** **paris-pantheon.fr**

When Louis XV recovered from illness in 1744, he was so thankful that he conceived a magnificent church to honour Ste Geneviève, the patron saint of the city. The French architect Jacques-Germain Soufflot planned the church in Neo-Classical style. Work began in 1764 and was completed in 1790 under the control of Guillaume Rondelet. But with the Revolution under way, the church was turned into a pantheon – a monument housing the tombs of France's great heroes.

Napoleon returned it to the Church in 1806, but it was secularized and then desecularized once more, before finally being made a civic building in 1885.

The façade, inspired by the Rome Pantheon, features a pediment relief that depicts the mother country granting laurels to her great men. Under the building, the vast crypt divides into galleries flanked by Doric columns. Many notable French people rest here, including Voltaire and Emile Zola.

 13

Fontaine de l'Observatoire

F7 **Place Ernest Denis, av de l'Observatoire 75006** **Port Royal**

Situated at the southern tip of the Jardin du Luxembourg, this is one of the finest of all

Pitti Palace in Florence. By the time it was finished, in 1631, Marie had been banished from Paris, but it remained a royal palace until the French Revolution. In World War II it became the Luftwaffe headquarters. The Musée du Luxembourg in the east gallery hosts art exhibitions.

St-Sulpice

📍 F5 🏠 2 rue Palatine, place St-Sulpice 75006 Ⓜ St-Sulpice 🕐 7:30am–7:30pm daily 🌐 pss75.fr/saint-sulpice-paris/

This imposing church, which was started during 1646, and took more than 100 years to be completed, has a simple façade consisting of two tiers of elegant columns with mismatched towers at the ends. Large windows fill the interior with light, and the fine organ fills it with sound when concerts are held. The chapel to the right of the entrance has murals by Eugène Delacroix, including *Jacob Wrestling with*

Beautiful gardens in
↓ front of the imposing
Palais du Luxembourg

the Angel. Tours of the crypt are given regularly, including one in English, on the first Sunday of the month.

Val-de-Grâce

📍 G7 🏠 1 pl Alphonse-Laveran 75005 Ⓜ Les Gobelins 🚆 Port Royal 🕐 Noon–6pm Tue–Thu, Sat & Sun 🔒 Aug 🌐 valdegrace.org

This church, one of the most beautiful in all of France, was designed by François Mansart and Jacques Lemercier, and forms part of a military hospital complex. Built for Anne of Austria (wife of Louis XIII) in gratitude for the birth of her son, young Louis XIV himself laid the first stone in 1645, when he was seven years old.

The church is noted for its grand, two-storey façade, and for the dome, a landmark on Paris' skyline. In the cupola is Pierre Mignard's enormous fresco, with over 200 triple-life-size figures. The six huge marble columns framing the altar are similar to ones in St Peter's in Rome. There is no charge if you only want to enter the nave.

DRINK

Monk le Taverne de Cluny
The place on the Left Bank for craft beer, with a great selection on tap and bottled. There's regular live music too.

📍 G5 🏠 51 rue de la Harpe, 75005 🌐 la tavernedecluny.com

Le Piano Vache
Students and locals hit the bar at this rowdy watering hole, which plays loud rock music.

📍 H6 🏠 8 rue Laplace 75005 🔒 Sun 🌐 lepianovache.com

Le Bombardier
Paris has few pubs worthy of the name, but this one has earned its stripes with draught and cask ales.

📍 H6 🏠 2 place du Panthéon 75005 🌐 bombardierpub.fr

The cobbled streets of Montmartre

Must Sees

1 Sacré-Coeur
2 Cimetière du Père-Lachaise

Experience More

3 La Défense
4 Bois de Boulogne
5 Fondation Louis Vuitton
6 Fondation Le Corbusier
7 Rue La Fontaine
8 Moulin Rouge
9 St-Alexandre-Nevsky
10 Musée Marmottan Monet
11 Parc Monceau
12 Musée Gustave Moreau
13 Canal St-Martin
14 Cimetière de Montmartre
15 Marché aux Puces de St-Ouen
16 Parc des Buttes-Chaumont
17 Cité de Sciences et de l'Industrie
18 Bercy
19 Cité Nationale de l'Histoire de l'Immigration
20 Château de Vincennes
21 Bibliothèque Nationale de France
22 Parc Montsouris
23 Musée National d'Histoire Naturelle
24 Grande Mosquée de Paris
25 Catacombes
26 Jardin des Plantes
27 Montparnasse

BEYOND
THE CENTRE

Once a largely rural area, the lands beyond Paris's city walls supplied the city with food for centuries. It was also home to those jettisoned from the city; a legacy of plague hospitals, leper colonies and cemeteries pepper the landscape. In 1860, the 11 villages were absorbed into the city as Napoléon reorganized the city's infrastructure. In the 18th century, low-cost housing in Montmartre attracted the working classes, as well as artists and intellectuals. In the 1970s, the final bastion of this past, the slaughterhouses of La Villette, became a park.

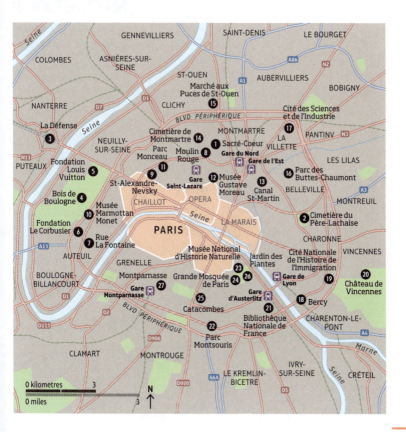

❶ 🧭 🎒

SACRÉ-COEUR

🏛 33–35 rue du Chevalier-de-la-Barre 75018 Ⓜ Abbesses (then funiculaire to steps of Sacré-Coeur), Anvers, Jules Joffrin, Pigalle 🚌 30, 31, 80, 85 Ⓒ Basilica: 6am–10:30pm daily; dome: 9am–6pm daily; vespers 4pm Sun Ⓦ sacre-coeur-montmartre.com

Situated atop the hill of Montmartre, the spectacular white basilica of the Sacré-Coeur watches over Paris from the city's highest point. It stands as a memorial to the 58,000 French soldiers killed during the Franco-Prussian War.

At the outbreak of the Franco-Prussian War in 1870, two Catholic businessmen made a private religious vow to build a church dedicated to the Sacred Heart of Christ, should France be spared the impending Prussian onslaught. The two men, Alexandre Legentil and Hubert Rohault de Fleury, lived to see Paris saved from invasion despite the war and a lengthy siege – and were able to witness the start of work on the Sacré-Coeur basilica. The project was taken up by Archbishop Guibert of Paris and construction began in 1875 to Paul Abadie's designs, which were inspired by the Romano-Byzantine church of St-Front in Périgueux. The basilica was completed in 1914, but its consecration was forestalled by World War I until 1919, when France was victorious.

THE SIEGE OF PARIS

Prussia invaded France in 1870. During the four-month siege of Paris, instigated by the Prusso-German statesman Otto von Bismarck, hungry Parisians were forced to eat the city's horses and other animals.

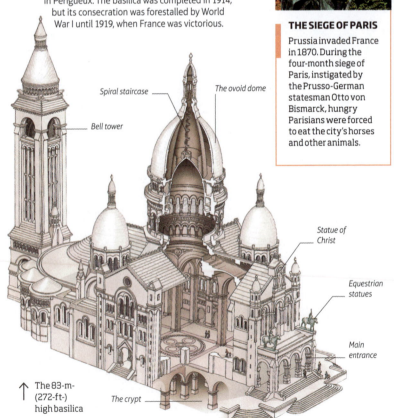

Spiral staircase

The ovoid dome

Bell tower

Statue of Christ

Equestrian statues

Main entrance

↑ The 83-m-(272-ft-) high basilica

The crypt

PICTURE PERFECT
The Basilica and the City

The best view of the Sacré-Coeur is from the gardens below, but for a 360-degree panorama of the city, climb the 300 steps to the top of the basilica dome.

↑ The beautiful basilica, crowned by its elegant ovoid dome

CIMETIÈRE DU PÈRE LACHAISE

🏠 Blvd de Ménilmontant Ⓜ Père Lachaise, Alexandre Dumas 🚌 60, 61, 64, 69, 26 to Pl Gambetta 🕐 8am–6pm Mon–Fri, 8:30am–6pm Sat, 9am–6pm (closes 30 min earlier daily Nov–mid-Mar)

This is the most visited cemetery in the world. It contains over 70,000 graves, including the tombs of numerous famous figures, such as the writer Honoré de Balzac, the composer Frédéric Chopin, the singer Jim Morrison and the actor Yves Montand.

Paris's most prestigious cemetery is set on a wooded hill overlooking the city. The land was once owned by Père de la Chaise, Louis XIV's confessor, but it was bought in 1803 by order of Napoleon to create a new cemetery. Père Lachaise, the first cemetery in France with a crematorium, became so popular that it was expanded six times during the 19th century.

Today the cemetery is a place of pilgrimage for rock fans, who come from around the world to see the grave of Jim Morrison of The Doors. With its moss-grown tombs and ancient trees, as well as striking funerary sculpture, Père Lachaise is an atmospheric and rather romantic place for a stroll.

Did You Know?

The remains of Molière were transferred here in 1817 to add some historic glamour to the new cemetery.

→ A visitor exploring the funerary art among the lanes of Père Lachaise

← Théodore Géricault's tomb, with a depiction of *The Raft of the Medusa*

MUR DES FÉDÉRÉS

Following France's defeat in the Franco-Prussian War in 1871, a left-wing group revolted, setting up the Paris Commune. After 72 days, government troops marched on the city and in a week of brutal street fighting, much of the city was burned and thousands were killed. Mur des Fédérés in Père Lachaise is where the last Communard rebels were shot by government forces.

Notable Residents

Allan Kardec

▷ Kardec was the founder of a 19th-century spiritual cult, which still has a strong following. His tomb is perpetually covered in pilgrims' flowers.

George Rodenbach

The monument to this 19th-century poet depicts him rising out of his tomb with a rose in the hand of his outstretched arm.

Oscar Wilde

◁ The Irish dramatist, aesthete and great wit was exiled from virtuous Britain to die of drink and dissipation in Paris in 1900. American-British artist Jacob Epstein sculpted his tomb.

Marcel Proust

The French novelist brilliantly chronicled the belle époque in *In Search of Lost Time*.

Sarah Bernhardt

▷ The great French tragedienne, who died in 1923 aged 78, was once the most famous actress in the world.

Edith Piaf

Known as the "Little Sparrow" because of her size, Piaf was the 20th century's greatest French popular singer. In her tragic voice, she sang of the sorrows and woes of the Paris working class.

Jim Morrison

▷ The Doors' lead singer died in Paris in 1971 at the age of 27. When he died, he was one of the most famous singers in the world. The circumstances of his death are still a big mystery.

Rowing boats for hire on Lac Inférieur, the largest lake in the Bois de Boulogne ↑

EXPERIENCE MORE

La Défense

🅰 La Grande Arche, 1 parvis de la Défense Ⓜ La Défense 🆁🅴🆁 La Défense 🚌 73, 141, 158, 159 🕐 10am–7pm daily 🌐 grandearche.fr

This skyscraper business city on the western edge of Paris is the largest office development in Europe. La Grande Arche is an enormous hollow cube that is large enough to hold Notre-Dame cathedral. Designed by Danish architect Otto von Spreckelsen in the late 1980s, the arch houses a video-game museum and a museum on computers, a gallery, and has superb views.

---

④

Bois de Boulogne

🅰 75016 Ⓜ Porte Maillot, Porte Dauphine, Porte d'Auteuil, Les Sablons 🕐 24 hrs daily

This 8.5-sq-km (3.3-sq-mile) park, located between the western edges of Paris and the River Seine, offers a vast belt of greenery for strolling, cycling, horse-riding, boating, picnicking or spending a day

at the races. The park was once part of the immense Forêt du Rouvre. In the mid-19th century Napoleon III had the Bois designed and landscaped by Baron Haussmann, along the lines of Hyde Park in London. One of several self-contained parks within the forest is the lush Jardin d'Acclimatation (a fun park for children), the Pré Catalan and the Bagatelle gardens, with architectural follies and an 18th-century villa famous for its rose garden. This otherwise family-friendly park is notoriously seedy after dark, when it is best avoided.

---

⑤

Fondation Louis Vuitton

🅰 8 av du Mahatma Gandhi, Bois de Boulogne, 75116 Ⓜ Les Sablons 🚌 Shuttle from pl Charles de Gaulle 🕐 Noon–7pm Mon & Wed, noon–9pm Fri, 11am–8pm Sat & Sun 🚫 1 Jan, 1 May, 25 Dec 🌐 fondationlouis vuitton.fr

Located close to the Jardin d'Acclimatation in the Bois de Boulogne, Frank Gehry's dramatic glass structure

consisting of twelve glass "sails" seems to float on the water. The building is a poetic example of modern architecture, containing a gallery of modern art, with space for huge installations and soundscape exhibitions. There is also a space for hosting contemporary art exhibitions and events, including classical concerts, and a range of activities for all ages, from art workshops to fun-filled hands-on games and wonderful storytelling events for younger visitors.

STAY

Grandes Écoles
Old-world charm.

 75 rue du Cardinal Lemoine 75005 hotel-grandes ecoles.com

€€€

Seven Hôtel
Swanky décor sets this modern hotel apart.

 20 rue Berthollet 75005 sevenhotelparis.com

€€€

Hôtel Saint Marcel
A great location, and the family's own wine.

 45 boulevard St-Marcel 75013 hotel saint-marcel-paris.com

€€€

Fondation Le Corbusier

🏠 8-10 square du Docteur-Blanche 75016 Ⓜ Jasmin
🕐 1:30–6pm Mon, 10am–6pm Tue-Sat ✖ Aug and public hols 🖥 fondation lecorbusier.fr

In a quiet corner of Auteuil stand the villas La Roche and Jeanneret, the first Parisian houses to be constructed by the influential 20th-century architect Charles-Edouard Jeanneret, better known as Le Corbusier. Built at the beginning of the 1920s, they demonstrate his revolutionary use of white concrete in Cubist forms, a defining Modernist style. The rooms flow into each other, allowing for the maximum natural light and acoustics to be enjoyed. The houses stand on stilts with windows along their entire length. Today, the villas can be visited (tours in English 4pm Tue, Thu & Fri), and provide apt venues for lectures about Le Corbusier and his work.

→

View over the park to the city from the Fondation Louis Vuitton

7

Rue la Fontaine

🏠 75016 Ⓜ Michel-Ange-Auteuil, Jasmin Ⓡ Gare d'Avenue du Pdt Kennedy

Rue la Fontaine and the surrounding streets act as a showcase for some of the most exciting early 20th-century Art Nouveau architecture, featuring sinuous decorative detail.

At No 14 stands the Castel Béranger, a stunning apartment block made from cheap building materials to keep the costs low, yet featuring eye-catching stained glass, mosaic decoration, convoluted ironwork and balconies. It firmly established the reputation of its architect, Hector Guimard, who went on to design the city's famous Art Nouveau Métro entrances. Other great examples of his work can be seen further along the street, such as the exterior of the Hôtel Mezzara at No 60.

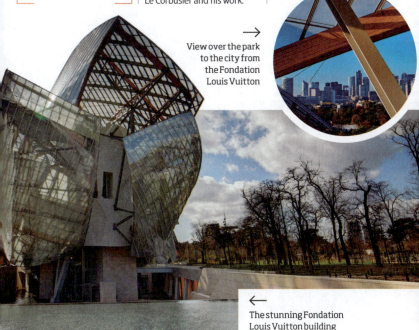

←

The stunning Fondation Louis Vuitton building in the Bois de Boulogne

The glass skyline of La Defense, Paris's financial district

SHOP

Maison Arnaud Demontel

Exquisite bread and pastries at this award-winning bakery.

🏠 39 rue des Martyrs
🌐 arnauddemontel.com

Mesdemoiselles Madeleine

All about multiple varieties of madeleines.

🏠 37 rue des Martyrs
🌐 mllesmadeleines.com

Popelini

Cream-filled *choux*, and nothing else – but what else could you want?

🏠 44 rue des Martyrs
🌐 popelini.com

Henri Le Roux

Salted-butter caramels and chocolate fill this boutique.

🏠 24 rue des Martyrs
🌐 chocolatleroux.com

8

Moulin Rouge

🏠 82 blvd de Clichy 75018
Ⓜ Blanche ⏰ Shows: 9 & 11pm daily; dinner: 7pm
🌐 moulinrouge.fr

Built in 1885, the Moulin Rouge was turned into a dance hall as early as 1900. Henri de Toulouse-Lautrec immortalized the wild and colourful cancan shows here in his posters and drawings of famous dancers such as Jane Avril and May Milton. The high-kicking routines continue today in glitzy, Las-Vegas-style revues.

9

St-Alexandre-Nevsky

🏠 12 rue Daru 75008
Ⓜ Courcelles, Ternes
⏰ By appt 3–5pm Tue, Fri & Sun 🌐 cathedrale-orthodoxe.com

With its five golden-copper domes, this imposing Russian Orthodox cathedral bears witness to the large Russian community in Paris. A designated historic monument, it was designed by members of the St Petersburg Fine Arts Academy, financed by Tsar Alexander II together with the local Russian community. The church also holds a place in secular culture. In July 1918, Picasso was married to Russian ballet dancer Olga Khokhlova here. The cathedral appears in the opening scenes of the 1956 film adaptation of Marcelle Maurette's *Anastasia*.

Inside, a whole wall of icons divides the church in two. The Greek-cross plan and the rich mosaics and frescoes that decorate the interior are Neo-Byzantine, while the exterior and gilt domes are traditional Russian Orthodox. Visits, including into the crypt, can be arranged by appointment.

10

Musée Marmottan Monet

🏠 2 rue Louis Boilly 75016
Ⓜ La Muette ⏰ 10am–6pm Tue–Sun (to 9pm Thu) 📅 1 Jan, 1 May, Aug, 25 Dec 🌐 marmottan.fr

Featuring one of the best collections of Impressionist art in France, this museum was created within the 19th-

Parc Monceau

📍 35 blvd de Courcelles 75017 📞 01 42 27 39 56 Ⓜ Monceau 🕐 7am-8pm daily (to 10pm in summer)

This lovely green haven dates back to 1778, when the Duc de Chartres commissioned the painter and amateur landscape designer Louis Carmontelle to create a magnificent garden. The result was an landscape enhanced by a range of architectural follies in the style of English and German gardens. In 1852 the garden became a chic public park, and a few of the original features can still be seen, such as the *naumachia* basin, an ornamental version of a Roman pool, and a pyramid. Today, the park also has playgrounds.

Musée Gustave Moreau

📍 14 rue de la Rochefoucauld 75009 Ⓜ Trinité-d'Estienne d'Orves 🕐 10am-5:15pm Wed-Mon 🕐 12:45-2pm Mon, Wed & Thu 🌐 musee-moreau.fr

The Symbolist painter Gustave Moreau (1826–98), known for his symbolic works depicting biblical and mythological scenes, lived and worked in this town house, now displaying a large number of his paintings across three floors. The collection includes *Jupiter and Semele*, one of the artist's most outstanding works.

century home of the famous art historian Paul Marmottan, in 1932. He had bequeathed his graceful mansion, as well as his fine collection of Renaissance, Consular and First Empire paintings and pieces of furniture, to the Institut de France.

In 1966 the museum acquired a fabulous collection of work by the Impressionist painter Claude Monet, which was the bequest of his son, Michel. Some of Monet's most famous paintings can be seen

↑ Some of the works on display at the Musée Marmottan Monet

here, including *Impression – Sunrise* (giving the genre its name, "Impressionist"), a painting of Rouen Cathedral *(p246)* and the Water Lilies series. Also here is the work painted at Giverny during the last years of Monet's life, including *The Japanese Bridge* and *The Weeping Willow*. The iridescent colours and daring brushstrokes make them some of the museum's most powerful works.

Part of Monet's personal art collection was passed on to the museum as well, including work by fellow Impressionists Camille Pissarro, Edgar Degas, Pierre-Auguste Renoir, Paul Gauguin and Alfred Sisley, and the museum does an excellent job of explaining the relationships between the artists. The space also has displays of medieval illuminated manuscripts and 16th-century Burgundian tapestries. Piano and chamber music concerts are held here on occasion.

← Boulevard de Clichy after dark, with the brightly illuminated Moulin Rouge

Did You Know?

Impressionist painters Monet and Renoir were great friends, and often painted the same scene side-by-side.

13 Canal St-Martin

M Jaurès, J Bonsergent, Goncourt

A walk along the quays of the Canal St-Martin gives a glimpse of how this working-class area of the city looked at the end of the 19th century. The 5-km (3-mile) canal was opened in 1825 to provide a shortcut for river traffic on the Seine. A few brick-and-iron factories and warehouses survive from this time, as well as the legendary Hôtel du Nord, made famous by Marcel Carné. Around it are tree-lined quays with quirky shops and cafés, iron footbridges and public gardens. The Canal de l'Ourcq, an offshoot, offers a pleasant stroll to Parc de la Villette.

14 Cimetière de Montmartre

A 20 av Rachel 75018
C 01 53 42 36 30 **M** Blanche
O 8am–6pm daily (from 8:30am Sat, from 9am Sun)

This cemetery is the third largest in Paris, and has been the resting place for many luminaries of the creative arts since the beginning of the 19th century. The composers Hector Berlioz and Jacques Offenbach (who wrote the renowned cancan tune), Russian dancer Vaslav Nijinsky and the film director François Truffaut are just a few of the notable people to have been buried here over the years.

There is also a Montmartre cemetery, the St-Vincent, near square Roland-Dorgelès, where you can find the grave of celebrated Dax-born painter Maurice Utrillo.

↑ The tomb of Vaslav Nijinsky in the Cimetière de Montmartre

↑ A stretch of pleasant tree-lined quays along the Canal St-Martin

EAT

Here are the four best coffee shops along the canal.

Ten Belles Coffee Bar
A 10 rue de la Grange aux Belles 75010
W tenbelles.com

€/€/€

——————

Holybelly
A 5 rue Lucien, Sampaix 75010 **W** holybellycafe. com

€/€/€

——————

Craft
A 24 rue des Vinaigriers 75010 **W** cafe-craft.com

€/€/€

——————

Radiodays
A 15 rue Alibert 75010
W radiodays.cafe

€/€/€

Marché aux Puces de St-Ouen

 Rue des Rosiers, St-Ouen 93406 M Porte-de-Clignancourt, Garibaldi 9am–6pm Sat, 10am–6pm Sun, 11am–5pm Mon (reduced hours in summer) W marcheauxpuces-saintouen.com

The oldest and largest Paris flea market spans around 6 ha (15 acres). In the 19th century, rag merchants and tramps would gather outside the fortifications that marked the city limits and offer their wares for sale. Today the area is divided into 15 separate markets, and mainly sells antiques. It is well known for its heavy Second Empire furniture and ornaments.

Parc des Buttes-Chaumont

1 rue Botzaris 75019 C 01 42 02 91 21 M Botzaris, Buttes-Chaumont Sep–Jun: 7am–9pm daily; Jul–Aug: 24 hrs daily

In the 1860s, urban planner Baron Haussmann converted this hilly site from a rubbish dump and quarry with gallows at the foot to English-style gardens. His colleague was landscape architect Adolphe Alphand, who was responsible for a vast 1860s programme to provide new pavement-lined Parisian avenues with benches, streetlights, kiosks and urinals. Others involved in the creation of this highly praised park were the engineer Darcel and the landscape gardener Barillet-Deschamps. They created a lake, made an island with real and artificial rocks, gave it a Roman-style temple, and added streams, a waterfall and footbridges leading to the island. Today, in the summer months, visitors will also find

a splendid puppet theatre (*guignol*) for the kids, and acres of beautiful lawns.

Cité des Sciences et de l'Industrie

30 av Corentin Cariou 75019 M Porte de la Villette 75, 139, 150, 152, 375 T3b 10am–6pm Tue–Sat, 10am–7pm Sun 1 Jan, 1 May, 25 Dec W cite-sciences.fr

This hugely popular science and technology museum occupies the largest of the former Villette slaughterhouses, which now form part of a massive urban park. Architect Adrien Fainsilber has created an imaginative interplay of light, vegetation and water in the high-tech, five-storey building. At the museum's heart is the

Explora exhibit, a fascinating guide to technology and science. Elsewhere there is a children's science city with interactive displays; children can play with machines that show how scientific principles work. The building is surrounded by a moat designed by Fainsilber to allow natural light to penetrate into the lower levels of the building. A series of walkways crisscross the moat, linking the various floors of the museum to the La Géode cinema and the park.

Did You Know?

La Géode, a giant entertainment sphere in Cité des Sciences, houses a 1-sq-km (1-sq-mile) hemispherical cinema screen.

Inside the futuristic Cité des Sciences et de l'Industrie ↑

18 Bercy

🏠 75012 📞 01 71 19 33 33
Ⓜ Bercy, Cour St-Emilion
🚍 24, 64, 87 Cinémathèque
Française: 51 rue de Bercy
🕐 Museum: noon–7pm
Wed–Mon; library: noon–
8pm Wed–Mon

This former wine-trading quarter just to the east of the city centre, with its riverside warehouses and pavilions, has been successfully rejuvenated. The hub of the quarter is the Cour Saint-Emilion, a pretty cobbled street lined by ochre-coloured former warehouses that have been converted to house shops, restaurants and wine bars.

Nearby is the modern Parc de Bercy, which is beautifully landscaped with lily ponds, rose gardens and even vineyards. Bordering the park, the striking Frank Gehry-designed Cinémathèque Française is worthy of a detour; it holds a fascinating arthouse cinema and accompanying museum.

19 Cité Nationale de l'Histoire de l'Immigration

🏠 Palais de la Porte Dorée,
293 av Daumesnil 75012
Ⓜ Porte Dorée 🚍 46
🕐 10am–5:30pm Tue–Fri,
10am–7pm Sat & Sun (Jun–
Aug: to 9pm Wed) 🚫 1 Jan, 1
May, 25 Dec 🌐 histoire-
immigration.fr

Housed in the Palais de la Porte Dorée, which was designed for the city's grand colonial exhibition in 1931, this museum is devoted to immigration in France. The museum's three thematic sections examine first the reasons for immigration itself, then issues of assimilation and finally the contribution of diverse cultures in the everyday life of the French people.

Did You Know?
—
Immigrants make up approximately 12 per cent of the population in France.

20 Château de Vincennes

🏠 1 av de Paris 94300
Vincennes Ⓜ Château de
Vincennes 🚉 Vincennes
🚍 46, 56, 86 🕐 10am–5pm
daily (to 6pm mid-May–Sep)
🚫 1 Jan, 1 May, 1 & 11 Nov,
25 Dec 🌐 chateau-
vincennes.fr

The Château de Vincennes was the permanent royal residence until the 17th century, before the court moved to Versailles. The keep, the tallest fortified medieval building in Europe, the Gothic chapel, 17th-century pavilions and moat are all worth seeing.

Beyond lies the Bois de Vincennes. Once a royal hunting ground, it is now a landscaped forest with ornamental lakes and a racecourse.

21 Bibliothèque Nationale de France

🏠 Quai François-Mauriac
75013 Ⓜ Bibliothèque
François-Mitterrand, quai
de la Gare 🚉 Bibliothèque
François-Mitterand 🚍 62,
64, 89, 132, 325 🕐 10am–
8pm Tue–Sat, 1–7pm Sun
🚫 Public hols, 1 week in Sep
🌐 bnf.fr

These four great book-shaped towers house some 10 million volumes, and the libraries here offer more than 400,000 titles. Other resources include

↑ The palatial interior of the huge Bibliothèque Nationale de France

sound archives and digitized illustrations. Temporary exhibitions are also held on a regular basis.

 Parc Montsouris

🏠 2 rue Gazan, blvd Jourdan 75014 📞 01 53 90 67 14 Ⓜ Pte d'Orléans 🚆 Cité Universitaire ⏰ Hours vary, call ahead

This lovely English-style park is the second largest green space in the city of Paris, and is a favoured spot of Parisians. It was laid out by Adolphe Alphand, an engineer under the direction of Baron Haussmann, between 1865 and 1878.

Sculptures dot the park's grassy expanse, and there is a large lake that's home to a variety of birds. Here, too, you can visit the Montsouris meteorological observatory and the *mire du Sud*, which marks the exact location of the Paris meridian.

The bandstand, puppet theatre, playgrounds and petting zoo are also on hand to keep all ages busy.

DRINK

Mini Pong Bar
This small bar screams fun through its decor and great cocktail list.

🏠 64 rue Jean-Baptiste Pigalle 75009 🕐 Sun 🌐 minipongbar.com

€€€

Lulu White
Made for long nights with friends over the best cocktails around.

🏠 12 Rue Frochet 75009 🕐 Tue 🌐 luluwhite.bar

€€€

Les Papilles
Wine bottles line the walls of this friendly local.

🏠 30 rue Gay-Lussac 75005 🕐 Sun, Mon 🌐 lespapilles paris.fr

€€€

← The bridge arching across the river towards the towering skyscrapers of Bercy

23

Musée National d'Histoire Naturelle

⌂ 36 rue Geoffroy Saint-Hilaire 75005 Ⓜ Jussieu, Austerlitz ⏰ 10am–6pm Wed-Mon 🚫 1 Jan, 1 May, 25 Dec 🌐 mnhn.fr

This museum's well-curated Grande Galerie de l'Evolution traces evolution on earth. The four other departments focus on palaeontology, featuring the evolution of bone structure; palaeobotany, devoted to plant fossils; mineralogy, including gemstones; and entomology, showing some of the oldest fossilized insects ever found.

24

Grande Mosquée de Paris

⌂ 2 bis place du Puits de l'Ermite 75005 Ⓜ Place Monge ⏰ 9am–noon & 2–6pm Sat-Thu 🚫 Muslim hols 🌐 mosqueedeparis.net

Built during the 1920s in the Hispano-Moorish style, as a token of gratitude for the Muslim *tirailleurs* who died

fighting in World War I, the Grande Mosquée features beautiful decoration and a striking, 33-m- (108-ft-) high minaret. These buildings are the centre of Paris's Muslim community. Once used exclusively by scholars, the mosque has expanded significantly over the years. It now houses some rather salubrious but fun Turkish baths, a lush and landscaped garden, a fine restaurant and a beautiful *salon de thé*.

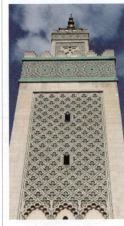

↑ The lofty minaret of the beautiful Grande Mosquée de Paris

25

Catacombes

⌂ 1 av du Colonel Henri Rol-Tanguy 75014 Ⓜ Denfert-Rochereau ⏰ 10am–8:30pm Tue-Sun 🚫 1 Jan, 1 May 🌐 catacombes.paris.fr

A long, labyrinthine series of quarry tunnels dug during the 13th century, the catacombs are lined with ancient bones and skulls, many arranged artfully into macabre mosaics. Thousands of rotting corpses were transported here in the 1780s to absorb the excess from the overflowing mass graves of Les Halles cemetery. Coats are recommended – the tunnels are chilly year-round.

26

Jardin des Plantes

⌂ 57 rue Cuvier 75005 Ⓜ Gare d'Austerlitz 🚆 Gare d'Austerlitz 🚌 24, 57, 61, 63, 67, 89, 91 ⏰ Early Feb-late Oct: 7:30am–8pm daily; late Oct-early Feb : 8am-5:30pm daily 🌐 jardindesplantes.net

The botanical gardens were established when Louis XIII's

HIDDEN GEM
Musée Zadkine

The former home of Russian-born sculptor Ossip Zadkine is now a well-curated museum devoted to his works (*www.zadkine.paris.fr*). The collection spans the development of the artist's style, from the Cubism of his early work to the Expressionism of his final pieces.

The evolution of animals, two by two in the Musée National d'Histoire Naturelle

physicians founded a medicinal herb garden in 1626. A school of botany, natural history and pharmacy followed. The garden was opened to the public in 1640, and now houses the natural history museum, a botanical school and the **Ménagerie le Zoo du Jardin des Plantes**, one of the oldest zoos in the world that houses a number of endangered species. As well as fine vistas and walkways flanked by statues, the park has an alpine garden and a display of herbaceous and wild plants. A cedar of Lebanon, originally from Britain's Kew Gardens, was the first to be planted in France.

Ménagerie le Zoo du Jardin des Plantes

⌖ 🏠 Avenue Daumesnil & route de la Ceinture du Lac 🕐 9am–6pm daily (to 6:30pm Sun & public hols) 🌐 zoodu jardindesplantes.fr

---

27

Montparnasse

🏠 75014 & 75015 Ⓜ Montparnasse, Vavin, Raspail, Edgar Quinet

The name Montparnasse was first used ironically, when 17th-century arts students performed on a "mount" of rubble that was left over from quarrying. In ancient Greece, the original Mount Parnassus was dedicated to poetry and music. By the 19th century, crowds were being drawn to the local cabarets and bars.

The mixture of art and high living was especially potent in the 1920s and 1930s, when creative residents like Ernest Hemingway, Picasso, Cocteau and Matisse called the area home. Today, the *quartier* is dominated by the disliked **Tour Montparnasse**, although the view from the top (the 56th floor) is just spectacular.

Tour Montparnasse

🏠 33 avenue du Maine 🕐 9:30am–11:30pm daily 🌐 tourmontparnasse56.com

Visitors strolling along a grand avenue of trees in the Jardin des Plantes ↓

A SHORT WALK
MONTMARTRE

Distance 1.5 km (1 mile) **Nearest metro** Abbesses
Time 20 minutes

The steep hill of Montmartre has proved a draw for Parisians and visitors for centuries. Artists Théodore Géricault and Camille Corot came here in the 19th century, while in the 20th Maurice Utrillo immortalized the streets in his works. The area was also home to artists such as Picasso, Matisse and Toulouse-Lautrec. Today, this picturesque district, which in places still preserves the atmosphere of prewar Paris, is a perfect place to wander. A stop at the place du Tertre is recommended: admire the works of street artists and relax with a coffee and pastry.

Au Lapin Agile, *a rustic café and cabaret, was a popular meeting point for artists including Picasso.*

Musée de Montmartre *features the work of artists who lived in the area. Look out for the* Portrait of a Woman *(1918), by the Italian painter and sculptor Amedeo Modigliani.*

Clos Montmartre *is one of the last surviving vineyards in Paris. The grape harvest is celebrated on the first Saturday in October.*

Metro Lamarck Caulaincourt

RUE ST VINCENT
RUE DE L'ABREUVOIR
RUE DES SAULES
RUE CORTOT
RUE ST-RUSTIO
RUE NORVINS
RUE LEPIC
P L J B CLEMENT
RUE POULBOT
RUE DE LA MIRE
RUE RAVIGNAN
RUE GABRIELLE
RUE BERTHE
RUE DREVET
RUE DES TROIS FRERES

↑ A passerby looks on as an artist paints in the lively place du Tertre

The **Espace Dalí Montmartre** *is France's only permanent collection of the Surrealist master's sculptures, paintings and graphic works.*

The bustling **place du Tertre** *is the tourist centre of Montmartre and is full of portraitists and other easel artists. Cafés and bars surround the square.*

0 metres	100
0 yards	100

N ↑

A La Mère Catherine *was a favourite eating place of Russian Cossacks in 1814. They would bang on the table and shout "Bistro!" (Russian for "quick") – hence the Paris bistro was born.*

St-Pierre de Montmartre *was made a Temple of Reason in the Revolution – this new cult was meant to replace Christianity*

BEYOND THE CENTRE
Montmartre

Locator Map
For more detail see p145

↑ The beautiful Sacré-Coeur illuminated at sunrise

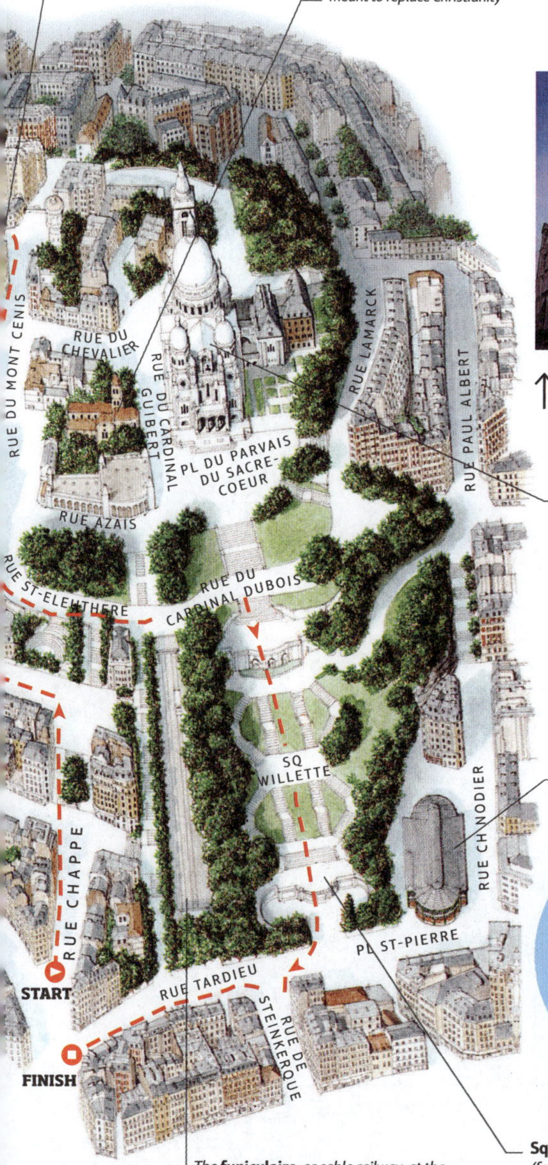

The Romano-Byzantine **Sacré-Coeur**, *started in the 1870s and completed in 1914, is a highlight of the area (p146).*

RUE DU MONT CENIS

RUE DU CHEVALIER

RUE DU CARDINAL GUIBERT

RUE LAMARCK

RUE PAUL ALBERT

PL DU PARVIS DU SACRÉ-COEUR

RUE AZAIS

RUE ST-ELEUTHÈRE

RUE DU CARDINAL DUBOIS

SQ WILLETTE

RUE CHNODIER

Halle Saint-Pierre *hosts exhibitions of Art Brut and Naïve Art.*

Did You Know?

Montmartre's name is ascribed to local martyrs tortured in around AD 250: *mons martyrium.*

RUE CHAPPE

PL ST-PIERRE

START

RUE TARDIEU

RUE DE STEINKERQUE

FINISH

The **funiculaire**, *or cable railway, at the end of Rue Foyatier takes you to the foot of the basilica of Sacré-Coeur. Metro tickets are valid on it.*

Square Willette *lies below the parvis (forecourt) of Sacré-Coeur. It is laid out on the side of the hill in a series of descending terraces with lawns, shrubs, trees and flowerbeds.*

EXPERIENCE
FRANCE

The abbey of Mont-St-Michel piercing the sky

ÎLE-DE-FRANCE

Set at the heart of France, with Paris as its hub, the Île-de-France extends well beyond the densely populated suburbs of the city. The region was a favourite with French royalty after François I transformed Fontainebleau into a Renaissance palace in 1528. Louis XIV kept the Île-de-France as the political axis of the country when he started building Versailles in 1661. This Neo-Classical château was created by the combined genius of Le Nôtre, Le Vau, Le Brun and Jules Hardouin-Mansart, and stands as a monument to the power of the Sun King. The excessive displays of opulence of such châteaux were brought to a violent end during the Revolution of 1789, but many were spared, including nearby Château de Rambouille, which gained prominence in the Naopleonic era. An industrial boom in the 19th century was followed by a number of large-scale construction projects in the 20th century, including blocks of social housing and the Périphérique. Today the varied neighbourhoods of the suburbs are home to the vast majority of Paris's citizens.

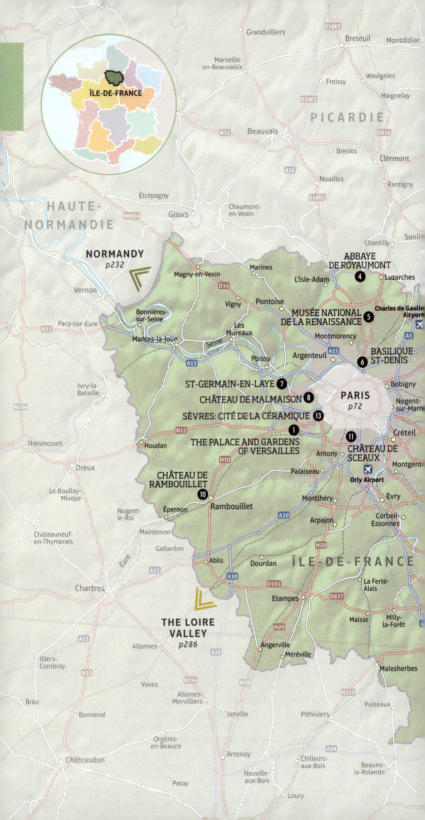

ÎLE-DE-FRANCE

Must Sees

1 The Palace and Gardens of Versailles
2 Disneyland® Paris
3 Château de Fontainebleau

Experience More

4 Abbaye de Royaumont
5 Musée National de la Renaissance

6 Basilique St-Denis
7 St-Germain-en-Laye
8 Château de Malmaison
9 Château de Vaux-le-Vicomte
10 Château de Rambouillet
11 Château de Sceaux
12 Provins
13 Sèvres: Cité de la Céramique

LE NORD AND PICARDY
p184

CHAMPAGNE
p204

BURGUNDY AND FRANCHE-COMTÉ
p312

2 DISNEYLAND® PARIS

CHAMPAGNE-ARDENNE

9 CHÂTEAU DE VAUX-LE-VICOMTE

12 PROVINS

3 CHÂTEAU DE FONTAINEBLEAU

0 kilometres 20
0 miles 20

N

THE PALACE AND GARDENS OF VERSAILLES

🅐 D2 🅐 Pl d'Armes, 78000 Versaille 🚌 Versailles Express from Eiffel Tower 🚆 Versailles-Château-Rive-Gauche, Versailles Chantiers ⏲ Opening hours vary; check website 📅 1 Jan, 25 Dec 🌐 chateauversailles.fr

This stunning royal residence is overwhelming in its scale and opulence. The spectacular, lavishly decorated palace and vast gardens, complete with fountains, landscaped topiary and even a model farm, make Versailles the top day trip from the centre of Paris.

The Palace

Staring in 1668 with his father's hunting lodge, Louis XIV built the largest palace in Europe, housing 20,000 people at a time. Architects Louis Le Vau and Jules Hardouin-Mansart designed the buildings, which grew as a series of "envelopes" around the lodge. The Opera House was added by Louis XV in 1770.

The sumptuous main apartments are on the first floor of the vast château complex. These were richly decorated by Charles Le Brun with coloured marbles, stone and wood carvings, murals, velvet, silver and gilded furniture. The climax is the glorious Hall of Mirrors, where 357 great mirrors face 17 tall arched windows.

TOP 5 STUNNING PALACE ROOMS

Salon de Vénus
A statue of Louis XIV stands amid this room's rich marble decor.

Salon d'Apollon
Designed by Le Brun and dedicated to the god Apollo, this was Louis XIV's throne room.

Salon de la Guerre
The room's theme of war is dramatically reinforced by the stuccoed relief of Louis XIV riding to victory.

Hall of Mirrors
This glittering room stretches 73 m (240 ft) along the west façade of this stunning palace.

Queen's Bedroom
In this room, the queens of France gave birth to the royal children in full public view.

The palace and gardens of Versailles, the epitome of royal grandeur ↓

1 The Marble Courtyard is decorated with marble paving, urns, busts and a gilt balcony.

2 Mansart's last great work, the two-storey Baroque Chapelle Royale was Louis XIV's final addition to Versailles.

3 The South Wing's original apartments for great nobles were replaced by Louis-Philippe's museum of French history.

The formal gardens, complete with geometric paths and shrubberies →

The Gardens

The grounds of Versailles are no less impressive than the palace. Designed by the great landscaper André Le Nôtre, the formal gardens are a masterpiece: sculptural fountains and secluded groves sit amid geometric flowerbeds and hedges. The 1.7-km- (1-mile-) long Grand Canal leads from the gardens to the enormous park, which features wooded areas and agricultural fields delineated by a network of footpaths. The grounds also encompass the Grand Trianon and Petit Trianon palaces, as well as the Queen's Hamlet – a life-size model village built for Marie Antoinette that was also a functioning farm.

The formal gardens are a masterpiece: sculptural fountains and secluded groves sit amid geometric flowerbeds and hedges.

↑ The Grand Trianon, built by Louis XIV in 1687 to escape the rigours of court life

EAT

Ore

This Alain Ducasse dining experience in the Pavillon Dufour is as luxurious as the château it occupies.

🏠 **Château de Versailles, 78000 Versailles**
Ⓦ **ducasse-chateauversailles.com**

€€€

Angelina

The iconic tea house has two outposts in Versailles – one in the Pavillon d'Orléans and one at the Petit Trianon – both serving a selection of snacks and delectable pastries.

🏠 **Château de Versailles, 78000 Versailles**
Ⓦ **angelina-paris.fr**

€€€

Did You Know?

One third of the estate's budget went to the fountains. Today they only go on during the summer months.

1

2

3

① The cottages in the Queen's Hamlet were inspired by rural French architecture. Although rustic on the exterior, inside they were richly furnished.

② During the Grands Eaux Nocturnes in the summer, the gardens of Versailles come alive with superb illuminations and installations.

③ Built in 1762 as a retreat for Louis XV, the Petit Trianon became a favourite of Marie Antoinette.

2 ⊘ ⓜ 🍴 💻 🛍️

DISNEYLAND®
PARIS

🅰️ E2 🏠 Marne-la-Vallée 77777 🚉 Disneyland® Paris
Express from Gare du Nord, Opéra and Châtelet 🚆 Marne-
la-Vallée/Chessy 🕐 Disneyland® Park: 10am–11pm in
high season (closes earlier in low season); Walt Disney
Studios® Park: 10am–9pm in high season (closes earlier
in low season) 🔲 disneylandparis.com

Unbeatable for complete escapism, combined with
vibrant excitement and sheer energy, Disneyland®
Paris offers extreme rides, gentle experiences and
phenomenal visual effects.

The resort is built on a massive scale, a 22-sq-km (8.5-sq-mile)
site which encompasses two theme parks; seven hotels; a
shopping, dining and entertainment village; an ice-skating
rink; a lake; two convention centres; and a golf course. The
theme parks are split into Disneyland® Park and the Walt
Disney Studios® Park. The former, with more than 60 rides
and attractions, celebrates Hollywood folklore and fantasies,
while the latter highlights the ingenuity involved in cinema,
animation and television production with interactive exhibits
and live shows.

DISNEY VILLAGE

The fun does not have
to end when the two
parks close. Disney
Village offers a whole
host of evening enter-
tainment options –
including a cinema,
concerts and Buffalo
Bill's Wild West Show –
as well as numerous
restaurants in which
to dine and plenty of
shops for retail ther-
apy. Seasonal events
take place all year,
including celebrations
for Easter, Halloween
and New Year.

Did You Know?

Sleeping Beauty's castle was designed to contrast with the grey Parisian skies.

↑ The view from Alice's Curious Labyrinth in Disneyland® Park

1 The entrance to Crush's Coaster® in Walt Disney Studios® Park.

2 The Mad Hatter's Tea Cups in Disneyland® Park's Fantasyland®.

3 The parade in Disneyland® Park features characters from films such as *Toy Story*.

DISNEYLAND® PARK

The Disneyland® Park comprises five areas. Main Street represents a fantasy small-town America, its Victorian façades fronting interesting stores and food outlets. Frontierland®, a homage to America's Wild West, hosts some of the park's most popular attractions, while wild rides and Audio-Animatronics are the draw at Adventureland®. The buildings in Fantasyland® are modelled on those in animated movies, and contain many attractions for younger children. Science fiction and the future are the themes at Discoveryland®, home to the popular multi-loop ride Star Wars Hyperspace Mountain.

TOP 3 RIDES IN DISNEYLAND® PARK

Star Wars Hyperspace Mountain
Formerly known as Space Mountain®, this iconic rollercoaster draws big crowds but towards the end of the day you can often walk straight onto the ride.

Big Thunder Mountain
This wild rollercoaster ride on a speeding runaway mine train is a crowd favourite.

Pirates of the Caribbean
This boat ride takes you on a thrilling journey through underground prisons and past fighting galleons.

Indiana Jones™ and the Temple of Peril *(below)* and *(inset)* the ↓ park illuminated at dusk

The entrance to Walt Disney Studios® Park, with the Earful Tower ↑

↑ The four-wheeled Cars Quatre Roues Rallye attraction

↑ The underwater animated world of Crush's Coaster®

WALT DISNEY STUDIOS® PARK

The four production zones at Walt Disney Studios® Park reveal the secrets of movie-making. Inside the giant studio gates on the Front Lot, Disney Studio 1 houses a film set boulevard, complete with stylized street façades and venues such as the 1930s-style Club Swankedero. Toon Studio® contains rides and exhibits inspired by various iconic Disney and Pixar characters, and includes La Place de Rémy, home to the 4D experience Ratatouille: A Recipe for Adventure. The Production Courtyard® offers the chance to go behind the scenes on the Studio Tram Tour®, among other attractions, while the Backlot focuses on special effects, film music recording and dare-devil stunts.

Mickey Mouse casting his magic over the Toon Studio® zone →

3 ⟨⟨⟩⟩ ⟨⟨⟩⟩ ⟨⟨⟩⟩ ⟨⟨⟩⟩ ⟨⟨⟩⟩

CHÂTEAU DE FONTAINEBLEAU

🅐 E3 🅐 Seine-et-Marne 🅒 Château: 9:30am–5pm Wed–Mon (to 6pm Apr–Sep);
gardens: 9am–5pm daily (to 6pm Mar, Apr & Oct; to 7pm May–Sep)
🆆 chateaudefontainebleau.fr

Fontainebleau is not the product of a single vision but rather a bewildering cluster of styles from different periods, as various French monarchs improved and added to the palace. Yet Fontainebleau's abiding charm comes not from this grandeur, but from its relative informality and spectacular forest setting.

Although Fontainebleau was first used by French kings in the 12th century – Louis VII built an abbey here that was consecrated by Thomas Becket in 1169 – only a medieval tower survives from this period. The present château harks back to François I, often considered France's first Renaissance king. He ordered a château be built in the Italian style, a decorative and romantic building that showcased the best art and artisans from this period. The most notable feature from this era is the François I gallery by Rosso Fiorentino, an ornate passageway featuring 12 spectacular frescoes that connected the king's chambers to the chapel. François I's mission of improving the château was continued by subsequent kings; the famous horseshoe staircase was added in 1634. It remained one of the principal palaces of the kings and emperors of France.

THE BARBIZON SCHOOL

Artists have been drawn to the glades of Fontainebleau since the 1840s, when a group of landscape painters who were determined to reject the orthodoxy of Neo-Classicism formed around Théodore Rousseau and Millet. Resolved to paint only from nature, as seen in the ethereal *Spring at Barbizon* by Jean-François Millet (1814–75) *(below)*, these painters settled in the hamlet of Barbizon. Today, the excellent Auberge Ganne, a museum found in the house that Rousseau used to occupy in Barbizon, tells the artistic story of the village.

Did You Know?

François I was said to have worn the key to his gallery around his neck; very few were allowed inside.

← The Plates Gallery, built in 1838, is decorated with over 120 porcelain plates

→ The orrnate stone carvings on the exterior of Fontainebleau showing skillful artistry

↑ The famous horseshoe staircase at the château, designed to let carriages pass underneath

EXPERIENCE MORE

4

Abbaye de Royaumont

D2 **Fondation Royaumont, Asnières-sur-Oise, Val-d'Oise** **10am-6pm daily (to 5:30pm Nov-Mar)** **royaumont.com**

Set in woods 35 km (22 miles) north of Paris, Royaumont is the finest Cistercian abbey in the Île-de-France. Chosen for its remoteness, the abbey has stark stonework and simple lines that reflect the austere teachings of St Bernard. Yet, unlike his Burgundian abbeys, Royaumont was founded in 1228 by Louis IX and his mother, Blanche de Castille. "St Louis" showered the abbey

with riches and chose it as a royal burial site. The abbey retained its royal links until the Revolution, when much of it was destroyed. It became a textiles mill then orphanage, until its revival as a cultural centre. The original pillars still remain, along with a gravity-defying corner tower and the largest Cistercian cloisters in France, which enclose a charming Classical garden. The monastic quarters border one side of the beautiful cloisters.

↑ The vaulted Cistercian cloisters *(inset)* at the Abbaye de Royaumont

Did You Know?

Louis XIII held one of his ballets, *La Merlaison*, at the Abbaye de Royaumont in 1635.

5

Musée National de la Renaissance

D2 **Rue Jean Bulant, Château d'Ecouen, Val-d'Oise** **9:30am-12:45pm & 2-5:15pm Wed-Mon (to 5:45pm mid-Apr-Sep)** **1 Jan, 1 May, 25 Dec** **musee-renaissance.fr**

The moated Château d'Ecouen, now a Renaissance museum, provides an authentic setting for a fine collection of paintings, stained glass, jewellery, tapestries, coffers, carved

doors and staircases salvaged from this and other châteaux. Ecouen was built in 1538 for Anne de Montmorency, adviser to François I and Commander-in-Chief of his armies. As the second most powerful person in the kingdom, he employed École de Fontainebleau artists and craftsmen to adorn his palace, most apparent in the painted fireplaces depicting biblical and Classical themes in mysterious landscapes. The most striking room is the chapel, containing a gallery and vaulted ceilings painted with the Montmorency coat of arms.

Upstairs is one of the finest series of 16th-century tapestries in France. Equally compelling are the princely apartments, the library of illuminated manuscripts, vivid ceramics from Lyon, Nevers, Venice, Faenza, and Iznik, and a display of early mathematical instruments. There are also 16th- and 17th-century engravings from France, Italy and Germany. The castle is set within lovely formal gardens.

Basilique St-Denis

D2 **1 rue de la Légion d'Honneur, 93200 Sain-Denis** **Line 13 Basilique de St-Denis** **Apr-Sep: 10am-6:15pm daily; Oct-Mar: 10am-5:15pm daily** **1 Jan, 1 May, 25 Dec** **saint-denis.basilique.fr**

Constructed between 1137 and 1281, this cathedral is set on the site of the tomb of St Denis, the first bishop of Paris, who was beheaded in 250. The building was the original influence for Gothic art. From Merovingian times, it was a burial place for rulers of France. During the French Revolution, many tombs were desecrated and scattered, but the best were stored, and now represent a collection of funerary art. Memorials include those of Dagobert, Louis XVI and Marie-Antoinette.

St-Germain-en-Laye

D2 **Yvelines** **Maison Claude Debussy, 38 rue au Pain; www.seine-saintgermain.fr**

Dominating place Général de Gaulle in this chic suburb is the legendary Château de St-Germain, birthplace of Louis XIV. Louis VI built the original stronghold in 1122, but only the keep and St-Louis chapel remain. Under François I and Henri II, the upper tiers were demolished, leaving a moated pentagon. Henri IV built the pavilion and terraces that run down to the Seine,

PARC DE MALMAISON

Josephine Bonaparte was a keen amateur botanist and took a great interest in the garden at the Château de Malmaison. She introduced several exotic plants and flowers, such as magnolia, camellia and hibiscus, which had never before been seen in the country. Josephine's rose garden was renowned and contained some 250 species. She also kept a menagerie with kangaroos and zebras. Neglected for many years, the gardens have been restored and extended by several hectares.

and Louis XIV had Le Nôtre landscape the gardens before leaving for Versailles in 1682.

Today the château houses the **Musée d'Archéologie Nationale**, with archaeological finds from prehistory to the Middle Ages. Inaugurated by Napoleon III, the collection includes a 22,000-year-old carved female, a megalithic tomb, a bronze helmet from the 3rd century BC and fine Celtic jewellery. The finest treasure is the Gallo-Roman mosaic pavement.

Musée d'Archéologie Nationale

Château de St-Germain-en-Laye, pl Charles de Gaulle **10am-5pm Wed-Mon** **1 Jan, 1 May, 25 Dec** **musee-archeologie nationale.fr**

Château de Malmaison

D2 **Rueil-Malmaison, Hauts-de-Seine, av du Château de Malmaison** **Hours vary, check website** **1 Jan, 25 Dec** **musees-nationaux-malmaison.fr**

Set 15 km (9 miles) west of Paris, this 17th-century estate is known for its Napoleonic associations. Attracted by its charming rural grounds, Empress Josephine purchased the estate as a tranquil retreat from the formality of the royal residences at the Tuileries and Fontainebleau. While she loved this country manor, Napoleon scorned its entrance as fit only

for servants, and so he had a curious drawbridge built at the back of the château. The finest rooms are the frescoed and vaulted library, the canopied campaign room and the sunny Salon de Musique. Napoleon's restrained, yellow canopied bedroom contrasts with the bedchamber in which Josephine died, a magnificent indulgence in red. Many of the rooms overlook the romantic "English" gardens and the rose garden that Josephine cultivated after her divorce. Memorabilia abounds, from imperial eagles to French artist Jacques-Louis David's moody portrait of Napoleon.

Set in the wooded grounds nearby, the Château Bois Préau houses a fascinating museum dedicated to Napoleon's exile and death.

↑ Empress Josephine's decadent bedroom at the Château de Malmaison

9

Château de Vaux-le-Vicomte

🅰 E2 🏠 Maincy, Seine-et-Marne 🚌 From Melun station (Mar-Nov: daily; Dec-Feb: Wed-Sun) 🕐 Hours vary, check website 🌐 vaux-le-vicomte.com

This château north of Melun enjoys a peaceful rural location. Nicolas Fouquet, a powerful court financier to Louis XIV, challenged the architect Le Vau and the decorator Le Brun to create the most sumptuous palace of the day. The result was Vaux-le-Vicomte – and Fouquet's downfall: Louis and his ministers were so enraged – because its luxury cast all the royal palaces into the shade – that they arrested the financier.

The château's interior is a gilded banquet of frescoes, stucco, caryatids and giant busts. The Salon des Muses boasts Le Brun's magnificent frescoed ceiling of dancing nymphs and poetic sphinxes. La Grande Chambre Carrée is decorated in Louis XIII style

with panelled walls and an impressive triumphal frieze. However, its many rooms feel intimate and the scale is not overwhelming. Outside, André Le Nôtre's gardens are truly stunning (and the main draw for visitors), with magnificent terraces, lakes and fountains descending to a formal canal.

> **Outside, André Le Nôtre's gardens are truly stunning, with magnificent terraces, lakes and fountains descending to a formal canal.**

10

Château de Rambouillet

🅰 D3 🏠 Domaine National de Rambouillet, 77120 Rambouillet 🕐 9:50am-noon & 1:50-5pm Wed-Sun (to 6pm Apr-Sep) 📅 1 Jan, 1 May, 1 Nov, 11 Nov, 25 Dec 🌐 chateau-rambouillet.fr

Bordering the deep Forêt de Rambouillet stands this beautiful ivy-covered red-brick château, flanked by five stone towers. Adopted variously as a feudal castle, country estate, royal palace and imperial residence, it is a composite of

French royal history. Since 1897, it has been the president's official summer home. Its oak-panelled rooms are adorned with Empire-style furnishings and Aubusson tapestries. The main façade overlooks Classical parterres.

Nearby is the Château de Thoiry, which has an innovative play area for children.

11

Château de Sceaux

🅰 D3 🏠 Domaine de Sceaux, Hauts-de-Seine 🚈 Bourg-la-Reine, Sceaux, Parc de Sceaux 🚌 192, 197 🕐 Nov-Feb: 1-5pm Tue-Sun; Mar-Oct: 2-6:30pm Tue-Sun 📅 1 Jan, 1 May, 25 Dec 🌐 domaine-de-sceaux.hauts-de-seine.fr

Built for Colbert in 1670, the original château was

ANDRÉ LE NÔTRE

As the greatest French landscape gardener, Le Nôtre (1613–1700) created exquisite château gardens all over France. His Classical vision shaped many gardens in the Île-de-France. At Vaux *(below)* he perfected the *jardin à la française*: avenues framed by statues and box hedges; water gardens with fountains and pools; graceful terraces and geometrical parterres "embroidered" with motifs. His genius lay in architectural orchestration and symmetry, typified by Versailles *(p170)*, his greatest triumph.

demolished and rebuilt in Louis XIII style in 1856. Since 2010, the stylish reconstruction has housed the Musée de l'Île-de-France, which celebrates the landscapes and châteaux of the region with an extensive collection from the painters of the School of Paris, plus various porcelain, furniture and sculpture.

The Parc de Sceaux, which is bounded by elegant villas, is an appealing mixture of formal gardens, woods and water. The gardens, designed by Le Nôtre, use water to stunning effect, with tiered waterfalls and fountains presenting a moving staircase that tumbles down into an octagonal basin. This then feeds into the Grand Canal and offers a poplar-lined view towards the Pavillon de Hanovre. This elegant pavilion is one of several that adorn the park, which also contains Mansart's Classical Orangerie. Today it hosts exhibitions and music concerts.

Standing to attention, an avenue of trees leading to the Château de Rambouillet

Provins

🅐E3 🅗Seine-et-Marne
🚃🚌 🛈4 Chemin de Villecran 77160; www.provins.net

As a Roman outpost, Provins commanded the border of Île-de-France and Champagne. Today, it offers a coherent vision of the medieval world. Ville Haute, the upper town, is clustered within 12th-century ramparts, complete with crenellations and defensive ditches. The ramparts to the west are the best preserved. Here, between the fortified gateways of Porte de Jouy and Porte St-Jean, the battlements are dotted with towers of all different shapes.

The town is dominated by Tour César, a keep with four corner turrets and a pyramid-shaped roof. The moat and fortifications were added by the English during the Hundred Years' War. A guardroom leads to a gallery and views over place du Chatel, a square of medieval gabled houses, and over the wheatfields beyond.

Provins is very proud of its crimson roses. In addition to a daily medieval show, a floral celebration is held in the rose garden every June, an event marked by a medieval festival with falconry and jousting.

Sèvres: Cité de la Céramique

🅐D2 🅗2 Place de la Manufacture, 92310 Sèvres 🕙10am–12:30pm & 1:30–5pm Wed–Sun 🗓1 Jan, 1 May, 25 Dec 🌐sevrescite ceramique.fr

With over 50,000 objects on display, this museum traces the history of porcelain around the world from antiquity onward. The building was erected in 1756 as a royal factory under Louis XV and has remained under state ownership ever since. In 1824 it became home to the world's first ceramics museum. The collections include the latest pieces by 21st-century designers. Explore objects from America, Japan and Europe and discover how techniques for making and decorating porcelain and ceramics have changed over the centuries.

← Potpourri vase, from the Cité de la Céramique

Amien Cathedral behind the bustling streets bordering the canal

LE NORD
AND PICARDY

The northern reaches of France were settled by tribes during the Stone Age, drawn by its coastal waters and dense forests. The small fishing villages and farming communities that evolved left behind evidence of flint-cutting and corn-grinding. These were absorbed into the Romans Empire around 1 AD. A frontierland, French Flanders, as Le Nord was known, was hotly disputed by the Counts of Flanders until the 13th century, while Picardy was held variously by French dukes and even the English, until 1477. Throughout this period, agriculture and small industry flourished; woven fabrics from Arras and delicate lacework from Chantilly were highly sought after in nearby Paris. In the 18th century, the rise of the coal-mining industry led to the creation of canals and made Calais and Dunkerque important port towns. The World Wars decimated great swathes of the region and, following World War II, stirring memorials of the fighting were erected, attracting those wishing to pay their respects. The opening of the Channel Tunnel in 1994 once again made Calais an economic hub.

LE NORD AND PICARDY

UNITED KINGDOM

Ashford
Dover
Folkestone

CHANNEL TUNNEL

CALAIS 4
Gravelin

Guînes   Ard

Cap Griz Nez

A16

Wimereux
BOULOGNE-SUR-MER 2

Desvres
D341
Samer
Fauquembergue
D901
Vallée de la Course

LE TOUQUET 18
Les Sept Vallées
Fressin
Montreuil-sur-Mer

Berck-sur-Mer
D1001 D939 Hesdin
D9

Fort-Mahon-Plage
A16
Vron
Authie
D928

Crécy-en-Ponthieu
Auxi-le Châtea
BAIE DE LA SOMME 6
Nouvion
Buigny-Saint-Maclou

Ault
Abbeville
VALLÉE L
Le Tréport
Fressenneville
Pont-Rémy
Somme

A28
Airaines

Biville-sur-Mer
Oisemont
D1001

Londinières
A28
Hornoy
A29

Neufchâtel-en-Bray
A29
D1029
Poix-de Picardi

Grandvilliers

NORMANDY
p232
Marseille-en-Beauvaisis
D901 D930

Buchy
Songeons

Vascoeuil
N31
BEAUVAIS 1

HAUTE-NORMANDIE
D981

D6014
Étrépagny
A

Les Andelys
Chaumont-en-Vexin

Seine
Marines

Vernon
Pontoise
Bonnières-sur-Seine
Les Mureaux

N13
Pacy-sur-Eure
Poissy

Saint-Germain-en-Laye

Ivry-la-Bataille
N12

English Channel

LE NORD AND PICARDY

Must see

1 Amiens Cathedral

Experience more

2 Boulogne-sur-Mer
3 St-Omer
4 Calais
5 Flandre Maritime
6 Baie de la Somme
7 Vallée de la Somme
8 Arras
9 Compiègne
10 Dunkerque
11 Noyon
12 Senlis
13 Lille
14 Parc Astérix
15 Laon
16 Chantilly
17 Château de Pierrefonds
18 Le Touquet
19 Beauvais

←

1 The beautiful beach at Le Touquet.

2 Amiens's awe-inspiring Gothic cathedral.

3 A delicious plate of *carbonnade flamade* stew.

4 Lille's charming Old Town.

3 DAYS
in Le Nord and Picardy

Day 1

Morning Arrive in Lille *(p200)* and head straight for the sublime Palais des Beaux Arts. Highlights of the collection include paintings by Rubens, Manet and Picasso; sculptures by Rodin and Claudel; medieval religious art; and scale models of fortresses in France and Belgium.

Afternoon Have lunch on one of the pretty pedestrianized streets radiating from place du Général de Gaulle, then take a taxi to the Maison Natale de Charles de Gaulle, where France's most renowned president grew up in bourgeois comfort. Walk southwest to the Old City, which has a distinct Flemish vibe, to check out the boutiques along rue de la Grande Chausée, then drop by Meert *(p197)* for a waffle.

Evening Have dinner in an *estaminet*, a traditional Flemish restaurant, and try the *carbonnade flamande* (beef stew made with onions and beer). After, mosey over to Château de Beaulieu *(p199)* and relax in one of its bright and spacious rooms.

Day 2

Morning Fuel up on *tartine* (baguette and conserves), then take a roundabout route to the seaside town of Le Touquet, past the poignant World War I memorial sites at Ypres and Dunkerque *(p198)*.

Afternoon Pull into Le Touquet *(p202)* in the early afternoon, in time for coffee at A L'Arome Colonial *(98 rue de Metz)* – its varied bean menu makes it the perfect spot to quell caffeine cravings. Officially known as Le Touquet-Paris Plage (Paris-by-the-Sea), this elegant beach resort has been popular with well-heeled tourists for over a century. Faded reflections of 1920s glamour can be spotted in its imaginative interwar buildings and at its wide, fine-sand beach, lined by huts with rainbow-coloured doors.

Evening Wander along the sandy shore for an aperitif at Le Sand *(www.lesand.fr)* next to the serene Dunes Nature Preserve, then dine on innovative French cuisine at the romantic Les 2 Moineaux *(www.restaurant-les2moineaux.com)*. Stroll back along the beach to reach Le Westminster *(p194)*; this luxury hotel's elegant pool is ideal for a late-night dip.

Day 3

Morning Follow the Somme River Valley to Amiens. Its Gothic cathedral *(p192)* is one of Europe's most magnificent. Visit the statue of the Ange Pleureur (Crying Angel) and the treasury, where the purported skull of John the Baptist is on display. If you don't mind facing 307 steps, climb the cathedral's north tower for spectacular views, before stopping for a mouth-watering vegan burger at La Maison à Vapeur *(22 Rue Dusevel)*.

Afternoon Spend the afternoon letting your imagination run wild at the truly extraordinary Maison de Jules Verne, longtime home of the uncannily prescient science fiction writer.

Evening Enjoy a gentle riverside walk, then duck into Leu Duo *(www.leuduo.fr)* for a plate of classic French fare in the charming St-Leu Quarter, with its picturesque canals. If you're visiting during summer or in December, don't miss Chroma, a sound-and-light spectacular projected on the façade of the cathedral. Fall asleep recalling memories of your trip at the luxurious Marotte *(p194)*, a tranquil getaway in the heart of the city.

Great Battlegrounds

One of the best ways to take in the battlegrounds is to pick up a road map and plot a course. Follow the route between the Marne, 50 km (31 miles) outside of Paris, where the German army was finally stopped on the river by French forces in 1914, to the Somme, where two years later more than 600,000 Allied soldiers and 465,000 Germans were killed. The Somme is just a 20-minute cycle from Amiens; here, hundreds of tanks and thousands of aircraft supported Allied infantry at the battle that launched the final offensive of World War I. To the northeast is Arras, scene of a major Allied offensive.

→

Sunset over Ovillers Cemetery with a section of the Somme battlefield in the distance

LE NORD AND PICARDY FOR
REMEMBRANCE

France's battle-scarred northern reaches have become a pilgrimage for military history buffs and the descendents of the fallen alike. Today, this peaceful region is awash with moving monuments, insightful museums and one of the most comprehensive ancestry databases in the country.

COMMONWEALTH WAR GRAVES COMMISSION

The Commonwealth War Graves Commission *(www.cwgc.org)* was set up in 1917 to manage the solemn task of commemorating the fallen soldiers of Britain and its colonial allies in World War I. Its guiding principles were remarkably egalitarian for this point in time, stating not only that each of the dead should be commemorated by name on a permanent headstone or memorial, but also that the war graves should make no distinction whatsoever on account of rank, race or creed.

A display in the poignant Historial de la Grande Guerre ↑

War Museums

Carefully curated and deeply sympathetic, some of the best World War I museums can be found across northern France. The deeply affecting Historial de la Grande Guerre *(www.historial. fr)* depicts World War I from the point of view of both Allied and Axis soldiers. While in Arras *(p197)*, visitors can explore the underground passages at Carriere Wellington *(carriere wellington.com)*, where Allied soldiers prepared for the Arras offensive in 1917. Just south in the forest of Compiegne *(p198)* is the railway carriage where German commanders signed the November 1918 armistice; it is now a memorial and museum.

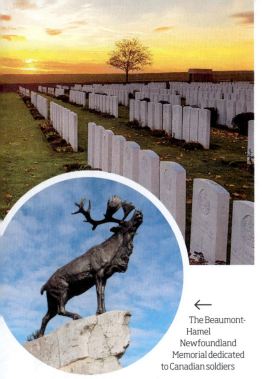

MEMORIAL SITES

Thiepval Memorial
Designed by Sir Edward Lutyens, this huge monument, commemorates the missing of the Somme.

Canadian National Vimy Memorial
A tribute to the Canadian soldiers who died in the battle for Vimy Ridge, 10 km (6 miles) north of Arras.

Beaumont-Hamel Newfoundland Memorial
Surrounding the largest unchanged section of the Somme battlefront, this cemetery is dedicated to this nearly decimated regiment.

← The Beaumont-Hamel Newfoundland Memorial dedicated to Canadian soldiers

Memorials and Cemeteries

Hundreds of thousands of war dead lie beneath simple white crosses in the cemeteries of the Western Front. For those seeking the grave of an ancestor who fell there, the database of the Commonwealth War Graves Commission holds details of the last resting places or memorials to all British and Commonwealth dead.

↑ The Thiepval Memorial, designed by Sir Edwin Lutyens

❶ ⊗ Ⓜ 🛍

AMIENS CATHEDRAL

🅐D2 🏠30 pl Notre-Dame 🕐Cathedral: 8:30am-6:30pm daily (to 5:30pm Oct-Mar:); towers: Mon, Wed-Sat & Sun pm 🌐amiens-cathedrale.fr

Work on France's largest cathedral started around 1220. It was built to house the head of St John the Baptist, brought back from the Crusades in 1206 and is still displayed here. Within 50 years, the cathedral, a masterpiece of Gothic architecture, was complete.

Restored in the 1850s by Viollet-le-Duc (p202), and having miraculously survived two world wars, Amiens's cathedral is famous for its statues and reliefs, which include scenes from the life of St Firmin and the Last Judgement, the inspiration for John Ruskin's *The Bible of Amiens* in 1884. La Cathédrale en Couleurs, a sound-and-light show, re-creates the original colours of the statuary around the west door, during the summer and at Christmas.

WHAT ELSE TO SEE IN AMIENS

The hub of Amiens, the capital of Picardy, is the picturesque St-Leu quarter, a pedestrianized area of low houses and flower-lined canals with waterside restaurants and artisans' shops. Further east are the colourful Les Hortillonnages, a patchwork of marshland market gardens, once tended by farmers using punts that now ferry visitors around the protected natural site. The Musée de Picardie has many fine sculptures and paintings. Maison de Jules Verne celebrates the famous author, who lived here from 1882 to 1900.

The west front towers are of unequal height.

The King's Gallery, a row of 22 colossal statues representing the kings of France.

St Firmin Portal is decorated with scenes from the life of St Firmin, first bishop of Amiens.

The calendar shows signs from the zodiac and their corresponding monthly labours.

→

A cutaway illustration of Amiens's great Gothic cathedral

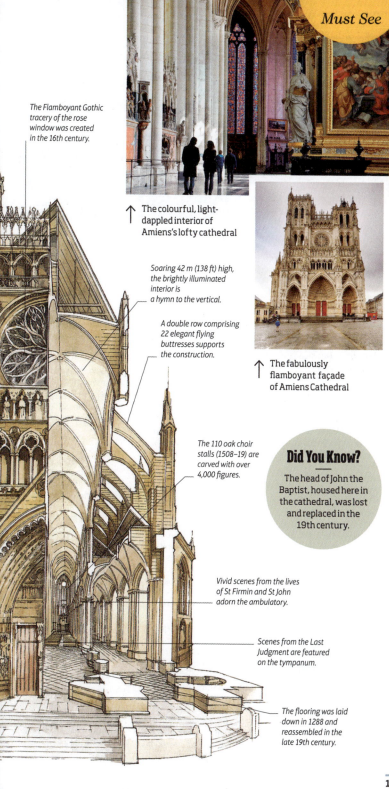

The Flamboyant Gothic tracery of the rose window was created in the 16th century.

↑ The colourful, light-dappled interior of Amiens's lofty cathedral

Soaring 42 m (138 ft) high, the brightly illuminated interior is a hymn to the vertical.

A double row comprising 22 elegant flying buttresses supports the construction.

↑ The fabulously flamboyant façade of Amiens Cathedral

The 110 oak choir stalls (1508–19) are carved with over 4,000 figures.

Did You Know?

The head of John the Baptist, housed here in the cathedral, was lost and replaced in the 19th century.

Vivid scenes from the lives of St Firmin and St John adorn the ambulatory.

Scenes from the Last Judgment are featured on the tympanum.

The flooring was laid down in 1288 and reassembled in the late 19th century.

Boats moored in the tranquil marina at the pretty fishing port of Boulogne-sur-Mer ↑

EXPERIENCE MORE

Boulogne-sur-Mer

🅐D1 🔼Pas de Calais 🖼️🚌
ℹ️Parvis de Nausicaa;
www.tourisme-
boulognesurmer.com

An important fishing port and busy marina, Boulogne's attractions come neatly boxed in a walled Haute Ville, with the Porte des Dunes opening onto a 17th- to 19th-century ensemble of the Palais de Justice, Bibliothèque and Hôtel de Ville.

The 19th-century Basilique Notre-Dame is capped by a dome visible for miles. Inside, a bejewelled wooden statue represents Boulogne's patroness, Notre-Dame de Boulogne. She is wearing a *soleil*, a headdress also worn by women during the *Grande Procession* held annually in her honour. Nearby, the moated

Did You Know?

Julius Caesar walked Boulogne-sur-Mer's streets when he visited his naval base around 55 BC.

13th-century **Château de Boulogne-sur-Mer**, built for the Counts of Boulogne, is now a historical museum.

In the centre of town, shops, hotels and fish restaurants line quai Gambetta on the east bank of the River Liane. To the north lie Boulogne's beach and **Nausicaa**, a vast, innovative aquarium and Sea Centre, the largest of its kind in Europe. A great option for families, the aquarium's exhibits invites visitors to "dive in" to shark-filled caves and coral lagoons.

North of town, the Colonne de la Grande Armée was erected in 1841 as a monument to Napoleon I's invasion of England in 1803–5. From the top there is a panoramic view along the coast. This is the most scenic stretch of the Côte d'Opale (Opal Coast).

Château de Boulogne-sur-Mer

♿ 🔼Rue de Bernet 📞0321 10 02 20 🕐May–Sep: 10am–6pm Wed–Mon; Oct–Apr: 10am–12:30pm & 2:30–5:30pm Wed–Mon 🚫1 May, 25 Dec, 1st week of Jan

Nausicaa

♿ 🔼Bd Sainte-Beuve 🕐9:30am–6:30pm daily (to 8pm Jul–Aug) 🚫3 weeks in Jan, 25 Dec 🌐nausicaa.fr

STAY

Marotte

A 19th-century mansion has been transformed into a luxurious and very romantic hideaway.

🅐D2 🔼3 rue Marotte, Amiens 🌐hotel-marotte.com

€€€

Meurice

Founded in 1771 and rebuilt after World War II, the Meurice has hardly changed since it was a favourite of postwar British high society.

🅐D1 🔼5-7 rue Edmond Roche, Calais 🌐hotel-meurice.fr

€€€

Le Westminster

Le Touquet's finest Art Deco hotel since the 1920s, with elegant rooms, a pool and a spa.

🅐D1 🔼Av du Verger, Le Touquet-Paris-Plage 🌐hotelsbarriere.com

€€€

❸
St-Omer

🅰 D1 🏛 Pas de Calais 🚉🚌
ℹ 7 pl Victor Hugo; www.
tourisme-saintomer.com

With cobbled streets and
17th- and 18th-century
buildings, St-Omer appears
untouched. The Hôtel
Sandelin houses a fine and
decorative arts museum.
The fascinating **Bibliothèque
d'Agglomération** contains
rare manuscripts from the
nearby 15th-century Abbaye
St-Bertin. Five km (3 miles)
from St-Omer, **La Coupole** is a
World War II museum located
inside a converted bunker.

Bibliothèque
d'Agglomération

🏛 40 rue Gambetta ⏰ Tue,
Wed, Fri & Sat 🚫 Public hols
🌐 bibliotheque-agglo-
stomer.fr

La Coupole

♿ 🏛 Rue Clabaux, 62570
Wizernes ⏰ 9am–6pm daily
(from 10am Jul–Aug)
🚫 2 weeks in Jan, 24 & 25 Dec
🌐 lacoupole-france.co.uk

↓ Full-scale exhibits at La
Coupole, a World War II
museum in St-Omer

❹
Calais

🅰 D1 🏛 Pas de Calais 🚉
🚌 ⛴ ℹ 12 bd Clémencea;
www.calais-cote
dopale.com

Calais is a busy port town
with a sandy beach to the
west. Many visitors never get
closer to it than the huge Cité
Europe shopping mall by the
Channel Tunnel exit. In town,
the **Musée des Beaux Arts**,
has an impressive collection
including studies for Auguste
Rodin's famous statue *The
Burghers of Calais* (1895). The
Cité de la Dentelle et de la
Mode recalls the town's lacemaking past. **Musée Mémoire**

↑ Fine artwork at
Calais's Musée des
Beaux Arts

1939–1945, in a battle-scarred
German blockhouse, examines
local events during the war.

Musée des Beaux-Arts

♿ 🏛 25 rue Richelieu
📞 03 21 46 48 40 ⏰ 1–5pm
Tue–Sun (to 6pm Apr–Oct)
🚫 Public hols

Musée Mémoire 1939-
1945

♿ 🏛 Parc St Pierre ⏰ Oct-
Apr: 11am–5pm Mon & Wed-
Sat; May–Sep: 10am–6pm
daily 🚫 Jan & Dec 🌐 musee-
memoire-calais.com

⑤

Flandre Maritime

🗺 D1 🚗 Nord ✈ Lille
🚌 Bergues 🚉 Dunkerque
ℹ Bergues, Le Beffroi,
pl Henri Billiaert; www.
bergues.fr

South of Dunkerque lies a flat, agricultural plain with narrow waterways and expansive skies – an archetypal Flemish landscape with canals, cyclists and ancient windmills. The Noordmeulen, built just north of Hondschoote in 1127, is thought to be the oldest windmill in Europe.

From Hondschoote the D3 follows the Canal de la Basse Colme west to Bergues, a fortified wool town with fine 16th- to 17th-century Flemish works in its **Musée du Mont-de-Piété**. Further south, the hilltop town of Cassel has a cobbled Grande Place with 16th- to 18th-century buildings, and views across Flanders from its Jardin Public.

Musée du Mont-de-Piété

 🏠 1 rue du Mont de Piété, Bergues ⏰ 2–6pm Thu–Mon 🚫 Nov–Apr 🌐 musees-bailleul-bergues.com

---

⑥

Baie de la Somme

🗺 D1 ℹ 2 pl Guillaume Le Conquérant, St-Valery-sur-Somme; www.tourisme-baiedesomme.fr

Although much of its salt marshes are submerged

↑ Aerial view of the salt marshes that distinguish the Baie de la Somme

during high tides, the vast estuary of the Somme River provides habitat for 300 species of birds. The best place to learn about the Baie de la Somme's avian life is the wild, open **Parc du Marquenterre Bird Sanctuary**, which has three walking trails where guides can help spot rare birds. Local experts offer guided walks across the estuary and seal-watching excursions. The seafront towns of Le Crotoy and St-Valery-sur-Somme offer places to stay and eat.

Parc du Marquenterre Bird Sanctuary

 🏠 25 bis chemin des Garennes, Saint-Quentin-en-Tourmont ⏰ Mid-Feb-Oct: 10am–5pm daily; Nov–mid-Feb: Sat & Sun 🌐 parcdumarquenterre.fr

---

⑦

Vallée de la Somme

🗺 D2 🚗 Somme ✈🚉 🚌 Amiens ℹ 16 pl André Audinot, Péronne; www. somme-tourisme.com

The name "Somme" is sadly synonymous with the slaughter and horror of trench warfare during World War I (*p68*). Yet the Somme Valley is home to pretty countryside, a vast estuary wetland and

abundant wildlife. Lakes and woods alongside provide enjoyable camping, walking and fishing.

Battlefields lie along the river and its tributaries north and northeast of Amiens, and extend north to Arras. Neat World War I Commonwealth cemeteries cover the area. The **Historial de la Grande Guerre** at Péronne gives a thoughtful introduction to the war. Parc Mémorial Beaumont-Hamel, near Albert, is a real battlefield left to disappear in its own time. Travel to Vimy Ridge Canadian Memorial, near Arras, to see a bloodbath battle site preserved as it was, and to Notre-Dame de Lorette, the French National Cemetery.

West of Amiens, **Samara** – the Gallo-Roman name for Amiens – is France's largest archaeological park. Taking visitors back 600,000 years, it features reconstructions of prehistoric dwellings, and exhibitions explaining early crafts such as flint-cutting and corn-grinding. Further downstream, Église St-Vulfran at Abbeville is noted for its Flamboyant Gothic west front with beautifully carved 16th-century door panels.

→

Pavement cafés on place des Héros facing the Hôtel de Ville, Arras

---

📷 PICTURE PERFECT
Flemish Style

Flemish-style buildings from the 17th and 18th centuries, topped by Dutch gables, surround Arras's main squares, the Grand Place and adjacent place des Héros – enchantingly illuminated at night.

Did You Know?

The waterfront villas at St-Valéry-sur-Somme were getaways for the likes of Victor Hugo.

St-Valéry-sur-Somme is a charming harbour resort with a historic upper town and a tree-lined promenade looking across the estuary. Birdwatchers should visit the Parc Ornithologique de Marquenterre on the far shore near delightful Le Crotoy, or the Maison de la Baie de Somme et de l'Oiseau nearby at Lanchéres.

Historial de la Grande Guerre

🎨 🎭 🅰 Château de Péronne ⏰ Apr–Oct: 9:30am–6pm daily; Nov–mid-Dec & mid-Jan–Mar: 9:30am–5pm Thu–Tue 🚫 Mid-Dec–mid-Jan 🌐 historial.fr

Samara

🎨 🅰 La Chaussée-Tirancourt ⏰ Hours vary, check website 🌐 samara.fr

---

8

Arras

🅰 D1 🅰 Pas de Calais 🚉 🚌 🛈 Hôtel de Ville, pl des Héros; www.explore arras.com

The centre of Arras is graced by two picturesque cobbled squares enclosed by houses with 17th-century Flemish-style façades. A triumph of postwar reconstruction, each residence in the Grand'Place and the smaller place des Héros has a slightly varying design, with some original shop signs still visible.

A monumental **Hôtel de Ville** rebuilt in the Flamboyant Gothic style stands at the west end of place des Héros – in the foyer are four giants, Colas, Dédé, Ami Bidasse and Jacqueline, who swagger round the town during local festivals. You can take a lift up to the belfry for superb views, or take a guided tour into the underground passages below that were cut in the limestone in the 10th century. They have often served as shelter, during World War I notably, as a subterranean army camp.

The huge Abbaye St-Vaast includes the **Musée des Beaux-Arts**. The museum contains some fine medieval sculpture, including a pair of beautiful 13th-century angels.

EAT

Le Bistrot de Flandre

In the centre of Compiègne, this buzzy bistro gives French classics a modern twist.

🅰 E2 🅰 16 quai de la République, Compiègne 🌐 bistrotdeflandre.fr

---

Meert

Almost unchanged since 1839, this patisserie is famous for its vanilla *gaufres* (waffles).

🅰 E1 🅰 27 rue Esquermoise, Lille 🌐 meert.fr

Hôtel de Ville

🎨 🎭 🅰 Pl des Héros 📞 03 21 51 26 95 ⏰ Building: Jul–Aug: Sun pm, Mon–Fri; tunnels: Feb–Dec: daily; belfry: daily 🚫 25 Dec, 1 Jan

Musée des Beaux-Arts

🎨 🅰 22 rue Paul Doumer 📞 03 21 71 26 43 ⏰ 11am–6pm Wed–Mon 🚫 Pub hols

↑ Sumptuous interiors in the private apartments at Château de Compiègne

⑨ Compiègne

Ⓐ D2 Ⓝ Oise 🚌🚆 ⓘ Pl de l'Hôtel de Ville; www.compiegne-tourisme.fr

Compiègne is where Joan of Arc was captured by the Burgundians in 1430. A 16th-century Hôtel de Ville with a towering belfry rules over the centre, but the town is most famous for its royal **Château de Compiègne**. Designed as a summer residence for Louis XV, the château was completed by Louis XVI, then restored by Napoleon and later became a residence of Napoleon III and Empress Eugénie. Tours of the Imperial Apartments take in the sumptuous bedrooms of Napoleon I and Marie-Louise.

Within the château, the Musée du Second Empire and Musée de l'Impératrice display furniture, memorabilia and portraits, while the Musée de la Voiture is an assembly of historic carriages, bicycles and early motor cars.

South and east of the town, the old hunting grounds of the Forêt de Compiègne spread as far as Pierrefonds, with ample space for walks and picnics beneath its oaks and beeches.

The Clairière de l'Armistice, north of the N31, marks the spot where the armistice of World War I was signed on 11 November 1918. The small **Musée Wagon de l'Armistice** has a replica of the railway carriage where the ceremony took place, which was used again in World War II by Hitler as a humiliating venue for the signing of the French surrender on 22 June 1940.

Did You Know?

Compiègne's famous railway carriage was destroyed by the Germans in 1945.

Château de Compiègne

⊕ Ⓐ Pl du Général de Gaulle Ⓒ Wed–Mon Ⓒ 1 Jan, 1 May, 25 Dec Ⓦ palaisde compiegne.fr

Musée Wagon de l'Armistice

⊕ Ⓐ Clairière de l'Armistice, Route de Soissons Ⓒ 10am–5:30pm daily (to 6pm Mar–Nov) Ⓒ 1 Jan, 25 Dec Ⓦ musee-armistice-14-18.fr

⑩ Dunkerque

Ⓐ D1 Ⓝ Nord 🚌🚆🚢 ⓘ Le Beffroi, rue de l'Amiral Ronarc'h; www.ot-dunkerque.fr

Though a major industrial port, Dunkerque has much Flemish character. Start a

→ Statue of local hero Jean Bart standing in Dunkerque's old centre

tour from place du Minck, with its fresh fish stalls. Nearby **Musée Portuaire** celebrates the town's maritime history. In the old centre, stands a statue that commemorates local hero Jean Bart, a 17th-century corsair, who lies in Eglise St-Eloi. Its belfry (1440) offers fine views.

Other noteworthy places include **Le Mémorial du Souvenir**, which features an exhibition of the dramatic evacuation of 350,000 British and French troops in 1940, and the **Lieu d'Art et d'Action Contemporaine (LAAC)**, housing a fine collection of ceramics and glassware.

Musée Portuaire

 9 quai de la Citadelle Hours vary, check website 1 Jan, 1 & 8 May, 25 Dec, 2 wks Jan museeportuaire.com

Le Memorial du Souvenir

Rue des Chantiers de France 03 28 66 79 21 Apr-Sep: 10am-noon & 2-5:30pm daily

Lieu d'Art et d'Action Contemporaine (LAAC)

Jardin de sculptures, 302 av des Bordées 9.30am-6pm Tue-Sun Public hols musees-dunkerque.eu

---

11

Noyon

E2 Oise pl Bertrand Labarre; www.noyon-tourisme.com

Noyon has long been a religious centre. The Cathédrale de Notre-Dame, dating from 1150, is the fifth to be built on this site and was completed by 1290. It provides a harmonious example of the transition from the Romanesque to the Gothic style.

A local history museum, the **Musée du Noyonnais**, occupies part of the former Bishop's Palace, and at the cathedral's east end is a rare half-timbered chapter library built in 1506.

Jean Calvin, the Protestant theologian and one of the leaders of the Reformation, was born here in 1509 and is commemorated in the small Musée Jean Calvin.

Musée du Noyonnais

 Ancien Palais Episcopal, 7 rue de l'Evêché 03 44 09 43 41 10am-noon & 2-5pm Tue-Sun (to 6pm Apr-Oct) 11 Nov, 24 Dec-2 Jan

---

12

Senlis

D2 Oise Pl du Parvis Notre-Dame; www.senlis-tourisme.fr

Senlis is worth visiting for its Gothic cathedral and the well-preserved historic streets. Cathédrale Notre-Dame was built during the 12th century and the sculpted central doorway of its west front, depicting the Assumption of the Virgin, influenced later cathedrals such as in Amiens (p192). The south tower's spire dates from the 13th century, while the south transept, built in the mid-16th century, makes an ornate contrast with the austerity of earlier years. Opposite the west front, a gateway leads to the ruins of the Château Royal and its gardens. Here the **Musée de la Vénerie**, in a former priory, celebrates hunting through paintings, old weapons and trophies.

Musée de la Vénerie

Pl du Parvis Notre-Dame 10am-1pm & 2-6pm Wed-Sun 1 Jan, 1 May, 25 Dec musees-senlis.fr

→

Paintings and hunting trophies in the main hall, Musée de la Vénerie

STAY

Au Vintage

In a 1920s mansion, this cosy, welcoming B&B is convenient to many of the most important Somme battlefield sites.

D2 19 rue de Corbie, Albert chambres-dhotes-albert.com

€€€

Château de Beaulieu

Ensconced in a 17th-century château, this hotel has bright, spacious rooms and a fine Michelin-starred restaurant.

E1 1098 rue de Lillers, Busnes lechateaudebeaulieu.fr

€€€

Les Tourelles

This unpretentious beachfront Baie de Somme hotel has an old-school maritime vibe and a good-value bistro.

D1 2-4 Rue Pierre Guerlain, Le Crotoy lestourelles.com

€€€

⑬ Lille

🅰E1 🅰Nord ✈🚗🚆
ℹ1 rue du Palais Rihour;
www.lilletourism.com

Lille has excellent shops and markets and a powerful sense of its historic Flemish identity – the Flemish name, Rijssel, is still used and some of the area's one million residents speak a Franco-Flemish patois. With heavy industry declining, the city has turned to high-tech. A modern commercial quarter, including the ultra-modern Euralille shopping complex, adjoins Lille Europe station, the TGV/Eurostar/Thalys rail interchange. The city's metro, VAL, is a driverless automatic train.

The city's charm lies in its historic centre, Vieux Lille – a mass of cobbled squares and narrow streets packed with stylish shops, cafés and restaurants. Place du Général de Gaulle forms its hub, with façades including the 17th-century Vieille Bourse (Old Exchange). Adjacent stand the Nouvelle Bourse and the Opéra, both built in the early 20th century. The moated Citadel by Vauban is also notable.

⑭ Parc Astérix

🅰E2 🅰Plailly 🕐Apr–early Nov (times vary, check website) 🌐parcasterix.fr

Near Charles de Gaulle airport a small fortified Gaulish village has its own customs controls, currency and radio station (Menhir FM). One of the most popular theme parks in France, it is dedicated to Asterix the Gaul and all the other characters in Goscinny and Uderzo's famous cartoon strip: Getafix, Obelix, Cacofonix et al. The Romans are driven crazy as they try to subdue these larger-than-life Gauls, who dodge patrolling Roman centurions. Hilarious battles take place.

The park is as much about French history as about the cartoons. Via Antiqua and the Roman City are lighthearted but still genuinely educational. The Rue de Paris shows this city through the centuries, including the construction of Notre-Dame cathedral.

There are non-historical attractions too, such as a dolphinarium and Zeus' Thunder high-speed roller coaster. Check out the latest rides – there's usually something new every year.

> ## Did You Know?
>
> Goscinny and Uderzo were inspired by Vercingetorix, who united the Gauls against Rome.

⑮ Laon

🅰E2 🅰Aisne 🚆 ℹHôtel-Dieu, pl du Parvis Gauthier de Montagne; www.tourisme-paysdelaon.com

The capital of the *département* of Aisne, Laon occupies a dramatic site on top of a long, narrow ridge surrounded by wide plains.

The pedestrianized rue Châtelaine leads to Laon's splendid Cathédrale de Notre-Dame. Completed in 1235, the cathedral lost two of its original seven towers in the Revolution but remains a fine monument to the early Gothic style.

Details include the deep porches of the west façade, the four-storey nave and the carved Renaissance screens enclosing its side chapels. The immense 13th-century

↑ Families enjoying a ride at the popular Parc Astérix amusement park

rose window in the apse represents the Glorification of the Church. Protruding from the cathedral's western towers are statues paying tribute to the oxen that were used to haul up stone for its construction.

The rest of medieval Laon rewards casual strolling: a promenade rings the 16th-century Citadelle further east, while to the south you can follow the ramparts past the Porte d'Ardon and Porte des Chenizelles to Eglise St-Martin. South of Laon is Chemin des Dames, named after Louis XV's daughters, who used to take this route; it is more often remembered as a World War I battlefield and is lined with cemeteries and memorials.

Chantilly

🅐 D2 🏛 Oise 🚆🚌 ℹ 73 rue du Connétable; www. chantilly-tourisme.com

The horse-racing capital of France, Chantilly offers a classy combination of château, park and forest that has long made it a popular excursion.

With origins in Gallo-Roman times, the château of today started to take shape in 1528, when Anne de Montmorency, Constable of France, had the old fortress replaced and the Petit Château added. During the time of the Great Prince of Condé (1621–86), renovation work continued and André Le Nôtre created a park and fountains that made even Louis XIV jealous. Destroyed in the Revolution, the Grand Château was again rebuilt and its receptions and hunting parties became crowded by the fashionable high society of the 1820s and 1830s. It was finally replaced by a Renaissance-style château in the late 19th century.

Today the Grand Château and the Petit Château form the **Musée Condé**, displaying art treasures collected by its last private owner, the Duke of Aumale. These include work by Raphael, Botticelli, Poussin and Ingres. Among the most precious items is the famous 15th-century illuminated manuscript *Les Très Riches Heures du Duc de Berry*, reproductions of which are on view. You can also tour the opulent stately apartments.

Both châteaux are upstaged by the magnificent stables (Grandes Ecuries), an equestrian palace designed by Jean Aubert in 1719 to house 240 horses and 500 dogs. It is occupied by the **Musée du Cheval**. Devoted to equine art and culture, it also presents various breeds of horses and ponies, riding displays and special events related to horses.

Musée Condé

♿♻🅿 🏛 Château de Chantilly 📞 03 44 27 31 80 🕐 Museum: Apr-Oct: 10am-6pm daily, Nov-Mar: 10:30am-5pm Wed-Mon; park: Apr-Oct: 10am-8pm, Nov-Mar: 10:30am-6pm 🕐 Jan

↑ Musée Condé, the art gallery of Chantilly, one of the largest in France

Musée du Cheval

♿ 🏛 Grandes Ecuries du Prince de Condé, Chantilly 🕐 Apr-Oct: 10am-6pm daily; Nov-Mar: 10:30am-7pm Wed-Mon; park to 8pm 🌐 domainedechantilly.com

---

CHANTILLY RACES

Chantilly is a shrine to the love affair between the French upper classes and equestrian sport. It held its first official race in 1834, and today some 2,000 horses are trained in the surrounding forests. Every June, the Chantilly racetrack becomes the focus of the flat racing season, when top riders and their thoroughbreds compete for prestigious historic trophies.

The splendid Château de Pierrefonds towering over the charming village ↑

17

Château de Pierrefonds

🅰 E2 🏠 Rue Viollet-le-Duc Oise 🕐 Sep-Apr: 10am-5:30pm daily; May-Aug: 9:30am-6pm daily 🕐 1 Jan, 1 May, 25 Dec 🌐 chateau-pierrefonds.fr

The immense Château de Pierrefonds dominates the small riverside village below.

An impressive castle was constructed here by Louis d'Orléans in the 14th century, but by 1813 it had become a picturesque ruin, which Napoleon I purchased for less than 3,000 francs.

In 1857, Emperor Napoleon III commissioned the architect Viollet-le-Duc to restore the castle, and in 1884 Pierrefonds was reborn as a museum of fortification. The exterior, with its moat, drawbridge, towers and double sentry walks, is a diligent reconstruction of medieval military architecture. The interior, by contrast, is enlivened by romantic fancies.

18

Le Touquet

🅰 D1 🏠 Pas de Calais 🚗🚆 🚉 Pavillon Cousteau, 370 Avenue Louis Aboudaram; www.letouquet.com

Properly known as Le Touquet Paris-Plage, this resort was created in the 19th century and became fashionable with the rich and famous between the two world wars. A vast pine forest spreads around the town sheltering stately villas. To the west, a grid of smart hotels, holiday residences and sophisticated shops and restaurants borders a long, sandy beach. A racecourse and two casinos are complemented by seaside amusements and sports facilities, including two excellent golf courses, horse riding and land yachting.

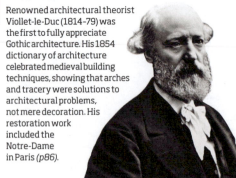

VIOLLET-LE-DUC

Renowned architectural theorist Viollet-le-Duc (1814–79) was the first to fully appreciate Gothic architecture. His 1854 dictionary of architecture celebrated medieval building techniques, showing that arches and tracery were solutions to architectural problems, not mere decoration. His restoration work included the Notre-Dame in Paris (p86).

Did You Know?

French rapper Sianna, one of the few women on the French scene, is from Beauvais.

 19

Beauvais

🅰D2 🅱Oise ✈🚗🚌
ℹ1 rue Beauregard;
www.visitbeauvais.fr

Heavily bombed in World War II, Beauvais is now a modern town with one outstanding jewel. Though never completed, the Cathédrale St-Pierre is a poignant, neck-cricking finale to the vaulting ambition that created the great Gothic cathedrals. In 1227, work began on a building designed to soar above all predecessors, but the roof of the chancel caved in twice from lack of structural support before its completion in the early 14th century. The transept was not completed until 1550. In 1573 its crossing collapsed after a tower and spire were added.

What remains today is nevertheless a masterpiece, rising 48 m (157 ft) high. In the transept much of the original 16th-century stained glass survives, while near the north door is a 90,000-part astronomical clock assembled in the 1860s. Displays take place daily at 30 minutes past the hour and cost €5.

The former Bishop's Palace is now home to **Le MUDO – Musée de l'Oise**. The collection includes archaeological finds, medieval sculpture, tapestries and local ceramics.

→

Exquisite decoration and gilt leaf on the astronomical clock in Beauvais's Cathédrale St-Pierre

Le MUDO – Musée de l'Oise

🅰Ancien Palais Episcopal, 1 rue du Musée 🕐11am–6pm Wed–Mon 🚫1 Jan, Easter, 1 May, 9 Jun, 1 Nov, 25 Dec Ⓦmudo.oise.fr

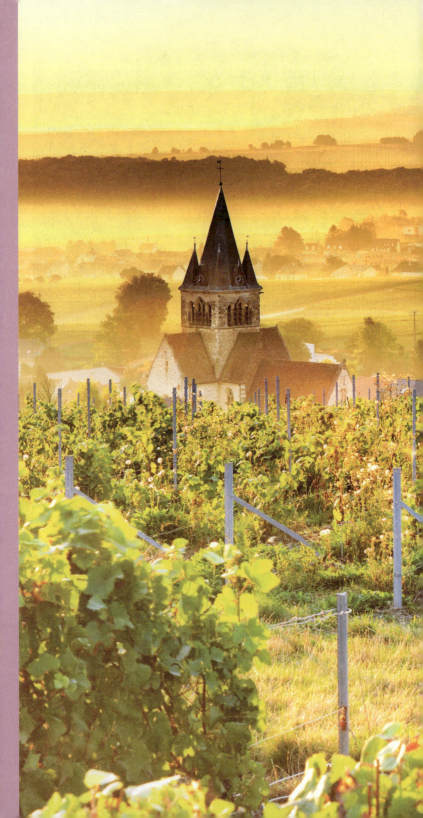

CHAMPAGNE

The Romans were the first to plant grape vines in the chalky hills of Champagne in the 5th century. During the early Middle Ages, Hugh Capet, crowned king at Reims in 987, and Pope Urban II spread the reputation of the region's vineyards by serving the pale white wine at ceremonies. The vineyards of Champagne, owned by popes and European royalty for centuries, continued to bring wealth, while trade fairs in Troyes and flourishing textile and metallurgical industries in Reims and St-Dizier respectively established the region as an economic powerhouse. In the 18th century, the British, followed by the French nobility, developed a taste for Champagne's sparkling wine, and winemaking became the region's primary industry.

When Champagne's sovereignty was abolished in 1790, along with the rest of the traditional French provinces, the region brought its prosperity into the France nation state. Its peace was always tenuous, however; for as a frontier region, Champagne was invaded whenever France was attacked by an eastern front. In 1870, during the Franco-Prussian War Napoleon III surrendered at Sedan, while the vineyards of the region became a battlefield throughout the both World Wars. Thankfully, the regions wine cellars have recovered and corks continue to pop into the 21st century.

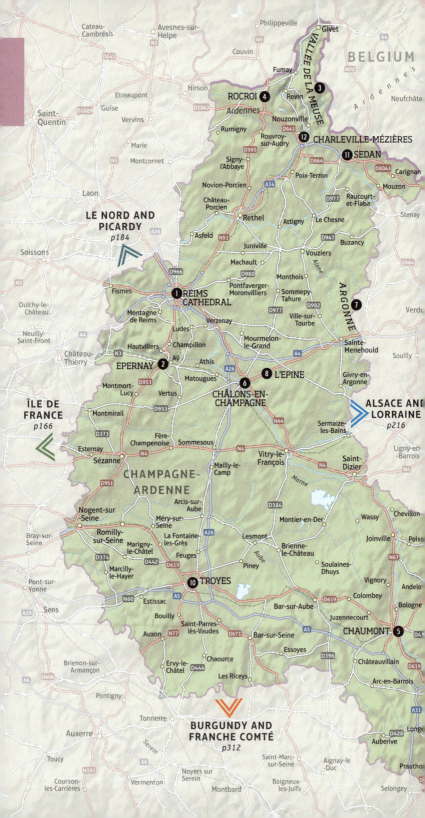

CHAMPAGNE

Must see

1 Reims Cathedral

Experience more

2 Epernay
3 Vallée de la Meuse
4 Rocroi
5 Chaumont
6 Châlons-en-Champagne
7 Argonne
8 L'Epine
9 Langres
10 Troyes
11 Sedan
12 Charleville-Mézières

EXPERIENCE Champagne

REIMS CATHEDRAL

🅰 E2 📍 Place du Cardinal Luçon 🚆🚌 Reims 🕐 Cathedral: 7:30am–7:30pm daily; towers: hours vary, check website 🌐 cathedrale-reims.fr

Noted for its monumental stature, Reims's magnificent Gothic Cathédrale Notre-Dame was the setting for coronations from medieval times till 1825, when Charles X was crowned. In 1429 the coronation of Charles VII here was attended by Joan of Arc. The Gallery of the Kings, with 56 statues of past monarchs, decorates its western façade.

A cathedral has stood on this site since 401, but the present building was begun in 1211. During the Revolution, the rood screen and windows were destroyed, but the stonework survived. World War I damage was fully restored in 1996, to coincide with the 1,500th anniversary of the baptism of Clovis, King of the Franks, at Reims – considered the first coronation of a French king. Rich in statuary, Reims is often called "the cathedral of angels" on account of the many statues of angels that grace the façade and flying buttresses. Angel musicians can also be seen in the glorious 13th-century rose window. Inside are beautiful stained-glass windows designed by Chagall.

> **World War I damage was fully restored in 1996, to coincide with the 1,500th anniversary of the baptism of Clovis, King of the Franks, at Reims.**

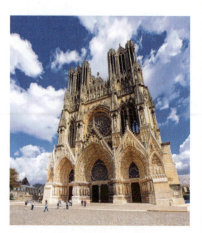

↑ The cathedral's majestic façade, a masterpiece of the French Gothic style

WHAT ELSE TO SEE IN REIMS

Reims's Roman past is recalled by the Porte de Mars, a richly decorated triple arch from the 3rd century. Basilique St-Rémi, a Benedictine abbey church, mixes Romanesque and early Gothic elements. The Musée des Beaux-Arts (*www.musees-reims.fr*) houses portraits by the Cranachs and landscapes by Corot. At the Musée Hôtel Le Vergeur (*www.museelevergeur.com*), the highlight is a set of original prints by Albrecht Dürer (1471–1528). The French HQ of Dwight D Eisenhower now forms the centrepiece of the Musée de la Reddition (*www.musees-reims.fr*).

Did You Know?
—
During World War I, Reims Cathedral was hit by around 300 German artillery shells.

↑ The soaring nave of Reims Cathedral, with its exquisite stained glass *(inset)*.

EXPERIENCE MORE

↑ A wooden cask on display at Epernay's house of Mercier

 2

Epernay

A E2 **A** Marne **B** **i** 7 av de Champagne; www.ot-epernay.fr

The main reason for visiting Epernay is to burrow into the chalky *caves* and taste the Champagne. The town lives off the fruits of its profitable Champagne industry. As proof, the avenue de Champagne quarter abounds in mock-Renaissance mansions. **Moët et Chandon**, dating back to 1743, is the largest and slickest *maison*. Its underground cellars stretch for 28 km (18 miles).

The group also owns other Champagne houses, such as Mercier, Krug, Veuve Clicquot and Ruinart. There is little to choose between a visit to the

 GREAT VIEW
Hautvillers

According to 19th-century marketing, Dom Perignon (1638–1715) invented Champagne in Hautvillers, a picture-perfect little village near Epernay with vine-covered hillsides all around.

cellars of Moët et Chandon or **Mercier** – both are in avenue de Champagne. Mercier has the distinction of displaying a giant tun (cask) created for the 1889 Paris Exhibition, and takes you through the *caves* in an electric train. **De Castellane** offers a more personalized tour, accompanied by a heady *dégustation*.

Moët et Chandon

⊘⊘ **A** 20 av de Champagne **C** By appt only, Apr–mid-Nov: daily; mid-Nov–Dec & Feb–Mar: Mon–Fri **w** moet.com

Mercier

⊘⊘ **A** 70 av de Champagne **C** Feb–26 Mar: Thu–Sun; 27 Mar–Nov: daily **w** champagnemercier.fr

De Castellane

⊘⊘ **A** 57 rue de Verdun **C** Mid-Mar–Dec: daily **w** castellane.com

 3

Vallée de la Meuse

A F2 **A** Ardennes **B** Monthermé **i** Pl Jean Baptiste Clément, Monthermé; www.tourisme-meuse.com

The Meuse meanders through the Ardennes among spectacular scenery of wild gorges, woods and warped rock formations of granite or schist.

Dramatically set on a double meander of the Meuse, Revin is a rather unremarkable town in an exceptional site, its Vieille Ville (Old Town) tucked into the north bend. From the quay, you can see wooded Mont Malgré Tout and a route dotted with observation points

> **The Meuse meanders through the Ardennes among spectacular scenery of wild gorges, woods and warped rock formations of granite or schist.**

and steep trails. Just south is Dames de la Meuse, a rocky outcrop over the river gorge.

The town of Monthermé lies on two banks, with its Vieille Ville clustered on the charming left bank. The rocky gorges around Roche à Sept Heures on the far bank entice climbers and ramblers. The jagged crest of Rocher des Quatre Fils d'Aymon suggests the silhouette of four legendary local horsemen.

 4

Rocroi

A F2 **A** Ardennes **B** Monthermé **i** 1 ter rue du Pavillon; www.otrocroi.com

Set on the Ardennes plateau, the star-shaped citadel of Rocroi was originally built under Henri II in 1555, and later made impregnable by military strategist Sébastien

→

The Château de Chaumont, a fairytale vision of plump turrets and piercing spires

Le Prestre de Vauban in 1675. The main attraction is the walk along the ramparts from the southern gateway. The nature reserve at Rièzes is home to carnivorous plants and orchids.

 5

Chaumont

🗺 **F3** 📍 **Haute-Marne** 🚉🚌
ℹ 7 av du Général de Gaulle; www.tourisme-chaumont-champagne.com

The former residence of the Counts of Champagne, this feudal town enjoyed great prestige in the 13th century. On the far side of a ravine, the old town sits on a rocky spur, with the Palais de Justice and the medieval castle dominating the view.

The keep is a reminder that this administrative centre had a formidable past. This is confirmed by the Renaissance town houses, which are bulging with *tourelles d'escaliers*, turreted staircases. Basilique St-Jean-Baptiste, a grey-stone Champenois church, is the most remarkable monument in Chaumont. The interior is enlivened by a spider's web of vaulting, a striking turreted staircase and Renaissance galleries. Near the entrance is a tiny chapel containing an unsettling *Mise au Tombeau* (1471), an

intense multicoloured stone group of ten mourners gathered around Christ laid out on a shroud in his tomb. In the left transept is a bizarre but beguiling *Tree of Jesse*. On this ill-lit Renaissance stone relief, a family tree sprouts from the sleeping Jesus.

Northwest of Chaumont, Colombey-les-Deux-Eglises is associated with General Charles de Gaulle (1890–1970). The de Gaulles bought their home, **La Boisserie**, in 1933, but had to abandon it during the war, when it was badly damaged. After its restoration, de Gaulle would return to La Boisserie from Paris at weekends to write his memoirs. He died

here on 9 November 1970. His house is now a museum. In the village churchyard, he lies in a simple tomb, but a giant granite cross of Lorraine, erected in 1972, dominates the skyline. At its foot is the **Mémorial Charles de Gaulle**, a museum dedicated to his life.

La Boisserie

🌐 📍Rue Général de Gaulle, Colombey-les-Deux-Eglises 📞 03 25 01 52 52 🕐 Apr–Sep: daily; Oct–Mar: Wed–Mon 🚫 Mid-Dec–Jan

Mémorial Charles de Gaulle

🌐 📍Colombey-les-Deux-Eglises 🕐 May–Sep: daily; Oct–Apr: Wed–Mon 🚫 Jan, 24, 25 & 31 Dec 🌐 memorial-charlesdegaulle.fr

---

MÉTHODE CHAMPENOISE

The secret to making bubbly is in its second fermentation. After *liqueur de tirage* (wine, sugar and yeast) is added, the wine is bottled and, over a year or more, the yeast converts the sugar to alcohol and carbon dioxide – the latter produces the sparkle. Cloudy yeast sediments are moved towards the cork by slowly elevating and turning each bottle in a process called *remuage*. The mouth of the bottle is frozen and the sediments removed (*dégorgement*). Finally, the sweetness is adjusted by adding liqueur *de dosage* (a mixture of wine and sugar) and the bottle is sealed with a high-pressure cork held on with a wire hood.

⑥ Châlons-en-Champagne

🄰 E2 🄰 Marne 🚇🚌
ℹ️ 3 quai des Arts; www.chalons-tourisme.com

Encircled by the River Marne and minor canals, Châlons has a sleepy bourgeois charm thanks to its half-timbered houses and gardens mirrored in canals. Nearby are vineyards producing Blanc de Blancs (Champagne made only from Chardonnay grapes).

From quai de Notre-Dame there are views of old bridges and the Romanesque towers of Notre-Dame-en-Vaux, a masterpiece of Romanesque Gothic. Behind the church is a well-restored medieval quarter and the **Musée du Cloître de Notre-Dame-en-Vaux**, containing the original Romanesque cloisters.

Cathédrale St-Etienne is a Gothic affair with a Baroque portal, Romanesque crypt and medieval windows. Beyond is Le Petit Jard, riverside gardens overlooking the Château du Marché, and a tollgate built by Henri IV. River tours are available from the tourist office.

Musée du Cloître de Notre-Dame-en-Vaux

⊗♿🄰 Rue Nicolas Durand 📞 03 26 69 38 53 🕐 10am–12pm & 2–6pm Wed–Mon 🚫 1 Jan, 1 May, 1 & 11 Nov, 25 Dec

⑦ Argonne

🄰 F2 🄰 Ardennes & Meuse 🚌 Châlons 🚌 Ste-Menehould ℹ️ 6 pl du la République, Clermont en Argonne; www.tourisme-argonne.com

East of Reims, the Argonne is full of picturesque valleys and forests, dotted with priories, trenches and war cemeteries. As a wooded border between the rival bishoprics of Lorraine and Champagne, the Argonne was home to abbeys and priories. Now a ruin, the abbey of Beaulieu-en-Argonne boasts a 13th-century wine press and has forest views. Just north is Les Islettes, known for its faïence pottery. The hilly terrain here was a battleground during the Franco-Prussian War and World War I. The disputed territory of Butte de Vauquois, north of Les Islettes, bears a war memorial.

TOP 5 TOP FIVE CHAMPAGNE HOUSES

Moët et Chandon
Offers some of Epernay's most elegant and impressive cellar tours (www.moet.com).

Mumm
Not far from the centre of Reims, informative tours take you deep into chalk cellars (www.mumm.com).

Pommery
From an entrance hall in Reims, 101 steps lead down to Gallo-Roman cellars, decorated with art (www.champagne-pommery.com).

Joseph Perrier
Based in Châlons-en-Champagne, this family house has 3 km of chalk caves to explore (www.josephperrier.com).

Tattinger
Cellar tours in Reims take you to Gallo-Roman quarries and a 13th-century abbey (www.taittinger.com).

⑧ L'Epine

🄰 E2 🄰 Marne 🚌 Châlons 🚌 ℹ️ 3 quai des Arts, Châlons en Champagne; 03 26 65 17 89

Surrounded by idyllic rural scenes and rolling countryside, L'Epine is worth visiting if only for a glimpse of the Basilique de Notre-Dame de l'Epine, surrounded by wheatfields. Designed on the scale of a cathedral, this 15th-century Flamboyant Gothic church has been a pilgrimage site since medieval times. Even French kings have come here to venerate a "miraculous" statue of the Virgin. On the façade, three

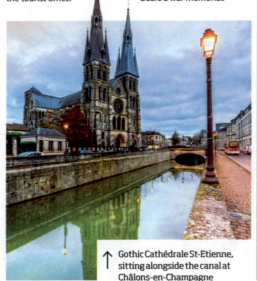

↑ Gothic Cathédrale St-Etienne, sitting alongside the canal at Châlons-en-Champagne

↑ Cafés spilling out on the cobbles at the centre of pretty Langres

gabled portals are offset by floating tracery, a gauzy effect reminiscent of Reims Cathedral. All around are gargoyles, symbolizing evil spirits and deadly sins, chased out by the holy presence within. Unfortunately, the most risqué sculptures were destroyed, judged obscene by 19th-century puritans. The subdued Gothic interior contains a 15th-century rood screen and the venerated statue of the Virgin.

CHAMPAGNE TIMBER CHURCHES

An hour south of L'Epine lies a region of woodland and water meadows, containing 12 Romanesque and Renaissance half-timbered churches with curious pointed gables and *caquetoirs*, rickety wooden porches. Set in rural spots, they feature intimate and often beautifully carved interiors with stained-glass windows designed in the vivid colours of the School of Troyes.

↑ The 16th-century timber church at Bailly-le-Franc

⑨

Langres

△F3 **⌂Haute-Marne**
🚌🚋 ℹ Square Olivier Lahalle; www.tourisme-langres.com

Set on a rocky spur, Langres lies beyond Chaumont, in the backwaters of southern Champagne. This ancient bishopric was one of the gateways to Burgundy and the birthplace of the encyclopedist Denis Diderot (1713–84). Langres promotes itself as a land of springs, claiming that its proximity to the sources of the Seine and Marne grant it

mystical powers. Virtually the whole town is enclosed by well-preserved medieval ramparts, undoubtedly Langres's best-known attraction. A succession of towers and parapets provide glimpses of the romantic town gates and sculpted Renaissance mansions, with panoramic views of the Marne Valley, the Langres plateau, the Vosges and, on a clear day, even Mont Blanc.

Near Porte Henri IV is the much-remodelled Cathédrale St-Mammès. In Burgundian Romanesque style, the gloomy vaulted interior is redeemed by the sculpted capitals in the apse, reputedly taken from a temple of Jupiter. The town's **Musée d'Art et d'Histoire** presents archaeological finds from the region, and has some interesting collections of paintings, engravings and sculpture.

Langres's lively summer season includes historical re-enactments, theatre and firework displays. Its nearby lakes, Lac de Charmes and Lac de la Vingeanne, offer excellent opportunities for fishing and birdwatching.

Musée d'Art et d'Histoire

⊗ **⌂Pl du Centenaire 52** **🕐Apr–Sep: 9am–noon & 1:30–6:30pm; Oct–Mar: 1:30–5:30pm 🚫1 Jan, 1 May, 1 Nov, 25 Dec 🌐musees-langres.fr

10 Troyes

E3 Aube
16 rue Aristide Briand;
www.tourisme-troyes.com

Troyes is a delight, a city of magnificent Gothic churches and charming 16th-century half-timbered houses, in a historical centre shaped like a champagne cork. The city is famous for its heritage of stained glass and *andouillettes* (sausages), as well as its long established hosiery industry and factory shops.

A splended vaulted interior opens out from the battered Flamboyant Gothic west front of the Cathédrale St-Pierre-et-St-Paul. The nave is bathed in mauvish-red rays from the 16th-century rose window, complemented by the discreet turquoise of the Tree of Jesse window and the intense blue of the medieval windows of the apse.

Nearby, Eglise St-Nizier glitters in the faded quarter behind the cathedral with its shimmering tiled Burgundian roof. Inside, it is lit by windows in a range of warm mauves and soothing blues.

The Gothic Basilique St-Urbain boasts grand flying buttresses and 13th-century windows. Eglise Ste-Madeleine is noted for its elaborate 16th-century rood screen that resembles lacy foliage, grapes and figs. Beyond is a wall of windows in browns, reds and blues. The quaint ruelle des Chats, a covered passageway, connects rue Charbonnet and rue Champeaux.

Set in one of the best-preserved quarters is the Eglise St-Pantaléon. Its Gothic and Renaissance interior houses an imposing collection of 16th-century statuary and severe *grisaille* windows. The 17th-century Hôtel de Vauluisant contains the Musée d'Art Champenois (Regional Art Museum) and the Musée de la Bonneterie, dedicated to hosiery.

11 Sedan

F2 Ardennes
32 rue du Menil; www.charleville-sedan-tourisme.fr

Just to the east of Charleville is the Château de Sedan, the largest fortified castle in Europe. There has been a bastion on these slopes since the 11th century, but each Ardennes conflict has spelled a new tier of defences for Sedan.

In 1870, during the Franco-Prussian War, with 700 Prussian cannons turned on Sedan, Napoleon III surrendered and 83,000 French prisoners were deported to Prussia. In May 1940, after capturing Sedan, German forces reached the French coast a week later. The seven-storey bastion contains sections dating from early medieval times to the 1550s. Its highlights include the 16th-century fortifications, the ramparts, and the magnificent 15th-century eaves in one tower.

←

An imposing Gothic aisle in Cathédrale St-Pierre-et-St-Paul, Troyes

↑ Cheerful flower beds in place Ducale at the heart of Charleville-Mézières

The **Musée du Château** has a fine collection of armour, brought here by Napoleon Bonaparte. There are also tableaux of wax figures illustrating medieval life.

The bastion is surrounded by 17th-century slate-roofed houses, which hug the banks of the Meuse. These reflect the city's earlier prosperity as a Huguenot stronghold.

Further south is Fort de Villy-la-Ferté, one of the few forts on the Maginot Line to have been captured in combat with the enemy in 1940.

Musée du Château

⊘ 🏛 Château Fort du Sedan, cours du Château 🕿 03 24 29 98 80 🕒 Daily

---

12

Charleville-Mézières

🅰 E2 🏛 Ardennes 🚉 📧
🚋 4 pl Ducale; www.charle-ville-sedan-tourisme.fr

This riverside ford used to be two towns. The medieval citadel of Mézières merged with the neat Classical town of Charleville in 1966. Mézières has irregular slate-covered houses curving around a bend in the Meuse. Battered fortifications and gateways are visible from the avenue de St-Julien. Tucked into the ramparts is the much remodelled Gothic Notre-Dame de l'Espérance.

A model of Louis XIII urban planning, the centrepiece of Charleville is place Ducale, which echoes place des Vosges in Paris (p99). The poet Arthur Rimbaud was born nearby in 1854. No 12 rue Bérégovoy, his modest birthplace is still there, along with his childhood home on the Meuse at what is now 7 quai Arthur Rimbaud.

Just along the quayside is the Vieux Moulin, the town house whose view inspired "Le Bateau Ivre", Rimbaud's greatest poem. Inside is the **Musée Rimbaud**, which has a collection of handwritten manuscripts and photographs by the poet.

Musée Rimbaud

 🏛 Quai A Rimbaud
🕿 03 24 32 44 65 🕒 Tue–Sun
🕒 1 Jan, 1 May, 25 Dec

EAT

La Cave à Champagne

Tasty classic Champenoise dishes and plenty of excellent local fizz at this buzzy local favourite.

🅰 E2 🏛 16 Rue Gambetta, Épernay
🌐 la-cave-a-champagne.com

€€€

Art Deco Café du Palais

Authentic bistro food and a great wine list served under an exquisite Art Deco stained-glass ceiling.

🅰 E2 🏛 14 Place Myron Herrick, Reims
🌐 cafedupalais.fr

€€€

> This riverside ford used to be two towns. The medieval citadel of Mézières merged with the neat Classical town of Charleville in 1966.

One of the colourful streets found in Colmar, Alsace

ALSACE AND LORRAINE

First settled by the Celts, Alsace was conquered in the 1st century BC by the Romans, who established vineyards here. The region was subsequently ruled by the Germanic Alemanni tribe, and then from the 5th century by the Franks. Although France took control of most of Alsace in 1648 following the end of the Thirty Years' War, provisions of the Treaty of Westphalia provided for local customs, including the use of German, to be respected. In 1681, the Alsatian capital, Strasbourg, at last came under the control of the French state. Neighbouring Lorraine, also at the intersection of Germanic and French cultures, was taken over by France in 1766.

Both Alsace and Lorraine's northern section were annexed by Germany following the Franco-Prussian War (1870–71); it was only after World War I that these regions re-joined France. Annexed yet again by Nazi Germany in 1940, they were returned to France once more in 1945. Since then, Strasbourg has become a symbol of post-war Franco-German reconciliation and serves as the seat of the the European Parliament, the Council of Europe and the European Court of Human Rights.

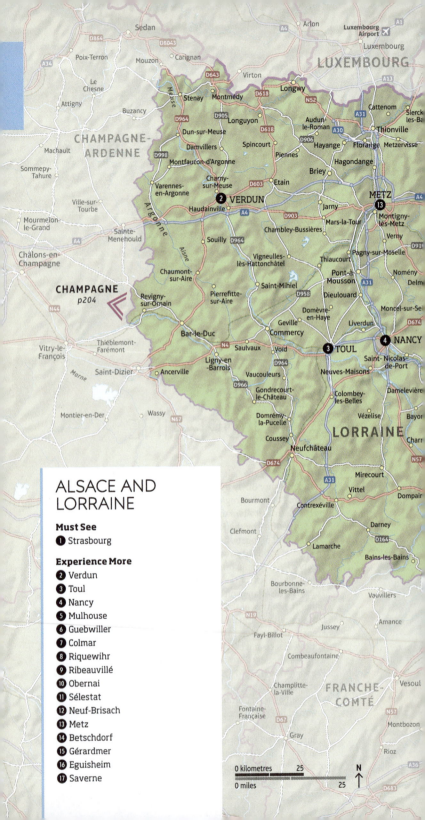

ALSACE AND LORRAINE

Must See

❶ Strasbourg

Experience More

❷ Verdun
❸ Toul
❹ Nancy
❺ Mulhouse
❻ Guebwiller
❼ Colmar
❽ Riquewihr
❾ Ribeauvillé
❿ Obernai
⓫ Sélestat
⓬ Neuf-Brisach
⓭ Metz
⓮ Betschdorf
⓯ Gérardmer
⓰ Eguisheim
⓱ Saverne

CHAMPAGNE
p204

0 kilometres   25
0 miles   25

N

↑ Traditional half-timbered houses in Strasbourg's scenic Old Town

① STRASBOURG

🅰 G2 🏠 Bas-Rhin ✈ 12 km (7.5 miles) SW Strasbourg 🚉 Place de la Gare 🚌 Pl des Halles 🛈 17 pl de la Cathédrale; www.otstrasbourg.fr

Located halfway between Paris and Prague, Strasbourg is, not surprisingly known as "the crossroads of Europe". The city wears its European cosmopolitanism with ease – after all, its famous cathedral has catered to both Catholic and Protestant congregations. The city is one of the capitals of the European Union, and the futuristic-looking European Parliament building is located in the Wacken district, outside the historic centre.

① Cathédrale Notre-Dame

🏠 Place de la Cathédrale ⏰ 8:30am–5:45pm Mon-Sat, 11:15–5:30pm Sun 🌐 cathedrale-strasbourg.fr

A masterpiece of stone lace work, the sandstone cathedral "rises like a most sublime, wide-arching tree of God", as frequent visitor Goethe marvelled. Construction began in the late 11th century and ended only in 1439, with the completion of the west façade. The three portals are ornamented with statues and topped with a rose window. At certain times, mechanical figures appear around the Astronomical Clock accompanied by chimes. There are wonderful views from the viewing platform.

② Palais Rohan

🏠 2 pl du Château ⏰ Wed-Mon 🚫 1 Jan, Good Fri, 1 May, 1 & 11 Nov, 25 Dec 🌐 musees.strasbourg.eu

Designed by Robert de Cotte in 1730, this grand Classical palace was intended for the prince-bishops of Strasbourg. It houses three museums: the Musée des Beaux-Arts; the Musée Archéologique; and the Musée des Arts Décoratifs, which contains an exquisite collection of ceramics and the sumptuous State Apartments.

③ Musée Historique

🏠 2 rue du Vieux-Marché-aux-Poissons ⏰ Tue-Sun 🚫 1 Jan, Good Fri, 1 May, 1 & 11 Nov, 25 Dec 🌐 musees.strasbourg.eu

The museum occupies the 16th-century city abattoir and focuses on Strasbourg's political and military history. There is a narrative-led audio tour and a range of interactive exhibitions and play areas for children.

Did You Know?

Rouget de Lisle wrote the French national anthem, "La Marseillaise", in Strasbourg.

(4) Musée Alsacien

⌂ 23 quai St-Nicolas ☎ 03 68 98 51 52 🕐 Wed–Mon 🗓 1 Jan, Good Fri, 1 May, 1 Nov, 25 Dec

This museum, housed in a series of interconnecting Renaissance buildings, has fascinating exhibits on local traditions, daily rural life, and popular arts and crafts. It also includes displays on the daily life of Alsatian Jews.

(5) Musée de l'Oeuvre Notre-Dame

⌂ 3 pl du Château ☎ 03 68 98 51 60 🕐 Tue–Sun 🗓 1 Jan, Good Fri, 1 May, 1 & 11 Nov, 25 Dec

The cathedral's impressive museum contains much of its original sculpture, as well as magnificent 11th-century stained glass. This sombre gabled house also displays a collection of Medieval and Renaissance Alsatian art.

(6) Musée d'Art Moderne et Contemporain

⌂ 1 pl Hans-Jean Arp ☎ 03 68 98 51 55 🕐 Tue–Sun 🗓 1 Jan, Good Fri, 1 May, 1 & 11 Nov, 25 Dec

Adrien Fainsilber's cultural flagship for the 21st century is a marvel of glass and light (particularly at night, when it appears to float on the river). Its superb collections run from 1860 to 1950 (modern) and from 1950 onwards.

(7) MM Park Museum

⌂ 4 rue Gutenberg, La Wantzenau 67610 🕐 Tue–Sun 🗓 1 Jan, Good Fri, 1 May, 1 & 11 Nov, 25 Dec 🌐 mmpark.fr

The largest private collection of World War II artifacts in Europe is housed in this lovely museum outside Strasbourg. The collection includes around 120 vehicles, plus numerous uniforms and weapons.

SLEEP

Régent Petite France

Housed in an old mill, this five-star hotel offers stylish rooms, a state-of-the-art spa and seasonal Alsatian cuisine at its riverside restaurant.

⌂ 5 rue des Moulins 🌐 regent-petite.france.com

€€€

Carpe Diem Home

Located in a historic property, these spacious apartments combine contemporary decor with classic old-fashioned Alsatian charm.

⌂ 28 rue des Orfèvres 🌐 bijoux-carpediem.fr

€€€

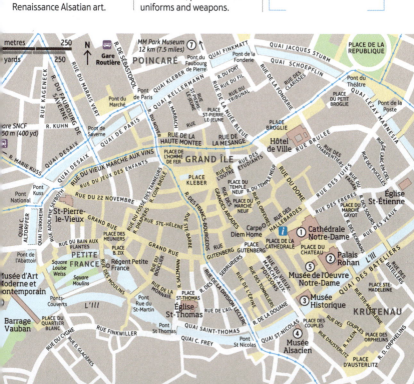

EXPERIENCE MORE

2

Verdun

⚑ F2 ◉ Meuse ▣▤ 🛈 Pl de la Nation; www.tourisme-verdun.com

Verdun is remembered for the horrors of the 1916 Battle of Verdun, when about a million men died over almost a whole year of continuous bloodshed. It is considered the worst single battle of the Great War.

Several poignant museums, memorials, battle sites and cemeteries can be visited in the hills just outside Verdun. In this devastated region, nine villages were obliterated without a trace. The Musée-Memorial de Fleury tells their story. Nearby, the Ossuaire de Douaumont contains the unidentified bones of over 130,000 French and German dead. One of the most striking monuments to the Battle of Verdun is Rodin's memorial in Verdun itself. It depicts the winged figure of Victory unable to soar triumphant because she has become caught in the remains of a dead soldier.

The town of Verdun was heavily fortified over the centuries. The crenellated Porte Chaussée, a medieval river gateway, still guards the eastern entrance to the town and is the most impressive of the remaining fortifications. The Citadelle de Verdun still retains its 12th-century tower, the only relic from the original abbey that engineer Vauban incorporated into his new military design. Now a war museum, the underground **Citadelle Souterraine** recreates life for soldiers going to the front in World War I. A moving display tells how the "Unknown Soldier" was chosen for the symbolic tomb under the Arc de Triomphe in Paris (p120).

The town centre is dominated by the cathedral, where Romanesque elements were rediscovered after the 1916 bombardments.

Citadelle Souterraine

♿ 🏠 Ave du Soldat Inconnu
📞 03 29 84 84 42 ⏰ Hours vary, call ahead 🚫 21 Dec–late Jan

3

Toul

⚑ F2 ◉ Meurthe-et-Moselle ▣▤ 🛈 1 pl Charles de Gaulle; www.lepredenancy.fr

Lying within dark forests west of Nancy, the octagonal fortress city of Toul is encircled by the Moselle and the Canal de la Marne. Along with Verdun and Metz, Toul was one of the 4th-century bishoprics. In the early 18th century, Vauban built the citadel, from which the ring of defensive waterways, the octagonal city ramparts and the Porte de Metz remain.

The Cathédrale St-Étienne, begun in the 13th century, took over 300 years to build. It suffered damage in World War II but its recognizable Champenois style has survived, notably in the arched, high-galleried interior. The imposing Flamboyant Gothic façade is flanked by octagonal towers. Rue du Général-Gengoult, behind the Gothic Église St-Gengoult, contains a clutch of sculpted Renaissance houses. North of the city, the local "grey" Côtes de Toul wines are produced.

South of Toul, near the town of Neufchâteau, is the birthplace of Joan of Arc at Domrémy-La-Pucelle. Next door to the house where she was born is an exhibition about her remarkable life.

Lying between Toul, Verdun, and Metz is the vast Parc Régional de Lorraine, which takes in red-tiled cottages, vineyards, forests, cropland, chaumes (high pastureland), marshes and lakes.

Did You Know?

Toul was the Iron Age capital of the Leuci tribe; its name is derived from the Leuci name Tullum.

←

The Citadelle Souterraine bringing World War I to life in a fascinating presentation

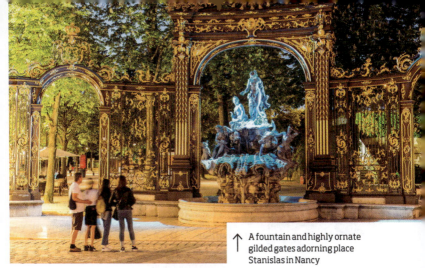

A fountain and highly ornate gilded gates adorning place Stanislas in Nancy

4

Nancy

🅰 F2 🏛 Meurthe-et-Moselle 🚆🚌 ℹ 14 pl Stanislas; www.nancy-tourisme.fr

Lorraine's historic capital, Nancy backs on to the Canal du Marne and the River Meurthe. In the 18th century, Stanislas Leczinski, Duke of Lorraine, transformed the city, making it a model of 18th-century town planning.

Nancy's second golden age was at the turn of the 20th century, when glassmaker Émile Gallé founded the École de Nancy, which was a forerunner of the Art Nouveau movement in France.

Nancy's principal and most renowned landmark is place Stanislas. Laid out in the 1750s, this elegantly proportioned square is enclosed by highly ornate gilded wrought-iron gates and railings, which have been beautifully restored. Lining the square are fine *hôtels particuliers* (town houses) and there are several chic restaurants.

An Arc de Triomphe leads to place de la Carrière, a gracious, tree-lined square. At the far end, flanked by semicircular arcades, is the Gothic Palais du Gouvernement.

Next door in the Parc de la Pépinière is Rodin's statue of Claude Lorrain, the landscape painter, born near Nancy.

Grande Rue provides a glimpse of medieval Nancy. Of the original fortifications the only one remaining is the Porte de la Craffe, which was used as a prison after the Revolution. The dukes of Lorraine are buried in the crypt of the **Église et Couvent des Cordeliers**, and the adjoining converted monastery contains the Musée Lorrain (closed for renovation until 2023), with displays of folklore, furniture, costumes and crafts.

A renovation and modern extension at the **Musée des Beaux-Arts** have enabled 40 per cent more of the museum's remarkable collection of 14th- to 20th-century European art to be seen, including superb works by Delacroix, Manet, Monet, Utrillo and Modigliani. Particularly stunning is the Daum glassware.

The exhibits at the **Musée de l'École de Nancy** are displayed in reconstructed Art Nouveau settings. Most noteworthy are the unique collections of furniture, fabrics and jewellery, as well as the extensive fanciful glassware and ceramics of Émile Gallé, founder of the École de Nancy.

Église et Couvent des Cordeliers

♿ 🏛 64 & 66 Grande Rue 📞 03 83 32 18 74 🕐 10am-12.30pm & 2-6pm Tue-Sun 🚫 Pub hols

Musée des Beaux-Arts

♿ 🎫 🏛 3 pl Stanislas 🕐 Wed-Mon 10am-6pm 🚫 Pub hols 🌐 mban.nancy.fr

Musée de l'École de Nancy

♿ 🎫 🏛 36-38 rue de Sergent Blandan 🕐 Wed-Sun 10am-6pm 🚫 Pub hols 🌐 ecole-de-nancy.com

---

WHITE STORKS

Long a symbol of Alsace, white storks were on the verge of local extinction in the mid-1970s, but due to an intensive campaign the region is now home to about 600 breeding pairs. Today, storks can be seen soaring through the sky – or standing in rooftop nests clattering their bills – along the Alsace Wine Route. You're sure to see them in the areas of Munster, Hunawihr and Eguisheim, as all three are home to stork reintroduction centres.

↑ Buzzy café tables outside Mulhouse's imposing town hall

5
Mulhouse

 G3 △ Haut-Rhin ⊠⊞⊟ ▮ 1 av Robert Schuman; www.tourisme-mulhouse.com

Close to the Swiss border, Mulhouse is an industrial city that was badly damaged in World War II, but rebounded with modern technical museums and shopping galleries, as well as Alsatian taverns and Swiss wine bars. Most visitors use the city as a base for exploring the rolling hills of the Sundgau on the Swiss border.

Of the museums, Musée de l'Impression sur Étoffes, at 14 rue Jean-Jacques Henner, is devoted to textiles and fabric painting, while the Cité du Train, at 2 rue Alfred Glehn, has a collection of steam and electric locomotives. Cité de l'Automobile, at 15 rue de l'Épée, boasts over 100 Bugattis, a clutch of Mercedes and Ferraris, and Charlie Chaplin's Rolls-Royce. In the Renaissance former town hall, on place de la Réunion, is the Musée Historique.

At Ungersheim, north of Mulhouse, the **Ecomusée d'Alsace** preserves the region's rural heritage. The 12th-century fortified house from Mulhouse is a dramatic building, complete with Gothic garden. Farms are run along traditional lines, with livestock such as the Alsatian black pig.

Ecomusée d'Alsace
⊗ ⊘ □ Chemin du Grosswald ⊙ Hours vary, check website ⊠ Jan-Mar & Nov ⊞ ecomusee.alsace

6
Guebwiller

 G3 △ Haut-Rhin ▯ ▮ 45 rue de la République; www.tourisme-guebwiller.fr

Surrounded by vineyards and flower-filled valleys, Guebiller is known as "the gateway to the valley of flowers". However, as an industrial town producing textiles and machine tools, it feels cut off from this rural setting. Even so, the caves and churches make it worth a visit.

Set on a pretty square, Église Notre-Dame combines Baroque theatricality with Neo-Classical elegance, while Église des Dominicains boasts Gothic frescoes. Église St-Léger, the Romanesque church, is the most rewarding, especially the façade, triple porch and portal.

The scenic Lauch valley, northwest of Guebwiller, is known as "Le Florival" because of its floral aspect. Lautenbach is used as a starting point for hikes. The village has a pink Romanesque church, with a portal depicting human

 HIDDEN GEM
Paper Museum

Mulhouse is something of an ugly duckling due to its long history as an industrial powerhouse, but the surprising Musée du Papier Peint (*www. museepapierpeint.org*) always has something colourful on show from the 18th century to the present day.

passion and the battle between Good and Evil. The square leads to the river, a small weir, *lavoir* (public washing place) and houses overlooking the water.

 7

Colmar

🅰 G3 🅰 Haut-Rhin 🚉 🚌
🄘 Pl Unterlinden; **www. tourisme-colmar.com**

As a trading post and river port, the well-preserved Colmar had its heyday in the 16th century, when wine merchants shipped their wine along the waterways running through the picturesque canal quarter, now known as Petite Venise. "Little Venice" is best seen on a boat trip from the tanners' quarter to rue des Tanneurs. The adjoining place de l'Alsacienne Douane is dominated by the Koïfhüs, a galleried customs house with a Burgundian tiled roof, overlooking half-timbered houses sporting sculpted pillars.

Did You Know?

Colmar's cityscape was the basis for the design of the 2005 Japanese animated film *Howl's Moving Castle*.

Nearby, place de la Cathédrale quarter is full of 16th-century houses. Église St-Martin, essentially Gothic, has a noted south portal. To the west, the place des Dominicains, busy with cafés, is dwarfed by the Gothic Église Dominicaine.

The adjoining square, place Unterlinden, has the Musée Unterlinden. Set in a Dominican monastery, it displays early Rhenish paintings. The highlight is the Issenheim altarpiece. A masterpiece of emotional intensity, it is part of an early 16th-century Alsatian panel painting by Matthias Grünewald. A three-storey wing houses modern and contemporary art.

In the historic centre, the quaint rue des Têtes has the former wine exchange, a Renaissance town house known as the Maison des Têtes because of the grimacing heads on the gabled façade.

The Musée Bartholdi, on rue des Marchands, is devoted to Colmar-born Frédéric-Auguste Bartholdi, designer of the Statue of Liberty.

EAT

Buerehiesel
Feast on Michelin-starred Alsatian cuisine in an old house north of the cathedral.

🅰 G3 🅰 4 parc de l'Orangerie, Strasbourg
🅦 **buerehiesel.fr**

Wistub Brenner
Traditional Alsatian dishes served in a convivial location.

🅰 G3 🅰 1 rue de Turenne, Colmar
🅦 **wistub-brenner.fr**

Le Magasin aux Vivres
Set in the citadel, this Michelin-starred restaurant is famed for its scrumptious dishes and superb wine list.

🅰 F2 🅰 A5 av Ney, Metz
🅦 **citadelle-metz.com**

Brasserie Excelsior
Oysters are a specialty at this glorious belle époque restaurant.

🅰 F3 🅰 50 rue Henri Poincaré, Nancy
🅦 **brasserie-excelsior-nancy.fr**

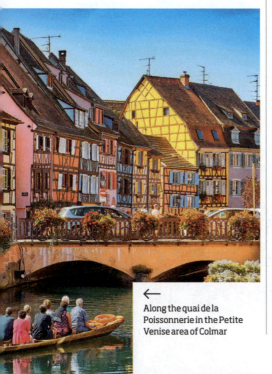

← Along the quai de la Poissonnerie in the Petite Venise area of Colmar

⑧

Riquewihr

🅐 G3 🅗 Haut-Rhin 🚌 🛈 2 rue de la 1ère Armée; www.ribeauville-riquewihr.com

Vineyards run right up to the ramparts of Riquewihr, the prettiest village on the Route des Vins (p230). Deeply pragmatic, Riquewihr winemakers plant roses at the end of each row of vines – both for their pretty effect and as early detectors of parasites. The village belonged to the counts of Wurttemberg until the Revolution and has grown rich on wine, from Tokay and Pinot Gris to Gewurztraminer and Riesling. Virtually an open-air museum, Riquewihr abounds in cobbled alleys, geranium-clad balconies, galleried courtyards, romantic double ramparts and watchtowers.

From the Hôtel de Ville, rue du Général de Gaulle climbs gently past medieval and Renaissance houses, half-timbered, stone-clad, or corbelled. Oriel windows vie with sculpted portals and medieval signboards. On the right lies the idyllic place des Trois Églises. A passageway leads through the ramparts to the vineyards on the hill. Further up lies the Dolder, a 13th-century belfry, followed by the Tour des Voleurs (both are museums, the latter with a medieval torture chamber), marking the second tier of ramparts. Beyond the

Did You Know?

Riquewihr's bright, cheery houses inspired the "Little Town" in Disney's *Beauty and the Beast*.

gateway is the cour des Bergers, where gardens are laid out around the 16th-century ramparts.

---

⑨

Ribeauvillé

🅐 G3 🅗 Haut-Rhin 🚉 🚌 🛈 1 Grand'Rue; www.ribeauville-riquewihr.com

Overlooked by three ruined castles, the beautiful town of Ribeauvillé is a favoured stop on the Route des Vins. This is in large part due to the ample opportunities to taste (and purchase) the *grands crus* of Alsace, especially Riesling at numerous places particularly near the park, in the lower part of town.

Alleys wind past the steep-roofed houses of artisans and *vignerons* in the upper part of the town. Beyond these are Renaissance fountains,

pretty painted façades and the Gothic parish church St-Grégoire-le-Grand. A path, which begins in this part of town, leads into the vineyards.

The town is also known for its festivals, among them Pfifferdaj (Fiddlers' Festival), the oldest festival in Alsace.

---

⑩

Obernai

🅐 G3 🅗 Bas-Rhin 🚉 🚌 🛈 Pl du Beffroi; www.tourisme-obernai.fr

At the north end of the Route des Vins, Obernai retains a flavour of authentic Alsace: residents speak Alsatian, at festivities women wear traditional costume, and church services are well attended in the cavernous Neo-Gothic Église St-Pierre-et-St-Paul. Place du Marché is well preserved, and features the gabled Halle aux Blés, a 16th-century corn hall (now a restaurant) above a former butcher's shop, with a façade adorned with cows' and dragons' heads.

Place de la Chapelle, the adjoining square, has a Renaissance fountain and the 16th-century Hôtel de Ville and the Kapellturm, the galleried Gothic belfry.

↑ Rare books on the shelves of the Beatus Rhenanus Room at the Bibliothèque Humaniste, Sélestat

Side streets have Renaissance and medieval timber-framed houses. A stroll past the cafés on rue du Marché ends in a pleasant park by the ramparts.

Odile, Alsace's 7th-century patron saint, was born in Obernai, and is venerated on Mont Sainte-Odile, to the west of the town.

Sélestat

🅰 G3 🅰 Bas-Rhin 🚋🚌
🚉 10 blvd Leclerc; www.selestat-haut-koenigsbourg.com

During the Renaissance, Sélestat was the intellectual centre of Alsace, with a tradition of humanism fostered by Beatus Rhenanus, a friend of Erasmus. The **Bibliothèque Humaniste** has a collection of editions of some of the earliest printed books, including the first book to name America, in 1507. Nearby are the Cour des Prélats, a turreted ivy-covered mansion, and the Tour de l'Horloge, a clocktower. Église Ste-Foy is 12th century, with an octagonal bell tower.

←

The picturesque village of Riquewihr, set among wine-making country

Opposite is Église St-Georges, glittering with green and red "Burgundian tiles".

Medieval Dambach-la-Ville, another pretty town about 9 km (6 miles) north of Sélestat, is linked to Andlau and red-tiled Ittersviller by a delightful rural road through vineyards.

Bibliothèque Humaniste
⊗ 🅰 1 pl Dr Maurice Kubler
🕒 Hours vary, check website
🚫 1 & 31 Jan, 1 May, 25 & 26 Dec 🌐 bibliotheque-humaniste.fr

Neuf-Brisach

🅰 G3 🅰 Haut-Rhin 🚌
🚉 Palais du Gouverneur, 6 pl d'Armes; www.selestat-haut-koenigsbourg.com

Situated near the German border, this octagonal citadel is military engineer Vauban's masterpiece. Built between 1698 and 1707, the citadel forms a star-shaped pattern, with symmetrical towers enclosing 48 equal squares. Straight streets radiate from the centre, where you'll find place d'Armes and the Église St-Louis, which was added in 1731–6. This was the usual homage to Louis XV, implying that the church was dedicated to the king, not the saint.

STAY

Hôtel Le Maréchal
In the heart of the romantic Petite Venise area, this riverside inn from 1565 has cheerfully colourful rooms.

🅰 G3 🅰 4/5 Place des Six Montagnes Noires, Colmar 🌐 hotel-le-marechal.com

€€€

Chambard
This chic hotel has luxurious rooms and a Michelin-starred restaurant to match. It's also home to a traditional *winstub* (wine lounge).

🅰 G3 🅰 9-13 rue du Général de Gaulle, Kayserberg 🌐 lechambard.fr

€€€

L'Oriel
This half-timbered hotel, in picturesque Riquewihr, has vibrant rooms overlooking a lovely courtyard.

🅰 G3 🅰 3 rue Ecuries Seigneuriales, Riquewihr 🌐 hotel-oriel.fr

€€€

The historic Porte de Belfort houses the **Musée Vauban**, which includes a model of the town, showing the outlying defences, now concealed by woodland. They represent Vauban's barrier to the fortress and it is to his credit that the citadel was never taken.

Musée Vauban
⊗ 🅰 7 pl de Belfort 🕒 Hours vary, check website 🌐 vaubanecomusee.org

⑬

Metz

🅰 F2 🚇 Moselle ✈ 🚉 🚌
ℹ Pl d'Armes; www.
tourisme.metz.com

An austere yet appealing city, Metz sits at the confluence of the Moselle and the Seille. Twenty bridges crisscross the rivers and canals, and there are pleasant walks along the banks. This Gallo-Roman city, now the capital of Lorraine, has always been a pawn in the game of border chess. It was annexed by Germany in 1871, but France regained it in 1918.

Located on a hill above the Moselle, the Cathédrale St-Étienne overlooks the historic centre. Inside, there are notable stained-glass windows, including some by Marc Chagall.

To the northwest of the cathedral, a narrow wooden bridge leads across to the island of Petit Saulcy, site of the oldest French theatre still in use. Located on the other side of the cathedral, the Porte des Allemands, spanning a river, resembles a medieval castle because of its bridge, defensive towers and 13th-century gate with pepper-pot towers.

In the Vieille Ville, the delightful place

St-Louis is bordered by arcaded 14th-century mansions. Église St-Pierre-aux-Nonnains claims to be one of France's oldest churches. The external walls and façade date from Roman times, while much of the rest belongs to the 7th century. Nearby is the 13th-century Chapelle des Templiers, built by the Knights Templar; it can be visited by guided tour.

The **Centre Pompidou Metz** is an annexe to the Centre Pompidou in Paris (p90). Modern European art is displayed inside an unusual hexagonal building.

Also known as the Musée d'Art et d'Histoire, the **Musée de la Cour d'Or** is set in the Petits-Carmes, a deconsecrated 17th-century monastery incorporating Gallo-Roman baths and a medieval barn. On display are Merovingian stone carvings; Gothic painted ceilings and German, Flemish and French paintings.

Centre Pompidou Metz

⊗ ⓣ ⓘ 🏢 1 parvis des Droits de l'Homme ⊙ 10am–6pm Wed–Mon 🚫 1 May
🌐 centrepompidou-metz.fr

Musée de la Cour d'Or

⊗ 🏢 2 rue du Haut-Poirier
⊙ 9am–12:30pm & 1:45–5pm Wed–Mon 🚫 Pub hols
🌐 musee.metzmetropole.fr

↑ Pretty sculptures marking the entrance to Betschdorf village

⑭

Betschdorf

🅰 G2 🚇 Bas-Rhin ℹ 1 rue des Francs, La Mairie;
www.betschdorf.com

The village of Betschdorf borders the Forêt de Haguenau, 45 km (28 miles) north of Strasbourg. Many residents occupy timber-framed houses dating from the 18th century, when pottery made the village prosperous. Generations of potters have passed down the knowledge of the characteristic blue-grey glaze to their sons, while the women have been entrusted with decorating it in cobalt blue. A pottery museum, with a workshop attached, displays

rural ceramics. Betschdorf is a good place to try tasty *tartes flambées* – hot, crispy bases topped with cheese or fruit.

Another pottery village, Soufflenheim, lies 10 km (6 miles) southeast. Its earth-coloured pottery is usually painted with bold flowers.

15

Gérardmer

 G3 🏔 Vosges 🚆🚌
i 4 pl des Déportés; www.gerardmer.net

Nestling on the Lorraine side of the Vosges, on the shore of a magnificent lake stretching out before it, Gérardmer is a setting rather than a city. In November 1944, just before its liberation, Gérardmer was razed by the Nazi scorched-earth policy, but has since been reconstructed. Sawmills and woodcarving remain local trades, though tourism is fast replacing the textile industry.

Gérardmer is now a popular holiday resort. In winter, the steep slopes of the Vosges Cristallines around the town turn it into a ski resort, while the lake is used for watersports in summer. The town's attractions also include walks

along the lakefront and boat trips, as well as Géromée cheese, similar to the more famous Munster, from just over the Alsatian border. Gérardmer also boasts the oldest tourist information office in the country, dating from 1875.

The scenic drives and mountain hikes in the Vosges attract adventurous visitors. Most leave the lakeside bowl to head for the Alsatian border and the magnificent Route des Crêtes, which can be joined at the mountain pass of Col de la Schlucht.

16

Eguisheim

 G3 🏔 Haut-Rhin 🚌
i 22a Grand'Rue; www.tourisme-eguisheim-rouffach.com

Eguisheim is an exquisite small town, laid out within three concentric rings of 13th-century ramparts. The ensemble of austere fortifications and elegance within makes for a harmonious whole.

In the centre of town is the octagonal feudal castle of the Counts of Eguisheim. A Renaissance fountain in front has the statue of Bruno Eguisheim, born here in 1002. He became Pope Léon IX and was later canonized.

Did You Know?

Protected by the Vosges, Alsace has a warm climate and France's lowest annual rainfall.

The Grand'Rue is lined with half-timbered houses. Close to the castle is the Marbacherhof, a monastic tithe barn and corn hall. On a neighbouring square, the modern parish church retains its Romanesque sculpted tympanum.

The rest of the town has its share of Hansel-and-Gretel atmosphere, while inviting courtyards offer tastings of *grands crus*. From rue de Hautvilliers, outside the ramparts, a marked path leads through scenic vineyards.

17

Saverne

 G2 🏔 Bas-Rhin 🚆🚌 *i* 37 Grand'Rue; www.tourisme-saverne.fr

Framed by hills, and set on the River Zorn and the Marne–Rhine canal, Saverne is a pretty sight. The town was a fief of the prince-bishops of Strasbourg and its sandstone Château des Rohan was a favourite summer residence. Today, it houses the fascinating **Musée du Château des Rohan**, with a collection that traces Saverne's past. On the far side of the château, the Grand'Rue is studded with buzzy restaurants and handsome, well-kept timber-framed Renaissance houses.

Musée du Château des Rohan

⊘ 🏛 Château des Rohan
☎ 03 88 71 63 95 🕐 Jan-mid-Jun & mid-Sep-Dec: 2-6pm Mon-Wed, 10am-noon & 2-6pm Sat & Sun; mid-Jun-mid-Sep: 10am-noon & 2-6pm daily 🔒 Pub hols

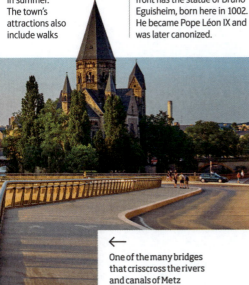

← One of the many bridges that crisscross the rivers and canals of Metz

A DRIVING TOUR
ALSACE ROUTE DES VINS

Length 180 km (110 miles) **Stopping-off points** Molsheim, Dambach-la-Ville, Ribeauvillé, Riquewihr, Turckheim and Guebwiller

This picturesque wine route takes in historic towns with cobbled streets, medieval timber-framed houses and Renaissance fountains. Romantically appointed *winstubs*, or cellars, offer traditional *choucroute garnie* and flowery white Alsatian wines. Dedicated wine lovers could spend several days covering the route at leisure. For a refreshing contrast from the unremitting charm of the towns and villages, escape occasionally into *sentiers viticoles* – lovely paths through the vineyards themselves.

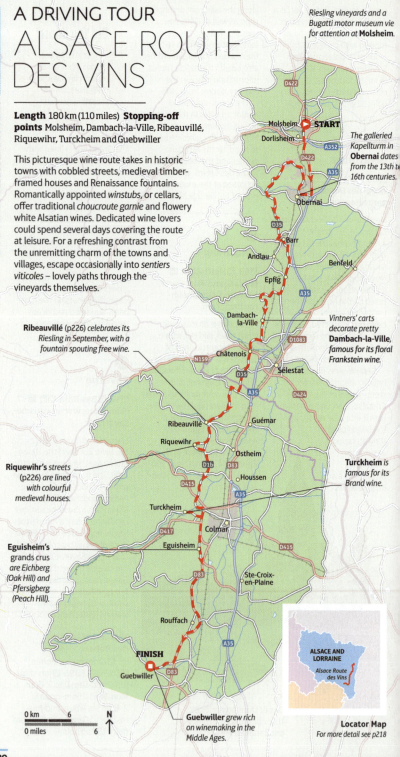

Riesling vineyards and a Bugatti motor museum vie for attention at **Molsheim**.

The galleried Kapellturm in **Obernai** *dates from the 13th to 16th centuries.*

Vintners' carts decorate pretty **Dambach-la-Ville**, *famous for its floral Frankstein wine.*

Ribeauvillé *(p226) celebrates its Riesling in September, with a fountain spouting free wine.*

Turckheim *is famous for its Brand wine.*

Riquewihr's *streets (p226) are lined with colourful medieval houses.*

Eguisheim's *grands crus are Eichberg (Oak Hill) and Pfersigberg (Peach Hill).*

Guebwiller *grew rich on winemaking in the Middle Ages.*

0 km   6
0 miles   6
N

ALSACE AND LORRAINE
Alsace Route des Vins

Locator Map
For more detail see p218

Did You Know?

It has been forbidden to cultivate anything other than "noble" vine stocks in Riquewihr, since 1575.

↑ Walking through the cobbled streets of colour-filled Riquewihr

NORMANDY

Settled first by Celtic tribes, then the Romans, Normandy was invaded by Vikings in the mid-800s. These pillaging Norsemen settled here, giving the region its name. In 1066 the Duke of Normandy earned a place in history as William the Conqueror following the defeat of the Anglo-Saxons at the Battle of Hastings. The Duchy of Normandy became part of France in the early 1200s, though it was occupied twice during the Hundred Years War. In the 1600s, explorers set sail from Normandy to establish colonies in North America, and sea-faring port-cities Le Havre and Honfleur became active in the trans-Atlantic slave trade.

Normandy was relatively peaceful during France's post-Revolutionary political upheavals, and during the 19th century, Impressionist painters flocked here, enchanted by the region's natural beauty. They were followed by tourists, leading to the establishment of elegant seaside resorts between Carboug and Étretat. This peace was shattered during World War II. The three-month Battle of Normandy claimed the lives of 20,000 French civilians and devastated cities such as Caen, but it paved the way for the liberation of France. Normandy's breathtaking landscapes and harbourside cities continue to attract visitors, as does the magnificent monastery of Mont St-Michel.

NORMANDY

Must Sees
1. Mont-St-Michel
2. Caen
3. Rouen

Experience More
4. Cherbourg
5. Cotentin
6. Coutances
7. Granville
8. Suisse Normande
9. Parc Naturel Régional de Normandie-Maine
10. Bayeux
11. Côte de Nacre
12. Côte Fleurie
13. Honfleur
14. Le Havre
15. Dieppe
16. Basse-Seine
17. Giverny
18. Evreux
19. Avranches
20. Côte d'Albâtre
21. Pays d'Auge
22. Haute-Seine

←

1 The magical Mont St-Michel, illuminated at dusk.

2 Rouen's Gothic catherdral.

3 Memorial on Omaha Beach, dedicated to American troops.

4 The port town of Honfleur.

5 DAYS

in Normandy

Day 1

Morning Arrive in Giverny *(p255)* for the 9:30am opening of Claude Monet's house (late-Mar–Oct only), and drift around the colourful blooms and beds of the artist's garden before the crowds descend.

Afternoon Head to the lively Norman city of Rouen *(p246)* and grab a late lunch in a city-centre bistro. Visit the city's magnificent Gothic cathedral *(p246)*, painted countless times by Monet, then enjoy a late afternoon stroll past the quays and along the Seine to Pont Jeane d'Arc.

Evening Buzzing place du Vieux Marché is the spot for dinner – dine on Norman classics at the Michelin-starred Gill *(p247)*.

Day 2

Morning Drive downriver to the Seine Estuary and the seaside town of Honfleur *(p252)*. Stroll around its Vieux Bassin harbour; a short walk carries you towards the extraordinary Église Ste-Catherine, built from massive shipbuilders' timbers in the late-15th and 16th centuries.

Afternoon After a hearty lunch of *galettes* and cider at La Cidrerie *(26 place Hamelin)*, drive south-west to chic Deauville. Walk along the beachfront boardwalk, with the sea on one side and the belle-époque-era Anglo-Norman architecture on the other.

Evening Enjoy refined Franco-Asian fusion at L'Essential *(p253)*, then fall asleep at the Hôtel Normandy Barrière *(p255)*, a charmingly converted palace.

Day 3

Morning Awake with a cup of coffee and a pastry in the hotel's flower-filled garden, then set off to Caen *(p244)*, to spend a few hours at its impressive World War II museum, Le Mémorial – Un Musée pour la Paix.

Afternoon After lunch at the museum's restaurant, drive to the sombre Normandy American Cemetery and Memorial *(www. abmc.gov/cemeteries-memorials)*, which overlooks Omaha Beach, site of D-Day's bloodiest battle. Visit the small museum and walk along the bluffs above the beach.

Evening Travel to Bayeux *(p251)* and spend the night at the marvellous, and well-located, Hôtel Churchill *(p255)*.

Day 4

Morning Admire the stunning Bayeux Tapestry *(p251)* and learn about the Battle of Hastings, then fast-forward to another trans-Channel invasion at the Musée Mémorial de la Bataille de Normandie.

Afternoon Stroll around Bayeux's quaint centre and lunch near the cathedral. Then visit the Bayeux War Cemetery, final resting place of British and Commonwealth soldiers who died in the Battle of Normandy.

Evening Drive to majestic Mont-St-Michel *(p240)* and check into Les Terrasses Poulard *(p255)*, a cosy spot with epic sea views.

Day 5

Morning Rise early and beat the crowds to the breathtaking abbey *(p242)*, spending a few hours exploring its innumerable nooks and crannies; if you really want to bring history to life, try the guided tour.

Afternoon Enjoy a picnic at the Tour du Nord (North Tower), then walk the ramparts and watch the galloping tides. After, explore the town's tightly packed alleys.

Evening Enjoy an early dinner in one of the restaurants on the Grand Rue (once the pilgrim's route). Next, admire stout La Porte du Roy, the King's Gate, then walk across the 3-km (2-mile) pedestrian bridge to watch the sunset cast a giant shadow of Mont-St-Michel – a picture-perfect sight.

Belle Époque Architecture

Normandy's coastline is peppered with swathes of gorgeous villas, lavish hotels, swanky casinos and picture-perfect beach huts, legacies of its late-19th- and early-20th-century resort towns on Côte Fleurie (p252). Deauville's lavish hotels and 1920s beach huts (each named after an actor) are unmissable, while in Houlgate, a number of sumptuous seaside villas are beautifully preserved. One of the coast's most alluring spots, Honfleur (p252) is known for its "Anglo-Norman"-style grand villas and opulent seafront hotels.

> 💬 **INSIDER TIP**
> **Star Struck**
>
> Each year thousands of visitors flock to this pretty town for the star-studded Festival du Film Asiatique de Deauville (www.deauvilleasia.com) and the Festival du Cinéma Américain de Deauville (www.festival-deauville.com).

The Hotel Normandy, one of Deauville's magnificent hotels ↑

NORMANDY'S
PARISIAN RIVIERA

Dubbed the "Parisian Riviera", due to its proximity to the capital, the pretty stretch of Normandy coastline between Étretat and Cabourg became a favourite summer spot for northern France's glitterati in the late 19th century – and it remains so to this day.

Suave Casinos

Elegant casinos bear witness to the Côte Fleurie's decadent past. Opened in 1912, the splendid Casino Barrière Deauville (www.casinos-barriere.com) is richly decorated with crystal chandeliers and marble. The Cabourg (www.casinocabourg.com), built in 1862, once played host to some of France's most famous chanteurs. Enjoy a drink in its bar, La Belle Époque, to follow in the footsteps of Edith Piaf.

←

The sumptuous seafront Casino Barrière Deauville

Beautiful Beaches

All along the coast, coves blossom into wide, sandy beaches brimming with technicolour umbrellas and pop-up bars. Le Havre's *(p253)* 2-km (1-mile) beach is known for the fantastic Point Plage, home to every watersport imaginable, while Étretat's *(p256)* shingle beach is surrounded by extraordinary cliffs, weathered by wind and sea.

← Boats on Étretat's pebbly beach

Picturesque Fishing Villages

Once popular with artists, the pretty fishing ports along Normandy's coast are utterly picturesque. Deauville's harbour, on the Côte Fleurie, is lined with colourful seafood restaurants offering fresh oysters, while down-to-earth Trouville-sur-Mer has an arty history going back over a century.

→ The charming town of Trouville-sur-Mer

❶

MONT-ST-MICHEL

△B3 △Manche ⊞To Pontorson, then bus ⊙9am–dusk daily ⊘1 Jan, 1 May, 25 Dec & periods of high tide ⊚abbaye-mont-saint-michel.fr

Shrouded by mist, encircled by sea, soaring above glistening sands – the silhouette of Mont-St-Michel is one of the most enchanting sights in France. This magnificent fortified abbey crowns the top of the island of Mont-Tombe (Tomb on the Hill), which stands at the mouth of the River Couesnon; the abbey is in fact double the island's height.

Lying strategically on the frontier between Normandy and Brittany, Mont-St-Michel grew from a humble 8th-century oratory to become a Benedictine monastery that had its greatest influence in the 12th and 13th centuries. Pilgrims known as *miquelots* journeyed from afar to honour the cult of St Michael, and the monastery was a renowned centre of medieval learning. The Grande Rue, once the pilgrim's route, climbs up past Église St-Pierre to the abbey gates. For many years the island was linked to the mainland by a causeway, but this was replaced in 2014 by a bridge which allows the water to flow freely once again, preventing the build-up of silt.

←

Visitors climbing the many narrow stairways up to the abbey of Mont-St-Michel

◉ **PICTURE PERFECT**
Ideal Island

The classic shot of Mont-St-Michel is taken from the causeway at the mouth of the River Couesnon. Check the tides to ensure that the island will be surrounded by water. Arrive at early dawn.

Timeline

708
△ St Aubert builds an oratory on Mont-Tombe.

966
Benedictine abbey founded by Duke Richard I.

1017
Work on abbey church starts.

1067–70
▽ Mont-St-Michel depicted in Bayeux Tapestry.

1434
△ Last assault by English forces; ramparts surround the town.

Did You Know?

Alleys barely wider than a person's shoulders lead up from Grande Rue to a tiny church.

↑ A floodlit Mont-St-Michel looking particularly atmospheric at sunset

1789

▽ French Revolution: abbey is a political prison.

1874

Abbey declared a national monument.

1877–9

△ Causeway built linking the island to the mainland.

1895–7

Belfry, spire and statue of St Michael added.

1922

Services again held in abbey church.

2014

▽ The causeway is demolished and a bridge is built connecting the island to the mainland.

Exploring the Abbey

The three levels of the abbey reflect the monastic hierarchy. The monks lived at the highest level. The abbot entertained his noble guests on the middle level. Soldiers and pilgrims further down on the social scale were received at the lowest level. The present buildings bear witness to the time when the abbey served both as a Benedictine monastery and, for 73 years after the Revolution, as a political prison. In 1017 work began on a Romanesque church at the island's highest point, building over its 10th-century predecessor, now the Chapel of Our Lady Underground. A monastery built on three levels, La Merveille (The Miracle), was added to the church's north side in the early 13th century.

VISITING THE ABBEY

The admission fee includes an optional guided tour, available in English and lasting just over an hour. Tours begin at the West Terrace at the church level and end in the almonry, where alms were dispensed to the poor. The almonry is now a shop.

Four bays of the Romanesque nave of this church survive. Three were pulled down in 1776.

Protected by high walls, the abbey and its church occupy an impregnable position.

The monks took their meals in the refectory, a long, narrow room, flooded with light.

The rib vaults in the Knights' Room are typically Gothic.

The small 15th-century St Aubert's Chapel was built on an outcrop of rock.

Three floors of cannons point in all directions from Gabriel Tower.

Entrance

1 The abbey's cloisters, with their elegant, slender columns in staggered rows, are a beautiful example of early 13th-century Anglo-Norman architecture.

2 The tranquil graveyard of St Pierre, set away from the bustle and crowds, belongs to the island's parish church of St Pierre.

3 The tiny 15th-century Chapel of St Aubert, perched on top of a rocky outcrop, is dedicated to St Aubert, the founder of Mont-St-Michel.

The abbot's lodgings, where he received visitors, were close to the abbey entrance.

Once the pilgrims' route, the Grand Rue is now crowded with restaurants.

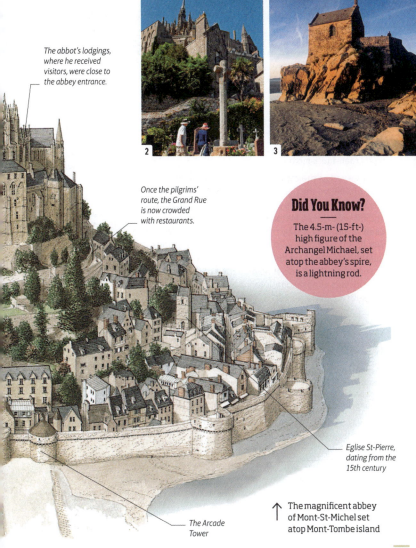

Did You Know?

The 4.5-m- (15-ft-) high figure of the Archangel Michael, set atop the abbey's spire, is a lightning rod.

Eglise St-Pierre, dating from the 15th century

The Arcade Tower

↑ The magnificent abbey of Mont-St-Michel set atop Mont-Tombe island

2

CAEN

🅰C2 🏠Calvados 🚂St-Pierre 🛈12 Place Saint-Pierre;
www.caen-tourisme.fr

Caen served as the capital of western Normandy in the time of William the Conquerer (1028-87), and to this day the city is graced by a fortress and two abbeys he and his wife Queen Matilda built. In 1346 and 1417 Caen was conquered by the English. During World War II, British forces, with help from Canadian troops, fought here yet again during the fierce Battle of Normandy in 1944, this time on behalf of the French. The city was almost completely destroyed in the war and subsequently rebuilt.

EAT

Ivan Vautier
Exquisite modern French food in stylish surroundings with wonderful service.

🏠3 ave Henry Chéron,
🕒Sun evening and Mon
🌐ivanvautier.com

€€€

①

Mémorial de Caen

🏠Esplanade Dwight-Eisenhower 🕒Hours vary, check website 🚫Jan, 25 Dec
🌐memorial-caen.fr

This fantastic museum walks visitors through the events leading up to the D-Day invasion of Normandy by Allied forces in 1944, telling the story through artifacts, photos and film. There is a particular focus on the Allied efforts to liberate France, and the suffering of French civilians. Allow 3 to 4

hours to explore the museum and its grounds, including the peaceful Souvenir Garden.

---

②

Château de Caen

🏠Esplanade du Château
🕒9:30am–6pm daily
🚫Main public hols

Built by William the Bastard shortly before he travelled to England and became the Conqueror, Caen's Norman castle is one of the largest

fortified enclosures in Europe, with massive ramparts and a gatehouse. Situated in the middle of the city, there are great views of Caen from the castle walls; these originally enclosed a keep that was used as a palace by the dukes of Normandy, but it was razed during the French Revolution.

Inside the castle are two small, worthwhile museums: **Musée de Normandie** and the **Musée de Beaux-Arts**. At the Musée de Normandie, exhibits illustrate the area's rich history. The Musée de Beaux-Arts has an excellent collection strong on 16th- and 17th-century European works.

↑ An aerial view over the rooftops and Norman churches of Caen

Musée de Normandie
🕐 9:30am–6pm Wed–Fri; 11am–6pm Sat & Sun
🌐 musee-de-normandie.fr

Musée de Beaux-Arts
🕐 9:30am–6pm daily 🚫 Main public hols 🌐 mba.caen.fr

③ 🚶 Ⓜ
Abbaye-aux-Hommes
🏠 Espl Jean-Marie Louvel
📞 02 31 30 42 81 🕐 9:30am–7pm daily 🚫 Main public hols

Now used as the city's town hall, the Abbey for Men was commissioned by William the Conquerer in 1063. The handsome abbey church, Eglise St-Etienne, is a masterpiece of Norman design, crowned with 13th-century spires.

④ 🚶 Ⓜ
Abbaye-aux-Dames
🏠 Pl de la Reine Mathilde
📞 02 31 06 98 45 🕐 8am–6pm daily (from 2pm Sat & Sun) 🚫 Main public hols

The Abbey for Women was founded by William the Conquerer's queen, Matilda, in 1060 and was consecrated six years later. Queen Matilda is buried here in the choir under a slab of black marble.

Must See

THE BATTLE OF NORMANDY

During World War II, the Allies had planned to capture Caen on D-Day, but in the end the city only fell to British and Canadian troops after a month of fighting. During the battle, the extensive bombing and ground combat destroyed 70 per cent of the city and killed about 2,000 French civilians, almost four per cent of the city.

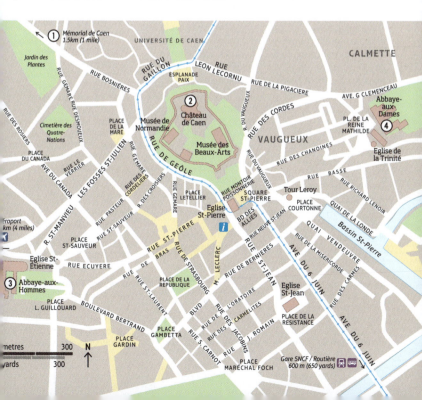

↑ The thriving historic port of Rouen, set on the mighty River Seine

③

ROUEN

Ⓐ D2 Ⓒ Seine Maritime ✈ 11 km (7 miles) SE of Rouen Ⓡ Gare Rive Droite, pl Bernard Tissot 🚌 25 rue des Charrettes (02 35 52 52 52) ⓘ 25 pl de la Cathédrale; Ⓦ rouentourisme.com

Founded at the lowest point where the Seine could be bridged, Rouen has prospered through maritime trade and industrialization to become a rich and cultured city. Despite the severe damage of World War II, it boasts a wealth of historic sights on its right bank.

①

Cathédrale Notre-Dame

Ⓐ Pl de la Cathédral Ⓒ 7am–7pm daily Ⓦ cathedral-rouen.net

This Gothic masterpiece is dominated by the famous west façade, often painted by Monet, and framed by two unequal towers – the northern Tour St-Romain, and the later Tour du Beurre. Above the central lantern tower rises a Neo-Gothic cast-iron spire. Both the 14th-century northern Portail des Libraires and southern Portail de la Calende stand out for their precise sculpting and

delicate tracery. Many of the cathedral's riches are accessible by guided tour only, including Richard the Lionheart's tomb; his heart was buried here. On summer nights a spectacular light show illuminates the cathedral façade.

②

Historial Jeanne d'Arc

Ⓐ 7 rue Saint Romain Ⓒ 10am–6pm Tue–Sun 🔒 Pub hols Ⓦ historial-jeannedarc.fr

Entertaining state-of-the-art multimedia displays trace the story of Joan of Arc at

this museum, in the former archbishop's palace where she was sentenced.

③

Eglise St-Maclou

Ⓐ 3 pl Barthélemy Ⓒ 02 32 08 13 90 Ⓒ 10am–6pm Mon, Sat & Sun

Behind this Flamboyant Gothic church, the Aître St-Maclou is a rare surviving example of a medieval cemetery for the burial of plague victims. The timbers of its buildings, set around the quadrangle, are carved with a macabre array of grinning skulls, crossed bones and gravediggers' implements.

④

Eglise St-Ouen

Ⓐ Pl du Général de Gaulle Ⓒ 02 32 08 13 90 Ⓒ 8am–8pm Tue–Thu, Sat & Sun

Once part of a formidable Benedictine abbey, St-Ouen is a Gothic church with a lofty, unadorned interior made all the more beautiful by its 14th-century stained glass.

Musée Le Secq des Tournelles

🏠 Rue Jacques-Villon
🕐 2–6pm Wed-Mon
🌐 museeelesecqdes
tournelles.fr

Located in a 15th-century church, this museum exhibits antique ironmongery ranging from keys to corkscrews and Gallo-Roman spoons.

---

⑥ Musée des Beaux-Arts

🏠 Esplanade Marcel Duchamp 🕐 10am–6pm Wed-Mon 🌐 mbarouen.frs

Major art works here include masterpieces by Caravaggio and Velázquez, and paintings by Normandy-born Théodore Géricault, Eugène Boudin and Raoul Dufy. Also on display is Monet's *Rouen Cathedral, The Portal, Grey Weather*.

⑦ Musée de la Céramique

🏠 1 rue Faucon 🕐 2–6pm Wed-Mon 🌐 Pub hols
🌐 museedelaceramique.fr

Exhibits of 1,000 pieces of Rouen faïence – the famed local colourful glazed earthenware – together with other pieces of French and foreign china are displayed in a fine 17th-century town house.

---

⑧ Musée Flaubert

🏠 1 rue de Lecat 📞 02 35 15 59 95 🕐 2–6pm Wed-Sat, 10am–6pm Tue

Flaubert's father was a surgeon at Rouen Hospital, and his former family home combines memorabilia from the author's life with an awesome display of 17th- to 19th-century medical equipment.

EAT

Gill
Norman classics and more, in a Michelin two-star place by the Seine.

🏠 8-9 quai de la Bourse
🕐 Sun & Mon
🌐 gill.fr.

€€€

Le 37
This attractive city-centre bistro serves modern cuisine. Find the daily specials on the chalkboard.

🏠 37 rue St-Etienne des Tonneliers
🕐 Sun & Mon
🌐 le37.fr

€€€

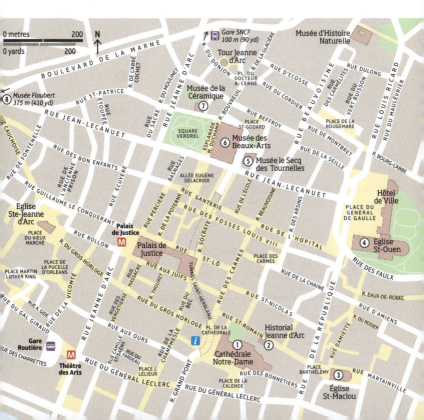

EXPERIENCE MORE

4

Cherbourg

[A] B2 **[A]** Manche **[X][A]**
[=][=] **[f]** 2 quai Alexandre III;
**www.cherbourg
tourisme.com**

Cherbourg has been a naval
base and strategic port since
the mid-19th century. The
French Navy still uses its
harbours, as do transatlantic
ships and the cross-Channel
ferries to and from England
and Ireland. For a good view
of the port, drive to the hilltop
Fort du Roule, which houses
the **Musée de la Libération**,
recalling the D-Day invasion

and the subsequent liberation
of Cherbourg. Most activity is
centred on the flower-filled
market square, place Général
de Gaulle, and along streets
such as rue Tour-Carrée and
rue de la Paix. Within the Parc
Emmanuel Liais are small
botanical gardens and the
Musée d'Histoire Naturelle.

The **Cité de la Mer** is a
bilingual centre with a deep-
sea aquarium and the world's
largest visitable submarine.

Musée de la Libération

[⊕] [▲] Fort du Roule **[☎]** 02 33
20 14 12 **[⏰]** 10am–6pm Tue–
Fri, 1–6pm Sat & Sun
[✕] Public hols

La Cité de la Mer

[⊕][⑦][☕] [▲] Gare Maritime
Transatlantique **[⏰]** Feb–Sep:
9:30am–7pm daily; Oct–Dec:
10am–6pm daily **[✕]** Jan,
25 Dec **[w]** citedelamer.com

5

Cotentin

[A] B2 **[A]** Manche **[X][A][=]**
[=] Cherbourg **[f]** 15 bis
**rue G Le Conquérant,
Barneville-Carteret;
www.otcdi.com**

Thrusting northward into
the English Channel, the
Cotentin Peninsula has a
landscape similar to Brittany's.
Its long sandy beaches have
wild and windblown head-
lands around Cap de la Hague
and Nez de Jobourg. The latter
is popular with birdwatchers –
gannets and shearwaters fly
by in large numbers. Along
the east coast stretches Utah
Beach, where some 23,000
American troops landed as
part of the World War II Allied
invasion on 6 June 1944.
Inland, Ste-Mère-Église

D-DAY LANDINGS

In the early hours of 6 June 1944, Allied troops, supported
by a staggering 13,000 aircraft and 6,000 ships and boats,
stormed the beaches of Normandy in the largest seaborne
invasion in history. Codenamed Operation Overlord, the
landings began the long-awaited battle to liberate northern Europe from Nazi occupation. American troops came
ashore at beaches codenamed Utah and Omaha, while
British, Canadian, Polish and the Free French troops landed
further to the east at Gold, Juno and Sword Beaches.

↑ The Great Gallery of Men and Machines at La Cité de la Mer in Cherbourg

commemorates the event with its **Musée Airborne** (Airborne Troops Museum). Just outside Ste-Mère-Église, the rewarding **Ferme-Musée du Cotentin** has farm animals and activities, which give an insight into rural life in the early 1900s, while further to the north, in Valognes is the **Musée Régional du Cidre**, which celebrates the thriving local industry.

Two fishing ports command the peninsula's northeast corner: St-Vaast-la-Hougue and Barfleur, the former famous for oysters and a base for boat trips to the Île de Tatihou. The Val de Saire is ideal for a scenic drive, with a viewpoint at La Pernelle, which boasts a stunning panorama of the coast. On the west side of the peninsula, the resort of Barneville-Carteret offers sandy beaches and summer boat trips over to the Channel Islands. The low-lying, marshy landscape east of Carentan forms the heart of the Parc Régional des Marais du Potentin et du Bessin.

Musée Airborne
⊘ 🅰 14 rue Eisenhower, Ste-Mère-Église 🕐 Feb–Nov: 10am–6pm daily 🚫 Jan & Dec
🅦 airborne-museum.org

Ferme-Musée du Cotentin
⊘ 🅰 1 Chemin de Beauvais, Ste-Mère-Église 📞 02 33 95 40 20 🕐 Jul & Aug: 11am–7pm daily; Apr–Jun, Sep & Oct: 2–6pm daily 🚫 Nov–Mar

Musée Régional du Cidre
⊘ 🅰 Rue du Petit-Versailles, Valognes 📞 02 33 40 22 73
🕐 Apr–Sep: 2–6:15pm Wed–Sun, from 11am Jul & Aug

6

Coutances

🅰 B2 🅰 Manche 🚊 🚌
 6 rue Milon; www. tourisme-coutances.fr

From Roman times until the Revolution, this hilltop town was capital of the Cotentin. The slender Norman Gothic Cathédrale Notre-Dame has a soaring 66-m (217-ft) lantern tower. Founded in the 1040s, it was financed by the local de Hauteville family using money gained in Sicily, where they had founded a kingdom. The town was badly damaged during World War II, but the cathedral, two churches and the public gardens, with their rare plants, all survived.

7

Granville

🅰 B2 🅰 Manche 🚊 🚌 🚌
 4 cours Jonville; www. ville-granville.fr

Ramparts enclose Granville's upper town, which sits on a spur above the Baie du Mont-St-Michel. The walled town developed from fortifications that were originally built by the English in 1439.

The chapel walls of the Église de Notre-Dame are lined with tributes from local fishermen to their patroness, Notre-Dame du Cap Lihou.

An old-fashioned seaside resort occupies the lower part of the town, complete with a casino, pleasant promenades and colourful public gardens.

Did You Know?

—

Christian Dior named one coat in every collection after Granville, the town where he was born.

From the picturesque harbour there are boat trips to the Îles Chausey, a scattering of low-lying granite islands that form part of the Channel Islands.

The **Musée d'Art Moderne Richard Anacréon** houses art from the early 20th-century. Amid a beautiful cliff garden, the **Musée Christian Dior** is in the lovely pastel-pink Villa Les Rhumbs, which was the renowned fashion designer's fine childhood home.

Musée d'Art Moderne Richard Anacréon
⊘ 🅰 Place de l'Isthme, La Haute-Ville 📞 02 33 51 02 94
🕐 11am–6pm Tue–Sun

Musée Christian Dior
⊘ 🅰 Villa Les Rhumbs
🕐 10am–6:30pm daily
🅦 musee-dior-granville.com

↑ Pink-painted Villa Les Rhumbs, home to the Musée Christian Dior

8
Suisse Normande

🅰 C2 🏠 Calvados & Orne
🚇 Caen 🚌🚆 Caen, Argentan
ℹ️ 2 place St-Sauveur, Thury-Harcourt; www.suisse-normande-tourisme.com

Though hardly the mountains of Switzerland, the cliffs and valleys carved out by the River Orne as it winds north to Caen have become a very popular destination for walking, with lovely trails through Grimbosq Forest and on the Suisse Normande Route along the Orne. Opportunities for rock climbing, camping and river sports are good, too. Its highest and most impressive point is the Oëtre Rock, where you can look down over the dramatic gorges created by the River Rouvre.

65 km
The length of the Suisse Normande Route that follows the River Orne.

9
Parc Naturel Régional de Normandie-Maine

🅰 C3 🏠 Orne & Manche
🚇 Alençon 🚌🚆 Argentan
ℹ️ Carrouges; www.parc-naturel-normandie-maine.fr

The southern fringes of central Normandy have been incorporated into what is now the largest of all of France's 49 regional parks. Charming towns include Domfront, on a spur overlooking the River Varenne; the spa town of Bagnoles-de-l'Orne, which has a casino and sports facilities; and Sées with its fine Gothic cathedral. The **Maison du Parc** at Carrouges has information on walks and other activities.

Just north of the park is the **Château d'O**, a Renaissance château with fine 17th-century frescoes. The **Haras national du Pin** is France's national stud, called "horses' Versailles" for its 17th-century architecture. Horse and dressage

↑ The long drive through the serene grounds of fairy-tale Château d'O

events take place through the year, and tours are available.

Maison du Parc
🏠 Carrouges 📞 02 33 81 13 33 🕐 Apr-mid-Oct & 6-21 Dec: 9am-6pm daily 🚫 1 May

Château d'O
♿ ⏰ 🏠 Rte d'Almenêches, Mortree 📞 02 33 12 67 46 🕐 10am-12pm & 1:30-4:30pm daily

Haras national du Pin
♿ ⏰ 🏠 Carrouges 🕐 Hours vary, check website 🌐 haras-national-du-pin.com

→
The remains of a Mulberry Harbour at Gold Beach, northwest of Bayeux

10
Bayeux

C2 **Calvados** 🏛️🚌
i Pont-St-Jean; www.
bayeux-bessin-tourisme.
com

In 1944, Bayeux was the first town to be liberated by the Allies and was fortunate to escape war damage. Today, an attractive nucleus of buildings from the 15th to 19th centuries remain around its central streets, rue St-Jean and rue St-Martin, both lined with shops and cafés.

Piercing the skyline are the spires of the fine Cathédrale Notre-Dame. Its crypt, which belonged to an 11th-century predecessor, is decorated with 15th-century frescoes of angels playing musical instruments. The original Romanesque church was consecrated in 1077, and it is thought likely that the Bayeux tapestry was commissioned by one of its key characters, Bishop Odo, for this occasion.

The exquisite and intricate 70-m- (230-ft-) long tapestry is displayed in a renovated seminary, now the **Centre Guillaume-le-Conquérant-Tapisserie de Bayeux**, which gives a detailed audio-visual explanation of events leading up to the Norman conquest.

On the southwest side of the town, the restored **Musée Mémorial de la Bataille de Normandie** traces the events of the Battle of Normandy in World War II, with

BAYEUX TAPESTRY

A lively comic strip of the story of the Norman Invasion of England from the partisan perspective of the victor, this embroidered hanging was ordered by Bishop Odo of Bayeux, half-brother of William the Conqueror. It is fascinating as a work of art, a portrayal of 11th-century life, a historical document, an entertaining yarn and an early example of spin.

an excellent film, made using contemporary newsreels. Other items on display here include vehicles, weapons, and equipment used by the British, American and German forces. Near the museum is a vast British military cemetery with the graves of 4,000 soldiers.

Centre Guillaume-le-Conquérant-Tapisserie de Bayeux

⊕ 🏠 13 rue de Nesmond
🕐 Mar-Oct: 9am-6:30pm daily (to 7pm May-Aug); Nov-Feb: 9:30am-12:30pm & 2-6pm daily 🕐 Jan, 24-26 Dec 🌐 bayeuxmuseum.com

Musée Mémorial de la Bataille de Normandie

⊕ 🏠 Blvd Fabian-Ware
🕐 Mid-Feb-Dec: 10am-6pm daily 🕐 Jan 🌐 bayeux museum.com

11
Côte de Nacre

C2 **Calvados** ✈️ Caen
🚆 Caen, Bayeux 🚌 Caen-Ouistreham **i** place St-Pierre, Caen; www.
caenlamer-tourisme.fr

The stretch of coast between the mouths of the rivers Orne and Vire was dubbed the Côte de Nacre (Mother-of-Pearl Coast) in the 19th century. More recently it has become known as the site of the D-Day landings, when Allied troops poured ashore at the start of Operation Overlord (p248). The cemeteries, memorials and museums, and the remnants of the Mulberry Harbour at Arromanches-les-Bains, provide focal points.

The coastline is equally popular for summer holidays, with long, sandy beaches and relaxed seaside resorts such as Courseulles-sur-Mer and Luc-sur-Mer.

↑ Part of the beach at the small resort of Houlgate, near the western end of the Côte Fleurie

12

Côte Fleurie

🅰C2 🅰Calvados
❌🚌Deauville ℹ112 rue Victor Hugo, Deauville; www.deauville.org

The Côte Fleurie (Flowery Coast), along the Channel coast west of the Seine estuary, between Villerville and Cabourg, is planted with chic resorts and buzzy beaches, and they burst into bloom every summer.

Trouville-sur-Mer was once a humble fishing village, but during the mid-19th century it caught the attention of writers Alexandre Dumas and Gustave Flaubert, and by the 1870s the town had acquired grand hotels, a railway station and pseudo-Swiss villas along the beachfront. Trouville has, however, long been outclassed by

its neighbour, Deauville, which was created by the Duc de Morny during the 1860s. This resort's attractions include a casino, racecourses, marinas and the famous beachside catwalk, Les Planches.

For something quieter, head west to smaller resorts, like Villers-sur-Mer or Houlgate. Cabourg, further west is dominated by the turn-of-the-20th-century Grand Hôtel, where novelist Marcel Proust spent many summers. He used the resort as a model for the fictional Balbec in his epic novel *À la recherche du temps perdu* (In Search of Lost Time).

13

Honfleur

🅰C2 🅰Calvados
🚌Deauville ℹQuai Lepaulmier; www.honfleur.tourism.co.uk

A major defensive port in the 15th century, Honfleur has become one of the region's most appealing harbours. At its heart is the 17th-century Vieux Bassin (Old Dock), with its pretty houses that extend as high as six or seven storeys.

Honfleur became a centre of artistic activity during the 19th century. Eugène Boudin, the painter, was born here in

1824, as was the composer Erik Satie in 1866. Courbet, Sisley, Renoir, Pissarro and Cézanne all visited Honfleur, often meeting at the Ferme St-Siméon, now a luxury hotel. Painters still work from the quayside, and exhibit their work in the **Greniers à Sel**, two salt warehouses built in 1670. These lie to the east of the Vieux Bassin in an area known as l'Enclos, which made up the fortified heart of the town in the 13th century.

In a narrow cobbled alley, within a fine old half-timbered building, the engaging **Musée d'Ethnographie et d'Art Populaire Normand** displays mementos of Honfleur's nautical past, with a warren of furnished Norman interiors next door within the former prison. Place Ste-Catherine has an unusual 15th-century church constructed by ship's carpenters. The **Musée Eugène-Boudin** documents the artistic appeal of Honfleur and the Seine estuary, with works from Boudin to Raoul Dufy. **Les Maisons Satie**, based in the composer's old home, gives you an audio guide which plays Satie's music as you explore the reconstructions of his rooms.

PICTURE PERFECT
Walk of Fame

Pretty Deauville's well-known beachfront promenade, Les Planches, leads to the colourful beach huts lining the sand. Each hut is named after a star who has visited the local film festival – get your angles right to capture all their names.

Greniers à Sel
 Rue de la Ville
Consult tourist office for guided tours (02 31 89 23 30)

Musée d'Ethnographie et d'Art Populaire Normand
Quai St-Etienne
Apr-Sep: 10am-6pm Tue-Sun; Oct, Nov & Mar: 2:30-5:30pm Tue-Fri, 10am-5:30pm Sat & Sun Dec-Feb
musees-honfleur.fr

Musée Eugène-Boudin
Pl Erik Satie, rue de l'Homme de Bois 10am-6pm Wed-Mon musees-honfleur.fr

Les Maisons Satie
67 blvd Charles V Mid-Feb-Dec: 10am-6pm Wed-Mon Pub hols musees-honfleur.fr

---

14

Le Havre
C2 Seine-Maritime 186 blvd Clemenceau; www.lehavretourisme.com

Strategically positioned on the estuary of the River Seine, Le Havre (The Harbour) was created in 1517 by François I after Harfleur's port, nearby, silted up. Home to the second-largest port in the country, it maintains its seafaring heritage and services container ships and Channel ferries.

During World War II the town was virtually obliterated by Allied bombing, but in spite of a vast industrial zone, which stands beside the port, it still has much appeal and attracts awards for its environmental record. It is an important yachting centre, and its beach has a two blue flag rating (very clean).

As a result of the bombing, much of the city centre was rebuilt by a team led by architect Auguste Perret, whose towering Église St-Joseph pierces the skyline. The result has earned the city a prestigious UNESCO World Heritage listing. On the seafront, the **Musée Malraux** showcases works by, among others, the local artist Raoul Dufy. The city also has France's biggest skatepark, on the seafront.

Musée Malraux
2 blvd Clemenceau 11am-6pm Tue-Sun (to 7pm Sat & Sun) Pub hols muma-lehavre.fr

---

EAT

Le Spinnaker
One of Normandy's finest fish restaurants, Le Spinnaker is an attractive modern spot.

 C2 52 rue Mirabeau, Deauville Mon & Tue spinnakerdeauville.com

€€€

Jean-Luc Tartarin
Imaginative dishes featuring local produce.

 C2 73 av Foch, Le Havre Mon & Sun jeanluc-tartarin.com

€€€

L'Essential
Fresh, light, fabulous Franco-Asian fusion.

 C2 29 rue Mirabeau, Deauville Tue & Wed lessentiel-deauville.com

€€€

← Natural light flooding in to illuminate paintings in the Musée Malraux

EXPERIENCE Normandy

15

Dieppe

▲D2 🏛Seine-Maritime
🚌🚏 ℹ️Pont Jean Ango;
www.dieppetourisme.com

Nestled in a break between chalky cliffs, Dieppe won prestige as a Channel fort, port and resort. Prosperity came during the 16th and 17th centuries, when the local privateer Jehan Ango raided the Portuguese and English fleets, and a trading post called Petit Dieppe was founded on the West African coast. Dieppe's population was already 30,000 by then, and included a 300-strong community of craftsmen who carved imported ivory. This maritime past is celebrated in **Le Musée de Dieppe**, located in the 15th-century castle crowning the headland to the west of the seafront. Here you can see historical maps and model ships,

Did You Know?

Dieppe's annual kite festival attracts over 500,000 visitors from all over the globe.

Dieppe ivories, and art that evokes the town's 19th-century development as a fashionable seaside resort. Boasting the closest beach to Paris, it was perfect place for promenading, seawater cures and bathing.

Today Dieppe's air above broad seafront becomes filled with colourful kites during a huge festival each September, that pulls in professional kite-flyers from around the world. For the rest of the year, the city's liveliest streets are around Eglise St-Jacques.

Le Musée de Dieppe

◉🏛 🏛Rue de Chastes 📞02 35 06 61 99 🕐10am-6pm Wed-Sun 🔒Pub hols

L'Estran-La Cité de la Mer

◉ 🏛37 rue de l'Asile Thomas 🕐Daily 🔒1 Jan, 25 Dec 🌐estrancitedelamer.fr

16

Basse-Seine

▲D2 🏛Seine-Maritime & Eure ✈️Le Havre, Rouen 🚌🚏Yvetot 🚢Le Havre ℹ️8 pl de Maréchal Joffre, Yvetot; 02 32 70 99 96

Meandering seaward from Rouen to Le Havre, the lower (basse) Seine is crossed by three spectacular road

TOP 3 **CIDER PRODUCERS**

Étienne Dupont
🏛Victot-Pontfoll 🌐calvados-dupont.com
The well-established Dupont family has been making delicious cider and calvados since 1887.

Manoir de Grandouet
🏛3 km (2 miles) from Cambremer 🌐manoir-de-grandouet.fr
The Grandval family's half-timbered farm produces calvados and award-winning ciders.

Calvados Pierre Huet
🏛5 avenue des Tilleuls, Cambremer 🌐calva dos-huet.com
The 1¼-hour tours (€3) here include the apple press, the alembic and the cellars, and finish with a tasting.

bridges: the Brotonne, the Tancarville and the Normandie. Their modern grace and daring echo the soaring aspirations of the abbeys founded in the 7th and 8th centuries, which are now good stepping stones for a tour of the Lower Seine valley.

West of Rouen is the lovely Église de St-Georges at St-Martin-de-Boscherville, which until the Revolution was the church of a small abbey. Its 12th-century chapterhouse has remarkable statues and carved capitals. From here the D67 runs south to the riverside village of La Bouille.

As you head northwest, an hourly car ferry at Mesnil-sous-Jumièges takes you over to the colossal ruins of the Abbaye de Jumièges. Founded in 654, it once housed 900

Elegant Pont de Normandie, spanning the expanse of the river Seine near Basse-Seine

↑ Claude Monet's famous inspirational garden at his home in Giverney

monks and 1,500 servants. The main abbey church was consecrated in 1067, a major event attended by William the Conqueror.

The D913 strikes through the woodland of the Parc Régional de Brotonne to the Benedictine Abbaye de St-Wandrille, founded in the 7th century. The Musée de la Marine de Seine at Caudebec-en-Caux gives an engrossing account of many aspects of life on the great River Seine since the late 19th century.

Giverny

▲D2 ◈Eure ℹ️80 rue Claude Monet, Giverny; www.giverny.fr

In 1883 Impressionist painter Claude Monet rented a house in this small village and lived and worked here until his death. The house, now known as the **Fondation Claude Monet**, is open to the public. The house is decorated in the colour schemes that Monet admired. The glorious gardens, made famous as the subject of some of Monet's studies, have been restored to their original glory. Only copies of Monet's work are on show here, but there is superb original 19th- and 20th-century art in the nearby **Musée des Impressionnismes**.

Fondation Claude Monet
◈◈◈ ▲84 rue Claude Monet ◷Apr–Oct: 10am–6pm daily ⓦfondation-monet.com

Musée des Impressionnismes
◈◈◈ ▲99 rue Claude Monet ◷Mar–Nov: 10am–6pm daily ⓦmdig.fr

Evreux

▲D2 ◈Eure ▲🚌 ℹ️11 rue de la Harpe; www.grandevreuxtourisme.fr

This pleasant cathedral town is set in wide, agricultural plains. It is home to the Cathédrale Notre-Dame, renowned for its 14th- to 15th-century stained glass and Renaissance screens adorning its chapel. Next door, the former bishop's palace houses the Musée de l'Ancien Evêché, with Roman statues and fine 18th-century furnishings.

STAY

Les Terrasses Poulard
On the slopes of Mont St-Michel with stunning sea and sunset views.

▲B3 ◈Grande rue, Mont-St-Michel ⓦle montsaintmichel.info

€€€

Hotel Churchill
A good town-centre spot, near the tapestry.

▲C2 ◈14–16 rue St-Jean, Bayeux ⓦhotel-churchill.fr

€€€

Hôtel Normandy Barrière
Large half-timbered palace, with lavish rooms and lots of charm.

▲C2 ◈38 rue Jean Mermoz, Deauville ⓦhotelsbarriere.com

€€€

Detective Hôtel
Each room is named and styled for a fictional detective.

▲C2 ◈6 ave George V, Étretat ⓦdetectivehotel.com

€€€

Aubert's skull in the treasury of St-Gervais church, Avranches

⑲
Avranches

🅐 C2 🏛 Manche 🚊🚌
ℹ️ 2 rue Général-de-Gaulle; www.ot.montsaintmichel.com

Avranches has been a religious centre since the 6th century; the final staging post for visitors to the abbey on Mont-St-Michel. According to legend, the Archangel Michael came to Aubert, the bishop of Avranches, one night in 708 and told him to build a church on the nearby island. Aubert's skull, supposedly with the fingerhole poked by by the angel, can be seen in the treasury of St-Gervais in Avranches. The best views of Mont-St-Michel are from the Jardin des Plantes. More than 200 illuminated manuscripts were rescued from Mont-St-Michel's abbey after the Revolution. These and many others are held in the **Musée des Manuscrits du Mont-St-Michel**. Multimedia displays show how monks copied and illuminated the texts. The **Musée d'Art et d'Histoire** highlights life in the Cotentin during World War II.

Musée des Manuscrits du Mont-St-Michel

♿ 🏛 Pl d'Estouteville
🕐 10am–6pm Tue–Sun (to 7pm Jul & Aug) 🚫 Public hols 🌐 scriptorial.fr

Musée d'Art et d'Histoire

🏛 Pl Jean de Saint-Avit
📞 02 33 58 25 15 🕐 Jun–Sep: Wed–Sun

⑳
Côte d'Albâtre

🅐 D2 🏛 Seine-Maritime
🚊🚌🚲 ℹ️ 28 rue Raymond Aron, Mont-Saint-Again; www.seine-maritime-tourisme.com

The Alabaster Coast gets its name from the chalky cliffs and milky waters that characterize the Normandy coastline between Le Havre and Le Tréport. It is best known for the Falaise d'Aval, west of Étretat, eroded into an arch. The author Guy de Maupassant, born near Dieppe in 1850, compared these cliffs to an elephant dipping its trunk into the sea. From Étretat, a chain of coastal roads runs east across a switchback of breezy headlands and wooded valleys to Dieppe.

Fécamp is the only major town along this route. Its Benedictine abbey was once an important pilgrimage centre after a tree trunk said to contain drops of Christ's blood was washed ashore here in the 7th century. This is enshrined in a reliquary at the entrance to the Lady Chapel of the abbey church, La Trinité.

The **Palais Bénédictine** is a vast Neo-Gothic and Renaissance homage to the ego of Alexandre le Grand, a local wine and spirits merchant who rediscovered the monks' recipe for Bénédictine, the famous herbal liqueur. Built in 1882, it incorporates a distillery and a museum packed with curios. The adjacent halls provide an aromatic account and tastings of the herbs and spices that make up the elixir.

 INSIDER TIP
Elephant Trunk

Étretat is famed for its 71-m- (233-ft-) high "elephant trunk" arch which leans out from the Falaise d'Aval cliff into the sea. For the best view, look left from the beach or climb up the Falaise d'Amont.

→
Sunrise over the towering chalky cliffs of Étretat, Côte d'Albâtre

Palais Bénédictine

 🏠 110 rue Alexandre Le Grand, Fécamp 📞 02 35 10 26 10 🕐 10am–5pm daily 🚫 Jan–mid-Feb, 1 May, 25 Dec

---

㉑

Pays d'Auge

🅰 C2 🏠 Calvados 🚉 Deauville 🚌 Lisieux 🛈 11 rue d'Alençon, Lisieux; www.lisieux-tourisme.com

Inland from the Côte Fleurie, the Pays d'Auge is lushly woven with fields, wooded valleys, cider orchards, dairy farms and manor houses. Its capital is Lisieux, a cathedral town devoted to Ste Thérèse of Lisieux, who was canonized in 1925 and who still attracts hundreds of thousands of pilgrims. Lisieux is an obvious base for exploring the region, but nearby market towns, such as St-Pierre-sur-Dives and Orbec, are smaller and more attractive.

The best way to enjoy the Pays d'Auge is to potter around its minor roads. There is a tourist route dedicated to promoting local cider, and

picturesque châteaux testify to the wealth of this fertile land. St-Germain-de-Livet can be visited, as can Crèvecoeur-en-Auge, and the charming half-timbered village of Beuvron-en-Auge.

㉒

Haute-Seine

🅰 G3 🏠 Eure 🚉 Rouen 🏠 Vernon, Val de Reuil 🚌 Gisors, Les Andelys 🛈 2 rue Grande, Les Andelys; www.cape-tourisme.fr

Southeast of Rouen, the river Seine follows a convoluted course, with most points of interest on its north bank. At the centre of the Forêt de Lyons, once the hunting ground for the dukes of Normandy, is the country town of Lyons-la-Forêt, with half-timbered houses and an 18th-century covered market.

The D313 follows the Seine south to Les Andelys. Above the town towers the ruins of Château Gaillard, built by Richard the Lionheart in 1197.

DRINK

Le Bar O Mètre
Picture-perfect views and good local cider on the beach.

🅰 D2 🏠 51 rue Alexandre Dumas, Dieppe 📞 02 32 90 12 31

Vous Êtes Ici
Locals come for handmade cocktails, while DJs set the scene on weekends.

🅰 C2 🏠 13 rue Saint-Sauveur, Caen 📞 02 50 50 26 02

Le Goeland 1951
A former World War I bunker serves up laid-back vibes and great sea views.

🅰 C2 🏠 82 Route du Phare, Reville 📞 02 32 90 12 31

BRITTANY

Little is known about Brittany's first inhabitants, bar their lasting imprint upon the landscape – the thousands of Neolithic megaliths that still stand mysteriously throughout the area. The region was later inhabited by the Celts, who knew it as Armorica, "land of the sea". In 56 BC, the Romans conquered Brittany, but could not retain control. In the 5th and 6th centuries Celtic tribes from Britain, seeking refuge from Anglo-Saxon invaders, settled in the area and gave Brittany its name. The region was united in the 9th century by Nomenoë, hero of the Bretons, who led a revolt against the Frankish Carolingian emperors. Following this it became an independent duchy, only joining France in 1532; despite this union, it continued to have a large degree of autonomy. The events of the French Revolution saw little support in the region, as it led to the duchy, with all its sovereign powers, being abolished. Following the Revolution, Brittany withstood a dramatic economic decline that affected its strong Breton culture; it was only in the 1960s that the region began to revive. Celtic ties today are, fondly, stronger than ever.

BRITTANY

Must Sees
1. St-Malo
2. Côte de Granit Rose

Experience More
3. Île d'Ouessant
4. Parc Naturel Régional d'Armorique
5. Douarnenez
6. Locronan
7. Cancale
8. Quimper
9. Pays Bigouden
10. Concarneau
11. Roscoff
12. Le Pouldu
13. Lampaul-Guimiliau
14. Guimiliau
15. Pointe du Raz
16. Île de Bréhat
17. St-Thégonnec
18. Combourg
19. Tréguier
20. Dinan
21. Carnac
22. Golfe du Morbihan
23. Presqu'île de Quiberon
24. Belle-Île-en-Mer
25. Vannes
26. Josselin
27. Forêt de Paimpont
28. Côte d'Emeraude
29. Vitré
30. Pont-Aven
31. Rennes

8 DAYS
in Brittany

▌ *Day 1*

Put your walking shoes on for your first morning in historic Rennes, the capital of Brittany *(p284)*. Wander past timber-framed houses on your way to the market in places des Lices, open on Saturday mornings, where you can pick up goodies for an al fresco lunch. Dive into Rennes's art scene with a visit to the Musée des Beaux-Arts and its Rembrandts and Picassos. As the sun sets, follow the thirsty crowds to rue de la Soif, or "Drinkers' Alley", where there's a bar every 7 m (23 ft); it's the place to try local cider.

▌ *Day 2*

Follow the River Rance to the enchanting town of Dinan *(p278)*, 40 minutes north. The setting is gloriously French, from the medieval cobbled streets to the half-timbered buildings. If it's a clear day, climb the 158 steps of the Tour d'Horloge for views of Mont Saint-Michel *(p240)*. Move on to St-Malo *(p268)* for a bracing walk around the city walls; the loop offers glorious views of nearby beaches and the islands of Bé just off the coast. Indulge in

gourmet seafood at Le Chalut *(p285)*, before an indulgent night at the elegant Symphonie des Sens *(3 rue du Chapitre)*.

▌ *Day 3*

Set off early for the buzzing village of Ploumanac'h on the wild Côte de Granit Rose *(p270)*. Stop for a quick café crème before stretching your legs with a hike along the coastal path past pink granite boulders to Tregastel beach. Reward yourself with a galette at Crêperie des Flots *(9 rue Anatole le Braz)* in Perros-Guirec – these crispy pancakes come with a choice of savoury fillings. Return to Ploumanac'h for a night in the colourful Castel Beau Site *(137 Rue Saint-Guirec)*.

▌ *Day 4*

Pack a picnic lunch before driving to the wild headlands of Parc Naturel Régional d'Armorique *(p272)*. Pause on the way in the forest of Huelgoat, a place of myth and legend. Arrive in the town of Quimper in time for a relaxing aperitif on the harbourfront; sip bols of cider before dinner at intimate Le Cosy *(2 rue du Sallé)*.

5

① Rose-gold boulders at the
Côte de Granit Rose.

② The charming town of Dinan.

③ Fairy-tale turrets in Josselin.

④ *Fruits de mer* on sale, St-Malo.

⑤ Huelgoat's mythical forest.

Day 5

Spend the morning exploring the
picture-book charm of Quimper *(p274)*,
before a coffee and a tasty tart at café-
bookshop Le Bistro à Lire *(18 Rue des
Boucheries)*. Continue on to Concarneau
(p275), 30 minutes south-east, with its
sunny beaches and 15th-century walled
city. The colourful Le Petit Chaperon
Rouge *(7 place du Guesclin)* is the spot for
galettes and crêpes. Finish the day at
Sleep Hotel Tumulus *(p279)* in Carnac, an
hour's drive east; this hotel has broad-
reaching coastal views and a range of
luxurious spa treatments.

Day 6

At Carnac *(p279)* 3,000 standing stones
are arranged in rows at the world's largest
megalithic site – a tour is essential. Come
afternoon, drive 35 minutes east to
medieval Vannes *(p281)* to peruse the
boutiques and snap up some Breton
biscuits. Stop for an aperitif on the quayside before heading to buzzy L'Eden
(p285) for a feast of fresh fruits de mer.
Le Clos du Gusquel B&B *(Lieu-dit le*

Gusquel) is a 15-minute drive west
of Vannes, but it's worth it for the
breakfast alone.

Day 7

Take a boat trip out to the Île aux Moines,
and hire bikes on the quayside. Spend the
day sampling the idyllic life on the island;
starting with a pedal into the village for a
café au lait. Point your wheels towards
Pointe du Trech for views of the Ile d'Arz
before lunch. Take the waters with a late-
afternoon dip at Le Grande Plage.
Refreshed, catch the ferry back to Vannes
for a seafood dinner at Le Vivier *(p285)*.

Day 8

From Vannes, turn inland and north to
visit the attractive château and gardens
at Josselin *(p282)*. The nearby Forêt de
Paimpont *(p282)* is a place of magic where
Merlin and King Arthur are said to have
lived. Spend the afternoon pottering
about the Arthurian Centre at Château de
Comper near Concoret. End your trip with
a Breton feast at Le Relais De Broceliande
(5 rue des Forges) in Paimpont.

Monumental Menhirs

Menhirs can be found across Brittany's interior from Saint Uzec to Belz – the most famous site is the town of Carnac *(p279)*. Here visitors flock to marvel at the thousands of ancient granite rocks arranged across three fields in mysterious lines and patterns by megalithic tribes as early as 4000 BC. Their original purpose remains obscure: the significance was probably religious, but the precise patterns also suggest they adhere to an early astronomical calendar. Celts, Romans and Christians have since adapted them to their own beliefs.

→

Standing sentry for millennia, the striking stones of Carnac guarding the secrets of the past

BRITTANY FOR
PREHISTORIC MONUMENTS

Here on the Atlantic fringe of Europe, mysterious arrangements of massive granite rocks bear witness to our earliest past. Those at Carnac are the best known, and as such they draw the most visitors, yet these Neolithic monuments, each with its own history, are found throughout the region.

↑ The Gavrinis passage grave, closed to the world for thousands of years

Mysterious Tombs

Often obscured by long grass, dolmen, passage graves carved with swirls and symbols, form portals to the underworld. Wander down the hairpin country lanes around Dinan and these "fairy houses" seem to pop out of nowhere. One of the most remarkable is found on the tiny island of Gavrinis in the Golfe du Morbihan *(p280)*. At the winter solstice, the sun shines directly down the passage to hit the back wall – a tantalizing clue to the belief systems and rituals of the ancient people who built it.

WHAT DOES THAT MEAN?

There are several different formations of megaliths. Words from the Breton language, such as *men* (stone), *dole* (table) and *hir* (long), are still used to describe them. Menhirs, the most common type of megalith, comprise upright stones that stand alone or arranged in lines, while cromlechs are menhirs that stand in a circle. Dolmen are usully formed of two upright stones roofed by a third; these were once used as a burial chamber. A tumulus is a dolmen covered with a cairn of stones and soil to form a burial mound, while *allée couverte* were placed to form a covered alley.

← Examining the menhirs near Camaret sur Mer

Coastal Megaliths

Prehistoric monuments have been found around the Breton coast. On the skinny Quiberon peninsula *(p280)*, drive or cycle down the "coast of Megaliths", which runs south from Carnac to the tip, to investigate each in turn. On the northern coastal path in Plouézoc'h, you'll find the largest, and oldest, burial chamber in Europe.

↑ The Cairn de Barnenez at Plouézoc'h, which predates the pyramids of Egypt

Islands to Explore

Brittany's coastline bubbles with pretty islands, some uninhabited. Just a ten-minute boat ride from Pointe de l'Arcouest, the Île de Bréhat *(p277)* is actually two small islands linked by a bridge. Wander down the lanes between summer cottages to the rocky beaches – ideal for paddling and rock-pooling.

A popular local getaway, the car-free Île de Bréhat

BRITTANY FOR
NATURAL WONDERS

Brittany's natural environment is spectacularly diverse, with plenty of ways to enjoy it. The coast has hiking trails with sensational views, glorious beaches, vertiginous cliffs and hidden coves. Inland, there is much to explore too, with rivers, canals, forests and mountains all offering adventure.

Colourful Coastlines

Brittany has named parts of its coastline according to the colours of the varied natural environments. The Côte d'Emeraude *(p282)* takes its name from the sparkling, emerald-green waters of the sea where it collides with the striking cliffs on the Cap Frehel and the awe-inspiring Fort La Latte. At the Côte de Granit Rose *(p270),* pink granite boulders have been carved over millennia into weird and wonderful shapes by the wind and sea, while the ancient coastline of the Parc Naturel Régional d'Armorique *(p272),* a riot of flowers in season, is an ideal stretch for ambling walks, horseback rides and touring by bicycle or car.

Did You Know?

Brittany's coastline measures 1,800 km (1,118 miles) – almost twice as long as the US Pacific Coast Highway.

Wild West

In Finistère – literally, "the end of the earth" – Île d'Ouessant *(p272)* is the most westerly point of continental France. An hour's boat trip from Le Conquet on the mainland, it's perfect for exploring by bike, past white-washed granite cottages out to the breathtaking Pointe de Pern, dotted with lighthouses. Here you can look down – from the safety of the cliff top – at the wild Atlantic waves that have sent countless ships crashing against the dark rocks to meet their fate.

→

Warning seafarers of danger, the lighthouses of windy Pointe de Pern

Scenic Pointe du Raz

On the far west coast of Finistère, the Pointe du Raz *(p277)* is a moorland peninsula that juts out into the sea. Heather- and gorse-lined paths lead to awe-inspiring cliff-faces pounded by the powerful Atlantic waves and spectacular views over the Raz de Sein, a perilous stretch of water between the mainland and the Île de Sein.

←

Gorgeous views westward over the Atlantic at sunset

The Long and Winding Odet River

One of Brittany's most beautiful rivers, the Odet runs from the Montagnes Noires. Catch a ferry and travel downstream through the stunning Stangala gorges to flow gently past Quimper *(p274)* before meeting the sea at Bénodet (Breton for "river mouth"), a pretty little fishing town with an expansive beach.

→

Taking the ferry across the Odet at Bénodet, much loved for family holidays

↑ Dawn glow suffusing the rounded boulders of the Côte de Granit Rose

Did You Know?

You can walk St-Malo's imposing ramparts all the way around the historic core.

1

ST-MALO

B2-B3 Ille-et-Vilaine Dinard Bretagne Esplanade St-Vincent; www.saint-malo-tourisme.com

Named after Maclou, a Welsh monk who came here in the 6th century to spread the Christian message, the buzzing town of St-Malo stands in a commanding position at the mouth of the River Rance. During the 16th–19th centuries the port grew in prosperity and power through the exploits of its seafarers.

HIDDEN GEM

Butterfingered!

Stop by the charming little La Maison du Beurre Bordier, the last buttermaker in the area to churn by hand. The front of the shop sells a range of flavoured butters and cheeses, while at the back is a bijou museum about Breton butter making *(9 Rue de l'Orme; 02 99 40 88 79)*.

Heavily bombed in 1944, St-Malo has since been scrupulously restored and is now an atmospheric destination. The old city is encircled by granite ramparts providing breathtaking views of St-Malo and its islands of Bé just off the coast. Take the steps up by the Porte St-Vincent and walk clockwise, passing the 15th-century Grande Porte. Within the city is a maze of narrow cobbled streets overlooked by tall 18th-century buildings housing *malouinières* (merchants' mansions), art galleries, boutiques and crêperies. Rue Porcon-de-la-Barbinais leads to Cathédrale St-Vincent, with its sombre 12th-century nave contrasting with the stained glass of the chancel. On cour La Houssaye, the 15th-century Maison de la Duchesse Anne has been carefully restored. When the tide is out, good beaches are revealed around St-Malo. Nearby, on the coast, Les Rochers Sculptés is a beguiling array of figures carved into the cliffs by a local priest, Abbé Fouré, at the end of the 19th century.

THE SEAFARERS OF ST-MALO

St-Malo owes its wealth to its mariners. In 1698 Breton sailors colonized the Îles Malouines, now known as Las Malvinas or the Falklands. By the 17th century St-Malo was France's largest port and famous for its corsairs. It was the riches won by trade and piracy that enabled the town's shipowners to build the great houses known as *malouinières*.

↑ The sun setting over the beautiful walled town of St-Malo

1 One of St-Malo's most illustrious corsairs was the intrepid Robert Surcouf (1773–1827), whose ships hounded vessels of the British East India Company.

2 In 1534 Jacques Cartier discovered the mouth of the St Lawrence and claimed the territory for France; he is buried in the 12th-century Cathédrale St-Vincent.

3 The Château de St-Malo houses the *mairie*, or town hall, and the city's museum.

CÔTE DE GRANIT ROSE

🅰B2 🏛Côtes d'Armor ✈🚉🚌Lannion 🅹Lannion; www.
bretagne-cotedegranitrose.com

**Brittany's extravagantly indented coastline is at its most
stunning along the Côte de Granit Rose, a landscape of
cliffs glowing with ruddy warmth and solitary offshore
outcrops that turn into islets with receding tides.**

INSIDER TIP
From the Water

While the views from
the coast are amazing,
a completely different
point of view is on offer
from a kayak or stand-
up paddle board (SUP).
You can explore hidden
coves, admire the rock-
scape from the water
and watch sealife under
the crystal clear waters.

Due to its rosy-hued cliffs, the lovely stretch of
coastline between Paimpol and Trébeurden is
known as the Côte de Granit Rose, or the Pink
Granite Coast. The rocks have been weathered
by wind and sea, with fanciful nicknames that
reflect their dreamlike shapes and curves. The
best spot to admire them is between Trégastel
and Trébeurden, where visitors can follow the
beautiful coastal path, passing huge piles of
blush-pink boulders, picturesque cottages
tucked away among the coves and the striking
lighthouse at Ploumanac'h. There are several
excellent beaches which are great for families,
with gentle, shallow waters that appear turquoise, making for an alluring sight. The village
of Ploumanac'h (called Ploum by locals) is
buzzing by day, but quieter in the evening as
the visitors disperse to other towns. Perros-
Guirec, a larger resort with golden beaches
and bigger waves, is also a popular hub.

Did You Know?

Originally a place of
prayer, Ploumanac'h
derives its name from
the Breton *poull* (pond)
and *manac'h* (monk).

← Perros-Guirec's medieval St-Jacques church, parts of which date from the 11th century

→ Walking the iconic GR34 Sentier des Douaniers (Customs Officers' Path), a long-distance coastal footpath, passing the boulders of the Pink Granite Coast

↑ The Mean Ruz lighthouse at Ploumanac'h, built of the same granite as the cliffs below it

EXPERIENCE MORE

❸ Île d'Ouessant

A3 ⬛ Finistère
✈ Ouessant 🚂 Brest
⛴ Le Conquet 🚌 ℹ pl de
l'Église, Lampaul; www.ot-
ouessant.fr

A well-known Breton proverb
suggests that "He who sees
Ouessant sees his own blood".
Also known as Ushant, this
island is notorious among
sailors for its fierce storms
and strong currents. However,
this westerly point of France
has a very pleasant climate in
summer and, though often
bleak and stormy, it can be
surprisingly mild in winter.
Part of the Parc Naturel
Régional d'Armorique, the
windswept island supports
migrating birds and a small
seal population, which may
be observed from the Pern
and Pen-ar-Roc'h headlands.

Two museums shed light
on the island's defiant history,
dogged by shipwrecks and
tragedy. At Niou Huella, the
Ecomusée Ouessant shows
furniture that was made from
driftwood and wrecks, often
painted blue and white in
honour of the Virgin Mary.
Nearby at Phare du Créac'h,
the **Musée des Phares et
Balises** explains the history
of the many lighthouses and
beacons in Brittany.

Ecomusée Ouessant
 ⬛ Niou Huella ⏰ Apr–Sep:
11am–5pm daily; Oct–Mar:
2–5pm Tue–Sun 🌐 pnr-
armorique.fr

Musée des Phares et Balises
 ⬛ Pointe de Créac'h
📞 02 98 48 80 70 ⏰ 10am–
6pm daily

---

❹ Parc Naturel Régional d'Armorique

A3 ⬛ Finistère ✈ Brest
🚂 Chateaulin, Landernau
🚌 Le Faou, Huelgoat, Car-
haix ℹ 15 pl aux Foires,
Le Faou; www.pnr-
armorique.fr

The Armorican Regional
Nature Park stretches from
the moorlands of the Monts

HIDDEN GEM
Musée du Loup

This museum dedicated
to wolves, within the
Armorique regional
park, allows its visitors
to learn about this
fascinating animal, from
its social structures and
place in nature to being
the big baddie of stories
(*www.museeduloup.fr*).

d'Arrée west to the Presqu'île
de Crozon and Île d'Ouessant.
Within this protected area lies
a mixture of farmland, heaths,
remains of ancient oak forest
and wild, open spaces. The
park and its scenic coastline
is ideal for walking, riding and
touring by bicycle or car.

Huelgoat is a good starting
point for inland walks, while
Ménez-Hom (330 m/1,082 ft),
at the beginning of the Crozon
Peninsula, has excellent views.
The main park information
centre is at Le Faou. Nearby
at Ménez-Meur is a wooded
estate with wild and farm
animals, and a Breton horse
museum. Scattered around
the park are 16 small specialist
museums, some of which pay
tribute to country traditions
such as hunting, fishing and
tanning. The Musée de l'École

Rurale (open Feb–Oct) at Trégarvan re-creates an early 20th-century rural school. Other museums deal with subjects such as medieval monastic life, rag-and-bone men and the lifestyle of a Breton country priest. The Ferme d'Antéa in Brasparts displays contemporary art and crafts.

 5

Douarnenez

△ A3 ⚑ Finistère 🚌
ℹ 2 rue du Docteur Mével; www.douarnenez-tourisme.com

A century ago Douarnenez was the leading sardine port in France; today, although it continues to be devoted to fishing, it is mainly a tourist resort with fine beaches lining

Did You Know?

Love story *Tristan and Isolde* likely has roots in the 11th-century Persian story *Vis and Rāmin*.

the Pouldavid estuary. Nearby is tiny Île Tristan, linked with the tragic 12th-century story of adulterous lovers Tristan and Isolde. In the 16th century it was the stronghold of the brigand, La Fontenelle.

The picturesque Port du Rosmeur offers cafés, fish restaurants and boat trips around the bay, with a lively early morning *criée* (fish auction) held in the nearby Nouveau Port. The Port-Rhu has been converted into a floating museum, **Le Port Musée,** with more than 100 boats and several shipyards. Some of the larger vessels can be visited.

Le Port Musée

♿ 🏛 pl de l'Enfer 🕐 Jul & Aug: 10am–6pm daily; Feb–Jun, Sep & Oct: 10am–6pm Tue–Sun 🚫 Nov–Jan 🌐 port-musee.org

←

Spring flowers blooming along coastal Parc Naturel Régional d'Armorique

↑ Locronan's rough-hewn stone buildings crowding St-Ronan church

 6

Locronan

△ A3 ⚑ Finistère ℹ Pl de la Mairie; www.locronan-tourisme.bzh

In the 15th–17th centuries Locronan grew wealthy from sailcloth manufacture. After Louis XIV ended the Breton monopoly on this trade, the town declined, but it still has elegant Renaissance buildings. In the central cobbled square is a late-15th-century church dedicated to St Ronan, an Irish missionary. On rue Moal is the delightful Chapelle Notre-Dame-de-Bonne-Nouvelle, with a calvary and a fountain. Every July, a hilltop pilgrimage, known as *Troménie, is* held in honour of St Ronan. The more elaborate *Grande Troménie* takes place every six years.

↑ Bright floral displays spilling across the bridges leading to Quimper's historic houses

⑦

Cancale

B2 🏠 Ille-et-Vilaine
🚌 𝒊 44 rue du Port; www. cancale-tourisme.fr

A small port with views across the Baie du Mont-St-Michel, Cancale is entirely devoted to the cultivation and consumption of oysters. Prized by the Romans, the acclaimed flavour of Cancale's oysters is said to derive from the strong tides that wash over them daily. You can survey the beds from a *sentier des douaniers* (custom officers' path) running along the cliffs. There are plenty of opportunities for sampling the local delicacy, in a multitude of bars and restaurants along the busy quays of the Port de la Houle, where the fishing boats arrive at high tide. Devotees should take the

> **Prized by the Romans, the acclaimed flavour of Cancale's oysters is said to derive from the strong tides that wash over them daily.**

tour at **La Ferme Marine** (Oyster Farm) with workshop tours, a documentary film and an exhibition.

La Ferme Marine

 🏠 Aurore ⏱ Only by tour: mid-Feb-Jun & mid-Sep-Oct: 3pm Mon–Fri (in French only); Jul-mid-Sep: 2pm daily (in English) 🌐 ferme-marine.fr

---

⑧

Quimper

🄰 A3 🏠 Finistère
🚆🚌🚌 𝒊 Pl de la Résistance; www. quimper-tourisme.com

The former ancient capital of Cornouaille, Quimper has a distinctly Breton character. Here you can buy Breton language books, music and traditional costumes, and tuck into some of the best *crêpes* and cider in Brittany. The city gets its name from the Breton *kemper*, meaning "confluence of two rivers", and the Steir and Odet still flow through it.

The pedestrianized area of Vieux Quimper is full of shops, *crêperies* and half-timbered houses. Rue Kéréon is the main thoroughfare, with place au Beurre and the picturesque *hôtels particuliers* (mansions) of rue des Gentilshommes to the north.

The cathedral is dedicated to the city's founder-bishop St Corentin. Begun in 1240, it is the earliest Gothic building in Lower Brittany, its colourfully painted interior now restored. It was constructed with its choir at a slight angle to the nave, perhaps to fit in with some since-disappeared buildings. Two spires were added to the west façade in 1856. Between them rides a statue of King Gradlon, the mythical founder of the drowned city of Ys. Legend has it he chose St Corentin as his spiritual guide and Quimper as his new capital.

The city's **Musée des Beaux Arts** is one of the best in the region, strong on *fin de siècle* artists, such as Jean-Eugène Buland, offering an insight into the way visiting painters perpetuated a romantic view of Brittany. There are works of the Pont-Aven School and by local artists such as Max Jacob and J-J Lemordant. The 16th-century bishop's palace houses the **Musée Départemental Breton**, with costumes, furniture and faïence, such as Cornouaille *coiffes*, ornately carved wardrobes, and turn-of-the-20th-century Breton tourist posters.

Quimper has produced elegant hand-painted faïence pottery since 1690. Designs often feature flowers and animals framed by blue and yellow borders. Faïence is today exported to collectors world-wide. In the southwest of the city Faïenceries HB-Henriot, the oldest factory, is open to visitors all year round.

Musée des Beaux-Arts

 40 place St-Corentin 10am–6pm daily Most public hols; Sep–Jun: Tue; Nov–Mar: Sun am mbaq.fr

Musée Départemental Breton

 1 rue de Roi-Gradlon 10am–7pm daily musee-breton.finistere.fr

---

⑨

Pays Bigouden

🅰A3 Finistère Pont l'Abbé Pont l'Abbé; www.destination-paysbigouden.com

This is the southwesternly point in Brittany, a windy peninsula with proud and ancient traditions. The region is famous for the women's tall *coiffes* (lace bonnets) still worn at festivals and *pardons* – the fascinating **Musée Bigouden**. has a collection of them.

Along the Baie d'Audierne is a brooding landscape of hamlets and isolated chapels; the 15th-century calvary at Notre-Dame-de-Tronoën is the oldest in Brittany. There are invigorating sea views from Pointe de la Torche (a good surfing spot) and from the Eckmühl lighthouse.

Musée Bigouden

sq de l'Europe, Pont l'Abbé Jul & Aug: 10am–6pm daily; Apr–Jun & Sep-Nov: 2–6pm Tue–Sun 1 May museebigouden.fr

---

⑩

Concarneau

🅰A3 Finistère Only for islands Quai d'Aiguillon; www.tourisme concarneau.fr

An important fishing port, Concarneau's main attraction is its 14th-century Ville Close (walled town), on an island in the harbour encircled by massive lichen-covered granite ramparts. It is accessed by bridge from place Jean Jaurès. Parts of the ramparts can be toured, and the narrow streets are full of independent shops and restaurants. The interesting little **Musée de la Pêche**, in the port's ancient barracks, explains the local techniques and history of fishing at sea.

Musée de la Pêche

3 rue Vauban Jul & Aug: 10am–6pm daily; Feb, Mar, Nov & Dec: 2–5:30pm Tue–Sun; Apr–Jun, Sep & Oct: 10am–6pm Tue–Sun Jan, pub hols musee-peche.fr

→

Concarneau's seafaring past on display at the Musée de la Pêche

EAT

Le Petit Chaperon Rouge

You can't miss the colourful façade of the kooky Little Red Riding Hood, with excellent savoury galettes and sweet crêpes, each with a fairy-tale name.

🅰A3 7 place Duguesclin, Concarneau 02 98 60 53 32

€€€

Auberge des Glazicks

Chef Olivier Bellin's gourmet menus feature carefully chosen local produce matched with excellent wines.

🅰A3 7 rue de la Plage, Plomodiern aubergedes glazick.com

€€€

Restaurant Patrick Jeoffroy

Jaw-dropping views of the coast are paired with inventive menus featuring seafood with Far Eastern influences.

🅰A2 20 rue du Kelenn, Carentec hoteldecarantec.com

€€€

11

Roscoff

A2 **Finistère**
i Quai d'Auxerre; www.
roscoff-tourisme.com

Roscoff is a thriving Channel port and beach resort with a wealthy seafaring past. Along rue Amiral Réveillère and in place Lacaze-Duthiers, the 16th- and 17th-century ship-owners' mansions, and the weatherbeaten caravels and cannon on the Église Notre-Dame-de-Kroaz-Baz testify to the days when its privateers were as ill-famed as those of St-Malo (p268).

The famous French onion sellers ("Johnnies") first crossed the Channel in 1828, selling plaited onions door to door. The **Maison des Johnnies et l'Oignon de Roscoff** (tours obligatory) tells their history.

The large industrial plant of **Algoplus** has tours showing how its products are made from seaweed. Boat trips from the harbour go to the peaceful Île de Batz.

Maison des Johnnies et l'Oignon de Roscoff

 48 rue Brizeux **02 98 61 25 48** Jun–Sep: 10am–6pm daily; Oct–May: 2:30–5pm daily

The idyllic Île de Batz, a 150-minute boat ride from Roscoff harbour ↑

Algoplus

 2 quai Charles de Gaulle Tours obligatory, check website algoplus-roscoff.fr

12

Le Pouldu

A3 **Finistère**
i Place Ocean Le Pouldu, Clohars; www.quimperle-terreoceane.com

A quiet port, Le Pouldu has a small beach. Its **Maison Musée du Pouldu** re-creates the inn where Paul Gauguin and other artists stayed and covered the dining room with self-portraits, caricatures and still lifes, later discovered beneath layers of wallpaper.

Maison Musée du Pouldu

10 rue des Grands Sables May–Oct: 11am–7pm Tue–Sun maisonmuseedupouldu.blogspot.com

13

Lampaul-Guimiliau

A3 **Finistère** **i** Place de l'Eglise; 02 98 68 76 67 9am–6pm daily

Within a monumental gate, the chapel and ossuary lie to the left, and the calvary to the

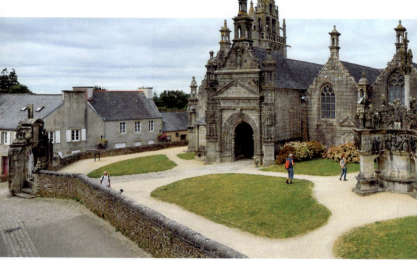

right. Its church demands most attention, with a zealously decorated interior, including some scenes from the Passion on the rood-beam dividing the nave and choir.

14

Guimiliau

🅰A3 🏠Finistére ℹ️53 rue du Calvaire; www.roscoff-tourisme.com

Almost 200 figures adorn the intensely decorated calvary (1581–8) here. One figure is that of a servant girl tortured by demons for stealing a consecrated wafer for her beau.

The church is dedicated to St Miliau and has a richly decorated south porch. The baptistry's elaborate carved oak canopy dates from 1675.

15

Pointe du Raz

🅰A3 🏠Finistère 🚉Quimper 🚌Quimper, then bus ℹ️Maison de la Pointe du Raz; www.pointeduraz.com

The dramatic Pointe du Raz, almost 80 m (262 ft) high, is a

headland that juts out into the Atlantic at the tip of Cap Sizun. The views of jagged rocks and pounding seas are breathtaking. Further west is the flat Île de Sein and the Ar Men lighthouse.

Despite being only 1.5 m (5 ft) above sea level, Île de Sein is nevertheless home to 260 people, and can be reached by boat from Audierne in an hour.

16

Île de Bréhat

🅰B3 🏠Côtes d'Armor 🚉🚌Pointe de l'Arcouest ℹ️Le Bourg; www.brehat-infos.fr

A 15-minute crossing from the mainland, the Île de Bréhat is actually two islands, joined by a bridge, which together are only 3.5 km (2 miles) in length. With a ban on all motorized traffic, and a climate so mild that mimosa and a variety of fruit trees flourish, it has a wonderfully laidback vibe that invites visitors to slow to the more civilized pace of its inhabitants. Bicycle hire and various boat tours are available in the main town, Port-Clos, and there's a very rewarding walk to the island's highest point, the Chapelle St-Michel.

17

St-Thégonnec

🅰A3 🏠Saint-Thégonnec Loc-Eguiner 🚉 ℹ️13 place de la Mairie; www.baiedemorlaix.bzh

This is one of Brittany's most complete parish closes. As you pass through its triumphal archway, the ossuary is to the left. The calvary illustrates the skills of Breton sculptors working with the local granite. Among the many animated figures that surround the cross, a small niche contains a statue of St Thégonnec with a cart pulled by wolves.

> ### PARISH CLOSES
>
> Reflecting the religious fervour of the Bretons, the Enclos Paroissiaux (parish closes) were built during the 15th–18th centuries, when Brittany had few urban centres but many rich rural settlements that profited from maritime trade and the manufacturing of cloth. Grand religious monuments, with cartoonish biblical figures carved in stone *(below)* created to inspire and instruct visitors, were built by small villages such as St-Thégonnec. Some of the finest lie in the Elorn Valley, linked by the signed Circuit des Enclos Paroissiaux.

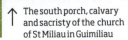

↑ The south porch, calvary and sacristy of the church of St Miliau in Guimiliau

18

Combourg

 B3 ⚑ Ille-et-Vilaine 🚌🚉
🛈 9 rue Notre Dame; www.
tourisme.bretagne
romantique.fr

A small, sleepy town set beside a lake, Combourg is completely overshadowed by the great, haunting **Château de Combourg**. The building we see today dates from the 14th and 15th centuries. In 1761 it was purchased by the Comte de Chateaubriand. The melancholic childhood spent there by his son, the author and diplomat François-René de Chateaubriand (1768–1848), is candidly described in his entertaining book *Mémoires d'Outre-Tombe* (Memoirs from Beyond the Grave).

Empty after the Revolution, the château was restored in the 19th century and is open for us. One room has the belongings of François-René de Chateaubriand.

Château de Combourg

♿🚫 ⚑ 23 rue des Princes
🕐 Apr-Oct: 10am-6pm Sun-Fri (daily in Jul & Aug:)
🌐 chateau-combourg.com

19

Tréguier

 B2 ⚑ Côtes d'Armor 🛈 11 rue Marcellin Berthelot; www.bretagne-cotedegranitrose.com

Overlooking the estuary of the Jaundy and Guindy rivers, Tréguier stands apart from the resorts of the Côte de Granit Rose (*p270*), nearby. It is a typically Breton market town, with one main attraction, the 14th- to 15th-century regal Cathédrale St-Tugdual. It has three towers: one Gothic, one Romanesque and the other 18th century. The latter, which was financed by Louis XVI with his winnings from the Paris Lottery, has holes in the shapes of playing-card suits.

The ancient stone Chapelle St-Gonery, in the centre of Plougrescant, 7 km (4 miles) to the north of Tréguier on the D8 road, has a leaning lead spire and a 15th-century painted wooden ceiling.

20

Dinan

 B3 ⚑ Côtes d'Armor 🚌🚉
🛈 9 rue du Château www.
dinan-tourisme.com

Situated on a hill above the forested Rance Valley, Dinan is a modern market town with a medieval heart. Surrounded by its substantial ramparts, the half-timbered houses and cobbled streets of its Vieille Ville (Old Town) retain an impressive, unforced sense of unity. Nearby, Basilique St-Sauveur contains the heart of Dinan's famous son, the 14th-century warrior and one-time Constable of France, Bertrand du Guesclin.

Behind the church, the peaceful Les Jardins Anglais enjoy good views of the River Rance and the viaduct span ning it. A couple of streets further to the north, the steep rue du Jerzual, bright with geraniums, winds down through the 14th-century town gate to the port. Once a busy harbour from which cloth was shipped, it is now a quiet backwater, where you can take a pleasure cruise, or walk along a towpath to the restored 17th-century Abbaye St-Magloire at Léhon.

The handsome **Château de Dinan** is flanked by the 14th-century Duc de Bretagne Jean IV keep and the 15th-century Tour de Coëtquen. Inside, in contrast to the military-style exterior, there is a kitchen, a chapel and various well-designed residential rooms that are most notable for their monumental fireplaces.

Dinan's surrounding country lanes are peppered with pre-historic dolmen (stone tombs).

Château de Dinan

♿ ⚑ Rue du Château 📞 02 96 87 58 72 🕐 May-Sep: 10am-6pm daily 🚫 Pub hols

---

 GREAT VIEW
Tour d'Horloge

It's a stiff climb up to the top of Dinan's Tour d'Horloge – 158 steps in all – but it is worth the effort for the far-reaching views to be enjoyed at the top, which can extend as far as Mont-St-Michel on a clear day.

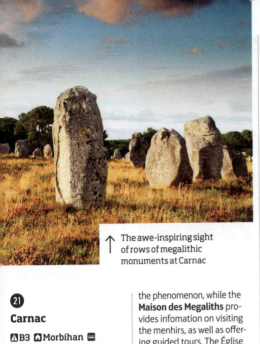

↑ The awe-inspiring sight of rows of megalithic monuments at Carnac

㉑

Carnac

🅰B3 🄰Morbihan 🚌
🛈 74 avenue des Druides; www.ot-carnac.fr

A popular seaside resort, Carnac is best known as one of the world's great prehistoric sites, with almost 3,000 menhirs (standing stones) set in formation in parallel rows by people and for reasons unknown. The excellent **Musée de Préhistoire** has more than 6,000 well-curated exhibits that attempt to explain

the phenomenon, while the **Maison des Megaliths** provides infomation on visiting the menhirs, as well as offering guided tours. The Église St-Cornély is dedicated to St Cornelius, patron saint of horned animals.

Musée de Préhistoire

🄰 10 de la Chapelle
🄾 Hours vary, check website
🅦 museedecarnac.fr

Maison des Megaliths

⏱ 🄰 Rue du Ménec
🄾 9:30am–6pm daily
📅 1 Jan, 1 May, 25 Dec
🅦 menhirs-carnac.fr

STAY

Sleep Hotel Tumulus
As if the views of Quiberon Bay weren't enough, this friendly and welcoming hotel offers an inviting outdoor swimming pool and an indoor spa area. It has 29 spacious and tastefully decorated rooms.

🅰B3 🄰 chemin du Tumulus, Carnac
🅦 hotel-tumulus.com

 €€€

Villa Reine Hortense
Overlooking Dinard's splendid stretch of pale sand beach, this elegant hotel was built for royalty. All but one of its seven spacious rooms have a sea view, and all are elegantly decorated, with pretty pops of vibrant colour.

🅰B2 🄰 19 rue de la Malouine, Dinard
🅦 villa-reine-hortense.com

 €€€

La Residence
This modern boutique hotel with a garden, in the heart of Roscoff, has 28 stylishly renovated rooms and is close to the seafront and the buzzing little town's shops and restaurants.

🅰A2 🄰 14 rue des Johnnies, Roscoff
🅦 hotelroscoff-la residence.fr

 €€€

← The spire rising above the bell tower of Cathédrale St-Tugdual in Tréguier

A tour guide illuminating the ancient stone carvings in a cave on the island of Gavrinis

24

Belle-Île-en-Mer

 A3 🗺 Morbihan
➕ Quiberon 🚌 ℹ Quai Bonnelle, Le Palais; www. belle-ile.com

Brittany's largest island, the "beautiful island" lies around 14 km (9 miles) off the coast of the Golfe du Morbihan and can be reached in 45 minutes by car ferry from Quiberon. There are several fine coastal paths popular with walkers, dramatic cliffs and a number of good beaches. Inland there are exposed highlands cut through by sheltered valleys.

In the main town, Le Palais, stands the Citadelle Vauban, a 16th-century star-shaped fortress, which now houses a restaurant-with-rooms and an interesting museum devoted to the island's history. The island hosts the internationally renowned Festival Lyrique en Mer each August.

22

Golfe du Morbihan

 B3 🗺 Morbihan
➕ Lorient 🚌🚢 Vannes
ℹ 1 quai Tabarly, Vannes; www.golfedu morbihan.bzh

Morbihan means "little sea" in Breton, an apt name for this landlocked expanse of water. Only connected to the Atlantic by a small channel between the Locmariaquer and Rhuys peninsulas, the gulf is dotted with islands. Around 40 of the islands are inhabited, the largest being Île d'Arz and the Île-aux-Moines. These are served by regular ferries that depart from Conleau and Port-Blanc respectively.

Around the gulf several small harbours earn a living from fishing, oyster cultivation and tourism to megalithic sites, notably on the island of Gavrinis, where stone carvings have been excavated. There are boat trips to the island of Gavrinis from Larmor-Baden and services around the gulf can be picked up from Auray, Locmariaquer, Vannes and Port-Navalo.

23

Presqu'île de Quiberon

 B3 🗺 Morbihan
➕ Quiberon 🗓 Jul-Aug
🚌🚢 ℹ 14 rue de Verdun, Quiberon; www.quib eron.com

Once an island, the slender Quiberon peninsula, barely connected to the rest of France by a sliver of sand bar, has a bleak west coast with craggy, sea-punished cliffs. It is appropriately known as the Côte Sauvage (Wild Coast). The east coast is a far more benign place. At the peninsula's southern tip is the fishing port and resort of Quiberon. The town is bright with blue-painted houses, and there are pubs aplenty, ideal for a refreshing cider after a walk along the wind-whipped coast.

The town is the point of departure for a ferry that carries vehicles to Belle-Île.

> 🟠 INSIDER TIP
> **The Plage du Gouret**
>
> On the Île-d'Houat, off the coast to the south of the Morbihan, the plage du Gouret (*Treac'h er Gouret* in Breton) is a wonderful 2-km (1-mile) stretch of golden sand, backed by dunes. Even in the high summer it is blissfully empty, and is one of the region's most beautiful, wild beaches.

25

Vannes

B3 **Morbihan**
**1 quai Tabarly; www.
tourisme-vannes.com**

Standing at the head of the Golfe du Morbihan, Vannes was the capital of the Veneti, a seafaring Armorican tribe defeated by Caesar in 56 BC. In the 9th century, Nominoë, the first Duke of Brittany, made it his power base. The city remained influential up until the signing of the union with France in 1532, when Rennes became the Breton capital. Today it is a bustling commercial city with a well-preserved medieval quarter, and makes a good base for explorations around the Golfe du Morbihan.

The impressive eastern walls of old Vannes can be viewed from promenade de la Garenne. Two of the city's old gates survive at either end: Porte-Prison in the north, and the southern Porte-Poterne, with a row of 17th-century washhouses close by.

Walking up from elaborate Porte St-Vincent, you come to the city's old market squares, which are still in use today. Place des Lices was once the location for medieval tournaments and the streets around rue de la Monnaie are lined by a wealth of well-maintained 16th-century houses. Begun in the 13th century, Cathédrale St-Pierre has been drastically remodelled and restored. The Chapel of the Holy Sacrament houses the tomb of the much revered Vincent Ferrier, a Spanish saint who died in Vannes in 1419. Opposite the western front of the cathedral is the old covered market, La Cohue (meaning "throng" or "hubbub"), once a central meeting place in the city. Parts of the building date from the 13th century, and a museum inside features contemporary art by Soulages, Genevieve and Tal-Coat, plus a small collection related to seafaring.

Within the 15th-century Château Gaillard, the **Musée d'Histoire** displays jewellery, pottery and weapons from Morbihan's many prehistoric sites. The **Musée de Beaux-Arts** has paintings from the 16th century and a collection of contemporary art.

Did You Know?

"Vannes and his wife", carved on the corner of a house in place Valencia, are the town's mascots.

To the south of the city the Parc du Golfe is a beautiful leisure park with waterfront attractions. These include a butterfly garden, a conservatory set in a tropical forest and an aquarium that boasts more than 400 species of fish.

Northeast of Vannes, off the N166, lie the romantic ruins of the imposing 15th-century castle, Tours d'Elven (Elven Towers).

Musée d'Histoire

Château Gaillard, 2 rue Noé 02 97 01 63 00 Jun-Sep: 1:30-4pm daily Public holidays

Musée des Beaux-Arts

La Cohue, place St-Pierre 02 97 01 63 00 Jun-Sep: 1:30-6pm daily

↑ The honey-stoned old city walls of historic Vannes, with canalside lawns

26

Josselin

🅰 B3 🏛 Morbihan 🚌
ℹ️ 21 rue Olivier de Clisson;
www.josselin-tourisme.fr

Overlooking the River Oust, Josselin is dominated by the medieval **Château de Josselin**, which has been owned by the de Rohan family since the end of the 15th century. Only four of its original nine towers survive. The elaborate inner façade incorporates the letter "A" – a tribute to the much-loved Duchess Anne of Brittany (1477–1514), who presided over the "Golden Age" of Brittany. Tours of the fine 19th-century interior are given, and include the former stables, where the Musée des Poupées has 600 dolls.

In the town, the Basilique Notre-Dame-du-Roncier contains the mausoleum of the château's most famous owner, Olivier de Clisson (1336–1407). West of Josselin, at Kerguéhennec, an 18th-century château, are the lovely landscaped grounds of with a modern sculpture park linked by a trail over lawns and beside a river.

Château de Josselin
⊘ 🅲 Apr–Sep: 2–6pm daily
🌐 chateaudejosselin.com

 27

Forêt de Paimpont

🅰 B3 🏛 Ille-et-Vilaine
🚆 Rennes 🏛 Monfort-sur-Meu 🚌 Rennes ℹ️ Place du Roi St-Judicael, Paimpont;
www.tourisme-broceliande.bzh

Also known as the Forêt de Brocéliande, this is a remnant of the dense primeval woods that once covered a large part of Armorica. It has long been associated with the legends of King Arthur, and visitors still come on a quest to search for the magical spring where the sorcerer Merlin first met the Lady of the Lake.

A good base for exploring both the forest and its myths is the pleasant little village of Paimpont.

 28

Côte d'Emeraude

🅰 B2 🏛 Ille-et-Vilaine & Côtes d'Armor 🛫 Dinard-St-Malo 🚉 🚌 ℹ️ Dinard;
www.ot-dinard.com

Between Le Val-André and the Pointe du Grouin sandy beaches, rocky headlands and a number of classic seaside resorts stretch along the north shore of Brittany.

Known as the Emerald Coast because of the colour of the sea, its most beautiful spot is the aristocratic resort of Dinard, "discovered" in the 1850s and still playing host to the international rich.

To its west are other resorts, including St-Jacut-de-la-Mer, St-Cast-le-Guildo, Sables d'Or-les-Pins and Erquy, all with tempting beaches. In the Baie

↑ Château Josselin reflected in the Oust, and *(inset)* one of its grand beamed room

↑ Fort La Latte on its rocky headland on the shores of scenic Côte d'Emeraude

> **Its splendid medieval Château de Vitré is complete with pencil-point turrets and has picturesque 15th- to 16th-century buildings in attendance.**

de la Frênaye, the medieval Fort La Latte provides good views from high in its ancient watchtower; the 30-m- (98-ft-) tall lighthouse that dominates Cap Fréhel nearby provides even more extensive vistas.

To the east of Dinard, the D186 runs onward to St-Malo, crossing the Barrage de la Rance. Built in 1966 it was the world's first dam to generate electricity by using the power of the tides. Beyond St-Malo, coves and beaches surround La Guimorais, while around the Pointe du Grouin the seas are often truly emerald.

29
Vitré

🅰 C2 🅱 Ille-et-Vilaine 🅲🅳
ℹ Place Général de Gaulle;
www.bretagne-vitre.com

The fortified town of Vitré, which is tantalizingly visible from the Laval to Rennes autoroute, is set high on a hill overlooking the lovely Vilaine Valley. Its splendid medieval **Château de Vitré** is complete with pencil-point turrets and has a range of picturesque 15th- to 16th-century buildings in attendance. The castle was rebuilt during the 14th–15th centuries and has a triangular plan. Some of its ramparts are walkable, and in the Tour St-Laurent there is a museum.

To the east, rue Beaudrairie and rue d'Embas are lined by some historic overhanging timber-frame houses that have remarkable patterning.

The Cathédrale Notre-Dame, built in Flamboyant Gothic style during the 15th to 16th centuries, has a south façade with an exterior stone pulpit. A little further along rue Notre-Dame is access to promenade du Val, which skirts around the town's 13th- to 17th-century ramparts.

To the southeast of Vitré on the D88 is the **Château des Rochers-Sévigné**, home of the Sévigné family from 1410 and home to Mme de Sévigné (1626–96), the famous letter-writer and chronicler of life at the court of Louis XIV. The park, chapel and some of her rooms are open to the public (guided tours only; book in advance).

Château de Vitré

✦ 🅰 Ille-et-Vilain 📞 02 99 75 04 54 🕐 8:30am-5:30pm Mon-Fri, 8:30am-12:30pm Sat & Sun 🚫 Pub hols

Château des Rochers-Sévigné

✦✦ 🅰 Ille-et-Vilain
📞 02 99 96 76 51 🕐 Apr-Sep: 11am-5pm daily

 PICTURE PERFECT
The Côte d'Emeraude

Running to the west of the River Rance, almost as far as fairy-tale Mont St-Michel, the Emerald Coast has deserted beaches and wild rocky headlands, such as those of the striking Cap Fréhel peninsula, and the dramatic Fort La Latte that clings to a rocky promontory over the grey-green sea.

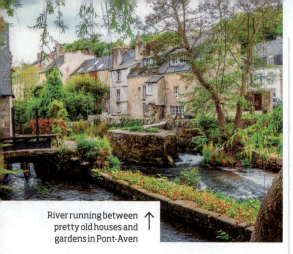

River running between pretty old houses and gardens in Pont-Aven ↑

 30

Pont-Aven

🅰A3 🏠Finistère 🚌 🚉5 pl Julia; www.pontaven.com

Once a tiny market town of "14 mills and 15 houses", Pont-Aven's picturesque location in the wooded Aven estuary made it attractive to many late 19th-century artists.

In 1888 Paul Gauguin, along with Émile Bernard and Paul Sérusier, developed a crude,

---

PAUL GAUGUIN IN BRITTANY

At the age of 35, Paul Gaugin (1848-1903) left his career as a stock-broker to become a full-time painter. From 1886 to 1894 he lived and worked in Brittany, at Pont-Aven and Le Pouldu, where he incorporated the landscape and its people into his work, and the intense, almost "primi-tive" quality of the Breton Roman Catholic faith. This is evident in *Le Christ Jaune* (The Yellow Christ), in which the Crucifixion is depicted as reality against the rural backdrop of contem-porary Brittany.

---

colourful Synthetism style. Drawing inspiration from the Breton landscape and people, the École de Pont-Aven (Pont-Aven School) worked here and in nearby Le Pouldu until 1896.

The town is devoted to art, with 50 private galleries, along with the informative **Musée de Pont-Aven**, which docu-ments the achievements of the Pont-Aven School. The surrounding woods offer pleas-ant walks – one leads to the Chapelle de Trémalo, where the wooden Christ in Gauguin's *Le Christ Jaune* still hangs.

Musée de Pont-Aven

♿🖼🎨 🏠Place Julia 📞02 98 06 14 43 🕐Feb, Mar, Nov & Dec: 2–5:30pm Tue–Sun; Apr–Jun, Sep & Oct: 10–6pm Tue–Sun; Jul & Aug: 10am–7pm daily 🚫Jan, 25 Dec

---

 31

Rennes

🅰B3 🏠Ille-et-Vilaine ✈🚆🚌 🚉11 rue St-Yves; wwww.tourisme-rennes.com

Founded by the Gauls and colonized by the Romans, Rennes is strategically sited where the Rivers Vilaine and Ille meet. Following Brittany's union with France in 1532, the town became regional capital.

In 1720 a fire that lasted for six days devastated the city. Today a small part of the medieval city survives, along with the neat grid of 18th-century buildings that arose from the ashes. Around this historic core cluster the tower blocks and high-tech factories of a modern and confident provincial capital, with two universities and a thriving cultural life.

Wandering through the streets that radiate from place des Lices and place Ste-Anne, it is very easy to imagine what Rennes was like before the Great Fire. Now mostly pedes-trianized, this area is the city's youthful heart with bars, *crêperies* and designer shops. At the western end of rue de la Monnaie stands the 15th-century Portes Mordelaises, once part of the ramparts.

Close by, the Cathédrale St-Pierre was completed in 1844, the third on this site. Note the carved 16th-century Flemish altarpiece. Nearby is the 18th-century Église St-Sauveur. In the place de la Mairie stands the early 18th-century Hôtel de Ville and the Neo-Classical Opéra de Rennes. Just south of the attractive rue St-George, the Église St-Germain has a typically Breton belfry and wooden vaulting. The Parc du

Thabor, once the grounds of a Benedictine monastery, is ideal for walks and picnics. Rennes's Law Courts, built in 1618–55, housed the **Palais du Parlement de Bretagne** until the Revolution. Severely damaged by fire during riots over fish prices in 1994, the major restoration work is all but complete, including the unique coffered ceiling and gilded woodwork within the Grande Chambre. Today, the Salle des Pas Perdus, with its vaulted ceilings, can again be admired by the public on a guided tour.

The **Musée des Beaux-Arts** has a wide-ranging collection of art from the 14th century to the present, including a room dedicated to Breton themes. There are works of the Pont-Aven School, including paintings by Gauguin, and works by Picasso, notably *Baigneuse* painted at Dinard in 1928.

In Rennes's cultural centre, with the Science Museum and Planetarium, the **Musée de Bretagne** includes examples of traditional Breton wares, displays on the growth of Rennes, rural crafts, the fishing industry and local prehistoric megaliths.

Just to the south of Rennes, the **Ecomusée du Pays de Rennes**, traces the history of a local farm since the 17th century, and is also a very popular destination for picnics. Further on, some 16 km (10 miles) to the southeast of Rennes is **Châteaugiron**, a charming medieval village, with an imposing castle and houses with wooden eaves.

Palais du Parlement de Bretagne

⊘ ⊘ 🏠 Place du Parlement 🎫 Book tickets for guided tour online via website 🌐 tourisme-rennes.com

Musée des Beaux-Arts

⊘ 🏠 20 quai Zola ⏱ 10am–5pm Tue–Fri, 10am–6pm Sat & Sun 🚫 public hols 🌐 mba. rennes.fr

Musée de Bretagne

⊘ 🏠 10 cours des Alliés ⏱ 1–7pm Tue–Fri, 2–7pm Sat & Sun 🚫 public hols 🌐 musee-bretagne.fr

Ecomusée du Pays de Rennes

⊘ 🏠 Ferme de la Bintinais, rte de Châtillon-sur-Seiche ⏱ 9am–6pm Tue–Fri, 2–6pm Sat & Sun 🚫 public hols 🌐 ecomusee-rennes-metropole.fr

Châteaugiron

⊘ ⊘ 🏠 Ille-et-Vilaine 📞 02 99 37 89 02 ⏱ Jul & Aug: 2–6pm Mon–Sat & Sun (call ahead)

EAT

Essentials
This friendly canalside bistro serves fresh, modern menus using produce from its own kitchen garden.

🅰B3 🏠 11 rue Armand Rebillon, Rennes 🌐 restaurant essentiel.com

€€€

L'Eden
A popular spot on the Canal St-Martin serving nicely presented seafood and meat dishes *par excellence*.

🅰B3 🏠 3 rue Pasteur, Vannes 📞 02 97 46 42 62

€€€

Le Chalut
One for seafood lovers – expect the freshest fish and seafood dishes amid fun maritime-inspired décor.

🅰B2 🏠 8 rue de la Corne de Cerf, St-Malo 📞 02 99 56 71 58

€€€

Le Vivier
Freshly caught seafood and breathtaking views of the Côte Sauvage are the major draws at this unpretentious local hangout.

🅰B3 🏠 3 rue Pasteur, Vannes 📞 02 97 46 42 62

€€€

←
Admiring paintings in Rennes's well-curated Musée des Beaux-Arts

THE LOIRE VALLEY

Colonized by the Romans in 52 BC, the peaceful Loire Valley has been blessed with long periods of stability, punctuated by short bursts of unrest or invasion. The Romans attempted to quell these periods of disruption by building walls around major towns, such as Le Mans and Angers. During the Hundred Years' War, the English invaded the Loire, bringing a long period of strife to the valley. In the midst of the struggle, Joan of Arc rallied the French at Orléans to free the city and oust the English from the Loire – a victory that would reawaken the French spirit. Leonardo di Vinci made the valley his home for the final years of his life, and his influence can be seen in the exquisite gardens and châteaux all along the Loire. Chambord and Chenonceau, the two greatest Renaissance châteaux, were created as prestigious symbols of royal rule, resplendent amid vast hunting forests and waterways. Industry, especially textiles, thrived as stability took hold of the region, even when the Wars of Religion divided the valley. The region's fortunes waivered as the effects of the French Revolution took hold, only to rebound in time for World War I. From 1917, the American Expeditionary Force set up its headquarters in Tours and served as a temporary base for the French government. Today, known for its easygoing atmosphere, tranquility again reigns across the fertile vineyards and valley of Loire.

THE LOIRE VALLEY

Must Sees

1. Tours
2. Château de Chenonceau
3. Château de Chambord
4. Chartres Cathedral

Experience More

5. Angers
6. The Vendée
7. Nantes
8. Le Mans
9. Saumur
10. Montreuil-Bellay
11. Abbaye Royale de Fontevraud
12. Chinon
13. Château de Villandry
14. Château de Langeais
15. Château d'Azay-le-Rideau
16. Château d'Ussé
17. Montrésor
18. Amboise
19. Loches
20. Vouvray
21. Beaugency
22. Vendôme
23. Blois
24. The Loir
25. Orléans
26. St-Benoît-sur-Loire
27. Bourges

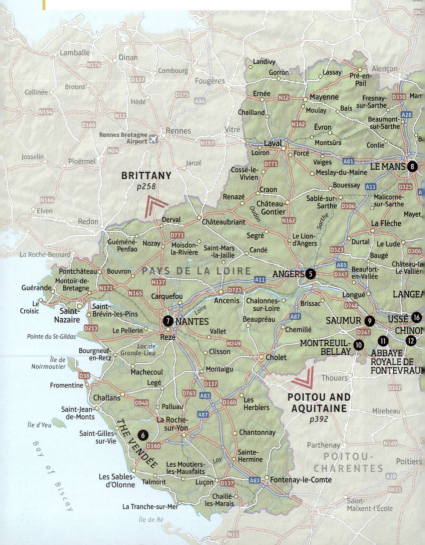

↑ The picturesque place Plumereau, nestled in Tour's medieval heart

❶

TOURS

 C3 ◆ Indre-et-Loire ✈🚇 ℹ 78 rue Bernard Palissy; www.tours-tourisme.fr

Built over a Roman town, Tours was once the capital of France. The city was bombarded by the Prussians in 1870, then bombed in World War II, suffering extensive damage. During the latter part of the 20th centry its historic centre underwent regeneration.

❶

Place Plumereau

This pretty pedestrianized square, found in the medieval heart of the city, is surrounded by fairy-tale half-timbered houses and cute pavement-side cafés, as well as a number of boutiques and galleries. The streets leading off from the square, such as the picturesque rue Briçonnet, reveal a selection of half-timbered façades, hidden courtyards and crooked towers. A gateway leads to the unusual place St-Pierre-le-Puellier, a square which contains sunken Gallo-Roman remains alongside a Romanesque church, which has been converted into a charming café.

❷

Église St-Julien

◆ 20 rue Nationale 📞 02 47 70 21 00 ⏰ Hours vary, call ahead

Once part of a Benedictine abbey, this church was named after St Julien, whose relics it houses. Its Gothic monastic cells and chapterhouse contain a small wine museum.

❸

Tour Charlemagne

◆ Place de Châteauneuf

In place de Châteauneuf lies the impressive Romanesque Tour Charlemagne. Standing

SLEEP

Château De Beaulieu

This grand château has splendid views, formal French gardens and a luxury spa.

◆ 67 rue de Beaulieu, Joué-les-Tours Ⓦ chateaude beaulieu37.com

€€€

Hôtel de Biencourt

Just outside of town, this charming hotel offers modern rooms and a pretty terrace.

◆ 7 rue de Balzac, Azay-le-Rideau Ⓦ hotelbiencourt.fr

€€€

56 m (183 ft) high, it is all that remains of St Martin's, the church which originally stood on this site. It was built to house the tomb of Luitgard, wife of Charlemange, who

> Its Flamboyant Gothic façade is blackened and crumbling but still truly impressive, as are the medieval stained-glass windows.

died while visiting the city in 800. Visits to the tower can be organized via the tourist office and include the chance to climb the 284 steps to the top of the tower.

West of here are the cute shops, hip bars and grand theatre of rue de la Scellerie.

---

④

Centre de Création Contemporain Olivier Debré

📍 Jardin François 1er
🕐 11am-7pm Tue-Sun (to 9pm Thu) 🌐 cccod.fr

Located just behind the Hôtel Goüin, with its truly stunning façade, is the Centre de Création Contemporain Olivier Debré, a contemporary art museum named after the 20th-century artist who was inspired by the Touraine region. Housed in an elegant modern building, it displays several of Debré's large-scale works and also hosts regular temporary exhibitions.

⑤

Cathédrale St-Gatien

📍 Place de la Cathédrale
📞 06 62 36 42 89
🕐 8:30am-8pm daily; call ahead to book guided tour

The Cathédrale St-Gatien, in the east of the city, was begun in the early 13th century and completed in the 16th. Its Flamboyant Gothic façade is crumbling but still impressive, as are the medieval stained-glass windows. It is open to the public daily, but guided tours must be booked in advance.

---

⑥

Musée des Beaux-Arts

📍 18 pl François Sicard
🕐 9am-6pm Wed-Mon
🚫 Public hols 🌐 mba.tours.fr

The Musée des Beaux-Arts, set in the former archbishop's palace, overlooks Classical gardens and a giant cedar of Lebanon. Its star exhibits are

Prayer in the Garden of Olives and *The Resurrection*, both by Andrea Mantegna.

---

⑦

Musée du Compagnonnage

📍 8 rue Nationale 🕐 Mid-Jun-mid-Sep: 9am-6pm daily; mid-Sep-mid-Jun: 9am-6pm Wed-Mon
🚫 Public hols 🌐 musee-compagnonnage.fr

Covering the history of *compagnonnage* – a mentoring network through which young craftsmen would learn a trade – This museum's fascinating displays contain hundreds of finely crafted works by master craftsmen of the guilds.

Did You Know?

It is widely believed that the French spoken by the people of the Touraine is the "purest" in France.

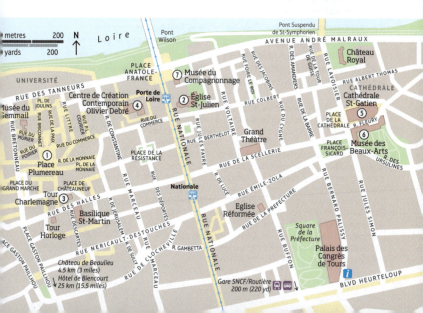

THE CREATION OF CHENONCEAU

The women who lived at Chenonceau each left their mark on it. Catherine Briçonnet, wife of the first owner, commissioned the turreted pavilion and one of the first straight staircases in France. Henri II's mistress, Diane de Poitiers, added the formal gardens and arched bridge over the river; the bridge was turned into an Italian-style gallery by Catherine de' Medici. Louise de Lorraine, bereaved wife of Henri III, painted the ceiling of her bedchamber black and white. In 1863, Madame Pelouze undertook a complete restoration in 1863.

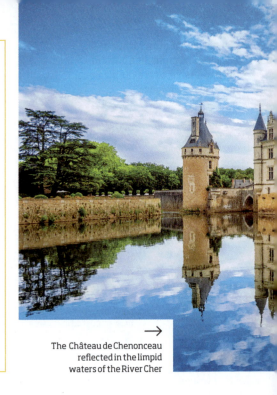

→

The Château de Chenonceau reflected in the limpid waters of the River Cher

2

CHÂTEAU DE CHENONCEAU

🅰D3 🏠Chenonceaux 🚉Chenonceaux 🚌From Tours 🕐Sep–Jun: 9:30am–5pm daily; Jul & Aug: 9am–7:30pm 🌐chenonceau.com

A romantic pleasure palace, Chenonceau was first built during the Renaissance and subsequently expanded and improved by a series of aristocratic women. A magnificent avenue bordered by plane trees leads to symmetrical gardens and the serene vision that Flaubert praised as "floating on air and water".

The château's distinctive feature is its Florentine-style 60-m (197-ft) gallery built over a series of arches, its elegant beauty reflected in the languid waters of the River Cher. The grandeur continues inside with splendidly furnished rooms, airy bedchambers and a wonderful collection of fine paintings and tapestries. The main living area was in the square-shaped turreted pavilion built over the foundations of an old water mill in the middle of the River Cher. Four principal rooms open off the Vestibule on the ground floor: the Salle des Gardes and the Chambre de Diane de Poitiers, both hung with 16th-century Flemish tapestries; the Chambre de François I, with a Van Loo painting; and the Salon Louis XIV. On the first floor, reached via the Italianate staircase, are other sumptuous apartments, including the Chambre de Catherine de' Médici.

 INSIDER TIP
Promenades Nocturnes

In July and August the grounds are lit up at night (9–11:30pm) and visitors can take a stroll through the illuminated gardens to the stirring sound of music by great Classical composers, from Handel to Corelli.

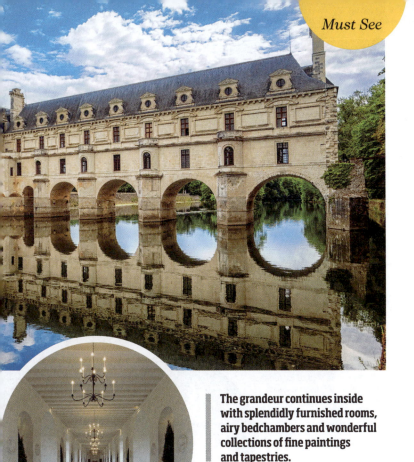

> **The grandeur continues inside with splendidly furnished rooms, airy bedchambers and wonderful collections of fine paintings and tapestries.**

← The elegant Grande Galerie where Catherine de' Medici held wild parties and lavish balls

---

Timeline

1513
▲ Thomas Bohier acquires medieval Chenonceau. His wife, Catherine Briçonnet, undertakes rebuilding it.

1533
Marriage of Catherine de' Medici (1519-89) to Henri II (1519-59). Chenonceau becomes a royal palace.

1575
Louise de Lorraine (1554-1601) marries Henri III, Catherine's third and favourite son.

1730–99
▼ Madame Dupin, a "farmer-general's" wife, makes Chenonceau a salon for artists, writers and philosophers.

1789
Chenonceau is spared in the bloody French Revolution, thanks to Madame Dupin.

1913
The château is bought by the Menier family, the chocolatiers who still own it today.

1941
Chenonceau chapel is damaged during a bombing raid.

3 🖊️ 🎨 💻 🛍️

CHÂTEAU DE CHAMBORD

🅰️D3 📍Loir-et-Cher 🚉Blois, then taxi, bus (2, 4) or shuttle to Chambord (shuttle Apr–early Sep only) 🕐Apr–Oct: 9am–6pm daily; Nov–Mar: 9am–5pm daily 🚫1 Jan, 1 May, 25 Dec 🌐chambord.org

Henry James once said, "Chambord is truly royal – royal in its great scale, its grand air, and its indifference to common considerations." One glimpse of the fairy-tale turrets and elegant gardens of this magnificent château proves him right.

The Loire's largest residence, brainchild of extravagant François I, began as a hunting lodge in the Forêt de Boulogne. In 1519 the original building was razed and the creation of present-day Chambord began, to a design probably initiated by Leonardo da Vinci. By 1537 the towers, keep and terraces had been completed, the work of 1,800 men and three master masons. At one point François I suggested diverting the Loire river to flow in front of the château, but he settled for redirecting the nearby Cosson instead. His son Henry II continued his work, and Louis XIV completed the 440-roomed edifice in 1685. Depictions of the salamander, François I's enigmatic symbol, appear over 800 times throughout the château.

→
Chambord's chapel, begun by François I shortly before his death

Timeline

1519–37
▲ The Count of Blois's hunting lodge is demolished by François I and the château created.

1547
François I dies at the Château de Rambouillet in Ile-de-France.

1547–59
Henri II adds the west wing and second storey of the chapel.

1669–85
▽ Louis XIV completes the building, then abandons it.

1670
▲ *Le Bourgeois Gentilhomme* by Molière is staged at Chambord.

LE BOVRGEOIS GENTILHOMME. Comedie . Ballet . Donné par le ROY à toute ſa Cour dans le Chaſteau de Chambord. L'OVVERTVRE Se fait par un grand aſſemblage d'inſtrumens. ...NS LE PREMIER AC...

32,500

The number of plants brought in to replant the gardens during a major renovation in 2017.

↑ Boats at rest on the canal beside the splendid château of Chambord

1725–33

Chambord is inhabited by Stanislas Leczinski, exiled king of Poland and duke of Lorraine

1840

▽ Chambord is declared a Monument Historique.

1748

The Maréchal de Saxe acquires Chambord. On his death, two years later, the château yet again falls into decline.

1970s

△ Chambord is restored and refurnished, and the moats once again dug out.

EXTENSIVE GROUNDS

Chambord's setting is as impressive as the château. Some 50 sq km (19 sq miles) of parkland, heath and forest surround the château – including the largest walled nature reserve in Europe, home to wild boar and deer. Explore the park with a forest guide or rent a bike to discover it by wheel.

4

CHARTRES CATHEDRAL

D3 **Pl de la Cathédrale** **8:30am–7:30pm daily** **cathedrale-chartres.org**

According to art historian Émile Male, "Chartres is the mind of the Middle Ages manifest." A true masterpiece of Gothic architecture, this monumental, double-spired cathedral towers over the old town. Visitors from all over the world come to visit its spectacular stained-glass windows and mysterious labyrinth.

Begun in 1020, the Romanesque cathedral was destroyed by fire in 1194. Rebuilt in just 25 years, few alterations were made to the church after 1250, and fortunately, Chartres was unscathed by the Wars of Religion and the French Revolution. The result is a Gothic cathedral with a true "Bible in stone" reputation. Donated by royalty, aristocracy, priests and the merchant brotherhoods between 1210 and 1240, its glorious collection of stained glass is world renowned. Around 176 windows illustrate biblical stories and daily life in the 13th century. During both World Wars the windows were dismantled and removed for safety. There is an ongoing programme, begun in the 1970s, to restore the windows in the cathedral.

Did You Know?

Some believe the cathedral's labyrinth represents the pilgrimage to the Holy Land.

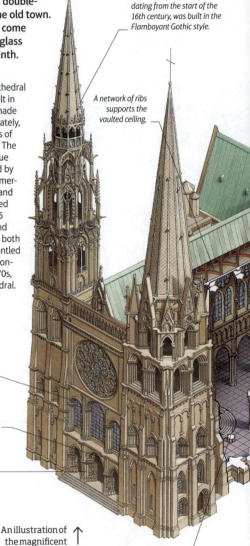

The taller of the two spires, dating from the start of the 16th century, was built in the Flamboyant Gothic style.

A network of ribs supports the vaulted ceiling.

Part of the original Romanesque church, the west front has three windows dating from the mid-12th century.

The central tympanum of the Royal Portal (1145–55) shows Christ in Majesty.

These statues on the Royal Portal represent Old Testament figures.

An illustration of the magnificent Chartres cathedral

Labyrinth

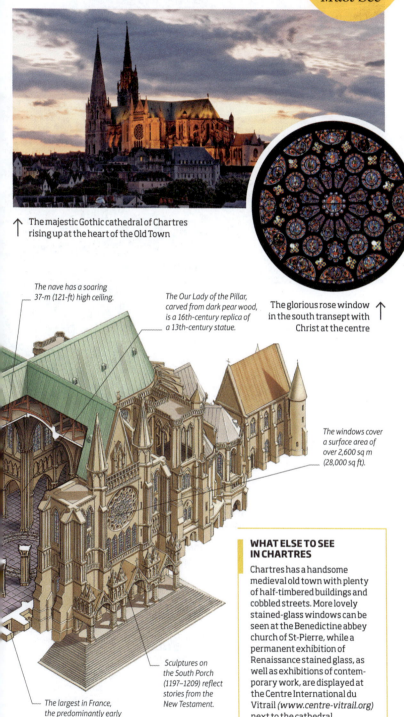

↑ The majestic Gothic cathedral of Chartres rising up at the heart of the Old Town

The glorious rose window in the south transept with Christ at the centre ↑

The nave has a soaring 37-m (121-ft) high ceiling.

The Our Lady of the Pillar, carved from dark pear wood, is a 16th-century replica of a 13th-century statue.

The windows cover a surface area of over 2,600 sq m (28,000 sq ft).

Sculptures on the South Porch (1197–1209) reflect stories from the New Testament.

The largest in France, the predominantly early 11th-century crypt houses the Veil of the Virgin relic.

WHAT ELSE TO SEE IN CHARTRES

Chartres has a handsome medieval old town with plenty of half-timbered buildings and cobbled streets. More lovely stained-glass windows can be seen at the Benedictine abbey church of St-Pierre, while a permanent exhibition of Renaissance stained glass, as well as exhibitions of contemporary work, are displayed at the Centre International du Vitrail *(www.centre-vitrail.org)* next to the cathedral.

EXPERIENCE MORE

 5

Angers

🄰 C3 🏠 Maine-et-Loire 🚉 🅿
🚌 🛈 7 pl Kennedy; www.
angersloiretourisme.com

Angers is the historic capital of Anjou and gateway to the Loire Valley. The town is home to the formidable 13th-century **Château d'Angers** with the longest (103 m/338 ft) medieval tapestry in the world. It illustrates the story of the Apocalypse, with battles between hydras and angels.

Nearby **Galerie David d'Angers**, housed in the glass-covered ruins of a 13th-century church, celebrates the sculptor born in Angers. Across the River Maine, the 12th-century Hôpital St-Jean, a hospital for the poor from 1174 to 1854, houses the **Musée Jean Lurçat**. Its prize exhibit is the exquisite *Chant du Monde* tapestry, which was created by Lurçat in 1957. In the same building is **Le Musée de la Tapisserie Contemporaine**, with displays of ceramics and paintings.

Château d'Angers

🎟 🚫 🚻 🕙 10am–5:30pm daily 🚫 1 Jan, 1 May, 1 & 11 Nov, 25 Dec 🌐 chateau-angers.fr

Galerie David d'Angers

🎟 🏠 33 rue Toussaint 🕙 10am–6pm Tue–Sun 🚫 Most public hols 🌐 musees.angers.fr

Musée Jean Lurçat/Le Musée de la Tapisserie Contemporaine

🎟 🏠 4 blvd Arago 🕙 10am–6pm Tue–Sun 🚫 Most public hols 🌐 musees.angers.fr

---

6

The Vendée

🄰 B4 🏠 Vendée and Maine-et-Loire 🛫 Nantes 🅿 🚌 La Roche-sur-Yon 🛈 7 place du Marché; www.vendee-tourisme.com

The counter-revolutionary movement that swept western France between 1793 and 1799 began as a series of uprisings in

↑ Black-and-white patterned Château d'Angers *(above)*, home to a medieval Apocalypse tapestry

the Vendée, and the region remains coloured by conservatism and religious fervour.

This local history is retraced just south of Cholet at France's popular theme park, **Le Puy du Fou**, which stays open late for its summer evening show, *Cinéscénie*. An account is given at the Musée du Textile in Cholet, the town whose flax and hemp textiles provided royalists with their kerchiefs: originally white, then blood red.

The tranquil Vendée offers green tourism inland, in the *bocage vendéen*, a wooded idyll with paths and nature trails. The stretch of the Atlantic coastline between the Loire

Did You Know?

Cinéscénie, at Le Puy du Fou, is the world's biggest nighttime show, staged by 2,400 actors.

and La Rochelle has beaches, yet the only sizable resort is Les Sables d'Olonne, with boat trips that head into the salt-marshes, out to sea or across to the nearby Île d'Yeu.

Le Puy du Fou

 Les Epesses Hours vary, check website for details puydufou.com

---

7

Nantes

 B4 Loire-Atlantique 9 rue des Etats; www.nantes-tourisme.com

Visually, Nantes is a city of variety, with high-tech towers overlooking the port, canals and Art Nouveau squares. Chic bars and restaurants cram the medieval nucleus, bounded by place St-Croix and the château.

The impressive **Château des Ducs de Bretagne** is where Anne of Brittany was born in 1477, and where the Edict of Nantes was signed by Henri IV in 1598, granting Protestants religious freedom. The château houses the lively, interactive Musée d'Histoire, which charts the history of Nantes itself.

Château des Ducs de Bretagne

 Pl Marc Elder Jul & Aug: daily; Sep–Jun: Tue-Sun 1 Jan, 1 May, 1 Nov, 25 Dec chateaunantes.fr

---

8

Le Mans

 C3 Sarthe 16 rue de l'Etoile; www.lemans-tourisme.com

Ever since Monsieur Bollée became the first designer to put an engine in a car, Le Mans has been synonymous with the motor trade. Bollée's son created an embryonic Grand Prix, and the event and the **Musée des 24 Heures du Mans** are star attractions.

The ancient fortified centre, with half-timbered houses and arcaded alleys, is wrapped by superb Roman walls. The crown is the Gothic Cathédrale St-Julien, with its Romanesque portal rivalling that of Chartres.

Musée des 24 Heures du Mans

9 pl Luigi Chinetti 10am–5pm daily lemans-musee24.com

EAT

L'U.Ni

The inventive cuisine at this buzzy spot reflects Nantes's creative vibe.

 B4 36 rue Fouré, Nantes 02 40 75 53 05

€€€

L'Atelier Gourmand

Innovative takes on traditional food served amid hip surroundings.

 C3 37 rue Etienne Marcel, Tours lateliergourmand.fr

€€€

Le Lièvre Gourmand

Offers delicious French-Asian fusion.

D3 28 quai de Chatelet, Orléans 02 38 53 66 14

€€€

Le Grand Monarque - Le Georges

Enjoy *grands crus* wines paired with Michelin-starred French cuisine.

 D3 22 pl des Epars, Chartres bw-grand-monarque.com

€€€

Mamie Bigoude

Galettes are a specialty at this kitschy family-friendly spot.

C3 22 rue de Châteauneuf, Tours www.mamie-bigoude.com

€€€

←

The 1964 Citroën HY S.E.V. Marchal at the Musée des 24 Heures du Mans

❾ Saumur

C4 Maine-et-Loire
8 quai Carnot; www.ot-saumur.fr

Saumur is celebrated for its fairy-tale château, cavalry school, mushrooms and sparkling wines. Its stone mansions recall the city's 17th-century heyday, when it was a bastion of Protestantism and vied with Angers as the intellectual capital of Anjou.

High above both town and river is the turreted **Château de Saumur**. The present structure was started in the 14th century by Louis I of Anjou and remodelled later by his grandson, King René. Collections include medieval sculpture, and equestrian exhibits.

The Military Cavalry School, established in Saumur in 1814, led to the creation of the Musée des Blindés, which features over 150 different armoured vehicles and the prestigious Cadre Noir horse-riding formation. Morning training sessions, stable visits and occasional evening performances, can be seen at the internationally renowned **École Nationale d'Equitation**.

Château de Saumur

Hours vary, check website
chateau-saumur.fr

Did You Know?

Saumur's walls once boasted a wooden parrot used for target practice by archers.

École Nationale d'Equitation

St-Hilaire-St-Florent Feb-mid-Nov: for guided tours; Apr-Oct: see website for show times Pub hols cadrenoir.fr

❿ Montreuil-Bellay

C4 Maine-et-Loire
2 pl de la Mairie; www.ville-montreuil-bellay.com

Montreuil-Bellay, set against the River Thouet, is one of the region's most gracious small towns. The towering roofline of the Gothic collegiate church overlooks walled mansions and surrounding vineyards. The Chapelle St-Jean was an ancient hospice and pilgrimage centre.

The **Château de Montreuil-Bellay**, established in 1025, is a veritable fortress with its 13 interlocking towers, barbican and ramparts. A 15th-century house lies beyond the gateway, with a vaulted medieval kitchen and an oratory decorated with 15th-century frescoes.

Château de Montreuil-Bellay

Place des Ormeaux
Apr-Nov: 10am-6pm Wed-Mon (Jul-Aug: daily)
chateau-de-montreuil-bellay.fr

⓫ Abbaye Royale de Fontevraud

C4 Maine-et-Loire
9:30-7pm daily Jan, 25 Dec

Abbaye Royale de Fontevraud is the largest and most intact medieval abbey in Europe. It was founded in the early 12th century by Robert d'Arbrissel, a visionary itinerant preacher, who set up a Benedictine community of monks, nuns, nobles, lepers and vagabonds. The radical founder entrusted the running of the abbey to an abbess, usually from a noble family, and the abbey became a favourite sanctuary for the female aristocracy.

Wandering around the abbey buildings and gardens gives a fascinating insight into monastic life. The focal point was the Romanesque abbey church, consecrated in 1119.

It boasts beautifully carved capitals and an immense nave with four domes, one of the finest examples of a cupola nave in France.

The abbey's nuns lived around the Renaissance Grand Moûtier cloisters, forming one of the largest nunneries in France. The leper colony was once housed in the St-Lazare priory, now a hotel and restaurant. Most impressive is the octagonal kitchen with its fireplaces and chimneys in the Tour Evraud, a rare example of secular Romanesque architecture. The abbey is now an arts centre, and regularly hosts concerts and exhibitions.

↑ Diners relaxing over a bottle of wine in the attractive centre of Chinon

Chinon

C4 ⌂ Indre-et-Loire ▭ ▭
ℹ 1 rue Rabelais; www. chinon-valdeloire.com

The Château de Chinon is an important shrine in Joan of Arc country and, as such, wheedles money from all passing pilgrims. It was here in 1429 that the saint first recognized the disguised dauphin (later Charles VII), and persuaded him to give her an army to drive the English out of France. Before that, Chinon was the Plantagenet kings' favourite castle. Although the château is now mostly in ruins, the ramparts are an impressive sight from the opposite bank of the Vienne river.

The town's bijou centre is like a medieval film set. Rue Voltaire, lined with 15th- and 16th-century houses and once enclosed by the castle walls, represents a cross-section of Chinonais history. At No 12 is the **Musée Animé du Vin**, where animated figures tell the story of wine making. Nearby, at 44 rue Haute St-Maurice, is the Musée d'Art et d'Histoire, a stone mansion, where, in 1199, Richard the Lionheart is said to have died. The grandest mansion is the Palais du Gouverneur, with its double staircase and loggia. More charming is the Maison Rouge in the Grand Carroi, studded with a red-brick herringbone pattern.

The 1900s market, with folk dancing, music and stallholders in period costume, , is a must (third Saturday of August).

Musée Animé du Vin
🜨 🜨 ⌂ 12 rue Voltaire
☏ 02 47 93 25 63 🕘 Mid-Mar-mid-Oct: 10am-10pm daily

↑ The château and church towering above the riverside town of Montreuil-Bellay

---

FRANÇOIS RABELAIS

Rabelais, born in 1494, was a priest, doctor and humanist scholar noted for his wisdom and tolerance. He is best remembered for his ribald satires (written as "medicine" for his patients), *Pantagruel* and *Gargantua*, set around his native Chinon. His writing, full of scatological humour, was judged obscene by the Sorbonne, but it was also rich and inventive, with many of his words passing into the French language.

FRANÇOIS RABELAIS

13

Château de Villandry

C4 Indre-et-Loire
Tours Château: mid-Feb–mid-Nov & mid-Dec–early Jan: 10am–6pm daily; gardens: hours vary, check website chateau villandry.fr

Villandry was the last great Renaissance château built in the Loire Valley, a perfect example of 16th-century architecture. The Château de Villandry's gardens were restored to their original splendour in the early 20th century by Dr Joachim Carvallo, whose grandson continues his work.

The result is a patchwork of sculpted shrubs and flowers on three levels: the *jardin potager* (kitchen garden), the *jardin d'ornement* (ornamental garden) and, on the highest level, the *jardin d'eau* (water garden). There are signs to explain the history and meaning behind each plant: the marrow, for instance, symbolized fertility; the cabbage, sexual and spiritual corruption. Plants were also prized for their medicinal properties. The humble cabbage was thought to help cure hangovers, while pimento was believed to aid digestion.

The delicate roots of the 51 km (32 miles) of box hedge mean that the 40,000 sq m (430,000 sq ft) of gardens must be weeded entirely by hand.

> The Château de Villandry's gardens were restored to their original splendour in the early 20th century by Dr Joachim Carvallo, whose grandson continues his work.

 INSIDER TIP
Loire by Bike

Ideal terrain for cycling, the Loire has extensive, well-maintained cycle paths and even a dedicated cycle trail, the well-signposted Loire à Vélo (*loireavelo.fr*), which follows over 900 km (559 miles) of paths, many along the river. Starting at Cuffy and ending at St Brévin-les-Pins, the route passes through rolling countryside lined with vineyards and pretty villages along the way.

14

Château de Langeais

C4 Indre-et-Loire
Langeais Jul & Aug: 9am–7pm; Sep–Jun 9:30am–5:30pm daily 1 Jan, 25 Dec chateau-de-langeais.com

Compared with neighbouring towns, Langeais is distinctly untouristy and has a laid-back, welcoming feel. Its château is fiercely feudal, built strictly for defence with a drawbridge, portcullis and no concessions to the Renaissance. It was constructed by Louis XI in just four years, from 1465 to 1469, and has hardly been altered since that time. The ruins of an impressive keep, built by Foulques Nerra in AD 994, stand in the château's small picturesque courtyard.

A *son-et-lumière* display in the Salle de Mariage represents the marriage of Charles VIII and Anne of Brittany in 1491. Many of the rooms have intricate designs on the tiled floors, and all of them are hung with caarefully restored Flemish and Aubusson tapestries.

A burbling canal carving its way through the Château de Villandry's *jardin d'ornement*

↑ The romantic turrets and terraced gardens of Château d'Usse

 15

Château d'Azay-le-Rideau

🅰C4 🅰Indre-et-Loire 🚉Azay-le-Rideau ⏰10am-6pm daily (to 11pm Jul & Aug) 🚫1 Jan, 1 May, 25 Dec 🌐azay-le-rideau.fr

Balzac called Azay-le-Rideau "a multifaceted diamond set in the Indre". Indeed, it is the most beguiling of the Loire châteaux, created in the early 16th century by Philippa Lesbahy, wife of François I's corrupt finance minister, and restored in the 19th century. Although Azay is superficially Gothic, it clearly shows the transition to the Renaissance: the turrets are purely decorative and the moats are picturesque pools. The interior is equally delightful, an airy, creaking mansion full

of lovingly re-created domestic detail. The first floor is furnished in the Renaissance style, with a fine example of a portable Spanish cabinet and exquisite tapestries. The four-storey grand staircase is unusual for its time, being straight as opposed to spiral. In July and August, from 9pm until midnight, a sound and light show takes place.

Wine tasting in the village is a welcome reminder that vineyards are all around.

 16

Château d'Ussé

🅰C4 🅰Indre-et-Loire 🚉Chinon, then taxi ⏰Mid-Feb–mid-Nov: 10am-6pm daily 🌐chateaudusse.fr

The illustrious Château d'Ussé enjoys a bucolic setting by

overlooking the rivers Loire and Indre. Its romantic turrets, pointed towers and chimneys inspired 19th-century writer and collector of French fairy-tales Charles Perrault to pen the now-famous story of *Sleeping Beauty*.

A fortification was built here in the 11th century, and replaced by the castle in the 15th century, which was gradually transformed into an aristocratic château. It has been privately owned by the same family for more than two centuries. The interior is perhaps a little lacklustre (and the *Sleeping Beauty* tableaux are a bit clumsily presented), but it is worth visiting for the delightful Renaissance chapel, framed by the oak forest of Chinon, and the exquisite gardens, designed by Le Nôtre, who also created the gardens of Versailles (*p170*).

Bold and bright, the colourful interiors of Château de Montrésor

 17

Montrésor

🅰️C4 🏠Indre-et-Loire ℹ️43 grande rue; 02 47 92 70 71

Classed as one of the most beautiful villages in France, Montrésor does not disappoint. Set on the River Indrois, it became a Polish enclave in the 1840s. In 1849 a Polish nobleman, Count Branicki, bought the 15th-century château, built on the site of 11th-century fortifications. One of the most charming castles in the Loire Valley, **Château de Montrésor** has remained in the family ever since, largely unchanged since the mid-19th century.

Château de Montrésor

🕙 ⊘ 🕙10am–6pm daily 🌐chateaudemontresor.fr

 18

Amboise

🅰️D3 🏠Indre-et-Loire 🚉🚌 ℹ️Quai du Général de Gaulle; www.amboise-valdeloire.com

Once the home of France's royals, few buildings are more

historically important than the **Château d'Amboise**. Both Louis XI and Charles VIII lived here; François I was brought up here, as were Catherine de' Medici's ten children. The château was also the setting for the Amboise Conspiracy of 1560, an ill-fated Huguenot plot against François II. Visitors are shown the metal lacework balcony that once served as a gibbet for 12 of the 1,200 conspirators who were put to death. The Tour des Minimes, the château's original entrance, is famous for its huge spiral ramp, which horsemen would ride up to deliver provisions.

On the ramparts is the beautifully restored Gothic Chapelle St-Hubert, best known for being Leonardo da Vinci's burial place. Under the patronage of François I, the artist lived in the nearby

manor house of **Clos-Lucé** between 1516 and 1519. The Clos-Lucé contains a museum exhibiting models of Leonardo's inventions, constructed from his sketches.

Château d'Amboise

🕙 ⊘ 🕙9am–7pm daily 🚫1 Jan, 25 Dec 🌐chateau-amboise.com

Clos-Lucé

⊘ 🏠2 rue du Clos-Lucé 🕙9am–7pm daily 🚫1 Jan, 25 Dec 🌐vinci-closluce.com

 19

Loches

🅰️D4 🏠Indre-et-Loire 🚉🚌 ℹ️Place de la Marne; www.loches-valdeloire.com

This picturesque, untouched medieval town is removed from the château trail in the Indre Valley. It is a tranquil refuge of late-Gothic gateways and sculpted façades. Its keep boasts the deepest dungeons in the Loire. The **Logis Royal de Loches** is associated with Charles VII and his mistress Agnès Sorel. It is also where Joan of Arc pleaded with

Did You Know?

Charles VIII met an early death at the age of 28 in 1498 after hitting his head on a door lintel in the Château d'Amboise.

Charles to go to Reims and be crowned. Anne of Brittany's chapel is decorated with ermines, and contains an effigy of Agnès Sorel.

Logis Royal de Loches

 Loches 9am–6pm daily 1 Jan, 25 Dec citeroyaleloches.fr

20

Vouvray

D3 Indre-et-Loire 12 rue Rabelais; www. tourismevouvray-valdeloire.com

Just east of Tours *(p290)* is the village of Vouvray, the home of the delicious white wine that Renaissance author Rabelais likened to taffeta.

The star vineyard is **Huet**, where, since 1990, grapes have been grown according to biodynamic methods, such as manual weeding and the use of natural fertilizers. In the

preface to his novel *Quentin Durward*, Sir Walter Scott sang the praises of its dry white wines, which are still matured in chestnut barrels. In 1990, Gaston Huet campaigned successfully against plans to build the tracks for the TGV train over Vouvray vineyards (instead tunnels were built under the hilly vineyards).

Overlooking the Loire, the **Château de Montcontour** sits on a hilltop. It is the place where monks first planted vines in the area in the 4th century. The château has its own winemaking museum in the 10th-century cellars hewn out of the tufa rock. Visits to the museum can be followed by wine tastings. Note both wine tastings and tours of the cellar are by reservation only.

Huet

 11–13 rue de la Croix-Buisée 02 47 52 78 87 9am–12pm, 2–6pm Tue–Sat Pub hols

Château de Moncontour

 Route de Rochecorbon 10am–5pm Mon–Fri moncontour.com

The verdant vineyards of Vouvray, and *(inset)* its delicious wines, aged in barrels
↓

STAY

Domaine des Hauts de Loire
An ivy-clad château with plush rooms, Michelin-starred restaurant and a spa.

D3 Rte d'Herbault, Onzain hautsde loire.com

€€€

Hôtel Anne d'Anjou
A grand staircase leads up to characterful rooms with river or castle views.

C4 32–34 quai Mayaud, Saumur hotel-anneanjou.com

€€€

Hôtel de l'Abeille
This grand building offers charming rooms, plus a relaxing rooftop terrace.

D3 64 rue Alsace Lorraine, Orléans hoteldelabeille.com

€€€

21
Beaugency

D3 ⬤ **Loiret** 🚃🚌 ℹ️ **3 pl
de Docteur-Hyvernaud;
www.tourisme-
beaugency.fr**

The compact medieval town
of Beaugency makes a peaceful base for exploring the
Orléanais region. Exceptionally
for the Loire, it is possible
to walk along its riverbanks
and stone levees. At quai de
l'Abbaye there is a good view
of the 11th-century bridge,
which, until relatively recently,
was the only crossing point
between Blois and Orléans.

Dominating the town centre
is a ruined 11th-century watchtower. It stands sentry on place
St-Firmin, along with a 16th-
century bell tower (the original church was destroyed in
the Revolution) and a statue
of Joan of Arc. Further down is
the **Château de Beaugency**,
built on the site of the feudal
castle by one of Joan of Arc's
compagnons d'armes, Jean de
Dunois. Highlights include the
16th-century kitchens and
the handsome seigneurial
lodgings. Facing the Château
de Beaugency is Notre-Dame,
a Romanesque abbey church
that witnessed, in 1152, the
annulment of the marriage
between Eleanor of Aquitaine
and Louis VII, leaving Eleanor
free to marry the future
Henry II of England.

Nearby is the medieval clock
tower in rue du Change and
the Renaissance Hôtel de Ville
(town hall), its façade adorned
with the town's arms.

Château de Beaugency

 ⬤ **3 pl Dunois** 🕙 **10am–
6pm daily (to 7pm Jul–Aug)**
🚫**Nov–mid-Feb** 🌐**chateau-
de-beaugency.com**

22
Vendôme

C3 ⬤ **Loir-et-Cher** 🚃🚌
ℹ️ **47 rue Poterie; www.ven
dome-tourisme.fr**

Once a valued stop for pilgrims
on the road to Compostela in
Spain, Vendôme is still popular
with modern pilgrims, thanks
to the TGV rail service. A desir-
able address for Parisian
commuters, the town still
retains its provincial charm.
Vendôme's old stone buildings
are encircled by the River Loir.
Its lush gardens invite exploration, especially Parc Ronsard.
Reached by a footbridge across
the Loir, this park has a plane
tree planted in 1759 and a
medieval *lavoir*.

The greatest monument of
the town is the abbey church
of La Trinité, founded in 1034.
Its Romanesque bell tower is
overshadowed by the church
portal, a masterpiece of
Flamboyant Gothic tracery.
The interior is embellished

with Romanesque capitals
and 15th-century choir stalls.
On a rocky spur above the Loir
is the ruined château, built by
the counts of Vendôme in the
13th–14th centuries. The tranquil garden around the château
is remarkable for its collection
of hydrangeas.

23
Blois

D3 ⬤ **Loir-et-Cher** 🚃🚌
ℹ️ **23 pl du château; www.
bloischambord.com**

Once a fief of the counts of
Blois, the town was a royal
domain in the 15th century,
retaining its historic façades
to this day. Architectural interest abounds in Vieux Blois, the
hilly, partially pedestrianized
quarter of Blois enclosed by the
château, cathedral and river.

Set back from the north
bank of the river, the grand
Château Royal de Blois was
the main royal residence until
Henri IV moved the court to
Paris in 1598. The château's
four contrasting wings make
a harmonious whole. The Salle
des Etats Généraux, the only
part of the building surviving
from the 13th century, housed
the council and court, and is
the largest and best-preserved
Gothic hall in all of France.
The adjoining Louis XII wing

↑ The peaceful River Loire near Beaugency, with
the town's medieval stone bridge in the distance

← Blois cathedral's spires against the glowing sky as the River Loire flows past

from the late 15th century, which houses the Musée des Beaux-Arts, infuses Gothic design with Renaissance spirit, sealed with the king's porcupine symbol.

The 16th-century François I wing is a masterpiece of the French Renaissance, containing a monumental spiral staircase in an octagonal tower.

Blois is hung with paintings interpreting its troubled past. These include a portrayal of the murder of the Duc de Guise in 1588. The most intriguing room is Catherine de' Medici's study lined with 237 carved wooden wall panels, four of which are secret cabinets said to have stored her poisons.

In the eastern sector of the city, the imposing Cathédrale St-Louis is a 17th-century reconstruction of a Gothic church, almost destroyed by a hurricane in 1678. Behind the cathedral the former bishop's palace, built in 1700, is the Hôtel de Ville.

Place Louis XII is overlooked by splendid 17th-century façades. Rue Pierre de Blois, a quaint alley straddled by a Gothic passageway, winds downhill to the medieval Jewish ghetto. Rue des Juifs boasts distinguished *hôtels particuliers* (mansions), including the galleried Hôtel de Condé, with its Renaissance archway and courtyard, and the Hôtel

Jassaud, with notable 16th-century bas-reliefs above the main doorway. Place Vauvert is the most charming square, with a fine example of a half-timbered house.

Château Royal de Blois

♦ ♦ 🏠 6 place du Château 📞 02 54 90 33 33 🕐 Jan–Mar, Nov & Dec: 10am–5pm daily; Apr–Jun, Sep & Oct: 9am–6:30pm daily; Jul & Aug: 9am–7pm daily 🚫 1 Jan, 25 Dec

---

㉔
The Loir

🅰 D3 🏠 Loir-et-Cher ✈ Tours 🚆 Vendôme 🚌 Montoire-sur-le-Loir 🛈 16 pl Clémenceau, Montoire-sur-le-Loir; www.otsi-montoire.fr

Compared with the royal River Loire, the tranquil Loir to the north has a more rural charm.

The stretch between Vendôme and Trôo is the most rewarding, offering walking trails, wine tasting, troglodyte caves, fishing and boat trips.

Les Roches-l'Évêque is a fortified village with cave dwellings. Just downstream is Lavardin, with its Romanesque church, half-timbered houses, Gothic bridge and ruined château ringed by ramparts. In Montoire-sur-le-Loir, the Chapelle St-Gilles, a former leper colony, has Romanesque frescoes. Trôo, the next major village, is known for its beautiful church and a labyrinth of troglodyte dwellings. Facing the village of Trôo, St-Jacques-des-Guérets has a frescoed Romanesque chapel, as does Poncé-sur-le-Loir, further downstream. On the slopes are vineyards producing Jasnières and Côteaux du Vendômois. Wine tastings enliven sleepy Poncé and La Chartre-sur-le-Loir.

TROGLODYTE DWELLINGS

For centuries, caves carved out of the *tufa* (soft limestone) of the Loire Valley – either hewn from cliff-faces or dug underground – have been a source of cheap, secure accommodation. Today they are used for wine storage, mushroom growing and even as hotels. For a glimpse into a way of life that existed as late as the 1930s, visit the troglodyte village of Rochemenier *(www.troglodyte.fr)*, which has been partly preserved as a museum.

㉕ Orléans

🛆 D3 🛈 Loiret 🚊🚗🚌
**🛈 2 pl Etape; www.
tourisme-orleans
metropole.com**

Orléans's dazzling modern bridge symbolizes the city's increasing importance as the geographic heart of both France and Europe. As a tourist, however, one is struck by the city's continued attachment to its past, most particularly to Joan of Arc. It was from here that the Maid of Orléans saved France from the English in 1429. Since her martyrdom at Rouen in 1431, Joan remains a presence in Orléans. Every 29 April and 1 and 7–8 May her liberation of the city is enthusiastically re-enacted in a pageant and a blessing is given in the city's Cathédrale Ste-Croix.

Though badly damaged in World War II, a faded grandeur lingers in reconstructed Vieil Orléans (Old Town), the quarter bounded by the cathedral, the River Loire and place du Martroi. The latter, a Classical but rather windswept square, has an equestrian statue of the city's heroine. Nearby the half-timbered **Maison de Jeanne d'Arc**, rebuilt in 1961 from period dwellings on the site where Joan had lodgings in 1429, has multimedia displays telling her story.

From place du Martroi, rue d'Escures leads past notable Renaissance mansions to the cathedral. **Hôtel Groslot** is the grandest, a 16th-century red-brick mansion, where kings Charles IX, Henri III and Henri IV all stayed. The 17-year-old François II died here in 1560 after attending a meeting of the États Généraux with his child bride, Mary, later Queen of Scots. The building served as Orléans's town hall from 1790 to 1982, and the sumptuously decorated interior, which contains fascinating Joan memorabilia,

is still used for marriages and official ceremonies. Virtually opposite the Hôtel Groslot and alongside the new town hall is the **Musée des Beaux-Arts**, displaying a collection of European works of art from the 16th to the 20th centuries.

Standing nearby, the Cathédrale Ste-Croix is an imposing edifice begun in the late 13th century. The building was destroyed by the Huguenots (Protestants) in 1568, and then rebuilt in supposedly Gothic style between the 17th and 19th centuries.

Maison de Jeanne d'Arc

🏛♿ 🛆 3 pl du Général de Gaulle ⏰ 10am–6pm Tue–Sun (from 2pm Oct–Mar)
🌐 jeannedarc.com.fr

Hôtel Groslot

🛆 Pl de l'Etape 📞 02 38 79 22 30 ⏰ Jul–Sep: 9am–7pm daily

Musée des Beaux-Arts

♿ 🛆 1 rue Fernand Rabier 📞 02 38 79 21 83 ⏰ 10am–6pm Tue–Sat, 10am–8pm Fri, 1–6pm Sun 🚫 Pub hols

THE HEROINE OF FRANCE

Joan of Arc is the quintessential French national heroine and woman martyr. Her divinely led campaign to "drive the English out of France" during the Hundred Years' War has inspired plays, poetry and films. She became champion of the uncrowned Charles VII, but was captured in 1430 and accused of witchcraft. She was burned at the stake in Rouen in 1431 at the age of 19. In 1920 she was canonized in recognition of her heroism and tragic martyrdom.

→

Statue of valiant Joan of Arc

㉖ St-Benoît-sur-Loire

**🛆 D3 🛈 Loiret 🚌 🛈 44 rue Orléanaise; www.
tourisme-loire-foret.com**

Situated along the River Loire between Orléans and Gien, St-Benoît-sur-Loire boasts one of the finest Romanesque abbey churches (1067–1108) in France. It is all that survives of an important monastery founded

→

People enjoying an open-air concert at Jardin des Prés Fichaux, Bourges in AD 650 and is named after St Benedict, patron saint of Europe. His relics were brought from Italy at the end of the 7th century.

The church's belfry porch is graced with carved capitals depicting biblical scenes. The nave is tall and light, and the choir floor is an amazing patchwork of Italian marble. Daily services with Gregorian chants are open to the public.

㉗

Bourges

Ⓐ D4 **Ⓐ Cher** **🚆🚌** **ℹ 21 rue Victor Hugo; www. bourges-tourisme.com**

Today Bourges flourishes as a university town and cultural mecca, renowned for its spring festival of music. This Gallo-Roman city still retains its original walls but is best known as the city of Jacques Coeur, who rose through the ranks to become financier and foreign minister to Charles VII. Coeur came from humble beginnings – his father was a furrier in the cloth trade – to become the greatest merchant of the Middle Ages and

was ennobled in 1441 and it was in his capacity as an arms dealer that he established a tradition maintained for four centuries, as Napoléon III had cannons manufactured here in 1862.

Built over part of the walls, the **Palais Jacques Coeur** is a Gothic gem and a lasting memorial to its first master. Finished in 1453, it incorporates Coeur's two emblems, scallop shells and hearts, as well as his motto: *"À cœur vaillant, rien d'impossible"* – to the valiant heart, nothing is impossible. The guided tour reveals a barrel-vaulted gallery, painted chapel and a chamber that had Turkish baths.

Rue Bourbonnoux leads to St-Étienne, a cathedral very similar to Paris's Notre-Dame. The grand west façade, the widest among France's Gothic cathedrals, has five sculpted portals, the central one depicting an enthralling Last Judgment. In the choir are vivid 13th-century stained-glass windows presented by the guilds. The crypt holds the tomb of the 14th-century Duc de Berry, who commissioned the illuminated manuscript the *Très Riches*

Did You Know?

In Bourges, in summer evenings, the medieval buildings are lit up with light, images and music.

Heures. From the top of the north tower stretch views of the beautifully restored medieval quarter and the marshes beyond. Beside the cathedral is a tithe barn and the remains of the Gallo-Roman ramparts. The Jardin des Prés Fichaux, set by the River Yèvre, contains pools and an open-air theatre. To the north lie the Marais de Bourges, where gardeners transport their produce by river boat.

About 35 km (22 miles) south of Bourges is the Abbaye de Noirlac. Founded in 1136, it is one of the best-preserved Cistercian abbeys in France.

Palais Jacques Coeur

♿🚫 **Ⓐ** Rue Jacques Coeur **🕒** Hours vary, check website **🚫** Pub hols **🌐** palais-jacques-coeur.fr

A DRIVING TOUR
CHÂTEAUX TOUR OF THE SOLOGNE

Length 60 kms (37 miles) **Stopping-off points** Château de Beauregard; Château de Villesavin **Terrain** Mainly flat

The mysterious Sologne is a secretive landscape of woods and marshes edged by vineyards. This ambling rural route takes in some of the Loire's most varied châteaux. The five on this tour – for which a couple of days is required – represent a delightful encapsulation of regional architecture.

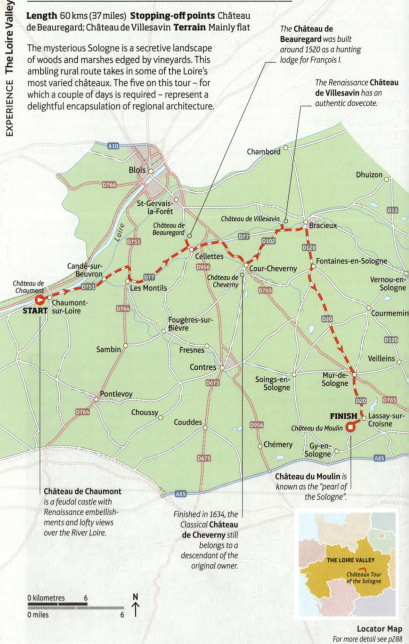

The **Château de Beauregard** *was built around 1520 as a hunting lodge for François I.*

The Renaissance **Château de Villesavin** *has an authentic dovecote.*

Château de Chaumont *is a feudal castle with Renaissance embellishments and lofty views over the River Loire.*

Finished in 1634, the Classical **Château de Cheverny** *still belongs to a descendant of the original owner.*

Château du Moulin *is known as the "pearl of the Sologne".*

THE LOIRE VALLEY
Châteaux Tour of the Sologne

Locator Map
For more detail see p288

Did You Know?

The Château de Chaumont was razed to the ground by Louis XI in 1465.

↑ The fairy-tale Château de Chaumont, built during the 9th century

The Roche de Solutré towering above the vineyards of Mâcon

BURGUNDY AND FRANCHE-COMTÉ

The gentle plains and lofty alpine forests made this region an attractive prospect to its earliest settlers, the Celtic Sequanis. When the Romans moved in, they repositioned Dijon on the road from Lyon to Paris. In the 5th century, the town was allied with the Burgundians, who would give Burgundy its name. Under the dukes of Valois in the 14th and 15th-centuries, Burgundy was France's most powerful rival, with territory extending well beyond its present boundaries. By the 16th-century, however, the duchy was ruled by governors appointed by the French king, though it still retained its privileges and traditions. Once a part of Burgundy, Franche-Comté – the Free County – struggled to remain independent of the French crown, and even joined forces with Spain in an effort to retain its sovereignty. It was annexed by Louis XIV in 1674, after a lengthy siege. A parliament and a university were established in Besançon, the new capital of the province, but separatist groups remained vocal until the 18th century. Today Burgundy considers itself the heart of France, a prosperous region with world-renowned wine, earthy cuisine and magnificent architecture, while Franche-Comté, to the east, remains somewhat untamed.

BURGUNDY AND FRANCHE-COMTÉ

Must Sees

1 Abbaye de Fontenay
2 Basilique Ste-Madeleine
3 Dijon

Experience More

4 Auxerre
5 Sens
6 Chablis
7 La Puisaye-Forterre
8 Tonnerre
9 Château de Tanlay
10 Château d'Ancy-le-Franc
11 Châtillon-sur-Seine
12 Alise-Ste-Reine
13 Morvan
14 Avallon
15 Saulieu
16 Nevers
17 Semur-en-Auxois
18 Côte d'Or
19 Beaune
20 Brionnais
21 Cluny
22 Autun
23 Paray-le-Monial
24 Tournus
25 Cascades du Hérisson
26 Dole
27 Arc-et-Senans
28 Mâcon
29 Arbois
30 Ronchamp
31 Champlitte
32 Ornans
33 Besançon
34 Belfort

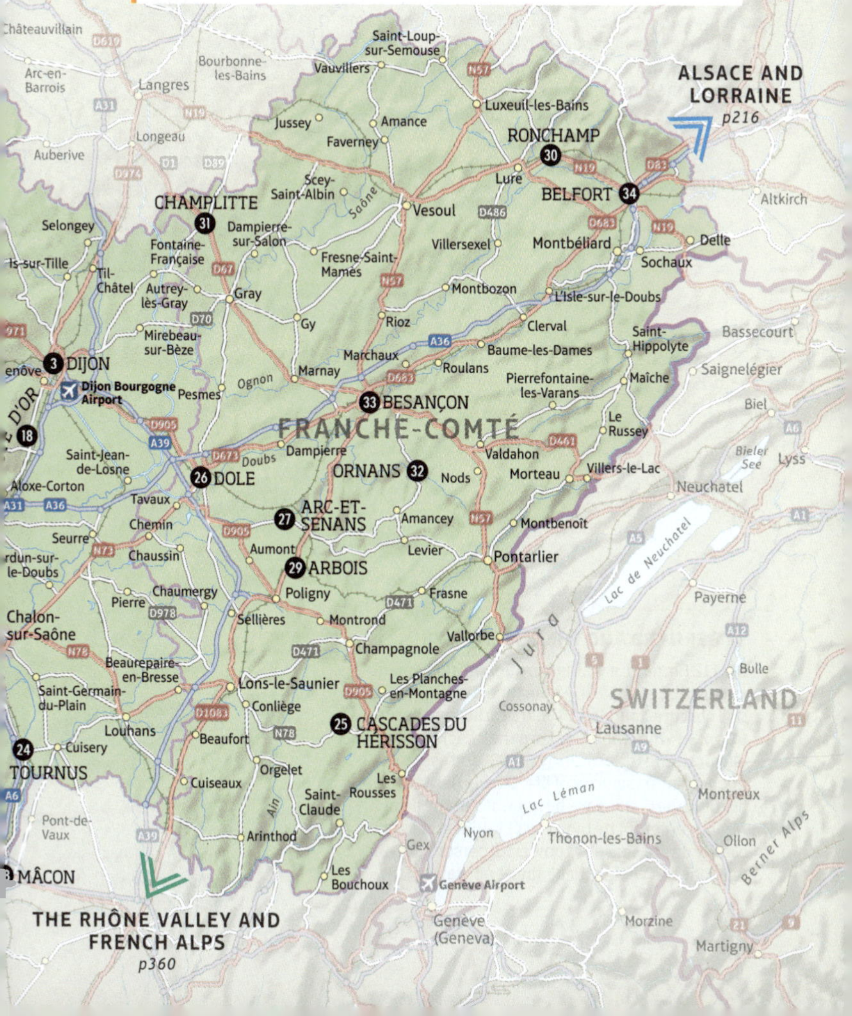

ALSACE AND LORRAINE p216

THE RHÔNE VALLEY AND FRENCH ALPS p360

❶ 🖉 🜋 🍴 🖵 🛍

ABBAYE DE FONTENAY

🅰 E3 📍 Côte-d'Or 🚉 Montbard ⏰ 10am–5pm daily (to 6pm Apr–Nov) 🌐 abbayedefontenay.com

Founded in 1118 by St Bernard of Clairvaux, the Abbey of Fontenay is the oldest surviving Cistercian foundation in France and offers a rare insight into the highly disciplined Cistercian way of life.

Situated deep in the forest, this site offered the peace and seclusion that the Cistercians sought for their abbey. The sublime gravity of the Romanesque church and its plain but elegant chapterhouse, built in early Gothic style, embody the austere discipline and spartan lifestyle of the Cistercian order. Supported by the local aristocracy, the abbey began to thrive and remained in use until the Revolution, when it was sold and converted into a paper mill. In 1906 the abbey came under new ownership and was restored to its original appearance. With its dormitory, bakery, prison, forge and many other outbuildings, it is one of the world's most complete surviving monastic complexes.

Did You Know?
—
Monks copying out manuscripts could come and warm their hands in the abbey's Warming Room.

The bakehouse is no longer intact, but the 13th-century oven and chimney have survived.

The visitors' hostel is where weary wanderers and pilgrims were offered board and lodging.

In the forge monks produced their own tools and hardware.

ST BERNARD AND THE CISTERCIANS

In 1112 Bernard, a young Burgundian nobleman, joined the Cistercians. At the time the order was still obscure, founded 14 years earlier by a group of monks who wanted to turn their back on the elaborate lifestyle of Cluny (p332) and espouse poverty and simplicity of life. During Bernard's lifetime the Cistercians became one of the most famous orders of its time. Part of this success was clearly due to Bernard's powerful personality and his skills as a writer, theologian and statesman.

↑ The expansive Abbaye de Fontenay, with its many outbuildings

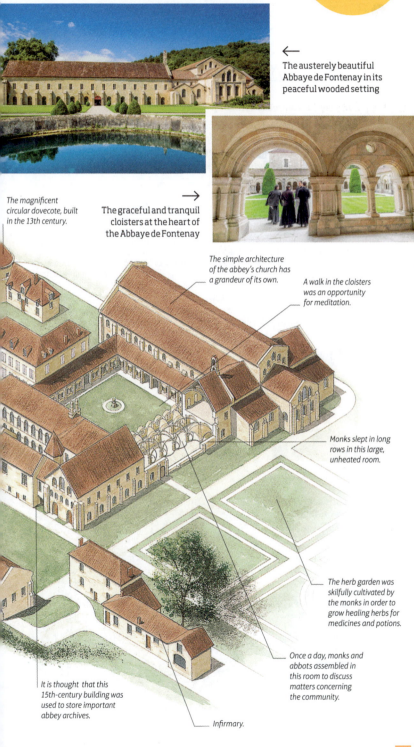

← The austerely beautiful Abbaye de Fontenay in its peaceful wooded setting

The magnificent circular dovecote, built in the 13th century.

→ The graceful and tranquil cloisters at the heart of the Abbaye de Fontenay

The simple architecture of the abbey's church has a grandeur of its own.

A walk in the cloisters was an opportunity for meditation.

Monks slept in long rows in this large, unheated room.

The herb garden was skilfully cultivated by the monks in order to grow healing herbs for medicines and potions.

It is thought that this 15th-century building was used to store important abbey archives.

Infirmary.

Once a day, monks and abbots assembled in this room to discuss matters concerning the community.

2

BASILIQUE STE-MADELEINE

🅰 E3 🅰 Vézelay 🅱 Sermizelles 🕐 7am–8pm daily 🅦 basiliquedevezelay.org

The golden glow of Vézelay's hilltop abbey church, Basilique Ste-Madeleine, is visible from afar. Today, tourists follow in the footsteps of medieval pilgrims, ascending the narrow street up to this magnificent abbey. In the 12th century, at the height of its glory, pilgrims flocked here to venerate relics believed to be those of Mary Magdalene.

The Basilique Ste-Madeleine was an important stopping point for pilgrims en route to Santiago de Compostela in Spain. It declined during the 16th century and suffered in the Wars of Religion and French Revolution. A Franciscan community has now been re-established and pilgrims once again come to pay respects to the relics of Mary Magdalene, kept in the atmospheric Romanesque crypt. The main draw though for most visitors is the Romanesque church itself with its magnificent sculpture and Gothic choir. Some of the most exquisite carvings are to be found in the narthex, added to the nave in 1150 to accommodate the growing number of pilgrims. The tympanum over the central portal bears a splendid carving of Christ on his throne, stretching out his hands, from which rays of light descend on to the apostles.

Superlatively carved, too, are the capitals in the narthex and nave, vividly rendering stories from classical antiquity and the Bible.

WHAT ELSE TO SEE IN VÉZELAY

Because of the abbey's importance, many pilgrims on the the road to Santiago de Compostela stayed in the charming hilltop village of Vézelay. Look down and you'll see shells inlaid in the roads – a symbol of the French pilgrims as they journeyed south. Next to the basilica, Maison Jules-Roy invites visitors into the home of the writer; its gardens also offer lovely views of the surrounding countryside and the River Cure.

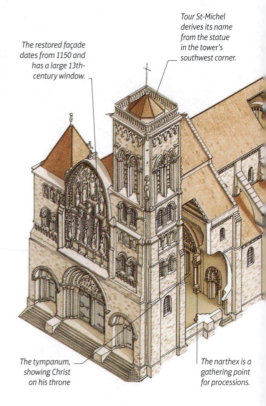

The restored façade dates from 1150 and has a large 13th-century window.

Tour St-Michel derives its name from the statue in the tower's southwest corner.

The tympanum, showing Christ on his throne

The narthex is a gathering point for processions.

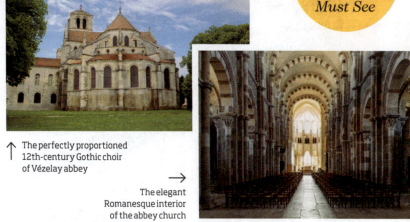

↑ The perfectly proportioned 12th-century Gothic choir of Vézelay abbey

→ The elegant Romanesque interior of the abbey church

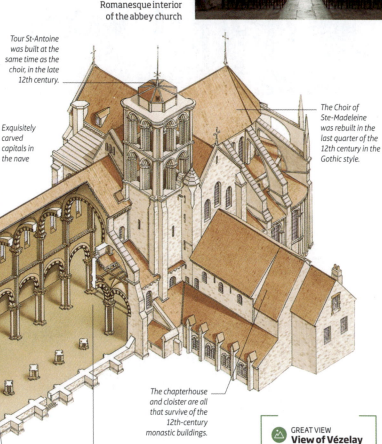

Tour St-Antoine was built at the same time as the choir, in the late 12th century.

Exquisitely carved capitals in the nave

The Choir of Ste-Madeleine was rebuilt in the last quarter of the 12th century in the Gothic style.

The chapterhouse and cloister are all that survive of the 12th-century monastic buildings.

The Crypt of Ste-Madeleine houses relics once thought to be Mary Magdalene's.

The Nave of Ste-Madeleine was rebuilt between 1120 and 1135, using alternate dark and light stone.

↑ The spectacular hilltop abbey church at Vézelay

△ GREAT VIEW
View of Vézelay

Rising up from its prominent hilltop position, the abbey dominates the area, offering splendid views of the red-rooves of Vézelay village and the surrounding countryside.

② Cathédrale St-Bénigne

🏠 Place Ste-Bénigne
🕐 8am–8pm daily
🌐 cathedrale-dijon.fr

Very little remains of this 11th-century Benedictine abbey, although beneath it lies a Romanesque crypt with a fine rotunda ringed by three circles of columns. Note that a fee applies to enter the crypt.

3

DIJON

🅰F4 🏠Côte d'Or 🚗🚌Cour de la Gare 🚊 🅹11 rue des Forges; www.destinationdijon.com

The capital of Burgundy, Dijon has a rich cultural life and a renowned university. Its centre is noted for its architectural splendour – a legacy from the dukes of Burgundy. The city is also famous for its mustard and *pain d'épices* (gingerbread).

① Musée des Beaux-Arts

🏠 Palais des Etats de Bourgogne, Cour de Bar
🕐 Oct–May: 9:30am–6pm Wed–Mon; Jun–Sep: 10am–6:30pm Wed–Mon 🔒 Public hols 🌐 beaux-arts.dijon.fr

This prestigious art collection is housed in the former Palais des Ducs, set on the magnificent place de la Liberation. The Salle des Gardes on the first floor is dominated by the giant mausoleums of the dukes, with tombs sculpted by Claus Sluter (c 1345–1405). Other exhibits include two gilded Flemish retables and a portrait of Philip the Good by Rogier van der Weyden. The collection contains a truly incredible variety of artworks: paintings by Dutch and Flemish masters; sculpture by Sluter and Rude; Swiss and German primitives; the Donation Granville of 19th-and 20th-century French art; 16th-to 18th-century French paintings; and sculptures by François Pompon. Note the ducal kitchens with six fireplaces, and the Tour Philippe le Bon, 46 m (150 ft) tall with a fine view of the city's Burgundian tiled roof tops. The museum is currently undergoing a huge restoration project; during this time some sections may be closed (see website for further details).

---

③ Musée Archéologique

🏠 5 rue du Docteur Maret 🕐 9:30am–6pm Wed–Mon 🔒 Public hols 🌐 archeologie.dijon.fr

This intriguing museum is housed in the old dormitory of the Benedictine Abbey of St Bénigne. The 11th-century chapterhouse, its stocky columns supporting a barrel-vaulted roof, houses a fine collection of Gallo-Roman sculpture. The ground floor, with its lovely fan vaulting, houses the famous head of Christ by Claus Sluter, originally from the Well of Moses.

← Dijon's elegant place de la Liberation, beautifully illuminated at sunset

STAY

Vertigo Hotel

A stylish hotel close to the city centre, with an excellent spa and a chic bar in which to wind down after sightseeing.

⌂ 3 rue Devosge
ⓦ vertigohoteldijon.com

€€€

Hostellerie du Chapeau Rouge

Set in a 19th-century building, this 28-room hotel has a superb two-star restaurant. Run by renowned chef William Frachot, the cuisine celebrates the produce of France's regions.

⌂ 5 rue Michelet
ⓦ chapeau-rouge.fr

€€€

④ Ⓜ

Chartreuse de Champmol

⌂ 1 blvd Chanoine Kir
☏ 08 92 70 05 58
🕑 10am–6pm daily

Once a Carthusian monastery built by Philip the Bold to service a dynastic burial site, this necropolis was all but destroyed during the Revolution. All that remains is a chapel doorway and the famous Well of Moses by Claus Sluter. It is located on the outskirts of the city, now in the grounds of a psychiatric hospital east of Dijon railway station – it is not very easy to find but worth the effort. The statue, representing Moses and five other prophets, is set on a hexagonal base above a basin. Sluter is renowned for his deeply cut carving and the work here is exquisitely lifelike.

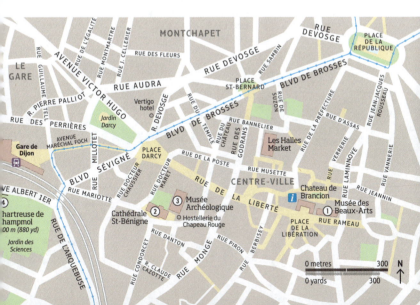

EXPERIENCE MORE

4

Auxerre

A E3 **Y** Yonne **B**
i 1-2 quai de la République
www.ot-auxerre.fr

Beautifully sited overlooking the Yonne river, Auxerre is justifiably proud of its fine churches and charming pedestrianized main square, place Charles-Surugue.

The fine Gothic Cathédrale St-Étienne took more than three centuries to build and was completed around 1560. It is famous for its intricate 13th-century stained glass. The choir, which has slender columns and *colonnettes*, represents the epitome of Gothic elegance, while on the western portals is some beautiful flamboyant sculpture sadly damaged by war and weather. The crypt is Romanesque, and adorned with 11th- to 13th-century frescoes, including one that depicts Christ riding a white horse. The severely pillaged treasury is less impressive, but does have an interesting collection of illuminated manuscripts. St Germanus, who was bishop of Auxerre during the 5th century, and mentor to St Patrick, was buried at the former

abbey church of St-Germain. The abbey was founded by Queen Clothilde, wife of Clovis, the first Christian King of France, and is an important shrine. This crypt has 11th- to 13th-century frescoes and tombs. The former abbey now houses the **Musée St-Germain** with local Gallo-Roman finds.

Musée St-Germain

⊙ **A** 2 place St-Germain
C 03 86 18 05 50 **⊙** 9am-6pm Wed-Sun (to 5pm Oct-Mar) **⊟** 1 & 8 May, 1 & 11 Nov, last week Dec

---

COLETTE

One of the greats of French literature, the avant-garde writer and actress was born in St-Sauveur-en-Puisaye, near La Puisaye-Forterre, in 1873. She is perhaps best known for her 1944 novella, *Gigi*, but it is her frank – and semi-autobiographical – treatment of married life and sexuality that launched her into notoriety. Her birthplace has now been transformed into a museum celebrating her life and work.

5

Sens

A E3 **Y** Yonne **B** ▭
i Place Jean-Jaurès; www.tourisme-sens.com

The little town of Sens, at the confluence of the rivers Yonne and Vanne, was important before Caesar came to Gaul. It was the Senones whose attempted sacking of the Roman Capitol in 390 BC was thwarted by a flock of geese.

The Cathédrale St-Étienne is the outstanding glory of Sens. Begun before 1140, it is the oldest of the great Gothic cathedrals, and its noble simplicity influenced other churches. Louis IX did the town the honour of getting married here in 1234.

The exquisite 12th- to 16th-century stained glass shows biblical scenes, including the Tree of Jesse, and a tribute to Thomas Becket, who was exiled here in 1164. His liturgical robes are in the Treasury, part of **Les Musées de Sens**, which has one of the finest collections in France.

The performing arts festival Musicasens draws crowds in July with music stages, art installations, dance classes and even a circus.

Les Musées de Sens

 135 rue des Déportés et de la Résistance ☎ 03 86 64 46 22 ⏰ 2–6pm Mon, Thu & Fri, 10am–6pm Wed, Sat & Sun ✖ Tue & public hols

Chablis

🅰 E3 🏠 Yonne 🚌 ℹ 1 rue du Maréchal de Lattre de Tassigny; www.tourisme-chablis.fr

There is no question that Chablis tastes best in Chablis. Although it is one of the most famous wine villages on earth, its narrow stone streets still have an air of sleepy prosperity. February processions in nearby Fyé, attended by the wine brotherhood of Piliers Chablisiens, honour St Vincent, patron saint of wine growers.

7

La Puisaye-Forterre

🅰 E3 🏠 Yonne, Nièvre 🚊 Auxerre, Clamecy, Bonny-sur-Loire, Cosne-Cours-sur-Loire 🚌 St-Fargeau, St-Sauveur-en-Puisaye ℹ Charny; 03 86 63 65 51

This secret forest country was immortalized by the famous author Colette (1873–1954), who was born at St-Sauveur-

↑ The Great Room in the Musée Colette in St-Sauveur-en-Puisaye

en-Puisaye in "a house that smiled only on its garden side". This 17th-century château is now the **Musée Colette**.

The best way to explore the region is on foot or by bike. Alternatively, take the *Transpoyaudin*, a 27-km (17-mile) train ride from St-Sauveur to Villiers St-Benoît.

Château de Guédelon is a 25-year project begun in 1997 to re-create a medieval castle, using only original building methods and local materials. Nearby, the real 13th-century Château de Ratilly has summer art exhibitions, concerts and music workshops. St-Amand is the centre of Puisaye stoneware, much of which was fired in the 18th-century kiln at Moutiers. The pottery and the frescoes in the churches at La Ferté-Loupière and Moutiers both used local ochre, a major export in the 19th century. The pink-brick Château de St-Fargeau housed the exiled Anne Marie Louise d'Orléans.

Musée Colette

 🏠 Château St-Sauveur-en-Puisaye ☎ 03 86 45 61 95 ⏰ Apr–Oct: 10am–6pm Wed–Mon

←

Boats on the River Yonne, in the heart of the historic town of Auxerre

STAY

Maison Lameloise
Impeccable, spacious rooms and three-Michelin-star dining.

🅰 F4 🏠 36 place d'Armes, Chagny lameloise.fr

€€€

La Montagne de Brancion
A countryside escape with Mâconnais views.

🅰 F4 🏠 Martailly-les-Brancion, Tournu lamontagne debrancion.com

€€€

Hotel Le Cep
This Old-Town-centre spot also has one of the city's best restaurants.

🅰 E4–F4 🏠 27 Rue Maufoux, Beaune hotel-cep-beaune.com

€€€

Hostellerie des Clos
Enjoy cheery rooms and Michelin-starred food in a converted almshouse.

🅰 E3 🏠 18 rue Jules Rathier, Chablis hostellerie-des-clos.fr

€€€

 The whirling waters of the Fosse gush through the centre of Tonnerre

corner tower, an intriguing painted ceiling (in the School of Fontainebleau), showing antique divinities as famous characters of the 16th century, such as Diane de Poitiers, the notorious mistress of Henry II, as Venus.

Château d'Ancy-le-Franc

🅰E3 🚗Yonne 🕐Apr–Nov: 10:30am–5pm Tue–Sun (Jul–Aug: to 6pm) 🌐chateau-ancy.com

The Renaissance façade of the Château d'Ancy-le-Franc gives an austere impression, but its inner courtyard has rich ornamentation. The château was built for the Duke of Clermont-Tonnerre during the 1540s by the Italian Sebastiano Serlio.

The interior was decorated by Primaticcio and others of the Fontainebleau School. Diane de Poitiers, who was the duke's sister-in-law, is portrayed in the Chambre de Judith et Holophernes. Diane's apartments, including her bedroom, can also be visited.

8

Tonnerre

🅰E3 🚗Yonne 🚉 ℹ️Pl Marguerite de Bourgogne; www.tourisme-tonnerre.fr

The mystical cloudy-green spring of Fosse Dionne is a good reason to visit the small town of Tonnerre. Here, an astonishing volume of water bursts up from the ground into an 18th-century washing place. Due to its depth and strong currents, it has never been thoroughly explored and local legend has it that a serpent lives on undisturbed.

The **Hôtel-Dieu**, the first of its kind in France, is 150 years older than its more famous counterpart in Beaune (p329). It was founded by Margaret of Burgundy in 1293 to care for

the poor. In the Revolution it lost its tiling, but the barrel-vaulted oak ceiling survived.

Hôtel-Dieu

🅰Place Marguerite de Bourgogne 📞03 86 55 44 23 🕐10am–6pm daily 🚫public hols

9

Château de Tanlay

🅰E3 🚗2 grande rue Basse, Tanlay 📞03 86 75 70 61 🕐Mar–Nov: 10am–5pm Wed–Sun (only via guided tour)

Built in the mid-16th century, the moated Château de Tanlay is a beautiful Renaissance edifice, with a trompe l'oeil in the Grande Galerie and, in the

11

Châtillon-sur-Seine

🅰E3–F3 🚗Côte d'Or 🚉 ℹ️Rue du Bourg; www.chatillonnais-tourisme.fr

World War II left Châtillon a ruin, hence the town's largely modern aspect. But the past is still present in the **Musée du Pays du Châtillonnais**, where the Vix treasure is displayed. In 1953, the tomb of a Gaulish princess, from the 6th century BC, was discovered near Vix at Mont Lassois. It held a trove of jewellery and artifacts of Greek origin that included a

> To the north is Château de Bussy-Rabutin, its highly individualistic decor created by the spiteful 17th-century soldier and wit Roger de Bussy-Rabutin.

GREAT VIEW
Flavigny-sur-Ozerain

Famous for its aniseed imperial sweets (and as the setting for the film *Chocolat*), this village's red roofs and church are a striking sight against the lush countryside.

stunning bronze vase, 164-cm-(66-in-) high, and weighing 208 kg (459 lb). Also of interest in the town is the Romanesque Église St-Vorles, containing an *Entombment* with a splendidly sculpted depiction of Christ and his mourners (1527).

Nearby are the sources of the River Seine, which rises between St-Seine-l'Abbaye and Chanceau, and its tributary, the River Douix. Each of the sources is marked by a beautiful grotto.

Musée du Pays du Châtillonnais

Rue de la Libération
Jul & Aug: 10am–5:30pm daily; Sep–Jun: Wed–Mon
Public hols musee-vix.fr

12
Alise-Ste-Reine

E3-F3 Côte d'Or 1 Av de la Gare, Venarey-Les Laumes 21150; www.alesia-tourisme.net

Above this village, Mont Auxois was the site of Caesar's final victory over the heroic Gaulish chieftain Vercingétorix in 52 BC after a six-week siege. The first excavations, undertaken in the mid-19th century, uncovered vestiges of a thriving Gallo-Roman town, with a theatre and forum. Within the **Alésia MuséoParc** is a good historical discovery centre with multimedia displays and reconstructions of siege engines.

Alise is dominated by Aimé Millet's gigantic moustachioed statue of Vercingétorix, placed here in 1865 to commemorate the first excavations. Cynics point out the uncanny resemblance to Napoleon III, who

A display showing medieval battle lines in the Alésia MuséoParc's discovery centre *(inset)* ↓

sponsored the dig. To the south lies the pretty village of Flavigny-sur-Ozerain, and to the north is **Château de Bussy-Rabutin,** its highly individualistic decor created by the spiteful 17th-century soldier and wit Roger de Bussy-Rabutin while exiled from Louis XIV's court. One room is dedicated to portraits of his many mistresses, as well as some made-up ones.

Alésia MuséoParc

Rue de l'Hôpital
Feb–Nov: 10am–5pm daily (to 6pm Jul & Aug)
alesia.com

Château de Bussy-Rabutin

Bussy-le-Grand
9:15am–5pm daily
Public hols chateau-bussy-rabutin.fr

⓭ Morvan

 E4 🐾 Yonne, Côte d'Or, Nièvre, Saône-et-Loire ✈ Dijon 🚉 Autun, Mombard 🚌 Château-Chinon, Saulieu, Avallon 🛈 6 blvd République, Château-Chinon; Maison du Parc, St-Brisson; www.tourisme.parcdu morvan.org

Morvan is a Celtic word for "Black Mountain", which is a good description of this area when seen from afar. The immense, sparsely inhabited plateau of granite suddenly appears in the centre of the Burgundy hills and farmland. Stretching roughly north to south, it gains altitude as it proceeds southwards, to a culminating point of 901 m (2,956 ft) at Haut-Folin.

The area's two sources of natural wealth are abundant water and dense forests of oak, beech and conifer. Lumber was once floated out of the area to Paris via a network of lakes and rivers. Today it travels by truck, and the Yonne, Cure and Cousin rivers are instead used for recreation and pro-ducing hydroelectric power.

The Morvan has always been a poor, remote area. Its largest towns, Château-Chinon in the centre and Saulieu on the outskirts, have barely 3,000 inhabitants. Its remoteness made it an ideal refuge for the French Resistance during World War II. Today it's a Regional Nature Park, and the main attraction is its wildness. Information on a wide variety of outdoor activities, including cycling, canoeing, skiing and horse trekking, is available from the Maison du Parc at St-Brisson, where there is also the very moving **Musée de la Résistance**. There are plenty of short walking trails, and two well-signed long-distance paths: the GR13 (Vézelay to Autun) and the Tour du Morvan par les Grands Lacs.

Musée de la Résistance

🚾 🐾 Maison du Parc, St-Brisson ⏰ Mar–Nov: 10am–6pm Wed–Sun (daily in July–Aug) 🆆 musee resistancemorvan.fr

---

⓮ Avallon

 E3 🐾 Yonne 🚉🚌 🛈 6 rue Bocquillo; www. avallon-morvan.com

This fine old fortified town is on a granite spur between two ravines by the River Cousin. The town is a quiet, peaceful place and full of charming details. The main

HIDDEN GEM
Château de Bazoches

Southwest of Avallon, this 12th-century castle was given by Louis XIV to the famed military strategist Maréchal de Vauban, who transformed it into a garrison.

monument is the 12th-century Romanesque Église St-Lazare, with two handsome, carved doorways. The larger of the two illustrates the 12 signs of the zodiac, the labours of the month, and the horsemen of the Apocalypse. The nave is decorated with sophisticated acanthus capitals and polychrome statuary.

The **Musée de l'Avallonnais** has an intricate Venus mosaic from the 2nd century AD, Georges Rouault's (1871–1958) Expressionist series of etchings, the *Miserere*, and pieces by the renowned silversmith Jean Després.

Musée de l'Avallonnais

🚾 🐾 🏛 5 rue du College ⏰ Mid-Feb–mid-Nov: 2–6pm Wed–Sun 🆆 musee avallonnais.com

↑ Statuary in the vaulted Musée de la Faïence et des Beaux Arts

version of the story of Balaam and his donkey waylaid by the Angel.

16

Nevers

A E4 **A** Nièvre **R R**
i Palais Ducal, rue Sabatier; www.nevers-tourisme.com

Like all Burgundian towns on the Loire, Nevers should be approached from the west side of the river to see the noble site at its best angle. Though lacking historical importance, the town has much to offer. Considered to be the earliest of the Loire

Did You Know?

Saulieu-born sculptor François Pompon gained fame at age 67 for his *L'Ours Blanc* (White Bear).

15

Saulieu

A E4 **A** Côte d'Or **R R**
i 24 Rue d'Argentine; www.saulieu.fr

On the edge of the Morvan, Saulieu has been a shrine of Burgundian cooking since the 17th century, when it was a staging post on the Paris to Lyon coach road.

Stylized animal sculptures of François Pompon feature among the exhibits at the Musée Pompon, which also houses a collection of Gallo-Roman stelae. The early 12th-century Romanesque Basilique St-Andoche has decorated capitals with representations of the Flight into Egypt and a comical

← A misty stroll on a path through the ancient woodland of Morvan

châteaux, the Palais Ducal has a long Renaissance façade framed by polygonal towers and a broad esplanade. The Romanesque 11th-century Église St-Étienne has graceful monolithic columns and a wreath of radiating chapels. In the crypt of the Gothic Cathédrale St-Cyr is a 16th-century sculpted *Entombment* and foundations of a 6th-century baptistry, discovered in 1944 after heavy bombing. The contemporary stained-glass is noteworthy.

The overlordship of Nevers passed to the Gonzaga family during the 16th century. They brought with them an Italian school of artists skilled in faïence-making and glass-blowing. The industry remains and modern pottery is still traditionally decorated in blue, white, yellow and green, with its curious trademark, the green arabesque knot, or *noeud vert*. It can best be seen at the **Musée de la Faïence et des Beaux Arts**.

Just south of Nevers, the 19th-century Pont du Guetin carries the Loire Canal across the Allier river. Industrial use has waned, but it is still used by pleasure craft. The church at St-Parize-le-Châtel has a jolly menagerie sculpted onto the capitals of the crypt.

Musée de la Faïence et des Beaux Arts
⊗ ⊙ **A** 16 rue St-Genest
◷ May-Sep: 10am-6pm Tue-Sun; Oct-Apr: 1-5:30pm Tue-Fri **w** musee-faiance. nevers.fr

---

THE GOLDEN AGE OF BURGUNDY

While the French Capetian dynasty fought in the Hundred Years' War, the dukes of Burgundy built up one of Europe's most powerful states, which included Flanders and some parts of Holland. From the time of Philip the Bold (1342-1404), the ducal court became a cultural force, supporting many of Europe's finest artists, such as the sculptor Claus Sluter and painter Rogier van der Weyden. The dominions of the duchy were, however, broken up following the death of Duke Charles the Bold in 1477, with most of Burgundy annexed to France, and the northernmost part of the empire taken by the Habsburgs.

Côte d'Or vineyards, stretching across the Burgundy landscape

17 Semur-en-Auxois

 E3 Côte d'Or 2 place Gaveau www. tourisme-semur.fr

Approached from the west, Semur-en-Auxois comes as a surprise on an otherwise uneventful road. Its massive round bastions, built in the 14th century (one with an unnerving gash in it) suddenly appear, towering over the Pont Joly and the peaceful River Armançon.

The Église Notre-Dame dates from the 13th and 14th centuries, and was modelled on the cathedral of Auxerre. The fragile high walls had to be restored in the 15th and 19th centuries. The church contains a tympanum with the legend of Doubting Thomas on the north doorway to the 15th-century *Entombment* by Antoine le Moiturier. The stained glass presents the legend of St Barbara, and the work of different guilds such as butchers and drapers.

Époisses is the site of the moated **Château d'Époisses**, its 11th- to 18th-century construction blending medieval towers with fine Renaissance details, and a huge dovecote. Époisses is also the home of one of Burgundy's most revered cheeses, available at the local café or fromagerie.

Château d'Époisses

 Epoisses Jul & Aug: 10am, noon, 3 and 6pm (via guided tours only) Wed–Mon chateau depoisses.com

18 Côte d'Or

F4 Côte d'Or Dijon Dijon, Nuits-St-Georges, Beaune, Santenay Dijon; www.cotedor-tourisme.com

In winemaking terms, the Côte d'Or includes the Côte de Beaune and the Côte de Nuits in a nearly unbroken line of vines from Dijon to Santenay.

The imposing façade of Eglise Notre-Dame in Semur-en-Auxois

> HIDDEN GEM
> **Maison Joseph Drouhin**
>
> This winemaker's *cave* in the Côte d'Or has Roman remains, and during World War II, its owner, a Resistance fighter, fled the gestapo through a tunnel here to the Hospices de Beaune.

Squeezed into the flat plain of the Saône to the southeast and a plateau of woodland to the northwest, this narrow escarpment is about 50 km (30 miles) long. The grapes of the foremost Burgundy vineyards grow in the golden reddish soil of the slope, which has given the area its name.

The classification of the characteristics of the land is fabulously elaborate, but for the layman a rule of thumb is that 95 per cent of the best vines are on the uphill side of the D974 thoroughfare. The placenames on the signposts here haunt the dreams of wine lovers the world over: Gevrey-Chambertin, Vougeot, Chambolle-Musigny, Vosne-Romanée, Meursault and Chassagne Montrachet.

→

The honey-stoned Old Town of Beaune in the golden glow of sunlight

19 Beaune

A E4-F4 **☐** Côte d'Or **☐☐**
ℹ 6 blvd Perpeuil; www.
beaune-tourisme.fr

The old centre of Beaune, snug within its ramparts and encircling boulevards, is very walkable. Its indisputable treasure is the Hospices de Beaune, while the Hôtel des Ducs de Bourgogne, built in the 14th–16th centuries, houses the **Musée du Vin de Bourgogne**. Behind its flamboyant façade is an interesting display of traditional winemaking equipment.

Further to the north lies the Collégiale Notre-Dame, begun in the early 12th century. The mainly Romanesque church contains five very fine 15th-century tapestries. With some hints of early Renaissance style, they delicately illustrate the life of the Virgin Mary in 19 scenes.

Musée du Vin de Bourgogne

⊘ **☐** Rue d'Enfer **☎** 03 80 22 08 19 **☐** 10am–6pm Wed–Sun (also Mon Apr–Sep) **☐** Dec–mid-Mar

---

20 Brionnais

A E4 **☐** Saône-et-Loire
✈ Mâcon **☐** Paray-le-Monial, Roanne **☐** Paray-le-Monial **ℹ** Marcigny; 03 85 25 39 06

A small, peaceful rural district, the Brionnais, grazed by white Charolais cattle, is squeezed between the River Loire and the Beaujolais foothills in the far south of Burgundy.

The area has an abundance of Romanesque churches, most built of the local ochre-hued stone. The 11th-century church of Anzy-le-Duc has a majestic three-tiered polygonal tower and exquisitely carved capitals. At Semur-en-Brionnais, the birthplace of Cluny's abbot St Hugues, the church was inspired by his

monastery, while the church at St-Julien-de-Jonzy has a very finely carved tympanum.

A small town by the River Genette, La Clayette is graced by a château (not open) set in a lake. In nearby Curbigny is the 18th-century Château de Drée, with its Louis XV and Louis XVI salons and chapel.

Southeast of La Clayette, lonely Montagne de Dun rises just over 700 m (2,300 ft) and offers a panoramic view. Full of sleepy corners and quiet byways, this is one of the best places to picnic in Burgundy.

ANNUAL CHARITY WINE AUCTION

Wine lovers will know of the Hospices de Beaune wine auction, which has been held at this famous medieval hospital each November since 1859. It is one of the most prestigious events in the wine calendar of France, and all of the proceeds go to the modern hospital and various charities. In the 2015 auction, the most expensive barrel ever sold went for €117,700 (£83,300).

Autumn mist rising from a vineyard on Burgundy's Côte d'Or

㉑

Cluny

F4 ⬜ Saône-et-Loire ⬚
ℹ 6 rue Mercière; www.
cluny-tourisme.com

The little town of Cluny is overshadowed by the ruins of its great abbey. The **Ancienne Abbaye de Cluny** was once the most powerful monastic foundation in Europe. It was founded by William the Pious, Duke of Aquitaine, in 910, and within 200 years Cluny had become head of a major reforming order with monasteries all over Europe. Its abbots were considered to be as powerful as monarchs or popes, and four of them are venerated as saints. But by the 14th century, the system was in decline. The abbey was closed in 1790 and the church was later dismantled.

The guided tour presents the abbey remains, notably the Clocher de l'Eau Bénite (Holy Water Bell Tower); the remains of figured capitals, displayed in the 13th-century flour store; and the **Musée d'Art et Archéologie**, in the former abbot's palace.

Also in the town is the lovely 12th-century Église St-Marcel. To the southwest, you'll find a chapel in Berzé-la-Ville decorated with numerous superb 12th-century frescoes, similar to those that would once have been seen at Cluny.

> Cluny had become the head of a major reforming order with monasteries all over Europe. Its abbots were considered to be as powerful as monarchs or popes.

Ancienne Abbaye de Cluny

♿ 🎫 🚻 ⬜ Place due 11 Août 1944 🕐 9:30am–6pm daily (to 7pm Jul & Aug) 🚫 Public hols 🌐 cluny-abbaye.fr

Musée d'Art et Archéologie

♿ ⬜ Palais Jean de Bourbon 🕐 9:30am–6pm daily (to 7pm Jul & Aug) 🚫 Public hols 🌐 cluny-abbaye.fr

㉒

Autun

E4 ⬜ Saône-et-Loire 🚆🚌 ℹ 13 rue Général Demetz; www.autun-tourisme.com

Augustodunum, the town of Augustus, was founded in the late 1st century BC. It was a great centre of learning, with a population four times what it is today. Its theatre, built in the 1st century AD, could seat 20,000 people.

Today Autun is still a delight, deserving of gastronomic as well as cultural investigation. The Cathédrale St-Lazare was built in the 12th century and is notable for its range of impressive sculptures, most of them the work of the mysterious 12th-century artist Gislebertus. He sculpted both the capitals inside the cathedral and the glorious Last Judgment tympanum over the main portal. This masterpiece, called a "Romanesque Cézanne" by André Malraux, survived destruction in the Revolution because it had been plastered over during the 18th century.

Inside, some of the capitals can be seen close up in the Salle Capitulaire. Look also for the sculpture of Pierre Jeannin and his wife. Jeannin was the president of the Dijon parliament that prevented mass anti-Huejonot violence from spreading, with the perceptive observation, "the commands of very angry monarchs should be obeyed very slowly".

The collection of medieval art in the **Musée Rolin** includes the bas-relief *Temptation of Eve* by Gislebertus, the 15th-century painted stone

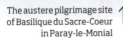

The austere pilgrimage site of Basilique du Sacre-Coeur in Paray-le-Monial ↑

Virgin of Autun and the *Nativity of Cardinal Rolin* by the Master of Moulins, from about 1480.

The Porte St-André and Porte d'Arroux, and the ruins of the Théâtre Romain and the Temple de Janus, recall Autun's glorious Roman past.

Musée Rolin

 3 rue des Bancs 03 85 52 09 76 10am–5pm Wed–Mon Dec–mid-Feb, public hols

---

23

Paray-le-Monial

E4 Saône-et-Loire 25 av Jean-Paul II; www.tourisme-paraylemonial.fr

Dedicated to the cult of the Sacred Heart of Jesus, the Basilique du Sacré-Coeur has made Paray-le-Monial one of the most important sites of pilgrimage in modern France. Marguerite-Marie Alacoque, who was born here in 1647, had rather gory visions, from which the cult later developed, and swept across France during the 19th century. The church is a small version of the now-lost abbey church of Cluny.

The **Musée du Hiéron** provides insight into industrial artistic tile production that took place here during the 19th and 20th centuries.

Situated on place Guignaud is the ornate Maison Jayet, dating from the 16th century, which houses the town hall.

Musée du Hiéron

13 rue de la Pais Mid-Mar–Dec paraylemonial.fr/le-musee-du-hieron

---

24

Tournus

F4 Saône-et-Loire Place de l'Abbaye; www.tournugeois.fr

Jewel of Tournus, the Abbaye de St-Philibert is one of Burgundy's oldest and greatest Romanesque buildings. It was founded by a group of monks from Noirmoutier, who had been driven from their island by invading Normans in the 9th century, and brought with them relics of their patron saint, Philibert (still in the choir). Rebuilt in the 10th–12th centuries, the well-fortified abbey church is made from pale pink stone, with black-and-white vaulting inside.

The 17th-century Hôtel-Dieu has its original rooms complete with the furniture, equipment and pharmacy on display. It also houses the **Musée Greuze**, dedicated to Tournus's most famous son, the artist Jean-Baptiste Greuze (1725–1805).

 Dusk falling on the towers of Abbaye de St-Philibert at Tournus

Southwest of Tournus lies the Mâconnais landscape of hills, vineyards, orchards, red-tiled farmhouses and Romanesque churches. Brancion is a pretty hill village, Chapaize has an 11th-century church and there is a sumptuous Renaissance château at Cormatin. The village of Taizé is the centre of a world-famous ecumenical community.

To the north, Chalon-sur-Saône features the Musée Niépce, dedicated to the inventor of photography, Nicéphore Niépce (1765–1833), who was born in the city.

Musée Greuze

21 rue de l'Hôpital Apr–Oct: 10am–1pm & 2–6pm Wed–Sun 1 May musee-greuze.fr.

 INSIDER TIP
St-Vincent Tournante

Each January a different Burgundy village hosts this celebration of all aspects of winemaking, with a procession of the 100 robed *confreries* (guilds) that then host wine tastings.

The glorious Cascade l'Eventail, which cuts the River Hérisson

quarter in the centre of town, full of winding alleys, houses that date back to the 15th century and quiet courtyards. Place aux Fleurs offers a good view of this part of town and the mossy-roofed, 16th-century Église Notre-Dame.

Southeast of Dole is the 18th-century Château d'Arlay, with immaculate gardens.

Arc-et-Senans

⚠F4 ⬆Doubs 🚉 ℹ3A rue de la Saline; www.destinationlouelison.com

A World Heritage Site since 1982, the Saline Royale (Royal Saltworks) at Arc-et-Senans were designed by the great French architect Claude-Nicolas Ledoux (1736–1806). He envisaged concentric circles around the main buildings, but the only ones to be completed (in 1775) were those used for the production of salt. Nevertheless, these show the staggering scale of his idea: salt water was to be piped from Salins-les-Bains

Cascades du Hérisson

⚠F4 ⬆Jura ℹClairvaux-les-Lacs; 03 84 25 27 47

The village of Doucier, at the foot of the Pic de l'Aigle, is the starting point for the valley of the River Hérisson, one of the finest natural settings in the Jura. Park by Moulin Jacquand and walk up the trail through the woods to a spectacular waterfall, the 65-m (213-ft) Cascade de L'Eventail, and beyond to view the equally impressive Cascade du Grand

> 📷 PICTURE PERFECT
> **Cliffs of Solutré**
>
> This gigantic limestone escarpment rises up over the Pouilly-Fuissé vineyards 8 km (5 miles) west of Mâcon. Long before there was wine here, it was inhabited during the Mousterian era, 52,000 years ago.

Saut. The walk, which takes about two hours there and back, is steep at times and can be slippery, so suitable footwear is essential.

Dole

⚠F4 ⬆Jura 🚉🚌 ℹ6 place Grévy; www.tourisme-paysdedole.fr

The busy town of Dole lies where the River Doubs meets the Rhine-Rhône canal. The former capital of the Comté was always a symbol of the region's resistance to the French. The people here were used to relative independence, first under the counts of Burgundy and then within the Holy Roman Empire. Though always French-speaking, its people did not appreciate the idea of the French absolute monarchy and during 1636 endured a very long siege; the town eventually submitted. There is a charming old nearby, and fuel to reduce it was to come from the Chaux forest. The enterprise was never a success and closed in 1895, but the buildings can be visited. The **Musée Ledoux Lieu du Sel** displays intriguing models of the grand projects.

Musée Ledoux Lieu du Sel

♻ ⊘ 🏠 Saline Royale 📞 03 81 54 45 45 🕐 9am–7pm daily 🚫 1 Jan, 25 Dec

---

28

Mâcon

🅰 F4 🚍 Saône-et-Loire ✈🚌🚗 ℹ 1 pl Saint Pierre; www.macon-tourism.com

At the frontier between the south and Burgundy, Mâcon is an industrial town and wine centre on the River Saône.

Its lack of churches is due to fervent anti-clericalism during the Revolution, when 14 were destroyed. A 17th-century convent, now the **Musée des Ursulines**, has Flemish and French paintings and exhibits on prehistoric Solutré. On the place aux Herbes, where the market is held, the Maison de Bois is a wooden building covered with bizarre carvings.

Outside of town, the Roche de Solutré rises dramatically above the Pouilly-Fuissé vineyards in the Mâconnais district. Below the rock, finds from the Stone Age have established it as a major archaeological site.

Mâconnais is also the land of Romantic poet Lamartine (1790–1869). Born in Mâcon, he spent his childhood at Milly Lamartine and later lived at Château de St-Point. Château de Pierreclos is associated with his epic poem *Jocelyn*.

Musée des Ursulines

⊘ 🏠 allée de Matisco 📞 03 85 39 90 38 🕐 10am–6pm Tue–Sat 🚫 Public hols

---

29

Arbois

🅰 F4 🚍 Jura 🚉 ℹ 17 rue de l'Hôtel de Ville; www. tourisme.arbois.com

This jolly wine town on the vine-covered banks of the Cuisance is famous for sherry-like *vin jaune* (yellow wine). On the north side of the town is the preserved house and laboratory of Louis Pasteur (1822–95), the first person to test vaccines on humans.

EAT

Les Deux Ponts
A friendly place with a sunny terrace, serving local produce and wine.

🅰 E3 🏠 1 Rte de Vézelay, Pierre-Perthuis 🌐 lesdeuxpoints.com

€€€

La Dame d'Aquitaine
Modern cuisine served in an atmospheric 13th-century crypt.

🅰 F3 🏠 23 Pl Bossuet, Dijon 🌐 ladame daquitaine.fr

€€€

Le Montrachet
Skilfully created and authentic local classics and haute cuisine.

🅰 E4–F4 🏠 10 pl du Pasquier de la Fontaine, Puligny-Montrachet 🌐 le-montrachet.com

€€€

↑ Maison de Louis Pasteur, in the town of Arbois, containing the great scientist's laboratory

→ Le Corbusier's winged, sculptural Chapelle Notre-Dame-du-Haut

 30

Ronchamp

[A] G3 **[A]** Haute-Saône **[□]**
[i] 25 rue Le Corbusier;
www.ot-ronchamp.fr

Le Corbusier's Chapelle Notre-Dame-du-Haut, built in 1954, dominates this former miners' town. More sculpture than building, its swelling concrete form was built on an old pilgrimage site, which had been destroyed during the Second World War, and has become one of his most iconic designs. The curved roof is held by support columns hidden in the walls; inside, light, shape and space form a unity.

There is also a Musée de la Mine evoking the industry and the lives of local miners.

31

Champlitte

[A] F3 **[A]** Haute-Saône **[□]**
[i] 2 allée du Sainfoin;
www.ot-champlitte.fr

In the small and charming town of Champlitte, the captivating **Musée des Arts et Traditions Populaires** was created by a local shepherd, who collected artifacts connected with disappearing local customs. One of the most poignant displays housed in this Renaissance château recalls the emigration of 400 citizens to Mexico in the mid-19th century.

Musée des Arts et Traditions Populaires

 [A] 7 rue de l'Église
[C] 03 84 95 76 50 **[O]** Apr-Sep: 9:30am-6pm Wed-Fri; Oct-Mar: 2-5pm Wed-Fri
[X] Dec-Feb

32

Ornans

[A] F4 **[A]** Doubs **[□]** **[i]** 7 rue Pierre Vernier; www.destinationlouelison.com

The great Realist painter Gustave Courbet was born at Ornans in 1819. Throughout his career, he painted the town in every possible light. His *Enterrement à Ornans* proved to be one of the most influential paintings of the 19th century. Courbet's work is displayed in three historic buildings, including his childhood home, which make up the **Musée Courbet**.

A canoeist's paradise, the Vallée de la Loue is the loveliest in the Jura. The D67 follows the river from Ornans eastwards to Ouhans, from where it is only a 15-minute walk to its magnificent source. Various belvederes along the way offer splendid views over the surrounding area.

Southwest of Ornans, the spectacular Source du Lison is a 20-minute walk from Nans-sous-Ste-Anne.

Musée Courbet

[A] Pl Robert Fernier
[O] 9am-5pm Wed-Mon
[X] Public hols **[w]** musee-courbet.doubs.fr

Did You Know?

Courbet's infamous painting, *A Burial at Ornans*, measures 3 m by 6 m (12 ft by 25 ft)

along the same street are the birthplaces of novelist Victor Hugo (1802–85) at No 140 and the Lumière brothers at place Victor Hugo. Behind Porte Noire, a Roman arch, is the 12th-century Cathédrale St-Jean. In its bell tower is the truly fascinating **Horloge Astronomique** with its automatons that pop out on the hour. The stunning **Musée des Beaux-Arts et d'Archéologie**, in the old corn market, houses a well-curated collection of works by world-renowned artists such as Rubens, Fragonard, Cranach, Ingres, Goya, Matisse and Picasso.

Vauban's impressive citadel, overlooking the River Doubs, has great views, plus three museums, including the wonderful **Musée Comtois**, with a collection of local artifacts, and a natural history museum with a "wild" insectarium and an aquarium.

33

Besançon

F4 🏛 Doubs 🚍 🛫 🛈 2 pl de la Première Armée Française; www.besancon-tourisme.com

Besançon supplanted Dole as the capital of the Franche-Comté in the 17th century. It began as an ecclesiastical centre and is now an industrial one, specializing in precision engineering. The stately architecture of the old town, with its elegant wrought-iron work, is a 17th-century legacy.

Behind the Renaissance façade of the Palais Granvelle, in the Grande Rue, is the **Musée du Temps**, a fine collection of time-pieces of all ages – a tribute to Besançon's renown as a clock- and watchmaking centre. An interactive exhibition on the third floor invites reflection on the relativity of the notion of time. Further

Musée du Temps

🕑 🅿 🏛 Palais Granvelle, 96 Grande Rue 🕒 9:15am–6pm Tue–Sun 🚫 Public hols 🌐 mdt.besancon.fr

Horloge Astronomique

🕑 🅿 🏛 Rue de la Convention 🕒 9:50am–5:30pm Wed–Mon 🚫 Nov, public hols 🌐 horloge-astronomique-besancon.fr

Musée des Beaux-Arts et d'Archéologie

🅿 🏛 1 pl de la Révolution 🕒 2–6pm Mon–Fri; 10am–6pm Sat & Sun (free Sun) 🌐 mbaa.besancon.fr

Musée Comtois

🕑 🅿 🏛 La Citadelle, rue des Fusillés de la Résistance 🕒 Sep–Jun: 10am–5pm daily; Jul & Aug: 9am–7pm daily 🚫 3 weeks in Jan 🌐 citadelle.com

---

A BURIAL AT ORNANS

Artist Gustave Courbet, born in Ornans in 1819, led the Realism movement. His *A Burial At Ornans* (1850) precipitated a change in French art. It depicts the funeral of his great uncle at Ornans with unflattering realism on an immense scale previously reserved for significant religious, heroic or mythological scenes. Its debut provoked outrage, but brought him instant fame. You can now see the painting at the Musée d'Orsay in Paris (*p136*).

34

Belfort

G3 🏛 Territoire de Belfort 🚍 🛫 🕒 Wed–Sun 🛈 2 bis rue Clemenceau; www.belfort-tourisme.com

The symbol of Belfort is an enormous pink sandstone lion. It was built (rather than carved) by Frédéric-Auguste Bartholdi (1834–1904), whose other major undertaking was the Statue of Liberty.

Belfort's immensely strong citadel, designed by Vauban under Louis XIV, withstood three sieges, in 1814, 1815 and 1870. Today this remarkable array of fortifications provides an interesting walk and extensive views of the surroundings. The well-presented Musée d'Histoire is housed in the citadel and displays models of the original fortifications, as well as regional art and local artifacts.

The great lounging lion of Belfort, a magnificent beast sculpted from pink sandstone

THE MASSIF CENTRAL

The Massif Central is an area of strange, wild beauty – a huge central plateau of ancient granite and crystalline rock that embraces the dramatic landscapes of the Auvergne, Limousin, Aveyron, and Lozère regions. The Averni, of which Auvergne was named after, was one of the most powerful and wealthy Gallic tribes in all of Gaul and established successful fortified communities here. The Romans took advantage of the local therapeutic springs in what would become Vichy, in the 1st century BC. In the 10th century, steep volcanic pinnacles were capped with Romanesque churches and medieval homes at Le Puy-en-Velay, a provincial city popular with pilgrims during the Middle Ages. In 1527, Auvergne united with the French crown, and 60 years later that unity was cemented with the crowning of Henry IV, the first of the Bourbons to be king of France. With the exception of the Napoleoonic era, his direct descendants ruled France until 1830, when Charles X was deposed. The region's many hot springs, at Vichy and Aubusson, became popoular once again with the wealthy in the 1860s. In 1907, local wine-growers protested poor sales and, in an effort to secure their own fortunes, began creating wine-making cooperatives, which continue to flourish.

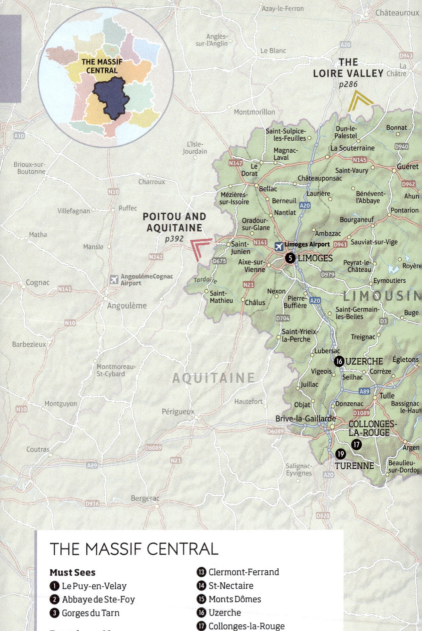

THE LOIRE VALLEY
p286

POITOU AND
AQUITAINE
p392

THE MASSIF CENTRAL

Must Sees
1. Le Puy-en-Velay
2. Abbaye de Ste-Foy
3. Gorges du Tarn

Experience More
4. Aubusson
5. Limoges
6. Montluçon
7. Moulins
8. Vichy
9. Château de La Palice
10. Issoire
11. Thiers
12. Orcival

13. Clermont-Ferrand
14. St-Nectaire
15. Monts Dômes
16. Uzerche
17. Collonges-la-Rouge
18. Turenne
19. Monts Dore
20. Monts du Cantal
21. La Chaise-Dieu
22. Salers
23. Vallée du Lot
24. Rodez
25. Parc National des Cévennes
26. Grands Causses

Did You Know?

Isabelle Romée, the mother of Joan of Arc, is said to have visited St-Michel d'Aighilhe in 1429.

Bird's-eye view of Le Puy, with the Chapelle St-Michel d'Aiguilhe soaring above the town ↑

❶

LE PUY-EN-VELAY

⚠ E5 🏠 Haute-Loire 🚇🚌📮 ℹ️ 2 pl de Clauzel; www.lepuyenvelay-tourisme.fr

Teetering on a series of rocky outcrops and basalt pillars within a volcanic cone, Le Puy-en-Velay is one of France's most dramatic sights and a UNESCO World Heritage Site. Each of the town's three peaks is topped by a landmark church or statue.

Le Puy is famous for its eponymous lentils, lacemaking and for being one of the starting points of the pilgrimage to Santiago de Compostela. Among the first pilgrims was the town's bishop, Gotescalk, who made the journey in 950 and built the Chapelle St-Michel d'Aiguilhe in 962. Seeming to grow out of a giant finger of lava rock and reached by a steep climb, the church is thought to be located on the site of a Roman temple to Mercury. Before setting off, pilgrims used to assemble at the Cathédrale de Notre-Dame, perched on the town's second peak, with its famous Black Madonna and "fever stone" – a Druidic ceremonial stone. Worth a visit is the Musée Crozatier, in the lower city, which has a collection of handmade lace from the 16th century to the present.

←

The 1860 Notre-Dame-de-France statue, set atop Le Puy's third hill, the Rocher Corneille

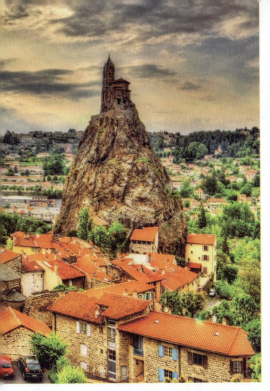

THE BIRD KING

In September, Le Puy transforms itself for its exuberant masked Renaissance carnival, the annual Bird King Festival *(www.roide loiseau.com)*. For four days the streets are given over to magic, theatre, music and food. At the heart of it all is a revival of an old festival from the days of François I: an archery contest whose winner is dubbed the Bird King.

 A Puy lacemaker demonstrating her craft, tatting fine threads with multiple bobbins, at her stall in the rue des Tables

 INSIDER TIP
Let There Be Light

On summer evenings a dazzling high-tech digital light show called the Puy de Lumières *(puydelumieres.fr)* sets six of the town's iconic sights ablaze with breathtaking colour.

↑ The statue of the revered Black Madonna at the Cathédrale de Notre-Dame

ABBAYE DE STE-FOY

A D5-6 **A** Aveyron **🚌** To St-Christophe, then a bus **ℹ** Pl de l'Eglise **🕐** Museum: 10am-noon & 2-6pm daily (from 9:30am & to 6:30pm Apr-Sep) **W** tourisme-conques.fr

The splendid Abbaye de Ste-Foy, in the village of Conques, is situated on a rugged site against the leafy hillside. Ste Foy was a young girl who was killed for refusing to participate in pagan rituals; she became an early Christian martyr. Her relics were first kept at a rival monastery in Agen, but in the 9th century a monk from Conques stole the relics, attracting pilgrims to this remote spot and establishing the site as a halt on the Camino de Santiago, en route to Santiago de Compostela.

The austerely simple Romanesque abbey church has beautiful modern stained-glass windows, added by noted French artist Pierre Soulages in 1994, and a tympanum that is a triumph of medieval sculpture. The treasury here holds the most important collection of medieval and Renaissance gold work in Western Europe, some of it even made in the abbey's own workshops. The treasures date from the 9th to the 19th century, and are prized for both their beauty and their rarity. The undoubted highlight is the gold-plated wood and silver reliquary of Ste-Foy, a statue-shaped shrine containing the remains of the saint. Other magnificent pieces include an "A"-shaped reliquary, said to be a gift from Charlemagne; the small but exquisite Pépin's shrine from AD 1000; and a late 16th-century processional cross. The precious contents of the Treasury were hidden by the townspeople to prevent their destruction during the French Revolution. Perhaps surprisingly, they were all returned.

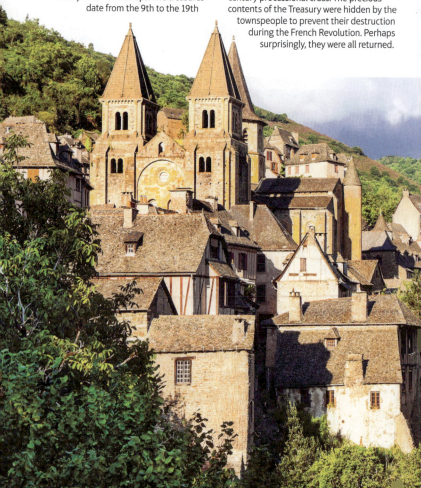

GREAT VIEW
Vista of the Village

The Chapelle St Roch, on a rocky spur just outside the village, provides one of the finest panoramas of Ste Foy and the surrounding houses with their distinctive *lauze* (flagstone) roof tiles.

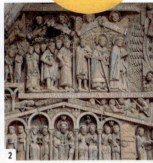

☐ The reliquary of Ste Foy, studded with gems and rock crystal, is over 1,000 years old and known for miracle cures.

② This sculpture from the early 12th century depicts the Last Judgment, with the Devil in Hell in the lower part of the sculpture and Christ in Heaven in the central position.

③ Pure and elegantly simple, the Romanesque interior dates from 1050–1135. The lovely nave has three tiers of arches.

Did You Know?

On summer evenings you can visit the abbey's upper gallery and see the intricate carvings up close.

THE ROAD TO COMPOSTELA

In the Middle Ages millions of Christians pilgrims trekked to Santiago de Compostela *(p406)* to pay homage at the shrine of St James (Santiago). The route, a series of connected ways, took them across the country into Spain. The pilgrims would stay in simple shelters or monasteries like Conques, and would return with a scallop shell as a souvenir. The route is still popular today and makes a great trek, as it takes in some of the finest landscapes in southern Europe.

←

The splendid Abbaye de Ste-Foy rising up above the village of Conques

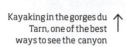

③

GORGES DU TARN

🅰 E6 🏠 Lozère, Aveyron 🆆 cevennes-gorges-du-tarn.com

For millions of years the Tarn river has carved its way through some of Europe's most spectacular gorges on its long journey to meet the River Garonne. Over this time, the Tarn and its tributary, the Jonte, have eaten their way down through the limestone plateaux of the Cévennes, creating a sinuous forked canyon some 24 km (15 miles) long and nearly 400 m (1,300 ft) deep.

The UNESCO-listed gorges are flanked by rocky bluffs and pine trees, and scaled by roads with dizzying bends and panoramic views, which are very popular during high season. The surrounding plateaux, or *causses*, are eerily different, forming an open, austere landscape that is dry in summer and snow-clad in winter, where wandering sheep and isolated farms are sometimes the only signs of life. One of the least populated parts of France, this area is well known for its wildflowers and birds of prey, and giant griffon vultures, once hunted nearly to extinction, are now being reintroduced. The best way to appreciate the scenery is to walk or follow the river's course by canoe or kayak.

←

Rounding up sheep on the rocky Causse Méjean, above the gorges du Tarn

GREAT VIEW
Point Sublime

Point Sublime, 870 m (2,855 ft) high, is a well-known lookout point located high up on the Causse de Sauveterre. From here there are stunning views of a major bend in the Tarn gorge, with the Causse Méjean visible in the distance.

Kayaking in the gorges du Tarn, one of the best ways to see the canyon ↑

900

The number of species of wildflower, including rare orchids, on the *causses* of the gorge.

↑ One of France's most dramatic gorges, cut by the River Tarn

↑ A wealth of local porcelain displayed at Limoges' Musée National Adrien-Dubouché

EXPERIENCE MORE

4

Aubusson

A D5 **A** Creuse 🚌 **i** Rue Vieille; www.tourisme-aubusson.com

Aubusson owes its renown to the exceptionally pure waters of the Creuse, perfect for making the delicately coloured dyes used for tapestries and rugs. Tapestry production was at its height in the 16th and 17th centuries, but by the end of the 18th century the rise of patterned wallpaper, and the Revolution, caused its decline.

↑ Tapestry restoration at the Manufacture St-Jean in Aubusson

In the 1940s, Aubusson was revived, largely due to the artist Jean Lurçat, who persuaded other modern artists to design for tapestry. The **Cité Internationale de la Tapisserie** houses a museum of these modern works. Workshops welcome visitors at the **Manufacture St-Jean**; watch tapestries and carpets being made by hand and restored.

Cité Internationale de la Tapisserie

♿ **A** Rue Williams-Dumazet ⏰ 10am–6pm Wed–Mon ❌ Jan **w** cite-tapisserie.fr

Manufacture St-Jean

♿♿ **A** 3 rue St-Jean ⏰ 10am–5pm daily **w** manufacture-saint-jean.fr

---

5

Limoges

A D5 **A** Haute-Vienne ✈🚌🚗 **i** 12 bd de Fleurus; www.limoges-tourisme.com

The capital of the Limousin has two hearts: the old Cité and the rival château, now the commercial centre of the modern city. The Cité is a quiet place of traditional half-timbered houses and narrow streets.

It was not until the 1770s that Limoges became synonymous with porcelain. The legendary local ware is on display at the **Musée National Adrien-Dubouché**. More than 10,000 exhibits trace the history of ceramics. The **Musée des Beaux-Arts de Limoges** houses an Egyptian collection, archaeological artifacts tracing the history of Limoges, over 600 Limousin enamels and Impressionist paintings. This area was a centre of Resistance operations in World War II; the **Musée de la Résistance et de la Déportation** has a collection of exhibits relating to these campaigns.

Resistance activity led to severe reprisals in Limousin. On 10 June 1944, SS troups shot the entire population of the village of Oradour-sur-Glane, 25 km (16 miles) northwest of Limoges. The ruins have been kept as a shrine, and a new village was built nearby.

Close by, St-Junien, a glove-making town since the Middle Ages, still supplies designers with luxury leather items.

> **PILGRIMAGES AND OSTENSIONS**
>
> Parishes in the Auvergne and the Limousin are renowned for honouring their saints in a series of popular outdoor processions that appear on the UNESCO Intangable Cultural Heritage list. Ascension Day sees the Virgin of Orcival carried above the village by night, accompanied by gypsies and their children for baptism. Every seven years a score of villages in the Limousin hold Ostensions, when the saints' relics are paraded through the streets into the surrounding woods. The Ostension season begins the Sunday after Easter and runs until June. The next event in the seven-year cycle will be held in 2023.

Musée National Adrien-Dubouché

 🏛 Pl Winston Churchill 🕙 10am–5:45pm Wed–Mon 🚫 1 Jan, 25 Dec 🌐 musee-adriendubouche.fr

Musée des Beaux-Arts de Limoges

🏛 1 pl de l'Évêché 🕙 9:30–6pm Wed–Mon 🚫 Public hols 🌐 museebal.fr

Musée de la Résistance et de la Déportation

🏛 Rue Neuve Saint-Étienne 🕙 9:30–5pm Wed–Sun 🚫 1 Jan, 1 May, 25 Dec 🌐 resistance-massif-central.fr

6

Montluçon

🅐 D4 🏛 Allier 🚌 🛈 67ter bd de Courtais; www.montlucontourisme.com

Montluçon is the economic centre of the region, a small town with a medieval core. At its heart there is a Bourbon château, which now houses temporary exhibitions. Jardin Wilson, a pleasant *jardin à la française* in the medieval quarter, sits on the original ramparts of the town. Mostly destroyed in the 18th century, little remains of the ramparts now. The stunning restored rose garden and spectacular flowerbeds are worth a visit. The 12th-century Église de St-Pierre is a surprise, with giant stone columns and a huge barrel-vaulted ceiling.

7

Moulins

🅐 E4 🏛 Allier 🚗🚌 🛈 Rue François Péron; www.moulins-tourisme.com

Capital of the Bourbonnais and seat of the Bourbon Dukes since the 10th century, Moulins flourished during the early Renaissance. Its most celebrated sight is the Flamboyant Gothic **Cathédrale Notre-Dame**, where members of the Bourbon court appear amid the saints in the 15th- and 16th-century stained-glass windows. The treasury contains a luminous 15th-century Virgin and Child triptych by the "Master of Moulins". Benefactors Pierre II, Duke of Bourbon, and his wife Anne de Beaujeu, bedecked in embroidery and jewels, are shown being introduced to a less richly dressed Madonna.

The tower keep and the single remaining wing of the Bourbon Vieux Château features a superb collection of sculpture, painting and decorative art from the 12th to the 16th centuries. Housed in the former cavalry barracks is a magnificent collection of 10,000 theatrical costumes.

Also worth a visit is the 19th-century Maison Mantin, a bourgeois town house which is now an interesting museum.

Cathédrale Notre-Dame

🏛 Pl des Vosges 📞 04 70 20 57 77 🕙 Treasury: 9am–6pm daily 🚫 25 Dec

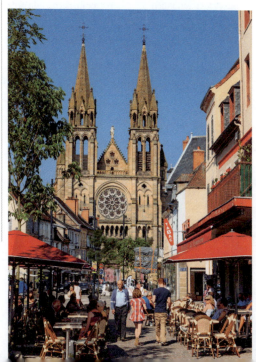

← A bustling outdoor café with a view of Moulins's Cathédrale Notre-Dame

8

Vichy

A E4 **A** Allier **R** **@** **i** 19 rue du Parc; www.vichy-destinations.fr

This small city on the River Allier has long been known for its hot and cold springs, and reputed cures for rheumatism, arthritis and digestive complaints. The letter-writer Madame de Sévigné and the daughters of Louis XV visited in the late 17th and 18th centuries – the former compared the showers to "a rehearsal for Purgatory". The visits of Napoleon III in the 1860s put Vichy on the map and made taking the waters fashionable. The small town was spruced up and became a favourite among the French nobility and the world's wealthy middle classes. These days, the grand old Thermal Establishment, built in 1900, lies abandoned, but it is possible to walk in and admire the pretty pastel-coloured architecture. The modern baths are state-of-the-art and strictly for medical purposes. A doctor's prescription and a reservation 30 days in advance are required for all treatments.

Vichy's fortunes changed for the better once again in the 1960s with the damming of the Allier, creating a huge lake in the middle of town, which rapidly became a thriving centre for water sports and international events. For a small fee, you can have a taste of sports from aikido to waterskiing, or learn canoeing on the 3-km- (2-mile-) long artificial river.

The focal point of life in Vichy is the Parc des Sources in the centre of town, with its turn-of-the-20th-century bandstand (afternoon concerts in season), *belle époque* glass-roofed shopping galleries, and the Grand Casino and Opera House. Here there is gambling every afternoon and musical performances in the evenings, and an atmosphere of gaiety pervades. Also open to the public are the beautiful bronze taps of the **Source Célestin**, in a riverside park containing vestiges of a convent bearing the same name. Only by making an effort to imagine the city in grainy black-and-white newsreel style is there the slightest reminder of the wartime Vichy government, which was based in the town from 1940 to 1944.

Source Célestin

A Blvd du Président Kennedy **Ⓞ** Apr-Sep: 8am-8:30pm daily; Oct-Mar: 8am-6pm daily **Ⓧ** Dec-Jan

---

9

Château de La Palice

A E4 **A** Allier **C** 04 70 99 37 58 **Ⓞ** Apr-Oct: 9am-6pm Wed-Mon

In the early 16th century, the Marshal of France, Jacques II de Chabannes, hired Florentine

---

VOLVIC SPRINGS

The Auvergne has over 100 spring and mineral waters, filtered through the volcanic rock. The best known include Vichy Célestins and Volvic. The latter has its source in the Chaine des Puys. Rainwater takes about five years to filter through 100 m (330 ft) of volcanic rock to reach the source, 90 m (300 ft) underground. From here it is pumped to the factory and bottled. You can find out more (and do some tasting) at the Volvic information centre (Apr-Nov; *www.volvic.fr*).

Magnificent Château de La Palice, set upon a hill overlooking the Besbre Valley

architects to reconstruct the feudal château-fort at Lapalisse, creating a refined Renaissance castle, which has been inhabited ever since by his descendants. The *salon doré* (gilded room) has a beamed ceiling panelled in gold, and two huge 15th-century Flemish tapestries showing the Crusader Knight Godefroy de Bouillon and Greek hero Hector, two of the nine classic braves of chivalric legend.

From Lapalisse, the D480 leads up through the beautiful Besbre Valley past a handful of other small, well-preserved châteaux, including Château de Thoury and Château Beauvoir. Though neither is open to the public, they can be admired from the outside.

🔟 Issoire

🅰 E5 🏠 Puy de Dôme
🚃🚌 ℹ 9 pl St-Paul; www. issoire-tourisme.com

Most of old Issoire was destroyed in the 16th-century Wars of Religion. The present-day town has been an important industrial centre since the end of World War II. Not only does Issoire have a thriving aeronautical tradition, it is also a mecca for glider pilots, who come from miles around to take advantage of the strong local air currents.

Issoire's colourful 12th-century abbey church of St-Austremoine is one of the great Romanesque churches of the region. The capitals depict scenes from the *Life of Christ* (one of the Apostles at the Last Supper has fallen asleep at the table), and imaginary demons and beasts. The 15th-century fresco of the *Last Judgment* shows Bosch-like figures of sinners being cast into the mouth of a dragon or carted off to hell. The nearby Tour de l'Horloge has scenes of Renaissance history.

⓫ Thiers

🅰 E5 🏠 Puy de Dôme 🚃🚌
ℹ Pl de Pirou; www.thiers-tourisme.fr

According to the writer La Bruyère, Thiers "seems painted on the slope of the hill", hanging dramatically as it does on a ravine over a sharp bend in the River Durolle. The city has been renowned for cutlery since the Middle Ages, when legend has it that Crusaders brought back techniques of metalwork from the Middle East. With grindstones powered by dozens of waterfalls on the opposite bank of the river, Thiers produced everything from table knives to guillotine blades, and cutlery remains its major industry today, much of it on display in the Cutlery Museum, the **Musée de la Coutellerie**.

The Old Town is filled with mysterious quarters including "the Corner of Chance" and "Hell's Hollow", honeycombed with tortuous streets and well-restored 14th- to 17th-century houses. Many have elaborately carved wooden façades, notably the Maison du Pirou in place Pirou. The view to the west from the rampart terrace, towards Monts Dômes and Monts Dore, is particularly splendid at sunset.

Musée de la Coutellerie

♿♻🚫 🏠 58 rue de la Coutellerie 📞 04 73 80 58 86 🕐 Apr–Sep: 10am–6pm daily; Mar & Oct by reservation only 🚫 Jan–mid-Feb

---

💬 INSIDER TIP
Artisan Knives

Home to more than 100 knife-making artisans, Thiers is the perfect place to pick up a pocket knife. The town's shops are full of handmade specimens from rare knives with mammoth-tooth handles costing thousands of euros to modest penknives costing around €50. The town's iconic knife is "Le Thiers", a hand-made folding knife that will last a lifetime.

The original Thermal Establishment building in the spa town of Vichy

⑫
Orcival

🅰 E5 🏠 Puy de Dôme ℹ Le Bourg; www.tourisme-sancy-artense.com

Crowded in summer, Orcival is nevertheless well worth visiting for its Romanesque church, the Basilique d'Orcival, which many would claim is the best in the region. It was completed at the beginning of the 12th century, and has changed little through the ages. It is typically Auvergne Romanesque in style; the apse is multi-tiered, and the side walls are supported by powerful buttresses and strong arches.

Inside the grand Basilique d'Orcival, the ornate silver and vermilion *Virgin and Child* (in the forward-facing position known as "in majesty") is enigmatic, with an unusual, rigid, square chair. With an interior lit by 14 windows and a spacious crypt, the proportions of the building itself are the most graceful aspect.

One of the walls of the church is hung with balls and chains, which were left as a sign of gratitude by prisoners, who believed they had been miraculously freed after praying to the Virgin of Orcival.

---

⑬
Clermont-Ferrand

🅰 E5 🏠 Puy de Dôme ✈🚆🚌 ℹ Pl de la Victoire; www.clermont-fd.com

Clermont-Ferrand began as two distinct cities, united only in 1630. Famous as the home of the Michelin tyre company and dramatically framed by volcanic mountains, the town has an appealing energy about it, lent partly by its thriving student population and large number of arts and music festivals; it is regularly ranked among France's best places to live in terms of quality of life.

Rising up at the heart of the medieval old town is one of the country's most striking cathedrals, the graceful 13th-century Cathédrale Notre-Dame-de-l'Assomption. The dark rock provides a foil for the jewel-like 12th- to 15th-century stained-glass windows, believed to be from the same workshop as Ste-Chapelle's in Paris (p92).

Northeast of the cathedral is Basilique Notre-Dame-du-Port, one of the most impor-

tant Romanesque churches in the region. The stone interior is beautifully proportioned, with a magnificent raised choir and carved capitals.

Clermont's ancient origins as a Celtic and then Roman settlement are well illustrated at the Musée Bargoin with its remarkable collections of locally found artifacts (closed Monday and Sunday morning).

> ### Did You Know?
> The International Short Film Festival in Clermont-Ferrand is the biggest of its kind in the world.

---

⑭
St-Nectaire

🅰 E5 🏠 Puy de Dôme 🚌 ℹ Les Grands Thermes; www.sancy.com

The Auvergne is noted for Romanesque churches. The Église St-Nectaire in the upper

↑ Soaring arches inside the 12th-century Basilique d'Orcival

→

Monts Dômes, an area of extinct volcanoes, topped by a telecommucations tower

Glowing lights of a traveling funfair in the centre of Clermont-Ferrand

village of St-Nectaire-le Haut, with its soaring, elegant proportions, is one of the most beautiful. The 103 stone capitals, 22 of them polychrome, are vividly carved, and the treasury includes a gold bust of St Baudime and a wooden Notre-Dame-du-Mont-Cornadore, both marvels of 12th-century workmanship. The lower village, St-Nectaire-le-Bas, has more than 40 hot and cold springs.

Nearby, the 12th-century citadel of **Château de Murol** has costumed guides demonstrating medieval life and knightly pursuits. It is wonderful for children.

Château de Murol
 Murol 10am–6pm daily (to 8pm Jun–Aug) 1 Jan, 14 Jul, 25 Dec murolchateau.com

---

15

Monts Dômes

E5 Puy de Dôme Clermont-Ferrand Aydat; www.parcdes volcans.fr

The youngest range of the Auvergne volcanoes at 4,000 years old, the Monts Dômes, or Chaîne des Puys, encompass 112 extinct volcanoes aligned over a 30-km (19-mile) stretch just west of Clermont-Ferrand. At the centre, the Puy de Dôme towers above a high plateau. A mountain railway spirals up the peak at a steady 12 per cent gradient, taking 15 minutes to reach the top, while the steeper Roman path is still used by hikers. (No cars or buses ascend the Puy de Dôme; phone 08 26 39 96 15 for train information.)

At the summit are the vestiges of the Roman temple of Mercury and a meteorological/telecommunications tower. On a clear day, the view across the volcano will take your breath away. The controversial, Parc Européen du Volcanisme, **Vulcania**, an educational amusement park built in the area, uses the latest technology to simulate volcanic activity in its underground circuit.

In the southwest corner of the Monts Dômes region is the **Château de Cordès**, a small, privately owned 15th-century manor house with formal gardens designed by Le Nôtre. Inside are well-furnished state rooms and a chapel, all Rococo in style.

Vulcania
 D941B, St-Ours-les-Roches Mid-Mar-mid-Nov: 10am–6pm vulcania.com

Château de Cordès
 Orcival Jul & Aug: guided tours at 11am, 2:30 & 4pm daily; gardens 10am–6pm daily Sep-Jun chateau-cordes-orcival.com

STAY

Hôtel Radio
This hilly Art Deco gem has original floor mosaics, mirrors and wrought-iron decor, side-by-side with radio memorabilia.

E5 43 av Pierre et Marie Curie, 63400 Clermont-Ferrant hotel-radio.fr

€€€

L'Auberge d'Aijean
High up in the Monts du Cantal, with a lovely terrace, this converted barn offers comfy rooms and delicious food.

E5 Le Gandilhon, Lavigerie auberge-puy-mary.com

€€€

Chateau St Saturnin
A 13th-century castle in beautiful grounds, with views of the mountains. Rooms have four-poster beds and tapestries.

E5 Pl de l'Ormeau, 63450 Saint-Saturnin chateaudesaint saturnin.com

€€€

16

Uzerche

 D5 Corrèze
Pl de la Libération; www.
uzerche-tourisme.com

Uzerche is an impressive sight: grey slate roofs, turrets and bell towers rising from a hill above the Vézère river. This prosperous town never capitulated during the conflicts of the Middle Ages, and earlier withstood a seven-year siege by Moorish forces in 732: the townspeople sent a feast out to their enemy – in fact, the last of their supplies. The Moors, thinking such lavish offerings meant the city had stores to spare, gave up.

The Romanesque Église St-Pierre crests the hill above the town. Beyond Uzerche, the Vézère cuts through the green gorges of the Saillant.

17

Collonges-la-Rouge

D5 Corrèze Brive, then bus to Collonges
Rue de la Barriere, Collonges; www.vallee-dordogne.com

There is something quite unsettling about Collonges' carmine sandstone architecture, beautiful in individual houses, though the overall effect is both austere and fairytale-like.

Founded in the 8th century, Collonges came under the rule of Turenne, whose burghers built the turreted houses in the surrounding vineyards. Look out for the communal bread oven in the marketplace, and the 11th-century church, later fortified with a tower keep. The church's unusual carved white limestone tympanum shows a man driving a bear, and other lively figures.

18

Turenne

E5 Corrèze
Brive-la-Gaillarde; 05 55 24 08 80

Turenne is one of the most appealing medieval towns in the Corrèze. Crescent-shaped and clustered on the cliff-side, the town has lots of unspoiled traditional Limousin houses. It was the last independent feudal fiefdom in France, under the absolute rule of the La Tour d'Auvergne family until 1738. Henri de la Tour d'Auvergne, their most illustrious member, was a marshal of France under Louis XIV, and one of the greatest soldiers of modern times.

GREAT VIEW
Cable Car

Since 1936 the cable car from Le Monts Dore has transported passengers up to the Puy de Sancy, the highest mountain in the Massif Central. From the cable car station it's a scenic climb to the summit, where fabulous views await.

Now the sole remains of the **Château de Turenne** are the 13th-century Clock Tower and 11th-century Tower of Caesar, from which there is a quite spectacular 360-degree view of the Cantal mountains across to the Dordogne Valley. Not far away is Turenne's 16th-century collegiate church and the unassuming Chapelle des Capucins, which dates from the 18th century. This chapel is closed to the public for much of the year, but it opens to host a series of popular music concerts and temporary exhibitions each summer.

Château de Turenne
Apr-Oct: 10am-6pm daily (to 7pm Jul-Aug)
chateau-turenne.com

⑲ Monts Dore

🅰E5 🏔 Puy de Dôme ✈ Clermont-Ferrand 🚆🚌 Le Mont-Dore ℹ Montlosier, Aydat; 04 73 65 64 26

Three giant volcanoes – the Puy de Sancy, the Banne d'Ordanche and the Puy de l'Aiguiller – and their secondary cones make up the Monts Dore: dark green, heavily wooded mountains laced with rivers and lakes and dotted with a range of summer and winter resorts that offer paragliding, sailing, canoeing, skiing and hiking. The 1,885-m (6,185-ft) Puy de Sancy is the highest point in central France. It can be

Red sandstone houses, the hallmark of Collonges-la-Rouge streets

reached by taking a shuttle from the town of Le Mont-Dore to the cable car, which goes up to the peak, followed by a long hike across open terrain. From Le Mont-Dore there is a scenic drive on the D36, which leads to the Couze-Chambon Valley, a beautiful stretch of high moorland threaded with waterfalls.

The area has two spa towns, La Bourboule, for children's ailments, with its casino, and

↑ Cyclist descending the mountain road weaving through the Monts Dore

Le Mont-Dore, with its grand turn-of-the-20th-century Établissement Thermal.

Below the Col de Guéry, on the D983, stand the eroded volcanic Roche Sanadoire and Roche Tuilière. From their peaks are extensive views over the Cirque de Chausse.

EAT

Le Haut Allier
Local produce is paramount at this hotel-restaurant. Set menus are great value.

📍E5 🏠 Pont d'Alleyras, 43580 Alleyras 📅 Mon & Tue; mid-Nov–Mar 🌐 hotel-lehautallier.com

€€€

Auberge des Montagnes
An idyllic mountain retreat where you can feast on a six-course menu.

📍E5 🏠 15800 Pailherols 📅 Mon & Tue 🌐 auberge-des-montagnes.com

€€€

Brasserie du Casino
In a stylish Art Deco salon, this Vichy institution has an excellent menu of classic upmarket brasserie fare. Impeccable service.

📍E4 🏠 4 rue du Casino, 03200 Vichy 📅 Tue & Wed 🌐 Brasserie-du-casino.fr

€€€

Chez Alphonse
There are good *prix-fixe* menus at this lively bistro serving regional cuisine using local ingredients.

📍D6 🏠 5 pl de la Motte, 87000 Limoges 📅 Sun 🌐 chezalphonse.fr

€€€

20

Monts du Cantal

 E5 Cantal Aurillac
Lioran Aurillac;
www.iaurillac.com

The Cantal mountains were originally one enormous volcano – the oldest and the largest in Europe, dating from the Tertiary period. The core of the Monts du Cantal is formed by the highest peaks, the Puy Mary at 1,787 m (5,863 ft), the Plomb du Cantal at 1,855 m (6,086 ft), and the Puy de Peyre-Arse at 1,686 m (5,531 ft), which are enclosed by numerous crests and deep river valleys.

Driving the narrow roads is a thrill, compounded by the views at every hairpin turn. Between peaks and gorges, rich mountain pastures provide summer grazing for red-gold Salers cows. From the Pas de Peyrol, the highest road pass in the country at 1,582 m (5,191 ft), it's about a 25-minute journey on foot

↑ Saler cows graze in front of Château d'Anjony; frescoes in the château's chapel (inset)

to the summit of the Puy Mary, a Grand National Site, which offers glorious views.

Château d'Anjony, one of the finest of the Auvergne châteaux, was built by Louis II d'Anjony, a supporter of Joan of Arc. Highlights are the 16th-century frescoes: in the chapel, scenes from the Life and Passion of Christ, and in the Salle des Preux (Knights' Room), a series of the nine heroes of chivalry. To the south lies the provincial town of Aurillac. With a centre of old streets and shops, it is a good base for exploring the Cantal region.

Château d'Anjony

 Tournemire 0471 476167 Jul & Aug: 11am–6:30pm daily; Sep–Jun: 2–5pm daily Dec–Jan

21

La Chaise-Dieu

E5 Haute-Loire
 Rue Saint-Esprit;
www.la-chaise-dieu.info

Sombre and massive, midway between Romanesque and Gothic, the 14th-century abbey church of St-Robert is the prime reason to visit the small village of La Chaise-Dieu. The building is an amalgam of styles; the choir, however, is sensational: 144 oak stalls carved with figures of Vice and Virtue. Above them, entirely covering the walls, are some of the loveliest tapestries in France. Made in Brussels and Arras in the early 16th century and depicting scenes from the Old and New Testaments, they are rich in colour and detail. On the outer walls of the choir the 15th-century wall painting of the Danse Macabre shows Death in

> The Cantal mountains were originally one enormous volcano - the oldest and the largest in Europe, dating from the Tertiary period.

the form of skeletons leading rich and poor alike to their inevitable end. Beyond the cloister is the Echo room, in which two people whispering in opposite corners can hear one another perfectly. A Baroque Music Festival from mid-August to September makes the abbey crowded.

22 Salers

 E5 ⚑ Cantal ⊟ Summer only ℹ Pl Tyssandier d'Escous; www.salers-tourisme.fr

A handsome town of grey lava houses and 15th-century ramparts, Salers sits atop a steep escarpment at the edge of the Cantal mountains. It is one of few virtually intact Renaissance villages in the region. The church has an admirable polychrome *mise au tombeau* (entombment), dated 1495, and five 17th-century Aubusson tapestries.

From the fountain, streets lead up to the cliff edge, and provide stunning views of the surrounding valleys, with the ever-present sound of cowbells in the distance. The town is very crowded in summer, but it makes a good starting point for excursions to the Puy Mary,

the huge barrage at Bort-les-Orgues, the nearby Château de Val and the Cère Valley to the south.

23 Vallée du Lot

 C5-6 ⚑ Aveyron ⊟ Rodez, Aurillac ⚑ Rodez, Séverac-le-Château ⊟ Espalion, Rodez ℹ Espalion; www.vallee dulot.com

From Mende and the old river port of La Canourgue all the way to Conques, the River Lot courses through its fertile valley past orchards, vineyards and pine forests. St Côme d'Olt, near the Aubrac mountains, is an unspoiled, fortified village with a 15th-century church surrounded by Medieval and Renaissance houses. At Espalion, the pastel stone houses and a 16th-century castle are reflected in the river, which runs beneath a 13th-century arched stone bridge. The town has one of the best markets in the region on Friday mornings. Just outside town is the 11th-century Perse Church, with carved capitals portraying knights and imaginary birds sipping from a chalice.

Estaing was once the fiefdom of one of the greatest

THE AUVERGNE'S BLACK MADONNAS

The cult of the Virgin Mary has always been strong in the Auvergne and this is reflected in the concentration of her statues in the region. Carved out of dark walnut or cedar, now blackened with age, the Madonnas are believed to originate from the Byzantine influence of the Crusaders. Perhaps the most famous Madonna is the one housed in the Cathédrale de Notre-Dame in Le-Puy-en-Velay (*p342*), which is a 17th-century copy of one that belonged to Louis IX in the Middle Ages.

families of the Rouergue, dating back to the 13th century. The pretty village nestles beneath its massive château (open May–mid-Oct) on the riverbank. The road passes through the Lot Gorge on the way to Entraygues ("between waters"), where the charming old quarter and 13th-century Gothic bridge are worth a visit. Beyond Entraygues, the river widens to join the Garonne.

→ Charming stone buildings in place de l'Église, Salers

㉔ Rodez

▲D6 ▲Aveyron ✈🚉🚌
ℹ Place de la Cité; www.
tourisme.grand-rodez.com

Like many medieval French cities, Rodez was politically divided: the shop-lined place du Bourg on one side of town and place de la Cité, near the cathedral, on the other, reflect conflicting secular and ecclesiastical interests. Rodez's commercial centre is the region's largest.

The huge 13th-century pink stone Cathédrale Notre-Dame is worth a look, with its fortress-like west façade and its magnificent bell tower. The 15th-century choir stalls show a panoply of creatures, including a winged lion and one naughty fellow exposing his derrière.

The striking steel **Musée Soulages** houses over 500 paintings and other works by the artist Pierre Soulages, who was born in Rodez in 1919. It also hosts temporary exhibitions of modern and contemporary art.

Southeast (45 km/28 miles) of Rodez lies Saint Léons, birthplace of Jean-Henri Fabre, the entomologist. Here is Micropolis, part interactive museum, part theme park, dedicated to the glory of insects (closed Nov–mid-Feb). Be sure to watch the excellent film of the same name, even if you don't have time for anything else.

Musée Soulages

♿🎟️🚻 🅿️ Jardin du Foirail, av Victor Hugo 📞 05 65 73 82 60 🕐 11am–7pm Tue–Sun (also from 2pm Mon in Jul & Aug)

STEVENSON TRAIL

The long-distance hiking path, the GR70, follows in the footsteps of the novelist Robert Louis Stevenson (1850–94), tracing the route that he took in 1878 through the Cévennes with only a small donkey, Modestine, for company. His classic account of this eventful journey, *Travels with a Donkey*, was published the following year. The two-week trail starts in Le Puy and takes in remote countryside.

Did You Know?

Fossils remains at St-Laurent-de-Trèves, on the Cévennes Corniche, suggest dinosaurs once roamed there.

㉕ Parc National des Cévennes

▲E6 ▲Lozère, Gard
🚉Alès 🚌St-Jean-du-Gard
ℹ 6bis pl du Palais, Florac 48400; www.cevennes-parcnational.fr

Lying between the Massif Central and the Mediterranean,

← Musée Soulages in Rodez, designed by Catalan architects

the Cévennes is a remote, mountainous region of wind-whipped plateaus, rivers and gorges. It was designated a national park in 1970, and is an excellent destination for hiking and other outdoor activities. The best-known walking path follows the route taken by author Robert Louis Stevenson. The Corniche des Cévennes is a dramatic drive from Florac to St-Jean-du-Gard, which was cut in the early 18th century by the army of Louis XIV in pursuit of the Camisards, Protestant rebels who had no uniforms but fought in their ordinary shirts (*camiso* in the langue d'oc). Florac is the main hub for hiking and other outdoor pursuits, and you can also explore charming traditional towns such as La-Garde-Guerin and Anduze.

↑ Striking underground rock formations found in the Grand Causses

26

Grands Causses

 E6 🅐 Aveyron 🚗 Rodez-Marcillac 🚌 Millau
ℹ Millau; www.millau-viaduc-tourisme.fr

The Causses are vast, arid limestone plateaus, alternating with green, fertile canyon valleys. The only sign of life at times is a bird of prey, or an isolated stone farm or shepherd's hut. The area makes for some desolate hiking. The four Grands Causses – Méjean, Sauveterre, Noir and Larzac – stretch out east of the city of Millau, which boasts the tallest vehicular bridge in the world. They extend from Mende in the north to the Vis river valley in the south.

Among the sights in the Causses are the *chaos* – bizarre rock formations reputed to resemble ruined cities, and named accordingly: there's the *chaos* of Montpellier-le-Vieux, Nîmes-le-Vieux and Roquesaltes. Aven Armand and the Dargilan Grotto are vast and deep natural underground grottoes.

A good place to head for in the Larzac Causse is the strange, rough-hewn stone village of La Couvertoirade, a fully enclosed citadel of the Knights Templar in the 12th century. The unpaved streets and medieval houses are an austere reminder of the dark side of the Middle Ages. Entry to the village is free, with a small fee for the tour of the surrounding ramparts.

The best-known village in the Larzac Causse is probably Roquefort-sur-Soulzon, a small grey town terraced on the side of a crumbled limestone outcrop. It has only one main street and one major product, Roquefort cheese. This is made from unpasteurized sheep's milk, seeded with a distinctive blue mould grown on loaves of bread, and aged in the warren of damp caves above the town.

 INSIDER TIP
Natural Swimming Holes

Scattered throughout the Auvergne are a number of natural lakes - some formed over the years in dormant volcano craters - that are appealing places to swim. Some have small beaches, such as Lac Chambon, with its two south-facing sandy stretches. A few have obtained Blue Flag status that guarantees exellent water quality.

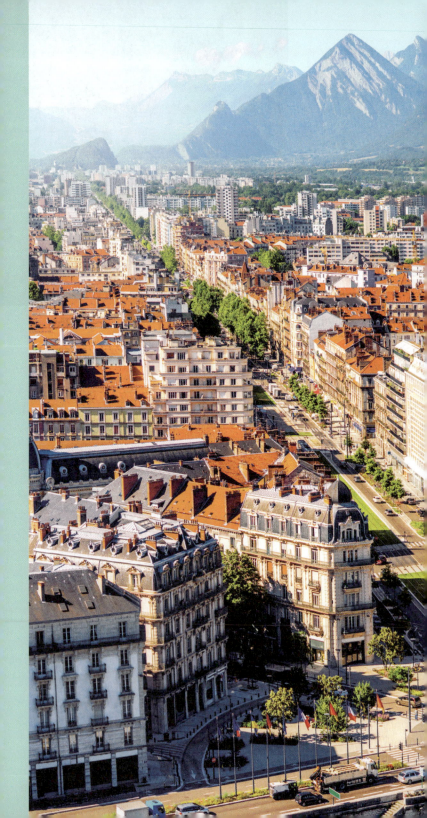

THE RHÔNE VALLEY AND FRENCH ALPS

The Romans recognized the strategic value of the the verdant rolling hills, mountainous reaches and, especially, the snaking Rhône River, France's most important north–south transport artery, 2,000 years ago. They established Lyon as a central trading station between the coast and Paris. During the late 1400s, the city became France's most important banking centre thanks to trade fairs that also attracted the silk trade. South-east of Lyon, the Alpine Dauphiné region was purchased by France in 1349, although it retained some autonomy until 1628. A stronghold of Protestantism in the early 1500s, it was devastated during the French Wars of Religion (1562–98). During this period, the region's famous Beaujolais vineyards, along with the Côtes du Rhône to the south, cemented the reputation of winegrowers along the Rhône corridor. Canals were used to transport bottles of wine to Paris and Nice. Railways arrived in the early 1800s, and in subsequent decades parts of the region – including Grenoble, the capital – became industrialized. The arrival of train travel also brought tourists to the region, and elegant *belle époque* spa towns proliferated all along the French shore of Lac Léman (Lake Geneva). Following Axis occupation during World War II, the French Alps rebounded in the 1950s and re-established the area's alpine landscapes as prime winter sports territory.

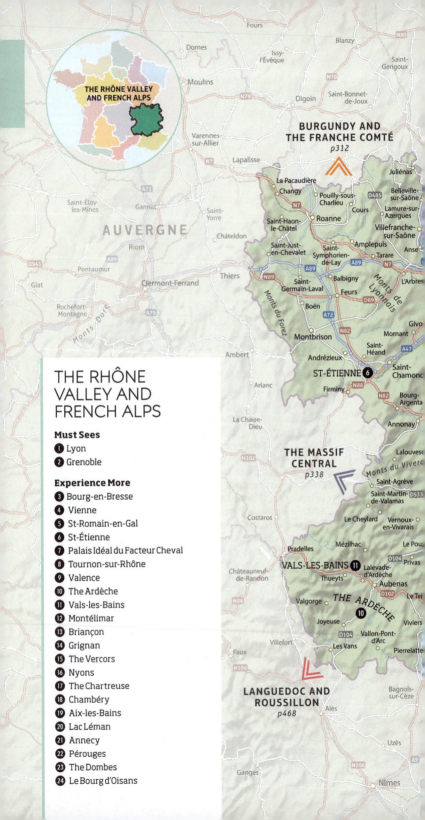

THE RHÔNE VALLEY
AND FRENCH ALPS

THE RHÔNE VALLEY AND FRENCH ALPS

BURGUNDY AND THE FRANCHE COMTÉ
p312

THE MASSIF CENTRAL
p338

LANGUEDOC AND ROUSSILLON
p468

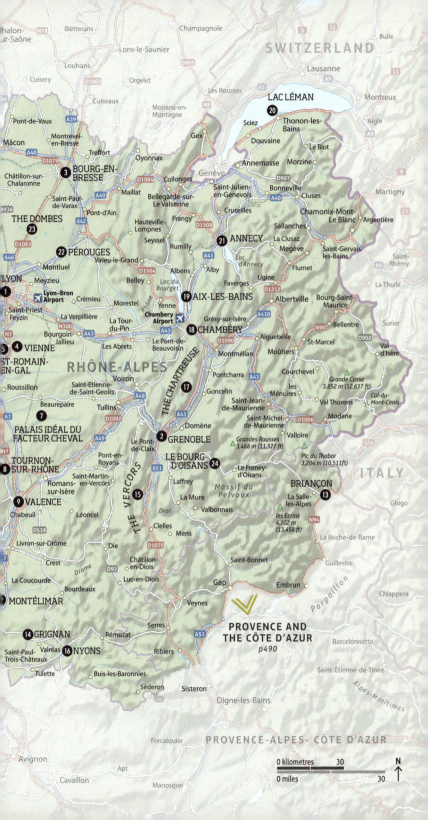

←

☐ Canoeing on Lake Annecy.

☐ The cable car up to Fort de la Bastille in Grenoble.

☐ A plate of *gratin dauphinois*.

☐ Dining outside overlooking a section of the Palais de l'Isle.

3 DAYS
in the French Prealps

Day 1

Morning Start your day in Grenoble *(p376)* at the Musée de Grenoble *(p377)*, working your way through 13th-century artifacts to paintings of the Middle Ages, the Renaissance and the Baroque, finishing with 20th-century masters. Stroll to atmospheric place St-Andre, stopping on the way to discover the city's history at the Musée de l'Ancien Evêché *(p377)*.

Afternoon After lunch in an outdoor café at place Grenette, visit the sobering Musée de la Résistance et de la Déportation de l'Isère *(p376)*, whose evocative exhibits illustrate the region's fierce resistance to the Nazis and the deportation of a thousand Jews. Then take the cable car up to Fort de la Bastille *(p377)*.

Evening Dine on the delectable local speciality *gratin dauphinois* (sliced potatoes baked in cream) at Une Semaine Sur Deux *(3 Rue Condorcet)*.

Day 2

Morning Drive north into the Chartreuse *(p386)*, a majestic massif that forms part of the French Prealps. Visit Monastère de la Grande Chartreuse, a Carthusian monastery famed for its yellowish-green liqueurs.

Afternoon Lunch in the Italianate centre of Chambéry *(p386)*, one-time capital of Savoy, then stroll around the narrow, cobbled streets of the old city. Don't miss place St-Léger and, on rue de Boigne, the Fontaine des Eléphants.

Evening Arrive in Annecy *(p388)* for a night in an individually styled room at the characterful, canalside Atipik Hôtel *(www. atipikhotel.fr)*, just up from the lake.

Day 3

Morning Stroll along the lakefront from the Champ de Mars, via Pont des Amours (Lovers' Bridge) over the crystal-clear waters of the Canal du Vassé, to Jardins de l'Europe. Then walk west along Canal du Thiou, through the Venice-like old city, to Palais de l'Isle, an impressively solid stone building that has stood at the tip of an islet since the 12th century.

Afternoon Take a boat ride around the lake to truly appreciate Annecy's idyllic setting. Bring a picnic aboard.

Evening Stroll around the old city and along the canals and lakefront in search of sparkling reflections of the city lights. Bring your trip to a fitting end with a delicious meal at L'Esquisse *(p379)*.

Feast at a Bouchon

Lyon's cuisine is renowned for its rich, rustic ingredients, many of which were traditionally used by the city's *canuts* (silk weavers) and are still served up in warm, homely *bouchons*. These, the city's traditional bistros, are usually family-owned, and are the perfect place to sample Lyon's specialities: *andouillette* (coarse offal sausage), *boudin noir* (blood sausage), *quenelles* (creamed fish dumplings) and *saucisson de Lyon* (a thick beef and pork sausage), all served on classic red-and-white-checked tablecloths beneath walls lined with decades of family photos.

→

Alfresco dining in summer at a *bouchon Lyonnaise*, serving local dishes and delicacies

LYON FOR
FOODIES

Lyon has the highest concentration of restaurants in France, and more Michelin-starred restaurants than any French city, except Paris. Quality is exceptional because of deep local traditions, intense competition and a highly sophisticated clientele, not forgetting top-quality ingredients.

Beaujolais Wine

On the third Thursday of November each year, place St-Jean turns itself over to the Beaujol'en Scène committee, in a brief but glorious festival that celebrates Beaujolais Nouveau (the new season's wine). Roll up to watch torch-lit processions and marching bands, then take part in tapping the barrels to discover Beaujolais's *terroir*. Don't be late – everything is recorked by midnight on the dot.

Beaujolais Nouveau barrels being rolled into the town centre by the winegrowers

↑ Pike *quenelles* in a rich sauce, a feature of many a Lyons *bouchon* menu

MÈRES LYONNAISES

Many of the women who cooked for Lyon's great bourgeois families went on to open their own restaurants, specializing in simple but perfectly executed local food. Known as the "mothers of Lyon", these chefs achieved great renown in this traditionally male-dominated field, and played a pivotal role in Lyon's transformation into a culinary force to be reckoned with.

Exploring Local Markets

Lyon's markets are a must for any gourmand. Lining the 1-km- (half-mile-) long boulevard de la Croix Rousse, part of Lyon's UNESCO World Heritage Site, is the La Croix Rousse market. Open every day but Monday, it is ideal for creating a gourmet picnic. The city's legendary indoor food market, Les Halles de Lyon, has won an international reputation for its finest-quality produce. Every gourmet speciality you could wish for can be found here: aromatic St-Félicien and St-Marcellin cheeses from nearby Isère; mouthwatering marbled beef from Charolais; and, of course, the sweet perfection of chocolate-and-marzipan *coussins de Lyon*. Book a spot on a walking tour with Lyon Food Tour *(www.lyonfoodtour.com)* and sample it all.

Produce and plants on sale at La Croix Rousse food market ↑

Take to the Slopes

Twice host of the Winter Olympics (Chamonix-Mont Blanc in 1924, Albertville in 1992), the slopes of the French Alps are legendary. Over 200 ski stations serve as warm, cosy gateways to some of the world's finest pistes, at elevations of up to 2,456 m (8,058 ft). In winter, take to the tow lines and gondolas, then fly back down on your skies or snowboard. In summer, some of the lifts can let you ski on glaciers.

 INSIDER TIP
Be Prepared

The weather in the Alps can change whatever the season. Whether you're skiing or hiking, check the forecast and always be prepared with a hat, warm clothing, rain gear, snacks and drinking water.

THE FRENCH ALPS FOR
THE GREAT OUTDOORS

Craggy peaks enveloped in blowing snow, separated by glaciers and snowfields, draw the eye ever upward, while down below sparkling Alpine snowmelt cascades through verdant valleys – in both winter and summer, the French Alps beckon visitors to explore.

Kids in the Snow

The pristine, powdery snow of the Alps creates a glorious winter wonderland for everyone, especially children. Head to Le Bourg d'Oisans *(p389)* and neighbouring L'Alpe d'Huez for a wealth of wintry activities just right for tots and teens, from building snowmen to sledging down snowy hills. Further north, Lac Léman *(p387)* is a gateway for families to try their hand at cross-country skiing. Most winter resorts offer a wide range of supervised activities for children, letting kids learn to ski with an instructor.

↑ A helmeted young skier following the instructor's lead on the snow

TOP 3 YEAR-ROUND RESORTS

Les Deux Alpes
Great high-altitude powder and renowned après-ski merriment in winter; glacier skiing, hiking and mountain biking in summer *(www.les2alpes.com)*.

Tignes and Val d'Isère
Also known as Espace Killy, this area has excellent ski touring, a snow park catering for freestylists and summer skiing on two glaciers *(www.valdisere.com)*.

Morzine
Straddling the Franco-Swiss border, the huge Les Portes du Soleil ski area includes this pretty village, with plenty of beginner and intermediate slopes *(www. portesdusoleil.com)*.

↑ Snowboarders and skiers taking to the slopes

← Paragliding over the mountains for epic views

When the Snow Melts
As the winter snows retreat, mountain passes reopen, trails thaw and wildflowers carpet the hillsides. Use the ski lifts in Le Bourg d'Oisans *(p389)* to reach the heights, then follow trails to walk or bike down. See it all from above, by paragliding or parasailing in Chamonix-Mont Blanc and Annecy *(p388)*. The Ardèche *(p382)*, with caves honeycombing its hills, is spelunking heaven.

→ Hiking towards the Giant's Tooth peak at Chamonix

LYON

🅵F5 🅰Indre-et-Loire ✈🚉🚌 ℹ78 rue Bernard Palissy;
www.lyon-france.com

**Dramatically sited on the banks of the Rhône and
Saône rivers, the city of Lyon boasts an atmospheric
old town and some of the country's finest restaurants.**

① The Presqu'île

At the heart of Lyon is the Presqu'île, a narrow peninsula north of the confluence of the Saône and Rhône rivers. Rue de la République, a pedestrianized shopping street, links the twin poles of civic life: the vast place Bellecour, with its equestrian statue of Louis XIV in the middle, and place des Terreaux. The latter is overlooked by Lyon's ornate 17th-century Hôtel de Ville (town hall) and the Palais St-Pierre, a former Benedictine convent and now the home of the Musée des Beaux-Arts (p372).

In the middle of the square is a monumental 19th-century fountain by Bartholdi, sculptor of the Statue of Liberty. Behind the town hall is architect Jean Nouvel's futuristic Opéra de Lyon, a black barrel vault of steel and glass encased in a Neo-Classical shell. A few blocks to the south, the enthralling **Musée de l'Imprimerie** illustrates Lyon's contribution to the early days of printing in the late 15th century. Both fabrics and decorative arts are on display at the **Musée des Tissus et des Arts Décoratifs**; its collections of sumptuous silks, including samples from the city's medieval *canuts* (silk weavers) and delicate, hand-finished porcelain are particularly outstanding. The other museum not to miss is the **Musée Lugdunum**, with its fine Gallo-Roman remains. For more on Lyon's history, as well as its long-held tradition

← Lyon's striking
ultra-modern Musée
des Confluences

↑ Lyon's Old Town with its many handsome Renaissance buildings

of puppetry, check out the **Musées Gadagne**. The city's most impressive architectural landmark is the contemporary steel-and-glass science centre and natural history museum, the **Musée des Confluences**.

Musée de l'Imprimerie
 🏛13 rue de la Poulaillerie ⏰10:30am–6pm Wed–Sun 🌐 imprimerie.lyon.fr

Musée des Tissus et des Arts Décoratifs
🏛34 rue de la Charité ⏰10am–6pm Tue–Sun 🌐mtmad.fr

Musée Lugdunum
🏛17 Rue Cleberg ⏰11am–6pm Tue–Sun 🌐lugdunum.grandlyon.com

Musées Gadagne
🏛1 place du Petit Collège ⏰10:30am–6:30pm Wed–Sun 🌐gadagne. musees.lyon.fr

Musée des Confluences
🏛86 quai de Perrache ⏰11am–7pm Tue–Sun 🌐museedes confluences.fr

②
La Croix-Rousse
This area north of Presqu'île became the centre of the city's silk-weaving industry in the 19th century. It is traced with covered passages known as *traboules*, once used by weavers to transport their finished fabrics. Enter at No 6 place des Terreaux and continue along to the Église St-Polycarpe. From here, it is a short walk to the Maison des Canuts, with its old silk loom.

③
La Part-Dieu
Once tranquil farmland, this modern business area on the east bank of the Rhône is home to a huge shopping complex and the Auditorium Maurice-Ravel, which hosts important cultural events. This is where some of the city's most interesting modern architecture is found, including the Tour Oxygène.

EAT

L'Auberge du Pont de Collonges
Paul Bocuse's temple of haute cuisine is a gourmet treat for all the senses. An unmissable foodie destination.

🏛40 rue de la Plage 🌐bocuse.fr

€€€

Têtedoie
Innovative French cuisine is served against panoramic Lyon views, in surprisingly intimate surrounds.

🏛4 rue Professeur Pierre Marion 🌐tetedoie.com

€€€

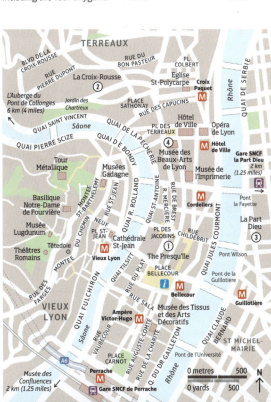

④ 🚲 Ⓜ️ 🍴

MUSÉE DES BEAUX-ARTS DE LYON

🏠 20 place des Terreaux Ⓜ️ Hôtel de Ville 🕐 10am–6pm Wed–Sun 🌐 mba-lyon.fr

Founded in 1801, the Musée des Beaux-Arts originally shared a buiding with Lyon's School of Fine Art. Today it is housed in the 17th-century Palais St-Pierre, a former Benedictine convent for the daughters of the nobility. The 70 rooms of the museum enclose the arches and columns of the former cloister.

Lyon's Musée des Beaux-Arts showcases the country's largest and, some say, most important collection of art after the Louvre. Its rooms display European paintings and sculpture, dating from the early medieval and Renaissance to the modern period, as well as extensive holdings of drawings and engravings, and ancient Egyptian and Near East artifacts. There is also a dazzling range of objets d'art featuring local Lyon silks, ceramics and stoneware from the Far East, and Islamic artworks. Unusually, the musuem is curated in chronological order rather than by artist, movement or theme.

💬 INSIDER TIP
Time Out

The interior courtyard garden is an ideal spot for respite between viewing galleries. Bring a snack to have on a bench or spread a picnic under one of the shade-giving trees, to refresh the senses and mull over all you've seen.

Admiring one of the rooms of sculpture inside the *(inset)* Musée des Beaux Arts ↑

European Paintings and Drawings

Sculpture

▷ The museum holds an exceptional collection of sculpture. It's particularly strong on works from the Middle Ages, where highlights include a 12th-century solemn-looking Virgin and Child from the Auvergne sculpted in wood. Also well represented is the French Romanesque period and the Italian Renaissance, and there are some striking late 19th- and early 20th-century pieces, including works by Rodin and Bourdelle (whose statues also appear in the courtyard), Maillol, Despiau and Pompon, among others.

Objets d'Art

The huge decorative arts collection ranges from Byzantine ivories and Limoges enamels to Lyon silks and Art Nouveau furnishings – as seen, for example, in "La Chambre de Madame Guimard", a collection of the furniture designed by Hector Guimard for his wife's bedroom in their Paris flat. Also on display is an important collection of ceramics from the Renaissance era, the Islamic world and East Asia. The museum alsi boasts an exceptional collection of coins and medallions.

Antiquities

◁ Included in this wide-ranging collection are nine rooms of objects from ancient Egypt as well as artifacts unearthed in Mesopotamia, Etruscan statuettes and 4,000-year-old Cypriot ceramics. Highlights include finely decorated funeral stelea and finds from Egyptian tombs, including the exquisite head of a boy carved from wood around 1400 BC.

Paintings

▽ The world-class collection of paintings includes works by Spanish and Dutch masters, among them Rembrandt; the French schools of the 17th, 18th and 19th centuries; and Impressionist-era paintings by the likes of Van Gogh, Manet and Renoir. The exquisite flower paintings of the Lyon School served as a source of inspiration for the designers of silk fabric. The museum's Cabinet d'Arts Graphiques isn't generally open to the public, but frequent temporary exhibitions showcase some of the collection's 4,000-plus drawings and etchings by such artists as Delacroix, Poussin, Géricault, Degas and Rodin.

A SHORT WALK
LYON

Distance 2.5 km (1.5 miles) **Nearest funicular** Fourvière **Time** 40 minutes

On the west bank of the River Saône, the restored old quarter of Vieux Lyon is an atmospheric warren of cobbled streets, *traboules* (covered passageways), bohemian shops, Renaissance palaces, first-class restaurants and lively *bouchons* (bistros). It is also the site of the Roman city of Lugdunum, the commercial and military capital of Gaul founded by Julius Caesar in 44 BC. Vestiges of this prosperous city can be seen in the Gallo-Roman museum at the top of Fourvière hill, while nearby two excavated Roman theatres still stage performances. At the foot of the hill is the finest collection of Renaissance mansions in France.

There are two Roman amphitheatres in this area. The **Grand Théâtre**, built in 15 BC, is the the oldest theatre in France and is still used for modern performances; the smaller **Odéon** has beautiful geometric tiled flooring.

The underground **Musée de la Civilisation Gallo-Romaine** contains a collection of statues, mosaics, coins and inscriptions evoking Lyon's Roman past.

Entrance to funicular

FINISH

Begun in the late 12th century, the **Cathédrale St-Jean** has a 14th-century astronomical clock that shows religious feast days.

↑ The peaceful interior of the Cathédrale St-Jean

Entrance to funicular

A gaudy mock-Byzantine creation, the 19th-century **Basilique Notre-Dame de Fourvière** is a riot of turrets and crenellations, marble and mosaic – it has become one of the symbols of Lyon.

The **Tour Métallique** was erected in 1893 and is now used as a television transmitter.

The **Chemin du Rosaire** is a beautiful path leading down from Notre-Dame de Fourvière, with spectacular views of the sprawling metropolis below.

Did You Know?

There are said to be 400 *traboules* (secret passages) concealed between buildings in the Old Town.

SSON

START

PL DE FOURVIERE

MONTEE SAINT BERTHELEMY

JF

SAC

RUE DU BOEUF

RUE JUIVERIE

RUE DE LA BOMBARDE

RUE SAINT JEAN

R DE LA BALEINE

R DES TROIS MARIES

ROLLAND

ROMAIN

Rue Juiverie boasts a number of truly splendid Renaissance mansions – look out for the Hôtel Paterin at No 4.

Rue St-Jean and rue du Boeuf are lined with Renaissance mansions, the former homes of bankers and silk merchants.

The 15th-century Hôtel Gadagne houses two museums: the **Musée Historique de Lyon** and the **Musée des Marionnettes du Monde**, which exhibits the famous Lyonnais puppets.

0 metres 100
0 yards 100

N

↑ An aerial view of the city of Grenoble, nestled among mountains

2

GRENOBLE

🅰F5 🅰Isère 🚉🚌 🅸14 rue de la République; grenoble-tourisme.com

The ancient capital of the Dauphiné region and site of the 1968 Winter Olympics, Grenoble is a thriving city surrounded by the soaring Vercors and Chartreuse mountain ranges.

① 🍴 🖥 🛍

City Centre

The focus of Grenoble's urban life is the pedestrian area surrounding the beautiful place Grenette, the city's main square since the 17th century. During the Middle Ages, livestock and grain fairs would be held here – the latter were what gave the square its name. Today, this pleasant paved area is surrounded by buzzing bars and eateries, and is home to a stunning 19th-century fountain, "Le château d'eau Lavalette".

Nearby, the medieval city's heart is place St-André, overlooked by Grenoble's oldest buildings, including the 13th-century Collégiale St-André and 16th-century Ancien Palais du Parlement du Dauphiné.

Did You Know?

Free vending machines in the city dispense short stories that take one, three or five minutes to read.

②

Musée de la Résistance et de la Déportation

🅰14 rue Hébert ⏰Hours vary, check website 🌐resistance-en-isere.fr

Spread over three floors, this enthralling museum looks at the events of World War II from the perspective of the maquis, local underground resistance groups who fought against both the Nazis and the Vichy government. The exhibits cover the beginnings of the maquis; their resistance activites and day-to-day life during the war years; the

SHOP

Fromagerie les Alpages
An award-winning cheese shop.

🅰4 rue de Strasbourg 🌐les-alpages.fr

Bensimon
A popular French chain famous for its elegant fashion.

🅰4 rue Millet 🌐bensimon.com

FAB
A great little place to pick up offbeat gifts.

🅰14 rue Lakanal 📞04 76 17 11 16

reprisals they were subject to under Marshall Pétain's government; and how the movement helped in the liberation of France. The museum also looks at what life was like for the city's Jews during this time.

Fort de la Bastille

📍 North bank of the Isère River ⏰ Hours vary, check website 🌐 bastille-grenoble.fr

Watching over Grenoble, this hilltop fort is one of the city's most iconic sights. While the current fort, with its imposing ramparts, dates from the 19th century, use of this area as a strategic stronghold goes back thousands of years. There are several ways to reach the summit, from being whisked effortlessly up via the cable car which starts at quai Stéphane-Jay, to strapping on some boots and hiking up – there's even a via ferrata route for real adrenaline junkies. However, you reach the top, get ready to enjoy superb views of the city and surrounding Chartreuse mountains.

The hilltop is also home to the Centre d'Art Bastille (CAB), a contemporary art museum, and to Le Musée des Troupes de Montagne (Museum of the Mountain Troops), as well as Acrobastille, a high-wire park.

④ Musée Dauphinois

📍 30 rue Maurice Gignoux ⏰ 10am-6pm Wed-Mon (to 7pm Sat & Sun) 🚫 1 Jan, 1 May, 25 Dec 🌐 musee-dauphinois.fr

This regional museum, housed in a 17th-century convent, is devoted to local history, arts and crafts. Two of its best exhibits are "The People of the Alps", a captivating portrayal of local rural mountain

life, and "The White Dream", a fascinating look at the history of winter sports.

⑤ Musée de l'Ancien Evêché

📍 2 rue Très-Cloîtres ⏰ Hours vary, check website 🌐 ancien-eveche-isere.fr

Located in Grenoble's former Bishops' Palace, nestled in the heart of the city, this museum recounts the history of Isère, and includes the remains of a 4th-century baptistry.

Musée de Grenoble

📍 5 pl de Lavalette ⏰ 10am-6:30pm Wed-Mon 🚫 1 Jan, 1 May, 5 Dec 🌐 museedegrenoble.fr

A veritable temple of art, this museum contains some 900 painting and sculptures dating from the 13th to the 21st centuries. Within its collection are works by Chagall, Giacometti, Picasso and Matisse. The museum also hosts temporary exhibitions.

↑ The exterior of the Musée de Grenoble, a treasure trove of art

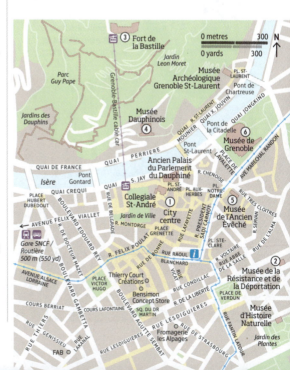

EXPERIENCE MORE

EXPERIENCE The Rhône Valley and French Alps

Vienne's Roman amphitheatre, built between 40 and 50 AD

3

Bourg-en-Bresse

⛰F4 🏛Ain 🚉🚌 ℹCentre Culturel Albert Camus, 6 avenue Alsace-Lorraine; www.bourgenbresse tourisme.fr

Bourg-en-Bresse is a busy market town, with some beautifully restored half-timbered buildings. It is best known for its tasty *poulet de Bresse* – chickens that have been bred and raised in the flat agricultural region of Bresse and have received the coveted designation of *appellation d'origine protégée*, or AOP – and for its abbey church of Brou out on the southeast edge of town. The church, no longer a place of worship, has become one of the most visited sites in France. Flamboyant Gothic in style, it was built between 1505 and 1536 by Margaret of Austria after the death of her husband Philibert, Duke of Savoy, in 1504.

The couple's finely sculpted Carrara marble tombs can be seen in the choir, along with the tomb of Margaret of Bourbon, Philibert's mother, who died in 1483. Notice also the beautifully carved choir stalls, stained-glass windows, and the rood screen, which features some elegant basket-handle arching.

The adjacent cloisters now house a small museum with a worthy collection of 16th- and 17th-century paintings by Dutch and Flemish masters, as well as contemporary works by local artists.

About 24 km (15 miles) north of Bourg-en-Bresse, at St-Trivier-de-Courtes, the restored **Ferme-Musée de la Forêt** offers a look at farm life in the region during the 17th century. The ancient house has what is known locally as a Saracen chimney, which has a brick hood in the centre of the room, similar to constructions found in Portugal and Sicily. The farm also has an interesting collection of antique farm implements.

Ferme-Musée de la Forêt
♿ 🏠1210 route de la Ferme-Musée, Courtes 📞04 74 30 71 89 🕐Apr-Oct: Sat & Sun (mid-Jun-Sep: Tue-Sun)

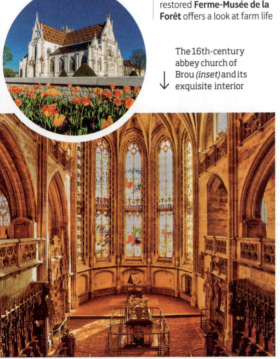

The 16th-century abbey church of Brou *(inset)* and its exquisite interior

4

Vienne

⛰F5 🏛Isère 🚉🚌 ℹCours Brillier; www.vienne-tourisme.com

No other city in the Rhône Valley offers such a notable concentration of architectural history as Vienne. Located in a natural basin of land between the river and the hills, this site was recognized for both its strategic and aesthetic advantages by the Romans, who vastly expanded an existing village when they invaded the area in the 1st century BC.

The centre of the Roman town was the handsome Temple d'Auguste et Livie, dating from 10 BC, which, thanks to various restorations, still stands on place du Palais,

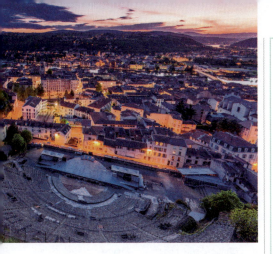

complete with its supporting Corinthian columns. Not far away, off place de Miremont, are the remains of the Jardin Archéologique de Cybèle, a temple dedicated to the goddess Cybele.

The Théâtre Romain, at the foot of Mont Pipet off rue du Cirque, was one of the largest amphitheatres built in Roman France, capable of accommodating in excess of 13,000 spectators. It was restored in 1938, and is now used for a variety of events, including an international jazz festival. From the very top seats the view across the town and river is spectacular. For an even loftier view, head up to the top of Mont Pipet, where you'll find a chapel dedicated to the Virgin.

Other interesting Roman vestiges include a fragment of Roman road in the public gardens and, on the southern edge of town, the Pyramide du Cirque, a curious structure about 20 m (65 ft) high that

was once the centrepiece of the chariot racetrack. The **Musée des Beaux-Arts et d'Archéologie** also has an interesting collection of Gallo-Roman artifacts, as well as 18th-century French faïence.

The city's most important medieval monument is the Cathédrale de St-Maurice, which was built between the 12th and 16th centuries and represents an unusual hybrid of Romanesque and Gothic architectural styles.

Two of Vienne's earliest Christian churches are the 12th-century Église St-André-le-Bas, which has richly carved capitals in its nave and in the cloister, and the even older Église St-Pierre, with parts dating from the 5th and 6th centuries. The latter houses the **Musée Lapidaire St-Pierre**, a museum of stone-carving, with Gallo-Roman bas-reliefs and statues.

Musée des Beaux-Arts et d'Archéologie

Place de Miremont
Apr-Oct: 9:30am-6pm Tue-Sun; Nov-Mar: 1pm-5:30pm Tue-Sun Public hols
musees-vienne.fr

Musée Lapidaire St-Pierre

Place St-Pierre
04 74 85 20 35 Apr-Oct: 9:30am-6pm Tue-Sun; Nov-Mar: 1pm-5:30pm Tue-Sun
Some public hols

Did You Know?

Beaujolais Nouveau Day, when the French wine hits the market shelves, is celebrated in November.

EAT

L'Esquisse
Fabulous gourmet dining in the centre of Annecy. Dishes are based on local, seasonal products and include super-fresh lake fish.

F5 21 rue Royale, 74000 Annecy
esquisse-annecy.fr

La Calèche
Alpine cuisine, including fondue, raclette and tartiflette, served amid warm, cosy chalet décor.

G4 18 rue du Docteur Paccard, 7440 Chamonix
restaurant-caleche.com

Le Restique
Tucked away on a narrow street, this restaurant is a local favourite in Vienne. The passionate chef serves up exquisite regional cuisine in a family-friendly atmosphere.

F5 16 rue Boson, Vienne
le-restique.fr

La Pyramide
Gorgeously presented gastronomic creations based on regional produce, with an excellent wine list. A classic establishment, with two Michelin stars.

F5 14 boulevard Fernand Point, Vienne
lapyramide.com

↑ A fine mosaic of Hylas and the Nymphs at the Musée Gallo-Romain

St-Romain-en-Gal

F5 **Rhône** **Vienne**
Vienne; 04 74 53 70 10

In 1967, building work in this commercial town directly across the Rhône from Vienne revealed extensive remains of a significant Roman community dating from 100 BC to AD 300.

The archaeological site, which extends over more than 3 ha (7.5 acres,) comprises the remnants of villas, public baths, shops and warehouses. Of particular interest is the House of the Ocean Gods, with a magnificent mosaic floor depicting the bearded Neptune and other images from the undersea world.

Much of what has been unearthed so far is housed in the **Musée Gallo-Romain** near the ruins. The collection includes household objects, murals and mosaics. The star exhibit is the *Châtiment de Lycurgue*, a mosaic discovered in 1907. This is a good spot for rainy days, with various family-friendly activities on offer.

Musée Gallo-Romain

⊗ ⓣ 🏛 **D502** ⏰10am–6pm Tue–Sun 🚫Some public hols 🖰musee-site.rhone.fr

6
St-Étienne

E5 **Loire** 🚆🚌🚉 **16 avenue de la Libération; www.saint-etienne tourisme.com**

The dour renown brought to this city by coal-mining and armaments is slowly being shaken off, with ongoing urban redevelopment well under way, an efficient tram-way network, and a lively central area around place du Peuple. Nearby, Jean-Michel Wilmotte has overhauled the **Musée d'Art et d'Industrie**, which covers St-Étienne's industrial history, including the development of the revo-lutionary Jacquard weaving loom, and world-class collec-tions of cycles and ribbon-making machines.

To the north of the city, the **Musée d'Art Moderne** has a collection of 20th-century art, including works by Andy Warhol and Frank Stella.

Musée d'Art et d'Industrie

⊗ ⓣ 🏛 **2 place Louis Comte** ⏰10am–6pm Wed–Mon 🚫Some public hols 🖰musee-art-industrie. saint-etienne.fr

Musée d'Art Moderne

⊗ 🏛 **Saint Priest en Jarez** ⏰10am–6pm Wed–Mon 🚫Some public hols & when exhibitions are changed 🖰mam-st-etienne.fr

Did You Know?

Feminist and World War II French Resistance leader Claudine Chomat was from St-Étienne.

7

Palais Idéal du Facteur Cheval

F5 **Hauterives, Drôme**
Romans-sur-Isère
9:30–dusk **1 & 15–31 Jan, 25 Dec** **facteur cheval.com**

At Hauterives, 24 km (15 miles) north of Romans-sur-Isère on the D538, is one of the greatest follies of France, an eccentric "palace" made of stones and evoking Egyptian, Roman, Aztec and Siamese styles of architecture. It was built by local postman Ferdinand Cheval, who collected the stones during his daily rounds. His neighbours considered him to be mad, but the project attracted the admiring attention of Picasso, the Surrealist André Breton and others.

The interior of the palace is inscribed with Cheval's numerous exhortations and mottoes, the most poignant of which refers to his assiduous efforts to realize his lifelong fantasy: "1879–1912: 10,000 days, 93,000 hours, 33 years of toil".

A variety of intimate concerts are held here regularly on summer evenings.

BRIDGES OF THE RHÔNE

The Rhône has played a crucial role in transporting military and commercial traffic between the north and south of France. It has always been dangerous, a challenge to boatmen and builders for centuries. In 1825, Marc Seguin (1786-1875) built the world's first wire suspension bridge across the Rhône, linking Tournon-sur-Rhône and Tain l'Hermitage. He built the pedestrian suspension bridge, still there today, in the late 1840s.

8

Tournon-sur-Rhône

F5 **Ardèche** **Hôtel de la Tourette; www. ardeche-hermitage.com**

Situated at the foot of a range of impressive granite hills, Tournon is a lovely town with gracious tree-lined promenades and an imposing 11th- to 16th-century château. The latter houses a museum of local history, and has fine views of the town and river from its terraces.

The adjacent Collégiale St-Julien, with its square bell tower and elaborate façade, is an interesting example of the Italian influence on the region's architecture during the 14th century. Inside is a powerful *Résurrection*, painted in 1576 by Capassin, who was a pupil of Raphael.

On quai Charles de Gaulle, the Lycée Gabriel-Fauré is the oldest secondary school in France, dating from 1536.

Directly across the Rhône from Tournon, the village of Tain l'Hermitage is famous for its steep-climbing vineyards, which produce both red and white Hermitage, the finest of all Rhône wines.

From Tournon's main square, place Jean Jaurès, the twisting Route Panoramique leads to St-Péray. This route offers breathtaking views around every corner, and at pretty St-Romain you are rewarded with a superb panorama.

←

The intricate and bizarre images covering the Palais Idéal du Facteur Cheval

A natural rock arch over the river in the Gorges de l'Ardèche

9

Valence

🄰 F5 🄰 Drôme 🚋🚌
🄸 11 bd Bancel; www.
valence-romans-
tourisme.com

Valence is a large, thriving market town on the east bank of the Rhône, looking across to the cliffs of the Ardèche. Its principal attraction is the Romanesque Cathédrale St-Apollinaire on place des Clercs, founded in 1095 and rebuilt in the 17th century.

Alongside the cathedral in the former bishop's palace, the small **Musée de Valence** contains a collection of late 18th-century chalk drawings of Rome by Hubert Robert.

A short walk from here are two Renaissance mansions. The Maison des Têtes at No 57

GREAT VIEW
The Ardèche

Sheer cliffs up to 300 m (984 ft) high line the 35-km (22-mile) Gorges de l'Ardèche, offering spectacular views. The best way to explore the area, including the Pont d'Arc, a 59-m- (194-ft-) wide natural bridge, is by canoe or kayak.

Grande Rue was built in 1532 and is embellished with the sculpted heads of ancient Greeks. On rue Pérollerie, the Maison Dupré-Latour has a finely sculptured porch and staircase.

The Parc Jouvet, south of avenue Gambetta, has lovely pools and gardens, with fine views across the river to the ruined Château de Crussol.

Musée de Valence

◈ 🄰 4 place des Ormeaux
🄲 04 75 79 20 80 🄾 10am–6pm Wed–Sun 🄲 12pm–2pm and some public hols

---

10

The Ardèche

🄰 E6 🄰 Ardèche
✈ Avignon 🚍 Montélimar
🚌 Montélimar, Vallon Pont d'Arc 🄸 Vallon Pont d'Arc;www.pontdarc-ardeche.fr

Over thousands of years, wind and water have endowed this southcentral region of France with a rugged landscape that

---

Wind and water have endowed this southcentral region of France with a rugged landscape that is more reminiscent of the American southwest.

is more reminiscent of the American southwest than the verdure commonly associated with the French countryside. This visible drama is repeated underground. The Ardèche is honeycombed by caves with enormous stalagmites and stalactites. Most impressive are the Grotte de la Madeline, on a signposted path from the D290, and the cave and museum La Cité de la Préhistoire (open February to mid-Nov) south of Vallon-Pont-d'Arc.

Above ground is the Gorges de l'Ardèche. Close to the head of the gorge, going west, is the Pont d'Arc, a limestone "bridge" over the river, created by erosion. Nearby is Grotte Chauvet, a replica of the oldest known decorated cave in the world, a UNESCO World Heritage site that is not open to the public. Painted up to 36,000 years ago, the cave contains hundreds of intricate animal paintings.

Canoeing and whitewater rafting are the two most popular sports here, and equipment can be rented;

CÔTES DU RHONE

Rising in the Swiss Alps and flowing into the Mediterranean, the Rhône is the thread linking the valley vineyards first planted by the Romans. Two-thirds of France's wine has the Côtes du Rhône label; this type of wine ages well. The best vineyards produce Côtes du Rhône Cru. Wines are named after individual vineyards such as Hermitage in the north and, in the south, Châteauneuf-du-Pape (*p513*).

operators at Vallon-Pont-d'Arc and other places rent canoes and organize transport.

The softer side of the region is found in its ancient and picturesque villages, gracious spa towns, vineyards and plantations of Spanish chestnuts (from which the delectable *marron glacé* is produced).

Some 13 km (8 miles) south of Aubenas, the 12th-century village of Balazuc is typical of the region. Its stone houses perch on a clifftop above a gorge of the Ardèche.

Neighbouring Vogüé is between the River Ardèche and a limestone cliff. A tiny but atmospheric village, its most commanding sight is the 12th-century **Château de Vogüé**, once the seat of the barons of Languedoc. Rebuilt in the 17th century, it houses a museum of the region.

Château de Vogüé

⊘ 🏠 2 impasse des Marronniers 🕐 Jun–Sep: 10am–6pm daily; Oct–May: 10:30am–6pm Wed–Mon 🔒 1st week Jun 🌐 chateaudevogue.net

 ①①

Vals-les-Bains

🅰 E5 🏠 Ardèche 🚌 Montélimar ℹ Rue Jean Jaurès; www.aubenas-vals.com

This small spa town, with a hint of past elegance, is in the Volane valley, which has at least 150 springs, all but two of them cold. Containing bicarbonate of soda and other minerals, the water is said to aid digestive problems, rheumatism and diabetes.

Discovered around 1600, this is one of the few spas in southern France to have been overlooked by the Romans. The town reached the height of its popularity in the late 19th century, and still retains something of the belle époque. It makes a good base for exploring the Ardèche.

Some 8 km (5 miles) east of Vals is the Romanesque church of St-Julien du Serre.

___

 ①②

Montélimar

🅰 F6 🏠 Drôme 🚆 🚌 ℹ Montée St-Martin, allées Provençales; www.montelimar-tourisme.com

Whether you choose to make a detour to Montélimar will largely depend on how sweet a tooth you might have. The main curiosity of this market town is its medieval centre, chock-full of shops selling almond-studded nougat. This splendid confection has been made here since the beginning of the 17th century, when the almond tree was first introduced into France from Asia.

The **Château des Adhémar**, a mélange of 12th-, 14th- and 16th-century architecture, surveys the town from the top of a high hill east of town.

The countryside to the east of Montélimar is full of picturesque medieval villages that are linked by scenic routes. La Bégude-de-Mazenc is a thriving little holiday centre, with its fortified Old Town perched on a hilltop. Further to the east is Le Poët Laval, a tiny medieval village set in the Alpine foothills.

Dieulefit is the capital of this beautiful region, and has a number of small hotels and restaurants, as well as sports facilities, including tennis, swimming and fishing.

To the south, the fortified village of Taulignan is known for its truffles.

Château des Adhémar

⊘ ⊘ 🏠 24 rue du Château 🕐 10am–6pm daily 🔒 Public hols 🌐 chateaux-ladrome.fr

→ A mural in Montélimar, boldly publicizing the town's main attraction

> The Vercors is one of France's most magnificent regional parks - a wilderness of pine forests, mountains, waterfalls, caves and deep, narrow gorges.

 13

Briançon

 G5 Hautes-Alpes 🚍🚌
ℹ️ 1 place du Temple; www.
serre-chevalier.com

The highest town in Europe, at 1,320 m (4,330 ft), Briançon has been an important stronghold since pre-Roman times, guarding as it does the road to the Col de Montgenèvre, one of the oldest and most important passes into Italy. At the beginning of the 18th century, the town was fortified with ramparts and gates, still splendidly intact, by Louis XIV's military architect, Vauban. If driving, park at the Champs de Mars, and enter the pedestrianized Old Town by way of the Porte de Pignerol.

This leads to the Grande Rue, a steep, narrow street with a stream running down the middle and bordered by lovely period houses. The nearby Église de Notre-Dame dates from 1718, and was also built by Vauban with an eye to defence. To visit Vauban's citadel, stop in at the tourist office, where you can arrange a guided tour.

Briançon is also a major centre for sport, with skiing in winter, and rafting, cycling and paragliding in summer.

Just to the west of town, the Parc National des Écrins is the largest of the French national parks, offering a range of lofty peaks and glaciers, and a magnificent variety of Alpine flowers.

The Parc Naturel Régional du Queyras is accessible from Briançon over the rugged Col de l'Izoard, a great wall of 3,000-m- (9,850-ft-) high peaks that separate this wild and beautiful national park from neighbouring Italy.

14

Grignan

F6 Drôme 🚍 ℹ️ Pl du Jeu de Ballon; www.
tourisme-paysde
grignan.com

Situated on a rocky hill surrounded by fields of lavender, this pleasant village owes its fame to Madame de Sévigné, who wrote many of her celebrated letters while staying at the **Château de Grignan**.

Built during the 15th and 16th centuries, the château is one of the finest Renaissance structures in this region of France. Its interior contains fine Louis XII furniture and Aubusson tapestries.

From the château's terrace, a panoramic view extends as far as the Vivarais mountains in the Ardèche. Directly below the terrace, the Église de St-Saveur was built in the 1530s, and contains the tomb of Madame de Sévigné, who died here in 1696 at the age of 70.

Château de Grignan
♿🚫 🕙 10am–6pm daily
🚫 Public hols 🌐 chateaux-ladrome.fr

 15

The Vercors

F5 Isère & Drôme
🚆 Grenoble 🚍 Romans-sur-Isère, St-Marcellin, Grenoble 🚍 Pont-en-Royans, Romans-sur-Isère
ℹ️ Maison du Parc: 255 chemin des Fusillés, Lans-en-Vercors 38250; www.
parc-du-vercors.fr

To the south and west of Grenoble, the Vercors is one of France's most magnificent regional parks – a wilderness of pine forests, jagged

→

The village of Château Bernard in the Vercors Regional Park

mountain peaks, spectacular waterfalls, caves and deep, narrow gorges.

The D531 out of Grenoble runs through Villard-de-Lans, a good base for excursions, and continues west to the dark Gorges de la Bournes. About 8 km (5 miles) further west, the hamlet of Pont-en-Royans is sited on a limestone gorge, its stone houses built into the rocks overlooking the River Bourne.

South of Pont-en-Royans along the D76, the Route de Combe-Laval snakes along a sheer cliff above the roaring

 INSIDER TIP
Olives of Nyons

As the southern Alps cascade into Provence, the climate and land are more Mediterranean. The Nyons area is famed for its Tanche olives and olive oil, with Protected Designation of Origin (PDO/AOC) status.

river. The Grands Goulets, 7 km (4 miles) to the east, is a gorge overlooked by sheer cliffs that virtually shut out the sky. The best-known mountain in the park is the Mont Aiguille, a soaring outcrop of 2,086 m (6,844 ft).

The Vercors was a key base for the French Resistance during World War II. In July 1944 the Germans launched an aerial attack on the region, flattening several of its villages. Resistance museums are at Vassieux and Grenoble.

 16

Nyons

🅰 F6 🅝 Drôme 🚍 🏛 Pl de la Libération; www. nyons.com

Nyons is synonymous with olives in France. All manner of olive products are sold at the Thursday-morning market, from soap to *tapenade*.

The Quartier des Forts is the town's oldest quarter, a warren of narrow streets and stepped alleyways, the most rewarding of which is the covered rue des Grands Forts. Spanning the River Aygues is a graceful 13th-century bridge; on its town side are several old mills turned into shops, where you can see the enormous presses once used to extract olive oil. The **Espace Vignolis – Musée de l'Olivier** further explains the industry.

There is a fine view from the belvedere above the town. Sheltered by mountains, Nyons has an almost exotic climate, with all the trees and plants of the Riviera to be found here.

From Nyons, the D94 leads west to the pleasant wine village of Suze-la-Rousse, which, during the Middle Ages, was the most important town in the area. Today, it is best known for its "university of wine", one of the most respected centres of oenology in the world, housed in the 14th-century **Château de Suze-la-Rousse**, the hunting lodge of the princes of Orange.

Espace Vignolis – Musée de l'Olivier

♿ 🕐 🅰 Place Olivier de Serres 🕐 9am–7pm daily 🅦 vignolis.fr

Château de Suze-la-Rousse

♿ 🕐 🅰 🕐 10am–6pm daily 🅞 Public hols 🅦 chateaux-ladrome.fr

> ### LIFE ON HIGH
>
> The sure-footed Alpine ibex lives high above the tree line for all but the coldest season. Until the Parc National de la Vanoise was created in 1963, it had become almost extinct in France, but conservation has seen the population rise to over 10,000. Both males and females have horns and those of the oldest males can be almost 1 m (3 ft) long.

17

The Chartreuse

F5 Isère & Savoie
Grenoble, Chambéry
Grenoble, Voiron
St-Pierre-de-Chartreuse
St-Pierre-de-Chartreuse; www.chartreuse-tourism.com

From Grenoble, the D512 leads north into the mountainous region of Chartreuse, where hydroelectricity was invented in the late 1800s. The Monastère de la Grande Chartreuse, west of St-Pierre-de-Chartreuse off the D520-B, is the main local sight.

Founded by St Bruno in 1084, the monastery owes its fame to the green and yellow Chartreuse liqueurs first produced by the monks in 1605. The recipe, based on a secret herbal elixir of 130 ingredients, is now produced in the town of Voiron.

The monastery itself is inhabited by about 40 monks, who live in seclusion. It is not open to visitors, but there is a museum at the entrance, the **Musée de la Correrie**, which depicts the daily routine of the Carthusian monks.

Musée de la Correrie

St-Pierre-de-Chartreuse Jun-Aug: 10am-6:30pm Fri-Wed; Apr-May & Sep-Nov: 2-6pm Fri-Wed musee-grande-chartreuse.fr

---

18

Chambéry

F5 Savoie
5 bis place Palais de Justice; www.chambery-tourisme.com

Once the capital of Savoy, this dignified city has aristocratic airs and a distinctly Italianate feel. Its best-loved monument is the extravagant Fontaine des Eléphants on rue de Boigne, erected in 1838 to honour the Comte de Boigne, who left to his home town some of the fortune he amassed in India.

The imposing 14th-century Château des Ducs de Savoie, at the opposite end of rue de Boigne, is now occupied by the Préfecture. Only certain parts of the building, such as the late Gothic Ste-Chapelle, can be visited, via guided tours arranged with the tourist office.

On the southeast edge of town is the charming 17th-century country house **Les Charmettes**, where the philosopher Jean-Jacques Rousseau lived with his mistress Madame de Warens. It is worth a visit for its peaceful gardens and small museum of memorabilia.

Les Charmettes

892 chemin des Charmettes
04 79 33 39 44
10am-6pm Tue-Sun
Public hols

19

Aix-les-Bains

F5 Savoie
Place Maurice Mollard; www.aixlesbains-rivieradesalpes.com

The Romantic poet Lamartine rhapsodized over the beauty of Lac du Bourget, site of the spa town of Aix-les-Bains. The heart of the town is the 19th-century **Thermes Nationaux**, thermal baths first enjoyed by the Romans over 2,000 years ago – in the basement are the remains of the original Roman baths. The ruins can be visited on a guided tour. Opposite the baths, the 2nd-century AD Temple of Diana contains Gallo-Roman artifacts. The tourist office runs guided tours (Feb–Nov). The nearby **Musée Faure** has some stunning Impressionist paintings by Degas and Sisley, 34 Rodin sculptures and fascinating Lamartine memorabilia.

The small town of Le Revard, just east of Aix on the D913, has spectacular views of the lake and Mont Blanc.

Thermes Nationaux

Pl Maurice Mollard
thermes-aixlesbains.com

← The ornate Fontain des Eléphants in Chambéry

↑ The idyllic medieval port of Yvoire, on the shores of Lac Léman

Musée Faure
◈ 🏛 Villa des Chimères, 10 blvd des Côtes 📞 04 79 61 06 57 🕐 May–Oct: 10am–6:30pm Wed–Sun 🚫 Public hols

---

20

Lac Léman

🏛 F4 🏛 Haute-Savoie & Switzerland ✈ Geneva 🚆🚌 Geneva, Thonon-les-Bains, Évian-les-Bains ℹ Thonon-les-Bains 🌐 thononlesbains.com

The stirring scenery and gentle climate of the French shore of Lake Geneva (Lac Léman to the French) has made it a fashionable resort area since the first spa buildings were erected at Évian-les-Bains in 1839.

Yvoire is a fine place to begin a visit to the area. This medieval port is guarded by a 14th-century castle, and its houses are bedecked with colourful flower boxes.

Further east along Lake Geneva is Thonon-les-Bains, a prosperous little spa town perched on a cliff overlooking the lake. A funicular takes you down to Rives, the harbour at the foot of the cliffs, where sailboats can be rented and excursion boats to the Swiss cities of Geneva and Lausanne call in. Just outside the town is the 15th-century Château de Ripaille, made famous by its one-time resident Duke Amadeus VIII, who later became antipope (Felix V).

Although it has been modernized and acquired an international reputation for its eponymous spring water, Évian-les-Bains still exudes a *vie en rose* charm. The tree-lined lakefront promenade is a lovely walk, while more energetic types can try tennis, golf, sailing and skiing. State-of-the-art spa treatments are available, and the exotic domed casino is busy at night.

> ### Did You Know?
> Evian water is mentioned in Agatha Christie's 1934 novel *Murder on the Orient Express*.

STAY

Hôtel Richemond
Rooms with plenty of period character in a grand town-centre hotel that's been owned by the same family since 1914.

🏛 G4 🏛 228 rue du Docteur Paccard, Chamonix Mont-Blanc 🌐 richemond.fr

---

Les Hospitaliers
Situated in a dreamy hilltop hamlet from the Middle Ages, this charming hotel offers spacious rooms and a top-notch restaurant.

🏛 F6 🏛 Vieux Village, Le Poët-Laval 🌐 hotel-les-hospitaliers.com

---

Hostellerie du Vieux Pérouges
Set in a hilltop village, this historic inn has rooms in four 13th-century timbered houses, clustered around a pretty cobblestone square.

🏛 F5 🏛 Village Médiéval, Pérouges 📞 04 74 61 00 88

Grand Hôtel des Alpes
Established in 1840, this supremely elegant establishment is famed for luxurious rooms and breathtaking views.

🏛 G4 🏛 75 rue du Docteur Paccard, Chamonix Mont-Blanc 🌐 grandhotel desalpes.com

21

Annecy

 F5 Haute-Savoie 1 rue Jean Jaurès; www.lac-annecy.com

Annecy is one of the most charming towns in the Alps, set at the northern tip of Lac d'Annecy and surrounded by snowcapped mountains. Its medieval quarter is laced with canals, flower-covered bridges and arcaded streets. Strolling around is the main attraction here, though there are a couple of sights worth having a look at more closely: the formidable Palais de l'Isle, a 12th-century prison in the middle of the Thiou canal; and the turreted Château d'Annecy, set high on a hill above with impressive views of Vieil Annecy and the crystal-clear lake beyond.

The best spot for swimming and water sports is at the eastern end of the avenue d'Albigny near the Imperial Palace hotel, while boat trips leave from quai Napoléon III.

One of the best ways to enjoy the area's breathtaking scenery is to take a boat from Annecy to Talloires, a tiny lakeside village celebrated for its hotels and restaurants. Facing Talloires across the lake is the 15th-century Château de Duingt (not open to visitors). On the west bank of the lake stands the Semnoz mountain and its summit, the Crêt de Châtillon, offers some of the most spectacular panoramic views of Mont Blanc and the peaks of the surrounding Alps.

22

Pérouges

 F5 Ain Meximieux-Pérouges Route de la cité; www.perouges.org

Pérouges is a fortified hilltop village of medieval houses and cobblestone streets. In the 13th century it was a centre of linen-weaving, but with the mechanization of the industry in the 19th century, the local population fell from 1,500 to 90.

Restoration of its buildings and an influx of craftspeople have breathed new life into Pérouges. The village has been used as the setting for historical dramas such as *The Three Musketeers* and *Monsieur Vincent*. The main square, place de la Halle, is shaded by a huge lime tree planted in 1792 to honour the Revolution.

23

The Dombes

F4 Ain Lyon Lyon, Villars-les-Dombes, Bourg-en-Bresse Villars-les-Dombes (from Bourg-en-Bresse) 3 pl de Hôtel de Ville, Villars-les-Dombes; www.dombes-tourisme.com

This flat, glacier-gouged plateau is located south of Bourg-en-Bresse is dotted with small hills, ponds and marshes, making it particularly popular with anglers and bird-watchers. In the middle of the area, at Villars-les-Dombes, is an ornithological and botanical park, the **Parc des Oiseaux**. Over 300 species of native and exotic birds live here, free to roam in their natural habitats, including tufted herons, vultures, and pink flamingoes, as well as emus and ostriches.

↑ Grey-crowned cranes found roaming around Villars-les-Dombes

Did You Know?

Created for fish-breeding, some of the rainwater ponds in the Dombes date from the 15th century.

→ A perfect snowy scene at the ski resort of Le Bourg d'Oisans

Parc des Oiseaux

⊘ ⓣ 🅰 Route Nationale 83, Villars-les-Dombes 🄲 04 74 98 05 54 🄾 Daily 🄲 Mid-Nov–Mar ⓦ parcdesoiseaux.com

Le Bourg d'Oisans

🅰 F5 🄾 Isère 🚌 To Grenoble 🚌 To Le Bourg d'Oisans
🄸 Quai Docteur Girard; www.bourg doisans.com

Le Bourg d'Oisans is an ideal base from which to explore the Romanche Valley, providing opportunities for cycling, rock-climbing and skiing in the resort of L'Alpe d'Huez. The town is often part of the Tour de France route; rent a bike and test your skills on some of the tricky paths.

Silver and other minerals have been mined here since the Middle Ages. The **Musée des Minéraux et de la Faune des Alpes**, squeezed into the attic of a church, is renowned for its collection of crystals and precious stones. Set to the sounds of nature, there is also a lively exhibition on the fauna of the Alps, where more than 140 species are presented in their natural environment.

Musée des Minéraux et de la Faune des Alpes

⊘ ⓐ 🅰 1 Pl de l'Eglise 🄲 04 76 80 27 54 🄾 2–6pm daily 🄲 Pub hols

📷 PICTURE PERFECT
Island Palais

Shaped like the prow of a ship, Annecy's Palais de l'Isle has stood on part of an island in the Canal du Thiou for about nine centuries. It's been a subject for many painters and photographers since the mid-1800s.

← Annecy's picturesque 12th-century Palais de l'Isle, in the middle of Thiou canal

A DRIVING TOUR OF
BEAUJOLAIS

Length 60km (37 miles) **Stopping-off points** Moulin-à-Vent; Fleurie; Brouilly **Terrain** Mainly flat

Beaujolais is the perfect place for wine tasting, offering delicious, affordable wine and glorious countryside. The south of the region produces most of the world-renowned Beaujolais Nouveau. In the north are the ten superior quality *cru* vineyards – among them Juliénas, Moulin-à-Vent, Fleurie, Chiroubles, Morgon and Brouilly – most of which can be visited in a day's drive. The distinctive *maisons du pays* have living quarters built over the wine cellar. Almost every village has its *cave* (wine cellar), offering tastings and a glimpse of the wine culture that dominates local life.

Locator Map
For more detail see p362

THE RHÔNE VALLEY AND FRENCH ALPS

Beaujolais

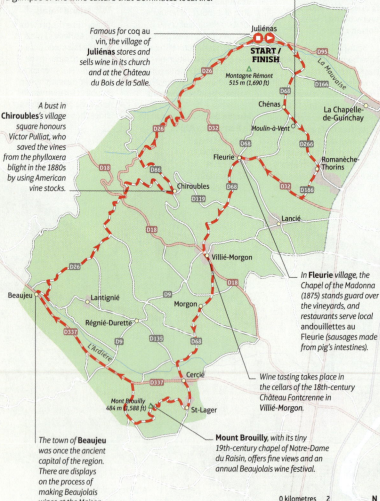

Moulin-à-Vent *is a 17th-century windmill with views of the Saône Valley; tastings of local wines are held in the caves next door.*

Famous for coq au vin, the village of **Juliénas** *stores and sells wine in its church and at the Château du Bois de la Salle.*

A bust in **Chiroubles's** *village square honours Victor Pulliat, who saved the vines from the phylloxera blight in the 1880s by using American vine stocks.*

START / FINISH

Montagne Rémont 515 m (1,690 ft)

In **Fleurie** *village, the Chapel of the Madonna (1875) stands guard over the vineyards, and restaurants serve local andouillettes au Fleurie (sausages made from pig's intestines).*

Wine tasting takes place in the cellars of the 18th-century Château Fontcrenne in Villié-Morgon.

The town of **Beaujeu** *was once the ancient capital of the region. There are displays on the process of making Beaujolais wines at the Maison du Terroir Beaujolais.*

Mount Brouilly, *with its tiny 19th-century chapel of Notre-Dame du Raisin, offers fine views and an annual Beaujolais wine festival.*

0 kilometres 2
0 miles 2

N

↑ The Chapel of the Madonna surrounded by rows of vines in Fleurie

POITOU AND AQUITAINE

With flat, fertile land and an accessible coastline, Poitou and Aquitaine were first inhabited more than 20,000 years ago. During the Iron Age, Celtic tribes grew immensely wealthy mining gold in the hills of Limousin, which they then turned into coins and beautiful ceremonial pieces. By the 1st century BC, Julius Caesar had transferred these riches to Roman coffers, and began building baths, arches and amphitheatres in Bordeaux and Saintes. During the Middle Ages, the exquisitely ornate cathedrals of Parthenay and Poitiers sprang up as the landscape became criss-crossed with pilgrimage routes, along which the devout journeyed to Santiago de Compostela in Spain. In 1152, Eleanor of Aquitaine added this province to England's Continental territories when she married Henry II; although Poitou was lost in 1259, Aquitaine would remain under English rule until 1453, when it was annexed by France. Many towns were destroyed during the Wars of Religion in the 16th century, but the region was largely spared by the French Revolution. In 1870, when Paris seemed under threat at the start of the Franco-Prussian war, the French capital was temporary moved to Bordeaux. History would repeat itself during World War I and very briefly during the World War II, when the government again relocated to Bordeaux before Paris was sieged.

POITOU AND AQUITAINE

Must Sees

1 Poitiers
2 Bordeaux

Experience More

3 Thouars
4 Parthenay
5 Niort
6 Marais Poitevin
7 Melle
8 Futuroscope
9 Abbaye de Nouaillé-Maupertuis
10 Chauvigny
11 Angles-sur-l'Anglin
12 Montmorillon
13 St-Savin
14 Aulnay de Saintonge
15 Charroux
16 Confolens
17 Pauillac
18 La Rochelle
19 Brouage
20 Talmont-sur-Gironde
21 Rochefort
22 Île d'Oléron
23 Cognac
24 Saintes
25 Aubeterre-sur-Dronne
26 Angoulême
27 Bassin d'Arcachon
28 St-Émilion
29 La Côte d'Argent
30 Les Landes
31 Mont-de-Marsan
32 Dax
33 Royan

Noirmoutier-en-l'Île
Île de Noirmoutier
Macheco

Fromentine
Challans

Saint-Jean-de-Monts

Île d'Yeu

Les Sables-d'Olonne

A t l a n t i c

O c e a n

Bay of Biscay

POITOU AND
AQUITAINE

Santander

Torrelavega
Laredo

Sopela
Bermeo

Saint-Jean-de-Lu

SPAIN

Bilbao

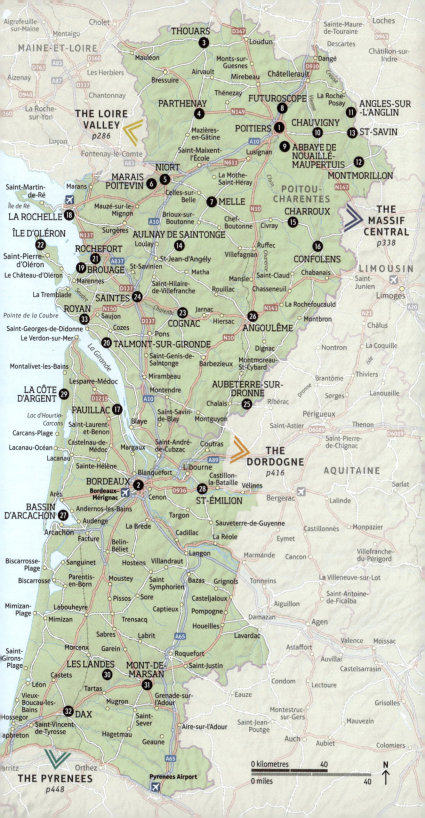

7 DAYS
in Poitou and Aquitaine

Day 1

Begin your week in the capital, Poitiers (*p398*), a vibrant town of varied architectural styles, such as the 11th-century façade of the elegant church, Notre-Dame-la-Grande (*p398*). For lunch, have delicious Moroccan-inspired food at Notre Dame de Pique (*185 Grand'Rue*). Spend the afternoon sketching out visions of the future at Futurescope (*p404*), just outside of town. Dinner is modern French dishes served in a former grand chapel at Les Archives (*14 rue Édouard-Grimaux*).

Day 2

Drive east to Chauvigny (*p404*), a pretty town that lies on the banks of the Vienne River and is surrounded by ancient castle ruins. Ramble about these before taking in the particularly fine columns at Église Saint-Pierre. Fortify yourself on crêpes at rustic La Bigorne (*25 Rue des Puys*) then head 10 km (6 miles) north of Chauvigny for a guided tour of romantic Château de Touffou (*p406*). Back in town, opt for burgers and a refreshing mojito at La Moustache (*www.la-moustache.fr*).

Day 3

Continue on to the historic sailor's city of La Rochelle (*p408*), a 2-hour drive west. Along the way, stop at Niort (*p402*) to pick up a bottle of angelica liquor – legend says it cures the plague. In La Rochelle, feast on fresh seafood down by the harbour before wandering through the cobbled streets on your way to climb the Tour de la Lanterne, with its 400-year-old graffiti. Tuck into a charcuterie plate and a pint of craft beer at Captain Houblon (*8 rue de la Ferté*), then take in the nightly street entertainment around the marina.

Day 4

Head an hour south to Saintes (*p411*), a 2,000-year-old city filled with historical treasures. There is a farmer's market here every day except Mondays, so stock up on local goodies for a picnic lunch amid the ruins of a 1st-century Roman amphitheatre. Rent a canoe and glide peacefully along the River Charente to finish off the day, then stretch out in comfort and simplicity at Hôtel des Messageries (*www.hotel-des-messageries.com*).

① Impressive harbour towers at La Rochelle.

② Local wines on display.

③ Roman ruins in Saintes.

④ The port in Cognac.

⑤ Miroir-d'Eau in Bordeaux.

Day 5

Upon arrival in Cognac *(p411)* wander the lovely old part of town, gazing up at the half-timbered and local white stone historic townhouses. By now it's probably late enough to indulge in some cognac tasting. One of the best places is the Royal Château de Cognac *(www.chateauroyaldecognac.com)*. For dinner, savour updated traditional fare at L'Atelier des Quais *(www.atelierdesquais.fr)* before another cognac as a nightcap in the tasting rooms at L'Yeuese *(www.yeuse.fr)*.

Day 6

Pick up some freshly baked breakfast treats from a boulangerie, then sally forth to Angoulême *(p412)*, a hilltop fortified town that abounds in historical sites, including a 12-century cathedral – but the town is now best known as a centre for comic book art. Each year, the art is celebrated at the noted Festival de la Bande Dessinée. If you're not in town for the show, head to Cité Internationale de la Bande-Dessinée et de l'Image to see

French comic strips and cartoons from as far back as 1946. A short drive east, just out of town, will take you to the charming country mansion Domaine du Châtelard *(1079 route du Chatelard)*, where you can eat a late lunch on the terrace overlooking a picturesque lake. Drive down to Bordeaux to be there when the sun sets on this ancient town.

Day 7

The final day is reserved for Bordeaux *(p400)*, one of France's finest cities. This industrial centre is also famed as one of the best wine regions in the country – so don't miss the opportunity to learn more about the drop at the spectacular La Cité du Vin museum *(p400)*, where tastings are also on the menu. Stroll off the cobwebs along the revitalized waterfront of River Garonne towards the famous Miroir d'Eau *(p401)* fountain. Shop for antiques and vintage wear along rue Notre-Dame in the Quartier des Chartrons. Join the locals for dinner accompanied by, of course, fine native wine, at the inviting Le Bouchon Bordelais *(2 rue Courbin)*.

❶

POITIERS

🅰C4 🚉Vienne ✈5 km (3 miles) W of Poitiers 🚌
ℹ45 pl Charles de Gaulle; www.ot-poitiers.fr

Three of the greatest battles in French history were fought around Poitiers, the most famous in 732, when Charles Martel halted the Arab invasion. The town thrived during the reign of Jean de Berry (1369–1416) and became a major centre of learning with the founding of its university in 1431. Today, Poitiers is a dynamic city with a rich architectural heritage.

↑ A beautiful statue gracing a side altar in Notre-Dame-La-Grande

Angevin kings, Henry II and Richard the Lionheart. This is thought to be the scene of Joan of Arc's examination by a council of theologians in 1429.

Cathédrale St-Pierre

🅰1 rue Sainte-Croix 📞05 49 41 23 76 🕒Summer: 9am-7:30pm daily; winter: 9am-5pm daily

Poitier's impressive Gothic cathedral dates from the 12th century. The 13th-century carved choir stalls are among the oldest in France. Note the huge 12th-century east window showing the Crucifixion; tiny figures of the cathedral's patrons (Henry II and Eleanor of Aquitaine) are crouched at the foot of the window. During renovation work in 2015 four amazingly well-preserved wall paintings dating from the cathedral's earliest days were discovered; they depict Christ in Majesty among other scenes. The organ (1787–91), made by François-Henri Cliquot, is one of the finest in Europe.

---

❷

Palais de Justice

🅰Pl Alphonse Lepetit 📞05 49 50 22 00 🕒9am-noon & 1:30-5pm Mon-Fri

Behind the bland Renaissance façade is the 12th-century great hall of the palace of the

---

❸

Notre-Dame-la-Grande

🅰53, place Charles de Gaulle 📞05 49 41 23 76 🕒9am-7pm daily

Notre-Dame-la-Grande is not a large church, despite its name. One of Poitiers's great pilgrim churches, it is most celebrated as a masterpiece of lively 12th-century Poitevin sculpture, notably its richly detailed façade. In the choir is a Romanesque fresco of Christ and the Virgin. Most of the chapels were added in the Renaissance.

Aerial view of Poitiers, with its imposing Gothic cathedral in the distance

Baptistère St-Jean

🏠 Rue Jean Jaurès 📞 05 49 41 21 24 🕐 Mid-Jun–Sep: 10am–12:30pm & 2–6pm daily; Oct–mid-Jun: 2–6pm Tue–Sun

This polygonal 4th-century building is one of the oldest Christian buildings in Western Europe. Now a museum, its displays include Romanesque frescoes of both Christ and the Emperor Constantine, and some Merovingian sarcophagi. It also preserves an ancient octagonal pool that was used for full-immersion baptisms up until the eighth century.

Musée Sainte-Croix

🏠 3 bis rue Jean Jaurès 📞 05 49 41 07 53 🕐 Hours vary, call ahead 🚫 Public hols

Musée Sainte-Croix exhibits prehistoric, Gallo-Roman and medieval archaeology, and a wide range of paintings and 19th-century sculpture. Seven bronzes by Camille Claudel are on show, including *La Valse*. There is also a collection of contemporary art.

Eglise St-Hilaire-le-Grand

🏠 26 rue Sainte Hilaire 📞 05 49 41 21 57 🕐 Apr–Nov: 9am–7pm daily; Dec–Mar: 9am–5:30pm daily

Fires and reconstructions have made St-Hilaire a mosaic of different styles. With its origins in the 6th century, the church still preserves intact an 11th-century bell tower and a 12th-century nave.

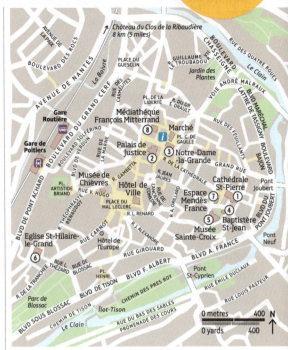

Espace Mendès France

🏠 1 pl de la Cathédrale 🕐 9am–6:30pm Tue–Fri, 2–6:30pm Sat & Sun 🚫 1 Jan; Sun in Jul–Aug 🌐 emf.fr

This museum contains a state-of-the-art planetarium, with laser shows explaining the mysteries of the universe, plus exhibitions.

Médiathèque François Mitterrand

🏠 4 rue de l'Université 🕐 11am–7pm Tue–Sat 🚫 Public hols 🌐 bm-poitiers.fr

This modern building, located in the historic quarter, is home to the Maison du Moyen Age, which displays a collection of medieval manuscripts, maps and engravings, and stages temporary exhibitions.

SLEEP

Château du Clos de la Ribaudière

A stately 18th-century mansion with heated outdoor pool and alfresco dining on the stone terrace during the summer months.

🏠 10 rue du Champ de Foire 🌐 ribaudiere.com

€€€

Hôtel de l'Europe

A modern hotel in the heart of the city, with an on-site car park and a good-value breakfast buffet.

🏠 39 rue Sadi Carnot 🌐 defiplanet.com

€€€

❷

BORDEAUX

 C5 10 km (6 miles) W of Bordeaux Rue Charles Domerq *i* 12 cours du 30 Juillet, bordeaux-tourisme.com

Built on a curve of the River Garonne, Bordeaux dates back to pre-Roman times. But little evidence of this ancient past remains, as the forward-looking industrial hub sprawls around a noble 18th-century centre.

① Place de la Bourse

This elegant square near the waterfront is flanked by two 18th-century buildings, Palais de la Bourse and Hôtel des Douanes. In front of them, next to the river, is the Miroir d'Eau water feature.

② Grand Théâtre

2 Pl de la Comédie By appointment only opera-bordeaux.com

Built by architect Victor Louis, the 18th-century Grand Théâtre is one of the finest Classical edifices of its type in France, with an auditorium known for its acoustics. The grand main staircase was later imitated by Garnier for the Paris Opéra.

③ La Cité du Vin

134 quai de Bacalan Hours vary, check website 1 Jan & 25 Dec lacitéduvin.com

Located in a purpose-built, architecturally striking building, the City of Wine Museum pays homage to Bordeaux's reputation as a wine-making centre – the immersive museum is the place to discover the world of wine from its origins to the present day. Visits include a tasting, and there are also restaurants on site.

④ CAPC Musée d'Art Contemporain

Entrepôt Lainé, 7 rue Ferrère 11am–6pm Tue–Sun (to 8pm Wed) Public hols capc-bordeaux.fr

One of the earliest museums of contemporary art in France, CAPC was founded in 1973 and moved to this converted 19th-century warehouse in 1974. It has a permanent collection of over a thousand works, including pieces by local and international artists, such as Nan Goldin and Gilbert & George. The museum also presents an often excellent programme of exhibitions throughout the year, and is well worth a visit.

⑤

Musée des Arts Décoratifs

⌂ 39 rue Bouffard ☎ 05 56 10 14 05 ⏰ 11am–6pm Wed–Mon ⊘ Public hols

Housed in the refined 18th-century Hôtel de Lalande, this museum has an exceptional collection of fine porcelain and elegant furnishings.

---

⑥

Cathédrale St-André

⌂ Pl Pey Berland ☎ 05 56 52 68 10

This gigantic church dates from the 11th century and is a mix of styles. Its fine medieval sculptures include scenes from the Last Judgment.

↑ Looking over the graceful 18th-century rooftops in the centre of Bordeaux

 Must See

EAT

Tante Charlotte
Traditional French food is served by candlelight in this inviting little restaurant, open late.

⌂ 7 rue des Bahutiers
☎ 33 9 82 60 13 12

€€€

Le Chapon Fin
Dating back to 1825, this fine-dining spot has a fabulous interior.

⌂ 5 rue Montesquieu
🌐 chapon-fin.com

€€€

↖ ⑤ *Musée des Arts Décoratifs (500m)*

The Eglise Notre-Dame was built in 1684–1707.

The Monument aux Girondins commemorates the Girondists sent to the guillotine by Robespierre during the Terror (1793–4).

← ⑥ *Cathédrale St-André (700m)*

Fine 18th-century buildings abound in this quarter.

③ *La Cité du Vin (2km)*

Terraces provide good views over the river.

The vast space of Esplanade des Quinconces features fine statues and fountains.

The quai, facing the waterfront, is lined with graceful façades.

EXPERIENCE MORE

Thouars

🅰 C4 🚉 Deux-Sèvres 🚌
ℹ 32 pl St-Médard; www.
tourisme-pays-thouar
sais.fr

On a rocky outcrop surrounded by the River Thouet, Thousars features as many roofs of northern slate as of southern red tiles. In the centre stands Église St-Médard. Its Romanesque façade is a perfect example of the Poitevin style that is typical of the region, although a splendid Gothic rose window has been added. Lined with half-timbered medieval houses, rue du Château leads up to the 17th-century château, which now houses a school and is open to the public from May to September.

East of Thouars lies the moated **Château d'Oiron**, which now hosts a rolling programme of contemporary art exhibitions. A masterpiece of Renaissance architecture, it was completed in 1549.

Château d'Oiron

♿ 🅟 🏠 10 rue du Château, Oiron 🕐 Daily 🚫 Some public hols 🌐 chateau-oiron.fr

Parthenay

🅰 C4 🚉 Deux-Sèvres 🚌
ℹ 22 blvd de la Meilleraye;
www.tourisme-gatine.com

Parthenay is a sleepy provincial town, except on Wednesdays, when France's second-biggest livestock market is held here. In the Middle Ages, the town was an important halt on the route to Santiago de Compostela and it is easy to imagine the processions of pilgrims in the medieval quarter. Steep and cobbled, rue de la Vau-St-Jacques winds up to the 13th-century ramparts, leading on from the

GREAT VIEW
Donjon de Niort

Climb the stairs to the battlements of the imposing Donjon de Niort for panoramic views across the city and beyond. A helpful map on the rooftop shows you what you're looking out at.

fortified Porte St-Jacques, which guards a 13th-century bridge over the River Thouet.

Niort

🅰 C4 🚉 Deux-Sèvres 🚌
ℹ 2 rue Brisson; www.
niortmaraispoitevin.com

Once a medieval port by the green waters of the Sèvre, Niort is now a prosperous industrial town specializing in machine tools, electronics, chemicals and insurance.

Its closeness to the marshes is evident in the local specialities that fill the stalls of the town's bustling Les Halles market – eels, snails and angelica. The last, a herb, is used in everything from liqueur to ice cream.

The huge 12th-century donjon overlooking the Vieux Pont was built by Henry II and Richard the Lionheart. It played an important role during the Hundred Years' War and was later used as a prison. The donjon is now a museum of local arts and crafts, and archaeology. The Musée d'Agesci in avenue de Limoges exhibits ceramics, sculpture and paintings from the 16th to 20th centuries.

Halfway to Poitiers is the tiny town of St-Maixent-L'École. A marvel of light and space, its abbey church is a Flamboyant Gothic reconstruction by

Niort's lively Les Halles market, thronging with visitors ↑

A flat-bottomed boat transversing the Venise Verte, Marais Poitevin

François Le Duc (1670) of a building destroyed during the Wars of Religion.

 6

Marais Poitevin

C4 **Charente-Maritime, Deux-Sèvres, Vendée** **La Rochelle** **Niort, La Rochelle** **Coulon, Arçais, Marans** **2 rue Brisson, Niort; www.niortmarais poitevin.com**

The Poitevin marshes, which have been slowly drained with canals, dykes and sluices for a thousand years, cover about 800 sq km (309 sq miles) between Niort and the sea. The area is now a regional park, divided into two parts. To the north and south of the Sèvre estuary is the Marais Desséché (dry marsh), where cereal and other crops are grown. The huge swathe of the Marais Mouillé (wet marsh) is upstream towards Niort.

The wet marshes, known as the Venise Verte (Green Venice), are the most interesting. They are crisscrossed by a winding labyrinth of weed-choked canals, adorned by irises and waterlilies, shaded by poplars and beeches, and support a rich variety of birds and other wildlife. The *maraîchins* who live here stoutly maintain that much of the huge, water-logged forest is unexplored. The pretty whitewashed villages hereabouts are all built on higher ground, and the customary means of transport is a flat-bottomed boat, known as a *platte*.

Coulon, St-Hilaire-la-Palud, La Garette and Arçais, as well as Damvix and Maillezais in the Vendée, are all convenient starting points for boat trips around the marshes.

 7

Melle

C4 **Deux-Sèvres.** **3 rue Émilien Travers; www.decouvertes. paysmellois.org**

A Roman silver mine was the origin of Melle, which in the 9th century had the only mint in Aquitaine. Later its fame derived from the baudet du Poitou, a sturdy mule bred in the area. Now Melle is better known for its churches of which the finest is St-Hilaire. It has a 12th-century Poitevin façade with an equestrian statue of the Emperor Constantine above the north door.

 TOP 4 **BIRDING SITES IN POITOU AND AQUITAINE**

Dune du Pilat
Europe's tallest sand dune and a haven for terns, oystercatchers and plovers *(p413)*.

Teich Bird Reserve
A vast and wild natural space, home to at least 323 bird species *(www. reserve-ornithologique -du-teich.com)*.

Parc Marais Poitevin
A paradise for migratory birds, plus owls and falcons *(www. parc-marais-poitevin.fr)*.

Gironde Estuary
Teeming with seabirds, birds of prey and migratory birds *(p414)*.

The Poitevin marshes, which have been slowly drained with canals, dykes and sluices for a thousand years, cover about 800 sq km (309 sq miles) between Niort and the sea.

The dynamic architecture, impressive water features and grounds of Futuroscope

8

Futuroscope

🅰C4 🔲 Av René Monory, Chasseneuil-du-Poitou, Jaunay-Clan 🚊 ⏱Hours vary, check website 🌐 futuroscope.com

Exploring visual technology in a futuristic environment, Futuroscope's attractions evolve yearly. Such attractions include simulators, 3D and 360-degree screens, and the "magic carpet" cinema, with one of its screens on the floor, creating the sensation of flying.

9

Abbaye de Nouaillé-Maupertuis

🅰C4 🔲 Vienne 05 49 55 35 69 ⏱Abbey church: 9am–6pm (to 7pm Jul & Aug)

Within a wooded valley, on the flowering banks of the River Miosson, lies the Abbaye de Nouaillé-Maupertuis. First mentioned at the end of the 7th century, the abbey became independent in the late 700s and followed the Benedictine rule. The church was built at the start of the 12th century and reconstructed several times. Behind the altar is the 11th-century sarcophagus of St-Junien, with three great eagles painted on the front.

More interesting is the nearby battlefield, scene of the great English victory at Poitiers Nouaillé by the Black Prince in 1356. The view has altered little since the 14th century. Drive down the small road to La Cardinerie (to the right off the D142), which leads to the river crossing at Gué de l'Omme, the epicentre of the battle. There is a monument commemorating the medieval battle halfway up the hill, where the heaviest fighting took place and where the French king Jean le Bon was captured.

10

Chauvigny

🅰C4 🔲 Vienne 🚌 ℹ5 rue St-Pierre; www.tourisme-chauvigny.com

Chauvigny, set on a steep promontory overlooking the broad River Vienne, displays the ruins of no fewer than four fortified medieval castles. Stone from the local quarry was so plentiful that nobody ever bothered to demolish these earlier castles for building material.

Nevertheless, the best thing in this town is the 11th- to 12th-century Église St-Pierre, whose decorated capitals are a real treasure – particularly those in the choir stalls. The carvings represent biblical scenes along

with monsters, sphinxes and sirens. Look for the one that says *Gofridus me fecit* (Gofridus made me), with wonderfully natural scenes of the Epiphany.

Nearby is the lovely **Château de Touffou**, a Renaissance dream on the banks of the Vienne, with terraces and hanging gardens.

Château de Touffou

 🔲Bonnes ⏱Apr–Sep: 10am–noon, 2–6pm Sat & Sun 🌐 touffou.com

11

Angles-sur-l'Anglin

🅰D4 🔲 Vienne ℹ2 rue du Four Banal; www.anglesuranglin.com

The village of Angles lies in a stunning riverside setting, dominated by its castle ruins. Adding to the charm is an old watermill by the slow-running River Anglin, graced by water-lilies and swaying reeds.

> PICTURE PERFECT
> **The Right Angle**
>
> Angles-sur-l'Anglin is considered one of the country's most beautiful villages. Capture its magic from the castle ruins, where they overlook the River Anglin.

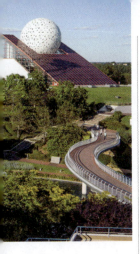

Angles is famous for its tradition of fine needlework, the *jours d'Angles*, which is determinedly maintained by the local women today.

Located just outside the village is the Roc-aux-Sorciers, a sculpted rock shelter that dates back 15,000 years and is the site of some of the world's most important Paleolithic cave art.

 Montmorillon

D4 🏛 **Vienne** 🚌 *i* **2 pl du Maréchal Leclerc, www. sudviennepoitou.com**

Montmorillon, built on the River Gartempe, has its origins in the 11th century. Like most towns in the region, it had a difficult time during the Hundred Years' War and the Wars of Religion. Some buildings survived, such as Église Notre-Dame, which has beautiful frescoes in its 12th-century crypt (contact the tourist office for the key). These include scenes from the life of St Catherine of Alexandria.

A short walk from the Pont de Chez Ragon, just south of

Montmorillon, is the Portes d'Enfer, a dramatically shaped rock perched high above the rapids of the Gartempe.

 St-Savin

D4 🏛 **Vienne** 🚌 *i* **20 pl de la Libération; www. sudviennepoitou.com**

The glory of St-Savin is its 11th-century abbey church with its slender Gothic spire and huge nave. The abbey had enormous influence until the Hundred Years' War, when it was burned down. It was later pillaged several times during the Wars of Religion. Despite restoration work by monks in the 17th century and again in the 19th century, the church appears quite untouched.

Its interior contains the most magnificent series of 12th-century Romanesque frescoes in Europe. These wallpaintings were among the very first in France to be classified as a *monument historique* in 1836.

ST-SAVIN WALL PAINTINGS

The great frescoes of St-Savin represent Old Testament history from the Creation to the Ten Commandments. The sequence starts to the left of the entrance with the Creation of the stars and of Eve. It continues with scenes from Noah's Ark to the Tower of Babel, the story of Joseph and the parting of the Red Sea. It is believed that all the frescoes were created by the same group of artists, due to the similarity in style.

→ The interior of St-Savin abbey, known for its extraordinary frescoes

THE PATH OF PILGRIMS

For centuries, thousands of dedicated pilgrims have made the months-long journey to the cathedral at Santiago de Compostela, following paths that criss-cross France.

CENTURIES OF PILGRIMAGE

The first recorded pilgrim was the bishop of Le Puy in 951. But pilgrims have probably been going to Santiago since 814, soon after St James's tomb was found. Legend has it that strange stars were seen hovering over a field in 814 and on 25 July, which now marks the feast of Santiago, the saint's remains were found (although subsequent evidence showed that St James's remains were never in Compostela after all). Throughout the Middle Ages, millions of Christians travelled to Santiago de Compostela in Spain to pay homage at the shrine of St James (Santiago). They came from across France, staying in monasteries or simple shelters and, so legend has it, carried back shells from the Spanish coast, proving that they had indeed completed the arduous journey. Most pilgrims went in hope of redemption and were often on the road for years. Today, there are 103 trails in Poitou and Aquitaine that are still used by pilgrims travelling between religious sights on the road to Compostela.

↑ Scallop shells, carried by pilgrims to prove they had completed the journey to Compostela

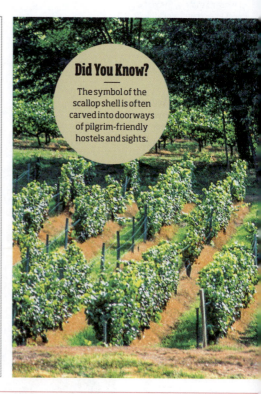

Did You Know?

The symbol of the scallop shell is often carved into doorways of pilgrim-friendly hostels and sights.

TOP 3 WALKING ROUTES

Dissay to Poitiers (GR655)
This 24-km (15-mile) stretch passes the church of St-Jacques, where an indent in the stone is, according to legend, the footprint of St James himself.

Gourgé to Parthenay (GR36)
An easy wander through fields and medieval pilgrim stopovers, past tiny shrines, covering 22.6 km (14 miles).

Angles-sur-l'Anglin to St-Savin (GR48)
Starting at a medieval junction, this 21-km (13-mile) route follows the river before ducking through fields to biblical frescoes of St-Savin.

PILGRIMAGE THROUGH POITOU AND AQUITAINE

There are four main routes across Europe that pilgrims took to get to Compostela. The Way of Tours is the westernmost route; stretching from Paris to Compostela, it snakes through Poitou and Aquitaine and picks up with the other three routes (the Way of St James) in the Pyrenees. In the medieval ages, pilgrims would have travelled along well-trodden paths to join the Way, as well as deviating from the main route to visit and pay homage to hermitages, shrines and relics as they went. In Poitou and Aquitaine, east of the Way, the abbey church of St-Savin *(p405)* was a popular diversion, for its extraordinarily rich narrative frescoes, which relay the history of the Old Testament, from the Creation to the Ten Commandments.

Pilgrims journeying from the west would have passed through 13th-century Porte St-Jacques, one of the four city gates of Parthenay *(p402)*, and along rue de la Vau St-Jacques, a narrow cobblestone street that climbs up to the centre of town, to rest before carrying on to Poitier *(p398)* to join the procession. Many pilgrims would have stayed in 13th-century Notre-Dame-la-Grande, the white jewel of Poitiers, with an incredibly intricate Romanesque façade, before heading south to Saintes to cross a Roman bridge, at the time the only bridge to cross the lower Charente river.

CODEX CALIXTINUS

Possibly the world's first tourist guidebook, the five-volume *Codex Calixtinus* was written by a French monk in the 12th century. Its intention was to provide information and advice for pilgrims following the Way of St James. The illustrated guide features routes and sights to see along the Way, as well as the history of St James, a letter by Pope Callixtus and reports on miracles.

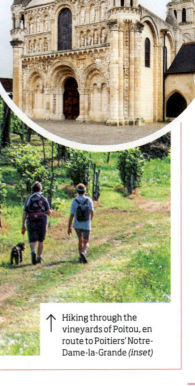

↑ Hiking through the vineyards of Poitou, en route to Poitiers' Notre-Dame-la-Grande *(inset)*

 Ascending angels around the cherry-red door to Église St-Pierre at Aulnay

14 Aulnay de Saintonge

 C4 Charente-Maritime
290 av de l'Église; www.saintongedoree-tourisme.com

Perhaps the most unusual fact about the lovely 12th-century Église St-Pierre at Aulnay is that it was all built at once; there is no ill-fitting apse or transept added to an original nave. The church is covered in glorious sculpture, particularly the outside of the south transept. It is a rare example of a complete Romanesque façade, with rank on rank of raucous monsters and graceful human figures. Note the donkey with a harp.

15 Charroux

E4 Vienne 2 rte de Chatain; www.civraisiencharlois.com

The 8th-century Abbaye St-Sauveur in Charroux was once one of the richest abbeys in the region. Today it is a ruin (go to the tourist office to visit). Its chief contribution to history was made in the 10th century, when the Council of Charroux declared the "Truce of God", the earliest-known attempt to regulate war in the manner of the Geneva convention. A huge tower marks what was once the centre of the church, and some superb sculpture from the original abbey portal can be seen in the small museum.

16 Confolens

C4 Charente
8 rue Fontaine des Jardins; www.mairie-confolens.fr

On the border with Limousin, Confolens, once an important frontier town, now suffers from rural exodus. Efforts to make the town more attractive include the annual folklore festival, held in August.

The medieval bridge that runs across the River Vienne was heavily restored in the early 18th century.

17 Pauillac

C5 Gironde
La Verrerie; www.pauillac-medoc.com

Situated on the west bank of the Gironde, this town was the

> 🔍 HIDDEN GEM
> ## Coriobona
> Just east of Confolens is Coriobona, a reconstructed Gallic village with thatched-roof houses. Here, actors in period clothing practicing various crafts such as weaving, forging and pottery.

bustling arrival point for transatlantic steamships in the 19th century. Today, this now sleepy port is mostly used by pleasure boats.

The commune of Pauillac is also one of the most famous areas in the Médoc wine region; three of its châteaux are Médoc premiers grands crus classés. Château Mouton Rothschild uses leading artists to create its wine labels and has a small museum of paintings on wine themes from all over the world. The Château Lafite Rothschild is of medieval origin and the Château Latour is recognizable by its distinctive stone turret. They can be visited by appointment (contact the tourist office well in advance).

18 La Rochelle

 B4 Charente-Maritime
2 quai Georges Simenon, Le Gabut; www.larochelle-tourisme.com

La Rochelle, a commercial centre and busy port since the 11th century, has suffered much from a distressing tendency to back the wrong side – the English and the Calvinists, for example. This led to the ruthless siege of the city by Cardinal Richelieu in 1628, during which 23,000 people

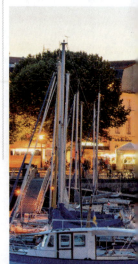

 Yachts moored in the peaceful harbour at La Rochelle, after sunset

starved to death. The walls were destroyed and the city's privileges withdrawn. The glory of La Rochelle is the old harbour, which is surrounded by stately buildings. It is now the biggest yachting centre on France's Atlantic coast. On either side of its entrance are **Tour de la Chaîne** and **Tour St-Nicolas**. A huge chain used to be strung between them to ward off attack from the sea.

La Rochelle's cobbled streets and arcades can be congested in high summer. To get an overview, climb the 15th-century **Tour de la Lanterne**. Its inner walls were covered in graffiti by prisoners, mostly mariners, from the 17th to the 19th century. The most common motif is ships.

The study of the acclaimed 18th-century French naturalist Clément Lafaille is preserved in the regularly updated **Muséum d'Histoire Naturelle**, complete with shell collection and display cabinets. The town's relation to the New World is treated in the moving **Musée du Nouveau Monde**. Emigration, commerce and the slave trade are explained through old maps, paintings and artifacts. The atmospheric

and fascinating **Bunker de la Rochelle** is well worth a visit. Constructed in secret for World War II submarine commanders, it has remained in its original condition for more than 70 years.

Next to the Vieux Port is the huge **Aquarium La Rochelle**. Transparent tunnels lead through tanks with different marine biotopes, including sharks and turtles.

Tours de la Chaîne, St-Nicholas, and Lanterne

 🏠 Rue des Murs, Le Port
🕐 Hours vary, check website
📅 1 Jan, 1 May, 25 Dec
🌐 tours-la-rochelle.fr

Muséum d'Histoire Naturelle

🏠 28 rue Albert Premier
🕐 Hours vary, check website
🌐 museum-larochelle.fr

Musée du Nouveau Monde

🏠 10 rue Fleuriau
🕐 Hours vary, check website
🌐 museum-larochelle.fr

Bunker de la Rochelle

🏠 8 rue des Dames
📞 05 46 42 52 89 **🕐** 10am–6pm daily **📅** 30 Dec–mid-Feb

Aquarium La Rochelle

 🏠 Bassin des Grands Yachts, quai Louis Prunier
🕐 Hours vary, check website
🌐 aquarium-larochelle.com

STAY

Hôtel Le Sénéchal
Near the beach, this charming hotel has rustic rooms and a lush courtyard with a pool.

🅐B4 **🏠**6 rue Gambetta, Île de Ré **🌐**hotel-le-senechal.com

€€€

––––––––––

Château Cordeillan-Bages
Set within a vineyard, modern rooms are spacious, and the restaurant has a Michelin star.

🅐C5 **🏠**Route des Châteaux, Pauillac **📞**33 5 56 59 24 24

€€€

––––––––––

Château de Saint-Loup
A restored castle with large rooms featuring period furnishings.

🅐C4 **🏠**1 rue Jacques de Boyer, St-Loup-sur-Thouet **🌐**chateaudesaint-loup.com

€€€

⑲ Brouage

🅰B5 🏠Charente-Maritime
ℹ️2 rue de l'Hospital; www.brouage-tourisme.fr

Cardinal Richelieu's fortress at Brouage once overlooked a thriving harbour, but its wealth and population declined in the 18th century, as the ocean receded. In 1659, Marie Mancini was sent into exile here by her uncle, Cardinal Mazarin, who did not approve of her liaison with Louis XIV. The king never forgot the beautiful Marie. On his way back from his wedding, he stayed alone at Brouage in the room once occupied by his first great love. Today the ramparts are a peaceful place to stroll and admire the view.

---

⑳ Talmont-sur-Gironde

🅰C5 🏠Charente-Maritime
ℹ️Rue de l'École; www.talmont-sur-gironde.fr

Talmont is a jewel of a village, packed full of little white houses and colourful hollyhocks in summer. The tiny Romanesque Église Ste-Radegonde is perched on a spit of land overlooking the Gironde. Built in 1094, the church's apse was designed to resemble the prow of a ship.

㉑ Rochefort

🅰B5 🏠Charente-Maritime
🚇🚌 ℹ️ Av Sadi-Carnot;
www.rochefort-ocean.com

The historic rival of La Rochelle, Rochefort was purpose-built by Colbert in the 17th century to be the greatest shipyard in France, producing over 300 sailing vessels per year. This maritime heritage can be traced in the beautifully restored 17th-century **Corderie Royale**. The building houses an exhibition on ropemaking. The **Musée National de la Marine** displays models of the ships built in the arsenal.

Rochefort is also the birthplace of the writer Pierre Loti (1850–1923) – his house, the stately Maison de Pierre Loti, is undergoing extensive renovations; some rooms are open.

Corderie Royale

🎨🏛️🍴🚻 🏠Centre International de la Mer, rue Audebert 🕐Hours vary, check website 🚫1, 7-25 Jan, 25 Dec 🌐corderie-royale.com

Musée National de la Marine

🎨🏛️ 🏠Pl de la Gallissonnière 🕐Apr-Sep: 10am-7pm daily; Oct-Mar: 1:30-6pm Wed-Mon 🚫Jan, 1 May, 25 Dec 🌐musee-marine.fr

> INSIDER TIP
> ### Cycling Île d'Oléron
>
> Île d'Oléron is ideal for exploring by bicycle. It has well-kept dedicated paths and the landscape is blissfully flat. Bikes for all ages can be hired from over a dozen shops on the island.

㉒ Île d'Oléron

🅰B4 🏠Charente-Maritime
🚈La Rochelle 🚉Rochefort, La Rochelle, Saintes then bus 🚌From La Rochelle (in summer) ℹ️22 rue Dubois Meynardie, Marennes; www.oleron-island.com

Accessible from the mainland by bridge, Oléron is France's second-largest island after Corsica, and a highly popular holiday resort. Its south coast, the Côte Sauvage, is beautifully lined with sweeping dunes and emerald green pine forest. There are some particularly excellent beaches at Grande Plage (found near La Cotinière) and Vert Bois, and a series of colourful ports. The town of Château d'Oléron is home to a magnificent citadel. The north of the island is used for winegrowing, farming and fishing.

Fishermen hoping for a catch at sunset, on the island of Oléron

㉓

Cognac

🅰C5 🚉Charente 🚌 ℹ️16 rue du 14 Juillet; www. tourism-cognac.com

Wherever you spot the black lichen stains from alcohol evaporation on the exterior of the buildings in this river port, you may be sure that you are looking at a storehouse of cognac.

All the great cognac houses run tours – one of the best is at **Château Royal de Cognac**, housed in the 15th- to 16th-century château where François I was born. The distillery was established in 1795 by a Scot named Otard. Much of the Renaissance architecture can be seen during the tour, which includes a cognac tasting.

Château Royal de Cognac

🎨🎭 🏠127 blvd Denfert-Rochereau ⏰Hours vary, check website 📅Jan, 1 May & public hols in winter 🌐chateauroyaldecognac.com

 Visiting the ruins of Saintes's open-air Roman amphitheater

㉔

Saintes

🅰C5 🚉Charente-Maritime 🚉 🚌 ℹ️Place Bassompierre; www.saintes-tourisme.fr

Saintes has an extraordinarily rich architectural heritage. It boasted the only bridge over the lower Charente, well used by pilgrims on their way to Santiago de Compostela. The Roman bridge no longer exists, but you can still admire the Arc de Germanicus (AD 19), which used to mark its entrance.

On the same side of the river is the fine Abbaye aux Dames. Consecrated in 1047, it was modernized in the 12th century. Be sure to stop to admire the decorated portal and the vigorous 12th-century head of Christ in the apse.

On the left bank is the 1st-century Roman amphitheatre. Further away lies the Église St-Eutrope. In the 15th century, this church had the misfortune to effect a miraculous cure of the dropsy on Louis XI. In a paroxysm of gratitude, he did his best to wreck it with ill-judged Gothic additions. Its rare Romanesque capitals survive.

EAT & DRINK

Chez Yvette

Local seafood joint since the early 1960s.

🅰B5 🏠59 blvd du General Leclerc, Arcachon 🌐restaurant-chez-yvette-arcachon.fr

 €€€

La Ferme aux Grives

Classic French restaurant in an old converted barn.

🅰C6 🏠334 rue René Vielle, Eugenie-les-Bains 🌐michelguerard.com

 €€€

Captain Houblon

Convivial pub offering craft beer and delicious charcuterie plates.

🅰B4 🏠8 rue de la Ferte, La Rochelle 🌐captainhoublon.com

 €€€

Villabordoh

Casual French bistro at a local inn.

🅰C5 🏠A5 rue de la Halle, Margaux ⏰Dinner 🌐villabordoh.com

 €€€

Did You Know?
—
Every major wine town has a Maison du Vin, which can provide information on visits to a château.

25 Aubeterre-sur-Dronne

C5 Charente
8 pl du Champ de Foine; www.sudcharente tourisme.fr

The chief ornament of this pretty white village is the staggering monolithic Église St-Jean. Dug out of the white chalky cliff that gave the village its name (*Alba Terra –* *White Earth*), some parts of it date back to the 6th century. Between the Revolution and 1860, it served as the village's cemetery. It contains an early Christian baptismal font and an octagonal reliquary.

The Romanesque Église St-Jacques is also of note for its fine sculpted façade.

The rest of the village is made up of white houses with honey-coloured roofs, built in terraces along the massif overlooking the Dronne valley.

26 Angoulême

C5 Charente
7 bis rue du Chat; www. angouleme-tourisme.com

The celebrated 12th-century Cathédrale St-Pierre, which dominates this industrial centre, is the fourth to be built on the site. One of its most interesting features is the Romanesque frieze on the façade. The cathedral's liturgical treasures are on show in a stunning display designed by contemporary artist Jean-Michel Othoniel. Some restoration work to the cathedral was carried out by the 19th-century architect Abadie. In his eagerness to wipe out all details added after the 12th century, he destroyed a 6th-century crypt.

Unfortunately, he was also let loose on the town's former château, transforming it into a Neo-Gothic Hôtel de Ville (town hall). However, the 15th-century tower, where Marguerite d'Angoulême, sister of François I, was born in 1492, still stands. Her statue can be seen in the garden. The ramparts offer a bracing walk with views over the Charente Valley.

Angoulême has become the capital of comic book (*bande dessinée*) art, hosting the prestigious Festival de la

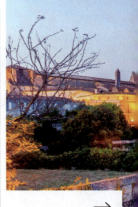

→

Medieval buildings at St-Émilion, a UNESCO World Heritage Site

Bande Dessinée, which takes place in January or February. The **Cité Internationale de la Bande-Dessinée et de l'Image** has a reference collection of French print and film cartoons dating back to 1946. From here, a footbridge leads to the Musée de la Bande Dessinée, where the history, techniques and aesthetics of the art form are explained.

Cité Internationale de la Bande-Dessinée et de l'Image

121 rue de Bordeaux 10am–6pm Tue–Fri, 2–6pm Sat & Sun Public hols citebd.orgz

27 Bassin d'Arcachon

B5 Gironde To Cap Ferret Espl Georges Pompidou; www.arcachon. com

In the middle of the Côte d'Argent the straight coastline suddenly forms a lagoon. Famous for its natural beauty,

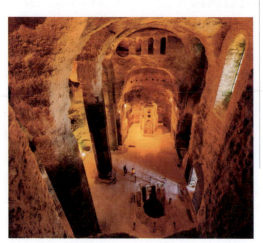

←

The atmospheric interior of the monolithic Église St-Jean at Aubeterre-sur-Dronne

fine beaches and oysters, the Bassin d'Arcachon is a protected area, perfect for holidaymakers, sailing enthusiasts and oyster-eaters.

The basin is dotted with smaller amorphous resorts, beaches and fishing/oyster villages, all worth exploring.

Cap Ferret, the northern headland that protects the basin from Atlantic winds, is home to the wealthy, whose luxurious villas stand among the pines. Look for the small road under the trees from Lège, which leads to the wild beach of Grand-Crohot.

Between Cap Ferret and Arcachon, near Gujan-Mestras, the **Parc Ornithologique du Teich** provides care and shelter for damaged birds and endangered species. There are two fascinating walks, each carefully marked: an introductory one, and another of greater length. Both provide concealed observation points from which people can watch the wildfowl without disturbing them.

Arcachon was created as a seaside resort in 1845. Its popularity grew and in the late 19th and early 20th centuries the elegant villas in Ville d'Hiver were built. The livelier Ville d'Eté, facing the lagoon, has a casino and sports facilities. The immense Dune du Pilat

is the largest sand dune in Europe. It is nearly 3 km (2 miles) long, 104 m (340 ft) high and 500 m (1,625 ft) wide. Aside from the view, the dune is a great vantage point in autumn for viewing flocks of migratory birds, as they pass overhead on their way to the sanctuary at Le Teich.

Parc Ornithologique du Teich

♿ 🚾 🅿 🅰 Le Teich, rue du Port 🕐 Hours vary, check website 🌐 reserve-ornithologique-du-teich.com

---

 28

St-Émilion

🅰 C5 🅰 Gironde 🚉 🚌 ℹ place des Créneau; **www.saint-emilion-tourisme.com**

This charming village in the middle of the red wine district to which it gives its name, dates back to an 8th-century hermit, Émilion, who dug out a cave for himself in the rock. A monastery followed, and by the Middle Ages Saint-Émilion had become a small town. Medieval houses still line the narrow streets, and parts of the 12th-century ramparts remain. The interior of the

church, dug out of the chalky cliff by followers of St Émilion after his death, is somewhat ruined by concrete columns put up to prevent its collapse.

Among the districts famous châteaux are the elegant Figeac, Cheval Blanc and Ausone, all of them St-Émilion premiers grands crus classés – vineyards of the higest quality.

BORDEAUX WINE

The first vineyards in the Bordeaux region were planted by the Romans as far back as the 1st century, including those found at St-Emilion. Today, there are thousands of wine producers, making it France's largest wine-growing region. While there are both red and white options, the most common is a red blend made from Merlot and Cabernet Sauvignon grape varieties. The term "château" in the context of Bordeaux wine means both the vineyard and the building, which can range from the most basic to the very grandest, or historic to modern.

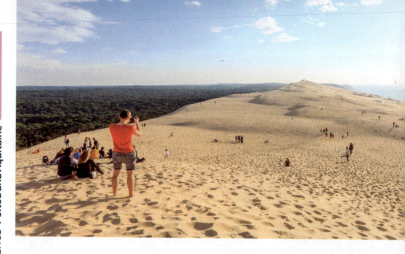

 29

La Côte d'Argent

🅰B5 🅰Gironde, Landes
✈Bordeaux, Biarritz
🚆Soulac-sur-Mer, Arcachon,
Labenne, Dax 🚌Lacanau,
Arcachon, Mimizan
ℹLacanau, 05 56 03 21 01;
Mimizan-Plag, 05 58 09 11
20; Capbreton, 05 58 72 12 11

The stretch of coast between
Pointe de Grave on the Gironde
estuary and Bayonne (p458) is
called La Côte d'Argent – the
Silver Coast. It is virtually one
vast beach of shifting sand
dunes. Tree-planting has now
slowed down their progress.

The coast is dotted with
seaside resorts renowned for
surfing, such as Soulac-sur-
Mer in the north, followed by
the big Lacanau-Océan and
Mimizan-Plage. Down in the
south is Hossegor, with its
salty lake, and Capbreton.

 30

Les Landes

🅰C6 🅰Gironde, Landes
✈Bordeaux, Biarritz
🚆Morcenx, Dax, Mont-
de-Marsan 🚌Mont-de-
Marsan ℹMont-de-Marsan;
www.tourismelandes.com

Almost entirely covered by
an immense pine forest, the
Landes area extends over the

two *départements* of Gironde
and Landes. The soil here is
uniformly sandy. Until the mid-
19th century the whole region
became a swamp in winter,
because of a layer of tufa
(porous rock) just under the
surface which retained water
from the brackish lakes. Any
settlement or agriculture close
to the sea was impossible
due to the constantly shifting
dunes. Furthermore, the
mouth of the Adour river kept
moving from Capbreton to
Vieux-Boucau and back, a
distance of 32 km (20 miles).

The Adour was fixed near
Bayonne by a canal in the
16th century. This was the
start of the slow conquest

of the Landes. The planting
of pine trees ultimately wiped
out the migrant shepherds
and their flocks. Today the
inner Landes is still very
underpopulated, but wealthy
from its pinewood and pine
derivatives. The coastal strip
also has a large influx of
holidaymakers each year.

In 1970, part of the forest
was made into a nature park.
At Marquèze, in the **Ecomusée
Marquèze**, a typical 19th-
century *airial* (clearing) has
been restored. It commem-
orates the vanished world
of Les Landes before the
draining of the marshes,
when shepherds still used
stilts to get about. There are a

LANDES FOREST

The vast, totally artificial
19th-century forest of Les
Landes was an ambitious
project to make use of an
area of sand and marshes.
Maritime pines and
grasses were planted to
anchor the coastal dunes,
and inland dunes were
stabilized with a mixture
of pines, reeds, and broom.
In 1855, the land was
drained. It is now covered
with tall pine groves and
undergrowth, preserving
a delicate ecological
balance, and is a popular
place for cycling.

The immense Dune du Pilat, south of the inlet to Bassin d'Arcachon

number of traditional *auberges landaises* (wooden houses with sloping roofs) found here.

Ecomusée Marquèze
 🚲☕🎫 🏠 Route de la Gare, 40630 Sabres
🕐 Hours vary, check website 🌐 marqueze.fr

31
Mont-de-Marsan

🅰 C6 🏠 Landes 🚆🚌
ℹ 1 pl Charles de Gaulle; www.visitmontde marsan.fr

A bullfighting mecca, this medieval town attracts all the great bullfighters of France and Spain in summer. A less bloodthirsty local variant of the sport is the *course landaise*, in which the object is to vault over the horns and back of a charging bull. The town is also home to a medieval keep. Sculpture from the first half of the 20th century can be seen at Musée Despiau-Wlérick, on place Marguerite de Navarre.

The administrative capital of the Landes is also known for its hippodrome, poultry farming and *foie gras* production.

Bathed in light, the spectacular interior of Église Notre-Dame at Royan

---

32
Dax

🅰 B6 🏠 Landes 🚆🚌 ℹ 11 cours Foch; www.dax-tourisme.com

The thermal spa of Dax is second only to Aix-les-Bains (*p386*) in importance. Its hot springs, with a constant temperature of 64° C (147° F) and tonic mud from the Adour, have been soothing aches and pains since the time of Emperor Augustus.

Apart from the 13th-century doorway of the otherwise 17th-century Cathédrale Notre-Dame, there isn't much of architectural interest in this peaceful town. But the promenade along the River Adour is charming and the bullring is world renowned.

33
Royan

🅰 B5 🏠 Charente-Maritime 🚆🚌 ⛴ To Verdon only ℹ 1 bd de la Grandière; www.royanatlantique.fr

Badly damaged by Allied bombing in World War II, Royan is now thoroughly modern and different in tone from the rest of the towns on

---

 GREAT VIEW
Royan Lighthouse

The historic Cordouan Lighthouse (Phare de Cordouan), off the coast of Royan, can be visited by boat at low tide, and offers incredible views of the Gironde estuary and coastline.

this weather-beaten coast. With five beaches of fine sand, here called *conches*, it becomes busy in the summer.

Built between 1955 and 1958, Eglise Notre-Dame is a remarkable early example of reinforced concrete architecture. Its interior is flooded with colour and light by the stained-glass windows.

The notable Renaissance Phare de Cordouan, visible in the distance from the coast, offers a change from all the modern architecture. Various lighthouses have been built on the site since the 11th century. The present one was finished in 1611, with a chapel inside, and was later reinforced and heightened. Since 1789, nothing has changed but the lighting method. Boat trips in summer ferry visitors to Phare de Cordouan from the harbour.

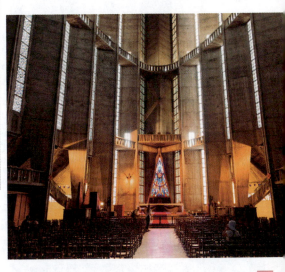

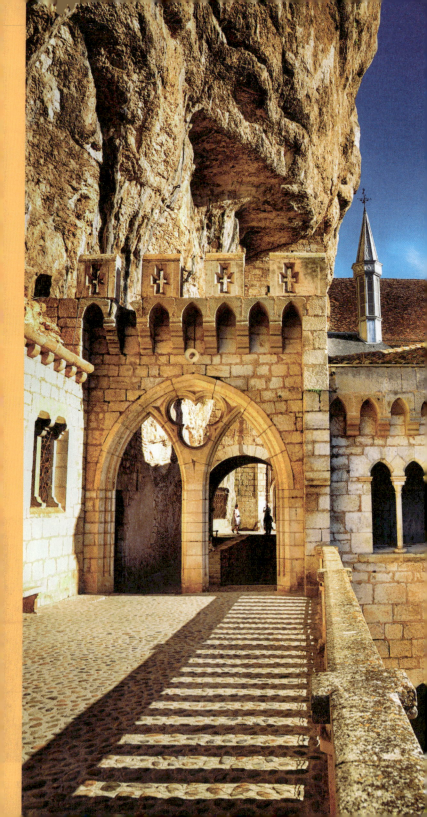

Rocamadour's abbey, clinging to the cliff face

THE DORDOGNE

Covering the old provinces of Périgord, Quercy and Gascony, the Dordogne is known as "the cradle of mankind". The region sheltered some of the first human settlers in Europe, 40,000 years ago. Among 147 surviving Paleolithic sites most famous are the Lascaux caves, with vibrant animal paintings dating back 17,000 years. The rolling terrain, crisscrossed with rich river valleys and oak forests, was an ideal home to hunter-gatherers. Julius Caesar conquered the region around 50 BC, and Vandals and Visigoths followed some 400 years later, seen off by the Franks in 507 AD. Viking raiders ousted the Franks in the 9th century, settling as farmers. Over the ensuing centuries, the landscape became dotted with impressive castles and medieval *bastides* (defensive towns), a legacy of the Hundred Years' War, fought and lost by the English, and the intermittent Wars of Religion, in which Catholics fought Huguenots (French Protestants). In 1844, the people of this region were immortalized in the swashbuckling D'Artagnan of Alexander Dumas's *The Three Musketeers*.

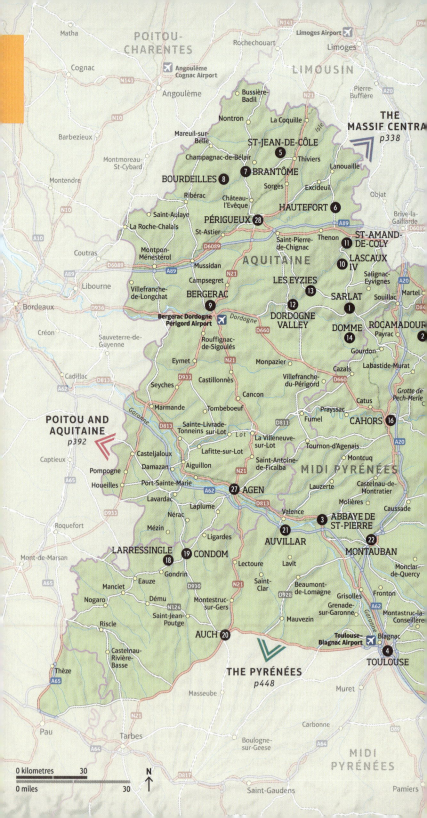

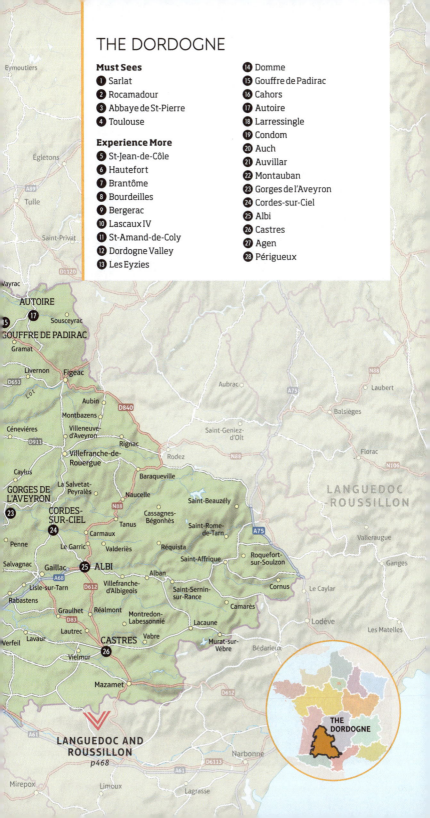

THE DORDOGNE

Must Sees

1. Sarlat
2. Rocamadour
3. Abbaye de St-Pierre
4. Toulouse

Experience More

5. St-Jean-de-Côle
6. Hautefort
7. Brantôme
8. Bourdeilles
9. Bergerac
10. Lascaux IV
11. St-Amand-de-Coly
12. Dordogne Valley
13. Les Eyzies
14. Domme
15. Gouffre de Padirac
16. Cahors
17. Autoire
18. Larressingle
19. Condom
20. Auch
21. Auvillar
22. Montauban
23. Gorges de l'Aveyron
24. Cordes-sur-Ciel
25. Albi
26. Castres
27. Agen
28. Périgueux

LANGUEDOC AND ROUSSILLON p468

THE DORDOGNE

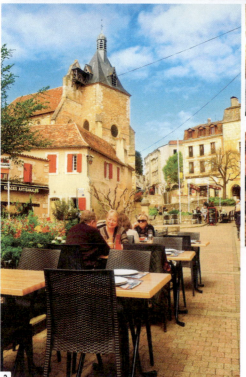

① Medieval Rocamadour.

② Dining al fresco in Bergerac.

③ Cave paintings at Lascaux.

④ Charcuterie at a market stand in Sarlat.

5 DAYS
in the Dordogne

Day 1

Morning There's no more dramatic way to start a tour of the Dordogne than at stunning Rocamadour (*p426*). Climb all 216 steps of the Grand Escalier to explore the cliff-side Cité Religeuse.

Afternoon Make your way to L'Hospitalet for fabulous views, then on to Gouffre de Padirac, where a boat trip takes visitors along a stream to the subterranean Lac de la Pluie (lake of rain).

Evening Drive an hour west to the hilltop town of Domme (*p436*). At L'Esplanade hotel-restaurant the terrace affords verdant countryside vistas (*p433*).

Day 2

Morning Set off early to Sarlat, where each Saturday, the town square fills with market stalls laden with fois gras, walnuts and truffles (*p424*).

Afternoon Travel into the tranquil Vézère Valley, famed for its prehistoric art. Marvel at spectacular cave paintings of horses, bison and deer in Lascaux (*p434*).

Evening Find a tasty dinner and cosy bed at Les Glycines (*p441*), a bijou hotel in glorious countryside on the way to Périgueux.

Day 3

Morning Just a short drive northwest lies Périgueux (*p444*), where you can strike out on foot to explore Roman remains and a Byzantine-style cathedral.

Afternoon Sample regional favourites at Pierrot Gourmet (*6 rue de l'Hôtel de Ville*) a delicatessen just steps from the Musée d'Art et d'Archéologie du Périgord (*p445*).

Evening Follow the River Isle northeast from Périgueux 20 minutes to Sorges and sample sumptuous truffles, a local delicacy, at Auberge de la Truffe (*p433*).

Day 4

Morning Drive west to Brantôme (*p432*), the "Venice of Périgord". Admire beautiful pieces at glass-blower Eric Simonin's workshop (*www.ericsimonin.fr*) and wander the leafy banks of the river Donne. Lunch on seafood at waterside Au Fil de l'Eau (*p433*).

Afternoon Leave the car behind and canoe downriver to Bourdeilles (*p433*), to tour the château and soak up the atmosphere of this lovely old village.

Evening Catch a taxi from Bourdeilles to Valeuil, then ride the 1A or 1B bus to return to Brantôme for the night.

Day 5

Morning Journey south to the market town of Bergerac (*p434*), surrounded by vineyards. The Maison des Vins can tell you more about the local terroir.

Afternoon Drive south of Bergerac, to sample wines at the idyllic 16th-century Château de Monbazillac (*www.chateaumonbazillac.com*). Explore the castle's attractive surrounding gardens.

Evening Return to Bergerac and Restaurant L'Imparfait (*www.imparfait.com*) for *café liégois* (coffee ice cream topped with chantilly cream) – a house specialty – a dreamy end to your trip.

Did You Know?

Research suggests that spotted horses, painted at Pech-Merle, were alive during the Ice Age.

THE DORDOGNE FOR
PREHISTORIC ART

Well-known for its advances in the art world, France is also home to some of the best preserved prehistoric art on the continent, especially in the Vézère valley. From the paintings at Lascaux to sculptures found around Les Eyzies, these works invite you to step back in time.

Incredible Carvings and Sculptures

Discovered in 1909, the rock shelter of Abri du Cap Blanc, just outside Les Eyzies *(p435)*, is home to a life-size frieze of horses sculpted in the rock. A display of the flint tools found at the site are on display at the on-site museum, which also shows a replica of the Magdalenian Woman and a several "Venuses". Finely carved throwing spears, found at Laugerie-Basse, near Les Eyzies, are on display at the visitor's centre there, and children can borrow a tablet to have a virtual "excavation" as they roam the site.

→

Frieze of a grazing horse, Abri du Cap Blanc

Inspiring Cave Paintings

The Dordogne boasts an extraordinary concentration of prehistoric art, some 20,000 years old. Visit a reconstruction of the Lascaux IV cave *(p434)*, where interactive displays recreate the original decorated cave's atmosphere and paintings. At Grotte de Pech-Merle, near Cahors *(p436)*, the "spotted horses" and handprints make the artists seem spine-tinglingly close. Learn the context at Les Eyzies's Musée National de Préhistoiret.

←

Exploring wall paintings in the lit-up Lascaux IV cave replica

ART FOR ART'S SAKE?

No one knows the exact significance of the cave paintings. Once believed they were created as part of a magic ritual designed to invoke a successful hunt, the common view now is that they were painted in a trance as part of a shamanic practice. Or they may simply have been attempts to capture fleeting beauty.

→

A room of reconstructions of Lascaux IV cave

Epic Etchings and Sketchings

Etchings, carvings, and sketchings, created by the stroke of a few lines, are seen in stunning detail at Grotte de Pech-Merle *(p437)*. Another chamber also contains etchings of female silhouettes and mammoths, and footprints chiselled into the rock. Children in particular enjoy a visit to Grotte de Rouffignac at Les Eyzies *(p435)*, and the journey into the cave on an underground electric train, stopping at various points to marvel at the 13,000-year-old engravings, many depicting mammoths. The highlight is the final chamber, the ceiling of which is decorated with animals.

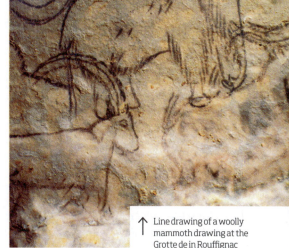

↑ Line drawing of a woolly mammoth drawing at the Grotte de in Rouffignac

1

SARLAT

🅐 D5 🏠 Dordogne 🚉 Ave de la Gare ℹ️ 3 rue Tourny; 05 53 31 45 45; www.sarlat-tourisme.com

Sarlat, which developed around a large Benedictine abbey in the 11th century, possesses the highest concentration of medieval, Renaissance and 17th-century façades of any town in France. Protected by law since 1962, Sarlat now feels like an open-air museum.

Sarlat was a prosperous town, a reflection of the privileged status it was granted in return for loyalty to the French crown during the Hundred Years' War. Behind nondescript rue de la République are narrow lanes and archways, and ancient, ochre-coloured stone town houses rich in ornamental detail and topped with roofs of heavy limestone *lauzes* (tiles). Rue des Consuls has some particularly fine examples of 15th-, 16th- and 17th-century mansions, built for the town's middle-class merchants, magistrates and church officials. The town is also famous for having one of the best food markets in France, while many of its old buildings house shops selling an abundance of foie gras, pâtés, sausissons, truffles and cheeses.

> **Behind nondescript rue de la République are narrow lanes and archways, and ancient, ochre-coloured stone town houses rich in ornamental detail.**

SARLAT MARKETS

Every Wednesday, the great Sarlat food market is held in place de la Liberté; every Thursday organic markets meet at 5pm; and every Saturday there is a full-scale fair that attracts locals from all around. A daily indoor market is held at Eglise Sainte-Marie. Sarlat lies at the heart of the nation's foie gras and walnut trades and also specializes in black truffles, dug up in the woods in January, and wild mushrooms.

STAY

Le Moullin Pointu
A charming B&B with large gardens and a pool.
 Ste-Nathalène
Ⓦ moulinpointu.com

€ € €

La Villa des Consuls
Modern rooms and apartments set in a historic building.
 3 rue Jean-Jacques Rousseau
Ⓦ villaconsuls.fr

€ € €

↑ Place de la Liberté, Sarlat's main square and site of its market

Rue des Consuls contains many fine old mansions.

Place de la Liberté is the heart of the Old Town.

Eglise Sainte-Marie houses an indoor local food market.

Soaring Cathédrale St-Sacerdos has a magnificent 18th-century organ.

RUE FENLON

RUE JEAN-JACQUES ROUSSEAU

RUE DE LA RÉPUBLIQUE

RUE DE LA LIBERTÉ

Lanterne des Morts

← A map of central Sarlat

The former Bishop's Palace is now the helpful tourist office.

RUE TOURNY

ue Jean-Jacques ousseau was the wn's main street.

Cour des Fontaines

2

ROCAMADOUR

🅰 D5 🅰 Lot 🅰 5 km (3 miles) SW of Rocamadour
🅾 Chapel of Notre-Dame: 9am–6:30pm daily
(to 9pm Jun–Sep) ℹ L'Hospitalet, Cour du Prieuré;
05 65 33 22 00; www.vallee-dordogne.com

Rocamadour, a famous pilgrimage site on the Way of St James, is best known for its Cité Réligieuse, accessed via the Grand Escalier staircase.

The Sanctuary at Rocamadour first attracted pilgrims following a series of miracles – each one heralded by the ringing of the bell in the Chapel of Notre-Dame. This was followed by the discovery in 1166 of an ancient grave containing an undecayed body, said to be that of the early Christian hermit St Amadour. Although the town suffered with the decline of pilgrimages in the 17th and 18th centuries, it was heavily restored in the 19th century. The best views of the town are to be had from the ramparts of the château, reached from the hamlet of L'Hospitalet.

💬 **INSIDER TIP**
Ascenseur

There is a lift dug into the rock face, which ascends (for a fee) from the base of the town to the sanctuaries and chapels that form the Cité Religieuse, though it does not go to the château at the top.

The château stands on the site of a fort that protected the sanctuary from the west.

St Michael's Chapel contains well-preserved 12th-century frescoes.

The Tomb of St Amadour once held the body of the hermit from whom the town took its name.

Pilgrims would climb this broad flight of steps on their knees as a penance.

↑ The spectacular town of Rocamadour lit up at night

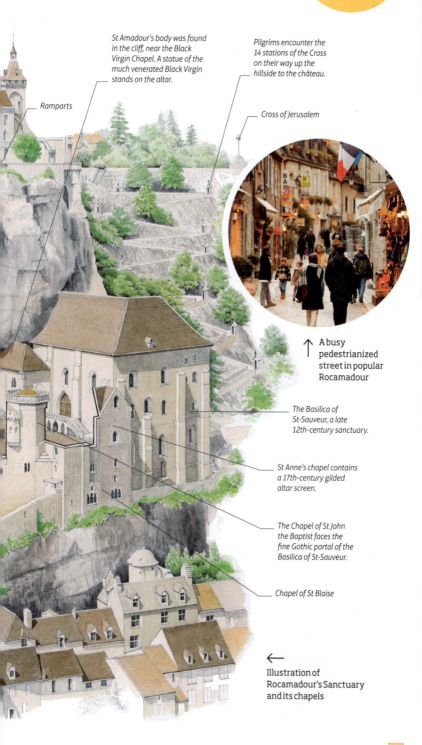

Ramparts

St Amadour's body was found in the cliff, near the Black Virgin Chapel. A statue of the much venerated Black Virgin stands on the altar.

Pilgrims encounter the 14 stations of the Cross on their way up the hillside to the château.

Cross of Jerusalem

A busy pedestrianized street in popular Rocamadour

The Basilica of St-Sauveur, a late 12th-century sanctuary.

St Anne's chapel contains a 17th-century gilded altar screen.

The Chapel of St John the Baptist faces the fine Gothic portal of the Basilica of St-Sauveur.

Chapel of St Blaise

← Illustration of Rocamadour's Sanctuary and its chapels

ABBAYE DE ST-PIERRE

⚐ D6 **🏠 Moissac, Tarn-et-Garonne** **🕐 Hours vary, check website** **ℹ 6 pl Durand de Bredon; www.tourisme.moissac.fr**

At the core of the otherwise unremarkable riverside town of Moissac is the exquisite abbey of St-Pierre, one of the undisputed masterpieces of French Romanesque architecture. Founded in the 9th century by a Benedictine monk, the abbey was subsequently ransacked by Arabs, Normans and Hungarians, before it became a pre-eminent monastery.

The abbey's exterior belongs to two periods: one part, in stone, is Romanesque; the other, in brick, is Gothic. The abbey is known above all for its superb south portal and tympanum, built over 30 years from 1100 to 1130, a masterful translation into stone of St John's dramatic vision of the Apocalypse (Book of Revelation). The Evangelists Matthew, Mark, Luke and John appear as "four beasts full of eyes". Moorish details on the door jambs and pillars reflect the contemporary cultural exchange between France and Spain. In 1998, the church and cloisters were bestowed UNESCO protection as part of the broader World Heritage Site, the "Routes of Santiago de Compostela in France".

FESTIVAL DES VOIX IN MOISSAC

This hugely popular world music festival (*www.moissac-culture. fr*) stages some 80 concerts every June in Moissac and in the surrounding villages. Many are free and held in the magical setting of Moissac's beautiful abbey cloisters, as well as in châteaux and town squares. The emphasis is on vocal music and ranges from *fado* and *chanson* to Italian folk music and Algerian *raï*.

1

2

3

① The late 11th-century cloister, occupied by monks until the Revolution, is lined with alternate columns in white, pink, green and grey marble.

② The fine, vaulted interior was remodelled in the 15th century in the Gothic style.

③ The church contains some notable 15th-century statuary. This remarkable grouping represents the Entombment of Christ.

Did You Know?

The abbey's "narrative" capitals depict scenes from the Bible and the lives of the saints.

↑ The dramatic entrance to Abbaye de St-Pierre, with intricate carved portals above

↑ A busy pedestrianized street in Toulouse's beautiful historic centre

④

TOULOUSE

Ⓐ D6 Ⓐ Haute-Garonne ✈ 6 km (4 miles) NW Toulouse Ⓖ Gare Matabiau 🚌 Blvd Pierre Semard ℹ Donjon du Capitole; 08 92 180 180; www.toulouse-welcome.com

This warm southern city, today a popular university town, was founded by the Roman on the Garonne. It flourished as a Visigoth city, then as a Renaissance town of towered brick palaces built with the wealth generated by the pastel (blue pigment) and grain trades. The Old Town centres around place du Capitole.

①

Les Abattoirs

Ⓐ 76 Allées Charles de Fitte Ⓒ 12–6pm Wed–Sun (til 7pm Thurs) Ⓦ lesabattoirs.orgr

The city's former abattoir has been superbly converted into a centre for modern and contemporary art, Les

Abattoirs. There is a rolling programme of exhibits, as well as installations and an outdoor sculpture park.

②

Les Jacobins

Ⓐ Rue Lakanal Ⓒ Tue–Sun Ⓦ jacobins.toulouse.fr

The Jacobins convent, with its church and cloisters, was begun in 1229 and completed over the next two centuries. The convent was founded by

the Dominicans to preach against Cathar heretics, and became the founding institution of Toulouse University. Its church, a Gothic masterpiece, features a soaring, 22-branched palm tree vault in the apse. The delicate Gothic Chapelle St-Antonin (1337) contains frescoes of the Apocalypse dating from 1341.

③

Fondation Bemberg

Ⓐ Hôtel d'Assézat, 7 pl d'Assézat Ⓒ Tue–Sun Ⓧ 1 Jan, 25 Dec Ⓦ fondation-bemberg.fr

This 16th-century palace houses the collection of local

→ Bright blue skies above the church and cloister of 13th-century Les Jacobins

Did You Know?

Toulouse is known as the "Pink City" because the sun turns its pale-brick buildings all shades of pink.

art lover Georges Bemberg, and covers Renaissance paintings, 19th- to 20th-century French artworks, including Impressionist, Post-Impressionist and Fauvist works and objets d'art.

Musée des Augustins

 21 rue de Metz Wed-Mon 1 Jan, 1 May, 25 Dec augustins.org

This museum of fine arts has Romanesque sculpture and cloisters from a 14th-century Augustinian priory. There are also 16th- to 19th-century French, Italian and Flemish paintings, including works by Ingres, Delacroix, Benjamin Constant and Laurens.

⑤

Basilique St-Sernin

Pl St-Sernin daily basilique-saint-sernin.fr

Built in the 11th–12th centuries to accommodate

pilgrims, this is the largest Romanesque basilica in Europe. Highlights are the octagonal brick belfry, with rows of decorative brick arches topped by an enormously tall spire. Beautiful 11th-century marble bas-reliefs of Christ and the symbols of the Evangelists by Bernard Gilduin are in the ambulatory.

⑥

Cité de l'Espace

Av Jean Gonord 10am-6pm Tue-Sun (Apr-Sep: daily) Jan cite-espace.com

Southeast of the city centre, this vast "space park" explores Toulouse's involvement in aeronautics and space travel. It includes two planetariums, an IMAX cinema and a lifesize replica of the Ariane 5 rocket. Interactive exhibits include a simulator that lets you run on the moon and an "anti-gravity" pod. A family-friendly place, there are great exhibits for children and plenty of space for down time.

STAY

Hôtel Saint-Sernin

Bright, stylish rooms near the basilica.

2 rue St-Bernard   hotelstsernin.com

€€€

Hôtel des Beaux Arts

Friendly staff and great views at this smart belle époque hotel.

1 pl du Pont-Neuf   hoteldesbeaux arts.com

€€€

La Cour des Consuls

Two 18th-century town houses combine at this stylish hotel, with spa.

46 rue des Couteliers sofitel.accor hotels.com

€€€

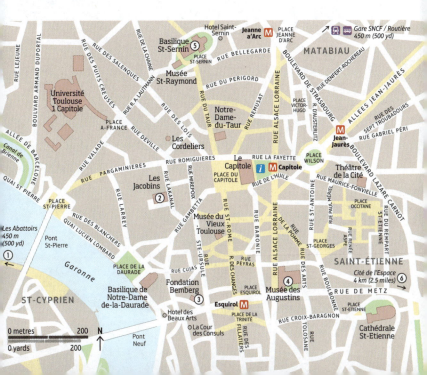

EXPERIENCE MORE

❺ St-Jean-de-Côle

🅰 D6 🏠 Dordogne
ℹ️ 19 rue du Château;
05 53 62 14 15

St-Jean-de-Côle's medieval, humpbacked bridge gives the best view of this lovely Dordogne village set in hilly countryside. Stone and half-timbered houses, roofed with the distinctive red-brown tiles of the region, cram the narrow streets around the main square. Here stand a covered marketplace, château and 12th-century church. The cupola of the church used to be the largest in the region – too large, it seems, for it fell down twice in the 18th and 19th centuries. The second time it happened, the builders gave up, and there has been a plank ceiling ever since.

❻ Château de Hautefort

🅰 D6 🏠 Dordogne
🕐 Hours vary, check website 🌐 chateau-hautefort.com

Hautefort clings to the sides of a steep hill topped by a massive 17th-century château, one of the finest in southwest France. Partially fortified and built as a pleasure palace in honour of King Louis XIII's secret love, the Marquis de Hautefort's sister Marie, the castle sits among French gardens on terraces with superb views of the rolling countryside of northeast Périgord. In the village, the hospice, of a similar date, has a fascinating museum of early medical implements.

❼ Brantôme

🅰 D6 🏠 Dordogne 🚌
ℹ️ Notre Dame church;
www.perigord-dronne-belle.fr

Surrounded by the River Dronne, Brantôme is often called the Venice of the Périgord Vert. Its medieval abbey and 11th-century belfry (reputedly the oldest in

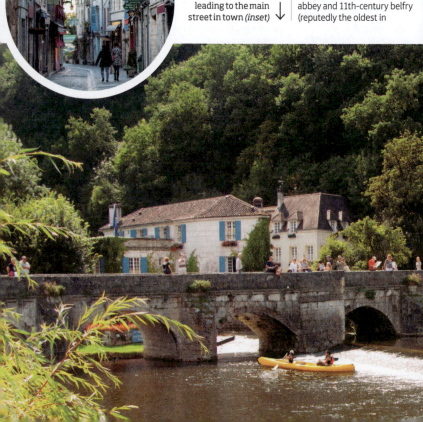

A picturesque river path in Brantôme, leading to the main street in town *(inset)* ↓

France), together with the verdant rockface behind, provide this picturesque town with a dramatic backdrop.

The poet Pierre de Bourdeille (1540–1614) was appointed abbot here in his youth. One of his lovers was allegedly Mary, Queen of Scots. After a crippling fall, Bourdeille retired here in 1569 to write his racy memoirs. It is possible to wander the stone staircases and cloisters, and walk through the main courtyard to the troglodyte dwellings in the cliff behind. In one of these dwellings are two scenes (the Last Judgment and the Crucifixion) that were cut into the stone between the 16th and 17th centuries.

Just 12 km (7 miles) northeast lies the Renaissance **Château de Puyguilhem**, set in lovely grounds at the foot of a wooded valley. Nearby is the **Grotte de Villars**. As well as spectacular rock formations, this underground network of caves house some marvellous cave paintings dating back some 19,000 years.

Château de Puyguilhem

 🅰 Villars ⏱ Hours vary, check website 📅 1 Jan, 1 May, 1 & 11 Nov, 25 Dec 🌐 chateau-puyguilhem.fr

Grotte de Villars

🅰 Villars ⏱ Hours vary, check website 🌐 grotte-villars.com

8
Bourdeilles

🅰 D6 🅰 Dordogne
ℹ️ 63 place Tilleuls; www.perigord-dronne-belle.fr

This town may be small, but it has much to offer – a Gothic bridge with cutwater piers over the River Dronne, a mill and the medieval **Château de Bourdeilles**. The 16th-century additions to the castle were designed in a hurry by the châtelaine Jacquette de Montbron, when expecting a visit from Queen Catherine de' Medici. After the royal visit was called off, so were the building works. The highlight is the gilded salon, decorated in the 1560s by the talented Ambroise le Noble, of the Fontainebleau School.

Château de Bourdeilles

📞 05 53 03 73 36 ⏱ Hours vary, call ahead 📅 Jan

EAT

Auberge de la Truffe
Truffles figure prominently in Périgord, and this inn is the ideal place to sample them.

🅰 D6 🅰 Le Bourg, Sorges 🌐 auberge-de-la-truffe.com

L'Esplanade
Sublime views from its terrace and superb cuisine make this hotel-restaurant a must.

🅰 D6 🅰 Domme 🌐 esplanade-perigord.com

Le Puits Saint-Jacques
Exquisite cuisine and wines are showcased at this restaurant set in a farmhouse.

🅰 D6 🅰 Ave Victor Capoul, Pujaudran 📅 Sun evening, Mon & Tue 🌐 lepuitssaintjacques.fr

---

Au Fil de l'Eau
A riverside setting makes this fish restaurant ideal for a summer evening meal. It can get busy, so book ahead.

🅰 D6 🅰 21 quai Bertin, Brantôme 📅 Mid-Oct-Apr 🌐 fildeleau.com

⑨ Bergerac

🅐D6 🏠Dordogne ✈🚗🚌
𝓲 97 rue Neuve d'Argenson;
www.pays-bergerac-
tourisme.com

This small port, a tobacco farming and commercial centre, spreads itself over both sides of the Dordogne. Chief attractions are its extraordinary **Musée du Tabac** (tobacco museum), and its food and wine, which are invariably excellent. Bergerac's most celebrated wine is Monbazillac, a sweet white wine, often drunk on cere-monial occasions. For an intro-duction to Bergerac's wines, visit the Maison des Vins, set in a former monastery.

Musée du Tabac

♿ 🏠Maison Peyrarède, pl du Feu 📞 05 53 63 04 13 🕑Mon-Sat 🚫Mon in winter, public hols

⑩ Lascaux IV

🅐D6 🏠Lascaux Centre International de l'Art Pariétal, Dordogne 🕑Daily 🚫1 Jan, 25 Dec 🌐lascaux.fr

Lascaux is the most famous of the prehistoric sites located on the River Vézère. Four boys came across the caves and their astonishing Palaeolithic paint-ings in 1940, and its importance as a prehistoric site was soon seen. Since 1963, Lascaux has been closed to the public due to deterioration, but

←

Statue of Cyrano de Bergerac in the town of Bergerac

the Centre International de l'Art Pariétal provides state-of the art replicas of the vivid cave paintings of bulls, high-antlered elk, bison and horses. It includes an interactive exhi-bition using digital touch-screens that retraces the history of the discovery of Lascaux, and a virtual reality tour of the caves. The café serves excellent regional food.

⑪ St-Amand-de-Coly

🅐D6 🏠Dordogne 🕑Daily 🌐saint-amand-de-coly.org

This abbey church is an outstanding example of fortress architecture, built in the 12th to 13th centuries by Augustinian monks to protect their monastery. There are two lines of defence: a high stone rampart and, behind it, the arched tower of the church itself, both built with very thick walls. The tower looks more like a castle keep, and was once pierced by arrow slits.

Inside, the church is beau-tifully simple, with pure lines, a flat ribbed vault, 12th-cen-tury cupola, a soaring nave and a stone floor sloping up to the altar. Yet even this interior was arranged for defence, with a gallery from which enemies within the building could be attacked. St-Amand was damaged

 GREAT VIEW
Aerial View

For amazing views of the Dordogne take off in a balloon with Périgord Dordogne Montgolfières (perigord-dordogne-montgolfieres.com).

during the Hundred Years' War. In 1575, it survived a siege by Huguenot cavalry and a six-day bombardment by cannon. Religious life here ended after the Revolution.

⑫ Dordogne Valley

🅐D6 🏠Dordogne 🚆Bergerac 🚌Bergerac, Le Buisson de Cadouin 🚌Beynac 𝓲Le Buisson de Cadouin; 05 53 22 06 09

Probably no river in France crosses so varied a landscape and such different geological formations as the Dordogne. Starting in deep granite gorges in the Massif Central, it continues through fertile lowlands, then enters the limestone Causse country around Souillac. By the time

→

Imposing Beynac castle, perched high above the Dordogne Valley

Replica of cave paintings at Lascaux Centre International de l'Art Pariétal

the Dordogne has wound down to the Garonne, it is almost 3 km (2 miles) wide.

Don't be put off by the valley's touristy image. It is a beautiful area for wandering. Several villages make good stopping-off points, such as Limeuil, Beynac and La Roque-Gageac, from where *gabarres* (river boats) ferry visitors (Easter–October).

Perched high above the river, southwest of Sarlat, is the 17th-century Château de Marqueyssac. Its exquisite topiary park offers panoramic views from Domme to Beynac, and of the medieval Château de Castelnaud on the opposite riverbank.

 13

Les Eyzies

A D6 **A** Dordogne **A** **i** 19 av de la Préhistoire; www. lascaux-dordogne.com

Four major prehistoric sites and a group of smaller caves cluster around the unassuming village of Les Eyzies. Head first for the **Musée National de Préhistoire**, in a modern building at the foot of a 16th-century castle overlooking the village. The exhibits are useful for putting the vast warren of prehistoric painting and sculpture into context.

The **Grotte de Font de Gaume** is the logical first stop after the museum. This cave, discovered in 1901, contains probably the finest prehistoric paintings still on public view in France.

Close by is the **Grotte des Combarelles**, with engravings of bison, reindeer, magic symbols and human figures. Further on, you reach the rock shelter of **Abri du Cap Blanc**, discovered in 1909, with a rare, life-size frieze of horses and bison sculpted in the rock.

On the other side of Les Eyzies is the cave system at **Rouffignac**, a favourite place for excursions since the 15th century. There are 8 km (5 miles) of caves here; 2.5 km (1.5 miles) are served by electric train. The paintings include drawings of mammoths, and a frieze of two bison challenging each other in combat.

Tickets for the caves sell out fast, so arrive early or book ahead. Tickets for Combarelles must be purchased at the Grotte de Font de Gaume.

Musée National de Préhistoire
⊛ 🏛 🕐 Hours vary, check website 🌐 musee-prehistoric-eyzies.fr

Grotte de Font de Gaume
🕐 Sun–Fri by appt 🕐 Some public hols, check website for details) 🌐 sites-les-eyzies.fr

REGIONAL DISHES

High-quality poultry, ducks and geese form the basis of the cuisine of this region, and their fat is a key ingredient in many meals from simple dishes such as *pommes sarladaises* (potatoes cooked in goose fat) to *confit*, where the entire duck legs are preserved in their own fat. The ultimate southwestern dish has to be *cassoulet*, a tasty stew containing either duck or goose, sausages, pork and white beans and topped with a crust of breadcrumbs.

Grotte des Combarelles
⊛ 📞 05 53 06 86 00 🕐 9:30am–5:30pm daily (book ahead for tours) 🔒 12:30pm–2pm Sep–May

Abri du Cap Blanc
⊛ 🏛 Marquay, Les Eyzies 📞 05 53 06 86 00 🕐 9:30–5:30pm daily 🔒 12:30pm–2pm Sep–May

Grotte de Rouffignac
⊛ 🏛 🕐 Mar–Oct: 10am–5pm; July & Aug: 9am–6pm daily (tickets at 9am and 2pm) 🌐 grottede rouffignac.fr

14
Domme

🅰 D6 🏠 Dordogne ℹ Pl de la Halle; www.perigord-noir-valleedordogne.com

American writer Henry Miller wrote: "Just to glimpse the black, mysterious river at Domme from the beautiful bluff… is something to be grateful for all one's life." Considered to be one of the most beautiful villages in France, Domme itself is a neat bastide of golden stone, with medieval gateways still standing.

Occupying a splendid position, people come here to admire the view, which takes in the Dordogne Valley from Beynac in the west to Montfort in the east, and to wander the maze of old streets inside the walls. There is also a large cavern under the 17th-century covered market, where the inhabitants hid at perilous moments during the Hundred Years' War and the 16th-century Wars of Religion. Despite a seemingly impregnable position, 30 intrepid Huguenots managed to capture Domme by scaling the cliffs under cover of night and opening the gates.

15
Gouffre de Padirac

🅰 D6 🏠 Lot 🕒 Mar–mid-Nov: hours vary, check website 🅦 gouffre-de-padirac.com

Formed by the collapse of a cave, this huge crater measures 115 ft (35 m) wide and 337 ft (103 m) deep. The underground river and stunning succession of galleries were discovered in 1889. The immense Salle du Grand Dôme chamber dwarfs the tallest of cathedrals. Visitors descend into the cave by stairs or lift and walk through a spectacular cave system, where punts await to take you along the underground river. An audio tour is also available.

INSIDER TIP
Visiting Gouffre de Padirac

The temperature in the Gouffre de Padirac cave is 13° C (55° F), so it's worth wearing warm clothes. A waterproof jacket for the boat ride is also a good idea after heavy rainfall in the area.

16
Cahors

🅰 D6 🏠 Lot 🚃🚌 ℹ Pl François Mitterrand; www.tourisme-cahors.fr

The capital of the Lot *département*, the small town of Cahors is renowned for its dark, heady red wine, which was produced as far back as Roman times. It is also famous for being the birthplace of the statesman Léon Gambetta (1838–82), who led France to recovery after the war with Prussia in 1870. The main street of Cahors – like many towns in France – is named after him.

Cathédrale de St-Étienne, entrenched behind the narrow streets of Cahors's Old Town, dates back to 1119. It has some fine medieval details: don't miss the lively figures of the Romanesque north door and tympanum, which depict the Ascension, or the huge cupola above the

←

Visitors taking a tour underground in the crater at Gouffre de Padirac

Sweeping views from the Cirque d'Autoire over the valley below

The capital of the Lot département, the small town of Cahors is renowned for its dark, heady red wine, which was produced as far back as Roman times.

nave (said to be the largest in France). They are covered in 14th-century frescoes that depict the stoning of St Stephen (St-Étienne). The Renaissance cloisters are decorated with some intricate, though damaged, carvings.

Also worth seeking out in the cathedral quarter is the ornate 16th-century Maison de Roaldès, its north façade decorated with tree, sun, and rose of Quercy motifs. It was here that Henri of Navarre (who later became Henri IV) stayed for one night in 1580 after besieging and capturing the town.

The landmark monument in Cahors is the Pont Valentré, a fortified bridge that spans the river. With seven pointed arches and three towers, it was built between 1308 and 1360, and has withstood many attacks since then. It is claimed that the bridge is one of the most photographed monuments in France. An alternative way to enjoy the scenery is to take a leisurely 90-minute boat trip through the lock from a wharf near the bridge (April–October).

Cahors makes a good base from which to explore the sights of the Lot. Visit the historic towns of Figeac – birthplace of Jean-François Champollion, who first deciphered Egyptian hieroglyphics – and the **Grotte de Pech-Merle** with its extraordinary painted walls.

Grotte de Pech-Merle
◈ 🅰 Cabrerets 🅲 Mar–Nov: 9:30am–5pm daily
🅦 pechmerle.com

---

⑰
Autoire

🅰 D6 🅰 Lot 🇫 Saint Céré; vallee-dordogne.com

This is one of the loveliest places in Quercy, the fertile area east of Périgord. There are no grand monuments or dramatic history, just an unspoiled site at the mouth of the Autoire gorge.

The Château de Limarque on the main square, and the Château de Busqueille overlooking it, are both built in characteristic Quercy style, with turrets and towers. Around the edge of the square are charming stone houses with steep brown roofs and mullioned windows. Elsewhere, elaborate dovecotes stand in fields or are attached to houses.

South of Autoire, past a 100-ft (30-m) waterfall, a path climbs to a limestone rock amphitheatre, the Cirque d'Autoire, giving panoramic views of Autoire and the lush valley below.

Did You Know?

Autiore is best visited in spring, when the flowers that fill the streets and gardens burst into colour.

The view of the Dordogne Valley from the village of Domme

The fortress gate concealing the fortified village of Larressingle

difference between the brandy of Armagnac and Cognac really is.

Musée de l'Armagnac

 📍2 rue Jules Ferry 📞05 62 28 47 21 🕐Apr–Oct: Wed–Mon ⛔Jan, public hols

18

Larressingle

🅰D6 🏛Gers 🚌To Condom ℹLarressingle; www.tourisme-condom.com

With its ramparts, ruined donjon (defence tower) and fortress gate, Larressingle is a particularly interesting, though rather tiny, fortified village in the middle of the Gascon countryside. It dates from the 13th century, and is one of the last remaining Gascon villages with its walls still intact. The state of preservation is unique, and gives an idea of what life must have been like for the small, embattled local communities who had to live for decades under conditions of perpetual warfare in the medieval period.

19

Condom

🅰D6 🏛Gers 🚌 ℹ5 pl St-Pierre; www.tourisme-condom.com

Long a centre for the Armagnac trade, Condom is a market town built around the late-Gothic Cathédrale St-Pierre. In 1569 during the Wars of Religion, the Huguenot (French Protestant) army threatened to demolish the cathedral, but Condom's citizens averted this by paying a huge ransom.

The river Baïse skirts the town centre. Notable among Condom's fine 17th- to 18th-century mansions is the Hôtel de Cugnac on rue Jean-Jaurès, with its ancient *chai* (wine and spirit storehouse) and distillery. On the other side of the town centre, the **Musée de l'Armagnac** is the place to find out, finally, what the

20

Auch

🅰D6 🏛Gers 🚌🚈 ℹ1 rue Dessoles; www.auch-tourisme.com

The ancient capital of the Gers department, Auch (said "Ohsh") has a rich heritage. It has long been a sleepy place which comes alive on market days. The new town by the station is not a place that encourages you to linger.

The interior and façade *(inset)* of Cathédrale Ste-Marie d'Auch

Head instead for the Old Town on the outcrop overlooking the River Gers. If you climb the 234 stone steps from the river, you arrive directly in front of the restored late Gothic Cathédrale Ste-Marie, begun in 1489. The furnishings of the cathedral are remarkable: highlights include the carved wooden choir stalls depicting more than 1,500 biblical, historical and mythological characters, and the equally magnificent 15th-century stained glass, attributed to Arnaud de Moles. The windows show a mix of prophets, patriarchs and apostles, with 360 individually characterized figures and exceptional colours. Three of these windows depict the key biblical events of the Creation, the Crucifixion and the Resurrection.

Auch went through an urbanization programme in the 18th century, when the allées d'Étigny, flanked by the grand Hôtel de Ville and Palais de Justice, were built. Some fine houses from this period line the pedestrianized rue Dessoles.

Auch's restaurants are known for their hearty dishes, including *foie gras de canard* (fattened duck liver).

Auvillar

🅰 D6 🏠 Tarn-et-Garonne 🛈 pl de la Halle; 05 63 39 89 82

A perfect complement to the high emotion of Abbaye de St-Pierre (*p428*), Auvillar is one of the loveliest hilltop villages in France. It has a marketplace lined with half-timbered arcades at its centre, and extensive views from the promenade overlooking the River Garonne. There are picnic spots along this panoramic path plus an orientation map. This includes all but the chimneys visible in the distance, belonging to the nuclear plant at Golfech.

> The ancient capital of the Gers department, Auch (said "Ohsh") has a rich heritage. It has long been a sleepy place which comes alive on market days.

STAY

Les Glycines
This small and mellow hotel combines a country location with boutique style. Lovely restaurant, pool and garden on site.

🅰 D6 🏠 4 av de Laugerie, Les Eyzies-de-Tayac 🌐 les-glycines-dordogne.com

 €€€

Hôtel Cuq en Terrasses
Set on a hilltop, this 18th-century manor house has a pool in lush gardens and glorious views from the terrace restaurant.

🅰 D6 🏠 Cuq le Château, Cuq-Toulza 🕐 Mid-Oct-mid-Apr 🌐 cuqenterrasses.com

 €€€

Le Pont de l'Ouysse
Rooms are bright and sunny at this indulgent retreat with a Michelin-starred restaurant.

🅰 D6 🏠 Lacave 🌐 lepontdelouysse.com

 €€€

Hostellerie le Vert
Rooms have heaps of character at this family-friendly, 17th-century house in wine country.

🅰 D6 🏠 Lieu dit "Le Vert", Mauroux 🕐 Nov-Mar 🌐 hotellevert.com

 €€€

㉒ Montauban

 D6 🏛 Tarn-et-Garonne 🚌🚆 🛈 4 rue du Collège; www.montauban-tourisme.com

Toulouse's little pink-brick sister and the capital of the 17th-century "Protestant Republic" of southern France, Montauban was the birthplace of the painter Jean-Auguste-Dominique Ingres (1780–1867). The town's great treasure is the **Musée Ingres**, a 17th-century palace with an exceptional bequest of paintings and 4,000 drawings, plus works by Van Dyck, Tintoretto, Courbet and sculptor Antoine Bourdelle, who was also born here.

Above all, Montauban has a pleasant shopping area, with a double-arcaded main square (place Nationale) built in the 17th and 18th centuries. A few streets away from here lies the stark white Cathédrale Notre-Dame, which was built on the orders of Louis XIV in 1692 in the backlash against Protestant heresy. It houses *The Vow of Louis XIII* painted by Ingres in 1824.

Musée Ingres

⊕ 🏛 Palais Episcopal, 19 rue de l'Hôtel de Ville 📞 05 63 22 12 91 🚫 Closed for renovation until end 2019

㉓ Gorges de l'Aveyron

 D6 🏛 Tarn-et-Garonne ✈ Toulouse 🚆 Montauban, Lexos 🚌 Montauban 🛈 10 rue de la Pélisserie; www.tourisme-saint-antonin-noble-val.com

At the gorges de l'Aveyron, the sweltering plains of Montauban change abruptly to cool, chestnut-wooded hills. Here the villages are of a different stamp from those of Périgord and Quercy, displaying an obsession with defence.

The château at Bruniquel, founded in the 6th century, is built over the lip of a precipice. Further along the D115, the village of Penne's position on the tip of a giant rock fang is even more extreme. The gorge then narrows and darkens and from St-Antonin-Noble-Val, beside the river, the valley turns towards Cordes.

㉔ Cordes-sur-Ciel

 D6 🏛 Tarn 🚌🚆 🛈 Maison Gaugiran, 38–42 rue Grand Raimond; www.cordessurciel.fr

Cordes-sur-Ciel ("Cordes in the Sky") is a fitting description as the town seems suspended against the skyline, built as a protective enclave for the local populace. During the 13th-century Cathar wars the entire town was excommunicated. Devastating

←

Bacchante aux raisins by Antoine Bourdelle, in the Musée Ingres, Montauban

TOP 3 **GORGES IN FRANCE**

France has some truly impressive gorges, and some great adventures are to be had exploring them either on foot, by canoe, paddleboard or paraglider.

Gorges de l'Aveyron
Where limestone cliffs tower over beautiful countryside.

Gorges du Tarn
Some of France's most spectacular natural scenery *(p346)*.

Gorges du Verdon
Constitutes one of the most dramatic natural sights in Europe *(p60)*.

epidemics of plague later sent it into decline, and the town was in an advanced state of decay at the beginning of the 20th century.

Restoration work began in the 1940s and the ramparts and many of the gates built in 1222 have been well preserved. Also intact are Gothic houses such as the 14th-century Maison du Grand Fauconnier.

Today, Cordes still exudes a sense of loss. The town of which Albert Camus wrote "Everything is beautiful there, even regret", is now dependent on tourism. Crafts aimed at visitors abound and a collection at the **Musée d'Art Moderne et Contemporain** evokes Cordes's former embroidery industry. The museum also houses works of modern art by such artists as Picasso and Miró. The Jardin des Paradis offers a corner of beauty and hope in which to reflect.

Musée d'Art Moderne et Contemporain

🕐 ⊕ 🏛 Maison du Grand Fauconnier 📞 05 63 56 14 79 🕐 Mid-Mar-mid-Nov: Wed-Mon

The exquisite interior of Cathédrale Ste-Cécile in Albi

26 Castres

A D6 **fi** Tarn **⊕** **fi** **i** 2 pl de la République; **www.tourisme-castres.fr**

A centre for the cloth industry since the 14th century, today Castres is also the headquarters of one of France's biggest pharmaceutical companies. The **Musée Goya – Musée d'Art Hispanique** has a large collection of Spanish art. Goya himself is well represented by a large, misty council scene and by a series of powerful prints, *Los Caprichos*.

Outside, the pretty formal gardens between the town hall and the River Agout were designed in the 17th century by André Le Nôtre, the landscape architect of Vaux-le-Vicomte and the Palace of Versailles.

Musée Goya – Musée d'Art Hispanique

⊗ **fi** Hôtel de Ville **C** 05 63 71 59 30 **O** Hours vary, check website **N** Mon & 1 Jan, 1 May, 14 Jul, 1 Nov, 25 Dec

---

BASTIDE TOWNS

Bastide towns were hurriedly built in the 13th century by both the English and the French to encourage settlement of empty areas before the Hundred Years' War. They are the medieval equivalent of "new towns", with planned grids of streets and fortified perimeters. Over 300 bastide towns and villages still survive between Périgord and the Pyrénées.

---

25 Albi

A D6 **fi** Tarn **fi** **i** Palais de la Berbie, pl Ste-Cécile; **www.albi-tourisme.fr**

Like many large towns in this region, Albi is not only red, but also can become red hot, and not ideal for afternoon visits in summer. You need to get up in the cool early morning to walk the streets around the market and the cathedral perched above the town.

Try to make for the **Musée Toulouse-Lautrec** in the Palais de la Berbie ahead of the crowds. The museum contains the most complete permanent collection of the Post-Impressionist artist's work in existence, including paintings, drawings and his famous posters for the Moulin Rouge. There are also canvases by famous artists such as Matisse, Dufy and Yves Brayer. After a stroll around the beautiful terraced gardens, step next door to the vast red-brick Cathédrale Ste-Cécile, built in the aftermath of the Albigensian crusade in 1265. It was intended as a reminder to potential heretics that the Church meant business. From a distance, its semicircular towers and narrow windows give it the appearance more of a fortress than a place of worship. Every feature, from the huge bell tower to the apocalyptic fresco of the Last Judgment, is on a giant scale, built deliberately to dwarf the average person. The effect is breathtaking, from outside and within.

Musée Toulouse-Lautrec

fi ⊗ **fi** Palais de la Berbie **O** Hours vary, check website **W** musee-toulouse-lautrec.com

27

Agen

 D6 ⬆ Lot-et-Garonne
🚆🚌🚗 ℹ 38 rue Garonne;
www.destination-agen.com

Vast orchards of regimented plum trees – producing the celebrated *pruneaux d'Agen* – characterize the landscape around this small provincial city. Crusaders returning from the Middle East brought the fruit to France in the 11th century, and monks in the Lot Valley nearby were the first to dry plums for prunes in commercial quantities.

Agen's **Musée Municipal des Beaux-Arts** has paintings by Goya, Sisley's *September Morning* and Corot's landscape *L'Étang de Ville d'Avray*. Jewel of the collection is the *Vénus du Mas*, a beautifully proportioned marble statue dating from the 1st century BC, discovered nearby in 1876.

The fortified village of Moirax, 8 km (5 miles) south of Agen, has a beautiful 12th-century Romanesque church. Two of the sculpted capitals depict biblical accounts of

↑ A self-portrait by Goya in the Musée Municipal des Beaux-Arts

Daniel in the lions' den, and Original Sin. The bastide town (p443) of Villeneuve-sur-Lot, 34 km (21 miles) south of Agen stands astride the River Lot. It has a tall 14th-century tower that once formed a defensive gateway. The red-brick Romano-Byzantine church of Ste-Catherine was built in 1909 but contains restored 15th-century stained-glass windows. Just to the east of Villeneuve is the pretty medieval hilltop village of Penne D'Agenais.

Musée Municipal des Beaux-Arts

⊘ 🏛 Pl du Docteur Esquirol
📞 05 53 69 47 23 🕐 Wed–Mon
🚫 1 Jan, Easter Mon, 1 & 8 May, 1 & 11 Nov, 25 Dec

28

Périgueux

🅰 D6 ⬆ Dordogne 🚆🚗🚌
ℹ 9bis, place du Coderc;
www.tourisme-perigueux.fr

The ancient and truly gastronomic city of Périgueux, like its neighbours Bergerac and Riberac, should be visited on market day, when stalls in the lively squares in the medieval part of town offer the pick of local specialities, including truffles (Nov–Mar), charcuterie and the succulent pies called *pâtés de Périgueux*.

Périgueux, now the busy regional capital, has long been the crossroads of Périgord. The earliest part remaining today is the quarter known as La Cité, once the important Gallo-Roman settlement of

→ Kayakers on the river at Périgueux, with Cathédrale St-Front in the background

> **Walking up the hill to Périgueux's dazzling white cathedral you pass through bustling streets and squares, each with its market activity.**

Vesunna. From Roman times to the Middle Ages, this was the focus of Périgueux. Most of the fabric of Vesunna was pulled down in the 3rd century, but some vestiges of a temple, a huge arena and a sumptuous villa remain. The Église St-Étienne nearby dates to the 12th century. La Domus de Vesonne, a Gallo-Roman museum, is also in La Cité.

Walking up the hill to Périgueux's dazzling white cathedral you pass through bustling streets and squares, each with its market activity. This is the medieval quarter of Le Puy St-Front, which began to flourish as pilgrims on their way to Santiago de Compostela visited the cathedral. As they brought prestige and wealth to the quarter, it gradually eclipsed La Cité. At the top is the imposing Cathédrale St-Front,

designed on the model of St Mark's Basilica in Venice and the largest in southwestern France. The Romanesque construction was heavily restored in the 19th century, when architect Paul Abadie added the fancy domes and cones. He later used St-Front as inspiration for the Sacré-Coeur in Paris *(p146)*.

Other gems of medieval and Renaissance architecture include Maison Estignard, at No 3 rue Limogeanne, with its unusual corkscrew staircase, and houses along rue Aubergerie.

Also in the cathedral quarter is the **Musée d'Art et d'Archéologie du Périgord**, which is one of the most comprehensive prehistory museums in France, with

remnants of burials dating back 70,000 years. Beautiful Roman glass, mosaics, earthenware and other artifacts from Vesunna are in the Gallo-Roman museum.

Musée d'Art et d'Archéologie du Périgord

⊘ 🏠 22 cours Tourny
🕐 Wed–Mon 🗓 Public hols
🅦 perigueux-maap.fr

 GREAT VIEW
Hot-air balloon rides from Périgueux

Seeing the Dordogne spread out underneath you as you soar on a hot-air balloon tour with Périgord Dordogne Montgolfières *(perigord-dordogne-montgolfieres.com)* is truly unforgettable.

A DRIVING TOUR OF
TWO RIVERS

Length 100 km (62 miles) **Stopping-off points** Figeac has
a number of excellent cafés for lunch and St-Cirq-Lapopie is a
must-stop for dramatic photos

Flanked by spectacular limestone cliffs, the
beautiful Lot and Célé valleys feature ancient
medieval villages and castles, narrow gorges
and rushing waterfalls along lazy stretches of
river. An unhurried tour of both valleys, around
160 km (100 miles), is best spread over two days,
to savour the gastronomic delights, the superb
views and cliffside towns .

From Cahors, the route meanders slowly up
the peaceful and picturesque Célé Valley to
reach Figeac, a handsome town full of charming
shops, cafés and restaurants. The return route is
via the busier Lot Valley, which has more sights,
including the spectacular village of St-Cirq-
Lapopie, one of the prettiest in France.

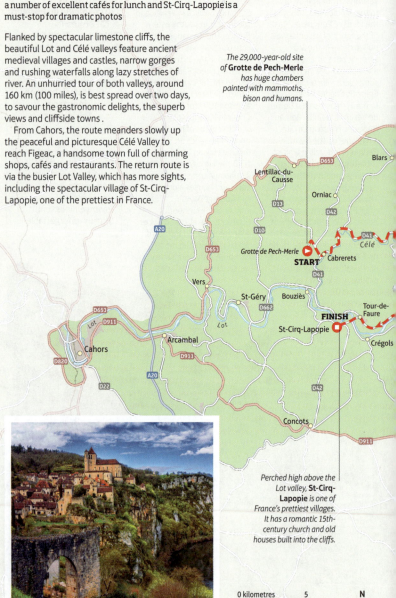

*The 29,000-year-old site
of **Grotte de Pech-Merle**
has huge chambers
painted with mammoths,
bison and humans.*

Blars

Lentillac-du-
Causse

Orniac

Célé

Grotte de Pech-Merle

START

Cabrerets

Vers

St-Géry

Bouziès

Tour-de-
Faure

FINISH

St-Cirq-Lapopie

Crégols

Arcambal

Lot

Cahors

Concots

*Perched high above the
Lot valley, **St-Cirq-
Lapopie** is one of
France's prettiest villages.
It has a romantic 15th-
century church and old
houses built into the cliffs.*

0 kilometres   5

0 miles   5

N

↑ The picturesque St-Cirq-Lapopie,
clinging to the cliffs above the valley

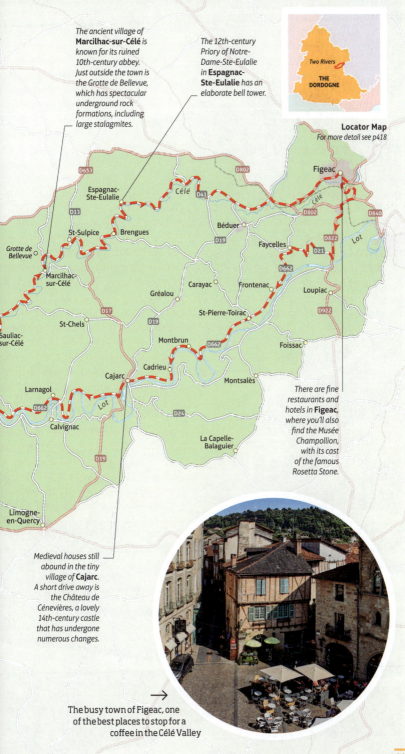

The ancient village of **Marcilhac-sur-Célé** is known for its ruined 10th-century abbey. Just outside the town is the Grotte de Bellevue, which has spectacular underground rock formations, including large stalagmites.

The 12th-century Priory of Notre-Dame-Ste-Eulalie in **Espagnac-Ste-Eulalie** has an elaborate bell tower.

Locator Map
For more detail see p418

Two Rivers

THE DORDOGNE

D653
Espagnac-Ste-Eulalie
Célé
D41
D802
Figeac
Célé
D802
D840
D13
St-Sulpice   Brengues
Béduer
D19
D822
Grotte de
Bellevue
Faycelles
D21
Marcilhac-
sur-Célé
Gréalou
Carayac
Frontenac
D662
Lot
Loupiac
Sauliac-
sur-Célé
St-Chels
D17
D19
St-Pierre-Toirac
D922
Montbrun
D662
Foissac
Cadrieu
Cajarc
Montsalès
Larnagol
D662
Lot
D24
Calvignac
La Capelle-
Balaguier
D19
Limogne-
en-Quercy

There are fine restaurants and hotels in **Figeac**, where you'll also find the Musée Champollion, with its cast of the famous Rosetta Stone.

Medieval houses still abound in the tiny village of **Cajarc**. A short drive away is the Château de Cénevières, a lovely 14th-century castle that has undergone numerous changes.

→
The busy town of Figeac, one of the best places to stop for a coffee in the Célé Valley

THE PYRÉNÉES

Clean water sources and bubbling hot springs enticed the first settlers to the rugged granite peaks of the Pyrénées some 10,000 years ago. A natural border between France and Spain, this mountain range lacks arable land, and so these early farmers instead herded sheep and cattle up and down the mountains. According to legend, Hannibal, more glamorously, tramped his elephants up and down the peaks in 218 BC. In the 1st century BC, Basque tribes assimilated with the Romans, but retained their culture. A confederacy of these tribes, with Bayonne as their capital, repelled invaders for a thousand years, but sank into feudalism in the 12th century, as politically canny families rose to prominence. By the 16th century, feuds between these families erupted into the bloody War of the Bands, which only ceased following royal intervention. In 1660, Louis XIV married Maria Theresa, the Infanta of Spain, in St-Jean-de-Luz, forming a tenuous relationship between the rival countries. The truce had dissolved by 1807, when the region was embroiled in the Franco-Spanish Peninsula Wars. Towards the end of the 19th century, peace reigned again. Coastal towns such as Biarritz and St-Jean-de-Luz became fashionable seaside resorts and, as tourism grew in the 1960s, Biarritz became a popular surfing spot.

Bay of Biscay

THE PYRÉNÉES

POITOU AND AQUITAINE *p392*

BIARRITZ

ST-JEAN-DE-LUZ

BAYONNE

Hendaye

Ustaritz

Espelette

Cambo-les-Bains

Saint-Martin-de-Seignanx

Labastide-Clairence

Hasparren

Saint-Palais

la Rhune
900 m (2,952 ft)

AÏNHOA

Saint-Étienne-de-Baïgorry

ST-JEAN-PIED-DE-PORT

FORÊT D'IRATY

Orhy
2,017 m
(6,617 ft)

Ezcároz

Lekunberri

Etxarri-Aranatz

Tolosa

Pamplona

Aoiz

Navascués

Lumbier

Yesa

Aragón

Tafalla

Puente la Reina

SPAIN

Bailo

Jaca

Tartas

Dax

Saint-Vincent-de-Tyrosse

Peyrehorade

Salies-de-Béarn

SAUVETERRE-DE-BÉARNT

ORTHEZ

Lacq

Mourenx

Navarrenx

AQUITAINE

Tardets-Sorholus

Aramits

Sainte-Engrace

Accous

Pic d'Anie
2,504 m (8,215 ft)

Saison

OLORON STE-MARIE

Arudy

Nay

PARC NATIONAL DES PYRÉNÉES

Balaïtous
3,144 m (10,314 ft)

Laruns

Pierrefitte-Nestalas

Argelès-Gazost

Vignemale
3,298 m
(10,820 ft)

Labouheyre

Trensacq

Morcenx

Garein

Labrit

Captieux

Houeilles

Roquefort

Mont-de-Marsan

Cazaubon

Nogaro

Saint-Sever

Grenade-sur-l'Adour

Castelnau-Rivière-Basse

Maubourguet

Pau Pyrénées Airport

Morlaas

Vic-en-Bigorre

PAU

Espoey

Nay

LOURDES

TARBES

LUZ-ST-SAUVEUR

Barèges

Castets

Saint-Martin-de-Seignanx

THE PYRÉNÉES

Must See

❶ Parc National des Pyrénées

Experience More

❷ Biarritz
❸ Bayonne
❹ Orthez
❺ Aïnhoa
❻ Sauveterre-de-Béarn
❼ St-Jean-Pied-de-Port
❽ Forêt d'Iraty
❾ Oloron-Ste-Marie
❿ Luz-St-Sauveur
⓫ Pau
⓬ Tarbes
⓭ Lourdes
⓮ St-Bertrand-de-Comminges
⓯ St-Lizier
⓰ Foix
⓱ Mirepoix
⓲ Arreau
⓳ St-Jean-de-Luz
⓴ Montségur

←

1 Colourful houses in the Old Town of Bayonne.

2 Shale cliffs at Pointe Sainte Barbe, outside St-Jean-de-Luz.

3 Bayonne *jambon* seller.

4 Espelette peppers.

3 DAYS
in the Basque Country

Day 1

Morning Explore Grand Bayonne *(p458)*, the area around the 13th-century Cathédrale Sainte-Marie, and stop for a glass of hot chocolate at one of the many chocolateries. Then cross the River Nive to Petit Bayonne to visit the Musée Basque to learn about this vibrant cross-border culture.

Afternoon Enjoy a light lunch at bustling Tarte Julie *(18 rue Thiers)* then spend the afternoon at a surf school on the Grande Plage. Try Jo Moraiz *(www.jomoraiz.com)*.

Evening Sample Bayonne ham at the Auberge du Cheval Blanc *(p465)*. Then head to the pier to stay in one of the spacious cabins aboard Peniche Djebelle *(www.djebelle.com)*, a small B&B in a barge.

Day 2

Morning Arrive in St-Jean-de-Luz *(p466)*, and browse the buzzing market (each Tuesday and Friday) for its charcuterie, cheese and seafood, then wander to the Église St-Jean-Baptiste to admire its glittering altar. Take care to look up – the wooden ship hanging from the ceiling is a witty nod to the town's seafaring tradition.

Afternoon Cross the Charles de Gaulle bridge, which overlooks the marina, to the village of Ciboure and wander its narrow, hilly streets lined with red-and-white Basque architecture. Further west, the historic Socoa district has fabulous views from the lighthouse on rue du Phare.

Evening Walk up to Pointe Ste-Barbe for sensational sunset views, then on to dinner at La Reserve *(1 rue Gaëtan de Bernoville)*. Spend the night in one of its luxurious rooms overlooking the water.

Day 3

Morning Travel inland through Aïnhoa *(p459)*, up to the lively village Espelette, famous for its red peppers. Try *axoa*, a veal stew, and local wines at Aintzina *(440 Karrika Nagusia)*.

Afternoon Further into the Pyrenees, St-Jean-Pied-de-Port *(p460)*, a stop on the Camino de Compostela pilgrim route, is famous as the last village in France before the route crosses to Spain. Climb the ramparts for panoramic views.

Evening Linger in St-Jean-Pied-de-Port for a sunset aperitif and then head to Café Ttipia *(2 place Floquet)*.

THE PYRÉNÉES FOR
BASQUE CULTURE

As piquant and vibrant as their famous cuisine, the Basques present an intriguing blend of culture, tradition and language that's utterly their own, in a region long squabbled over by their Spanish and French neighbours. Red is the colour of their spirit of independence, and you'll see it everywhere.

Fêtes de Bayonne

Bayonne is the capital of the French Basque country and each July sees the city come alive with five days of festivals *(fetes.bayonne.fr)* that see the red-and-white-clad locals party hard. Join the throngs lining the streets to watch parades through the city, dance and sing along at concerts, cheer on *pelota* matches and light up at the eruption of fireworks each night.

→

Locals celebrating the Fêtes de Bayonne

Bastions of Everyday Basque Life

For a true Basque experience, start with Bayonne *(p458)*, the capital of Basque culture and home to the Musée Basque, then dip into one of the fishing villages that dot the coast, such as St-Jean-Pied-de-Port *(p460)*, for bowls of *marmitako* (fish stew, typically tuna), eaten to the sound of *pelota* balls being smacked across a court, or to the border towns Aïnhoa *(p459)* and Espelette, where the annual pepper festival has been celebrated for centuries. If there is only time to visit one village, make it St-Jean-de-Luz *(p466)*. This proud fishing port, with its red timber-framed architecture set against the breathtaking backdrop of the Pyrénées, is a quintessential Basque gem.

←

Fishing and pleasure boats bobbing in front of St-Jean-de-Luz's charming and colourful harbourfront.

→

Axoa aux piments d'Espelettes, a typically spicy Basque veal stew

PELOTA

A traditional Basque ballcourt game, *pelota* pits players against each other using their bare hands, different kinds of bats or a *chistera* – a narrow curved basket on the end of a glove. It can be played in a number of ways, generally against a wall, like a cross between squash and handball; you'll see a high-walled court or *fronton* in most Basque towns and villages.

Zingy Cuisine

The food in this region is distinctly different from the rest of French cuisine. Basque dishes are generally spicy, with their central ingredient being the *piment d'Espelette*, a mild pepper. You'll see strings of these peppers adorning buildings throughout the region, but most evidently in the village of Espelette, from which they take their name.

→

Stringing Espelette peppers into *ristras* (chains) to dry

❶

PARC NATIONAL DES PYRÉNÉES

🗺 C7 🏠 Hautes-Pyrénées & Pyrénées-Atlantiques 🕐 Year-round, except for the high passes ℹ Cauterets; www.pyrenees-parcnational.fr/en

With peaks rising to over 3,000 m (9,850 ft), 230 high-altitude lakes and the Cirque du Gavarnie – the colossus of the Pyrénées – this national park is a stunning collection of natural wonders.

The Pyrénées National Park, designated in 1967, extends 100 km (62 miles) along the Franco-Spanish border. It boasts some of the most spectacular scenery in Europe, ranging from meadows glimmering with butterflies to high peaks snowcapped even in summer. Alongside the Cirque du Gavarnie, unmissable sights include the jagged peaks of the Vallée d'Aspe, the formidable Pic du Midi d'Ossau and the Pic d'Anie, which soars over meadows ablaze in spring with Pyrenean varieties of gentian and columbine found nowhere else. Variations in altitude and climate make the park rich in flora and fauna, and one of the most enjoyable ways to explore it is on foot, along its 350 km (217 miles) of well-marked trails.

THE GR10 TRAIL

The 866-km (538-mile) GR10 walking trail runs along the length of the Pyrénées, connecting Hendaye on the shores of the Atlantic ocean to Banyuls-sur-Mer on the Mediterranean coast. One of the toughest GR (Grande Randonnée) routes, it takes around 52 days to walk and showcases some magnificent landscapes, including dry garrigue, lush meadows and glacial valleys. If lucky, hikers may even spot a Pyrenean brown bear.

←

The Brèche de Roland, the famous breach in Gavarnie's crest, forming a gateway between France and Spain

→
Pyrenean brown bear, close to extinction but still found in this park, especially in the west

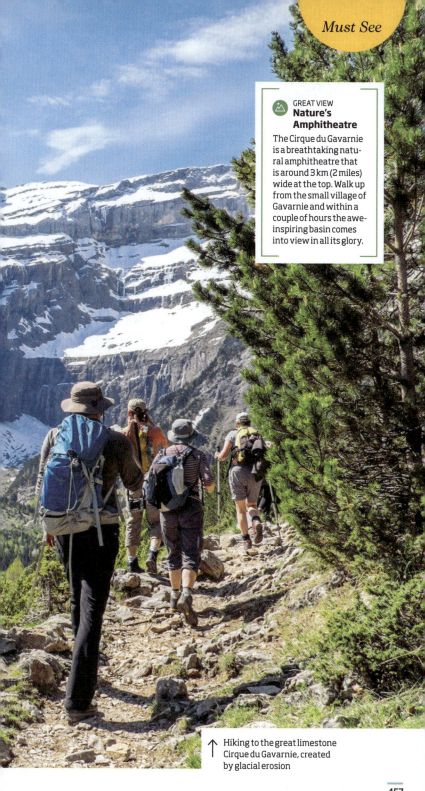

GREAT VIEW
Nature's Amphitheatre

The Cirque du Gavarnie is a breathtaking natural amphitheatre that is around 3 km (2 miles) wide at the top. Walk up from the small village of Gavarnie and within a couple of hours the awe-inspiring basin comes into view in all its glory.

↑ Hiking to the great limestone Cirque du Gavarnie, created by glacial erosion

→

Walkway to the rock of La-Basta at Biarritz and (inset) a surfer riding the waves

EXPERIENCE MORE

2

Biarritz

🅰B6 🄰Pyrénées-Atlantiques ✈🚃📧 ℹJaval quinto, square d'Ixelles; www.tourisme.biarritz.fr

Biarritz, west of Bayonne, has a grandiose centre, but has been developed along the coast by residential suburbs. The resort began as a whaling port but was transformed into a playground for Europe's elite in the 19th century. Its popularity was assured by Empress Eugénie, who discovered its mild winter climate during the 1852–70 reign of her husband, Napoleon III. With some of the best surfing in Europe, the town has three good beaches, two casinos and one of the last great luxury hotels in

> **INSIDER TIP**
> ### Surfing Biarritz
>
> The whole south French Atlantic coast draws surfers and in Biarritz, most catch the waves either on Grand Plage, the town's main beach, or the Côte des Basques, where the beach totally disappears at high tide.

Europe, the Palais, which was formerly the winter residence of Eugénie.

In the port des Pêcheurs, the **Aquarium de Biarritz** is home to some of the marine life of the Bay of Biscay. Below it, there is a narrow causeway leading across to the Rocher de la Vierge, with far-reaching views along the whole of the Basque coast. The Musée Asiatica is fine compensation for a rainy day.

Aquarium de Biarritz

♿😊🕐 🄰Esplanade du Rocher-de-la- Vierge, 14 plateau de l'Atalaye 🕐Hours vary, check website 🌐aquariumbiarritz.com

---

3

Bayonne

🅰B6 🄰Pyrénées-Atlantiques 🚃📧 ℹPl des Basques; www.bayonne-tourisme.com

Bayonne, capital of the French Basque country, lies between two rivers: the turbulent Nive, which arrives straight from the mountains, and the wide, languid Adour. An important town since Roman times because of its command of

one of the few easily passable roads to Spain, it prospered as a free port under English rule from 1154 to 1451. Since that time it has successfully withstood 14 sieges, including a particularly bloody one that was directed by the Duke of Wellington in 1813.

Grand Bayonne, the district around the cathedral, can be easily explored on foot. The 13th-century **Cathédrale Ste-Marie**, begun under English rule, is in the northern Gothic style. Look for the handsome cloister and the 15th-century knocker on the north door – if a fugitive could put a hand to this, he was entitled to receive sanctuary. The pedestrianized streets around form a lively shopping area, especially the arcaded rue Port Neuf, with cafés serving hot chocolate, a Bayonne speciality. Fine-quality chocolate-making was introduced by the Jews who fled Spain at the end of the 15th century, and the town has been renowned for it ever since. Immerse yourself in the chocolate-making process by visiting the museum within **L'Atelier du Chocolat** and follow a tour of the factory, with tastings included, finishing at the shop. Bayonne is also famous for its ham.

Petit Bayonne lies on the opposite side of the quay-lined River Nive. The **Musée Basque** gives an excellent introduction to Basque customs and traditions, with reconstructed house interiors and exhibits on seafaring.

L'Atelier du Chocolat
 🏠 7 allée de Gibéléou
🕐 9:30am–7pm Mon–Sat
🚫 Public hols 🌐 atelierdu-chocolat.fr

Musée Basque
🏠 37 quai des Corsaires
🕐 Hours vary, check website
🚫 Public hols 🌐 musee-basque.com

---

❹
Orthez

🄰 C6 🄰 Pyrénées-Atlantiques 🚉🚌
ℹ️ 1 rue des Jacobins; www.coeurdebearn.com

Orthez is an important Béarn market town, and its 13th- to 14th-century fortified bridge

> ## From here you can enjoy the best vantage point in the Pays Basque, and the walk back through the fields is just as picturesque.

was a vital river-crossing point over the Gave de Pau during the Middle Ages. On every Saturday morning between November and February, it has a spectacular market selling *foie gras*, smoked and air-cured Bayonne hams, and all kinds of fresh produce.

Fine buildings line rue Bourg Vieux, especially the house of Jeanne d'Albret, the mother of Henry IV, on the corner of rue Roarie. Jeanne's enthusiasm for the Protestant faith alienated both her own subjects and Charles X, and ultimately caused the Béarn region to be drawn into the Wars of Religion.

---

❺
Aïnhoa

🄰 B6 🄰 Pyrénées-Atlantiques 🚌 ℹ️ Maison du Patrimoine; www.ainhoa-tourisme.com

A tiny township on the road to the Spanish border, Aïnhoa

was founded during the 12th century as a waystation for pilgrims travelling the road to Santiago de Compostela *(p406)*. The main street still has the 17th-century white-washed Basque houses and the galleried church.

There is a similar church in the village of Espelette nearby. Typically Basque, the galleries boosted the seating capacity and separated the men from the women and children. Espelette is the trading centre for pottocks, an ancient local breed of pony, auctioned here at the end of January. It is also the shrine of the local crop, red pimento peppers, especially during October when a pepper festival is held here.

At the foot of the St-Ignace pass lies the mountain village of Sare. From the pass you can reach the summit of La Rhune by cog railway. From here you can enjoy the best vantage point in the Pays Basque, and the walk back through the fields is just as picturesque.

→
The patchwork of fields and woods around Aïnhoa, watched over by table-topped La Rhune mountain

6

Sauveterre-de-Béarn

⚑C6 **⌂**Pyrénées-Atlantiques **▣** **🛈**Pl Royale; www.tourisme-bearn-gaves.com

An attractive market town, Sauveterre is well worth a night's stay. It has stunning views southward over the Gave d'Oloron, the graceful single arch of the fortified bridge over the river, and the 16th-century Château de Nays. Fishermen gather in the town for the annual salmon-fishing championships in the fast-flowing Oloron, which take place from April to July.

Be sure to visit the **Château de Laàs**, 9 km (6 miles) along the D27 from Sauveterre. It has an excellent collection of 18th-century decorative art and furniture – most notably the bed in which Napoléon slept the night after his defeat at Waterloo, as well as a fine display of Aubusson and Gobelins tapestries and paintings by the Old Masters. There is also a pretty park with romantic Italian- and English-style gardens.

Château de Laàs
⊘ **⌂** **☏**05 59 38 91 53
◷Hours vary, call ahead

Did You Know?

St-Jean-Pied-de-Port translates to mean "at the foot of the pass".

7

St-Jean-Pied-de-Port

⚑B7 **⌂**Pyrénées-Atlantiques **▣▣** **🛈**14 pl du Général de Gaulle; www.saintjeanpieddeport-pays basque-tourisme.com

The historic capital of Basse-Navarre, St-Jean-Pied-de-Port lies at the foot of the Ronces-valles Pass. Here the Basques crushed Charlemagne's rear guard in 778 and killed its commander, Roland, who was later glorified in the epic poem, *Chanson de Roland*.

Throughout the Middle Ages this red sandstone fortress town was famous as the last rallying point before entering Spain on the pilgrim route to Santiago de Compostela (*p406*). Tall booths were erected next to the gates for additional security. Visitors and pilgrims in all

→

The junction of the wild Aspe and Ossau valleys at Oloron-Ste-Marie

seasons still provide St-Jean with its income, entering the narrow streets of the upper town on foot from the Porte d'Espagne, and passing cafés, hotels and restaurants on the way up. The ramparts are worth the steep climb, and the citadel has spectacular panoramic views. On Mondays the town hosts a popular craft market and Basque *pelota* matches.

8

Forêt d'Iraty

B7 🏔Pyrénées-Atlantiques 🚌St-Jean-Pied-de-Port 🚉 ℹ️St-Jean-Pied-de-Port, 05 59 37 03 57; Larrau, 05 59 28 62 80

A plateau clothed in beech woods and moorland, the Forêt d'Iraty is famous for its opportunities for walking and cross-country skiing. Here the ancient breed of Basque ponies, the *pottocks*, run half-wild. These creatures have not changed since the prehistoric inhabitants of the region traced their silhouettes onto the walls of local caves.

The tourist office at St-Jean-Pied-de-Port publishes maps of local walks. The best begins at the Chalet Pedro car park, south of the lake on the Iraty plateau, and takes you along the GR10 path to a group of 3,000-year-old standing stones on the western side of the Sommet d'Occabé.

←

The winding route down from medieval Sauveterre-de-Béarn to the Oloron river

9

Oloron-Ste-Marie

🅰B7 🏔Pyrénées-Atlantiques 🚉🚌 ℹ️Allées du Comte de Tréville; www.tourisme-oloron.com

A small town at the junction of the Aspe and Ossau valleys, Oloron grew from a Celtiberian settlement. It is famed for producing the famous classic French berets and for huge agricultural fairs in May and September. The town's great glory is the doorway of the Romanesque Cathédrale Ste-Marie, with its biblical and Pyrenean scenes, while the Église Sainte-Croix has Spanish-influenced carvings and Moorish-style vaulting.

Head up the Aspe Valley to try one of the famous cheeses. A side road leads to Lescun, beyond which is a spectacular range of saw-toothed peaks topped by the Pic d'Anie at 2,504 m (8,215 ft), one of the most beautiful sights in the Pyrénées. This is also one of the last refuges of the Pyrenean brown bear, their numbers diminished particularly by hunting and road- and house-building.

SLEEP

Hotel-Restaurant Euzkadi

Its façade adorned with Espelette peppers, this family-run three-star hotel offers 27 rooms, a friendly restaurant and a swimming pool.

🅰B6 🏠285 Karrika Nagusia, Espelette 🌐www.hotel-restaurant-euzkadi.com

€€€

___

Hotel de l'Ocean

This immaculate three-star hotel near the Port des Pêcheurs has contemporary rooms with balconies and lovely views of Le Grande Plage

🅰B6 🏠9 place Sainte-Eugénie, Biarritz 🌐biarritz-hotel-ocean.co.uk

€€€

Luz-St-Sauveur

🅐C7 🅐Hautes-Pyrénées
🚌To Lourdes 🚌 🅘Pl du
8 Mai 1945; www.luz.org

Luz-St-Sauveur is a small but attractive spa town. Its rather unusual church was built during the 14th century by the Hospitaliers de Saint Jean de Jérusalem, an order established to protect pilgrims.

The church is fortified and has gun slits from where the knights could watch over the pilgrims on their way to Santiago de Compostela (*p406*). The elegant spa town of Cauterets is a good base for climbing, skiing and walking.

Gavarnie is a former stop on the pilgrim route to Santiago de Compostela. A track leads from here to the spectacular natural rock amphitheatre known as the Cirque de Gavarnie. Here the longest waterfall in France, at 420 m (1,378 ft), drops off the mountain, encircled by eleven 3,000 m (9,800 ft) peaks.

Tourists can now share much of the **Observatoire Pic du Midi de Bigorre** with scientists. There's an area where visitors can learn about space through experiments and a planetarium show in the dome. It is even possible to spend the night here. Access is by cable car from La Mongie or on foot via one of a number of walks up to the summit, which takes a minimum of four hours.

The French are justly proud of the observatory, which has supplied some of the clearest images of Venus and other planets so far obtained from Earth. The 1-m (3.2-ft) telescope also mapped out the surface of the moon prior to NASA's Apollo missions.

Observatoire Pic du Midi de Bigorre

🅐 🅣 🅢 🅓Daily 🅒Mid-Apr–May & mid Nov–Dec 🅦picdumidi.com

↓ The scenic road into the Cirque de Gavarnie, and *(inset)* the observatory

Pau

🅐C6 🅐Pyrénées-Atlantiques 🚌🚌🚌 🅘Pl Royale; www.pau-pyrenees.com

A lively university town, with streets of elegant belle époque architecture and shady parks, Pau is the capital of the Béarn region, and the most interesting big town in the central Pyrénées. The weather during autumn and winter is mild, so the town has been a favourite resort of affluent foreigners, especially the English, since the early 19th century.

Pau is primarily famous as the birthplace of Henry IV. His mother, Jeanne d'Albret, travelled for 19 days from Picardy, in the eighth month of her pregnancy, just to have her baby here. She sang during her labour, convinced that if she did so, Henry would grow up as tough as she was. As soon as the infant was born, his lips were smeared with garlic and local Jurançon wine, in keeping with the traditional local custom.

The town's principal sight is the **Château de Pau**, first remodelled in the 14th century for the ruler of Béarn, Gaston

Phoebus. It was entirely restored 400 years later. Marguerite d'Angoulême, sister of the King of France, lived here in the late 16th century, and transformed the town into a centre for the arts and free thinking. The château's 16th-century Gobelin tapestries, woven by Flemish craftsmen in Paris, are stunning.

Outside, the boulevard des Pyrénées has glorious views of some of the highest peaks, often snow-capped year round. The **Musée des Beaux-Arts** has a splendid Degas, the *Cotton Exchange, New Orleans*, and two works by Rubens.

The Maison Carrée in Nay, 18 km (11 miles) towards Lourdes, exhibits the former Musée Béarnais's collection of artifacts, which traces the history, traditions and culture of the Béarn.

Château de Pau

🎨🎨🎨 🏠 Rue du Château
🕐 Hours vary, check website
🚫 1 Jan, 1 May, 25 Dec
🌐 chateau-pau.fr

Musée des Beaux-Arts

🎨 🏠 Rue Mathieu Lalanne
📞 05 59 27 33 02 🕐 Hours vary, call ahead 🚫 Some public hols

THE MIRACLE OF LOURDES

In 1858 young Bernadette Soubirous experienced 18 visions of the Virgin at the Grotte Massabielle near the town. She was guided to a spring with miraculous healing powers, endorsed by the Church in the 1860s. Many people have since claimed cures, and shrines, churches and hospices (and a dynamic tourism industry) have grown up around the spring.

12

Tarbes

🅰 C6-7 🏔 Hautes-Pyrénées
✈🚗🚌 ℹ 3 cours Gambetta; www.tarbes-tourisme.fr

Known as Turba in Roman times, Tarbes is the capital of the Bigorre region and hosts a major agricultural fair each year. Agriculture is such a part of Tarbes that the town is known locally as "market town".

The **Jardin Massey**, in the middle of town, was designed at the turn of the 19th century and is one of the loveliest parks in the southwest of France. It features a variety of many rare plants such as the North American sassafras, as well as a 14th-century cloister with finely carved capitals and a wonderful domed glass greenhouse.

Within the glorious gardens is the **Musée Massey**, which is home to a unique collection of items relating to the history of French and international hussars. It also contains a well-curated collection of fine paintings and sculpture.

Musée Massey

🎨🎨 🏠 Jardin Massey
🕐 Mid-Apr-mid-Oct: 10am-12:30pm & 1:30-7pm Wed-Mon; mid-Oct-mid-Apr: 10am-noon & 2-5pm
🚫 1 Jan, 1 May, 25 Dec
🌐 musee-massey.com

13

Lourdes

🅰 C7 🏔 Hautes-Pyrénées
✈🚗🚌 ℹ Pl Peyramale; www.lourdes-info tourisme.com

Lourdes, one of the great shrines of Europe, owes its fame to visions of the Virgin experienced by 14-year-old Bernadette Soubirous in 1858. Six million people annually visit Grotte Massabielle, where the visions occurred, and rue des Petits-Fossés where Bernadette lived, in search of a miracle cure. The **Musée du Petit Lourdes** gives information about Bernadette.

Visit the **Grottes de Bétharram** for underground rides by boat and train, or the Musée Pyrénéen, to find out about the pioneers who opened up these ranges.

Musée du Petit Lourdes

🎨 🏠 68 avenue Peyramale
🕐 Mid-Apr-mid-Oct: 10am-7pm daily; mid-Oct-mid-Apr: 10am-5pm Mon, 10am-6pm Tue-Sun 🚫 1 Jan, 1 & 11 Nov, 25 Dec 🌐 chateaufort-lourdes.fr

Grottes de Bétharram

🎨 🏠 St-Pé-de-Bigorre
🕐 Feb-late Mar: Mon-Thu at 2:30 & 4pm, Fri 2:30pm; late Mar-Oct: 9am-noon & 1:30-5:30pm daily (to 6pm early Jul-late Aug) 🌐 betharram.com

The picturesque town of
St-Bertrand-de-Comminges,
perched on a hilltop

15

St-Lizier

D7 ◪ Ariège ▦ **i** Pl de
l'Eglise; www.tourisme-
stgirons-stlizier.fr

St-Lizier is located in the
Ariège, a department of the
Occitan region that is famous
for its steep-sided valleys and
wild mountain scenery. The
village dates back to Roman
times, and by the medieval
period it had become an
important religious centre.

The town still boasts two
cathedrals; the finer of them,
with an interesting cloister,
is the 12th- to 14th-century
Cathédrale St-Lizier, which is
in the lower town, but the
Cathédrale de la Sède, in the
upper town, is the one with
the best view. Nearby is the
Bishop's Palace, which houses
a museum of local history.

14

St-Bertrand-
de-Comminges

C7 ◪ Haute-Garonne
▦ Montrejeau, then taxi
▦ **i** Les Olivetains, parvis
de la Cathédrale; www.
tourisme-stgaudens.com

The pretty hilltop village
of St-Bertrand is the most
remarkable artistic and
historic site in the Central
Pyrénées and the venue for
Festival du Comminges, an
acclaimed music festival
held in the summer.

Some of the best sculpture
in the region can be seen on
the portal of the **Cathédrale
Ste-Marie**, and the adjoining
Romanesque and Gothic
cloisters contain sarcophagi,
carved capitals and statues
of the four Evangelists.

St-Bertrand's origins lie on
the plain below, in the city
founded by the great Roman
statesman Pompey in 72 BC.

At that time it consisted of
two thermal baths, a theatre,
a temple, a market and a
Christian basilica. All were
destroyed by Gontran, the
grandson of Clovis in 585,
and six centuries were
to pass before the Bishop
of Comminges, Bertrand
de l'Isle, saw the site as a
potential location for a new
cathedral and monastery.
Thereafter, the town, which
was relatively unimportant
in political terms, became
a major religious centre.

Inside the cathedral,
highlights include the 66
magnificent carved choir
stalls and the 16th-century
organ case. Also worth
seeking out is the tomb of
Bertrand de l'Isle, situated
at the far end of the choir,
with an altar beside it; the
beautiful marble tomb in
the Virgin's chapel just off
the nave is that of Hugues
de Châtillon, a bishop who
provided the funds for the
completion of the cathedral
during the 14th century.

Cathédrale Ste-Marie
♿ **C** 05 61 95 44 44
⏰ Daily ⏰ Sun am

Did You Know?
—
St-Bertrand is part of
Les Plus Beaux Villages
de France (The Most
Beautiful Villages of
France) association.

→
Medieval timbered buildings
lining one side of the large
town square in Mirepoix

Foix

 B7 Ariège 29 rue Théophile Delcassé; www.foix-tourisme.com

With its battlements and towers, Foix stands four-square at the junction of the rivers Arget and Ariège. In the Middle Ages, Foix's dynasty of counts ruled the whole of the Béarn area. Count Gaston Phoebus (1331–91) was the most flamboyant, a poet who wrote a famous treatise on hunting. He was a ruthless politician, who had his brother and his son put to death.

Some medieval pleasures are re-created in the summer fair, the largest in the south-west. At any time, the 15th-century keep of the **Château de Foix** is worth climbing just for the view. The restored 14th-century Église de St-Volusien is delightful in its simplicity and grace.

The **Grotte de Niaux**, 15 km (9 miles) south of Foix, has prehistoric cave paintings.

Château de Foix

Hours vary, check website 1 Jan, 25 Dec sites-touristiques-ariege.fr

Grotte de Niaux

Hours vary, check website sites-touristiques-ariege.fr

Mirepoix

D7 Ariège Pl du Maréchal Leclerc; www.tourisme-mirepoix.com

Mirepoix is a solid country *bastide* town *(p443)* with a huge main square surrounded by beamed 13th- to 15th-century arcades and half-timbered houses.

The cathedral, begun in 1317 with the last additions in 1867, has the widest Gothic nave (22 m/72 ft) in France.

The best times to visit the town are on market days, when stalls in the square sell a mass of local produce.

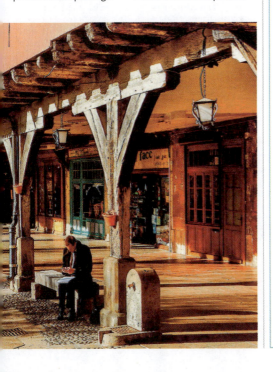

EAT

Le Phoebus
With excellent views of the château's towers, this elegant restaurant offers local dishes with foie gras and duck.

D7 3 cours Irénée Cros, Foix
05 61 65 10 42

La Tantina de Burgos
This local favourite serves traditional Basque dishes. Friendly staff bring plates of freshly caught fish and hearty stews, including *axoa de piment d'espelette*.

B6 2 pl Beau Rivage, Biarritz
03 55 59 23 24 47

Auberge du Cheval Blanc
This atmospheric Basque restaurant dates from 1715, and offers traditional dishes including locally caught hake and the town's speciality, cured ham.

B6 63 rue Bourgneuf, Bayonne www.cheval-blanc-bayonne.com

Chez Simone
A welcoming family restaurant with a lovely terrace overlooking the countryside. Choose from a select menu of tasty local dishes.

C7 Le Village, St-Bertrand-de-Comminges
5 61 94 91 05

18

Arreau

△C7 **⌂**Hautes-Pyrénées
⛍ **ℹ**9 place de la Fontaine;
www.pyrenees2
vallees.com

Arreau is at the confluence of the rivers Aure and Louron. It is a bustling village of historic half-timbered buildings with slate roofs. Despite its small size, Arreau has a range of good shops and restaurants, making it the perfect place to buy supplies for alpine hiking and fishing trips.

The town is centred on its town hall, which features a covered marketplace beneath it. Next door is the 16th-century Maison de Lys, which has a façade ornamented with the fleur-de-lys motifs.

Did You Know?

Basque is a language isolate, meaning it does not have its roots in any other language.

↑ Skiers heading for the slopes of St-Lary Soulan in the Pyrénées

Nearby St-Lary Soulan is a family-friendly ski resort, with an interesting National Park Centre, and it makes a good base for exploring the entire Massif du Néouvielle. Head for the village of Fabian and the smattering of lakes above it, where the GR10 and other well-marked trails crisscross the peaks. Up here there's a very good chance of sighting golden eagles or a lammergeier soaring overhead.

19

St-Jean-de-Luz

△B6 **⌂**Pyrénées-
Atlantiques **✈**Biarritz
⊞⛍ **ℹ**20 blvd Victor
Hugo; www.saint-jean-
de-luz.com

St-Jean is a quiet fishing town out of season and a scorching tourist resort in August, with shopping to rival the chic rue du Faubourg St-Honoré in Paris. During the 11th century whale carcasses were towed here to feed the whole village. The natural harbour protects the shoreline, making it one of the few beaches safe for swimming along this stretch of coast.

An important historical event took place in St-Jean: the wedding of Louis XIV and the Infanta Maria Teresa of Spain in 1660, a union that had the effect of sealing the long-anticipated alliance between France and Spain. In the long run, it ended up with the two countries ultimately embroiled in the War of the Spanish Succession. This wedding took place at the Eglise St-Jean-Baptiste, and it is still the biggest and best of

↑ The town of Montségur and its historic castle, high up in the Pyrenees

all the great Basque churches, a triple-galleried marvel with a glittering 17th-century altarpiece and an atmosphere of gaiety and fervour. The gate through which the Sun King led his new bride was walled up immediately by masons: a plaque now marks the spot. The **Maison Louis XIV**, which is

furnished with contemporary pieces, is where the king stayed in 1660, and is worth taking a look.

The port is busy during the summer, while the restaurants behind the covered markets serve sizzling bowls heaped up with the local specialty of *chipirons* (squid cooked in their own ink). Place Louis XIV is a lovely place to relax and watch the world go by.

On the opposite side of the River Nivelle from St-Jean-de-Luz, Ciboure was the birthplace in 1875 of the composer, pianist and conductor Maurice Ravel. It is characterized by its steep narrow streets of 18th-century merchants' houses and its seafood restaurants.

From here, there's a very pleasant coastal walk of an hour or so, which leads to the neighbouring village of Socoa. The lighthouse on the clifftop there offers a splendid view north along the coast all the way to Biarritz (*p458*).

Maison Louis XIV

 🏠 Place Louis XIV
🕐 Hours vary, check website
Ⓦ maison-louis-xiv.fr

←

Colourful traditional Basque houses lining the pretty port of St-Jean-de-Luz

Montségur

🅰 D7 🏠 Ariège 🕐 Hours vary, check website
Ⓦ montsegur.fr

Montségur is famous as the last stronghold of the Cathars (*p482*). From the car park, a pathway leads up to the small castle, occupied during the 13th century by *faidits* (dispossessed aristocrats) and some Cathars, who lived outside the fortress in houses clinging to the rock. Opposing Catholic authority, the Cathar troops marched on Avignonnet in 1243 and massacred members of the Inquisitional tribunal. In retaliation, an army of 10,000 laid siege to Montségur for ten months. When captured, 205 Cathars refused to convert and were burned alive.

💬 INSIDER TIP
Mount Pog

The 30-minute hike up Mount Pog to Château de Montsegur is challenging, and there aren't any facilities on the way. Ensure you wear appropriate footwear and take plenty of water with you.

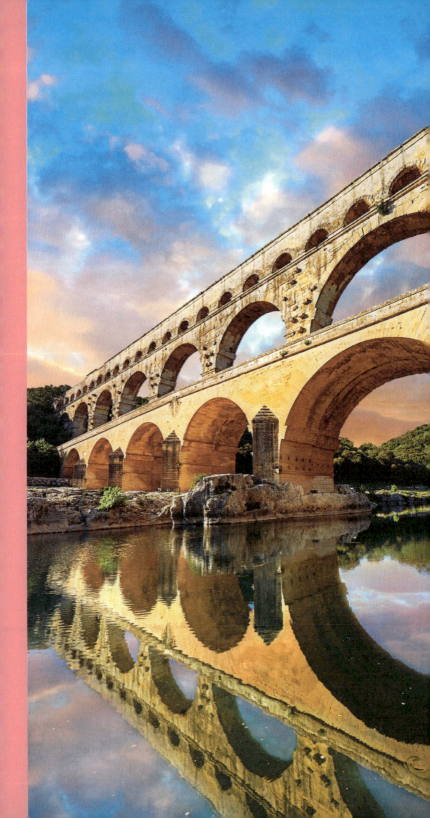

The magnificent Pont du Gard crossing the Gardon River

LANGUEDOC AND ROUSSILLON

More than 2,000 years ago, the southwest of France was an important Roman foothold in Celtic Gaul. As they cut a swathe through the land, taking over vineyards planted centuries earlier by Greek colonizers, the Romans erected monuments, such as the majestic Pont du Gard, as testaments to the might of the Roman empire. By the 12th century, the spirit of chivalry between knights and noblewomen developed at Narbonne, and was soon spread across the country by bards and moony romantics. The Canal du Midi was carved through the heart of the region 500 years later; it was intended to provide a passage for merchants and ships between the Atlantic and the Mediterranean but, following the advent of the more efficient railway system, it was soon co-opted by pleasure-seekers and never quite served its purpose. Disaster stuck this region of winegrowers in 1872 by the spread of phylloxera, an aphid-like infestation that destroyed centuries-old grape vines in their thousands. By World War I, wine production was sufficient that the region was given responsibility of supplying the daily wine ration to French soldiers. The region shot into prominence again in the 1970s with discovery of Tautavel Man, which proved that the region has been inhabited since 450,000 years BC.

LANGUEDOC AND ROUSSILLON

← The beautiful stained-glass Gothic interior of Basilique St-Nazaire, Carcassonne's cathedral

Basilique St-Nazaire contains the Siege Stone, said to depict the 1209 siege by crusaders.

Bishop's Tower

The ramparts were built in the 13th century.

1

CARCASSONNE

📍 D7 🏠 Aude ✈ 4 km (2 miles) W Carcassonne ⚓ Port du Canal du Midi 🚌 30 rue Georges Brassens ℹ 28 rue de Verdun; tourisme-carcassonne.fr

The huge and impressive citadel of Carcassonne is a perfectly restored medieval town, and is protected by UNESCO. It crowns a steep bank above the River Aude, a fairy-tale sight of turrets and ramparts overlooking the Basse Ville ("lower town") below.

The strategic position of Carcassone between the Atlantic and the Mediterranean, and on the corridor between the Iberian peninsula and the rest of Europe, led to its original settlement, consolidated by the Romans in the 2nd century BC. The city became a key element in medieval military conflicts. At its zenith in the 12th century, it was ruled by the Trencavels, an important noble family in the Languedoc, who built the spectacular château and cathedral. Military advances and the Treaty of the Pyrenees in 1659, which relocated the French–Spanish border, hastened its decline and the citadel fell into decay. In the mid-19th century, the attentions of architectural historian Viollet-le-Duc *(p202)* led to the restoration of Carcassonne, work which continued into the 1960s.

Did You Know?

Kate Mosse's best-selling thriller *Labyrinth* is set in Carcassonne.

↑ The enchanting medieval town of Carcassonne, with its defensive walls

Must See

EAT

La Marquiere
A family-run favourite with an Occitan menu.

🏠 13 rue St-Jean
🕐 Wed & Thu
🌐 lamarquiere.com

€€€

L'Escargot
Wine-and-tapas eatery in the heart of the city.

🏠 7 rue Viollet le Duc
🌐 restaurant-lescargot-carcassonne.fr

€€€

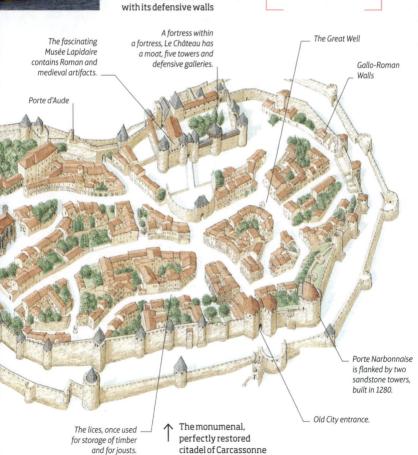

The fascinating Musée Lapidaire contains Roman and medieval artifacts.

A fortress within a fortress, Le Château has a moat, five towers and defensive galleries.

The Great Well

Gallo-Roman Walls

Porte d'Aude

Porte Narbonnaise is flanked by two sandstone towers, built in 1280.

Old City entrance.

The lices, once used for storage of timber and for jousts.

↑ The monumenal, perfectly restored citadel of Carcassonne

Did You Know?

To raise awareness of breast cancer, each year the city's Fontaine des Trois Graces is decorated in pink.

②

MONTPELLIER

 E6 ⬆ Hérault ✈🚗🚌 ℹ 30 place de la Comédie; montpellier-france.com

Montpellier developed in the 10th century as a result of the spice trade with the Middle East. Today, it is one of the liveliest cities in the south, thanks to its large student population. The city's medical school, founded in 1220, remains one of the most respected in France.

①

Place de la Comédie

This egg-shaped square, known affectionately as "l'Oeuf" ("the egg"), is a regular haunt of the city's students. One of the biggest pedestrian spaces in Europe, this expansive square is lined with grand buildings, among them the city's elegant 19th-century opera house fronted by the beautiful Fontaine des Trois Graces. This buzzing square is usually packed with local musicians, street artists and people relaxing on the terraces of its many cafés.

___

②

CORUM

⬆ Esplanade Charles De Gaulle ⏰ For performances 🌐 montpellier-events.com/Le-Corum

An esplanade of plane trees and fountains leads to this extraordinary opera and conference centre. Built from pink granite and metal, this innovative space is typical of the city's brave new architectural projects. Within the centre, the Opéra Berlioz is one of Montpellier's biggest entertainment venues. The auditorium can seat up to 2,000 people, boasts extraordinary moving wooden roof and is renowned for its acoustic qualities. It hosts both classical and contemporary music events, and festivals.

___

 GREAT VIEW
City Sights

Walk through the place du Peyrou gardens to the pavilion that marks the end of the 18th-century Aquéduc St-Clément; from here are stupendous views of the city nestled between mountains and sea – on a clear day you can see the far-off Pyrénées.

The city's expansive Place de la Comédie, with the Opéra Comédie in the distance

 ③

Cathédrale St-Pierre

📍 43 rue de l'Aiguillerie
📞 04 67 45 49 61 🕐 Hours vary, call ahead

This mammoth cathedral was originally the chapel of a Benedictine monastery; it only became a cathedral in 1536 when the archbishopric of Maguelone was transferred to the city of Montpellier. The building is more like a fortress than a cathedral thanks to the two tower-shaped pillars – measuring over 4.5 m (15 ft) in diameter – which support a monumental arched porch. The cathedral suffered extensive damage during the Wars of the Religion.

Nearby is the 18th-century Notre-Dame des Tables, a former Jesuit chapel, home to a splendid painted ceiling and impressive organ. Its crypt contains an exhibition on the city's history.

④

Musée Fabre

📍 39 blvd Bonne Nouvelle
🕐 10am–6pm Tue–Sun
🌐 museefabre.montpellier3m.fr

Housed in a 17th-century building, the Musée Fabre's collection is composed mainly of French artworks. Highlights include Courbet's *Bonjour M. Courbet* and Berthe Morisot's *L'Eté*, as well as a selection of evocative paintings of the region by Raoul Dufy. Look out for the paintings of local Impressionist artist Frédéric Bazille, who died tragically young at the age of 29.

---

⑤

Jardin des Plantes

📍 Blvd Henri IV 🕐 Noon–8pm Tue–Sun (to 6pm Oct–May) 🌐 umontpellier.fr/patrimoine/jardin-des-plantes

Created in 1593 to aid the studies of Montpellier's medical students, these are France's oldest botanical gardens. In fact, the Jardin des Plantes was used as a model for designing other botanical gardens in France, including the world-famous one in Paris.

The gardens cover nearly 5 hectares (12 acres) and, among other things, contain a tranquil lotus pond, an English garden and an aboretum. The gardens are also home to a 400-year-old mock privet tree, where locals make wishes by inserting notes bearing their heart's desires into indents in its trunk.

Must See

TOP 3 **BEACHES NEAR MONTPELLIER**

Carnon-Plage
This long sandy stretch is where the locals go.

Plage du Couchant
La Grande Motte's "sunset beach" lives up to its name at dusk.

Plage du Petit Travers
Powder-fine white sand, rolling dunes and pristine woodland.

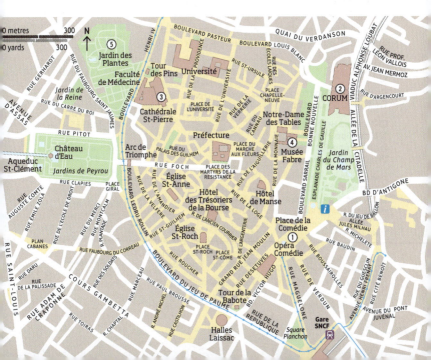

Nîmes's famous Roman amphitheatre, the scene of concerts and bullfights ↑

 3

NÎMES

🅰 E6 🅰 Gard ✈ 9 km (5.5 miles) SE of Nîmes 🚌 Blvd Talabot 🚈 Rue St Félicité 🛈 Blvd des Arenes; nimes-tourisme.com

An important crossroads in the ancient world, Nîmes is known for its Roman antiquities such as the amphitheatre, the best preserved of its kind. The city is also renowned for innovative architecture, from a Philippe Starck-designed bus stop to a glittering arts complex.

① Cathédrale Notre-Dame-et-St-Castor

🏠 Place aux Herbes
🕐 11am–6pm Mon, Wed–Fri, 9am–6pm Sat & Sun
🌐 cathedrale-nimes.fr

Built in 1096, the Romanesque Cathédrale Notre-Dame-et-St-Castor was badly damaged during the Wars of Religion in the 16th-century and was almost completely rebuilt during the 19th. Despite its turbulent history, this imposing cathedral still retains a Romanesque frieze, depicting Old Testament scenes, on the upper part of its façade.

A short stroll from the cathedral is a Roman gate, the Porte Auguste, once part of one of the longest city walls in Gaul. Several of its original arches are still standing.

---

② Les Jardins de la Fontaine (Tour Magne)

🏠 Quai de la Fontaine
📞 04 66 21 82 56 🕐 7:30am–6:30pm daily (to 8pm Mar & Sep; to 10pm Apr–Aug)

When the Romans arrived in Nîmes, they found a town established by the Gauls, centred on the source of a spring. They named the town Nemausus, after their river god. In the 18th century, beautifully elegant formal gardens were constructed; today a network of limpid pools and cool stone terraces remains. High above the garden on Mont Cavalier is the octagonal Tour Magne; once a key part of the Roman walls, this striking tower now offers a great view over the city. For guided tours of the gardens book ahead at the tourist office.

TOP 3 **ROMAN SITES**

Maison Carré
One of the world's best preserved pre-Christian Roman buildings.

Les Arènes
The huge oval arena seated 20,000 in its Roman heyday.

Tour Magne
Enjoy fabulous views from this bastion.

③
Les Arènes (L'Amphithéâtre)

🏛 10 bd des Arènes
🕐 Hours vary, check website 📅 Performance days, Feria de Vendanges, Feria de Pentecôte
🌐 arenes-nimes.com

All roads lead to Les Arènes, Nîmes's spectacular amphitheatre. Built at the end of the 1st century AD, this oval arena with its tiers of stone seats accommodated huge crowds of up to 20,000 spectators. Today it is a perfect venue for concerts and sporting events, not to mention Les Grands Jeux Romains, a fun-filled three-day re-enactment of Roman games at the end of April. Facing Les Arènes, the **Musée de la Romanité** houses ancient Roman statues, ceramics, glass and mosaics.

Musée de la Romanité

🏛 16 blvd des Arènes
🌐 museedelaromanite.fr

④
Maison Carrée

🏛 Pl de la Maison Carrée
🕐 Hours vary, check website 🌐 maisoncarree.eu

This elegant Roman temple built around AD 2 is one of the best preserved in the world. Inside, a multimedia experience, "Nemausus", illustrates the birth of the city.

---

⑤
Musée des Beaux-Arts

🏛 Rue de la Cité Foulc 📞 04 66 76 71 82 🕐 10am–6pm Tue-Sun

This fine arts museum houses a collection of 16th–19th-century French, Italian and Flemish works, notably Jacopo Bassano's *Susanna and the Elders* and the *Mystic Marriage of St Catherine* by Giambono. The Gallo-Roman mosaic *The Marriage of Admetus*, discovered in 1882, is also here.

⑥
Carré d'Art

🏛 Pl de la Maison Carrée
🕐 10am-6pm Tue-Sun
📅 1 Jan, 1 May, 1 Nov, 25 Dec
🌐 carreartmusee.com

Nîmes's glass-and-steel arts complex was designed by Sir Norman Foster. Five of its floors lie underground. The complex houses the Musée d'Art Contemporain, covering the main European art movements from the 1960s on.

 PICTURE PERFECT
Les Arènes

For the best morning light, shoot the arches of Les Arènes from the corner of rue de la République and place des Arènes. For warm afternoon light, take a snap from the foot of Boulevard Victor Hugo.

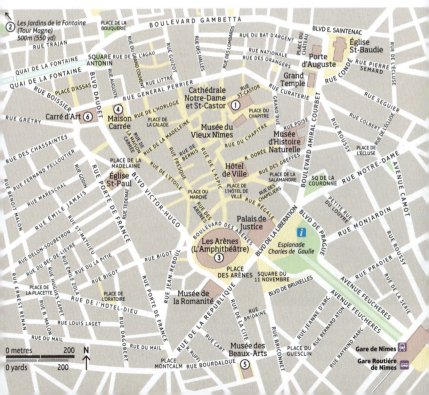

The ancient stone cloisters of the abbey of St-Michel-de-Cuxa, near Prades ↑

EXPERIENCE MORE

4

St-Martin-du-Canigou

🅐D7 🅐Casteil 🕐Only via guided 1-hour tours; hours vary, check website 🗓Jan, Good Friday 🅦stmartin-ducanigou.org

St-Martin-du-Canigou occupies a spectacularly remote site a third of the way up the Pic du Canigou. Perched atop a

↑ St-Martin-du-Canigou abbey, perched high up in the Pyrénées Orientales

jagged spur of rock, this abbey is only accessible by undertaking a 40-minute climb on foot from Casteil. To reach the start of the walk, take the special shuttle that runs daily from July to August, or hire a taxi.

Built at the beginning of the 11th century, the abbey was financed by Guifred, Count of Cerdagne, who entered the monastery during 1035. He was buried there 14 years later in a tomb that he had carved from the rock himself, and which can still be seen. The early Romanesque church is based on a simple basilican plan. Two churches are built quite literally one on top of the other, which makes the lower church the crypt for the building above.

The abbey complex is best viewed from above, by continuing up the path. From this vantage point, its irregular design, clinging to the rock, is dramatically framed by the isolated mountain setting, the whole ensemble a fitting tribute to the ingenuity and extraordinary vitality of its early builders.

5

St-Michel-de-Cuxa

🅐D7 🅐Rte de Tourinya Codalet, Prades, Pyrénées-Orientales 🕐Apr-Sep: 9:30-11:50am & 2-6pm daily; Oct-Mar: 2-5pm daily 🗓1 Jan, Easter Sunday, 25 Dec 🅦abbaye-cuxa.com

The small, pink marble town of Prades, in the Têt Valley, is distinguished by this pre-Romanesque abbey, which lies 3 km (2 miles) further up the valley. It was founded by Benedictine monks in 878 and rapidly became renowned throughout France and Spain. Distinctive, Moorish-influenced keyhole arches pierce the massive walls of the abbey church, which was consecrated in 974. The mottled pink marble cloisters, with their superbly carved capitals, were added in the 12th century. After the Revolution the building was abandoned, and its famous carvings looted.

In 1913, visiting American artist George Grey Bernard began to discover some of the

hairpin bends on the D618 approach road reveals the simple square tower and round apse of this remote Romanesque structure, which is surrounded by a botanical garden of indigenous herbs and woodland plants, clinging to the mountainside.

Inside the cool and austere 12th-century building there is a surprisingly elaborate chapel tribune, its columns and fine arches glowing from the local red-veined marble, artistically carved by the anonymous Master of Cuixà, whose work can be seen in many buildings throughout the region. Note the strange beasts and the verdant flora featured in the capital carvings, especially the rose of Roussillon.

 7

Céret

E7 **Pyrénées-Orientales** **5 rue Saint Ferréol; www. vallespir-tourisme**

Surrounded by a cloud of pink blossom in the early spring, Céret produces the very first cherries of the year. Th annual cherry festival, held over a weekend in May or early June, with music, dancing and cherry-related events.

There's a Spanish feel to the tiled and painted façades and loggias of the buildings. The town was popular with artists including Picasso, Braque and Matisse, and the sophisticated **Musée d'Art Moderne** houses a remarkable collection. It has works by the Catalan artists Tapiès and Capdeville; 50

Did You Know?

Torches lit at a midsummer bonfire atop Pic du Canigou are used to light fires all over Catalonia.

capitals incorporated in local buildings. In 1925 he sold the carvings to the Metropolitan Museum of Art in New York, where they were used to form the basis of the remarkable Met Cloisters museum – an accurate re-creation of a Romanesque abbey in the unlikely setting of Manhattan.

Down in the town of Prades, the Eglise St-Pierre has a southern Gothic wrought iron belfry and a Baroque Catalan interior. The town is also well-known for the legacy of the Spanish cellist Pablo Casals, who spent many years here in exile from Franco's Spain; the town's popular annual Festival Pablo Casals, featuring around 35 concerts of classical and chamber music is held in the abbey in his memory.

 6

Prieuré de Serrabone

D7 **Boule d'Amont** **04 68 84 09 30 (tourist office)** **10am–6pm daily** **1 Jan, 1 May, 1 Nov, 25 Dec**

Perched high up on the northern flanks of Pic du Canigou, the sacred mountain of the Catalans, is the priory of Serrabone. A final lap of

---

TOP 3 PLACES TO TAKE THE WATERS

Amélie-les-Bains
Found near Céret, these mineral springs fill thermal baths famed since Roman times for relieving skin issues.

Vernet-les-Bains
The sub-tropical microclimate here has attracted visitors since the belle époque. Kipling was a big fan *(www. vernet-les-bains.fr/)*.

St-Thomas-les-Bains
Naturally-heated to 58ºC (136ºF), these sulphur springs enable you to dip in the outdoor pools even in winter *(www.bains-saint-thomas.fr)*.

pieces donated by Picasso, including a series of ceramic bowls painted with scenes of bullfighting; and paintings by Matisse, Chagall, Juan Gris and Salvador Dalí.

The town's Catalan heritage is evident in regular bullfights that are held in the arena, and in its Sardana dance festivals, which take place in July.

Around Céret the mineral waters have long been used for their restorative properties. A short drive from Céret is the spa town of Amélie-les-Bains, where fragments of its Roman baths have been discovered.

Beyond, in Arles-sur-Tech, the charming Eglise de Ste-Marie has some fine frescoes from the 12th-century and a sarcophagus, which, according to local lore, produces drops of unaccountably pure water every year.

Musée d'Art Moderne

8 blvd Maréchal Joffre **10am–5pm Tue-Sun (to 7pm daily Jul-Sep)** **Oct-Jun: Tue, 1 Jan, 1 May, 1 Nov & 25 Dec** **musee-ceret.com**

Grapevines growing on a rocky slope on the Côte Vermeille

8

Côte Vermeille

E7 Pyrénées-Orientales Perpignan Collioure, Cerbère Collioure, Banyuls-sur-Mer Collioure; www.collioure.com

Here the Pyrénées meet the Mediterranean, the coast road winding around secluded coves and rocky outcrops. The *vermeille* (vermilion-tinted) rock gives this stretch of coast, the region's loveliest, its name.

The Côte Vermeille extends to the Costa Brava in northern Spain and, with its Catalan character, it is as redolent of Spain as of France. Argelès-Plage, with its three beaches, is Europe's largest camping centre. The small resort of Cerbère, the last French town before the border, flies the Catalan flag to signal its true allegiance. Terraced vineyards cling to rocky hillsides, producing strong, sweet wines such as Banyuls and Muscat. Vines were first cultivated here by Greeks in the 7th century BC, and Banyuls has *caves* dating back to the Middle Ages.

Banyuls is also famous as the birthplace of Aristide

Maillol, the 19th-century sculptor, whose work can be seen all over the region.

Port Vendres, with fortifications that were built by the indefatigable Vauban (the military architect to Louis XIV), is a fishing port, renowned for anchovies and sardines.

9

Collioure

E7 Pyrénées-Orientales Place du 18 juin; www.collioure.com

The colours of Collioure first attracted Matisse in 1905: brightly stuccoed houses sheltered by cypresses and gaily painted fishing boats, all bathed in the famous light, and washed by a gentle sea.

Other artists, including André Derain, worked here under Matisse's influence and were dubbed *fauves* (wild beasts) for their experiments with colour. Galleries and souvenir shops now fill the cobbled streets, but this small fishing port has changed little, and anchovies are still its main business. Three sheltered beaches of pebble and sand, nestle round the harbour, dominated by **Château Royal**, which forms part of the harbour wall. It was first built by the Knights Templar in the 13th century, and Collioure became the main port of entry for Perpignan, remaining under the rule of Spanish Aragon until France took over in 1659. The outer fortifications were reinforced ten years later by Vauban, who demolished much of the original town in the process. The château hosts exhibitions of modern art.

The quayside Église Notre-Dame-des-Anges was built in the 17th century to replace the one destroyed by Vauban. Inside the church are five Baroque altarpieces by Joseph Sunyer and other Catalan masters of the genre. Collioure is very popular in

Picturesque Collioure, with its pebble beach and historic church

STAY

Chateau de Riell
Mini-chateau with fabulous views and spa.

 D7 Molitg-les-Bains chateauderiell.com

€€€

Relais des Trois Mas
The pool and terrace overlook one of area's most beautiful bays.

E7 Rte de Port-Vendres, Collioure relaisdestroismas.com

€€€

Hôtel de l'Amphitheatre
A pretty boutique hotel in medieval mansions.

 E6 4 rue des Arenes, Nîmes hotel delamphitheatre.com

€€€

Hôtel de la Cité
Secluded within a medieval citadel.

 D7 Pl August-Pierre Pont, Carcassonne hoteldelacite.com

€€€

July and August, when its tiny streets and pretty pebbled beach are usually crammed with visitors.

Château Royal
 04 68 82 06 43 Hours vary, call ahead 1 Jan, 1 May, 15 & 16 Aug, 25 Dec

---

Forteresse de Salses

E7 Pyrénées-Orientales Salses-le-Château 66600 Daily 1 Jan, 1 May, 1 & 11 Nov, 25 Dec; www.forteresse-salses.fr

With the appearance of a giant sandcastle set against the ochre-coloured earth of the Corbières vineyards, the imposing Forteresse de Salses stands sentry at the old frontier of Spain and France. It guards over a narrow defile between the Mediterranean lagoons and the mountains, and was built by Francisco Ramiro Lopez for King Ferdinand of Aragon between 1497 and 1506 to defend what was at the time Spain's possession of the Roussillon region. The fort's massive walls and rounded towers are typical of Spanish military architecture, designed to deflect the then new threat posed by gunpowder. Inside, there were underground

Did You Know

A former lighthouse was incorporated as the Eglise Notre-Dame-des-Anges's bell tower at Collioure.

---

stables large enough to house 300 horses, and a subterranean passageway.

Elne

E7 Pyrénées-Orientales 14 bd Voltaire; www.elne-tourisme.com

This ancient town housed Hannibal and his elephants in 218 BC on his epic journey to Rome, and was one of the most important towns in the region until the 16th century. The 11th-century **Cathédrale de Ste-Eulalie et Ste-Julie** has a superb marble cloister and fine sculpted capitals embellished with flowers.

Cathédrale de Ste-Eulalie et Ste-Julie

Plateau des Garaffes 04 68 22 05 07 Oct-Apr: Tue-Sun; May-Sep: daily 1 Jan, 1 May & 25 Dec

12

Minerve

 E6 Hérault **i** 9 rue des Martyrs; www.minervois-tourisme.fr

In the parched, arid hills of the Minervois, surrounded by vines and not much else, Minerve appears defiant on its rocky outcrop at the confluence of the rivers Cesse and Briant. It is defended by the "Candela" (Candle), an octagonal tower which is all that remains of the medieval château. In 1210, the small town resisted the vengeful Simon de Montfort, scourge of the Cathars, in a siege lasting seven weeks. This culminated in 140 Cathars being burned at the stake.

Today visitors enter Minerve by a high bridge spanning the gorge. Turn right and follow the route of the Cathars past the Romanesque arch of the Porte des Templiers to the 12th-century Église St-Étienne. Outside the church is a crudely carved dove, symbol of the Cathars, and within is a 5th-century white marble altar table, one of the oldest artifacts in the region.

A rocky path follows the riverbed below the town, where the water has cut out caves and two bridges from the soft limestone.

 13

Béziers

E6 Hérault **i** Place du Forum; www.beziers-mediteranee.com

Famous for its bullfights and rugby, and the wine of the surrounding region, Béziers has several other points of interest. The town seems turned in on itself, its roads leading up to the massive 14th-century Cathédrale St-Nazaire, with its fine sculpture, stained glass and frescoes. In 1209, several thousand citizens were massacred in the crusade against the Cathars. The papal legate's troops were ordered not to discriminate between Catholics and Cathars, but to "Kill them all. God will recognize his own!" The **Musée du Biterrois** holds exhibitions (in French only) on local history, wine and the Canal du Midi, engineered in the late 17th century by Paul Riquet, Béziers's most famous son. His statue is on Allées Paul Riquet, which is lined by rows of plane trees and several large canopied restaurants, adding a civilized focus to this otherwise business-like town.

Overlooking the Béziers plain and the mountains that lie to the north is Oppidum d'Ensérune, a superb Roman site. The **Musée de l'Oppidum d'Ensérune** has a good archaeological collection, including Celtic, Greek and Roman vases, jewellery and weapons. The **Château de Raissac** (between Béziers and Lignan) houses an unusual 19th-century faïence museum in its stables.

Musée du Biterrois

Ramp du 96ème, Caserne St-Jacques 04 67 36 81 61 10am-6pm Tue-Sun (to 5pm Tue-Fri Oct-May) 1 Jan, Easter, 1 May, 25 Dec

Musée de l'Oppidum d'Ensérune

Nissan-lez-Ensérune Sep-Apr: 9:30am-5:30pm daily; May-Aug: 9:30am-6:30pm Public hols enserune.fr

Château de Raissac

Rte de Lignan sur Orr By appt raissac.com

14

Narbonne

E7 Aude **i** 31 rue Jean Jaurès; www.narbonne-tourisme.com

Narbonne is a cheerful town amid a booming wine region. The town is bisected by the tree-lined Canal de la Robine; to the north is the restored medieval quarter with good shops and restaurants. One of the town's most intriguing tourist attractions, the Roman **Horreum** is here, an underground warehouse dating back to the 1st century BC, when Narbonne was a major port and capital of the largest Roman province in Gaul.

The town prospered in the Middle Ages until the 15th century, when the harbour silted up and the course of the River Aude altered, taking Narbonne's fortunes with it. A grandiose cathedral was under construction, but the full design was abandoned, and just the chancel, begun in 1272, became the Cathédrale

---

CANAL DU MIDI

The first of the *grands projets* to have shaped modern France was the brainchild of Bézier-based salt-tax baron Paul Riquet. His 240-km (149-mile) waterway, completed in 1681 and linking the Atlantic to the Mediterranean, was the greatest engineering feat of its time. Revolutionizing local economies, it was the lifeblood of trade in the region. It still plays a key role, carrying tourists.

People strolling and relaxing in an attractive square in the heart of pretty Narbonne

St-Just et St-Pasteur. It is still enormous, with 14th-century sculptures, an 18th-century carved organ and fine stained-glass. Aubusson and Gobelin tapestries adorn the walls, and it is possible to visit a treasury of manuscripts and jewelled reliquaries.

Between the cathedral and the Palais des Archevêques (Archbishops' Palace) lies a cloister with four galleries of 14th-century vaulting.

This huge palace and cathedral complex dominates the centre of Narbonne. Between the Palais des Archevêques's massive 14th-century towers is the town hall, with a 19th-century Neo-Gothic façade by Viollet-le-Duc (p202), the architect who so determinedly restored medieval France. The palace is divided into the Palais Vieux (Old Palace) and the Palais Neuf (New Palace). Narbonne's most important

> **The town is bisected by the tree-lined Canal de la Robine; to the north is the restored medieval quarter with good shops and restaurants.**

museums are in the Palais Neuf, on the left through the low medieval arches of the passage de l'Ancre. The **Musée d'Archéologie** has remarkable Roman frescoes, milestones and parts of the original town walls plus an assemblage of domestic objects, coins, tools and glassware. Those with a head for heights can climb to the top of the 42-m (138-ft) Donjon Gilles Aycelin.

In the archbishops' former apartments is the **Musée d'Art et d'Histoire**, which is as interesting for its luxurious furnishings and richly decorated ceilings as for its fine art collection. This includes a number of paintings by the likes of Canaletto, Brueghel, Boucher and Veronese as well as a large selection of local earthenware. There is also an outstanding collection of Orientalist paintings.

South of the Canal de la Robine are a number of fine mansions, including the Renaissance Maison des Trois Nourrices on the corner of rue des Trois-Nourrices and rue

Edgard Quinet. Nearby is the **Musée Lapidaire**, housing architectural fragments from Gallo-Roman Narbonne. The collection will transfer to the new Narbo Via museum when it opens in 2020.

Southwest (13 km/8 miles) the Abbaye de Fontfroide is in a serene position, surrounded by cypress trees.

Horreum
ue Rouget-de-l'Isle
04 68 32 45 30 Oct-May: 10am-5pm Wed-Mon; Jun-Sep: 10am-6pm daily 1 Jan, 1 May, 1 & 11 Nov, 25 Dec

Musée d'Archéologie/ Musée d'Art et d'Histoire
Palais des Archevêques 04 68 90 30 65 Hours vary, call ahead 1 Jan, 1 May, 1 & 11 Nov, 25 Dec

Musée Lapidaire
Église Notre-Dame de Lamourguier 04 68 90 30 65 Hours vary, call ahead 1 Jan, 1 May, 1 & 11 Nov, 25 Dec

Did You Know?

Narbonne Plage, found close to the city, has won the European Blue Flag every year since 1988.

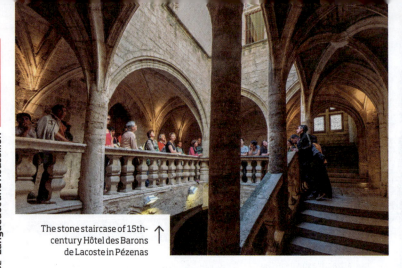

The stone staircase of 15th-century Hôtel des Barons de Lacoste in Pézenas ↑

 Pézenas

 E6 Hérault 🚍 🛈 Pl des Etats de Languedoc; www.pezenas-tourisme.fr

Pézenas is a charming little town, easily appreciated in a gentle stroll of its main sights, and abounding in evidence of its past brilliance as the seat of local government in the 16th–17th centuries. Then the town also played host to many troupes of musicians and actors, including Molière.

The narrow streets in the old town are beautifully preserved, with glimpses of fine houses through courtyard doorways: seek out the Hôtel des Barons de Lacoste, at 8 rue François-Oustrin, with its fine stone staircase, and the Maison des Pauvres at 12 rue Alfred Sabatier, with three galleries and staircase.

💬 INSIDER TIP
The Passa Pais

Following an old railway, this marked green trail winds through the southern fringes of Parc Naturel Régional du Haut-Languedoc, past some of the region's prettiest villages and riverside scenery.

Look for the medieval shop window on rue Triperie-Vieille and, within the 14th-century Porte Faugères, the Jewish quarter (rue Juiverie and rue des Litanies), with a chilling feeling of enclosure. Shops selling antiques, second-hand goods and books abound. All around the town, vines stretch as far as the eye can see.

⑯ **Sète**

E6 Hérault 🚉🚍🚌 🛈 60 grande rue Mario Roustan; www.tourisme-sete.com

Sète is a major fishing and industrial port, with a gutsier, more raffish air than much of the more leisure-oriented Mediterranean, with shops selling ships' lamps and propellers, and quayside restaurants full of hungry sailors eating platters of mussels and oysters straight off the boat. Most of Sète's restaurants can be found in a stroll along the Grand Canal, with its Italianate houses painted in pastel colours and with wrought-iron balconies overlooking Sète's canals and bridges. Boisterous water jousting tournaments on Canal Royal, dating back to 1666, form part of the patron saint's festival in August.

To the west of the town, next to the open-air Théâtre de la Mer, is the **Musée de la Mer**, exploring Sète's maritime and water jousting history from the 18th century to today.

Nearby is the Cimetière Marin, where Sète's famous poet Paul Valéry (1871–1945), is buried. There is a small art museum and breathtaking views of the coast and the mountains from the lookout on Mont St-Clair.

Musée de la Mer

 🏛 1 rue Jean Vilar 📞 04 99 04 71 55 🕐 Hours vary, call ahead 🚫 1 Jan, 1 May, 25 Dec

⑰ **St-Guilhem-le-Désert**

E6 Hérault 🚍 🛈 2 pl de la Liberté; www.saintguilhem-valleeherault.fr

Tucked away in the Celette mountains, St-Guilhem-le-Désert is no longer as remote as when Guillaume of Aquitaine retired here as a hermit in the 9th century. After a lifetime as a soldier, he received a fragment of the True Cross from Emperor Charlemagne and established a monastery here, above the River Hérault.

Vestiges of the first 10th-century church have been discovered, but it is mostly

EAT

L'Entre-Pots

An atmospheric old *vigneronne* serving delicious seasonal, regional food.

 E6 🏠 8 ave Louis-Montagne, Pezenas 🕐 Jul & Aug 🌐 restaurantentrepots.com

€€€

Le Divil

With Dalí-inspired décor and a menu to delight carnivores, Le Divil has few rivals in Perpignan.

 D7-E7 🏠 9 rue Fabriques d'en Nabot, Perpignan 🕐 Sun & Mon 🌐 restaurant-le-divil-66.com

€€€

Atelier & Co

Treat your tastebuds with Bouzigues oysters and mussels fresh from the Étang de Thau.

 E6 🏠 98 zone Conchylicole Ouest, Loupian 🕐 Oct-Mar

€€€

---

a superb example of 11th- to 12th-century Romanesque architecture. Its lovely apsidal chapels dominate the heights of the village, behind which a doorway leads to a square.

In the church is a sombre barrel-vaulted central aisle leading to the central apse. Two galleries of the cloisters remain: the rest are in New York, along with carvings from St-Michel-de-Cuxa.

→

Sunset over the tranquil Parc Naturel Régional du Haut-Languedoc

18 Parc Naturel Régional du Haut Languedoc

🅰 E6 🏠 Hérault, Tarn 🚆 Béziers 🚌 Béziers, Bédarieux 🚏 St-Pons-de-Thomières 🛈 St-Pons-de-Thomières; www.parc-haut-languedoc.fr

From the Montagne Noire, a mountainous region between Béziers and Castres, up into the Cévennes is a landscape of remote sheep farms, eroded rock formations and plunging river gorges. Much of it is now the Parc Naturel Régional du Haut Languedoc, one of the largest French regional parks.

You can enter the park at St-Pons-de-Thomières, with access to a wildlife research centre with mouflons (wild mountain sheep), eagles and wild boar, once a common sight around the region. Other access points are St-Chinian, Revel, Castres and Lodève.

Taking the D908 from St-Pons, you pass the village of Olargues with its 12th-century bridge over the River Jaur. To the east, Lamalou-les-Bains is a small spa town that has a soporifically slow pace.

To the northeast of the park are some spectacular natural phenomena. At the Cirque de Navacelles, the River Vis encircles an entire island and the peaceful village of Navacelles. The **Grotte des Demoiselles** is one of the best in the area with an abundance of caves. A funicular train takes visitors to the top of the mountain.

The **Grotte de Clamouse** is also extraordinary, with its underground rivers and pools reflecting flickering light onto the cavern roofs. The Spéléopark offers caving.

Grotte des Demoiselles

♿🅿️📷🕐 🏠 St-Bauzille-de-Putois, Ganges 🕐 Hours vary, check website 🔒 Jan, 25 Dec 🌐 demoiselles.com

Grotte de Clamouse

♿🅿️📷🕐 🏠 Route de St-Guilhem-le-Désert, St-Jean-de-Fos 🕐 By appt 🌐 clamouse.com

Pyramid-style buildings beside the popular marina at La Grande Motte

La Grande-Motte

🅰 E6 🏠 Hérault 🚌
ℹ 55 rue du Port; www.
lagrandemotte.com

The bizarre white ziggurats of this marina, one of several on the lagoons south of Montpellier, exemplify the development of the southwest coast. Every kind of sport is available, from tennis and golf to water sports. To the east lie Le Grau-du-Roi, once a tiny fishing village, and Port-Camargue, with its expansive marina.

Aigues-Mortes

🅰 E6 🏠 Gard 🚌🚌 ℹ Pl St
Louis; www.ot-aigues
mortes.fr

The best approach to this perfectly preserved walled town is across the salt marshes of the Camargue

GREAT VIEW
Pont du Gard

For the best view in Aigues-Mortes, climb up the spectacular Tour de Constance, an impressive tower erected in 1242 by Louis IX. From atop its walls you can enjoy splendid views over the Camargue.

Gardoise. Now marooned 5 km (3 miles) from the sea, the imposing defences of this once-important port have become a popular sight with visitors. Aigues-Mortes ("Place of Dead Waters") was established by Louis XI in the 13th century to consolidate his power on the Mediterranean, and built according to a strict grid pattern.

To the northeast St-Gilles-du-Gard, also once an important medieval port, is worth a detour to see the superbly sculpted 12th-century façade of its abbey church. Originally established by the monks of Cluny abbey as a shrine to St Gilles, it was a resting place on the route to Santiago de Compostela (p406).

Perpignan

🅰 D7–E7 🏠 Pyrénées-
Orientales 🚂🚌🚌 ℹ Place
de la Loge; www.perpignan
tourisme.com

Catalan Perpignan has a distinctly southern feel, with palm trees lining place Arago, house and shop façades painted vibrant turquoise and pink, and the streets of the Arab quarter selling aromatic spices, couscous and paella. Today, it is the vibrant capital of Pyrénées-Orientales, with an important position on the developing Mediterranean

sunbelt, but its zenith was in the 13th and 14th centuries under the kings of Majorca and Aragón, who controlled great swathes of what is now northern Spain and southern France. Their vast Palais des Rois de Majorque still spans much of the southern part of the city. One of the finest buildings, the Loge de Mer at the head of the square, was built in 1397 to house the Maritime Exchange; the eastern section keeps to the original Gothic design. The rest was rebuilt in Renaissance style in 1540. It remains the hub of Perpignan life, amid elegant cafés with a constant buzz of activity.

Next door is the Hôtel de Ville; sections of its arcaded courtyard date back to 1315, and at its centre is Aristide Maillol's allegorical sculpture, *The Mediterranean* (1950).

To the east, the labyrinthine cathedral quarter of St-Jean contains fine 14th- and 15th-century buildings. Topped by a fine wrought-iron belfry, the **Cathédrale St-Jean** was built from 1324 to 1509, mostly from river pebbles layered with red brick. In the gloomy

Did You Know?

Salvador Dalí insisted, with cosmic certainty, that Perpignan was the centre of the universe.

interior the nave is flanked by gilded altarpieces, painted wooden statues and a large font. A Chapel of the Devout Christ in the adjacent cemetery contains a poignantly realistic medieval wooden Crucifixion. Some areas may be restricted due to ongoing restorations.

Access to the vast 13th-century fortified **Palais des Rois de Majorque** is as circuitous today as it was intended to be for invaders, with flights of steps zigzagging within the sheer red-brick ramparts. Eventually, the elegant gardens and castle within are entered by way of the Tour de l'Hommage, with a panoramic view of city, mountains and sea.

The palace is built around a central arcaded courtyard, flanked on one side by the Salle de Majorque, a great hall with a triple fireplace and giant Gothic

arched windows. Two royal chapels, one above the other, show southern Gothic style at its best. The fine rose marble doorway of the upper King's Chapel is typical of the Roussillon Romanesque style, although the capitals are Gothic. Today the courtyard is sometimes used for concerts.

The brick tower and pink belfry of the Castillet, built as the town gate in 1368, was at one time a prison and is all that remains of the town walls. It now houses **Casa Pairal**, a traditionally furnished and equipped Catalan kitchen.

Two magnificent mansions dating from the 17th and 18th centuries house the **Musée d'Art Hyacinthe Rigaud**, with an eclectic collection dominated by the work of Hyacinthe Rigaud (1659–1743), born in Perpignan and court painter to Louis XIV and Louis XV. There's also some medieval art, its *chef d'oeuvre* the 15th-century *Retable de la Trinité* by the Master of the Loge de Mer.

One of the rooms is dedicated to Aristide Maillol and a number of his contem-

poraries, including Picasso, who had several prolonged stays here; his studio on the second floor is open to the public.

Cathédrale St-Jean

Pl de Gambetta 8am–6pm Mon–Sat (to 7pm in summer), 2–6pm Sun cathedrale perpignan.fr

Palais des Rois de Majorque

2 rue des Archers 04 68 34 96 26 Oct–May: 9am–5pm; Jun–Sep: 10am–6pm 1 Jan, 1 May, 1 Nov & 25 Dec

Casa Pairal

Place de Verdun, Le Castillet 04 68 35 42 05 Oct–May: 11am–5:30pm Tue–Sun; Jun–Sep: 10:30am–6:30pm daily Public hols

Musée d'Art Hyacinthe Rigaud

21 rue Mailly Oct–May: 11am–5:30pm Tue–Sun; Jun & Sep: 10:30am–7pm daily; Jul & Aug: 10:30am–9pm daily Public hols musee-rigaud.fr

← Courtyard and churches of the Palais des Rois Majorque in Perpignan

Did You Know?

The Golfe du Lion got its name from the roaring gales that often batter this area.

 22

Golfe du Lion

🗺️ E6 🏛️ Aude, Hérault
✈️🚗🚌 Montpellier
🚆 Sète ℹ️ 55 rue du Port,
La Grande-Motte; www.
lagrandemotte.com

Part of a lagoon complex, Languedoc and Roussillon's shoreline forms an almost unbroken sweep of sandy beach. Only at its southern limits does it break into the rocky inlets that punctuate the Côte Vermeille. Several resorts have been created since the 1960s, with a strong emphasis on environmentally friendly, low-rise family accommodation, some of them in local styles.

La Grande-Motte marina has distinctive ziggurat-style buildings, Cap d'Agde has Europe's largest naturist quarter and, inland, Agde is built of black basalt and has a fortified cathedral. Port Leucate and Port Bacarès are ideal for water sports. An older town is Sète (p484).

The *étangs*, large shallow lagoons near to the Camargue region, support thousands of wading birds.

23

Cerdagne

🗺️ D7 🏛️ Pyrénées-Orientales ✈️ Perpignan
🚗🚌 Mont Louis, Bourg
Madame, Latour de Carol
Enveitg ℹ️ 1 pl de Roser,
Saillagouse; Mont Louis;
www.pyrenees-cerdagne.
com or www.mont-louis.net

The remote Cerdagne, which was an independent state during the Middle Ages, is today divided between Spain and France. Its high plateaus provide superb winter skiing and summertime walking among clear mountain lakes and pine and chestnut forests. The Little Yellow Train (www.ter.sncf.com), one of the most scenic routes in France, which has been running since 1909 and includes the country's highest railway station, is an excellent way to sample it in a day. Stops include Mont Louis, a town fortified by Vauban, Louis XIV's military architect, and which still accommodates French troops; the huge ski resort of Font-Romeu; and Latour-de-Carol and the tiny village of Yravals below it.

Nearby Odeillo is the site of a solar furnace, the world's largest at 45 m (150 ft) tall and 50 m (165 ft) wide – its giant curved mirrors create a remarkable sight in the valley. Built in the 1960s, it is used for scientific research and to test various materials at extremely high temperatures. There's an information centre onsite for visitors.

Pont du Gard

F6 **400 route du Pont du Gard-La Bégud, Gard** **From Nîmes** **Hours vary, check website** **pontdugard.fr**

No amount of fame can diminish the first sight of the 2,000-year-old Pont du Gard, a UNESCO World Heritage Site. The Romans considered it the best testimony to the greatness of their empire, and, rising 49 m (160 ft), it was the highest bridge they ever built.

It is made from blocks of stone, which were hauled into place by enslaved peoples – an estimated 1,000 men over a five-year period – using an ingenious system of pulleys. The huge build-up of calcium in the water channels suggests the aqueduct was in continuous use for some 400 to 500 years, carrying water to Nîmes along a 50-km (31-mile) route from the springs at Uzès, a charming town boasting an arcaded marketplace.

Corbières

D7–E7 **Aude** **Perpignan** **Narbonne, Carcassonne, Lézignan-Corbières** **Narbonne, Carcassonne, Lézignan-Corbières** **2 rue Guynemer; www.tourisme-corbieres-minervois.com**

Still one of the wildest parts of France, the Corbières is best known for its wine and the great craggy hulks of the Cathar castles, which perch precariously on hilltops. Much of the land is untamed *garrigue* (scrubland), fragrant with honeysuckle and broom, while the south-facing slopes are planted with vines.

To the south are the spectacular medieval castles of Peyrepertuse and Quéribus, the latter being one of the last strongholds of the Cathars. The guided visits around the remarkable Cathar château at Villerouge-Termenes reveal some details surrounding its turbulent past.

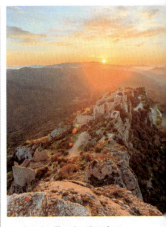

↑ Sunrise illuminating the castle of Peyrepertuse, near Corbières

To the west is the barren Razès area in the upper Aude Valley. Its best-kept secret is the village of Alet-les-Bains, with beautifully preserved half-timbered houses and the remains of a Benedictine abbey, battle-scarred from the Wars of Religion.

The spectacular Roman-built Pont du Gard aqueduct across the beautiful River Gardon ↓

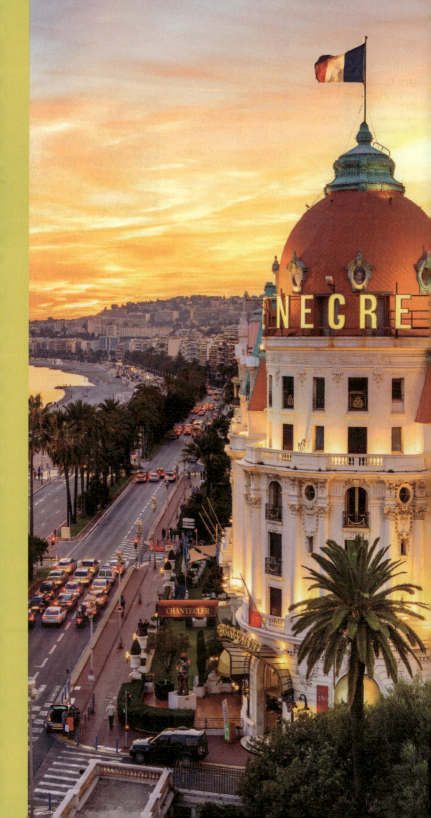

PROVENCE AND THE CÔTE D'AZUR

A region of monuments and art, the sun-kissed Côte d'Azur was decorated by prehistoric peoples, who painted caves with intricate scenes from their lives some 22,000 years ago. In the Vallée des Merveilles, 4,000-year-old petroglyphs were left at at Mont Bégo, while in Orange and Arles colourful mosaics and frescoes adorned the public baths, amphitheatres and coliseums that flourished across the landscape of Roman Provincia. The riches of the area drew frequent attacks by Saracen pirates, who plagued the coast in the 6th century. As a result, fortified villages such as Eze were built to withstand raiding parties. From the 17th century, experimental painters began to trickle into the region, drawn by the magnificent light and intense colour along the coast, and by the 1880s, Nice especially had become a hotbed of Impressionist painters. In the 19th century, rich Europeans sought winter warmth on the Riviera; by the 1920s, high society was in residence all year round, and their elegant villas, casinos and hotels remain.

PROVENCE AND
THE CÔTE D'AZUR

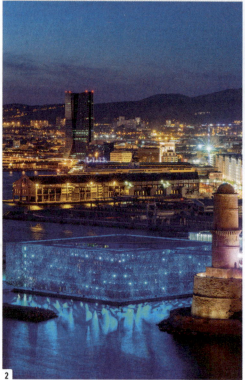

① The bustling market square of Aix-en-Provence.

② The Museé des Civilisations de l'Europe et de la Méditerrannée, Marseille.

③ *Pastis*, beer and canapés.

④ Les Alyscamps necropolis.

5 DAYS
in Western Provence

Day 1

Morning Start your trip in Orange *(p512)* with coffee and a croissant in a café on place George Clemenceau. Once refreshed, stroll up rue Victor Hugo for your first taste of Orange's Roman heritage at the massive Arc de Triomphe.

Afternoon A la Maison *(4 Place des Cordeliers)* is a pleasant spot for lunch, before exploring the Théatre Antique and tracing the city's history at the Musée d'Art et d'Histoire d'Orange.

Evening For a sunset panorama, climb through the leafy park to the top of the Colline St-Eutrope. Finish your evening at Le Parvis *(55 Cours Pourtoules)*; the six-plate degustation menu is a revelation and surprisingly affordable.

Day 2

Morning By car, Chateauneuf-du-Pape *(p513)* is just 15 minutes from Orange, a drive that takes you through some of France's most revered vineyards.

Afternoon The ruins of a papal château, built in the 14th century, dominate the village. After a ramble, visit the Caves du Verger des Papes *(2 Rue Montée du Château)* for a tasting session in cellars stocked with hundreds of the region's vintages.

Evening Dine on the terrace of Le Verger des Papes in the grounds of the château, with a fabulous view over the Rhône and a menu of dishes like Bigorre *porc noir*.

Day 3

Morning After breakfast, head back to Orange, where you can catch a short train to Arles *(p498)*. First stop is Les Arenes, the 20,000-seat Roman theatre still used for concerts and other events. Next, tour the Cryptoportiques, a Roman-era labyrinth carved 20 m (60 ft) beneath the city.

Afternoon Wander the vast necropolis at Les Alyscamps *(p499)*. Romans believed it was haunted and shunned it at night, so it became a secret nocturnal meeting place for persecuted early Christians.

Evening Visit the place du Forum to dine at the Restaurant-Café Van Gogh, still decorated as it was when it inspired the artist to paint *Café Terrace at Night* in 1888.

Day 4

Morning Start early to make your way to Marseille *(p528)*. After settling into your hotel, stroll along the Canebiere to find a bistro where you can sip a glass of *pastis*, the city's signature aperitif.

Afternoon Spend a couple of hours at the Musée des Civilisations de l'Europe et de la Méditerrannée, then hop on a boat from the Vieux Port to Chateau d'If *(p529)*, an island prison of literary legend.

Evening Sample *bouillabaisse*, Marseille's ultimate traditional dish, at Michelin-starred L'Epuisette *(Vallon des Auffes)*.

Day 5

Morning After a leisurely breakfast, head north to Aix-en-Provence *(p516)*. Upon arrival, stretch your legs with a stroll through the historic centre to visit L'Atelier de Cézanne. The artist's studio is preserved as it was when he died in 1906. The Terrain des Peintres is nearby, the vantage point from which Cézanne often painted the summit of Montagne Ste-Victoire.

Afternoon For art of a different kind, visit Fondation Vasarely, where works by the king of Op Art, Victor Vasarely (1908–97), are on show in a futuristic building.

Evening Dine along the elegant Cours Mirabeau at brasserie Les Deux Garcons *(53 Cours Mirabeau)*, a one-time favourite of Cézanne, Picasso and other artists.

1

2

3

7 DAYS
on the Côte d'Azur

Day 1

Start your trip in laid-back coastal Menton (*p528*) with a visit to the town hall – the Salle des Mariages (registry hall) was decorated with Provencal motifs by Jean Cocteau in 1957. Continue the art-themed exploration at the Musée Jean Cocteau: Collection Severin Wunderman, which has a stunning collection of the artist's works. Afterwards, visit the Musée des Beaux-Arts to view pieces by British artist Graham Sutherland (1903–80), an honorary citizen of Menton. Dine at Michelin-starred Le Mirazur (*30 avenue Aristide Briand*), where dishes are delectable works of art.

Day 2

Cocteau also left his imprint on Villefranche-sur-Mer (*p526*); after breakfast, catch a train to this unspoiled harbour town, where you can see more of his work at the Chapelle St-Pierre. Find a bistro on the lively waterfront for lunch, before taking another train to nearby Nice (*p506*). Stroll through Nice's Old Town to the excellent Musée d'Art Moderne et d'Art Contemporain, where stars of the

show include Yves Klein and other artists of the École de Nice. Make your way to the summit of the Colline du Chateau for stunning sunset views over the glittering Baie des Anges.

Day 3

Head for the Cimiez district to gaze at pieces by two great artists who lived and worked in Nice at the Musée Matisse (*p507*) and the Musée National Marc Chagall (*p506*). Next it's on to the Musée Internationale d'Art Naif Anatole Jakofsky to admire works by self-taught artists like Fréderic Lanovsky and Henri ("Douanier") Rousseau. Enjoy an aperitif and dinner at the famous Cours Saleya food market, before treating yourself to a cocktail in the bar of the iconic Hotel Negresco (*p507*).

Day 4

Grab a quick breakfast, then board a local train to Cagnes-sur-Mer (*p525*) where the Chateau-Musée Grimaldi is first on your agenda. This eclectic complex of museums includes 40 paintings of 1930s chanteuse

5

1 Colourful houses in Menton. ↑
2 Villefranche-sur-Mer.
3 Musée Jean Cocteau, Menton.
4 A narrow steet in
St-Paul-de-Vence.
5 La Siesta nightclub, Antibes.

Suzy Solidor. Before leaving Cagnes, visit the former home of Pierre-Auguste Renoir (1841–1919), another great artist who was inspired by Provence. Catch local bus 400 from Cagnes-sur-Mer train station to St-Paul de Vence (*p504*), a gorgeous medieval *village perché*. Dine at the legendary Colombe d'Or (*place du Général de Gaulle*), graced by an eye-catching private art collection, including paintings by Picasso, Braque and Miro.

Day 5

Wake early to admire another of the village's gems: the collection of modern art at the Fondation Maeght (*p502*). Sculptures by Miro, Calder and Giacometti stand in the gardens, and indoor galleries display works by Léger, Chagall and other stars of 20th-century art. Next, head to Vence (*p526*) to be wowed by the luminous colours of Henri Matisse's Chapelle du Rosaire, regarded by the artist as his greatest work. Take a wander around the old town centre before dining at La Maison du Frene (*1 place du Frêne*), a restaurant with a fine modern collection.

Day 6

Catch bus 400 to Antibes (*p522*), where you can take a break on Cours Masséna and watch the morning market bustle from your café table. Afterwards, take a 90-minute guided tour that includes the Musée Picasso in the Chateau Grimaldi, where Pablo Picasso had his studio in 1946. Spend an evening bar-hopping around the vibrant streets off Boulevard Aguillon, or head for the glitzy La Siesta nightclub at the Casino JOA.

Day 7

Walk to the Musée de l'Annonciade to admire works by Signac, Camoin and other 20th-century greats, before ascending to the rampart of the Citadelle de Saint-Tropez to admire the view. Take some time to relax and mull over the week's experiences at one of the beach clubs or bar-restaurants on the golden strand at Baie de Pampelonne, each of which has an array of loungers and umbrellas. Glam up for a final night at one of St-Tropez's legendary nightspots, such as Les Caves du Roy or the Bar du Port.

↑ The exterior of the impressive Roman amphitheatre, les Arènes

---

①

ARLES

⚐ F6 **🏠 Bouches-du-Rhône** **✈ 25 km (16 miles) NW of Arles** **🚍 Av Paulin Talabot** **ℹ Blvd des Lices; www.arles tourisme.com**

Like a miniature version of Rome, charming Arles spreads out around a massive arena, and remnants of its Roman heyday are scattered all around its narrow streets. The town is even better known for its connection with Vincent Van Gogh, who, inspired by the bright light and rich colours, enjoyed the most creative period of his short life here. Arles is also the gateway to the unique wetlands of the Camargue (*p500*).

---

①

Les Arènes

🏠 Rond-point des Arènes **🕐 9am–6pm daily** **🎫 Events** **🌐 arenes-arles.com**

The largest Roman building in Gaul is as impressive now as when it was built around 90 AD. Able to seat 20,000, today it is used for concerts and other spectacles. The top tier of seating provides an excellent panoramic view of Arles. To the southwest is the elegant Théâtre Antique, another beautifully preserved Roman-era stadium with 2,000 tiered seats.

---

②

Église St-Trophime

🏠 Place de la République **🕐 10am–6pm Wed–Mon** **🌐 patrimoine.ville-arles.fr**

This is one of Provence's great Romanesque churches. The ornately sculpted portal and beautiful cloisters (for which there is an admission fee) are decorated with biblical scenes. St Trophime, thought to be the first bishop of Arles in the early 3rd century, appears with St Peter and St John on the carved northeast pillar. The nave of the church is hung with Aubusson tapestries.

---

③

Cryptoportiques

🏠 Hôtel de Ville, place de la République **🕐 10am–6pm Wed–Mon** **🔒 Tue and public holidays** **🌐 patrimoine.ville-arles.fr**

Beneath the site of the Roman Forum and accessed via the Hôtel de Ville, these huge, horseshoe-shaped underground galleries – up to 10 m (33 ft) wide and ventilated by air shafts – were probably used as granaries or possibly as a barracks for slaves. Constructed in the 1st century AD, then buried beneath later church buildings, these impressive structures were left forgotten and inaccessible until archaeologists began the task of re-opening them in 1935.

> PICTURE PERFECT
> **Following Van Gogh**
>
> Visit the atmospheric place du Forum in the evening for a snap of the Restaurant-Café Van Gogh, still looking just as it did when it inspired his *Café Terrace at Night* (1888).

④
Les Alyscamps

🅰 Ave des Alyscamps
🕐 9am–6pm daily

Christ is claimed to have appeared to early Christians who met in secret at this vast necropolis, which was one of the largest and most famous cemeteries in the western world. An avenue of marble sarcophagi marks the site where many of the city's dignitaries were buried. Christians were often buried by the tomb of Genesius, a beheaded Christian martyr.

⑤ 🏛 Ⓜ 🍴 🖥 🏵
Luma Foundation

🅰 45 chemin des Minimes
🕐 11am–6pm Tue–Sun
🌐 luma-arles.org

Soaring above the old town like a starship ready for lift-off, architect Frank Gehry's gleaming metallic landmark opened in summer 2018, endowing Arles with a brand-new venue for world-class contemporary art and performance. The Luma Foundation, led by Swiss art collector Maja Hoffmann, forms a 20-acre complex of galleries, theatres, studios and workshops dedicated to producing new and adventurous work in photography and conceptual art. The collection is split between Gehry's building and six former factory and warehouse spaces.

⑥ 🏛 Ⓜ 🏵
Musée Départementale de l'Arles Antique

🅰 Rue du Grand-Prieuré
🕐 10am–6pm Wed–Mon
🌐 patrimoine.ville-arles.fr

A marble statue of the Emperor Augustus, a statue of Venus and a massive altar dedicated to Apollo are just

↑ Artists painting in the gardens of Fondation Vincent Van Gogh

some of the highlights of this museum's collection of Roman sculptures, which date from pre-Christian times to the period that followed Constantine's conversion of the Empire in AD 312. A new wing opened in 2013 to house the Arles Rhône 3, a fantastically well-preserved Roman 31-m- (102-ft-) long flat-bottomed wooden river barge that was retrieved from the bed of the Rhône.

⑦ 🏛 Ⓜ 🏵
Fondation Vincent Van Gogh Arles

🅰 35 rue du Dr Fanton
🕐 11am–6pm Tue–Sun (to 7pm Apr–Sep) 🌐 fondation-vincentvangogh-arles.org

Housed in a 15th-century mansion, the Hôtel Léautaud de Donines, this foundation aims to put Van Gogh's work in context and highlights the artist's influence on his contemporaries and successive generations of painters. Today artsist and students can gain permission to paint onsite.

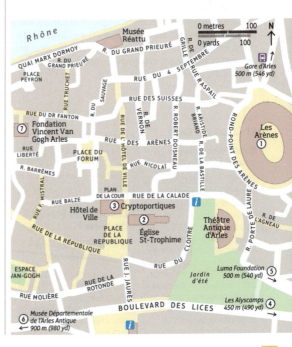

→

Flamingos wading
through the lagoons
of the Camargue

②

THE CAMARGUE

⬛F6 ✈ Montpellier-Méditerranée, 90 km (56 miles) E 🚆
🚌 Av Paulin Talabot, Arles 🛈 Mas du Pont de Rousty; parc-camargue.fr

The mighty Rhône meets the Mediterranean in the
Camargue, a delta of reedbeds, wetlands and marshland
pastures where half-wild white horses and black cattle
roam. At its heart is the vast Étang de Vaccarès, part of a
network of channels and lagoons edged by a seemingly
endless arc of beaches.

St-Gilles-du-Gard

🛈 1 pl F Mistral; www.
tourisme.saint-gilles.fr

Perched on the northern edge
of the delta, the small town
of St-Gilles-du-Gard is the
12th-century gateway to the
Camargue. It is noted for its
many festivals devoted to
local music, culture, produce
(including fruit from its famed
apricot and peach orchards)
and black bulls. In the heart of
the old town, the Abbaye de
St-Gilles is a UNESCO-listed
étape on the Santiago de
Compostela pilgrimage route.

The lovely carved façade is all
that remains of the original
building, which was founded
by Raymond IV, Count of
Toulouse, in the 12th century.

Les Saintes-Maries-de-la-Mer

🛈 5 ave Van Gogh; www.
saintesmaries.com

Miles of long sandy beaches
stretch either side of this easygoing seaside village, full of
restaurants and shops selling
colourful Camargue ceramics
and textiles. The 9th-century

Église de Notre-Dame-de-la-
Mer, with its black Madonna,
is the focus of a huge and
colourful gypsy festival in
May. Parades, horse races and
flamenco dances celebrate
the village's three patron
saints, Mary Magdalene, Mary
Jacobe (sister of the Virgin)
and Mary Salome (mother of
the apostles James and John).

Parc Ornithologique de Pont-de-Gau

⬛RD570, Pont-de-Gau
🕙10am–6pm daily
🚫Weekends in Jan, 1 May
🌐parcornithologique.com

Viewing platforms and
aviaries let visitors get close to
flocks of wading flamingos
and herons, as well as many
unusual birds, in this 24-ha
(60-acre) expanse of lagoons,
pastures and reedbeds.

Did You Know?

The salt pans in the
southeast corner of
the Camargue produce
800,000 tonnes
of salt a year.

Displays include video footage and slide shows, and provide an excellent introduction to the people, environment and wildlife of the wetlands. Among the many subjects covered are the lives of the Camargue cowboys and story of Frédéric Mistral, who won the Nobel Prize for literature in 1904.

---

⑤

Étang de Fangassier

🛈 Rte d'Arles, 13129 Salin de Giraud ⏱ For guided tours only 🗓 Oct–Mar 🌐 guides-nature.com

The Étang de Fangassier is home to France's only breeding colony of flamingos. Between 10,000 and 15,000 pink-plumaged pairs raise their young on and around a lagoon island that was used for salt production until 2008. The flamingos feed on shrimp and other tiny creatures that thrive in the lagoon. During the breeding season you can hear the birds from hundreds of metres away.

④

Musée de la Camargue

🏠 Mas pont de Rousty, D570, Arles ⏱ Hours vary, check website 🌐 musee delacamargue.com

The customs and lifestyles of the Camargue are the focus of this museum, housed in the huge barn of a traditional Provençal *mas*, or farmhouse.

Must See

STAY

L'Auberge Cavalière du Pont des Bannes

Stay in luxury rooms in these lovely waterside farmhouse-style villas. Guest perks include swimming pools, a spa, riding stables and an excellent restaurant.

🏠 Rte d'Arles, Les Saintes Maries-de-la-Mer 🌐 auberge cavaliere.com

€€€

Mas Saint Germain

Accommodation in spacious self-catering *gîtes* and guesthouse rooms among Camargue fields and pastureland.

🏠 Villeneuve-Camargue, Arles 🌐 massaint germain.com

€€€

3

ST-PAUL-DE-VENCE

🅰 G6 ✈ Nice 🚊 Nice, Cagnes sur Mer 🚌 Cagnes sur Mer, Vence, Nice ℹ 2 rue Grande; www.saint-pauldevence.com

Set in alpine hinterland with panoramic views of the Riviera coast, the breathtaking location of St-Paul-de-Vence first drew painters in the 1920s. The outstanding art collection of the Fondation Maeght is St-Paul-de-Vence's most powerful magnet, and a stroll through the town's maze of medieval streets is a real delight.

 1

Place du Jeu de Boules

Venerable plane trees spread their leaves over the place du Jeu de Boules. Any visit to St-Paul-de-Vence must start in this atmospheric space, where locals still like to meet for a friendly game of *pétanque* when the square is not crammed with visitors.

 2

Porte de Vence and Ramparts

A 14th-century tower stands guard over the Porte de Vence, an impressive gateway that leads through St-Paul-de-Vence's formidable ring of 16th-century ramparts into the heart of the village. From here, you can walk around the ramparts – originally built to resist assault from Savoy and Piedmont – for a panoramic view of the vineyards and olive groves that cloak the hilly countryside around the village.

 3

Rue Grande

Lined with the studios and workshops of local artists and artisans, the rue Grande is St-Paul's main thoroughfare. Running between the Porte de Vence and Porte de Nice, it resembles an open-air art museum where you can ogle the work of cutting-edge talents in the windows of upscale commercial galleries.

4

Folon Chapel (Chapelle des Pénitents Blancs)

🏠 Place de l'Église
📞 04 66 28 18 32
🕐 10:30am–12:30pm & 2–4pm (to 6pm May–Sep)
🚫 Public holidays

Belgian-born artist Jean-Michel Folon (1934–2005) spent much of his life in St-Paul-de-Vence and worked with local artisans to adorn this historic 17th-century chapel with vividly coloured, joyous stained-glass windows, graceful sculptures, murals and rich mosaics. The enchanting chapel is immaculately preserved as a celebration of his life and work.

↑ Place de la Grande Fontaine in St-Paul-de-Vence

resident of the village's cemetery. His modest, cedar-shaded grave is a place of pilgrimage for admirers, who leave coins in a growing pile as visible tribute to a great artist.

Musée d'Histoire Locale

🏠 Monté de la Castre 📞 04 66 28 18 32 🕐 7:30am–5:45pm daily (to 6:45pm Apr–Sep)

St-Paul's dramatic history is evoked by waxwork tableaux and life-size effigies created by Paris's Musée Grévin in this small museum. One of the main historic figures featured is Sébastien Le Prestre de Vauban (1633–1707), Francois I and Louis XIV's great military architect, who reinforced much

of the village's formidable fortifications to resist attack by France's enemies in 1543–7. A combined ticket for entrance to both the museum and the Folon Chapel is available.

⑦
Place de la Grande Fontaine

A gushing 17th-century central fountain lends its name to this charming square which was once the village's marketplace and communal laundry. Until the 1960s, laundresses would wash clothes and bed linen in stone troughs here within an open-sided washhouse. The square has long been a favourite subject with artists working in St-Paul-de-Vence.

↑ The medieval village of St-Paul-de-Vence, perched high on a hilltop

⑤
Cimetière

Marc Chagall, who made St-Paul-de-Vence his home from 1966 until his death in 1985, is the most famous

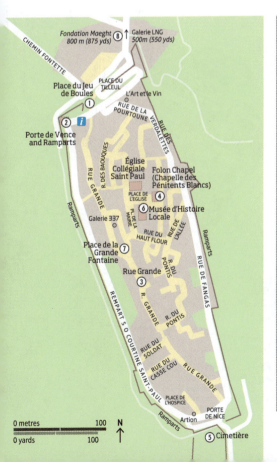

TOP 4 — ART GALLERIES IN ST-PAUL-DE VENCE

L'Art et le Vin
🏠 1 rue de la Pourtune
This wine bar and gallery is a perfect spot to savour local vintages and work by local artists.

Artion
🏠 1 pl de l'Église
A Provençal offshoot of a famous Swiss gallery, Artion exhibits work by old masters and world-class modern artists.

Galerie LNG
🏠 11 rempart Ouest
A gallery showcasing colourful pop art and work by 21st-century street artists.

Galerie 337
🏠 29 rue Grande
This modern art gallery features exceptional sculptures, prints and paintings by leading contemporary artists.

⑧ 🖊 🖥 🛍

FONDATION MAEGHT

📍 623 chemin Gardettes, St-Paul-de-Vence ⏰ 10am–6pm daily (to 7pm Jul–Sep) 🗓 24 & 31 Dec 🌐 fondation maeght.com

Nestling amid the umbrella pines in the hills above St-Paul-de-Vence, this small foundation houses one of Europe's largest collections of 20th-century art.

The Fondation Maeght was established in 1964 by Cannes art dealers Aimé and Marguerite Maeght, who numbered the likes of Chagall, Matisse and Miró among their clients. Their private collection formed the basis of the foundation, and they enlisted the help of their artist friends when designing the grounds: highlights include a courtyard filled with stick-thin Giacometti sculptures, an elaborate sculpture-filled maze designed by Miró, a bold swimming pool by Braque and a large mural mosaic by Chagall. The Maeghts intended the foundation not as an art museum, but as a forum to present modern art – a place for artists to gather, exchange ideas and exhibit their work. Today, just a fraction of the vast permanent collection is on display at any one time, with a changing programme of popular temporary exhibitions.

These slender bronze figures by Alberto Giacometti inhabit their own shady courtyard.

Georges Braque designed Les Poissons *mosaic in this swimming pool.*

Cowled roofs allow indirect light to filter into the galleries.

↑ Bold exterior of the Fondation Maeght

Alexander Calder's Les Renforts *(1963) is what he called a "stabile" – a counterpart to his more familiar mobiles.*

Joan Miró's Le Cadran Solaire (1973) is one of many statues in his multi-levelled maze of trees, water and gargoyles.

↑ Temporary Giacometti exhibition inside the Fondation Maeght

Did You Know?

The foundation drew Duke Ellington, Samuel Beckett, André Malraux and a galaxy of artists to its early events.

The Chapelle St-Bernard was built in memory of the Maeghts' son, who died in 1953, aged 11. Above the altarpiece is a stained-glass window by Braque.

← Illustration of the building and grounds of the Fondation Maeght, seen from above

↑ L'Oiseau Lunaire (1968), a sculpture in Miró's maze

↑ Nice's promenade des Anglais, stretching along the coast

4

NICE

🅰 G6 ✈ 7 km (4 miles) SW of Nice 🚆 Av Thiers 🚌 4 blvd Jean Jaurès 🛈 5 promenade des Anglais; nicetourism.com

With the blue curve of the Baie des Anges in front and the white summits of the Alpes-Maritimes as a backdrop, glittering Nice has enchanted visitors since the 19th century, when British, German and Russian aristocrats wintered here, revelling in its mellow climate. Painters, too, have been drawn here, endowing the city with a rich artistic legacy that the numerous visitors enjoy.

①

Villa Masséna

🅰 65 rue de France 🄲 04 93 91 19 10 🄾 11am–6pm Wed–Mon

The golden age of aristocratic tourism in Nice is brought to life in this museum, which is located within a beautiful 19th-century Italianate villa set in landscaped gardens. Religious works, paintings by Niçois "primitive" painters, and white-glazed faïence pottery are among the exhibits. The villa was built for Prince Victor D'Essling, grandson of Nice-born André Masséna, one of Napoleon's greatest marshals, whose bust has pride of place in the Empire-style main hall.

②

Musée d'Art Moderne et d'Art Contemporain (MAMAC)

🅰 Place Yves Klein 🄾 11am–6pm Tue–Sun 🆆 mamac-nice.org

The *enfants terribles* of Pop Art, New Realism and the modernists of the École de Nice find a fitting home in this strikingly original complex of marble-faced towers, steel arches and transparent walkways. Andy Warhol and

→

The *Loch Ness Monster* by Niki de Saint Phalle at MAMAC

Yves Klein are among the stars of a collection that celebrates the avant-garde from the 1960s to the 21st century.

③

Musée National Marc Chagall

🅰 36 ave Docteur Ménard 🄾 Nov–Apr: 10am–5pm Wed–Mon; May–Oct: 10am–5pm daily 🆆 musees-nation aux-alpesmaritimes.fr

Paintings from Marc Chagall's *Biblical Message* series, which includes five versions of *The Song of Songs*, form the core of this museum, home to the world's largest portfolio of the his work. Three stained-glass windows depict the *Creation of the World*, and a shallow pool reflects a mosaic of Elijah.

(4) Musée Matisse

🏠 164 av des Arènes de Cimiez 🕐 10am–5pm Wed-Mon (to 6pm May-Oct) 🌐 musee-matisse-nice.org

Matisse spent many years in Nice. This museum, housed in and below the 17th-century Arena Villa, includes *Still Life With Pomegranates* and Matisse's last completed work, *Flowers and Fruits*.

---

(5) Musée des Beaux-Arts

🏠 33 av des Baumettes 🕐 10am–6pm Tue-Sun 🌐 musee-beaux-arts-nice.org

Oil paintings and ceramics by Raoul Dufy steal the show in this charming museum, which is housed in a 19th-century villa. Other highlights include sculptures by Rodin, as well as works by 16th- and 17th-century Flemish masters.

(6) Musée des Arts Asiatiques

🏠 405 prom des Anglais 🕐 10am–5pm Wed-Mon 🌐 arts-asiatiques.com

An outstanding collection of ancient and modern art from China, Japan, Southeast Asia and India is displayed in Kenzo Tange's dazzling marble-and-glass building.

---

(7) Hotel Negresco

🏠 37 promenade des Anglais 🌐 hotel-negresco-nice.com

Built in 1912 by gypsy-violin star Henri Negresco, this landmark hotel is even more lavish today than in its heyday. Louis XIII grandeur meets modern amenities in the decadent rooms. The atmospheric bar is open to everyone, as is the Michelin-starred restaurant.

NICE JAZZ FESTIVAL

Louis Armstrong and his All Stars headlined at the first Nice Jazz Festival in 1948, as the Riviera emerged from the grim years of World War II and postwar poverty. It was the first big international jazz festival, and more than 70 years on it is still a major event.

The Théâtre de Verdure is the main venue and the six-day event kicks off with a lively carnival parade through the city centre.

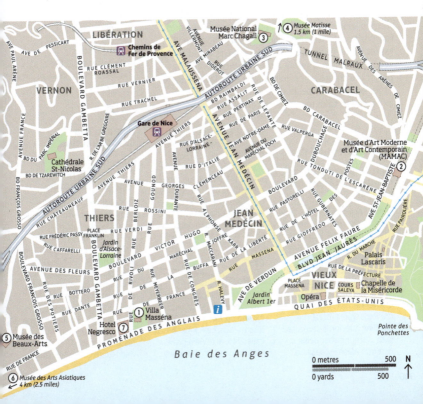

5

MONACO

 G6 Nice, 15 km (9 miles) SW of Monaco Monaco-Monte Carlo, pl Ste-Dévote Place des Moulins 2A blvd des Moulins; www.visitmonaco.com

The mega-yachts of the world's richest men and women weigh anchor at Port de Monaco, and world-famous sports stars and their consorts hog the VIP tables in the exclusive nightspots of the world's second smallest country. An ambitious €2 billion project to create a new millionaire's enclave on sand dredged from the seabed began in 2016 and is expected to take ten years to complete.

①

Casino de Monte Carlo

 Place du Casino 2pm–4am daily casinomontecarlo.com

Monaco owes much of its fame to this glorious monument, which harkens back to the late 19th century, when this tiny principality came to be seen as *the* place to frolic, flirt and play games of chance for high stakes. Renovated in 1878 by Charles Garnier, architect of the Paris Opéra (*p111*), the dazzling interior is decorated with glittering chandeliers, ostentatious frescoes and gilded bas-reliefs. The slot machines now in the Salle des Amériques and Salle Renaissance have made this once-exclusive venue more egalitarian, and full evening dress is no longer de rigueur, but the casino still strives to maintain a certain decorum.

②

Le Rocher

Set on the Rock, a sheer-sided, flat-topped finger of land extending 792 m (2,600 ft) into the sea, Le Rocher (also called Monaco-Ville) is the historic quarter of Monaco where Europe's oldest ruling family, the Grimaldis, founded their principality in the 13th century. Today, in contrast to the flashy modern city, it is a warren of narrow medieval lanes set around the **Palais Princier**, where the Grimaldis still live, which has wonderful frescoes and a dramatically opulent throne room.

Palais Princier

 Place du Palais Mar–Oct: 10am–6pm daily palais.mc

---

③

Monaco Top Cars Collection

 Les Terrasses de Fontvieille 10am–6pm daily mtcc.mc

This petrolheads' paradise began as the personal collection of Prince Rainier III. It is one of the world's greatest collections of classic cars, from a quaint 1903 De Dion Bouton to sleek thoroughbreds bearing the hood ornaments and badges of Maserati, Rolls Royce and the like. There are also important race and rally contenders from historic Monaco Grand Prix and Monte Carlo Rally events.

The glittering lights and flashy yachts of Monaco's harbour

Must See

EAT

Café de Paris

This classic brasserie serves refined French cooking and local dishes like *stockfish à la monégasque* under white umbrellas on a flowery terrace opposite the casino.

Place du Casino
 fr.montecarlosbm.com

€€€

Quai des Artistes

A classy, contemporary but unpretentious harbourside brasserie that bustles with locals and serves a great selection of seafood and an above-average children's menu.

Quai Antoine 1
quaidesartistes.com

€€€

---

 ④

Nouveau Musée National de Monaco

Villa Sauber, 17 ave Princesse Grace; Villa Paloma, 56 blvd du Jardin Exotique 10am–6pm daily for exhibitions only 19 Nov nmnm.mc

Two spectacular villas house this museum charting the cultural, historical and artistic heritage of the Principality. The Villa Sauber (currently closed) hosts a series of entertainment exhibits. Villa Paloma, with its lovely Italian garden, displays a fantastic collection of modern and contemporary art and design.

---

⑤

Jardin Exotique

62 bd du Jardin Exotique Hours vary, check website 19 Nov, 25 Dec jardin-exotique.mc

Clinging to the steep limestone hillside, with spectacular views over Monaco, this garden is filled with weird and wonderful tropical and sub-tropical cacti and other plants imported from arid native environments in the Americas, Africa and Asia. It boasts one of the largest collections of petrophile succulents (plants that grow on bare rock) in the world. But its biggest secret lies beneath the surface. In the Grotte de l'Observatoire, eerie caverns filled with dripping stalactites, palaeontologists have found evidence of early hominid people from around 1,000,000 years BC.

6 ⬡ⓂⒹ🛍

PALAIS DES PAPES

🅰F6 📍Pl du Palais, Avignon 🕐Mar: 9am-6:30pm daily; Apr-Jun: 9am-7pm daily; Jul: 9am-8pm daily; Aug: 9am-8:30pm daily; Sep & Oct: 9am-7pm daily; Nov-Feb: 9:30am-6:30pm daily 🔗palais-des-papes.com

One of the largest Gothic structures in Europe, the dramatic fortified walls of the Palais des Papes loom intimidatingly over visitors. This palace dates back to when, confronted with factional strife in Rome and encouraged by the scheming of Philippe IV of France, Pope Clement V moved the papal court to Avignon in 1309, where it remained undisputed until 1377.

Originally a modest episcopal building, Palais des Papes was transformed into a grand papal residence for the nine popes who ruled from here, its heavy fortifications a vital defence against bands of mercenaries. In its day, it would have been full of the luxurious trappings of 14th-century court life, particularly in the time of Clement VI, who added the flamboyant Palais Neuf to the original Palais Vieux. Clement VI felt luxury was the best way to honour God but, over the centuries, most of the art and furniture in the palace was destroyed.

EAT

Carré du Palais

The two-course menu at this restaurant and wine bar in a historic building on place de Palais is a bargain. The excellent wine list is long and ever-changing.

🅰1 pl du Palais 🔗carredupalais.fr

€€€

La Cabane d'Oléron

Tucked away in a corner of Avignon's extra-ordinary covered market, this eatery has a handful of tables and surprisingly affordable connoisseur's choice of fruits de mer.

🅰Rue de l'Olivier, Les Halles 📞0698 29 10 88

€€€

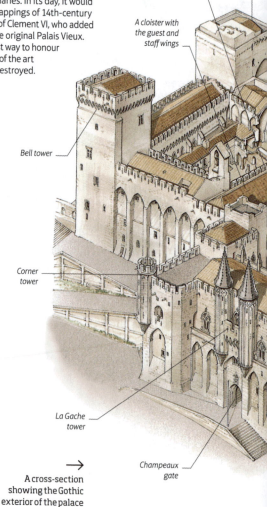

Trouillas tower

Consistory Hall

A cloister with the guest and staff wings

Bell tower

Corner tower

La Gache tower

Champeaux gate

→ A cross-section showing the Gothic exterior of the palace

← Moulded biblical scenes on display in the Sacristie Nord of the Palais Neuf

↑ The twin turrets above the entrance of the heavily fortified Palais des Papes

WHAT ELSE TO SEE IN AVIGNON

North of the Palais is the 13th-century Musée du Petit Palais *(www. petitpalais.paris.fr)*, with Romanesque and Gothic sculpture and medieval paintings. In contrast, two major art collections, the Musée Angladon and the Collection Lambert *(collectionlambert.fr)*, have combined their weight to provide a burst of modern and contemporary culture. Run under the same banner, the former has works by Degas, Picasso and Modigliani, while the latter features minimalist and conceptual art. Avignon hosts France's largest annual arts festival *(www. festival-avignon.com)*, including ballet, drama and classical concerts.

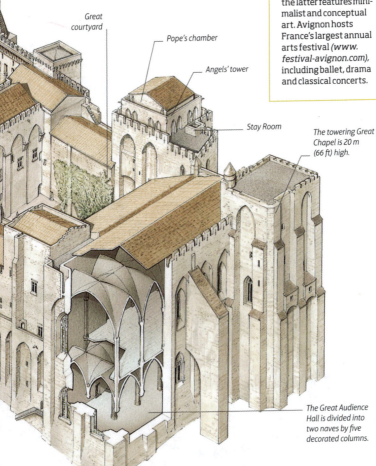

Great courtyard

Pope's chamber

Angels' tower

Stay Room

The towering Great Chapel is 20 m (66 ft) high.

The Great Audience Hall is divided into two naves by five decorated columns.

EXPERIENCE MORE

7

Orange

F6 **Vaucluse**
**5 cours Aristide Briand;
www.orange-tourisme.fr**

Orange is a thriving regional centre in the Rhône Valley, an important marketplace for local produce such as grapes, olives, honey and truffles. Explore the area around the 17th-century Hôtel de Ville, where attractive streets open on to some lovely quiet and shady squares. Orange is also blessed with two of the greatest Roman monuments in Europe, the Roman Theatre and the Arc de Triomphe. Dating back to the 1st century AD, the well-preserved **Roman Theatre (Théâtre Antique)**, a UNESCO World Heritage Site, still has perfect acoustics and continues to be regularly used for performances. The back wall soars up to a height of 37 m (120 ft) and is 103 m (338 ft) wide. In 2006 an immense glass roof, built high above the theatre so it would not affect the acoustics, replaced the original roof, destroyed in a fire. The triple-arched Arc de Triomphe was built around AD 20. It is decorated with scenes of battles, inscriptions and trophies honouring Tiberius and the conquest of Rome. Relics in the **Musée d'Art et d'Histoire d'Orange** reflect the Roman presence in Orange, some of which date to the 1st century BC.

Roman Theatre (Théâtre Antique)

1 rue Madeleine-Roch **Hours vary, check website** **theatre-antique.com**

Musée d'Art et d'Histoire d'Orange

1 rue Madeleine-Roch **Hours vary, check website** **theatre-antique.com**

8

Vaison-la-Romaine

F6 **Vaucluse**
**Pl du Chanoine Sautel;
www.vaison-ventoux-tourisme.com**

This site has been settled since the Bronze Age, but the

Did You Know?

Vaison only got its full name in 1924, after excavations unearthed the remains of a Roman city.

name stems from five centuries as a Roman town. Although the upper town, which is dominated by the ruins of a 12th-century castle, has some charming narrow streets, lined with fine stone houses and fountains, Vaison's principal attractions are to be found across the river.

The **Roman City** is split in two districts: Puymin and La Villasse. At Puymin, the Villa du Paon, an opulent mansion, and a Roman theatre have been uncovered.

Also at Vaison is the stout Cathédrale Notre-Dame-de-Nazareth, which includes medieval cloisters.

Roman City

Fouilles de Puymin & Musée Théo Desplans, pl du Chanoine Sautel **Hours vary, check website** **www.vaison-la-romaine.com**

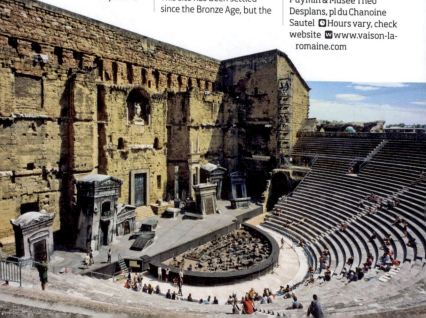

Seemingly endless rows of vines at Châteauneuf-du-Pape, with some of the resulting wine *(inset)*

 Mont Ventoux

⒜ F6 ⌂ Vaucluse ⟶ Avignon ⌂ Avignon ▭ Carpentras ⓘ Avenue de la Promenade, Sault-en-Provence; www.ventoux-sud.com

The name Mont Ventoux means "Windy Mountain" in the Provençal language, and it really does hint at conditions visitors might expect up there, but, at 1,912 m (6,273 ft), it's also known as "the giant of Provence". A variety of flora and fauna may be found on the lower slopes, but only moss survives at the summit, where the temperature can drop to -27° C (-17° F). The bare white scree at the peak makes it look snowcapped even in the depths of summer.

The legendary British cyclist Tommy Simpson died during 1967's Tour de France on Mont Ventoux. In spite of this, it remains a popular challenge for some cyclists, and guided rides are available from local tour operators. A road leads upward to the radio beacon pinnacle, but even in a car the trip should not be attempted

Preparing to enjoy the perfect acoustics in the Roman Theatre at Orange

in bad weather. At other times, though, the spectacular views from the top make the effort very worthwhile.

⒑ **Châteauneuf-du-Pape**

⒜ F6 ⌂ Vaucluse ▣ Sorgues, then taxi ▭ From Avignon or Orange ⓘ 3 rue de la République; www.chateauneuf-du-pape-tourisme.fr

Here, in the 14th century, the popes of Avignon chose to build a new castle *(château neuf)* and plant the vineyards from which one of the finest wines of the Côtes du Rhône is produced. These days, almost every doorway in this attractive little town seems to open into a *vigneron*'s cellar where tastings – and, if you're lucky, some worthwhile bargains – may be offered.

After the Wars of Religion, all that remained of the papal fortress were a few fragments of walls and tower, but the ruins look spectacular and offer magnificent views across to Avignon and the Vaucluse uplands beyond.

Wine festivals punctuate the year, including the Fête de la Véraison in August, when the grapes start to ripen, and the wonderful Châteauneuf-du-Pape Spring Wine Fair, hosted by local growers.

FÊTE DE LA VÉRAISON

Chateauneuf-du-Pape celebrates its medieval roots and its fabulous wines with the annual Fête de la Véraison, on the first weekend of August. Highlights of the event include a grand medieval-style banquet, a huge bonfire party on the place de la Fontaine, a medieval market, complete with costumed jongleurs and troubadours, and a lively procession by re-enactors dressed in the period costumes of the Avignon pontiffs and their courtiers.

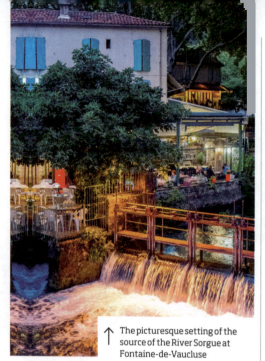

↑ The picturesque setting of the source of the River Sorgue at Fontaine-de-Vaucluse

1640. The Criminal Court has 17th-century carved tablets of local towns. In the Hôtel-Dieu pharmacy, the 18th-century cupboards have painted figures of monkey "doctors". More regional art and history is on show at the **Musée Sobirats**, renovated in 2018.

Synagogue

🏠 15 pl Maurice Charretier
🕐 Hours vary, check website
🌐 synagoguedecarpentras.fr

Musée Sobirats

 🏠 112 rue du Collège
📞 04 90 63 04 92 🕐 Apr–Sep: 10am–12pm & 2–6pm Wed–Mon 🚫 Pub hols

---

13

Luberon

🅰 F6 🏠 Vaucluse
✈ Avignon 🚍 Cavaillon, Avignon 🚍 Apt 🛈 Place François Tourel, Cavaillon; www.luberon-coeurde provence.com

The huge limestone range of the Montagne du Luberon is one of the most appealing areas of Provence. Rising to 1,125 m (3,690 ft), it combines wild areas with picturesque villages. Most is designated as a regional nature park, with more than 1,000 plant species and dense forests. The varied wildlife includes eagles, wild

11

Fontaine-de-Vaucluse

🅰 F6 🏠 Vaucluse
🚍 Avignon 🛈 Av Robert Garcin, Residence Jean Garcin; www.oti-delasorgue.fr

The main attraction here is the source of the River Sorgue. It is the most powerful spring in France, gushing at up to 90,000 litres (19,800 gallons) per second from an underground river at the foot of a cliff. It powers the Moulin à Papier Vallis Clausa (paper-mill), which produces handmade paper using the same methods that were employed in the 15th century, and now produces maps, prints and lampshades for sale. There are also a number of museums in the town. One is devoted to the poet Petrarch (Francesco Petrarca, 1304–74), who lived and wrote in the town, and another exhibits material related to the work of the French Resistance during World War II.

12

Carpentras

🅰 F6 🏠 Vaucluse 🚍
🛈 Maison de Pays, 97 place du 25 Août 1944; www.carpentras-ventoux.com

In 1320, Carpentras became capital of the papal county of Venaissin, and remained so until 1791. Modern boulevards follow the former ramparts, with one original gate, the Porte d'Orange, surviving.

In the Middle Ages the town was home to a sizeable Jewish community and the 1367 **Synagogue** is the oldest in France. While they were not openly persecuted under papal rule, many Jews changed faith, and they would enter the Cathédrale St-Siffrein by the Porte Juive (Jews' Door).

The Law Courts were built as the episcopal palace in

→

Colourful rows of blooming lavender by the Abbaye de Sénanque in Gordes

boar, vultures, snakes, beavers and Europe's largest lizards. The park headquarters are in Apt. Once a haunt of highwaymen, the Luberon hills now hide luxury holiday homes. The major village is Bonnieux, with its 12th-century church and 13th-century walls. Also popular are Roussillon, with red ochre buildings, Lacoste, with the ruins of the Marquis de Sade's castle, and Ansouis, with its 14th-century church and 17th-century castle. Ménerbes became world-famous through writer Peter Mayle's tales of life here.

Gordes

△F6 **🏠Vaucluse** **🛈Pl du Château; www.gordes-village.com**

This hilltop village, with its arcaded medieval lanes, is dominated by the 16th-century **Château de Gordes**

Just south lies the **Village des Bories**, a primitive habitat of tiny beehive-shaped huts. The construction techniques are thought to date back to Neolithic times, although the village was still occupied in the 19th-century.

The **Abbaye de Sénanque**, to the north, is a fine Romanesque Cistercian monastery.

Château de Gordes

🚻 🏠Pl du Château **📞**04 90 72 98 64 🕐Apr–Sep: Tue–Sun 🚫1 Jan, 25 Dec

Village des Bories

🚻 🏠Route de Gorde 🕐9am–5:30pm daily (open later in summer) 🚫1 Jan, 25 & 31 Dec 🌐levillagedesbories.com

---

St-Rémy-de-Provence

△F6 **🏠Bouches-du-Rhône** **🚌Avignon** **🛈Pl Jean Jaurès; www.saintremy-de-provence.com**

For centuries St-Rémy, with its boulevards, fountains and narrow streets, had two claims to fame. One was that Vincent van Gogh spent a year here, in 1889–90, at the St-Paul-de-Mausole hospital. *Wheat Field with Cypress* and *Ravine* are among the 150 works he produced here. The town was also, in 1503, the birthplace of Nostradamus, known for his prophecies. In 1921 it found new fame when Roman ruins were unearthed at the **Site Archéologique de Glanum**. Little remains of the ancient city, but the site impresses. Around the ruins of a Roman arch is a mausoleum, with scenes like the death of Adonis.

Site Archéologique de Glanum

🚻 😊 🏠 🕐Hours vary, check website 🚫1 Jan, 1 May, 1 & 11 Nov, 25 Dec 🌐site-glanum.fr

STAY

Pastis Hotel St-Tropez
A palm-fringed outdoor pool is a highlight of this intimate spot with sea and garden views.

△G6 **🏠**6 av du Général Leclerc, St-Tropez 🌐pastis-st-tropez.com

€€€

Hotel du Soleil & SPA
A peaceful haven with a pool, high-end spa, and top-quality linens and toiletries.

△F6 **🏠**35 av Pasteur St-Rémy-de-Provence 🌐hotelsoleil.com

€€€

Labastide de Voulonne
This Provençale farm house has family-friendly suites and gardens with a pool.

△F6 **🏠**2133 rte des Baumettes, Cabrieres d'Avignon, Gordes 🌐bastidevoulonne.com

€€€

16

Aix-en-Provence

🅰 F6 🏠 Bouches-du-Rhône
🚍🚌 ℹ Les allées proven-
çales, 300 av Giuseppe
Verdi; www.aixen
provence tourism.com

Founded by the Romans in
103 BC, Aix was frequently
attacked, first by the Visigoths
in AD 477, later by Lombards,
Franks and Saracens. Despite
this, the city prospered. By the
end of the 12th century it was
the capital of Provence. A centre of art and learning, it
reached its peak in the 15th
century during the reign of
"Good King" René. He is shown
in Nicolas Froment's *Triptych
of the Burning Bush* in the
13th-century Cathédrale St-
Sauveur, also noted for its
16th-century walnut doors,
baptistry and cloisters.

Aix is still a centre of art and
learning, and its museums
include the **Musée Granet** of
fine arts and archaeology in
the Palais de l'Archevêché.

Aix has been called "the city
of a thousand fountains" and
three of the best are on cours
Mirabeau. On one side are
some 17th- and 18th-century
buildings with wrought-iron
balconies; on the other are
cafés. The Old Town is centred
on place de l'Hôtel de Ville,
which has a colourful flower
market. The **Caumont Centre
d'Art**, in one of the city's most
stunning mansions, is an art
gallery and cultural centre.

Aix's most famous son is
Paul Cézanne (1839–1906).
The **Atelier de Cézanne** has
been kept as it was when he
died. Montagne Ste-Victoire,
inspiration for many of his
paintings, is 15 km (9 miles)
east of Aix.

 HIDDEN GEM
Going to Market

Aix-en-Provence is
famed for its astound-
ing variety of markets:
sample fresh, seasonal
produce daily at place
Richelme, snack on
delectable Provençal
cuisine at the Grand
Marché, or get literary
at the city's monthly
book market.

Musée Granet

🚻🅿 🏠 Pl St-Jean de Malte
🕐 Noon–5:30pm Tue–Sun 🚫 1
Jan, 1 May, 25 Dec 🌐 musee
granet-aixenprovence.fr

Caumont Centre d'Art

🚻🅿🍴 🏠 3 rue Joseph
Cabassol 🕐 Oct–Apr 10am–
6pm daily (to 7pm May–Sep)
🌐 caumont-centredart.com

Atelier de Cézanne

🚻🅿🍴 🏠 9 av Paul Cézanne
🕐 10:30am–12:30pm, 2–5pm
daily 🚫 Dec–Feb: Sun; 1–10
Jan, 1 May, 25 Dec 🌐 atelier-
cezanne.com

17

Tarascon

🅰 F6 🏠 Bouches-du-Rhône
🚍🚌 ℹ 62 rue des Halles;
www.tarascon.org

According to legend, the town
was named for the Tarasque,
a monster, half-mammal and
half-fish, which terrorized the
countryside. It was tamed by
Ste Marthe, who is buried in
the church here. An effigy of
this monster is still paraded
through the streets each June.

The striking 15th-century
Château Royal de Provence
on the banks of the Rhône is
one of the finest examples of
Gothic military architecture in

 ←

The colourfully lit apse
in the Cathédrale St-
Sauveur, Aix-en-Provence

Provence. Its sombre exterior gives no hint of the beauties within – a Flemish-Gothic courtyard, a spiral staircase and the painted ceilings of the grand banqueting hall.

Opposite is Beaucaire, a ruined castle and gardens.

Château Royal de Provence (Tarascon)

 Blvd du Roi René ⏱ Hours vary, check website 🌐 chateau.tarascon.fr

---

18

Fréjus

🅰 G6 ⏱ Var 🚌🚆 ℹ 249 rue Jean Jaurès; www.frejus.fr

The modern town of Fréjus is dwarfed in importance by two historic sites. Though not as complete as those at Orange or Arles, the remains of the Roman **Amphithéâtre** (founded by Julius Caesar in 49 BC) are of exceptional variety. As well as the great amphitheatre, fragments of an aqueduct and part of a rampart gateway remain. The sea has receded over the centuries and there are few traces of the original harbour.

The cathedral on rue de Fleury marks the entrance to the **Groupe Episcopal**. The fortified enclave includes the 5th-century baptistry, one of the oldest in France, and the cloister, its coffered medieval roof ornately decorated with a spectacular bestiary.

In 1959 Fréjus was hit by a wall of water, as the Malpasset Barrage burst. To the north of the town, the ruined dam can still be seen.

Did You Know?

The River Rhône is home to some monster catfish that eat pigeons.

↑ Les Baux-de-Provence, beautifully framed by a natural window in the cliff face

Amphithéâtre

🏛 Rue Henri Vadon 📞 04 94 51 34 31 ⏱ Hours vary, call ahead 📅 1 Jan, 1 May, 25 Dec

Groupe Episcopal

🏛 48–58 rue du Cardinal Fleury ⏱ Hours vary, check website 📅 1 Jan, 1 May, 1 & 11 Nov, 25 Dec; cloisters 🌐 cloitre-frejus.fr

---

19

Les Baux-de-Provence

🅰 F6 🏛 Bouches-du-Rhône 🚌 Arles ℹ La Maison du Roy; www.lesbauxde provence.com

One of the strangest places in Provence, the deserted citadel of Les Baux is like a natural extension of a huge rocky plateau. The ruins overlook the Val d'Enfer (Infernal Valley), with its weird rocks.

In the Middle Ages this was home to powerful lords, who claimed to descend from the Magus Balthazar. It was the most famous of the Provençal Cours d'Amour, at which troubadours sang the praises of high-born ladies. The ideal of everlasting but unrequited courtly love contrasts with the warlike nature of the lords.

The glory days ended in 1632. It had become a Protestant stronghold and Louis XIII ordered its destruction. The ruins are a reminder of a turbulent past and offer spectacular views. The village below has a pleasant little square, a 12th-century church and Chapelle des Pénitents Blancs, decorated by local artist Yves Brayer, whose work is in the Musée Yves Brayer.

Bauxite was discovered here in 1821 and named after the town. Deposits ran out at the end of the 20th century.

To the southwest are ruins of the Abbaye de Montmajour with a 12th-century church.

TOP 3 WALKS NEAR LES BAUX

Val d'Enfer
Explore a valley full of twisted rock formations.

Flânerie entre les Oliviers
Stroll through the area's famous olive orchards.

Le Rocher des Deux Trous
Hike to the "Rock with Two Holes", which offers panoramic views.

Umbrella pines and wild flowers on the Massif des Maures nature reserve ↑

20

Massif des Maures

G6 Var Toulon-Hyères Hyères, Toulon or Fréjus Bormes-les-Mimosas Toulon 1 pl Gambetta, Bormes-les-Mimosas; www.bormesles mimosas.com

The dense wilderness of pine, oak and chestnut covering nearly 65 km (40 miles) of the Maures mountains probably gave rise to its name, meaning "dark" or "gloomy". The D558 gives access. Along the way is La Garde-Freinet, well-known for its bottle-cork industry.

Northwest of Cannet-des-Maures lies the Abbaye de Thoronet. This, and abbeys at Sénanque, in Vaucluse, and Silvacane, in the Bouches-du-Rhône, are known as the "Three Sisters" of Provence.

 HIDDEN GEM
Port Pin

A beautiful one-hour hike west of Cassis will bring you to the idyllic pine-shaded calanque of Port Pin, blessed with blissfully clear waters. Bring water, a picnic and a parasol – there are no facilities on the beach.

21

Cassis

F7 Bouches-du-Rhône Quai des Moulins, Le Port; www.ot-cassis.com

Many of the villages along this coast have been built up and have all but lost their original charm, but Cassis is still much the same little fishing port that attracted artists such as Dufy, Signac and Derain. This is a place in which to relax at a waterside café, watching the fishermen at work or the street performers, while enjoying a meal of seafood fresh from the boat and a bottle of the local dry white wine for which Cassis is noted.

From Marseille to Cassis the coast forms narrow inlets, the Calanques, their jagged white cliffs (some as high as 400 m/1,312 ft) reflected in dazzling turquoise water. Abundant wildlife includes seabirds, foxes, stone martens, bats, large snakes and lizards.

The plant life is no less impressive, with more than 900 species, of which 50 are classified as rare. The Sormiou and En-Vau calanques are particularly lovely, and both the wonderful Massif de Calanque and the Cap Canaille have deservedly been designated as national parks.

22

Hyères

G7 Var Rotonde du Park Hotel, 16 av de Belgique; www. hyeres-tourisme.com

Towards the end of the 18th century, Hyères became one of the first health resorts of the Côte d'Azur. Subsequent visitors included Queen Victoria and writers Robert Louis Stevenson and Edith Wharton.

The main sights are in the Vieille Ville's medieval streets, leading past flagstoned place Massillon to a ruined castle and views over the coast.

Modern Hyères is imbued with a lingering belle époque charm, which has become popular with experimental film-makers. It continues to attract a health-conscious crowd and is a major centre for aquatic sports.

23

Toulon

F7 Var 12 pl Louis-Blanc; www.toulontourisme.com

In 1793 this naval base was captured by an Anglo-Spanish fleet, but was retaken by the young Napoleon Bonaparte. The impressive collection of the **Musée National de la Marine** explores its maritime history. The **Musée d'Art de Toulon**, housed in an Italian Renaissance building, has a collection representing Fauvism, Minimalism and Realism. In the Old Town few original buildings remain, but its fish market is worth a visit. For lovely views, take the boat trip around the bay and the cable car ride up to Mont Faron.

Musée National de la Marine

 ⬛ Pl Monsenergue
🕐 10am–6pm Mon & Wed–Sun 🚫 Tue, 1 May, 25 Dec, Jan
🌐 musee-marine.fr

Musée d'Art de Toulon

⬛ 113 blvd Mar Leclerc 📞 04 94 36 81 01 🚫 Closed for restoration until end of 2019

24

Îles d'Hyères

⬛ G7 ⬛ Var 🚆 Toulon-Hyères ⬛🚌 Hyères
ℹ Rotonde du Park Hôtel, ave de Belgique, Hyères; www.hyeres-tourisme.com

Locally known as the Îles d'Or ("Golden Islands"), after the gold colour of their cliffs, this lovely trio of islands can be reached by boat from Hyères, Tour Fondue, Le Lavandou, La Croix Valmer, Cavalaire and St Tropez.

Porquerolles, the largest of the three, measures 7 km (4 miles) by 2.5 km (1.5 miles). It is covered in rich vegetation, much of which – for instance the Mexican bellombra tree – was introduced from a variety of exotic foreign climes.

The island's main town, also known as Porquerolles, has an appearance more like a North African colonial settlement than a Provençal village. It was established in 1820 as a retirement town for Napoleon's most honoured troops.

All the island's beaches lie along the northern coastline, the best being the lengthy sands of Plage Notre-Dame. One of the finest beaches in Provence, it sits in a sheltered bay about an hour's walk from Porquerolles village.

A stroll around lush Port-Cros, which covers 2.5 sq km (1 sq mile), takes the best part of a day. It rises up to 195 m (640 ft), which is the highest point on any of the islands.

Both Porquerolles and Port-Cros have been designated as national parks for their unique reserves of flora and fauna, and their offshore waters are also protected. There is even a scenic swimming route of around 300 m (984 ft); you can buy a waterproof guide to the area's underwater wildlife, which will make exploring this route even more enjoyable.

The wild, virtually treeless Île du Levant is reached by boat from Port-Cros. Its main draw is the oldest naturist resort in France, Héliopolis, founded in 1931. The eastern half of the island, which is under the control of the French navy, is permanently closed to the public.

↑ Porquerolles town on the island of the same name, one of the Îles d'Hyères

EAT

L'Escourtin

Idyllically located and filled with antiques and flowers, the focus here is on fresh garden produce, game and subtly sauced seafood.

⬛ G6 ⬛ 159 ch de Notre Dame des Cypres, Fayence 🚫 Mid-Oct–mid-Nov 🌐 camandoule.com/en/restaurant-escourtin

 €€€

Aubergine

Excellent Provençale dishes, many based, as the name implies, on the aubergine.

⬛ G6 ⬛ 7 rue Sade, Antibes 📞 04 93 34 55 93 🚫 Wed

 €€€

Vague d'Or

Wild ingredients foraged from the slopes of the Massif des Maures are paired with local seafood and organic produce from their own garden.

⬛ G6 ⬛ Plage de la Bouillabaisse, St-Tropez 🌐 vaguedor.com

 €€€

 25

St-Tropez

G6 **Var** **Quai Jean Jaurès; www.sainttropez tourisme.com**

The geography of St-Tropez kept it untouched by the earliest development of the Côte d'Azur. Tucked away at the tip of a peninsula, it is the only north-facing town on the coast and so did not appeal to those seeking a warm and sheltered winter resort. In 1892 the painter Paul Signac was among the first outsiders to respond to its unspoiled charm, encouraging friends, such as the painters Matisse and Bonnard, to join him. In the 1920s the Parisian writer Colette also made her home here. St-Tropez also began to attract star-spotters, hoping for a glimpse of such celebrities as the then Prince of Wales.

 INSIDER TIP
L'Aiguille

Head for lovely Pointe de l'Aiguille, to the west of Théoule-sur-Mer, to escape the crowds and discover gorgeous little bays and pine-scented woodland walks on the lower slopes of the Massif de l'Esterel.

In World War II the beaches saw Allied landings and some heavy bombing. Then, during the 1950s, young Parisians began to arrive, and the Bardot-Vadim film helped to create the reputation of modern St-Tropez as a play-ground for gilded youth. The wild public behaviour and turbulent love affairs of Roger Vadim, Brigitte Bardot, Sacha Distel and others left fiction far behind. Mass tourism fol-lowed, with visitors eager to spot celebrities.

Today, there are far more luxury yachts than fishing boats in St-Tropez harbour. Its cafés are ideal for people- and yacht-watching. Another hub is place des Lices, both for the Harley-Davidson set and the morning market. The **Musée de l'Histoire Maritime**, in the tower of the citadel, with great views, recounts the village's impressive seafaring past. There's also the **Musée de l'Annonciade** with its out-standing collection of works by Signac, Derain, Rouault, Bonnard and others.

The best beaches are out of town, including the golden curve of Pampelonne, with its beach clubs and restaurants – *the* place to see and be seen. St-Tropez has no train sta-tion, so driving and parking can be a nightmare in summer. It is best to get the boat from St Raphaël or St Maxime.

Did You Know?

Sandales tropéziennes, sandals hand-made in St-Tropez, are treated to resist salt water.

St-Tropez is said to be named for a Roman soldier martyred as a Christian by the Emperor Nero. Each May a *bravade* in his honour takes place, with an effigy of the saint carried through town accompanied by musket fire.

Nearby are two small towns. Port-Grimaud was only built in 1966, but the traditional archi-tecture makes it seem older. Most of its "streets" are canals. Up in the hills, Ramatuelle has been restored by the largely celebrity population.

Musée de l'Histoire Maritime

Citadelle de Saint Tropez
04 94 97 59 43 10am-5:30pm daily (to 6:30pm Apr-Sep) 1 Jan, 1 & 17 May, 11 Nov, 25 Dec

Musée de l'Annonciade

2 rue l'Annociade, pl Grammont 04 94 17 84 10 10am-6pm Tue-Sun Mon, 1 Jan, Ascension, 1 & 17 May, Nov, 25 Dec

St-Tropez after sunset, with its lights reflected in the calm waters of the bay

 26

Digne-les-Bains

🗺️ G6 📍 Alpes-de-Haute-Provence 🚉🚌 ℹ️ Le Rond Point; www.dignelesbains tourisme.com

This charming spa town in the foothills of the Alps features in Victor Hugo's *Les Misérables*. A trip on the Train des Pignes from Nice offers superb views. Apart from the spa, Digne-les-Bains also has an annual lavender festival and **Le Jardin des Papillons**, a butterfly garden with over 120 species.

Le Jardin des Papillons

🦋🐛🚻🏛️ 📍 St Benoît
📞 04 92 36 70 70 🕐 Apr-Jun 9am-5:30pm daily; Jul & Aug 9am-7pm daily

 27

Cannes

🗺️ G6 📍 Alpes-Maritimes 🚉🚌 ℹ️ 1 blvd de la Croisette; www.cannes-destination.com

Just like Grasse (p522) is synonymous with the perfume industry, Cannes is known for its many festivals, especially the Film Festival, but there is much more to the city than

CANNES FILM FESTIVAL

Film stars, directors, paparazzi, and other movers and shakers descend on Cannes each May for the Cannes Film Festival, the movie industry's foremost international marketplace, and the home of the annual Palme d'Or awards. Launched in 1946, the event really took off as a major media circus during the mid-1950s, when such starlets as Brigitte Bardot provocatively posed and pouted for the cameras – a tradition that lives on in the 21st century.

these glittering events. It was Lord Brougham, the British Lord Chancellor, who put it on the map, though Prosper Mérimée allegedly visited Cannes two months before. Brougham came in 1834 when he was unable to reach Nice. Struck by the beauty and mild climate of what was then just a small fishing port, he built a villa here, and others followed.

The Old Town, centred in the district of Le Suquet, is on the slopes of Mont Chevalier. Part of the old city wall can still be seen on place de la Castre, which is dominated by the Notre-Dame de l'Espérance, built in the 16th and 17th centuries in the Provençal Gothic style. Another attractive feature is the 11th-century watchtower. The castle keep houses the **Musée de la Castre**, home to the eclectic finds of 19th-century Dutch explorer Baron Lycklama.

The famed boulevard de la Croisette is lined with gardens and palm trees. One side is occupied by luxury boutiques and hotels such as the belle-époque Carlton, with twin cupolas modelled on the breasts of La Belle Otero, a famous member of the 19th-century *demi-monde*. Opposite are some of the finest sandy beaches on the coast. The glamour of the Croisette, once one of the world's grandest thoroughfares, seems to have faded amid the noise and fumes of summer.

Musée de la Castre

♿ 📍 Le Suquet 📞 04 89 82 26 26 🕐 Oct-Mar: 10am-5pm Tue-Sun (to 6pm Apr-Jun & Sep); Jul-Aug: 10am-7pm daily 🚫 1 Jan, 1 May, 1 & 11 Nov, 25 Dec

Summertime strolling along the boulevard de la Croisette on the Cannes seafront

→

 HIDDEN GEM
Stop and Smell the Jasmine

From August, the fields around Grasse bloom with white jasmine flowers, their sweet scent permeating the air. The Fête du Jasmin celebrates their arrival, with petal-covered floats and music.

28

Grasse

🅰 G6 🚉 Alpes-Maritimes 🚌
ℹ️ Pl de la Buanderie; www. paysdegrassetourisme.fr

Cradled by hills, Grasse is surrounded by fields of lavender, mimosa, jasmine and roses. It has been at the centre of the world's perfume industry since the 16th century, when Catherine de' Medici set the fashion for scented leather gloves. At that time, Grasse was also known as the main centre for leather tanning. The tanneries have gone, but the perfume houses founded in the 18th and 19th centuries are still in business, although Grasse perfumes are now made from imported flowers or chemicals. The Fragonard and Molinard companies have museums, but the best place to learn all about the history of perfume is at the fascinating **Musée Internationale de la Parfumerie**, which has a garden of fragrant plants.

Grasse was the birthplace of the artist Jean-Honoré Fragonard (1732–1806). The late 17th-century **Villa-Musée Fragonard** is decorated with murals by his son. Fragonard's only religious work is in the Cathédrale de Notre-Dame-du-Puy in the Old Town, which also has paintings by Rubens. Lined with Renaissance balconies, the streets around Place aux Aires and place du Cours typify Grasse's charm.

Musée International de la Parfumerie

♿🔵👜 🏠 2 blvd de Jeu du Ballon 🕐 10am–7pm daily 🚫 1 Jan, 1 May, 25 Dec 🌐 museesdegrasse.com

Villa-Musée Fragonard

♿👜 🏠 23 blvd Fragonard 🕐 10am–7pm daily 🌐 museesdegrasse.com

 Swimmers and small boats in the pretty little rocky harbour at Cap d'Antibes

29

St-Raphaël

🅰 G6 🚉 Var 🚆🚌
ℹ️ 99 quai Albert 1er; www.saint-raphael.com

In a truly delightful location, St-Raphaël is a charming, old-style Côte d'Azur resort with belle époque architecture and a palm-fronded promenade. Apart from its beaches, it has a picturesque marina, a casino, a Neo-Byzantine basilica, a 12th-century church and an archaeology museum with treasures from prehistoric underwater wrecks.

It was here that Napoléon Bonaparte landed in 1799 on his return from Egypt.

30

Antibes

🅰 G6 🚉 Alpes-Maritimes
🚆🚌 ℹ️ 42 avenue Robert Soleau; www. antibes juanlespins.com

The lively town of Antibes was founded by the Greeks as Antipolis and settled by the Romans. In the 14th century,

Perfumery equipment and bottles of fragrances (inset) in the museum at Grasse ↑

Savoy's possession of it was contended by France until it fell to them in 1481. Fort Carré was then built and the port, now the base of many luxury superyachts, was remodelled by military architect Vauban.

The Château Grimaldi, built during the 12th century, was a residence of the ruling family of Monaco. It now houses the **Musée Picasso**. In 1946 the artist used part of the castle as a studio and, in gratitude, donated 23 paintings and 44 drawings, including *The Goat*. Over the years, the collection has grown to encompass more than 150 works.

The pottery on show in the **Musée d'Archéologie** includes many objects salvaged from shipwrecks, spanning the period from the Middle Ages to the 18th century.

Musée Picasso

 🏛 Château Grimaldi 📞 04 92 90 54 28 🕐 10am–6pm Tue-Sun 🚫 1 Jan, 1 May, 1 Nov, 25 Dec

Musée d'Archéologie

🏛 Bastion St-André 📞 04 93 95 85 98 🕐 Nov-Jan: 10am-5pm Tue-Sat; Feb-Oct: 10am-6pm Tue-Sun 🚫 1 Jan, 1 May, 1 Nov, 25 Dec

31 Cap d'Antibes

🗺 G6 🏛 Alpes-Maritimes ✈ Nice 🚌 Antibes 🚍 Nice ℹ 42 avenue Robert Soleau, Antibes; www.antibes juanlespins.com

With its sumptuous villas, this rocky peninsula has been a symbol of luxury life on the Riviera since it was frequented by F Scott Fitzgerald and the rich American set in the 1920s. The magnate Frank Jay Gould invested in Juan-les-Pins, and it became the focus of the high life. Today, memories of the Jazz Age live on at the Jazz Festival, featuring international stars, here and in Antibes.

At the peninsula's highest point, the sailors' chapel of **La Garoupe** has votive offerings and a 14th-century icon. The **Jardin Botanique de la Villa Thuret** nearby was created in 1856 to acclimatize tropical plants. Much of the region's exotic flora originated here.

Jardin Botanique de la Villa Thuret

🏛 90 ch Raymond, Antibes Juan-les-Pins 📞 04 97 21 25 00 🕐 Hours vary, call ahead 🚫 Sat & Sun, pub hols

EAT

Angelina
The freshest fish, with glorious harbour views.

 🗺 F7 🏛 7 ave Victor Hugo, Cassis 🌐 restaurant-angelina-cassis.com

€€€

―――――――

Le Café des Epices
Imaginative yet unpretentious gourmet dishes in the city centre.

 🗺 G6 🏛 4 rue du Lacydon, Marseille 🌐 lecafedesepices-by-acdg.com

€€€

―――――――

Le Parvis
Farm-to-table Provençale soul food at its finest.

 🗺 F6 🏛 55 Cours Pourtoules, Orange 🌐 leparvisorange.com

€€€

← The River Loup plunging over the Cascade de Courmes into a pool in the Gorge du Loup

In 1951, the village authorities commissioned the artist to paint a mural on a wall in the deconsecrated chapel next to the castle, and his *War and Peace* (1952) is the principal exhibit of the **Musée National Picasso**: In the main square there is a larger-than-life bronze statue, *Man with a Sheep* (1943), which Picasso donated to the town.

Musée National Picasso
⊛ 🏛 🏠 Place de la Libération
🕐 Hours vary, check website
🅦 musees-nationaux-alpesmaritimes.fr

34
Biot

🔺 G6 🏠 Alpes-Maritimes
🚆🚌 *i* 4 Chemin Neuf;
www.biot-tourisme.com

A typical hill village, charming Biot has always attracted artists and artisans. The best known is Fernand Léger, the French painter and sculptor, who made his first ceramics here in 1949. Some of these and other works by him are in the **Musée National Fernand Léger**, housed in a striking modern building outside the town, which has the world's largest collection of his works. Biot is also famous for its

---

32
Gorges du Loup

🔺 G6 🏠 Alpes-Maritimes
🚇 Nice 🚌 Cagnes-sur-Mer
🚌 Grasse 🚌 Nice *i* 2 pl de la Libération, Tourrettes-sur-Loup; www.tourrettes surloup.com

Rising in the Pre-Alps behind Grasse, the River Loup cuts a deep path down to the sea, with dramatic cascades and spectacular views along the way. The superb countryside is crowned by the region's famous perched villages.

Gourdon owes much of its appeal to its ancient houses, which are grouped round a 12th-century château built on the site of an earlier Saracen stronghold, perched high on the cliffside. Its lovely terraced gardens were laid out by the famous French landscape architect André Le Nôtre (p183).

Tourrettes-sur-Loup, a fortified village, is famous for its fields of violets, grown for use in perfume and sweets. The **Bastide aux Violettes** museum considers the role of the flower in the village's history.

Bastide aux Violettes
⊛ 🏛 🏠 La Ferrage 🕐 Oct–Mar: 10am–5pm Mon–Fri; Apr–Sep: 10am–6pm Tue–Sat 🅦 tourrettessurloup.com

---

33
Vallauris

🔺 G6 🏠 Alpes-Maritimes
🚆🚌 *i* 67 avenue Georges Clémenceau; Golfe Juan Vieux Port; www.vallauris-golfe-juan.fr

Vallauris owes its fame to Pablo Picasso, who was instrumental in rescuing the town's pottery industry.

 HIDDEN GEM
Ceramics in Vallauris
Browse the stalls and studios of local potters in Provence's ceramics capital of Vallauris. One of the best is Les Petites Porcelaines (*www.les petitesporcelaines.com*) offering beautiful hand-crafted homewares.

Did You Know?

After its population was decimated by the Black Death, Biot became a refuge for thieves.

bubble-flecked glassware, in which bubbles of air are trapped within the glass. The craft of the glassblowers can be seen (and purchased) at **La Verrerie de Biot**.

Musée National Fernand Léger

🏛️ 📱 📷 🅿️ **316 ch du Val-de-Pome** ⏰ 10am–5pm Mon, Wed–Sun (to 6pm May–Oct) 📅 1 Jan, 1 May, 25 Dec 🌐 musees-nationaux-alpesmaritimes.fr

La Verrerie de Biot

📱 📷 🅿️ **5 chemin des Combes** ⏰ Hours vary, check website 🌐 verreriebiot.com

Cagnes-sur-Mer

🅰️ G6 🏠 Alpes-Maritimes 📱💻 📷 6 blvd Maréchal Juin; www.cagnes-tourisme.com

The picturesque town of Cagnes-sur-Mer is divided into three districts. The oldest, Haut-de-Cagnes, is also the most interesting part, with its steep streets, covered passageways and ancient buildings, including a number of arcaded houses designed in the Renaissance style. The other districts are Cagnes-Ville, the modern town where hotels and shops are concentrated, and Cros-de-Cagnes, a seaside fishing resort and yachting harbour with a pebble beach and seafront promenade where summer entertainment takes place.

The **Château Grimaldi** in Haut-de-Cagnes was built during the 14th century and reworked in the 17th by Henri Grimaldi. Behind the fortress walls is a shady courtyard. The surrounding marble columns conceal a museum devoted to the olive tree and a small collection of modern art of the Mediterranean. There is also a fine collection of paintings bequeathed by *chanteuse* Suzy Solidor. The 40 works, all portraits of her, are by artists such as Lolita Lempicka and Kees van Dongen. Up on the ceiling of the banqueting hall is a vast illusionistic fresco of the *Fall of Phaeton*, attributed to Carlone in the 1620s.

The last 12 years of Pierre-Auguste Renoir's life were spent in Cagnes, at the house that is now the **Musée Renoir**. The house has been kept almost exactly as it was when he died in 1919 and contains 14 of his paintings as well as 17 plaster sculptures. The views from the garden across the countryside down to the sea are stunning.

Château Grimaldi

🏛️ 🅿️ Place du Château 📞 04 92 02 47 35 ⏰ 10am–5pm Mon, Wed–Sun (to 6pm Apr–Sep) 📅 1 Jan, 25 Dec

Musée Renoir

🏛️ 🏞️ 📷 🅿️ 📞 04 93 20 61 07 ⏰ Hours vary, call ahead 📅 1 May, 1 Jan, 25 Dec

→ The hilly town of Cagnes-sur-Mer, topped by the 14th-century Château Grimaldi

EXPERIENCE Provence and the Côte d'Azur

36
Villefranche-sur-Mer

 G6 Alpes-Maritimes Jardin François Binon; www.tourisme-villefranche-sur-mer.com

One of the most perfectly situated towns on the coast, Villefranche lies at the foot of a group of hills forming a natural sheltered amphitheatre. The town overlooks a beautiful natural harbour, which is deep enough to be a naval port of call.

The bright and animated waterfront is lined by Italianate façades, with cafés and bars that are perfect places to sit and watch the fishermen. Here, too, is the **Chapelle de St-Pierre**, which, after years of service storing fishing nets, was restored in 1957 and decorated by Jean Cocteau. His frescoes here depict non-religious images and the life of St Peter.

The 16th-century Citadelle St-Elme is also worth a visit. It incorporates three museums, a congress room, an exhibition room and a garden.

Behind the harbour, the streets are narrow, winding and frequently stepped, and walking through them you will be treated to the odd glimpse of the harbour. The vaulted 14th-century rue Obscure has always provided shelter from bombardment, right up to World War II.

Chapelle de St-Pierre

1 ave Sadi Carnot 04 93 76 90 70 9:30am–6pm Wed–Sun mid-Nov–mid-Dec, 25 Dec

---

37
Vence

G6 Alpes-Maritimes Place du Grand Jardin; www.vence-tourisme.fr

The gentle climate enjoyed by this historic market town has always been its main attraction and today it is surrounded by holiday villas. It was an important religious centre during the Middle Ages. The Cathédral was restored by the most famous of Vence's bishops, Antoine Godeau. A 5th-century Roman sarcophagus serves as its altar and there are Carolingian wall carvings. Note, too, the fine 15th-century carved choir stalls and Godeau's tomb.

Within the ramparts of the Old Town, which retains its 13th- to 14th-century town gates, is place du Peyra, once a Roman forum. Its fountain, built in 1822, still provides fresh water.

Found on the edge of town, and worth seeking out, the **Chapelle du Rosaire** was built between 1947 and 1951. It was decorated by Henri Matisse, in gratitude to the nuns who nursed him during an illness. On its white walls, biblical scenes are reduced to simple black lines tinted by splashes of coloured light filtering through the blue and yellow stained-glass windows.

Chapelle du Rosaire

466 ave Henri Matisse Hours vary, check website chapelle matisse.com

> **Within the ramparts of the Old Town, which still retains its 13th- to 14th-century town gates, is place du Peyra, once a Roman forum.**

38
Eze

 G6 Alpes-Maritimes Place Général de Gaulle; www.eze-tourisme.com

For many, Eze is the ultimate perched village, balancing on a rocky pinnacle high above the Mediterranean Sea. Every summer, thousands of visitors stream through the village's 14th-century fortified gate. The flower-decked buildings are almost all shops, galleries and craft workshops. At the top of the village, the château is surrounded by the lush tropical plants that thrive in the **Jardin Exotique**, which is arranged down the cliffside.

Further along the Upper Corniche is the Roman Alpine **Trophée d'Auguste à La Turbie**. This enormous structure, dating from 6 BC, dominates the surrounding village, and offers fine views towards Monaco and Italy.

Jardin Exotique

Rue du Château Hours vary, check website jardinexotique-eze.fr

Trophée d'Auguste à La Turbie

Avenue Albert 1er Hours vary, check website trophee-auguste.fr

39
Roquebrune-Cap-Martin

G6 Alpes-Maritimes Nice 218 avenue Aristide Briand; www.rcm-tourisme.com

Medieval Roquebrune overlooks the wooded cape where villas of the rich and famous still stand, once occupied by the likes of Coco Chanel and Empress Eugenie. The cape has not always been kind. The poet W B Yeats died here in 1939 and renowned French architect Le Corbusier was drowned off the coast in 1965.

In 1467 townsfolk believed that by performing scenes from the Passion they would escape the ravages of plague, and every August this ancient tradition is continued.

40
St-Jean- Cap-Ferrat

G6 Alpes-Maritimes Nice Nice Beaulieu-sur-Mer 5/59 av Denis Semeria; www.saint jeancapferrat-tourisme.fr

Some of the most sumptuous villas on the Riviera are on this peninsula. From 1926 until his death, the best-known was Somerset Maugham's Villa Mauresque, where he hosted celebrities like Noël Coward.

Possibly the best villa is open to the public. The **Villa Ephrussi de Rothschild** is a terracotta and marble mansion set in themed gardens on the crest of the cape. It once

 ←

Villefranche-sur-Mer, curving around the deep, clear waters of its bay

↑ The golden interior of the Villa Ephrussi de Rothschild

belonged to the Baroness Ephrussi de Rothschild, and is furnished as she left it, with her collections of priceless porcelain, items previously owned by Marie Antoinette and a unique set of drawings by Fragonard.

Beaulieu-sur-Mer lies where the cape joins the mainland. With an exceptionally mild climate and very fine hotels, it is the site of another unique house, the extraordinary **Villa Grecque Kérylos**. Built from 1902 to 1908 for archaeologist Theodore Reinach in imitation of an ancient Greek residence, it holds reproduction mosaics, frescoes and furniture.

Villa Ephrussi de Rothschild

1 av Ephrussi de Rothschild, Cap Ferrat Feb-Oct: 10am-6pm daily (to 7pm Jul & Aug); Nov-Feb: 2-6pm Mon-Fri, 10am-6pm Sat, Sun & school hols) villa-ephrussi.com

Villa Grecque Kérylos

Imp Gustave Eiffel, Beaulieu Jan-Apr & Sep-Dec: 10am-5pm daily; May-Aug: 10am- 7pm daily 1 Jan, 1 May, 1 & 11 Nov, 25 Dec villakerylos.fr

 41

Menton

 G6 Alpes-Maritimes
8 avenue Boyer;
www.tourisme-menton.fr

Menton's beaches, with the Alps and *belle époque* villas of the Old Town as a backdrop, would be enough to lure most visitors. Tropical plants thrive in the town's glorious climate, mild even in February for the lemon festival.

The Basilica St-Michel is a superb example of Baroque architecture. The **Salle des Mariages** in the Hôtel de Ville was decorated in 1957 by Jean Cocteau. Housed in a striking building, the **Musée Jean Cocteau Collection Séverin Wunderman** contains art and stage designs by the famed artist. In the Palais Carnolès the **Musée des Beaux-Arts** has works from the Middle Ages to the 20th century.

Salle des Mariages

Hôtel de Ville, place Ardoino 04 92 10 50 00
Hours vary, call ahead

Musée Jean Cocteau Collection Séverin Wunderman

2 quai de Monléon
Hours vary, check website
museecocteaumenton.fr

Musée des Beaux-Arts

Palais Carnolès, 3 av de la Madone 04 93 35 49 71
Hours vary, call ahead

42

Alpes-Maritimes

G6 Alpes-Maritimes
Nice Peille 15 rue Centrale, Peille; www.peille.fr

In the hinterland of the Côte d'Azur, it is still possible to find quiet, unspoiled villages off the tourist track, such as the tiny twin villages of Peille and Peillon. Changed little since the Middle Ages and perched on outcrops over the Paillon river, their streets contain a mass of steps and arches. Peille even still has its own dialect. The countryside is also unspoiled, with craggy gorges, tumbling rivers and windswept plateaux. Of note are the ancient rock carvings of the Vallée des Merveilles and rare wildlife in the Parc National du Mercantour.

43

Marseille

G6 Bouches-du-Rhône 11 La Canebière; www.marseille-tourisme.com

A Greek settlement, founded in the 7th century BC, then called Massilia, Marseille

↑ The mosaic-paved parvis in front of the Basilica-St-Michel in Menton

was seized by the Romans in 49 BC. It became the "Gateway to the West" for most Oriental trade. France's largest port and lively second-largest city has close links with the Middle East and North Africa. It was a European Capital of Culture in 2013, and has renovated its old harbour and port terminal.

Marseille has excellent museums, including several in the old harbour area. The Musée Cantini, to the south, is one of the best and houses the 20th-century art collection of sculptor Jules Cantini.

The **Musée des Beaux-Arts** is in the handsome 19th-century Palais Longchamp. Works include Michel Serre's graphic views of Marseille's plague of 1721, Pierre Puget's town plans for the city and murals depicting it in Greek and Roman times.

The **Château d'If** (Castle of Yew) stands on a tiny island 2 km (1 mile) to the southwest

of the port. A formidable fortress, constructed in 1529 to house artillery, it later became a prison, made famous by Alexandre Dumas's novel *The Count of Monte Cristo*.

Completed in 1864, the Neo-Byzantine Basilique de Notre-Dame-de-la-Garde dominates the city, its 46-m- (151-ft-) high belfry capped by a huge gilded statue of the Virgin. Abbaye de St-Victor was rebuilt in the 11th century and has an intriguing crypt, with an original catacomb chapel and pagan and Christian tombs. Annually, on 2 February, this becomes a place of pilgrimage celebrating the legendary arrival of St Mary Magdalene, Lazarus and St Martha nearly 2,000 years ago.

In 1640, construction of a shelter "for the poor and beggars" of Marseille was begun by royal decree. A hundred years later, Pierre Puget's **La Vieille Charité** hospital and church opened. The restored building houses the Musée d'Archéologie Méditerranéenne; the Musée des Arts Africains, Océaniens et Amérindiens (MAAOA) is on the second floor.

Linking Marseille's harbour, a former port terminal and the 17th-century Fort St-Jean, the fascinating **Musée des Civilisations de l'Europe et de la Méditerranée (MuCEM)** focuses on the enthralling history of civilization in Europe, specifically the Mediterranean region with over 500,000 ethnographical items, plus art and books.

300

The average number of days of sunshine that Marseille gets per year.

Musée des Beaux-Arts

◈ 🏛 Palais Longchamp, pl Aile Gauche (left wing) 📞 04 91 14 59 30 🕒 9:30am-6:30pm Tue-Sun 🚫 1 Jan, 1 May, 1 & 11 Nov, 25 & 26 Dec

Château d'If

◈ 🌳 🍽 🛍 🏛 Vieux Port 🕒 Jan-Mar & Oct-Dec: 10am-5pm Tue-Sun; Apr-Sep: 10am-6pm daily 🌐 chateau-if.fr

La Vieille Charité

◈ 🍽 🏛 2 rue de la Charité 🕒 Hours vary, check website 🌐 vieille-charite-marseille.com

Musée des Civilisations de l'Europe et de la Méditerranée (MuCEM)

◈ 🍽 🛍 🏛 1 esplanade de J4, 201 quai du Port (VJ4 and Fort Saint-Jean) 🕒 Hours vary, check website 🌐 mucem.org

JEAN COCTEAU

Born near Paris in 1889, Cocteau spent much of his very public life around the Côte d'Azur. A man of powerful intellect and great *élan*, he became a member of the Académie Française in 1955. Among other talents, Cocteau was a dramatist (*La Machine Infernale*, 1934); the writer of *Les Enfants Terribles* (1929); and a surrealist film director. *Orphée* (1950) was partly shot against the barren landscape at Les Baux (*p517*). He died before his museum opened in 1967.

A DRIVING TOUR
THE ROUTE DES CRÊTES

Length 120 km (75 miles) **Stopping-off points**
La Palud-sur-Verdon has several cafés and Moustiers-Ste-Marie is a good place to stop for lunch.

A driving tour of the Gorges du Verdon takes at least a day, and this route, made up of two loops, encompasses its most striking features. At its east and west points are the towns of Castellane and Moustiers-Ste-Marie. Parts of the tour are very mountainous, so drivers must be aware of hairpin bends and narrow roads with sheer drops. Weather conditions can also be hazardous and roads can be icy until late spring.

Locator Map
For more detail see p492

Set on craggy heights, **Moustiers-Ste-Marie** is famed for its faïence.

Organized walking trips start at the village of **La Palud-sur-Verdon**.

A beautifully restored 17th-century château crowns the village of **Aiguires**, with fine views down to the Lac de Sainte-Croix.

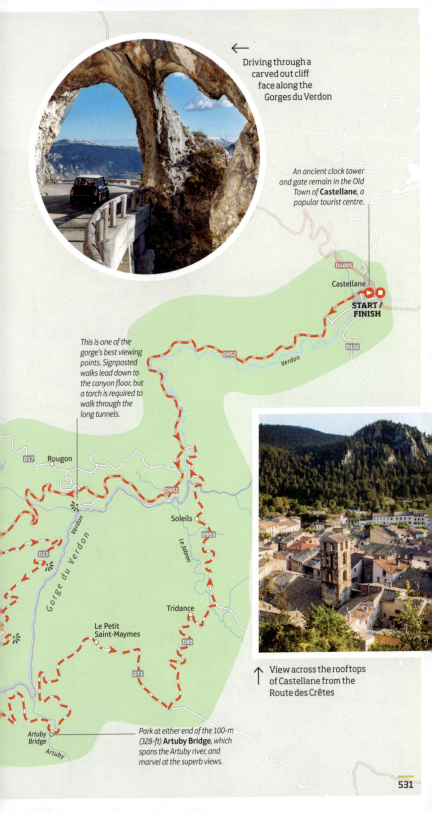

Driving through a carved out cliff face along the Gorges du Verdon

An ancient clock tower and gate remain in the Old Town of **Castellane**, a popular tourist centre.

This is one of the gorge's best viewing points. Signposted walks lead down to the canyon floor, but a torch is required to walk through the long tunnels.

D4085

Castellane

START / FINISH

D102

D952

Verdon

D17

Rougon

D952

Gorge du Verdon

Verdon

Soleils

D955

Le Jabron

D23

Tridance

D90

Le Petit Saint-Maymes

D71

Artuby Bridge

Artuby

View across the rooftops of Castellane from the Route des Crêtes

Park at either end of the 100-m (328-ft) **Artuby Bridge**, which spans the Artuby river, and marvel at the superb views.

CORSICA

Evidence shows that the craggy, wild shores and limestone cliffs of Corsica have sheltered seafaring inhabitants since 6570 BC. The Phocaeans wrote of the mountainous island in about 560 BC, when they founded the town of Alalia, and in the 8th century BC, Bonifacio was immortalized in Homer's *Odyssey*. Invasions between 450 and 1050 AD forced the island's inhabitants to abandon their coastal settlements, including Aléria and Calvi, and flee inland. Tenuous stability came with Pisan colonizers, who spent the next 200 years crafting beautifully proportioned Romanesque churches in towns such as St-Florent. The Corsican people enjoyed 14 years of independence under elected president Pasquale Paoli, who founded a university in Corte and printing press, before the island was sold in 1769 to Louis XV by the Genoese for 40 million francs. The ensuing discontent may have inspired Ajaccio-born Napoléon Bonaparte to declare himself Emperor of France in 1804, but his government neglected his homeland. During the 19th century, poverty on the island sent Corsicans in their thousands into the French colonies. Known as USS Corsica during World War II, thanks to the number of American military bases, Corsica has since developed a thriving tourism industry, drawing visitors and immigrants to its shores.

CORSICA

Ligurian Sea

Desert des Agriates

D81

Lozari

L'ILLE ROUSSE **14**

Belgodère

CALVI **13**

Muro

Calvi-Sainte-Catherine Airport

Calenzana

Balagne

Asco   D147   Ponte-Leccia

D81

Tartagine

THE NIOLO   Francardo

N193

Monte Cinto
2,706m (8,877 ft)   **7**

Girolata

Parc   Calacuccia

Golo

CORTE

GOLFE DE PORTO **5**

Porto

Naturel   D84

Gorges de la Restonica   **8**

Piana   D84   Evisa

Monte Rotondo
2,622m
(8,602 ft)

Regional

Venaco

Soccia

Vivario

D81   Vico

D70   CARGÈSE **16**

Golfe de Sagone

Vizzavona

de

Bocognano

Corse

Sari-d'Orcino

N193

Bastelica

AJACCIO **9**

Cauro

Gravona   D27

D69

Ajaccio Napoleon
Bonaparte Airport

Zicavo

Golfe d'Ajaccio

Santa-Maria-Siché

M e d i t e r r a n e a n

N196

D89   Petreto-Bicchisano

S e a

D155

Capo di Muro

FILITOSA **10**   Casalabriva

Zonza

Golfe de Valinco   Olmeto

Propriano

Sante-Lucie-de-Tallano

D368

SARTÈNE **11**

N196   *Ortolo*

Figari-Sud Corse
Airport   D859

Pianotolli-Caldarello   Figari

N198

BONIFACIO   **1**

CORSICA

Must See
1 Bonifacio

Experience More
2 Cap Corse
3 St-Florent
4 Bastia
5 Golfe de Porto
6 The Castagniccia
7 The Niolo (Niolu)
8 Corte
9 Ajaccio
10 Filitosa
11 Sartène
12 Côte Orientale
13 Calvi
14 L'Île Rousse
15 Lavezzi Islands
16 Cargèse
17 Porto-Vecchio
18 Plage de Palombaggia

0 kilometres 15
0 miles 15

N

7 DAYS
in Corsica

Day 1

Start your day in Ajaccio's *(p546)* palm-shaded main square, from where you can explore the town's historic core. Highlights include Maison Bonaparte, the birthplace of Napoléon, Corsica's most famous son. In the afternoon, ease your way into Corsican time with a couple of hours lolling on the beach. The aptly-named plage de Mare e Sole ("beach of sea and sun") is exactly what you're looking for. At sunset, go for dinner in the lesser-known Quartier des Étrangers.

Day 2

Head north to the hilltop town of Cargèse *(p549)*, pulling in at Les Calanches: these soaring, salmon-pink cliffs are the island's most photogenic pitstop. In Cargèse itself, its fresh seafood and fabulous views for lunch at A Volta *(www.a-volta.com)*. In the afternoon, take half a day's boat trip out to snorkel around the rocky shore of the mesmerizing Scandola Nature Reserve. Then, as evening falls, make for Calvi *(p548)*, stopping in at Piana – which locals maintain is France's prettiest village – for dinner at La Voûte *(place de la Fontaine)*. At Calvi, check into 18th-century La Signoria *(www.hotel-la-signoria.com)*.

Day 3

Go to the hotel's private beach for a paddle before breakfast, then spend a couple of hours exploring the nooks and crannies of Calvi's citadel – Horatio Nelson lost his right eye trying to capture this fortress. Later, tour the wine estates and vineyards around neighbouring villages Sant'Antonino and Montemaggiore. As evening descends, step onto the decked terrace at Octopussy *(www.plage-octopussy.com)* to enjoy French classics, given a Corsican twist, and panoramic views of Calvi's pretty port.

Day 4

The northernmost tip of Corsica is the off-grid option for those serious about their peace and quiet. Start on the beach at Barcaggio, where you'll have little more than cattle for company. The interior hides a number of tumbledown villages

1 The narrow streets of Calvi.
2 A beach on Corsica's east coast.
3 A bustling market stall in Ajaccio.
4 The citadel and town of Corte.
5 Cows basking on a beach in northern Corsica.

that haven't had a dust down in decades. Rogliano is ideal for getting your bearings, with stunning, wide-angle views of the coast. Finish your day with sunset cocktails and seafood at Le Pirate (p547) in the village of Erbalunga, poised on a natural balcony between sea and mountain on the Cap Corse (p542). Stay the night at the impeccable Hôtel Demeure Castel Brando (p543).

Day 5

Defiantly Corsican – rather than French – Bastia (p543) has plenty of spirit. To see a snapshot of this northern stronghold at its liveliest, check out the Terra Vecchia weekend market, which features stalls groaning with local cheese, wine and oils. As the day wears on and the crowds disperse, make a beeline for the Musée de Bastia, which is located inside the city's stark Terra Nova citadel – it's an excellent spot for a history lesson. Later, saunter along the old harbour to admire the pretty quayside buildings and lighthouses. As the sun starts to set, grab a table at one of the waterside restaurants or bars.

Day 6

Rise early and make a beeline for Corte; for a short time during the mid 18th-century, this mountainous town was the capital of Corsica. Take a stroll to the National Palace, then visit the citadel, perched dramatically atop a rocky outcrop. Next, drive down to Etang de Diane (Diane Pond), where tiny islands made of discarded oyster shells belie the long-time industry of the area. Then it's over to Porto-Vecchio to indulge in a dinner of delectable Italian flavours at Michelin-starred Le Casadelmar (p547).

Day 7

Corsica's southeast coast is all about the beach; build sandcastles and splash about in the shallows at Palombaggia, a gorgeous ellipsis of sea and sand. From here, drive west to Bonifacio (p540), for an afternoon exploring the limestone citadel and its jumbled array of fortress-houses and churches. Swing northwards along the coast to spend your final night in one of the rustic shepards' huts lining Domaine de Murtoli (p543), a beautiful private beach overlooking the Strait of Bonifacio.

Epic Hiking

In the hidden heights of Corsica's interior lies one of the world's most testing long-distance mountain trails: the GR20. This 180-km (112-mile) hike follows the Continental Divide from Calenzana to Conca, taking in valleys, glacial lakes and pine forests, as well as knee-trembling summits and ravines *(p545)*. Self-sufficient trekkers bivouac their way along the track every year, but the southern end around L'Alta Rocca has myriad trails offering day walks of varying length and for all abilities.

→

Hiking on the GR20 trail, known locally as Fra Li Monti ("Between the Mountains")

CORSICA FOR
THE GREAT OUTDOORS

The first surprise for new visitors to Corsica is its diverse landscape. An awesome backdrop of needle-like peaks, cleft valleys and almost-Alpine plateaus makes it a wonderland for hikers, bikers, climbers and viewpoint chasers. In the spaces between are quiet villages and gorgeous beaches.

→

Inviting beaches and turquoise waters at Palombaggia

Breathtaking Beaches

Many of Corsica's loveliest coves hide behind the island's rocky red *calanques*, the sharply defined west coast valleys that run down to the sea. The easiest way to access them is to go by kayak or boat, hopping from bay to bay. Discover golden sands around Porticcio, excellent for snorkelling in crystalline waters and exploring rock pools. On the east coast, head to the St-Tropez-esque resort of Porto-Vecchio *(p549)*, where the favourite beaches for sun-worshippers include Palombaggia and Tamaricciu.

> ### 💬 INSIDER TIP
> **Camping on Corsica**
>
> Temperatures can hit 40°C (104°F) in summer, so choose a shaded spot no matter how tempting the alternative. On the GR20 hike, camping is only permitted in designated areas, and not on the trail itself.

Rock Climbing in Corsica

With favourable conditions year-round, bouldering, canyoning and other cliff sports are all the rage. The reason? There are more 2,500-m (6,560-ft) peaks here than on any other Mediterranean island, plus countless granite towers and crags to shimmy up and abseil down. The Via Ferrata route outside Porto-Vecchio yields panoramic views across the Gulf of Porto-Vecchio and the lake of Ospedale, while the Col de Bavella pass is where you'll find the trickiest routes.

→ Not for the novice – climbing thrills at Col de Bavella

CORSICAN FAUNA

Corsican deer
The emblem of the island, reintroduced with great success.

Wild Boar
Snuffly creatures that populate the island's forests and thickets.

Greater Noctule
Europe's largest and rarest bat.

Hermann Tortoise
This land tortoise has almost disappeared from the rest of France.

Corsican Nuthatch
A blue-grey-winged bird, always seen near the Corsican pine.

↑ Getting back to nature in the Parc Naturel

Parc Naturel Régional de Corse

When it comes to outdoor thrills, this vast park has little competition. Dive into Corsica's interior to see forested gorges with hidden pools and waterfalls, then take to the trees to zipline through the canopy. To see nesting ospreys in the protected coastal reserve, you'll need to take a boat trip.

❶ BONIFACIO

⛰ A7 🏠 Corse-du-Sud 🚌🚃 ℹ 2 rue Fred Scamaroni; bonifacio.fr

Known as the "Citadel of Cliffs", Bonifacio is dramatically perched atop a limestone and granite cliff at the end of a peninsula. The southernmost town in Corsica, this seculded settlement is home to a charming harbour and an ancient citadel, and is surrounded by an array of beautifully secluded beaches.

Bonifacio's handsome harbour at the foot of the cliffs is the focus of local life: cafés, restaurants and boutiques abound and boats depart regularly for neighbouring Sardinia and the uninhabited Lavezzi islands. From here, steps lead up to Bonifacio's fortified Old Town. The citadel is a maze of sardine-tight alleyways, Renaissance churches and red-roofed, slender houses. Built by the conquering Genoese at the end of the 12th century, it has long been the town's main defensive post, and from 1963 to 1983 was the headquarters of the French Foreign Legion. From the citadel a narrow stone staircase winds down towards the matchbox-sized, stony Sutta Rocca Beach, overlooking the Grain de Sable. South of here, cut into the cliffs, is the King of Aragon's Stairway, 187 very steep steps leading down to the sea.

It's worth exploring the rest of the promontory, including the Capo Pertusato lighthouse, dating from 1838; this improbable building affords spectacular views across the Strait of Bonifacio and the Lavezzi islands. At the tip of the promontory stand three old windmills and the ruins of a Franciscan monastery.

The town of Bonifacio, spectacularly located atop eroded limestone cliffs ↑

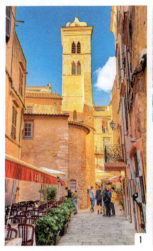

1 Bonifacio's fortified, medieval Old Town is a delight to wander.

2 Overlooked by the Citadel, the town's harbour is peppered with yachts and lined with buzzing cafés and restaurants.

3 Some of the town's shops are built into the cliff's walls.

GREAT VIEW
On a Cliff's Edge

Protruding like a giant thumb on the south-eastern coast, the Grain de Sable is a huge plug of rock set against a back-drop of white limestone cliffs. From here, on a clear day, you can see Sardinia in the distance.

→ The picturesque fishing village of Erbalunga on the eastern coast of Cap Corse

EXPERIENCE MORE

 ②

Cap Corse

🅰 A6 🏠 Haute-Corse
✈ Bastia 🚢 Bastia 🚌 Bastia
ℹ Port de Plaisance, Macinaggio; Port Toga, Pietrabugno; www.macinaggio
rogliano-capcorse.fr

Cap Corse is the northern tip of Corsica, 40 km (25 miles) in length but seldom more than 12 km (7 miles) wide, pointing like an accusatory finger towards Genoa.

There are two roads out of Bastia to the cape: the D81 leading west across the mountains and joining up with the D80 after the charming wine village of Patrimonio; and the D80 travelling north along the eastern shore to Erbalunga and Macinaggio. The road is narrow and twisting, giving a taste of what awaits in the rest of Corsica.

From the pretty coastal village of Lavasina, the D54 leads left off the D80 to Pozzo; from here it is a 5-hour round trip on foot to the 1,307-m- (4,288-ft-) summit of Monte Stello, the cape's highest peak. The 360-degree view from the top takes in St-Florent to the west, the massif of central Corsica to the south and the Italian island of Elba to the east.

Further up the coast, the restored Tour de Losse is one of a significant number of 16th-century Genoese towers along the coast – part of an elaborate defence system that enabled all Corsican towns to be warned within two hours of impending barbarian raids.

The 18th-century fishing port of Centuri, near the tip of the peninsula on the west coast, is an ideal spot to stop for a delicious seafood feast. Pino, a pretty village straggling down the mountainside further to the south, has no hotel, only a little church dedicated to the Virgin, which is full of model ships placed there by mariners who were grateful for her protection.

Did You Know?

Cap Corse was first named by Greco-Roman geographer and astronomer Ptolemy.

On the way south along the vertiginous lower corniche, be sure to turn left up the hill to Canari, which is one of the larger villages in this area. It has a jewel of a 12th-century Pisan church, Santa Maria Assunta, a magnificent view across the sea and a convivial hotel-restaurant. All of the byroads in this thickly wooded area seem to lead somewhere interesting. There are dozens of picturesque hamlets in the vicinity, and it also should be borne in mind that from this point onwards the landscape becomes steadily less attractive, as the road winds on past the old asbestos workings and beaches of black sand below the village of Nonza.

---

③

St-Florent

🅰 A6 🏠 Haute-Corse 🚌
ℹ Bâtiment Administratif, BP 53; www.corsica-saintflorent.com

St-Florent is almost a Corsican St-Tropez – chic, affluent and packed with yachts. Its citadel, which mounts photography exhibitions, dates from 1439, and is a splendid example of Genoese military architecture. The town itself is a pleasant place for a stroll, but its main attraction, the 12th-century Pisan Cathédrale de Santa Maria Assunta, lies just inland en route to Poggio-d'Oletta.

A leisurely four-hour driving circuit of the Nebbio region, which extends in an amphitheatre shape around the town of St-Florent, might take in the following: Santo-Pietro-di-Tenda; Murato, famous for its magnificent 12th-century Église de San Michele de Murato, a Pisan Romanesque construction built of white and green stone. Drive on, via the San Stefano pass, with the sea on either side, to Oletta, which produces a blue cheese made from sheep's milk. Then comes the Teghime pass and, finally, the wine village of Patrimonio, where there is a strange, big-eared menhir dating from 900–800 BC.

Along the coast to the west of St-Florent lies the barren, uninhabited Désert des Agriates.

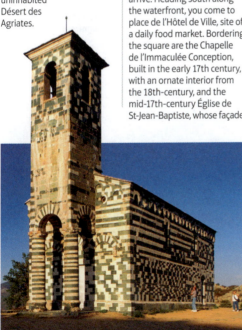

↑ The decorative exterior of Eglise de San Michele de Murato in St-Florent

If you can face the 10-km (6-mile) haul to the sea – on foot, by bike or by motorbike – the Saleccia beach is the most beautiful on the island.

Bastia

🄰A6 🄷Haute-Corse
�✈🚌🚆 🛈North end of place St-Nicolas; www.bastia-tourisme.com

A bustling, thriving port and the administrative capital of Upper Corsica, Bastia is utterly different in character from its more sedate west coast rival, Ajaccio. The Genoese citadel and colourful 19th-century Italianate buildings around the old port are quintessentially Mediterranean and look much the same as they did half a century ago.

The centre of Bastia's life is **place St-Nicolas**, facing the wharf where the ferries from mainland France and Italy arrive. Heading south along the waterfront, you come to place de l'Hôtel de Ville, site of a daily food market. Bordering the square are the Chapelle de l'Immaculée Conception, built in the early 17th century, with an ornate interior from the 18th-century, and the mid-17th-century Église de St-Jean-Baptiste, whose façade

dominates the Vieux Port. From here it is a short walk up to the 16th-century citadel housing the **Musée de Bastia**, which recounts the history of the town from medieval days.

Musée de Bastia
♿ 🄿Place du Dujon
🕙May-Sep: 10am-6:30pm Tue-Sun; Jul & Aug: 10am-6:30pm daily; Oct-Apr: 9am-12pm & 2pm-5pm Tue-Sat
🆆musee-bastia.com

STAY

Hôtel des Etrangers
A friendly family-run spot near the port for all budgets.

🄰A7 🄿Av Sylvère Bohn, Bonifacio 🆆hoteldesetrangers.fr

Hôtel Demeure Castel Brando
A fine old mansion with a lovely garden.

🄰A6 🄿Erbalunga, Brando 🆆castelbrando.com

Château Hôtel La Signoria
A jaw-dropping 18th-century manor with private beach club.

🄰A7 🄿Route de la Forêt de Bonifato, Calvi 🆆hotel-la-signoria.com

€€€

Domaine de Murtoli
Stunning villas and stone houses, within a protected wilderness.

🄰A7 🄿Av Sylvère Bohn, Bonifacio 🆆hoteldesetrangers.fr

450

The number of different types of seaweed found in the Réserve Naturelle de Scandola.

 5

Golfe de Porto

▲A6 🏠Corse-du-Sud
✈🚌🚢Ajaccio 🚌Porto
ℹ️Quartier la Marine;
www.porto-tourisme.com

Porto is sited at the head of the Golfe de Porto, one of the most beautiful bays in the Mediterranean, which for the sake of its fauna and flora has been designated a UNESCO World Heritage Site. The town has a Genoese watchtower – the perfect spot for admiring the sunset – and regular boat excursions (from April to October) to the Calanche, Scandola and Girolata.

The Calanche begin 8 km (5 miles) out of Porto, on the road to Piana. These 300-m (1,000-ft) red-granite cliffs plunge sheer to the sea, and are quite simply breathtaking. They are accessible by boat or on foot: well-defined trails start from the Tête du Chien

and the Pont de Mezanu, and boat tickets are available at Porto's Le Cyrnée restaurant and various other places in the marina.

East of Porto, the Gorges de la Spelunca are accessed by a mule route punctuated by Genoese bridges. Just to the south of Porto, along a spectacular corniche drive that passes beneath granite arches, lies the pretty village of Piana, a good base for the whole area, with information on recommended walks. One worthwhile destination is the cove at Ficajola, just below Piana, a truly delightful beach.

The mountain road from Porto to Calvi offers no more than a taste of this grandiose corner of Corsica – take to the sea to view it properly (ferries from Porto and Galéria). The tiny hamlet of Girolata, north of Porto, can be reached only by sea or on foot via a mule track (four hours round trip) from a clearly marked point 23 km (14 miles) north of Porto on the D81.

At the mouth of the Golfe de Girolata, the Réserve Naturelle de Scandola, instituted in 1975, is France's first land and sea reserve, covering

 PICTURE PERFECT
Golfe de Porto

Spectacular red cliffs, a skirt of eucalyptus, and sand beaches on either side of a watchtower define this idyllic bay. Hike the trails to see it from above, or take to the water in a yacht for a wind-in-your-hair-type experience.

over 10 sq km (4 sq miles) of sea, and a similar area of cliffs, caves and maquis. Marine life is abundant within these clear, protected waters; the birds include ospreys, puffins and falcons.

_____

6

The Castagniccia

▲A6 🏠Haute-Corse
✈Bastia 🚌Corte, Ponte Leccia 🚌Piedicroce, La Porta, Valle-d'Alesani
ℹ️Maison des Enterprises, Folelli, Piedicroce; www.castagniccia.fr

To the east of Corte is the hilly, chestnut-covered region of

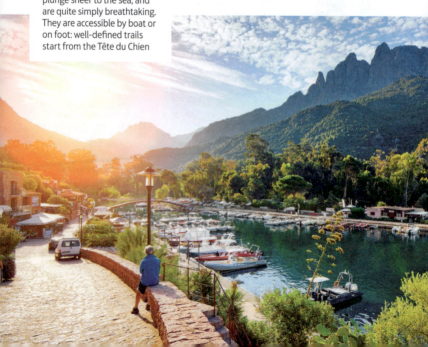

↑ Corte's medieval citadel, housing a museum, perched on a vertigo-inducing rocky summit

Castagniccia (literally "small chestnut grove"), which most Corsicans agree is the very heart and kernel of the island. It was here that independence leader Pasquale Paoli was born in 1725, and where the revolts against Genoa and then France began in earnest in 1729. Alas, many of the villages in this beautiful, remote area are all but empty, their inhabitants having joined the 800,000 or so Corsicans (almost three times the present population) who live and work in mainland France or Italy. It seems hard to believe that during the 17th century, when the great chestnut forests introduced here by the Genoese were at the height of their production, this was the most prosperous and populated region in Corsica.

The D71 from Ponte Leccia (north of Corte) to the east winds through Castagniccia, and to see the region at leisure will take the best part of a week. Stock up on essentials first, as there is little in the way of supplies en route.

---

⑦

The Niolo (Niolu)

 A6 ⬛ Haute-Corse ▦ Corte ⬛ Rte de Cuccia, Calacuccia; www.office-tourisme-niolu.com

The Niolo extends west from Corte to the Vergio pass and the upper Golo basin, and to the east as far as the Scala di Santa Regina. Corsica's highest mountain, the 2,706-m (8,878-ft) Monte Cinto is here, and its biggest river, the Golo.

← Boats tied up in lovely Porto village, at the head of the stunning Golfe de Porto

The Niolo is Corsica's only region to still farm livestock for its economic mainstay.

The main town, Calacuccia, is suitable for excursions to Monte Cinto. The nearby former ski resort of Haut Asco is best reached by the D147 from Asco, but enthusiasts can walk from Calacuccia (8–9 hours). To the south is the forest of Valdu Niello.

---

⑧

Corte

 A6 ⬛ Haute-Corse ▦ ▦ ⬛ La Citadelle; www.corte-tourisme.com

In the geographical centre of Corsica, Corte was the chosen capital of the independence leader Pasquale Paoli from 1755 to 1769, and today is the seat of the island's university. In the Old Town is the 15th-century citadel, housing the **Musée de la Corse** relating traditional Corsican life and anthropology.

Corte, exactly halfway along the GR20, the legendary 220-km (137-mile) trail from Calenzana to Conca, is the best base for the nearby mountains. Don't miss the Gorges de la Restonica, 12 km (7 miles) out of town via the D623. Above these beautiful gorges keen walkers can follow a well-marked climb to snow-fed Lac de Melo (60–90 minutes); or Lac de Capitello 30 minutes further, where snow can still remain in early June.

South of Corte, the Forêt de Vizzavona is crisscrossed by tumbling, trout-filled streams and pleasant walking trails (notably the GR20). A fine refuge from summer heat, it is also a good excuse to take the small-gauge train up from Ajaccio or Bastia.

Musée de la Corse
⊘ ⊘ ⬛ La Citadelle ⬛ Hours vary, check website ⬛ Public holidays ⬛ musee-corse.com

↑ Marble statue of a toga- and laurel-wreath-clad Napoléon Bonaparte, on place Foch in Ajaccio

A Cupulatta park, with over 170 species of tortoises and turtles (open April to October).

Musée National de la Maison Bonaparte
  Rue St-Charles
🕐 Hours vary, check website
🌐 musees-nationaux-malmaison.fr

Musée des Beaux-Arts
🕐 50–52 rue Cardinal Fesch 🕐 Hours vary, check website 🌐 musee-fesch.com.

⑩

Filitosa
A7 Station Préhistorique de Filitosa, Sollacaro, Corse-du-Sud 🕐 Apr–Oct: 9am–sunset daily 🌐 filitosa.fr

The 4,000-year-old, life-size stone warriors of Filitosa are the most spectacular relics of megalithic man in Corsica. Discovered in 1946, these phallus-like granite menhirs represent an interesting progression from mere outlines to detailed sculpture etched with human features.

The five most recent figures (about 1500 BC) stand around a 1,000-year-old olive tree, in the field below a tumulus. Other finds can be seen in the site's museum.

⑪

Sartène
A7 Corse-du-Sud 14 cours Soeur Amélie; www.lacoursedes origines.com

A medieval fortified town of narrow cobbled streets and granite houses rising above the Rizzanese Valley, Sartène

→

One of many charming narrow alleys in the medieval town of Sartène

⑨

Ajaccio
A7 Corse-du-Sud 3 boulevard du Roi Jérôme; www.ajaccio-tourisme.com

A noisy, busy town by Corsican standards, this was the birthplace of Napoléon Bonaparte in 1769. After crowning himself emperor of France in 1804, he never returned to Corsica, but the town, the modern capital of nationalist Corsica, celebrates his 15 August birthday.

The 16th-century Cathédrale Notre-Dame de la Miséricorde, where Napoléon was baptized in 1771, houses Delacroix's painting *Vierge du Sacré-Coeur*.

A few streets away the **Musée National de la Maison Bonaparte**, where Napoléon was born and spent his childhood, has memorabilia, family portraits and period furniture.

Much more extraordinary is the art collection assembled by Napoléon's unscrupulous uncle, Cardinal Fesch, who merrily looted churches, palaces and museums during the Italian campaign and brought the swag home to Ajaccio. Housed in the 19th-century **Palais Fesch**, the **Musée des Beaux-Arts** has the finest collection of Italian primitive art in France after the Louvre. Among its masterpieces are works by Bellini, Botticelli, Titian, Veronese, Bernini and Poussin. Next to the Palais Fesch stands the Chapelle Impériale, built in 1855 by Napoléon III to accommodate the tombs of the Bonapartes. From here, walk back along the quay to the Jetée de la Citadelle, which offers superb views of the town, marina and Golfe d'Ajaccio. From the quai de la Citadelle, daily excursions go to the Îles Sanguinaires found at the mouth of the Golfe d'Ajaccio.

At Vero, 21 km (13 miles) northeast on the N193, is the

Did You Know?

French novelist Prosper Mérimée once described Sartène as "the most Corsican of Cosica's towns".

was founded by the Genoese in the 16th century. It survived endless attacks and kidnappings by Barbary pirates and centuries of feuding by the town's leading families.

Despite all this, Sartène has a reputation for deep piety, and Good Friday's Catenacciu ("chained one") is the island's oldest and most intense ceremony, reenacting Christ's ascent to Golgotha.

In the town centre, the **Musée Départemental de la Préhistoire et d'Archéologie** has a collection of Neolithic, Bronze and Iron Age artifacts.

Connoisseurs praise the town's satisfying wine which is famous in the region.

Musée Départemental de la Préhistoire et d'Archéologie

⊛ Ⓐ Blvd Jacques Nicolaï Ⓞ Oct–May: 10am–5pm Tue–Sat; Jun–Sep: 10am–6pm Tue–Sat) Ⓦ prehistoire-corse.org

---

⑫

Côte Orientale

Ⓐ A7 Ⓗ Haute-Corse & Corse-du-Sud Ⓧ Bastia Ⓔ Bastia, Porto-Vecchio Ⓘ 80 av St-Alexandra, Aléria; rue Maréchal Leclerc, Porto-Vecchio; www.oriente-corsica.com

The flat alluvial plain which stretches from Bastia to Solenzara has been rich farmland since 1945, the year it was finally drained and rid of malaria. More recently, resorts and high-rise hotels have mushroomed along the coast, cashing in on its long beaches.

The best sight in Mariana is the early 12th-century cathedral of Mariana known as La Canonica. Nearby is the older Église de San Perteo, surrounded by meadows.

About halfway down the coast, the port of Aléria, originally a Greek colony and the base for Rome's conquest of Corsica in 259 BC, has a rich archaeological heritage. Just outside town, a museum housed in the 15th-century Fort de Matra chronicles daily life in Roman Aléria.

Near the southern tip of the island is an extremely popular resort, perfect for a seaside holiday, with white-sand beaches notably at Palombaggia and Pinarello.

EAT

Le Pirate

Local seafood and produce, with second-to-none harbour views.

Ⓐ A6 Ⓗ Le Port, Erbalunga Ⓦ restaurantlepirate.com

€€€

Le Week End

Family-run favourite serving just-landed fish and lobster from a tank.

Ⓐ A7 Ⓗ Route des Sanguinaires, Ajaccio Ⓦ hotel-le-weekend.com

€€€

Pozzo di Mastri

Regional French cuisine served with style in a beautiful farmhouse.

Ⓐ A7 Ⓗ Lieu dit Pozzo di Mastri Figari Ⓦ pozzodimastri.com

€€€

Le Casadelmar

Two Michelin stars, one creative Italian chef and many memorable dishes.

Ⓐ A7 Ⓗ Porto-Vecchio Ⓦ casadelmar.fr

€€€

13

Calvi

A6 Haute-Corse ◻◻◻
97 Port de Plaisance, chemin de la Plage; www.balagne-corsica.com

This is where Nelson lost his eye in an "explosion of stones" in 1794. Today it is half military town and half cheap holiday resort, but its 15th-century Genoese citadel, perched high above Calvi port, from where it towers over the sea, is one of the most beautiful sights on the island.

The town makes rather a half-hearted case for being the birthplace of Christopher Columbus, but no hard evidence has been put forward to support this, other than the ruins of his apparent house. A much better claim to fame is the very good and reasonably priced food. There is also a respected jazz festival here towards the end of June.

Outside the town, the 19th-century Chapelle de Notre-Dame de la Serra is gloriously sited on a hilltop, from where it commands extensive views in all directions.

> **Calvi's 15th-century Genoese citadel, perched high above Calvi port, from where it towers over the sea, is one of the most beautiful sights on the island.**

14

L'Île Rousse

A6 Haute-Corse ◻◻◻
Avenue Calizi; www.balagne-corsica.com

Founded in 1758 by Pasquale Paoli, leader of independent Corsica, L'Île Rousse is today a major holiday resort and ferry terminal. The centre of town is dominated by a marble statue of Corsica's national hero, Paoli. On the north side of the square is the covered market, with the Old Town beyond.

In summer it becomes overcrowded, its beaches a mass of bodies. It is worth travelling 10 km (6 miles) up the coast to Lozari, which offers a magnificent, virtually unspoiled stretch of sand.

One very pleasant way to discover the Balagne region is to take the tram-train from L'Île Rousse to Calvi and back. This odd little service (more frequent in summer) keeps to the coastline and stops at Algajola, Lumio and various villages along the way.

15

Lavezzi Islands

A7 Corse-du-Sud

With delightful shell beaches, brilliant blue sea and an uninhabited, sun-soaked archipelago, these islands 10km (6 miles) off Bonifacio are legion and ripe for fun. Snorkel among the resident grouper colony, or dive deeper with a scuba guide to see moray eels, rays and shoals of barracuda. The islands are an easy-access natural haven,

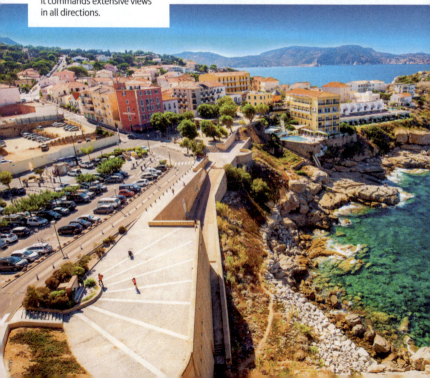

protected since 1982 and without a kiosk or cabin in sight: take all essentials with you. To get here, join one of the daily boat trips from Bonifacio, use the shuttle service or a private charter.

---

16 Cargèse

 A7 **Corse-du-Sud** ▣ **Rue du Docteur Dragacci; www.cargese.net** or **www.ouestcorsica.com**

Cargèse overlooks the sea from a promontory between Sagone and Pero bays. The town has an interesting history, and many of its people are the descendants of 17th-century Greek refugees. A few still speak Greek, and their icon-filled church faces its Catholic counterpart in an attitude that must once have seemed confrontational. Nowadays old rivalries have vanished, and the Orthodox priest and Catholic *curé* often stand in for one another.

There are splendid beaches in the vicinity, notably at Pero and Chiuni to the north, and at Ménasina and Stagnoli to the south.

---

17 Porto-Vecchio

A7 **Corse-du-Sud** ▣ **Avenue du Maréchal Leclerc; www.ot-portovecchio.com**

One of Corsica's medieval coastal cities, and brimming with history, sophisticated and splashy Porto-Vecchio is the closest thing the island has to the glamour of the French Riviera.

Start at the marina on quai Pascal Paoli, before window-shopping along avenue du Maréchal Leclerc for a retail fix with plenty of sparkle.

Above this, you'll find the picturesque walled Old Town, where backstreets cuddle up with creaky restaurants, then go beyond the city to stretch out on dazzling beaches. Three to choose from are Cala Rossa, to the north, A-list hangout Palombaggia or U-shaped Santa Giulia bay, with shallow tidal waters that are tailor-made for families.

---

18 Plage de Palombaggia

A7 **Corse-du-Sud**

Corsica doesn't get more idyllic than this: crystal clear lagoon waters wrapped by a wide strip of squeaky-soft sand. Add to that a low-rise shoulder of pink hills and shadow-casting umbrella pines, shallows for kids and oven-hot rocks for sun lizards. Beach time on this strand is a cinch if you get there early,

The historic town and rocky coastline of Calvi, both with beautiful sea views

 Corsica's stunningly beautiful Plage de Palombaggia beach

but remember it's incredibly popular for a reason and in the high season a parade of yachts can be seen skimming in and out of the bay. Every visit to Corsica should include at least one beach, and if you are short on time, be sure to make it this one.

TOP 5 BEACHES IN CORSICA

Palombaggia
The pin-up of Corsica's beach scene: sugary sands and clear water.

Arinella
Family heaven, with a water playground and views of Bastia Citadel.

Bodri
Soft, sloping sand, with excellent snorkelling and better swimming.

Roccapina
On the west coast, with calm waters that are perfect for kids and gorgeous sands.

Ostriconi
Quiet and isolated, this wild stretch without the crowds is a short drive from L'Île Rousse.

NEED TO KNOW

A train crossing the Séjourné bridge

BEFORE YOU GO

Forward planning is essential to any successful trip. Be prepared for all eventualities by considering the following points before you travel.

AT A GLANCE

CURRENCY
Euro (€)

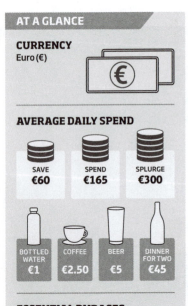

AVERAGE DAILY SPEND

SAVE
€60

SPEND
€165

SPLURGE
€300

BOTTLED WATER
€1

COFFEE
€2.50

BEER
€5

DINNER FOR TWO
€45

ESSENTIAL PHRASES

Hello	Bonjour
Goodbye	Au revoir
Please	S'il vous plait
Thank you	Merci
Do you speak English	Parlez-vous anglais?
I don't understand	Je ne comprends pas

ELECTRICITY SUPPLY

Power sockets are type C and E, fitting C and E plugs with two or three prongs. Standard voltage is 230v/50Hz.

Passports and Visas

For a stay of up to three months for the purpose of tourism, EU nationals and citizens of the US, Canada, Australia and New Zealand do not need a visa. For visa information specific to your home country, consult the French **Ministry of Foreign Affairs** website or your nearest French embassy.
Ministry of Foreign Affairs
W diplomatie.gouv.fr

Travel Safety Advice

Visitors can get up-to-date travel safety information from the **US Department of State**, the **UK Foreign and Commonwealth Office**, the **Australian Department of Foreign Affairs and Trade** and France's **Vigipirate** system.
Australia
W smartraveller.gov.au
UK
W gov.uk/foreign-travel-advice
US
W travel.state.gov
Vigiparate
W gouvernement.fr/vigipirate

Customs Information

An individual is permitted to carry the following within the EU for personal use:
Tobacco products 800 cigarettes, 400 cigarillos, 200 cigars or 1 kg of smoking tobacco.
Alcohol 10 litres of alcoholic beverages above 22 per cent strength, 20 litres of alcoholic beverages below 22 per cent strength, 90 litres of wine (60 litres of which can be sparkling wine) and 110 litres of beer.
Cash If you are carrying €10,000 or more in cash (or the equivalent in other currencies) you must declare it to the customs authorities.
Limits vary if travelling outside the EU, so always check restrictions before travelling.

Insurance

It is wise to take out an insurance policy covering theft, loss of belongings, medical problems, cancellation and delays. To receive discounted or free emergency medical care in France, EU citizens should ensure they have an **EHIC** (European Health Insurance Card). Visitors from outside the EU must arrange their own private medical insurance.

EHIC
W gov.uk/european-health-insurance-card

Vaccinations

No specific vaccinations are required for France.

Money

Most establishments accept major credit, debit and prepaid currency cards, but it's always a good idea to carry some cash too (which may be expected for purchases under €15). Contactless payments are widely accepted in all major cities.

Booking Accommodation

France offers a huge variety of accommodation, comprising luxury five-star hotels, family-run B&Bs, budget hostels and private apartments. The country is busiest during Christmas, New Year and France's school breaks. It is wise to book ahead during these peak seasons and in ski resorts and seaside towns. Hotels offer substantial discounts for advance online bookings. Local tourist offices are helpful for accommodation on farms and *gîtes*.

Travellers with Specific Needs

A number of organizations are working to improve accessibility across the country. The **Office du Tourisme et des Congrès** has a useful guide that lists easily accessible sights and routes for visitors with mobility issues, while **Jaccede** has details of accessible museums, hotels, bars, restaurants and cinemas in Paris and other cities. **Vianavigo** provides detailed information on accessible public transport, including a route planner that can be tailored to your specific needs. Rail operator **SNCF** provides information about train travel (including booklets at train stations) and a booking service for free assistance on TGVs. **Les Compagnons du Voyage** will provide an escort for persons with limited mobility or visibility on any form of public transport, for a small fee. For further

information on accessibility, contact the French disability advocacy group **GIHP**.

GIHP
W gihpnational.org
Jaccede
W jaccede.com
Les Compagnons du Voyage
W compagnons.com
Office du Tourisme et des Congrès
W parisinfo.com
SNCF
W accessibilite.sncf.com
Vianavigo
W vianavigo.com

Language

French is the official language, but English is increasingly understood, especially among the young. A few niceties will go a long way – try to say at least *"bonjour"* before switching to English.

Closures

Lunchtime Some shops and businesses close for an hour or two from around noon.
Mondays Some museums, small shops, restaurants and bars are closed for the day.
Tuesdays Most national museums are closed for the day, except Versailles and the Musée d'Orsay, which are closed on Monday.
Sundays Most shops are closed.
Public holidays Public services, shops, museums and attractions are usually closed.

PUBLIC HOLIDAYS	
1 Jan	New Year's Day
Apr	Easter Day and Easter Monday
1 May	Labor Day/May Day
8 May	Victory 1945
30 May	Ascension Day
10 Jun	Whit Monday
14 Jul	Bastille Day
15 Aug	Assumption of Mary
1 Nov	All Saints' Day
11 Nov	Armistice Day
25 Dec	Christmas Day
31 Dec	New Year's Eve

GETTING
AROUND

Whether you are visiting for a short city break or rural country retreat, discover how best to reach your destinations and travel like a pro.

PUBLIC TRANSPORT COSTS

PARIS

€1.90

Single journey
Metro, tram, bus, funicular

LYON

€1.90

Single journey
Metro, tram, bus

MARSEILLE

€1.60

Single journey
Metro, tram, bus

SPEED LIMIT

AUTOROUTE	DIVIDED HIGHWAY
130 km/h (81 mph)	**110** km/h (68 mph)

RURAL ROADS	URBAN ROADS
80 km/h (50 mph)	**50** km/h (31 mph)

Arriving by Air

Charles de Gaulle outside Paris is Europe's busiest continental airport and France's main international hub. Orly airport outside Paris is a hub for domestic, European and North African routes. About 40 regional airports, including Nice, Lyon, Marseille and Toulouse, handle budget airlines and charters.

Train Travel

International Train Travel

You can travel from France to any major city in Europe by regular rail or on the celebrated 300 km/h (186 mph) high-speed TGVs, which now link London, Brussels, Frankfurt, Munich, Luxembourg and Geneva. **Eurail** and **Interrail** sell passes (to European non-residents and residents respectively) for international journeys lasting from five days up to three months. Both passes are valid on TGVs but do not include the mandatory seat reservation fee.
Eurail
w eurail.com
Interrail
w interrail.eu

Domestic Train Travel

The state-owned **SNCF** serves all regions of France and Monaco. SNCF's regional TER trains cannot be booked, while the longer Intercity and night trains require reservations. All TGVs require numbered seat bookings. Tickets can be bought online at SNCF or **Loco2** and printed out or stored as QR codes on mobiles. Machines at stations also sell tickets, which must be inserted into yellow validating machines (located on every platform) before boarding to avoid fines.

Railway buffs will also enjoy France's steam locomotive routes and scenic tours; one of the most spectacular is the **Chamonix** cog railway.
Chamonix
w chamonix.net
Loco2
w loco2.com
SNCF
w en.oui.sncf

GETTING TO AND FROM THE AIRPORT

Airport	Distance to City	Taxi Fare	Public Transport	Journey Time
Paris Charles De Gaulle	25 km (16 miles)	€59	Bus/rail	45 mins
Paris Orly	19 km (12 miles)	€35	Bus/rail	26 mins
Nice	8 km (5 miles)	€41	Bus	16 mins
Lyon Saint Exupéry	34 km (21 miles)	€55	Bus/rail	27 mins
Marseille Provence	27 km (17 miles)	€60	Bus/rail	25 mins
Toulouse Blagnac	11 km (7 miles)	€48	Bus	25 mins
Bâle Mulhouse	31 km (20 mile)	€50	Bus	30 mins
Bordeaux Mérignac	11 km (7 miles)	€48	Bus	30 mins
Nantes Atlantique	12 km (7 miles)	€35	Bus	22 mins
Beauvais	6 km (4 miles)	€15	Bus	14 mins
Lille Lesquin	10 km (6 miles)	€35	Bus	16 mins

RAIL JOURNEY PLANNER

This map is a handy reference for travel on France's main scenic and passenger lines. Journey times given below are for the fastest available service on each route.

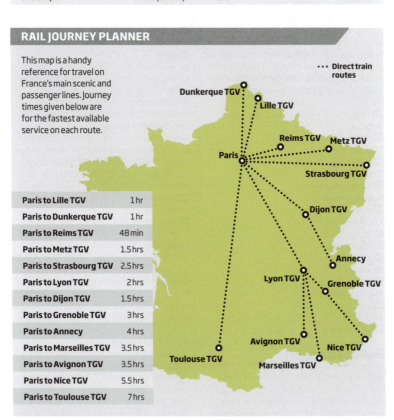

••• Direct train routes

Dunkerque TGV
Lille TGV
Reims TGV
Metz TGV
Paris
Strasbourg TGV
Dijon TGV
Annecy
Lyon TGV
Grenoble TGV
Avignon TGV
Nice TGV
Toulouse TGV
Marseilles TGV

Paris to Lille TGV	1 hr
Paris to Dunkerque TGV	1 hr
Paris to Reims TGV	48 min
Paris to Metz TGV	1.5 hrs
Paris to Strasbourg TGV	2.5 hrs
Paris to Lyon TGV	2 hrs
Paris to Dijon TGV	1.5 hrs
Paris to Grenoble TGV	3 hrs
Paris to Annecy	4 hrs
Paris to Marseilles TGV	3.5 hrs
Paris to Avignon TGV	3.5 hrs
Paris to Nice TGV	5.5 hrs
Paris to Toulouse TGV	7 hrs

Long-Distance Bus Travel

Deregulation in 2015 invigorated the previously almost non-existent long-haul coach business in France. SNCF now operates **Ouibus**, a low-cost bus network which travels as far as Amsterdam and London and includes several major French cities. Local bus companies in each region of France run frequent services between nearby cities. **Flixbus** has an extensive network across Europe and all over France.

Flixbus
w flixbus.fr
Ouibus
w ouibus.com

Boats and Ferries

For generations companies such as **P&O Ferries**, **DFDS Seaways**, **Condor Ferries** and **Brittany Ferries** have plied between Britain and French ports such as Calais, St-Malo, Le Havre, Dieppe and Cherbourg. **Aferry** has regular crossings to Tunisia, Algeria and Morocco while **Manche-Îles Express** connects to the Channel Islands and **Corsica Ferries** to Corsica. Inland, barges and narrow boats trace leisurely paths down France's waterways at walking pace. **En-Peniche** rent out a range of barges for use on the canals. It is not even necessary to leave Paris to take to the water – the city's **Batobus** riverboat shuttle runs every 20–45 minutes (more frequently in the spring and summer), while **Bateaux-Mouches** offer sightseeing cruises down the Seine.

Aferry
w aferry.fr
Batobus
w batobus.com
Bateaux-Mouches
w bateaux-mouches.fr
Brittany Ferries
w brittany-ferries.co.uk
Condor Ferries
w condorferries.co.uk
Corsica Ferries
w corsica-ferries.fr
DFDS Seaways
w dfdsseaways.co.uk
En-Peniche
w en-peniche.com
Manche-Îles Express
w manche-iles.com
P&O Ferries
w poferries.com

Public Transport

While the most rewarding way to take in any French city is on foot, public transport is highly developed, integrated and affordable. Each major city has a system of underground trains, commuter trains and city buses, including the **RATP** in Paris, Lyon's **TCL-SYTRAL**, **Tisséo** in Toulouse, Marseille's **RTM/Le Pilote**, Lille's **Ilévia** and Rennes's **Star**.

Buses are more affordable in France than in most of Europe, although not air-conditioned and often overcrowded. Costs can be reduced by buying tickets online rather than from the driver on board the bus. Get on the bus in the front and exit at the back or middle.

France is second only to Italy in the number of cities with underground metros. French metros are renowned for being efficient and affordable, although note that not all metro stations will have step-free access. Tickets for both buses and metro trains must always be stamped in the validating machine.

Ilévia
w ilevia.fr
RATP
w ratp.fr
RTM/Le Pilote
w rtm.fr
Star
w star.fr
TCL-SYTRAL
w tcl.fr
Tisséo
w tisseo.fr

Taxis

Official taxis are clearly identified. They can be hailed in passing, but not within sight of an official taxi stand. A number of apps have sprung up for summoning taxis, which can also be ordered by phones at taxi ranks. Billing begins from the moment of booking. **Uber** is popular throughout France, but beware of rogue drivers in private vehicles. **Heetch** is a late-night app-based service running in nine cities.

Heetch
w heetch.com
Uber
w uber.com

Driving

The French love driving, and fast and spacious *autoroutes* (motorways) fan out to every region. Driving in cities is not recommended – traffic is heavy, there are many one-way streets and parking is notoriously difficult and expensive.

Driving to France

For those driving from Britain to France, the simplest way is to use the Eurotunnel shuttles between Folkestone and Calais, both of which have direct motorway access. It is possible to drive from London to Paris in eight hours and to forge deep into the French Alps in one day. Paris from Frankfurt is about seven hours and from Rome 14 hours. When driving to Paris motorists should take time to check their destination address. The city is surrounded by the Boulevard Périphérique outer ring road, and all motorways leading to the capital link to this. Each former city gate, called a *porte*, now corresponds to a Périphérique entrance/exit. Consult a map of central Paris to find the closest *porte*.

To take your own foreign-registered car into and around France, you will need to carry the vehicle's registration and insurance documents, a full and valid driving licence, and valid passport or national ID at all times. EU driving licences are valid. If visiting from outside the EU, or if your licence is not in French, you may need to apply for an International Driving Permit (IDP).

Driving in France

Road markings can be confusing. Roads crossing frontiers are numbered as European Routes, the longest of which is the E40 connecting Calais to Kazakhstan. These routes may also have national markings: A for *Autoroute* or N for *Nationale* (National Highway). Small country roads are marked D for *Département*. Autoroutes have blue signs and are also marked *Péage*, with significant tolls. Toll-free National Highways are marked in green.

All diesel and petrol cars produced before 1997 are banned from Paris 8am–8pm on week-days. By 2020, only cars built after 2011 will be allowed to circulate. Paris has promised a ban on all petrol and diesel vehicles by 2030, with the entire country following by 2040. France has more electric cars than almost any European country, with about 10,000 charging stations.

Ten French cities now require all vehicles to display a **Crit'Air** pollution index sticker. Emergency pollution alerts may be issued at any time, closing districts to certain types of vehicles. The latest conditions are posted on **Urban Access Regulations in Europe**.

In most cities, you can park in areas with a large "P" or *payant* sign on the pavement or road. In Paris, drivers can pay at the meter with La Paris Carte (available from kiosks), a credit or debit card or via the PaybyPhone app *(p559)*.

Crit'Air
W certificat-air.gouv.fr
Urban Access Regulations in Europe
W urbanaccessregulations.eu

Car Rental

To rent a car you must be 21 or over and have held a valid driver's licence for at least a year. You will also need a credit card for the rental deposit. Rental cars with automatic transmission are rare, and must be booked in advance. Hire cars gene-rally cannot be taken on ferries. Returning a car to a different location will incur surcharges.

Rules of the Road

Drivers must be over 18, have had a valid licence for at least one year and must carry the car's registration and insurance documents and their licence at all times.

Always drive on the right. Unless otherwise signposted, vehicles coming from the right have right of way. Cars on a roundabout usually have right of way, although the Arc de Triomphe is a hair-raising exception as cars give way to traffic on the right. Seatbelts are compulsory, and it is prohibited to sound your horn in the city. Helmets and protective gloves are mandatory for motorcyclists and scooter riders. In the city centre, it is against the law to use the bus lanes at any time of day. Using a mobile phone while driving can result in an immediate loss of licence. France strictly enforces a blood alcohol content limit of 0.05 per cent. By law, drivers must carry a breathalyser device (€1 at petrol stations). French police can demand on-the-spot payment of traffic fines up to €750, and drugs tests can be applied even for minor infractions.

Bicycles and Scooters

Citywide bike app schemes include Avignon's **Vélopop**, Nice's **Vélobleu**, Marseille's **Le Vélo** and Lyon's **Vélo'V**. **Allo Vélo** is a Paris cycle rental firm with e-bikes. Scooters are a fun way to negotiate city traffic or soak up atmosphere at minimal cost. Try **Paris by Scooter**, **Riviera Scooter** or the Loire Valley's **Ride in Tours**. The rental will usually come with helmets, a lock and insurance. By law all children under 12 must wear helmets, even if passengers.

Allo Vélo
W allovelo.com
Le Vélo
W en.levelo-mpm.fr
Paris by Scooter
W parisbyscooter.com
Ride in Tours
W ride-in-tours.com
Riviera Scooter
W rivierascooter.com
Vélobleu
W velobleu.org
Vélopop
W velopop.fr
Vélo'V
W velov-grandlyon.com

Hitchhiking

Hitchhiking is forbidden on *autoroutes* and not recommended anywhere in France. Ride sharing with **Bla Bla Car** is a safer, more popular alterna-tive. Fees are about a third of bus fares.
Bla Bla Car
W blabla.fr

PRACTICAL
INFORMATION

A little local know-how goes a long way in France. Here you will find all the essential advice and information you will need during your stay.

AT A GLANCE

EMERGENCY NUMBERS

EMERGENCY OPERATOR	POLICE
112	**17**

AMBULANCE	FIRE SERVICE
15	**18**

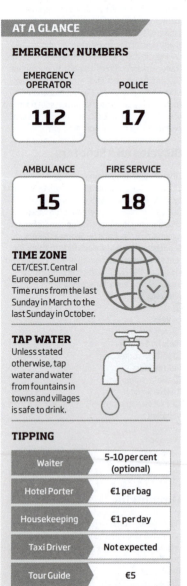

TIME ZONE
CET/CEST. Central European Summer Time runs from the last Sunday in March to the last Sunday in October.

TAP WATER
Unless stated otherwise, tap water and water from fountains in towns and villages is safe to drink.

TIPPING

Waiter	5–10 per cent (optional)
Hotel Porter	€1 per bag
Housekeeping	€1 per day
Taxi Driver	Not expected
Tour Guide	€5

Personal Security

France is generally a safe country and most visits are trouble-free. However, when travelling late at night, avoid long transfers in metro and bus stations. Beware of pickpockets in major tourist areas and on the metro and city buses during rush hour. If anything is stolen, report it as soon as possible to the nearest police station, and bring ID with you. Get a copy of the crime report in order to claim on your insurance. Contact your embassy if you have your passport stolen, or in the event of a serious crime or accident.

Health

If you fall sick during your visit, pharmacists are an excellent source of advice – they can diagnose minor ailments and suggest appropriate treatment. For English-speaking visitors, private hospitals with bilingual staff and doctors can be found in major cities, with the **American Hospital of Paris** and the **Franco-Britannique Hospital** in Paris being the best known. The **Centre Médical Europe** is an inexpensive private clinic with a dental practice.

All EU nationals holding an EHIC (*p553*) are entitled to use the French national health service. Patients must pay for treatment and can then reclaim most of the cost from the health authorities. The process may be lengthy and travellers should therefore consider purchasing private travel insurance. For visitors from outside the EU, payment of hospital and other medical expenses is the patient's responsibility. It is therefore important to arrange comprehensive medical insurance before travelling.

American Hospital of Paris
W american-hospital.org
Centre Médical Europe
W centre-medical-europe.fr
Franco-Britannique Hospital
W ihfb.org

Smoking, Alcohol and Drugs

Smoking is prohibited in all public places, but is allowed on restaurant, café and pub terraces, as

long as they are not enclosed. The possession of narcotics is prohibited and could result in a prison sentence. Unless stated otherwise, alcohol consumption on the streets is permitted. France has a strict limit of 0.05 per cent BAC (blood alcohol content) for drivers.

ID

There is no requirement for visitors to carry ID, but in the event of a routine check you may be asked to show your passport. If you don't have it with you, the police may escort you to wherever your passport is being kept.

Local Customs

Etiquette (la politesse) is important to the French. On entering and leaving a store or café, you are expected to say "bonjour" and "au revoir" to staff. Be sure to add "s'il vous plaît" (please) when ordering, and "pardon" if you accidentally bump into someone. The French usually shake hands on meeting someone for the first time. Friends and colleagues who know each other well greet each other with a kiss on each cheek. If you are unsure about what's expected, wait to see if they proffer a hand or a cheek.

Visiting Churches and Cathedrals

Dress respectfully. Cover your torso and upper arms; ensure shorts and skirts cover your knees.

Mobile Phones and Wi-Fi

With a part of its ambitious 5G network already operating, France offers strong mobile signals throughout. Visitors on EU tariffs will be able to use their devices without being affected by data roaming charges. Free Wi-Fi hotspots are widely available in public spaces. Cafés and restaurants usually permit the use of their Wi-Fi to customers who make a purchase.

Post

Stamps (timbres) can be bought at post offices and tabacs (tobacconists). Most post offices have self-service machines to weigh and frank your mail. Yellow post boxes are ubiquitous. France's

La Poste also runs the mail services in Andorra and Monaco.
La Poste
🌐 laposte.fr

Taxes and Refunds

VAT is around 20 per cent in France. Non-EU residents can claim back tax on certain goods and purchases over €175. Look out for the Global Refund Tax-Free sign, and ask the retailer for a form for a détaxe receipt. Present the goods receipt, détaxe receipt and passport at customs when you depart to receive your refund.

Discount Cards

Entry to some national and municipal museums is free on the first Sunday of each month. Under-18s and EU passport holders aged 18–26 years are usually admitted free of charge to national museums, and there are sometimes discounts for students and over-60s who have ID showing their date of birth. The **Paris Pass** offers access to 60 sights for two, four or six days, fast-track Louvre access, unlimited travel on the metro, buses and RER within central Paris and a hop-on hop-off bus tour. The **French Riviera Pass** allows free access to many sights, tours and activities, plus free public transport throughout the Nice-Côte d'Azur metropolitan area.
French Riviera Pass
🌐 en.frenchrivierapass.com
Paris Pass
🌐 parispass.com

WEBSITES AND APPS

France Tourism
Find information and inspiration on www.francetourism.com.
Happy Hours Paris
A fun app which guides you to the most convivial bars and the cheapest drinks.
PaybyPhone
Pay for on-street parking quickly and easily with this app.
RATP
The official app from RATP, Paris's public transport operator.

INDEX

Page numbers in **bold** refer to main entries

PHRASE BOOK

IN AN EMERGENCY

Help!	Au secours!	oh sekoor
Stop!	Arrêtez!	aret-ay
Call a doctor!	Appelez un médecin!	apuh-lay uñ medsañ
Call an ambulance!	Appelez une ambulance!	apuh-lay oon oñboo-loñs
Call the police!	Appelez la police!	apuh-lay lah poh-lees
Call the fire brigade!	Appelez les pompiers!	apuh-lay leh poñ-peeyay
Where is the nearest telephone?	Où est le téléphone le plus proche?	oo ay luh tehlehfon luh ploo prosh
Where is the nearest hospital?	Où est l'hôpital le plus proche?	oo ay l'opeetal luh ploo prosh

COMMUNICATION ESSENTIALS

Yes	Oui	wee
No	Non	noñ
Please	S'il vous plaît	seel voo play
Thank you	Merci	mer-see
Excuse me	Excusez-moi	exkoo-zay mwah
Hello	Bonjour	boñzhoor
Goodbye	Au revoir	oh ruh-vwar
Good night	Bonsoir	boñ-swar
Morning	Le matin	matañ
Afternoon	L'après-midi	l'apreh-meedee
Evening	Le soir	swar
Yesterday	Hier	eeyehr
Today	Aujourd'hui	oh-zhoor-dwee
Tomorrow	Demain	duhmañ
Here	Ici	ee-see
There	Là	lah
What?	Quoi, quel, quelle?	kwah, kel, kel
When?	Quand?	koñ
Why?	Pourquoi?	poor-kwah
Where?	Où?	oo

USEFUL PHRASES

How are you?	Comment allez-vous?	kom-moñ talay voo
Very well, thank you.	Très bien, merci.	treh byañ, mer-see
Pleased to meet you.	Enchanté de faire votre connaissance.	oñshoñ-tay duh fehr votr kon-ay-sans
See you soon.	A bientôt.	byañ-toh
That's fine	C'est bon	say bon
Where is/are...?	Où est/sont...?	ooay/soñ
How far is it to...?	Combien de kilometres d'ici à...?	kom-byañ duh keelo-metr d'ee-see ah
Which way to...?	Quelle est la direction pour...?	kel ay lah deer-ek-syoñ poor
Do you speak English?	Parlez-vous anglais?	par-lay voo oñg-lay
I don't understand.	Je ne comprends pas.	zhuh nuh kom-proñ pah
Could you speak slowly please?	Pouvez-vous parler moins vite s'il vous plaît?	poo-vay voo par-lay mwañ veet seel voo play
I'm sorry.	Excusez-moi.	exkoo-zay mwah

USEFUL WORDS

big	grand	groñ
small	petit	puh-tee
hot	chaud	show
cold	froid	frwah
good	bon/bien	boñ/byañ
bad	mauvais	moh-veh
enough	assez	assay
well	bien	byañ
open	ouvert	oo-ver
closed	fermé	fer-meh
left	gauche	gohsh
right	droite	drwaht
straight on	tout droite	too drwaht
near	près	preh
far	loin	lwañ
up	en haut	oñ oh
down	en bas	oñ bah
early	de bonne heure	duh bon urr
late	en retard	oñ ruh-tar
entrance	l'entrée	l'on-tray
exit	la sortie	sor-tee
toilet	les toilettes, le WC	twah-let, vay-see
free, unoccupied	libre	leebr
free, no charge	gratuit	grah-twee

MAKING A TELEPHONE CALL

I'd like to place a long-distance call.	Je voudrais faire un appel á l'étranger.	zhuh voo-dreh fehr uñ apel a laytroñ-zhay
I'd like to make a reverse charge call.	Je voudrais faire une communication en PCV.	zhuh voo-dreh fehr oon komoonikah-syoñ oñ peh-seh-veh
I'll try again later.	Je rappelerai plus tard.	zhuh rapeleray ploo tar
Can I leave a message?	Est-ce que je peux laisser un message?	es-keh zhuh puh leh-say uñ mehsazh
Hold on.	Ne quittez pas, s'il vous plaît.	nuh kee-tay pah seel voo play
Could you speak up a little please?	Pouvez-vous parler un peu plus fort?	poo-vay voo parlay uñ puh ploo for
local call	la communication locale	komoonikahsyoñ low-kal

SHOPPING

How much does this cost?	C'est combien s'il vous plaît?	say kom-byañ seel voo play
I would like...	Je voudrais...	zhuh voo-dray
Do you have?	Est-ce que vous avez	es-kuh voo zavay
I'm just looking.	Je regarde seulement.	zhuh ruhgar suhlmoñ
Do you take credit cards?	Est-ce que vous acceptez les cartes de crédit?	es-kuh voo zaksept-ay leh kart duh kreh-dee
Do you take travellers' cheques?	Est-ce que vous acceptez les cheques de voyages?	es-kuh voo zaksept-ay leh shek duh vwayazh
What time do you open?	A quelle heure vous êtes ouvert?	ah kel urr voo zet oo-ver
What time do you close?	A quelle heure vous êtes fermé?	ah kel urr voo zet fer-may
This one.	Celui-ci	suhl-wee-see
That one.	Celui-là	suhl-wee-lah
expensive	cher	shehr
cheap	pas cher, bon marché	pah shehr, boñ mar-shay
size, clothes	la taille	tye
size, shoes	la pointure	pwañ-tur
white	blanc	bloñ
black	noir	nwahr
red	rouge	roozh
yellow	jaune	zhohwn
green	vert	vehr
blue	bleu	bluh

TYPES OF SHOP

antique shop	le magasin d'antiquités	maga-zañ d'oñteekee-tay
bakery	la boulangerie	booloñ-zhuree
bank	la banque	boñk
bookshop	la librairie	lee-brehree
butcher	la boucherie	boo-shehree
cake shop	la pâtisserie	patee-sree
cheese shop	la fromagerie	fromazh-ree
chemist	la pharmacie	farmah-see
dairy	la crémerie	krem-ree
department store	le grand magasin	groñ maga-zañ
delicatessen	la charcuterie	sharkoot-ree
fishmonger	la poissonnerie	pwasson-ree
gift shop	le magasin de cadeaux	maga-zañ duh kadoh
greengrocer	le marchand de légumes	mar-shoñ duh lay-goom
grocery	l'alimentation	alee-moñta-syoñ
hairdresser	le coiffeur	kwafuhr
market	le marché	marsh-ay
newsagent	le magasin de journaux	maga-zañ duh zhoor-no
post office	la poste, le bureau de poste, le PTT	pohst, booroh duh pohst, peh-teh-teh
shoe shop	le magasin de chaussures	maga-zañ duh show-soor
supermarket	le supermarché	soo pehr-marshay
tobacconist	le tabac	tabah
travel agent	l'agence de voyages	l'azhoñs duh vwayazh

SIGHTSEEING

abbey	l'abbaye	l'abay-ee
art gallery	la galerie d'art	galer-ree dart
bus station	la gare routière	gahr roo-tee-yehr
cathedral	la cathédrale	katay-dral
church	l'église	l'aygleez
garden	le jardin	zhar-dañ

library	la bibliothèque	beebleeo-tek
museum	le musée	moo-zay
railway station	la gare (SNCF)	gahr (es-en-say-ef)
tourist information office	les renseignements touristiques, le syndicat d'initiative	roñsayn-moñ tooree-teek, sandee-ka deenee-syateev
town hall	l'hôtel de ville	lohtel duh veel
closed for public holiday	fermeture jour férié	fehrmeh-tur zhoor fehree-ay

STAYING IN A HOTEL

Do you have a vacant room?	Est-ce que vous avez une chambre?	es-kuh voo-zavay oon shambr
double room, with double bed	la chambre à deux personnes, avec un grand lit	shambr ah duh pehr-son avek un gronñ lee
twin room	la chambre à deux lits	shambr ah duh lee
single room	la chambre à une personne	shambr ah oon pehr-son
room with a bath, shower	la chambre avec salle de bains, une douche	shambr avek sal duh bañ, oon doosh
porter	le garçon	gar-soñ
key	la clef	klay
I have a reservation.	J'ai fait une réservation.	zhay fay oon rayzehrva-syoñ

EATING OUT

Have you got a table?	Avez-vous une table de libre?	avay-voo oon tahbl duh leebr
I want to reserve a table.	Je voudrais réserver une table.	zhuh voo-dray rayzehr-vay oon tahbl
The bill please.	L'addition s'il vous plaît.	ladee-syoñ seel voo play
I am a vegetarian.	Je suis végétarien.	zhuh swee vezhay-tehryañ
Waitress/ waiter	Madame, Mademoiselle/ Monsieur	mah-dam, mah-demwahzel/ muh-syuh
menu	le menu, la carte	men-oo, kart
fixed-price menu	le menu à prix fixe	men-oo ah pree feeks
cover charge	le couvert	koo-vehr
wine list	la carte des vins	kart-deh vañ
glass	le verre	vehr
bottle	la bouteille	boo-tay
knife	le couteau	koo-toh
fork	la fourchette	for-shet
spoon	la cuillère	kwee-yehr
breakfast	le petit déjeuner	puh-tee deh-zhuh-nay
lunch	le déjeuner	deh-zhuh-nay
dinner	le dîner	dee-nay
main course	le plat principal	plah prañsee-pal
starter, first course	l'entrée, le hors d'oeuvre	loñ-tray, or-duhvr
dish of the day	le plat du jour	plah doo zhoor
wine bar	le bar à vin	bar ah vañ
café	le café	ka-fay
rare	saignant	say-noñ
medium	à point	ah pwañ
well done	bien cuit	byañ kwee

MENU DECODER

apple	la pomme	pom
baked	cuit au four	kweet oh foor
banana	la banane	banan
beef	le boeuf	buhf
beer, draught beer	la bière, bière à la pression	bee-yehr, bee-yehr ah lah pres-syoñ
boiled	bouilli	boo-yee
bread	le pain	pan
butter	le beurre	burr
cake	le gâteau	gah-toh
cheese	le fromage	from-azh
chicken	le poulet	poo-lay
chips	les frites	freet
chocolate	le chocolat	shoko-lah
cocktail	le cocktail	cocktail
coffee	le café	kah-fay
dessert	le dessert	deh-ser
dry	sec	sek
duck	le canard	kanar
egg	l'oeuf	luf
fish	le poisson	pwah-ssoñ
fresh fruit	le fruit frais	frwee freh
garlic	l'ail	leye
grilled	grillé	gree-yay

ham	le jambon	zhoñ-boñ
ice, ice cream	la glace	glas
lamb	l'agneau	lanyoh
lemon	le citron	see-troñ
lobster	le homard	omahr
meat	la viande	vee-yand
milk	le lait	leh
mineral water	l'eau minérale	loh meeney-ral
mustard	la moutarde	moo-tard
oil	l'huile	lweel
olives	les olives	leh zoleev
onions	les oignons	leh zonyoñ
orange	l'orange	loroñzh
fresh orange juice	l'orange pressée	loroñzh press-eh
fresh lemon juice	le citron pressé	see-troñ press-eh
pepper	le poivre	pwavr
poached	poché	posh-ay
pork	le porc	por
potatoes	les pommes de terre	pom-duh tehr
prawns	les crevettes	kruh-vet
rice	le riz	ree
roast	rôti	row-tee
roll	le petit pain	puh-tee pañ
salt	le sel	sel
sauce	la sauce	sohs
sausage, fresh	la saucisse	sohsees
seafood	les fruits de mer	frwee duh mer
shellfish	les crustaces	kroos-tas
snails	les escargots	leh zes-kar-goh
soup	la soupe, le potage	soop, poh-tazh
steak	le bifteck, le steack	beef-tek, stek
sugar	le sucre	sookr
tea	le thé	tay
toast	pain grillé	pan greeyay
vegetables	les légumes	lay-goom
vinegar	le vinaigre	veenaygr
water	l'eau	loh
red wine	le vin rouge	vañ roozh
white wine	le vin blanc	vañ bloñ

NUMBERS

0	zéro	zeh-roh
1	un, une	uñ, oon
2	deux	duh
3	trois	trwah
4	quatre	katr
5	cinq	sañk
6	six	sees
7	sept	set
8	huit	weet
9	neuf	nerf
10	dix	dees
11	onze	oñz
12	douze	dooz
13	treize	trehz
14	quatorze	katorz
15	quinze	kañz
16	seize	sehz
17	dix-sept	dees-set
18	dix-huit	dees-weet
19	dix-neuf	dees-nerf
20	vingt	vañ
30	trente	tront
40	quarante	karoñt
50	cinquante	sañkoñt
60	soixante	swasoñt
70	soixante-dix	swasoñt-dees
80	quatre-vingts	katr-vañ
90	quatre-vingt-dix	katr-vañ-dees
100	cent	soñ
1,000	mille	meel

TIME

one minute	une minute	oon mee-noot
one hour	une heure	oon urr
half an hour	une demi-heure	oon duh-mee urr
Monday	lundi	luñ-dee
Tuesday	mardi	mar-dee
Wednesday	mercredi	mehrkruh-dee
Thursday	jeudi	zhuh-dee
Friday	vendredi	voñdruh-dee
Saturday	samedi	sam-dee
Sunday	dimanche	dee-moñsh

ACKNOWLEDGMENTS

The publisher would like to thank the following for their kind permission to reproduce their photographs:

Key: a-above; b-below/bottom; c-centre; f-far; l-left; r-right; t-top

123RF.com: Jon Bilous 156t; Francesco Bucchi 177br; Ildefonso Martin Burguillo 345tr; Olivier Cretin 364bl; Pavel Dudek 482bl, 483t, 516bl, 521bl; freeartist 344-5b; Jakub Gojda 513t; Philippe Halle 208cra, / American War Memorials Overseas (uswarmemorials.org) 236crb; Melanie Lemahieu 397tl; Luciano Mortula 208-9; stevanzz 11cr, 514-5b; Boris Stroujko 208bl, 292-3tr.

4Corners: Matteo Carassale / © The Estate of Alberto Giacometti (Fondation Annette et Alberto Giacometti, Paris and ADAGP, Paris), licensed in the UK by ACS and DACS, London 2019 505tl; Antonino Bartuccio 94-5b; Francesco Carovillano 18t, 21t, 204-5, 312-3; Susanne Kremer 25t, 330-1, 490-1; Maurizio Rellini 498t.

Alamy Stock Photo: 7Horses 408-9b, 444-5b; A1 images / Brian Lawrence 282b; Abbus Acastra 442bl; ACTIVE MUSEUM 294bc; age fotostock 264bl, 277br, / Ian Cook 357b, / J.D. Dallet 444tc, / Linh Hassel 529br / Javier Larrea 329b, 455b, / M&G Therin-Weise 29tr; AGF Srl / Charles Mahaux 447br, / Giuseppe Masci / architect COOP HIMMELB(L)AU 370bl; Sarah Akad 180cra, 183cla; Jerónimo Alba 345tc, 396tr, 412bl; All Canada Photos / Ian Cook 250-1b, 420bl; Todd Anderson 108cr; Andia 240crb, 264-5t, 434tr, / © Mucem / Architects Rudy Ricciotti & Roland Carta / Lighting : Yann Kersalé-SNAIK 494bl; Andrzej Gorzkowski Photography 173bl; Martyn Annetts 267br; Antiqua Print Gallery 295bc; Jon Arnold Images Ltd 294-5t; ART Collection 293clb, 301br; Art Collection 2 293bc; Arterra Picture Library 34bl, 243ca, 267cl, 269bl, 478bl, / Clement Philippe 275br; Ashley Cooper pics 472cla; ASK Images / Compagnon Michel 386-7t;Aurelian Images 251tr; B&Y Photography 513cra; Ian Badley 494cr; David Bagnall 383br, / statue of Cyrano de Bergerac by Mauro Corda © ADAGP, Paris and DACS, London 2019 434bl; Fraser Band/ Foster + Partners 56b; D A Barnes 181br; Barrey 44-5t; Peter Barritt 107cr; Martin Beddall 177bl; Nancy Hoyt Belcher 44bl; Biosphoto / Oscar Diez Martinez 460-1t; blickwinkel 53bl, 517tr, 539cl; Eva Bocek 548-9b; Ceri Breeze 537tl; Eden Breitz 45cl, 121cb; Ed Buziak 59br; Ryan Carter 368-9t; Marco Cattaneo 243tr; Peter Cavanagh / © Architects Rudy Ricciotti & Roland Carta / Mucem 57tl;Christophe Agence73bis 159tl; Chronicle 86br, 149tr; Classic Image 64bc; ClickAlps Srls / Roberto Moiola 541ca; Jonathan Cohen 67clb; Sorin Colac 220t; David Cooper 463tr, Steven Cottam 41cl, 190-1t; CTK Photo / Martin Sidorjak 43crb; Ian Dagnall 430t, 499tr, 511tl; Ian G Dagnall 28tl, 197b; Dan Burton Photo 436bl; DanieleC 320-1t; Danita Delimont 140tl, / Walter Bibikow 549tr; David Noton Photography 528-9t; David R. Frazier Photolibrary, Inc. 228tr; DE ROCKER 146cra; Stephane Debove 420t; DirectphotoCollection 46-7t; dpa picture alliance 497tr, 521cra; Andrew Duke 511cla; edpics 224tl; Chad Ehlers 176cla; Tor Eigeland 428bl; Elenaphotos 376t; John Elk III 294clb; Julian Elliott 214bl, 295cb; EmmePi Travel 150-1b; Sherry Epley 318cl; Keith Erskine 420crb; Everett Collection Inc 68crb; Factofoto 10cla; Findlay 188crb; Mick Flynn 303t; FORGET Patrick 255t; Peter Forsberg 138-9b; Peter Noyce FRA 415br; freeartist 226b, 300-1b, 545tl; French Connection 462-3b; Garden Photo World / David C Phillips 432clb; Jorge Garrido 241br; Christine Gates 236bl; GAUTIER Stephane 180t, 210tl; GFC Collection 334tl, 369br; GL Archive 149ca; Elly Godfroy 195b; Godong 373clb; Roger Goodwin 546tl; Paul Christian Gordon 406tr; Manfred Gottschalk 298t, 301tr, 308tr, 474t; Granger Historical Picture Archive 68bc, 294crb, 358tr, 423br, / Nadar 202bc; Olivier Parent / architects Olivier Félix-Faure, Antoine Félix-Faure and Philippe Macary from Grenoble Groupe6 377cr; Tony Gwynne 440c; HEITZ Lucas 538-9t; hemis.fr / AZAM Jean-Paul 49crb, 359tr, 467t; / BARRERE Jean-Marc 466tc, 485br; / BERTHIER Emmanuel 262cra, 271tl, 282crb; / BLANCHOT Philippe 405br; / CAVALIER Michel 518t; /

CEGALERBA-SZWEMBERG 525b; / CHAREL Franck 325crb; / CHICUREL Arnaud 40tl, 130bl, 139tr; / CORMON Francis 353b; / DEGAS Jean-Pierre 484t; / DOZIER Marc 41tl, 422br; / ESCUDERO Patrick 240clb, 328bl; / GARDEL Bertrand 43bl, 252tl, 155tl, 239cl; / GERAULT Gregory 411t; / GUIZIOU Franck 17bl, 184-5, 203br, 378clb, 440tl; / GUY Christian 64cb, 317cra, 325b, 326b, 327tl, 348t, 348clb, 351tl, 494crb; / HOUZE Philippe 195tr; / HUGHES Hervé 337br; / JACQUES Pierre 223t; / LECLERCQ Olivier 190crb, 192cl; / LEMAIRE Stephane 343clb; / MAISANT Ludovic 284-5b; / MATTES René 227tl, 252-3b, 271cra, 276-7b, 372-3b; MOIRENC Camille 196tr, 522b; / RIEGER Bertrand 28-9c, 222bl, 256tl, 522clb; / SOBERKA Richard 215t; / SONNET Sylvain 53cr, 97b, 115tl, 157b, 193tr, 398cra; / SPANI Arnaud 464-5b, 478-9t; / SUDRES Jean-Daniel 452bl; hitandrun / Greg Meeson / © Succession Brancusi - All rights reserved. ADAGP, Paris and DACS, London 2019 91crb; Oliver Hoffmann 254bl; Horizon Images / Motion 129trc; Peter Horree 109br, 183br, 373br; Kevin Howchin 279bl, 280tl; Michael Howes 306bl; Anthony Hucks 194t; Ian Dagnall Commercial Collection 149crb; IanDagnall Computing 149crb; Iconotec 239b; imageBROKER 24cb, 41br, 61cr, 98-9b, 297t, 311, 468-9; imageBROKER / Mara Brandl 539crb, / Christian GUY 346-7, 352clb, / Bernard Jaubert 430br, / Martin Moxter 304t, / Martin Dr.Schulte-Kellinghaus 213bc, 333tr; imageimage 58-9t; Imageplotter 527tr; Images & Stories 519bl; Images of Birmingham Premium 424-5t; incamerastock 31tl, 274t, 428-9b; INTERFOTO 241bl; isogood 198t; Ivoha 332-3b; Jam World Images 48bl; Eric James 407crb; Brian Jannsen 231; JAUBERT French Collection 49tr, 352tr, 355t; Joly / Andia 328-9t; Jon Arnold Images Ltd / Doug Pearson 464tl, / Walter Bibikow 427cra; Juice Images 432-3b; Michael Juno 263cla; John Kellerman 26crb, 179tl, 408tl; Keystone Pictures USA 149br; Gareth Kirkland 438-9; Elena Korchenko 171t; Russell Kord 305clb; Art Kowalsky 364crb; Andriy Kravchenko 12clb; Les. Ladbury 250t; Emmanuel LATTES 458t; Hervé Lenain 213t, 302bl, 305b, 308-9b, 324tl, 346clb, 349br, 350b, 396-7ca, 412-3t, 414-5t, 429tr, 437t, 489tr; LOOK Die Bildagentur der Fotografen GmbH, / Thomas Peter Widmann 543bl, / Konrad Wothe 547b; David Lyons 290t; Cro Magnon 345cra; Stefano Politi Markovina 480-1b; Regis Martin 367b; mauritius images GmbH 265b, 266-7b, / Ausloos 456-7b, / Steve Vidler 201tr, 298cra; Mavenvision 54b; Gareth McCormack 52bl; MeloDPhoto 228-9b; Tuul and Bruno Morandi 151crb, / Head of a Woman (1931) by Pablo Picasso © Succession Picasso / DACS, London 2019 98tr; Luciano Mortula 212bl, / Centre Pompidou in Paris: Studio Piano & Rogers; courtesy of Fondazione Renzo Piano and Rogers Stirk Harbour + Partners 90-1b; David Murphy 273tr; National Geographic Image Collection 101tl; Newscom 62cla; NielsVK 537tr, 542t; nobleIMAGES / David Noble 459b; Nathaniel Noir 96cra; North Wind Picture Archives 67br; Alexander Novikov 520t; Samantha Ohlsen 62cr; Sylvain Oliveira 249br; Pacific Press 69cr; Panther Media GmbH 49cla; Pawel Libera Images 174-5b; Doug Pearson 502-3t; Peter Adams Photography Ltd 283t; Martin Philpott 381cra; Photo 12 65bc; PhotoCuisine RM 364cr; Photononstop 113tr, / Daniele Schneider 182b, 406-7b; picturesbyrob 458cra; beatrice preve 240-1t; Prisma / Fiedler Bernd J. 334-5b, / Raga Jose Fuste 435b, / © FLC / ADAGP, Paris and DACS, London 2019 336-7t; Profimedia.CZ a.s. / Bauer Media / Kulinarni Studio 455cl; Stefano Ravera 142tl; Realy Easy Star / Claudio Concina 243cra, / Alberto Fozzi 269crb, / Silvio Massolo / Picasso Museum; Antibes Ulysse et les sirènes (1947) by Pablo Picasso © Succession Picasso / DACS, London 2019 45br; Simon Reddy 188cr; Mervyn Rees / Museum of Modern Art in the Pompidou Centre; Paris; France / Le Rhinocéros by Xavier Veilhan © Veilhan / ADAGP, Paris and DACS, London 2019 91cra; Fabrizio Robba 488-9b; robertharding 36-7t, 262tl, / Julian Elliott 398t; Maurice Rougemont 21cra; SAGAPHOTO.COM / FORGET Patrick 199br; Yolanda Perera Sánchez 66-7t; Maurice Savage 191cla; Norbert Scanella 443tl, 514tl; Peter Schickert 374bl; Richard Semik 480tl; shapencolour 429tl; Shawshots 121crb; SJH Photography 175bl; Kristen Soper 414bc; Jacek Sopotnicki 202-3t; Richard Splash 34cr; Kumar Sriskandan 63crb; STOCKFOLIO 697 40-1b, 512b; Boris Stroujko 466-7b; Sueddeutsche Zeitung Photo 238bl; Thibaut 343tr; travellinglight 278-9t;

Reinhold Tscherwitschke 294cr; Yuri Turkov 67tr; Frédéric VIELCANET 200b; Robin Weaver 263tr, 266tl; Don White 74cb, 82cb; Stefan van der Wijst 299bl; John G. Wilbanks 150t; Scott Wilson 262-3t; Jan Wlodarczyk 210-1b, 224-5b, 388-9b, 536tl, 536-7t, 540-1b, 541tl, 541tr, 544-5b; World History Archive 66cr, 240bc; www.thierryrambaud.fr 248-9t; Xavier Fores - Joana Roncero 386bl; Zoonar GmbH 265cl, / Konstantin Kalishko 306-7t.

AWL Images: Jon Arnold / Tour Eiffel- Illuminations Pierre Bideau 76tl, 116-7; Jan Christopher Becke 75, 102-3, 137tr; Walter Bibikow 179cra; Marco Bottigella 21bl, 338-9; Danita Delimont Stock 171cl; GUY Christian 456-7; Hemis 403t; Interfoto / Jean-Francois Hagenmuller 60-1t; Pierre Jacques 358-9bc; Tom Mackie 472-3t; Carlos Sanchez Pereyra 74, 82-3, 376t; SPANI Arnaud 550-1; George Theodore 4.

Bridgeman Images: Bibliotheque Nationale, Paris, France / Archives Charmet 66cb; Musee d'Orsay, Paris, France 178bl.

Clermont-Ferrand International Short Film Festival: Baptiste Chanat 51bl.

Commonwealth War Graves Commission (www.cwgc.org): 190-1.

Depositphotos Inc: gevision 506t; packshot 173clb; wjarek 128tr; Xantana 446bl.

Disneyland® Paris: 177t; © Disney / Pixar 175clb, 175br; Bertrand Guay 52-3t.

Dorling Kindersley: Jules Selmes 131cr.

Dreamstime.com: Adisa 100bl; Alexirina27000 / Loch Ness Monster © Niki de Saint Phalle Charitable Art Foundation / ADAGP, Paris and DACS, London 2019 506br; Aliaumesouchier 246t; Anitasstudio 62cra; Antonel 496tl; Anyaberkut 81cl; Valentin Armianu 112-3b; Valery Bareta 496-7t; Bargotiphotography 120; Jennifer Barrow 32-3t; Ilona Melanie Bicker 78t; Stephane Bidouze 19cb, 258-9; Eva Bocek 538bl; Braniffman 211tr; Theodor Bunica 188bl; Buurserstraat386 354-6b; Franck Camhi 63tr; Daliu80 272-3b, 284tl; Delstudio 454br; Demerzel21 12-3b; Dennis Van De Water 160-1t, 161b; Davide Lo Dico 293cl; Matthew Dixon 128b; Dennis Dolkens 93cra, 170-1b; Pierre Jean Durieu 373tr; Sergey Dzyuba 13t; Eddygaleotti 497cla; Emicristea / Hero, sculpture of Nimeño II by Serena Carone © ADAGP, Paris and DACS, London 2019 476t; Evolove 126-7t; Eyewave 193cra; Felis 55br; Fotografiecor 531clb; Ed Francissen 269br; Prochasson Frederic 34t, 366-7t; Eugeniu Frimu 140-1b; Giovanni Gagliardi 244-5t; Gawel 391; Giuseppemasci 241cb; Rostislav Glinsky 28cl; goga18128 26bl; Gornostaj 163cra; Grafner 536-7ca; Ioana Grecu 125tr; Guillohmz 172br; Dieter Hawlan 176b; Alan Hill 20t, 286-7; Hornet83 494t; Imladris 402bl; Irina88w / L'Oiseau Lunaire (1968) by Joan Miró © Successió Miró / ADAGP, Paris and DACS London 2019 505br; Izanbar 530tl; Valerijs Jegorovs 110b; Jojjik 10-1b; Jorisvo 26cr; Juliengrondin 19tl, 48-9t, 232-3; Aliaksandr Kazlou 149tl; Kloeg008 319tr; Kmiragaya 142-3b; Sergii Kolesnyk 78tl; Maryna Kordiumova 107crb; Jan Kranendonk 198br; Laudibi 367tr; Bo Li 107bl; José Lledó 78crb; Madrabothair 80br, 96t; Markwatts104 42-3t; Maurizio De Mattei 106-7t; Oxana Medvedeva 32cr; Meinzahn 11t, 57cla; MilaCroft 23t, 416-7; Milosk50 380-1b; Minnystock 317tl; Luciano Mortula 76cb, 132-3; MrFly 122cl; Christian Müller 18bl, 216-7; Olgacov 268-9t, 370-1; Outcast85 256-7b; Dennis Van De Water / American War Memorials Overseas 236cr; William Perry 92bl, 93tr, 95tr; Philippehalle 378bl; Photobac 368br; Photofires 172-3t; Beatrice Preve 60bl; Sharad Raval 396tl; Santi Rodriguez 65cla; Rosshelen 22t, 55tl, 238-9t, 360-1; Eq Roy 112t; Scaliger 8clb; Pramote Seemak 372clb; Siraanamwong 137cla; Darius Strazdas 148-9b; Travelling-light 426bl; Anibal Trejo 33tr; Trudywsimmons 297cra; Tupungato 160bc; Ukrphoto 136cra; Ivan Varyukhin 177cl, 319tl; Iryna Vlasenko 13br; Xantana 276tr, 452t, 454-5t; Jason Yoder 89bl; Zatletic 93c.

Futuroscope, France: Calune 404-5t.

Getty Images: Waring Abbott 89tr; AFP / Fred Dufour 62cl, 63clb, / Mehdi Fedouach 10clb, / Eric Feferberg 63tl, / Bertrand Guay 39crb, / Francois Guillot 62clb, / Boris Horvat 121cl, / Bertrand Langlois 50-1t, / Xavier Leoty 38-9t, / Philippe Lopez 62crb, / Ludovic Marin 69tr, / Jean-Pierre Muller 63cr, / Fred Tanneau 51cr, / Charly Triballeau 55cr; 420cr; / Nicolas Tucat 47cl, 47b; Ayhan Altun 89cr; Archive Photos 65tr; Atlantide Phototravel 57br; Patrick Aventurier 65tl; Bettmann 269br; Busà Photography / Centre Pompidou in Paris: Studio Piano & Rogers; courtesy of Fondazione Renzo Piano and Rogers Stirk Harbour + Partners 91c; Guillaume Chanson 136-7b; Christophel Fine Art 66tl, 68tl; De Agostini DEA / Biblioteca Ambrosiana 121bl, / G. Dagli Orti 17t, 67cra, 166-7, / C. Sappa 86bl, 380tl; P Deliss 89cra; Chuck Fishman 507tl; Owen Franken 36-7b; French Select / Bertrand Rindoff Petroff 110-1t; Gamma-Rapho / Paul Charbit 50bl, / Jean-Patrick DEYA 504bl, / Raphael GAILLARDE 323tr, / Pierre Marcellesi 58bl; Chris Graythen 63cl; hemis.fr / JACQUES Pierre 346bc, / SONNET Sylvain 343br; Heritage Images 66br, 121cra; Historic Map Works LLC and Osher Map Library 64t; Hulton Archive 122bl; Hulton Deutsch 86fbl; Icon Sport / Dave Winter 42bl; Julian Elliott Photography 77, 144; Keystone-France 69clb; Reg Lancaster 39cl; Linda Goodhue Photography 26t; Raimund Linke 500-1t; Peter Macdiarmid 245tr; MathieuRivrin 122-3; National Geographic Image Collection / Sisse Brimberg 422-3t; Tu xa Ha Noi 2-3; NurPhoto / Nicolas Liponne 366bl; Ocni Design 342bl; Pierre Ogeron 440-1b; Pacific Press 69br; Paris Match / Philippe Petit 46bl, 59cb, / Julien Weber 38bl; Photo Josse / Leemage 108bl; Photononstop / Daniele SCHNEIDER 462cla; Patrick Aventurier / architect Rudy Ricciotti 496-7ca; Frank Scherschel 68cla; Pakin Songmor 54tl; UIG / Andia 369cl, / Kike Calvo 452crb; Ian Waldie 68-9s; Westend61 508-9t; WireImage / Pascal Le Segretain 111cla.

iStockphoto.com: AleksandarGeorgiev 397tl; AlexKozlov 162bl; Alphotographic 30tl; aluxum 8-9; Leonid Andronov 342-3t; aprott 524tl; asab974 78cr; bbsferrari 526-7b; bluejayphoto 6-7, 322-3b; Eric Cowez 22bl, 392-3; DaLiu 280-1b; davidf 80-1t; DawidKasza 37crb; eddygaleotti 502br; espiegle 114-5b; Pawel Gaul 32tl; gui00878 384-5t; Infografick 25bl, 532-3; instamatics 147; Jag_cz 34crb; Janoka82 389tr; JohanSjolander 28-9t; JonathanNicholls 191b; JoselgnacioSoto 30-1c, 86crb; JurgaR 236t; KenWiedemann 240cl; Augustin Lazaroiu 152-3; LeoPatrizi 8cl; Maica 12t; MarcelloLand 158-9b; MargaretClavell 424br; Maximastudio 364t; mtoome 11br; NDStock 13cr; Howard Oates 24tl, 448-9; olrat 164-5; Pascal_p10 388tr; PictureReflex / La Grande Motte by Jean Balladur © ADAGP, Paris and DACS, London 2019 486tl; PJPhoto69 400-1t; RicoK69 270-1b; Juergen Sack 382t; Sasha64f 460b; Sean38t0 86cra; serts 16c, 70-1t; stock_colors 61crb; syolacan 33cl; thehague 81br; Tolga_TEZCAN 87; TomasSereda 124-5b; Natalia Van Doninck 8cla; Wailingwailers12 188t; zefart / Studio Piano + Rogers; courtesy of Fondazione Renzo Piano and Rogers Stirk Harbour + Partners 56tl; ZU_09 65br.

Musée de Louvre: © Pyramide du Louvre, arch I.M. Pei 26crb, 106-7t, 107bl,

RMN: Grand Palais (Musée du Louvre) / Peter Willi / Trésor de l'abbaye de Saint-Denis 109tl.

Robert Harding Picture Library: Barbara Boensch 429cla; Stuart Dee 137cl; Julian Elliott 31tr; Javier Larrea 452cr; Nick Servian 30tr; Colin Sinclair 523t.

Shutterstock: Alexander Tolstykh 154-5b; trabantos 486-7b.

SuperStock: 4X5 Collection 108tl; age fotostock / Heinz-Dieter Falkenstein 93br, / Danuta Hyniewska 178-9b, / Javier Larrea / With the black Arc (1912) by Vassily Kandinsky, Centre George Pompidou, Paris, France 91tl; hemis.fr / / AZAM Jean-Paul 456clb, / CAVIGLIA Denis 356cra, / DEGAS Jean-Pierre 356t, / GUIZIOU Franck 378-9t, / GUY Christian 410b, / LEMAIRE Stéphane 171cra; imageBROKER / Joachim Hiltmann 156bc; robertharding / Godong 86fbr; Universal Images 173crb.

Front flap:
123RF.com: Jakub Gojda t; **Alamy Stock Photo:** hemis.fr
/ GUIZIOU Franck br; **AWL Images:** Hemis bl; Interfoto /
Jean-Francois Hagenmuller cra; **Dreamstime.com:**
Christian Müller c; **Getty Images:** Westend61 cla;

Cover images:
Front and spine: **4Corners:** Francesco Carovillano.
Back: **4Corners:** Francesco Carovillano bc; **Alamy Stock
Photo:** imageBROKER c; **AWL Images:** Jon Arnold cla;
Dreamstime.com: Felis tr;

Mapping:
Colourmap Scanning Ltd; Contour Publishing;
Cosmographics; European Map Graphics; Meteo-France;
ERAMaptec Ltd (Dublin), adapted with permission from
original survey and mapping by Shobunsha (Japan).

For further information see: www.dkimages.com

Penguin
Random
House

Main Contributors Mary-Ann Gallagher,
Carolyn Boyd, Robin Gauldie, Mike MacEacheran,
Ruth Reisenberger, Daniel Robinson, Doug Sager,
Lisa Voormeij, John Ardagh, Rosemary Bailey,
Judith Fayard, Lisa Gerard-Sharp, Colin Jones,
Alister Kershaw, Alec Lobrano, Anthony Roberts,
Alan Tillier, Nigel Tisdall

Senior Editor Ankita Awasthi Tröger

Senior Designer Owen Bennett

Project Editor Emma Grundy Haigh

Project Art Editors Tania da Silva Gomez,
Sophie State, Mark Richards, Ian Midson,
Stuti Tiwari Bhatia, Bharti Karakoti,
Ankita Sharma, Priyanka Thakur,
Vinita Venugopal

Designer William Robinson

Factchecker Jennifer Geraghty, Doug Sager,
Lisa Voormeij

Editors Rachel Laidler, Lucy Sara-Kelly,
Lauren Whybrow, Sophie Adams,
Alice Fewery, Lucy Sienkowska, Louise Abbot,
Matthew Grundy Haigh, Penny Phenix, Ruth
Reisenberger, Jackie Staddon, Rachel Thompson

Proofreader Ben Ffrancon Davis

Indexer Hilary Bird

Senior Picture Researcher Ellen Root

Picture Research Sophie Basilevitch,
Sumita Khatwani, Susie Watters, Harriet Whitaker

Illustrators Stephen Conlin, John Lawrence,
Maltings Partnership, John Woodcock

Cartographic Editor James Macdonald

Cartography Simonetta Giori,
Subhashree Bharati

Jacket Designers Bess Daly,
Maxine Pedliham, Simon Thompson

Jacket Picture Research Susie Watters

Senior DTP Designer Jason Little

DTP George Nimmo, Azeem Siddiqui

Producers Samantha Cross, Igrain Roberts

Managing Editor Hollie Teague

Art Director Maxine Pedliham

Publishing Director Georgina Dee

MIX
Paper from
responsible sources
FSC
www.fsc.org   **FSC™ C018179**

The information in this
DK Eyewitness Travel Guide is checked regularly.
Every effort has been made to ensure that this book
is as up-to-date as possible at the time of going to
press. Some details, however, such as telephone
numbers, opening hours, prices, gallery hanging
arrangements and travel information, are liable to
change. The publishers cannot accept responsibility
for any consequences arising from the use of this
book, nor for any material on third party websites,
and cannot guarantee that any website address
in this book will be a suitable source of travel
information. We value the views and suggestions
of our readers very highly. Please write to: Publisher,
DK Eyewitness Travel Guides, Dorling Kindersley,
80 Strand, London, WC2R 0RL, UK, or email:
travelguides@dk.com

First edition 1995

Published in Great Britain by Dorling Kindersley Limited,
80 Strand, London, WC2R 0RL

Published in the United States by DK Publishing,
1450 Broadway, 8th Floor, New York, NY 10018

Copyright © 1995, 2019 Dorling Kindersley Limited
A Penguin Random House Company
19 20 21 22 10 9 8 7 6 5 4 3 2 1

All rights reserved.

No part of this publication may be reproduced, stored in
or introduced into a retrieval system, or transmitted, in any form,
or by any means (electronic, mechanical, photocopying,
recording, or otherwise), without the prior written permission
of the copyright owner.

A CIP catalog record for this book
is available from the British Library.

A catalog record for this book is available
from the Library of Congress.

ISSN: 1542 1554
ISBN: 978 0 2413 6536 6

Printed and bound in China.

www.dk.com